TAB 5 ■ Researching [P9-EDM-889] ...ting for Clarity

pages 147–200

17. Understanding Research
18. Finding Print and Online Sources
19. Evaluating Sources
20. Doing Research in the Archive, Field, and Lab
21. Working with Sources
22. Writing the Paper
23. Discipline-Specific Resources in the Library and on the Internet

pages 337–84

38. Wordy Sentences
39. Missing Words
40. Mixed Constructions
41. Confusing Shifts
42. Faulty Parallelism
43. Misplaced and Dangling Modifiers
44. Coordination and Subordination
45. Sentence Variety
46. Active Verbs
47. Appropriate Language
48. Exact Language
49. Dictionary and Thesaurus
50. Glossary of Usage

TAB 6 ■ MLA Documentation Style

pages 201–42

24. MLA Style: In-Text Citations
25. MLA Style: List of Works Cited
26. MLA Style: Explanatory Notes
27. MLA Style: Paper Format
28. STUDENT PAPER IN MLA STYLE

TAB 11 ■ Editing for Grammar Conventions

pages 385–430

51. Sentence Fragments
52. Comma Splices and Run-on Sentences
53. Subject-Verb Agreement
54. Problems with Verbs
55. Problems with Pronouns
56. Problems with Adjectives and Adverbs

TAB 7 ■ APA Documentation Style

pages 243–72

29. APA Style: In-Text Citations
30. APA Style: References
31. APA Style: Paper Format
32. STUDENT PAPER IN APA STYLE

TAB 12 ■ Editing for Correctness:
Punctuation, Mechanics, and Spelling

pages 431–96

57. Commas
58. Semicolons
59. Colons
60. Apostrophes
61. Quotation Marks
62. Other Punctuation Marks
63. Capitalization
64. Abbreviations and Symbols
65. Numbers
66. Italics (Underlining)
67. Hyphens
68. Spelling

TAB 8 ■ Other Documentation Styles: *Chicago,* CSE, and COS

pages 273–309

33. *Chicago* Documentation Style
34. CSE Documentation Styles
35. Columbia Online Style (COS)

TAB 9 ■ Document and Web Design

pages 311–35

36. Document Design
37. Writing for the World Wide Web

TAB 13 ■ Basic Grammar Review, with Tips for Multilingual Writers

pages 497–532

69. Parts of Speech
70. Parts of Sentences
71. Phrases and Dependent Clauses
72. Types of Sentences

Further Resources for Learning

Index

A Writer's
Resource

A Handbook for Writing and Research

Elaine P. Maimon
Arizona State University West

Janice H. Peritz
Queens College,
City University of New York

Boston   Burr Ridge, IL   Dubuque, IA   Madison, WI   New York
San Francisco   St. Louis   Bangkok   Bogotá   Caracas   Kuala Lumpur
Lisbon   London   Madrid   Mexico City   Milan   Montreal   New Delhi
Santiago   Seoul   Singapore   Sydney   Taipei   Toronto

McGraw-Hill Higher Education ☒

A Division of The **McGraw-Hill** Companies

A Writer's Resource
A Handbook for Writing and Research

1 2 3 4 5 6 7 8 9 0 KGP/KGP 0 9 8 7 6 5 4 3 2

ISBN 0-07-040055-5

Vice president and Editor-in-chief: *Thalia Dorwick*
Executive editor: *Lisa Moore*
Director of development, English: *Carla Kay Samodulski*
Senior marketing manager: *David S. Patterson*
Lead production editor: *David M. Staloch*
Manager, New book production: *Sandra Hahn*
Senior designer: *Jean Mailander*
Interior and cover designer: *Linda Robertson*
Photo research coordinator: *Alexandra Ambrose*
Photo researcher: *Christine Pullo*
Art editor: *Emma Ghiselli*
Compositor: *Thompson Type*
Typeface: *9/11 New Century Schoolbook*
Paper: *45# Publishers Matte*
Printer and binder: *Quebecor World, Kingsport*

Cover images (*top to bottom*): © Visual Landscape; Image #5618(2). Photo by Lynton Gardiner, American Museum of Natural History Library; © Bettmann/Corbis; © Will & Deni McIntyre/Photo Researchers, Inc.; © Eric Lessing/Art Resource, NY

Text and photo credits begin on page C-1 and constitute an extension of the copyright page.

LIBRARY OF CONGRESS CATALOGING-IN-PUBLICATION DATA

Maimon, Elaine P.
   A writer's resource / Elaine P. Maimon, Janice H. Peritz.—1st ed.
     p. cm.
   Includes index.
   ISBN 0-07-040055-5
    1. English language—Rhetoric—Handbooks, manual, etc. 2. English language—Grammar—Handbooks, manuals, etc. 3. Report writing—Handbooks, manuals, etc. I. Peritz, Janice. II. Title.

PE1408.M3366 2002
808'.042—dc21   2002016650

www.mhhe.com

IMPORTANT:

HERE IS YOUR REGISTRATION CODE TO ACCESS
YOUR PREMIUM McGRAW-HILL ONLINE RESOURCES.

For key premium online resources you need THIS CODE to gain access. Once the code is entered, you will be able to use the Web resources for the length of your course.

If your course is using **WebCT** or **Blackboard**, you'll be able to use this code to access the McGraw-Hill content within your instructor's online course.

Access is provided if you have purchased a new book. If the registration code is missing from this book, the registration screen on our Web site will tell you how to obtain your new code.

Registering for McGraw-Hill Online Resources

To gain access to your McGraw-Hill web resources, simply follow the steps below:

(1) USE YOUR WEB BROWSER TO GO TO: **http://www.mhhe.com/maimon**

(2) CLICK ON **FIRST TIME USER**.

(3) ENTER THE REGISTRATION CODE* PRINTED ON THE TEAR-OFF BOOKMARK ON THE RIGHT.

(4) AFTER YOU HAVE ENTERED YOUR REGISTRATION CODE, CLICK **REGISTER**.

(5) FOLLOW THE INSTRUCTIONS TO SETUP YOUR PERSONAL UserID AND PASSWORD.

(6) WRITE YOUR UserID AND PASSWORD DOWN FOR FUTURE REFERENCE.
KEEP IT IN A SAFE PLACE.

TO GAIN ACCESS to the McGraw-Hill content in your instructor's **WebCT** or **Blackboard** course simply log in to the course with the UserID and Password provided by your instructor. Enter the registration code exactly as it appears in the box to the right when prompted by the system. You will only need to use the code the first time you click on McGraw-Hill content.

Thank you, and welcome to your McGraw-Hill online Resources!

REGISTRATION CODE

typologies-37940979

McGraw-Hill
ONLINE RESOURCES

0-07-040055-5 MAIMON: A WRITER'S RESOURCE, 1/E

The personal passcode on the other side of this card gives you access to *Catalyst: A Tool for Writing and Research* (<www.mhhe.com/maimon>), the companion Web site to *A Writer's Resource*. This code gives you access to a wealth of online resources that will help you throughout your college career. You can test your knowledge and skills, learn more about what constitutes plagiarism and how to avoid it, search the Web and evaluate potential sources using an interactive Web research tutorial, use step-by-step guides to help you write your papers, format your list of works cited or references automatically, and more!

Preface

As we wrote *A Writer's Resource*, our students were in our minds, acting as our chief consultants. We knew that their perspectives on college life were different from those of previous generations of students, and so were their expectations. We understood that they needed a handbook for the twenty-first century, with state-of-the-art resources on writing, researching, and graphic design in cyberspace. They might be using a handbook in an English composition class at 9:00 AM, but at 10:00 AM they might be preparing PowerPoints for a speech course, and at 11:00 AM they might need the handbook to help with a history assignment. More than any other textbook, their handbook was their guide, not just to writing, but also to learning in college.

To meet these requirements, we present a student-centered text, designed as a resource for achieving excellence in writing and learning in the ever-changing digital environment that students confront in college. *A Writer's Resource* responds to this environment in a number of ways:

- **A guide for success in college through writing**
  Tab 1: Learning across the Curriculum introduces students to the new territory of college and to college writing. In this unique section, we define concepts such as *discipline* and explain how to use writing as a tool for learning.

  An innovative final section, Further Resources for Learning, also introduces students to college discourse through a glossary of selected terms across the curriculum (for example, *variable, control group, postcolonialism*). Additional resources, such as a quick reference for multilingual writers, a timeline, and a world map, are truly related to college learning and will help students become connected to college life.

- **A focus on critical thinking and effective writing**
  Although instructors in various disciplines may approach subject matter differently, thinking critically and writing logically are underlying expectations across the curriculum. For this reason, Tab 2: Writing Papers, begins with a chapter on critical reading, thinking, and writing. Reading and thinking critically lead to writing critically and presenting persuasive arguments.

- **Support for conducting research and managing information**
  The library's shelves are only the beginning of research for students today. The process continues on the Internet and in the field, the archive, and the lab. To assist students in these varied venues, we offer a directory of sources from different disciplines. In addition, we provide guidance on posing research questions, the role of ethics in research, conducting effective keyword searches, and thinking critically about sources.

- **Documentation styles for the disciplines**
  In addition to full tabbed sections on MLA and APA, with model research papers on Louis Armstrong in Tab 6 and the German economy in Tab 7, *A Writer's Resource* includes a tabbed section with coverage of the documentation styles provided by the *Chicago Manual of Style*, the Council of Science Editors (CSE, formerly CBE, Council of Biology Editors), and Columbia Online Style (COS). The section on COS tells students how to use this system with other documentation styles instead of treating it as a stand-alone style.

- **Guidelines for college writing assignments**
  Although the advice in Tab 2 on writing papers and in Tab 5 on researching applies to papers across the curriculum, Tab 3: Common Assignments across the Curriculum gives students step-by-step advice on writing the three most commonly assigned types of papers: informative, interpretive, and argumentative essays, as well as guidance on other common assignments, including case studies, lab reports, oral reports, the use of PowerPoint, and writing in-class essay exams. Three full student papers are included as models: an informative paper on the stock market, an interpretive paper on Flannery O'Connor's short story "Everything That Rises Must Converge," and an argument on injuries in the NFL.

- **Real student writing**
  Students learn best from practical models that relate to their actual experience. We emphasize real student writing to provide attainable examples on relevant topics. We provide plenty of student examples, including examples from sample student papers, to show the realities of the writing and research process. *A Writer's Resource* offers five student papers, including samples of informative, interpretive, and argumentative writing as well as full MLA and APA papers. We have also used student examples in the editing sections, so they illustrate the kinds of problems and concerns that students are most likely to have.

- **Grammar in the context of editing**
  Today's students need to see how grammar fits into the writing process, so they can learn to become effective editors of their own work. For this reason, each tab on the conventions of English usage, grammar, and mechanics starts with the word "Editing." These tabs give students a helpful way to organize their editing and proofreading by using a three-tier approach, beginning with issues of clarity (Tab 10), moving to grammar conventions (Tab 11), and ending with the surface concerns of mechanics, punctuation, and spelling (Tab 12). For many of the most serious problem areas, we provide students with practical strategies that will help them improve their style or recognize and correct their errors.

- **Strong support for multilingual writers**
  Starting in the very first tab, *A Writer's Resource* offers multilingual writers support for learning in college and for every stage of the writing process. Chapter 5 provides advice to multilingual students on how they can use writing to deal with the unique challenges they often face. In addition, boxes with guidance for multilingual students appear in most of the tabs, and tips for multilingual writers are integrated throughout the basic grammar review in Tab 13. Listed for easy reference under the tab contents on page 498, these tips address special writing problems such as prepositions and articles. A separate index is provided for multilingual writers following the main index, and the handy grammar tips in the pull-out section in Further Resources for Learning give them a quick reference that is easy to carry as they attend classes or work in the library.

- **Writing in college and in life**
  Writing has never been confined to the composition classroom, and today's student has more opportunities to write than ever

before. E-mails, Web sites, and chat rooms all supplement the traditional occasions for writing offered by college coursework. Because we recognize that writing in college and in the world of work has become less and less a matter of the writer alone at a desk and more and more a matter of using technology effectively, we give full attention (throughout the text) to technology, interactive learning and writing, and the uses of writing to build communities.

In Tab 1, *A Writer's Resource* provides a chapter on writing online, with advice on using e-mail and learning netiquette. Tab 2 provides specific, practical suggestions for using online resources to collaborate with peer reviewers and to revise. Tab 4 includes advice on writing résumés, applying for jobs, and expressing praise or complaint in personal and business contexts as well as a chapter on service learning and community-service writing—to make students aware of the opportunities they have to use writing to make a difference. Tab 9 provides a full section on document and Web design. Our goal is for this text to become a life-long resource, much like a good desk dictionary.

- **Boxes that offer support for today's diverse student population**
  The boxes in *A Writer's Resource* supplement the text discussion with important information and helpful advice.

    Learning in College: Featured throughout the text, these boxed tips offer students information and strategies that will help them become better learners and writers.

    Charting the Territory: Throughout *A Writer's Resource,* these boxes present relevant information on such topics as interpretive assignments in different disciplines and the function of the passive voice in scientific and business writing. They give students a sense of how requirements and conventions vary across the curriculum.

    TextConnex: These boxes offer advice on using electronic resources and composing on a computer, as well as lists of useful Web sites, helping today's hyper-connected students take full advantage of the technology that is available.

    Writing Connections: Found in Tabs 3 and 4, these boxes alert students to a variety of related writing situations beyond college.

    Boxes for Multilingual Students: These boxes offer advice on learning in college, writing, and research. They are featured throughout the book.

Ancillaries

- **Comprehensive Web support:** Throughout *A Writer's Resource,* Web references in the margin let students know where they can find additional resources on the text's comprehensive Web site *Catalyst: A Tool for Writing and Research* (<www.mhhe.com/maimon>), which provides extensive technological support, including over 3,000 grammar exercises; diagnostic tests; an online handbook; an interactive Web research tutorial; access to the *Northern Light* search engine, with 7,000 premium research sites, all evaluated by experts for credibility; a Bibliomaker for the MLA, APA, *Chicago,* CSE, and COS documentation systems that automatically formats bibliographic source information; instruction in how to avoid plagiarism; access to the *New York Times* archives on language; and step-by-step advice for writing informative, interpretive, and argumentative papers.

- **Electronic versions:** Because today's students expect handbook materials to be available whenever and wherever they need them—on CD, online, on campus, and at home—the full text of *A Writer's Resource* is also available on CD-ROM, and the documentation and editing tabs are available for use on a personal digital assistant (PDA).

- **Teaching Composition Faculty Listserv at <www.mhhe.com/tcomp>:** Moderated by Chris Anson at North Carolina State University and offered by McGraw-Hill as a service to the composition community, this listserv brings together senior members of the college composition community with newer members—junior faculty, adjuncts, and teaching assistants— through an online newsletter and accompanying discussion group to address issues of pedagogy, both in theory and in practice.

- **PageOut:** McGraw-Hill's own PageOut service is available to help teachers get their courses up and running online in a matter of hours—at no cost. Additional information about the service is available online at <http://www.pageout.net>.

- **Webwrite:** This online product, available through our partner company MetaText, makes it possible for writing teachers and students to, among other things, comment on and share papers online.

For further information about these and other electronic resources, contact your local McGraw-Hill representative, visit the English pages on the McGraw-Hill Higher Education Web site at <www.mhhe.com/catalogs/hss/english>, or visit McGraw-Hill's Digital Solutions pages at <www.mhhe.com/catalogs/solutions>.

Acknowledgments

When we wrote *A Writer's Resource,* we started with the premise that
it takes a campus to teach a writer. It is also the case that it takes a
community to write a handbook. This text has been a major collabo-
rative effort for the two of us. And over the years, that ever-widening
circle of collaboration has included reviewers, editors, librarians, faculty colleagues, and family members.

Let us start close to home. Mort Maimon did line editing, checked
sources, and brought to this project his years of insight and experience as a secondary and post-secondary English teacher. Rudy Peritz
and Lynne Haney reviewed drafts of a number of chapters, bringing
to our cross-curricular mix the pedagogical and writerly perspectives
of, respectively, a brilliant law professor and a brilliant sociologist.
Jess Peritz, a current college student, was consulted on numerous
occasions for her expert advice on making examples both up-to-date
and understandable. Finally, Janice wants to express her gratitude
to Deborah Luepnitz for the much needed personal assistance that
made it possible for her to undertake this project and see it to a conclusion six years later.

At Arizona State University West, Beverly Buddee, executive
assistant to the provost, worried with us over this project for six
years. Bev coordinated student assistants and, when they could not
find the answer, found it herself. It should also be clear from text
materials reprinted from documents created by reference librarians
at ASU West that one of the world's most creative, resourceful, and
knowledgeable teams of librarians blesses this Phoenix campus.
Their talents inform the work of all faculty members and students at
ASU West. Our deepest gratitude goes to Lisa Kammerlocher, Dennis
Isbell, and Sharon Wilson. Thanks, too, go to C. J. Jeney and Cheryl War-
ren for providing assistance. ASU West professors Thomas McGovern
and Martin Meznar shared assignments and student papers with us.

At Queens College, several colleagues in the English department
not only shared their astute reflections on teaching and writing but
also gave us valuable classroom materials to use as we saw fit. Our
thanks go to Fred Buell, Nancy Comley, Ann Davison, Joan Dupre, Hugh
English, Sue Goldhaber, Marci Goodman, Eric Lehman, Norman
Lewis, Charles Molesworth, Beth Stickney, Amy Tucker, and Stan
Walker. We are especially grateful to the mutlitalented Steve Kruger,
who let us use writing from his prior life as an undergraduate biolo-
gist and to the pedagogically gifted Stuart Cochran, who tested some
of the common assignments and editing chapters in his undergraduate courses and faculty workshops. The Queens College librarians
also gave us various kinds of help with the researching and documentation chapters, and we thank them, especially Sharon Bonk, Alexandra DeLuise, Izabella Taler, and Manny Sanudo.

At Queens, faculty from across the curriculum sent us material to consider for the book and, in some cases, also filled out questionnaires about their own practices as researchers and writers; our thanks go to David Baker, Linda Edwards, Ray Erickson, Peg Franco, Vivian Gruder, Marty Hanlon, Elaine Klein, Michael Krasner, Joel Lidov, Jacqueline Newman, Barbara Sandler, Dean Savage, and John Troynaski. We would also like to thank countless other faculty and administrative colleagues at ASU West and at Queens College, whose commitment to learner-centered education informs this text.

We are also grateful to the following faculty from other institutions who contributed valuable materials and advice: Jane Collins, Jane Hathaway, Jan Tecklin, Christine Timm, Scott Zaluda, Dianne Zannoni, and Richard Zeikowitz.

We want to give special thanks to the students whose papers we include in full: Joseph Smulowitz, Rajeev Bector, Nick Buglione, Esther Hoffman, and Jennifer Koehler. We also want to acknowledge the following students who allowed us to use substantial excerpts from their work: Ilona Bouzoukashvili, Wilma Ferrarella, Jacob Grossman, Umawattie Roopnarian, and Cheryl Pietrocarlo. Our thanks also go to Judy Williamson and Trent Batson for contributing their expertise on writing and computers as well as for sharing what they learned from the Epiphany Project. We are grateful to Harvey Wiener and the late Richard Marius for their permission to draw on their explanations of grammatical points in the *McGraw-Hill Handbook*. We also appreciate the work of Andras Tapolcai, who collected most of the examples used in the documentation chapters, and the contributions of Leslie Taggart and of John Chapman, who wrote the boxes for multilingual students. Thanks also go to librarians Debora Person, University of Wyoming, and Ronelle K. H. Thompson, Augustana College, who provided us with helpful comments on Tab 5: Researching, and to instructors Cherry Campbell, Sonoma State University, and Christine Francisco, City College of San Francisco, who gave us useful advice on the material for multilingual students. Our colleague Don McQuade has inspired us, advised us, and encouraged us throughout the years of this project.

Within the McGraw-Hill organization, many wonderful people have been our true teammates. Tim Julet believed in this project initially and signed us on to what has become a major life commitment. From 1999, Lisa Moore, the executive editor for the composition list, has creatively, expertly, and tirelessly led the group of development editors and in-house experts who have helped us find the appropriate form to bring our insights as composition teachers to the widest possible group of students. We have learned a great deal from Lisa. As an editor, Margaret Manos was a true collaborator, working to condense and clarify the first draft of the manuscript. So, too, was Carla Samodulski, director of development for composition and advanced writing; as the chapters on editing show, the book has benefited enormously from her care and intelligence, as did the production process, which she expertly managed. Laura Barthule, a development editor, led focus groups on the design and concept, checked Web references, and found many of the visual examples. James Marquand made major contributions to the Further Resources for Learning section, and Alexis Walker, sponsoring editor, helped develop and edit this section. Victoria Fullard, e-content development editor, checked and double-checked documentation models, coordinated the reviewing, and, working with Paul Banks, e-content manager, and Todd Vaccaro, senior media tech producer, oversaw the development of the Web content. David Staloch, lead production editor, monitored every detail of production; Jean Mailander, senior designer, supervised every aspect of the striking text design and cover. David Patterson, senior marketing manager, and Ray Kelley, Paula Radosovich, and Lori DeShazo, field publishers, have worked tirelessly and enthusiastically to market *A Writer's Resource.* We also appreciate the hands-on attention of McGraw-Hill senior executives Phil Butcher, publisher; Thalia Dorwick, editor-in-chief of the Humanities, Social Science, and Languages group; and Steve Debow, president of the Humanities, Social Science, and Languages group.

Finally, many, many thanks go to the reviewers who read various versions of this text, generously shared their perceptions, and had confidence in us as we shaped this book to address the needs of their students.

Harriet Arnold, University of the Pacific

Jim Baker, Texas A & M University

Jerry Ball, Arkansas State University

Cynthia Bascom, Butler University

Cynthia Bates, University of California, Davis

Anne Beaufort, American University

David Blakesley, Southern Illinois University at Carbondale

Gary Blank, North Carolina State University

Robinson Blann, Trevecca Nazarene University

Philip Blosser, Lenoir-Rhyne College

William Boggs, Slippery Rock University of Pennsylvania

Virginia Bracket, Triton College

William Breedlove, College of Charleston

Karen S. Burge, Wichita State University

Jeff Cain, Sacred Heart University
Patricia Cearley, South Plains College
John Clark, Bowling Green State University
Sandra Clark, Anderson University
Micael Clarke, Loyola University of Chicago
Lauren Sewell Coulter, University of Tennessee, Chatanooga
Michael Delahoyde, Washington State University
Mike DeLong, Oklahoma State University—Oklahoma City
John E. Doyle, Quinnipiac College
William Durfee, University of Minnesota
Deborah Fleming, Ashland University
Shelli Fowler, Washington State University
Lynee Lewis Gaillet, Georgia State University
Ellen Gardiner, University of Mississippi
Sara Garnes, Ohio State University
Susanmarie Harrington, Indiana University—
    Purdue University Indianapolis
Andrew Harvey, University of North Carolina at Charlotte
Sharon Hatton-Montoya, University of Southern Colorado
Sharon Roger Hepburn, Radford University
Michael Hogan, Southeast Missouri State University
Kathy Houff, University of Georgia
Jodee Hunt, Grand Valley State University
Ronald B. Jenkins, Georgia College and State University
Jim Jeremiah, University of Phoenix
Joan Johnson, Hagerstown Community College
Eunice Johnston, North Dakota State University
Enoch Jordan, Norfolk State University
Bennett M. Judkins, Lenoir-Rhyne College
Rodney D. Keller, Ricks College
Beth Kemper, Campbellsville University
Mary Lynch Kennedy, State University of New York at Cortland
Linda Cooper Knight, Coastal Carolina University
Bill Lamb, Johnson County Community College
David LeNoir, Western Kentucky University

Barbara Liu, Eastern Connecticut State University
Sonia Maasik, University of California at Los Angeles
Mike Mackey, Community College of Denver
Wanda Martin, University of New Mexico
Jonathan Mauk, Owens Community College
Lisa McClure, Southern Illinois University at Carbondale
Angela McGlynn, Mercer County Community College
John David Moore, Eastern Illinois University
Mike Moran, University of Georgia
Ed Nagelhout, University of Nevada, Las Vegas
R. Gerald Nelms, Southern Illinois University at Carbondale
Phillip F. O'Mara, Bridgewater College
C. R. Orchard, Indiana University of Pennsylvania
Virginia Polanski, Stonehill College
George Pullman, Georgia State University
Claude Reichard, Stanford University
Kelly Ritter, University of Illinois at Chicago
Mike Rose, University of California at Los Angeles
Alison Russell, Xavier University
David R. Russell, Iowa State University
Peter Sattler, Lakeland College
Cathy Sewell, Chesapeake College
Ernest J. Smith, University of Central Florida
Kathleen Sole, University of Phoenix
Madeleine Sorapure, University of California, Santa Barbara
Margot Soven, LaSalle University
Ernest Stromberg, University of Oregon
Lou Suarez, Lorain County Community College
John W. Taylor, South Dakota State University
Christopher Thaiss, George Mason University
Emily Thrush, University of Memphis
Rebecca Umland, University of Nebraska at Kearney
Jeffery Vail, University of Delaware
Beverly Wall, Trinity College
Amy Walsh, University of South Dakota

Frank Walters, Auburn University
Randal Woodland, University of Michigan—Dearborn
Diane Zannoni, Trinity College
Mary Zdrojkowski, Eastern Michigan University

Elaine P. Maimon
Janice H. Peritz

The adequate study of culture, our own
and those on the opposite side of the
globe, can press on to fulfillment only
as we learn today from the humanities
as well as from the scientists.

—RUTH BENEDICT

Learning
across
the Curriculum

1 Learning across the Curriculum

1. Your College Experience 3
   a. Charting your course 3
   b. Choosing your itinerary 4
   c. Learning the language 4

2. Writing to Learn 4
   a. Writing to aid memory 5
   b. Writing to sharpen observation 5
   c. Writing to clarify thought 5
   d. Writing to uncover connections 6
   e. Writing to strengthen argument 6

3. Writing in College 6
   a. Learning about common college assignments 8
   b. Learning how to understand assignments 8

4. Writing Online 9
   a. Exploring the virtual landscape 9
   b. Making use of e-mail 11
   c. Learning the netiquette of cybercultures 11
   d. Benefiting from online learning 13

5. Learning in English as a Second Language 14
   a. Becoming aware of cultural differences in communication 15
   b. Using writing to learn more about English 16
   c. Using the tools that are available for multilingual students 16

Your college campus is a place for exploration. As you travel its terrain and navigate its waterways, use this book as your compass, map, and guide.

1 Your College Experience

During your studies, you will travel through many courses, participating in numerous conversations—oral and written—about nature, society, and culture.

- As a compass, this text will help you get oriented to college and find a direction for your studies.
- As a map, this text will help you see the larger picture and understand the different approaches you may encounter as you move from course to course.
- As a guide, this text will help you write everything from notes to exams to research papers—the record of your participation in the culture of your campus.

1a Chart your course.

Navigators use the term *course* to mean onward movement in a particular direction. Charting a course means mapping the coastlines, water depths, and tides. Likewise, colleges use the term **course of study** to refer to your curriculum, your progress toward a college degree. The college's course catalog describes the units—the courses—in that curriculum, but it does more than simply list courses. In its mission statement and its explanations of various itineraries, the course catalog charts the culture of the campus.

Certain parts of your college journey may be largely predetermined. Some courses fulfill distribution or general education requirements. Just as travel guidebooks highlight places that most tourists want to visit, these requirements send you to a variety of places from which to view the territory. For example, you may be asked to take one or two courses in the arts and humanities (literature, art, music, philosophy), the social sciences (sociology, economics, history), and the natural sciences (biology, geology, astronomy). In doing so, you will be learning to see and think about the world from different vantage points.

At some point during your travels, it will be time to get to know one of these ways of seeing and thinking in more depth. In other words, you will be asked to choose a major. If general education requirements give you an academic grand tour, major requirements offer opportunities to explore one country more closely and to get to know the people, the customs, and the best cafés.

1b Choose your itinerary.

The academic territory is usually divided into areas of inquiry called **disciplines.** Disciplines share a history, a terminology, and some common concerns. The discipline of sociology, for example, is concerned with the conditions, patterns, and problems in groups and societies. Sociologists collect, analyze, and interpret data; they also debate its reliability and the credibility of various interpretations. These debates occur in journals, books, conferences, and classrooms—sites where knowledge is produced and communicated.

When you take a course, your purpose is not just to amass information about this or that topic. Your purpose is to learn about the discipline that has produced this mass of information:

- What topics and questions structure the discipline?
- How do researchers in this discipline collect data?
- What principles and terms guide the interpretation of data?
- What debates animate the discipline?

1c Learn the language.

Countries are composed of diverse communities or social groups. So, too, are disciplines. All economists do not see and say things in the same way. Although they belong to the same discipline—the discipline of economics—economists identify with various groups within their discipline based on the different ways in which they talk about economic theory.

Diversity and debate within a discipline can be both intimidating and confusing. You have guides, however: college professors who are willing to help you understand the discipline and its various groups. You also have guidebooks: course texts and this reference book. You will need to do more than listen to professors and read texts, though, to make sense of things. You will need to write if you want to understand and feel at home in the academic world.

2 Writing to Learn

Writing is not something reserved for novelists, playwrights, and poets. In the world of the twenty-first century, everyone writes. The technology may have changed from quill pens to typewriters to computer keyboards, but the need to put down words to discover, express, and record thoughts has not changed.

Scientists write proposals to gain support for their laboratories; bankers write descriptions of new investment products; physical therapists write notes on a patient's progress. Although we live in a world of cell phones and voice mail, when something is important, we still need to put it in writing.

We use writing not only when we need to go public with a proposal or report but also to help us remember, understand, and create. Think of the way a simple shopping list aids your memory once you get to the store, or recall the last time you were asked to keep the minutes of a meeting. Because of your heightened attention, you undoubtedly knew more about what happened at that meeting than did anyone else who attended it. Writing actively involves you in what you are seeing and hearing.

2a Writing aids memory.

From shopping lists to class notes to ideas for later development, writing things down helps you get things done. When you are writing something that others will eventually see, don't try to keep all your ideas in your head until you are ready to go public with them. That is like trying to do long division in your head. Write down your ideas—in any form or order—so that you won't forget them. Once your preliminary ideas are down on paper, you can shape what is there and cross out what you don't want.

2b Writing sharpens observation.

When you record what you see, hear, taste, smell, and feel, you increase the powers of your senses. Write a description of the taste of rosemary or the smell of lilacs, and you will be more alive to those experiences. Write down each place where a flute is heard in a piece of music, and you will hear the instrument more clearly.

2c Writing clarifies thought.

"How do I know what I think until I see what I say?" E. M. Forster's oft-quoted question reminds us that we frequently write our way into a topic. Writing and then carefully reading your own early drafts helps you pinpoint what you really want to say. It is often the case that the last paragraph of a first draft becomes the first paragraph of the next draft.

2d Writing uncovers connections.

Maybe a character in a short story reminds you of your next-door neighbor, or an image in a poem makes you feel sad. What is it about your next-door neighbor that is similar to the fictional character? What is it about the poetic image that evokes memories of loss? If you write down answers to these questions, you will learn more about the short story or poem, and possibly more about yourself.

2e Writing strengthens argument.

Often when you start out to persuade others of something you believe, you begin by writing as if only like-minded people were going to read your argument. As you review your draft, write down questions that those who disagree with you might ask. Answer these questions when you revise for a stronger piece of persuasive writing.

3 Writing in College

Most college courses require at least some writing, including one or more formal papers. Your writing projects might be case studies in the social sciences, lab reports in the hard sciences, texts for oral presentations in business studies, and reviews in the humanities, to name a few possibilities.

As you go from course to course, you will find particular ways to use writing as an aid to learning. Travelers often keep journals and write letters to record what they have seen, heard, and done; to react to their experiences; and to reflect on the meaning of it all. During your academic explorations, use writing to learn about the conventions of different disciplines and to make sense of your intellectual experiences.

- **If you are writing a paper on conflict resolution** among four-year-olds for a course in human development, observe and record the play activities of one child during several play periods in a nursery school class. How many instances do you note of conflict with other children? Observe the child's strategies for dealing with these incidents. Your careful written observations will help you understand principles in the course text and may later contribute to a case study paper.
- **If you are writing an article on journalistic styles** for a news reporting class, read an account of the same event in the *New York Times,* the *Arizona Republic,* and *Time* magazine.

Tips LEARNING in COLLEGE

Whether academic pursuits are a struggle or come easily to you, whether you are fresh out of high school or are returning to school many years after high school graduation, college is a challenge. Here are a few hints and strategies for taking on some of the challenges you will encounter.

- **Make the most of your time by setting clear priorities.** Deal with surprises by saying "no," getting away from it all, taking control of phone and e-mail interruptions, and leaving slack in your schedule to accommodate the unexpected.

- **Recognize how you prefer to learn.** *Tactile learners* prefer hands-on learning that comes about through touching, manipulating objects, and doing things. *Visual learners* like to see information in their mind, favoring reading and watching over touching and listening. *Auditory learners* favor listening as the best approach. Work on improving your less-preferred learning styles.

- **Evaluate the information you gather.** Consider how authoritative the source is, whether the author has any potential biases, how recent the information is, and whether anything important is missing from the research. In college, critical thinking is essential.

- **Take good notes.** The central feature of good note taking is listening and distilling important information—not writing down everything that is said.

- **Build reading and listening skills.** When you read, identify the main ideas, prioritize them, think critically about the arguments, and explain the writer's ideas to someone else. Listen actively: focus on what is being said, pay attention to nonverbal messages, listen for what is not being said, and take notes.

- **Improve your memory.** Rehearsal is the key strategy in remembering information. Repeat the information, summarize it, associate it with other memories, and above all, think about it when you first come across it.

Source: Based on Robert S. Feldman, *P.O.W.E.R. Learning: Strategies for Success in College and Life,* 2nd ed., New York: McGraw-Hill, 2003.

Keep notes on the style and point of view in each publication. Analyzing the treatment of similar material in different publications will help you identify stylistic differences.

- **If you are reviewing an art exhibit** for an art history course, take notes on the shape, color, line, and subject matter of one painting. Use these notes to help you better understand the other paintings in the exhibit.

3a Learn about common college assignments.

No matter what your course of study, writing will be an important part of your college experience. Understanding what is being asked of you as a writer is a critical ingredient in your success.

Although writing assignments can differ from one discipline to another, from one course to another, and from one part of a course to another, all writing has elements in common. There are also common writing assignments—types of writing required by courses in many different disciplines. The three most common types of papers are informative reports, interpretive analyses, and arguments. (*See Tab 3: Common Assignments across the Curriculum, pp. 75–129.*)

- **Informative reports** occur in all disciplines. In an informative report, the writer passes on what he or she has learned about a topic or issue. For example, a professor of music history writes a chapter explaining three distinctive characteristics of Renaissance music for a music appreciation textbook.

- **Interpretive analyses** explore the meaning of written documents, cultural artifacts, social situations, and natural events. For example, a professional cultural critic explores Freud's anecdotes, showing how they are used both to control and to dramatize the uncanny.

- **Arguments** are valued in all fields of study. These types of papers prove a point or support an opinion through logic and concrete evidence. For example, a political scientist critiques the idea that the prospects for Russian democracy depend on the economy, not on the quantity and quality of political participation.

3b Learn how to understand assignments.

From a journal entry to an essay exam to a research report, college writing assignments aim to enhance your knowledge. Assignments can also challenge your creativity: some may ask you to imagine situations outside the classroom; others may allow you to choose your own topic, purpose, and audience. Even when an instructor provides explicit and specific directions, you still need to make the assignment your own in order to write an effective response to it.

The following questions and suggestions will help you begin figuring out your assignments:

- **What has the professor said in class about the purpose of the assignment?** Check your notes and consult with classmates.

- **What type of project are you being asked to write?** Is it one of the common assignments, or is it particular to a discipline?

- **What are some key terms in the assignment that might give you a clue about what is being asked of you?** Terms like *comment, consider,* and *discuss* do not point to a particular purpose. *Classify, illustrate, report,* and *survey* are frequently associated with the task of **informing.** *Analyze, compare, explain,* and *reflect* are often associated with **interpreting.** *Agree, assess, defend,* and *refute* go with the task of **arguing.**

- **How long is the paper supposed to be, and when is it due?** Many topics must be narrowed to be completed on time within the specified number of pages. Some instructors may note due dates for progress reports or first drafts. The length of the paper and the amount of time you are given to complete it are good indications of the importance of the assignment.

- **What format is required for the assignment?** Some assignments, like a laboratory report, must follow a conventional form. When research is assigned, instructors generally will prefer a particular style of documentation. Check with your instructor. (*See the documentation sections, Tabs 6–8.*)

4 Writing Online

Until recently, the college classroom was the primary site of learning in higher education. It is true that in ancient Greece, Socrates's students followed him through Athens, and even in the twenty-first century, instructors may hold classes outdoors on a fine spring day. In the history of education, however, nothing has revolutionized the place where education happens like the computer. Technology now makes it possible to transcend the constraints of the clock, the calendar, and the car and to engage in educational activities twenty-four hours a day, seven days a week (24/7).

4a Explore the virtual landscape.

Computers are creating new possibilities for communication and inquiry, for commerce, and even for building community. All of these activities are taking place in an unmapped virtual landscape of computer networks called **cyberspace.**

Making the Best Net Connection

Try to select an Internet service provider (ISP) that offers full Internet access with services, one that is more than simply a connection to the Internet. A real Net connection makes it much easier to receive campus mail on a home computer and to use campus courseware. Some students have problems working at home with ISPs that limit access in certain ways, and some courseware packages work well with one browser (software that allows you to view pages on the World Wide Web) but not another.

Although we can map the academic territory of the university with courses, departments, and majors, it is difficult to map cyberspace, or the **Internet,** which is a vast international network of computers. Within the imaginative spaces of the Internet, we create **virtual realities**—places that are almost real, or real as media for communication but not as physical locations. It is within this virtual reality of cyberspace that people are creating new rhetorical forms and new cultural spaces: e-mail, chat rooms, MUDs and MOOs, news groups, discussion lists, and the World Wide Web, to name a few.

If you own a computer or have access to one at home but are not already connected to the Internet, the following Web sites can help you choose an Internet service provider (ISP), which can connect you to this important new resource. Most ISPs charge a fee for their services.

- *C/Net Internet Services* <http://www.cnet.com/Content/Reports/ Special/ISP/checklist.html>: This resource offers reviews of Internet service providers and helps you find the ones available in your area.

- *The List of ISPs* <http://thelist.internet.com/us.html>: This resource provides a comprehensive list of Internet service providers, with links to more information and the providers' Web sites.

It takes time to learn about using computers and about the countless opportunities that are available online. Be patient with your learning process, and remember that even expert users experience computer glitches. Rely on friends and classmates to share their knowledge. Take a playful approach, and don't be afraid to ask questions or try something new. Save your work often, and remember that if you make a mistake, there's usually an "Undo" command.

Here are three informational sites for newcomers to the Net:

- *Learn the Net* <http://www.learnthenet.com/english/index.html>.

- *Centerspan Internet Tutorial* <http://www.centerspan.org/tutorial/net.htm>.

- *Online Glossaries and Acronyms* <http://www.freeality.com/glossari.htm>. Find out what those alphabet soup letters mean!

4b Make use of e-mail.

E-mail, messages that are sent over the Internet, is the common currency of the electronic frontier and the most frequently used method of written communication in the world today. Once you are connected to the Internet and have learned a few simple procedures, you are ready to send e-mail to

- ask your professor a question between classes.

- continue an interesting conversation after class.

- request clarification about a writing assignment.

- send documents created using a word processor or other software as attachments.

- submit a draft of a paper to a classmate for his or her comments (peer review) or to a consultant in your school's writing center.

Remember, however, that although technology is always available, people are not. Just as your professor may schedule office hours in a campus building, she or he may tell you that you can send e-mail any time but that you should expect an answer only during certain periods of time.

4c Learn the netiquette of cybercultures.

As with any writing where your audience does not know you personally, in cyberspace you are what you write. Others get to know you through words and words alone. Don't underestimate the power of electronic text to convey who you are, to construct your writerly presence or ethos. (*For more on ethos, see Tab 2, p. 33.*)

Social encounters on the Internet are often conducted through text alone, without seeing faces or hearing voices. But don't forget that out there on the Internet, real people and real communities are involved in creating a shared culture. A culture consists of languages, values, artifacts, beliefs, behaviors, customs, history, arts, and folklore. In this section, we invite you to consider some of the cultural aspects of cyberspace.

The term **netiquette** combines the words *Internet* and *etiquette* to form a new word that stands for good manners in cyberspace. Knowing what constitutes good conduct in cyberspace will help you feel more at ease using the Internet. Here are a few tips to keep in mind as you move from one virtual space to another:

- **Remember that you are interacting with real humans,** not machines, and practice kindness, patience, and good humor.

- **Use accurate subject headers to indicate your topic.**

- **Limit each e-mail to a single topic,** particularly if you are sending e-mail to lists, news groups, or conferences. Two or three short, one-topic e-mails often have more impact than one overloaded message.

- **Use words economically, and edit carefully.** Readers' eyes tire fast when they encounter all lowercase letters or text that lacks appropriate punctuation.

- **Bear in mind that without cues such as facial expressions, body language, and vocal intonation, it is easy to be misunderstood in a virtual setting.** When you are writing to a friend, go ahead and use slang ("whatcha think?"), abbreviations (BTW, LOL), and smiley face symbols like :-). However, if you are inquiring about a job, for example, your e-mail should be less like a casual phone conversation and more like a formal business letter. Be extra careful about humor that could be misread as sarcasm. Misunderstandings can escalate quickly into flaming, the sending of angry, inflammatory posts that use heated language. A good writer does what is necessary to show consideration to readers.

- **Avoid ALL CAPS.** Typing in all caps is considered shouting. (If italics or underlining is not available, though, it is acceptable to use all caps for titles.)

- **Remember that your e-mail message can be reproduced.** Don't say anything you don't want attributed to you or forwarded to others. You are not really anonymous online. E-mail comes marked with the route it took to get to a receiver. More and more people are reporting e-mail abuse and offensive e-mails to their ISPs, and ISPs are taking action to enforce their appropriate-use policies. You can almost always be traced. Even if you intend a practical joke, your words online can backfire.

TextConnex

Emoticons

In informal online messages, writers often use emoticons, sideways faces created by typing marks of punctuation: :-) for happy, :-(for sad, ;-) for a wink, and so on. Emoticons add emphasis to your online message, letting readers know how you want your comments to be taken. They are fun, but like the exclamation point, their effectiveness decreases if they are used too often.

- **Include a sufficient portion of the previous text** when responding to an e-mail to keep the conversation flowing and to provide context.
- **Always seek permission to use other people's ideas.** Electronic text makes sharing ideas easy. If you use another person's online thoughts or words, seek permission first, and always acknowledge the other person properly. Never forward another person's words without consent.
- **Never copy other people's words and present them as your own.** This practice, known as **plagiarism,** is always wrong, whether the pilfered text comes from an electronic or a printed source. Sources of information found on the Internet must be cited accurately and properly. (*See the documentation sections, Tabs 6–8, for help with citing Internet sources.*)
- **Include your name and contact information at the end of every e-mail you send.** Not all e-mail applications display the sender's name as well as the e-mail address, so your reader may not know who is writing unless you identify yourself. Putting your contact information at the end of every message or post also makes it easier for others to give you credit for your words and ideas.

4d Take advantage of opportunities for online learning.

You may be taking this course online or in a computer lab, but even in a traditional classroom, the Internet can support learning.

- **Course Web sites.** Your professor may have a Web site for your course. If so, check it out for late-breaking announcements, course assignments (and their due dates), and Web resources.

TEXTCONNEX

Online Resources for Learning across the Curriculum

Netiquette <http://www.albion.com/netiquette/book>: A comprehensive text on netiquette by journalist Virginia Shea.

Simplified Plans of Action for Common Types of Question Words <http://www.coun.uvic.ca/learn/program/hndouts/simple.html>: Actions to take when you come across certain words in essay or test questions.

- **Networked classrooms.** A networked classroom allows for real-time discussion and is designed to facilitate class interaction. Unlike an oral discussion, an online discussion allows all students to "talk" at the same time in class. Because you are discussing a topic in writing, you can save your ideas and comments and use them in the first draft of a paper more easily than if you were discussing the subject orally. Online interactive class sessions also help you become more aware of audience and purpose in your writing because the audience is talking back to you and can ask you to clarify your purpose.

  In addition to offering opportunities for real-time interaction, a networked classroom makes it possible for the teacher to post a daily assignment. Students can log on, join the discussion, and complete the assignment online. Archiving, or logging, enables you to save and print a conversation in its entirety. This function can be helpful if you are getting feedback on a piece of writing or if you are discussing a topic you will need to explore more fully in writing.

- **Online collaboration.** As in the networked classroom, e-mail, online chats, bulletin boards (online forums where people can post comments), and other discussion resources enable you to talk about assignments and course texts with your peers. These discussions can help you test the water and clarify your thoughts as you respond to assignments and work through writing projects.

5   Learning in English as a Second Language

To some extent, the university presents everyone with an unfamiliar culture and its languages. The language of anthropology, for example, probably sounds strange and new to most students, including those who

For MULTILINGUAL STUDENTS

Online Resources

- *Dave's ESL Café* <http://www.eslcafe.com>
- *SchMOOze University* <http://schmooze.hunter.cuny.edu:8888>

have been speaking English all their lives. If you spoke another language before learning English, you already have experience trying to feel at home in a new culture and working to acquire a new language.

Asking questions of your professors and others, as well as consulting guidebooks like your course textbooks, can help with your learning. So too can recognizing specialized vocabulary, including common English words that have a special meaning when they are used within a discipline. Like all students, you will have to engage in writing to learn and in critical reading and thinking to succeed in college.

5a Become aware of cultural differences in communication.

Because you are familiar with at least two languages and cultures, you already know that there is more than one way to interact politely and effectively with other people. In fact, you may wonder about the way people communicate in U.S. college classrooms. Your classmates may pride themselves on being direct, yet you may think that they sound almost impolite in their enthusiasm to make a point. They may consider themselves to be explicit and precise; you may wonder why they are explaining things that attentive people should be able to figure out for themselves.

U.S. colleges place particular emphasis on openly exchanging views, clearly stating opinions, and explicitly supporting judgments with examples, observations, and reasons. You may be reluctant to participate because you are worried about an "accent" or about the fine points of grammar or pronunciation. Don't worry. Communication is your first priority, so gather up your confidence and join the conversation. As a student, you are expected to do the following:

- Participate actively in small group discussions.
- Ask and answer questions during class discussions.
- Approach instructors and fellow students outside of class when you need additional help.

5b Use writing to learn more about English.

To develop your fluency in English, get into the habit of writing every day.

- **Write a personal journal.** Using English to explore your thoughts, feelings, and questions about your studies and your life in college will help make you feel more at home in the language.

- **Keep a writer's notebook.** Every day, write down a quotation from something you have read, and then either comment on it or put the idea into your own words. Write down bits of dialogue you overhear. Make lists of words and phrases that are new to you; many of these will turn out to be English **idioms,** words and phrases with a special meanings not necessarily included in a simple dictionary definition. Go over these lists with your writing group, a friend, or a tutor in the writing center.

- **Write letters in English.** Letters are a good way to practice the informal style used in conversation. Write to out-of-town acquaintances who don't speak your first language. Write a letter to the college newspaper about some change you think needs to be made at the college or about what someone else has suggested in a letter to the editor. You can also write brief notes either on paper or through e-mail to instructors, tutors, librarians, secretaries, and other native speakers of English. Write notes to your roommates, dorm manager, repair person, and others whom you encounter on campus and off. Written communication will sometimes help you achieve your purpose more efficiently than leaving telephone messages.

5c Use the tools that are available for multilingual students.

The style of written communication favored in U.S. colleges is often referred to simply as "good writing." This handbook explains this academic style and its variations. This style—which is sometimes described as analytical and argumentative—reflects the Western cultural tradition, one of many traditions in the world.

The following reference books can also help you as you write papers for your college courses. You can purchase them in your college's bookstore or find copies in the reference room of your college's library.

1. ESL dictionary. A good dictionary designed especially for second-language students can be a useful source of information about word meanings. Ordinary dictionaries frequently define difficult words with other difficult words. In the *American Heritage Dictionary*, for example, the word *haze* is defined as "Atmospheric moisture, dust, smoke, and vapor suspended to form a partially opaque condition." An ESL dictionary defines it more simply as "A light mist or smoke."

Do not confuse ESL dictionaries with bilingual or "translation" dictionaries. Translation dictionaries frequently oversimplify word meanings. So too do abridged dictionaries because they do not indicate shades of meaning.

Like all standard English dictionaries, an ESL dictionary includes instructions for its use. These instructions explain the abbreviations used in the entries. They also list the special notations used for words classified as *slang, vulgar, informal, nonstandard,* or another category worthy of special attention. In the ESL/Learner's Edition of the *Random House Webster's Dictionary of American English* (1997), you will find "pig out" as the sixth entry under the word *pig:*

> **Pig out** (no obj) Slang. to eat too much food: *We pigged out on pizza last night.*

The entry tells you that "pig out" does not take a direct object ("no obj") and that its use is very informal ("Slang"), appropriate in talking with classmates but not in writing formal papers. You will hear a great deal of slang on your college campus, on the radio, and on TV. Make a list of slang phrases, and look them up later. If you don't find them listed in your standard or ESL dictionary, check for them in a dictionary of American slang.

The dictionary will help you with spelling, syllabication, pronunciation, definitions, word origins, and usage. The several meanings of a word are arranged first according to part of speech and then from most common to least common meaning. Examine the entry for the word *academic* in the ESL/Learner's Edition:

> **ac.a.dem.ic** /ˌækəˈdɛmɪk/ *adj.* **1.** (before a noun) of or relating to a school, esp. one for higher education: *an academic institution.* **2.** Of or relating to school subjects that teach general intellectual skills rather than specific job skills: *academic subjects like English and mathematics.* **3.** Not practical or directly useful: *Whether she wanted to come or not is an academic question because she's here now.—n.* (count) **4.** A student or teacher at a college or university —**ac'a.dem'i.cal.ly,** *adv.*

Note that nouns are identified as count or noncount, indicating whether you can place a number in front of the noun and indicate a plural. You can say "Four academics joined the group," so when *academic* is used as a noun, it is a count noun. *Honesty* is a noncount noun.

When you look up words or phrases in the dictionary, add them to your personal list. Talk the list over with classmates. They will be happy to explain particular, up-to-date uses of the words and phrases you are learning. To expand your vocabulary, consult a thesaurus for synonyms and use the most precise term. (*For more on the thesaurus, see Tab 10: Editing for Clarity, p. 375.*)

2. Dictionary of American idioms.   As we explained earlier, an idiom is an expression that is peculiar to a particular language and cannot be understood by looking at the individual words. "To catch a bus" is an idiom.

3. Desk encyclopedias.   You will find one-volume encyclopedias on every subject from U.S. history to classical or biblical allusions in the reference room of your college's library. You may find it helpful to look up people, places, and events that are new to you for a quick identification, especially if the person, place, or event is referred to often in U.S. culture.

I like to do first drafts at night, when
I'm tired, and then do the surgical
work in the morning when I'm sharp.

—ALEX HALEY

Writing Papers

2 Writing Papers

6. Reading, Thinking, Writing: The Critical Connection 21
   a. Reading critically 21
   b. Thinking critically 24
   c. Writing critically 29

7. Planning 34
   a. Learning how to approach assignments 34
   b. Exploring your ideas 37

8. Drafting 42
   a. Developing your thesis 43
   b. Preparing an outline 45
   c. Developing your ideas 47
   d. Writing purposeful paragraphs 52
   e. Using online tools for drafting 58

9. Revising 59
   a. Focusing on the purpose of your writing 59
   b. Testing your thesis 60
   c. Reviewing the whole paper and its parts 61
   d. Revising and editing sentences 62
   e. Collaborating with readers online and in print 69
   f. Using online tools for revising 73

6   Reading, Thinking, Writing: The Critical Connection

Critical readers, thinkers, and writers get intellectually involved. They recognize that meanings and values are made, not found, so they pose pertinent questions, note significant features, examine relationships, and consider the credibility of what they read, see, and hear. The strategies in this chapter will help you read, think, and write critically.

6a   Read critically.

1. Preview. Critical reading begins with **previewing:** a quick review of the author, publication information, title, headings, visuals, first and last paragraphs, and first sentences of the body paragraphs. As you preview, be skeptical: just because something is in print does not mean that it is true. Whenever possible, speculate about the following:

- **Author:** Who wrote this piece? What are the writer's credentials? Who is the writer's employer? What is the writer's occupation? Age? What do you know about his or her interests and values?
- **Context:** Where, when, and by whom was this piece of writing published? What are the facts of its publication?
  - **For a book:** Are you looking at the original publication, or is this a reprint from another source? What is the reputation of the publisher? University presses, for example, are very selective about the books they publish, whereas a vanity press—one that requires authors to pay for their own publication—is not selective at all.
  - **For an article in a periodical:** Look at the list of editors and their affiliations. What do you know about the journal, magazine, or newspaper in which this writing appears?
  - **For a Web page:** Who created the page? A Web page named for a political candidate, for example, may actually have been put on the Web by his or her opponents. (*See the box, "Critically Evaluating Web Resources" on pp. 173–74.*)
- **Purpose:** What do the title and first and last paragraphs tell you about the purpose of this piece? What might have provoked the writer to write it? Do you think the main purpose will be to entertain, to teach, to persuade, or something else? Are there visuals in this piece? What do the pictures or other

visual aids suggest about the frame of reference for this piece of writing? What do the headings tell you?

- **Audience:** Whom do you suspect the writer is trying to entertain, teach, persuade, or influence? Is the writer addressing you or people like you?

2. Annotate.   Imagine yourself in a dialogue with the writer. **Annotate** by underlining or circling words, phrases, and sentences as you read and by writing notes in the margin.

- Underline or circle words and phrases that capture the point of the text—the equivalent of a joke's punch line.

- Record your reactions. Agree or disagree with the writer. Ask "why?" or "how?"

Sounds more like idealism— and ideals are important.   Once upon a time I held these beliefs about divorce: that everyone who does it could have chosen not to do it. That it's a lazy way out of marital problems. That it selfishly puts personal happiness ahead of family integrity. Now I tremble for my (ignorance.) It's easy, in fortunate times, to forget about the ambush that could leave your head reeling: serious mental or

Why would anyone divorce a sick spouse?   physical illness, death in the family, abandonment, financial calamity, humiliation, violence, despair.

—BARBARA KINGSOLVER, "Stone Soup"

- At important intervals, pause and put into your own words what the writer is doing and saying:

Kingsolver used to believe that only selfish people got divorced; now she thinks that bad events may lead to divorce.

3. Analyze.   You **analyze** a text by identifying its significant parts and examining how those parts are related to each other to make a whole. Ask and answer questions about the *what, how,* and *why* of a text:

- **Topic and point:** Identify what the text is about and the main point the writer makes about that topic. Usually writers state the main point at the beginning and end of their text, often as a response to some question or issue the topic raises. Sometimes the point is signaled by such words as *in short, hence, therefore,* or *my point is.*

- **Writer's stance and voice:** A writer's **stance**—where he or she stands in relation to the audience and subject—involves his or her style, values, and way of establishing credibility. Does the writer seem to be speaking *at, to,* or *with* the audience? What about the writer's **voice**? How does the writer sound—like a reasonable judge, an enthusiastic preacher, a thoughtful teacher, or a reassuring friend?

- **Purpose:** To what extent is the writer's purpose informative? Interpretive? Argumentative?

- **Development of ideas:** What kind of support does the writer rely on to develop the main point? Does the writer define key terms? Tell relevant stories? Provide logical reasons? (*For more on ways of developing ideas, see Chapter 8, Drafting, pp. 47–52.*)

- **Appeals to emotion:** Does the text use any words, phrases, clichés, images, or examples that are emotionally charged? How much does the writer depend on emotional appeals to support his or her point?

- **Effect:** What is the text's effect on your images, ideas, beliefs, and actions?

4. Summarize.   A **summary** communicates what you have learned from analyzing a text. Writers often use a one-paragraph summary of the topic, main point, and major supporting points to report their understanding of a text to others. Writing a clear and accurate summary of a complex text is a difficult task. These suggestions may make that task a bit easier:

- **Write down the text's main point.** Compose a sentence that identifies the text, the writer, what the writer does (reports, explores, analyzes, argues), and the most important point the writer makes about the topic.

- **Divide the text into sections.** To develop the main point, writers move from one subtopic to another or from the statement of an idea to the reasons, evidence, and examples that support it.

- **In one or two sentences, sum up what each of the text's sections says.** When you summarize, you in effect compose your own topic sentence for each major section of the text.

- **Combine your sentence stating the writer's main point with the sentences summarizing each of the text's major sections.** Now you have a first draft of a summary. Read the draft to see if it makes sense. Add, remove, or change parts as needed.

5. Synthesize.   Whether you realize it or not, you **synthesize** material every day. When you hear contrasting accounts of a party from two different people, you assess the reliability and potential bias

CHARTING the TERRITORY

Mapping Your Topic

When you are analyzing a text within the framework of a particular discipline, you might begin your analysis by comparing the text you are studying with other texts written on the same topic but from different perspectives—from different places on the disciplinary map.

- **What issues might the topic raise for members of different disciplines?** For historians, the reunification of Germany might raise issues about top-down versus bottom-up modes of change. For economists, the interesting issue might be something else, such as the increased unemployment caused by privatizing East Germany's industry.
- **How would members of different disciplines investigate the issues that interest them?** What data would historians or economists want? Where and how would they get the data?
- **What kinds of conclusions do members of different disciplines tend to expect and accept?** Historians expect and accept arguments about how people have or have not changed their lives, conditions, or ideas over time. Economists tend to expect and accept conclusions based on some more or less unchanging law or principle, such as the law of supply and demand.

of each source; you select the information that is most pertinent to you; you evaluate the story that each one tells; and you finally create a composite, or synthesis, of what you think really went on. When you synthesize information from two or more texts, you follow the same process.

6b   Think critically.

Critical thinking is fundamental to all college work and to life in a democratic society. Thinking critically means getting involved, not necessarily finding fault. Critical thinkers never simply gather information and present it without question. They pose questions about what they see, hear, and read.

Evaluating a text's argument is not a game of "gotcha," an attempt to catch the bad guys in order to be seen as a good guy. Its purpose is more critical and thoughtful: to figure out a text's promise and limitations, strengths and weaknesses.

1. Recognizing an argument. The word *argument,* when used in the context of critical thinking, does not mean a shouting match. In the college classroom and in reasoned debate outside the classroom, an **argument** means a path of reasoning aimed at demonstrating the truth or falsehood of an assertion. The assertion must be arguable: it must be on an issue about which reasonable people can disagree.

For example, a journalism student writing for the school paper might make the following assertion:

> As Saturday's game illustrates, the Buckeyes are on their way to winning the Big Ten title.

2. Analyzing and evaluating an argument. There are a number of ways to analyze an argument and evaluate its effectiveness. Two common methods are (1) to concentrate on the type of reasoning the writer is using and (2) to question the logical relation of a writer's claims, grounds, and warrants, using the Toulmin method.

Type of reasoning Writers may use either inductive or deductive reasoning to make an argument. When writers use **inductive reasoning,** they do not prove that the argument is true; instead they convince reasonable people that it is probable by presenting evidence (facts and statistics, anecdotes, and expert opinion). When writers use **deductive reasoning,** on the other hand, they make two or more assertions (called *premises*) and then draw a conclusion.

CHARTING the TERRITORY

The Scientific Method

Inductive reasoning is also called the **scientific method.** Scientists gather data from experiments, surveys, and careful observations and formulate hypotheses—arguments— to explain these data. They then test their hypotheses by collecting additional information.

If the journalism student who is writing about the football team is reasoning inductively, she will present a number of facts—her evidence—and then draw the conclusion that seems probable:

FACT 1 With three games remaining, the Buckeyes have a two-game lead over the second-place Badgers.

FACT 2 The Buckeyes' final three opponents have a combined record of 10 wins and 17 losses.

FACT 3   The Badgers lost their two star players to season-ending injuries last week.

FACT 4   The Buckeyes' last three games will be played at home, where they are undefeated this season, giving them the home-field advantage.

LEARNING in COLLEGE

Assessing Evidence in an Inductive Argument

- **Is it accurate?** Make sure that any facts presented as evidence are correct.
- **Is it relevant?** Check to see if the evidence is clearly connected to the point being made.
- **Is it representative?** Make sure that the writer's conclusion is supported by evidence gathered from a sample that accurately reflects the larger population (for example, it has the same proportion of men and women, older and younger people, and so on). If the writer is using an example, make sure that the example is typical and not a unique situation.
- **Is it sufficient?** Evaluate whether there is enough evidence to satisfy questioning readers.

A reader would evaluate this student's argument by judging the quality of her evidence, using the criteria listed in the box above.

If the journalism student is using deductive reasoning, however, the reasonableness of her conclusion will depend on the accuracy of her premises.

PREMISE   Football teams with a two-game lead in their conference in early November usually go on to win their division.

PREMISE   As of November 8, the Ohio State Buckeyes have a two-game lead in the Big Ten.

CONCLUSION   The Buckeyes are probably on their way to winning the title.

A reader would evaluate this argument by deciding whether to accept the two premises. For example, a reader might question whether most football teams with two-game leads go on to win their conference.

In college, deductive reasoning predominates in philosophy and in other humanities disciplines. However, you should be alert to both types of reasoning in all your college courses and in your life.

LEARNING in COLLEGE

Evaluating Claims

- Are the terms in the claim clear and precise?
- Is the claim too absolute to be considered fair, or does it include qualifying words such as *might* or *possibly*?
- Is the claim merely a statement of fact or a statement that few would argue with?
- To what extent does the claim respond to a question or raise an issue of real concern to its audience (for example, the members of a discipline)?

Toulmin method Philosopher Stephen Toulmin has developed another useful way to understand and implement logical thinking. His analysis of arguments is based on *claims* (assertions about a topic), *grounds* (reasons and evidence), and *warrants* (assumptions or principles that link the grounds to the claims). Consider the following sentence from an argument by a student in an American literature class:

As *Death in the Afternoon* shows, Ernest Hemingway treats bullfighting as the essence of manliness.

This example, like all logical arguments, has three facets:

- **Logical arguments make a claim.** A **claim** is the same thing as a *point* or a *thesis:* it is an assertion about a topic. It is important to remember that a thesis says something arguable about a topic. A weak thesis does not make a claim and therefore cannot be argued. (*For more on theses, see pp. 29–32 and Chapter 8, Drafting, pp. 43–45.*)

  WEAK CLAIM   Hemingway writes about bullfighting.

  STRONG CLAIM   Hemingway writes about bullfighting as an equal contest between man and nature.

- **Logical arguments present grounds for the claim.** **Grounds** consist of the reasons and evidence (facts and statistics, anecdotes, and expert opinion) that support the claim. In literary criticism, for example, a literary work often serves as the grounds for a claim. In the claim "As *Death in the Afternoon* shows . . . ," the book itself is the source of the grounds, the reasons and evidence, for the critic's claim that Hemingway's writing identifies bullfighting as the essence of manliness.

Evaluating the Grounds for a Claim

- To support his or her assertions, does the writer present data, cite statistics, quote authorities, or tell anecdotes (brief narratives)?
- Does the writer use different kinds of evidence, or does he or she rely on only one type?
- Are the writer's reasons and evidence relevant to the claim or offtrack?
- Does the writer present enough evidence?
- What methods did the writer use to collect data? (*Also see p. 26 for more on assessing evidence.*)

- **Logical arguments depend on assumptions to link the grounds to the claim.** When you analyze an argument, you should be aware of the unstated assumptions, or **warrants,** that underlie both the claim and the grounds that support it. For example, by selecting *Death in the Afternoon* to support the claim that "Hemingway treats bullfighting as the essence of manliness," the student writer assumes that in a particular text, an action like bullfighting can function as a symbol.

  Warrants differ from discipline to discipline and even from one school of thought to another within a single discipline. If you were studying the topic of bullfighting and its place in Spanish society in a sociology course, for example, you would probably make different arguments with different warrants than would the writer of a literary analysis. You might argue that bullfighting serves as a safe outlet for its fans' aggressive feelings. Your warrant would be that sports can have socially useful purposes.

Evaluating Hidden Assumptions

- What does the reader have to assume—take for granted—to accept the reasons and evidence offered in support of the claim?
- Does this assumption reflect bias—a negative or positive attitude—on the part of the writer?

As you read the writing of others and as you write yourself, look for unstated assumptions and bring them to the surface. Be aware as well that hidden assumptions sometimes show **bias,** positive or negative inclinations that can manipulate unwary readers.

3. Recognizing common logical fallacies.

Even expert logicians can drift off course in their enthusiasm to make a point. These errors in direction are called **fallacies,** or mistakes in logic. Use the box on pages 30–31 to help you identify fallacies when you read and avoid them when you write.

6c Write critically.

Sharpening your ability to think critically and to express your views effectively is the main purpose of undergraduate study. When you write critically, you gain a voice in the important discussions and major decisions of our society. Writing can make a difference.

In every classroom, you will gain practice in addressing issues that are important in the larger community. Selecting a topic that you care about will give you the energy to think matters through and to make cogent arguments. Of course, you will have to go beyond your personal emotions about an issue to make the most convincing case. You will also have to empathize with potential readers who may disagree with you about a subject that is close to your heart.

1. Find a topic worth writing about. Arguments occur in a context of debate and usually concern one or more of the following questions:

- What is true?
- What is good?
- What is to be done?

People seek answers to these questions, but they often disagree about which answers are best. To enter into the debate, you have to figure out what is at issue in these disagreements, where you stand on the issue, and why your position is reasonable.

Your purpose in presenting your position to others is not to win but to take part in the ongoing conversation. As you present your argument, keep in mind that reasonable people can see things differently. Acknowledge and respect the views of others. Negotiating differences should become part of your purpose.

2. Make a strong claim. Advancing a strong, debatable thesis on a topic of interest to the discipline or to the public is key to writing a successful argument. Keep in mind, however, that writing itself is a

COMMON LOGICAL FALLACIES

Non sequitur: A conclusion that does not logically follow from the evidence presented or one that is based on irrelevant evidence.

> EXAMPLE Assistance to single mothers is provided under Aid to Families with Dependent Children, thereby encouraging out-of-wedlock births. [*Are unwed mothers really motivated by government programs?*]

Red herring: An argument that diverts attention from the true issue by concentrating on something irrelevant.

> EXAMPLE Hemingway's book *Death in the Afternoon* is not successful because it glorifies the brutal sport of bullfighting. [*Why can't a book about a brutal sport be successful? The statement is irrelevant.*]

Bandwagon: An argument that depends on going along with the crowd, on the false assumption that truth can be determined by a popularity contest.

> EXAMPLE Everybody knows that Hemingway is preoccupied with the theme of death in his novels. [*How do we know that "everybody" agrees with this statement?*]

Ad hominem: A personal attack on someone who disagrees with you rather than on the person's argument.

> EXAMPLE The district attorney is a lazy political hack, so naturally she opposes streamlining the court system. [*Even if the district attorney usually supports her party's position, does that make her wrong about this issue?*]

Circular reasoning: An argument that restates the point rather than supporting it with reasonable evidence.

> EXAMPLE The wealthy should pay more taxes because taxes should be higher for people with higher incomes. [*Why should wealthy people pay more taxes? The rest of the statement doesn't answer this question; it just restates the position.*]

tool for thinking through your position on a wide variety of issues. As you think, write, and learn about your topic, you will develop, clarify, and sometimes entirely change your views. Think of yourself as a potter working with soft clay. Your thesis is still forming as you work with the topic.

Begging the question: A form of circular reasoning that assumes the truth of a questionable opinion.

EXAMPLE   The president's poor relationship with the military has weakened the armed forces. [*Does the president really have a poor relationship with the military?*]

Hasty generalization: A conclusion based on inadequate evidence.

EXAMPLE   Temperatures across the United States last year exceeded the fifty-year average by two degrees, thus proving that global warming is a reality. [*Is this evidence enough to prove this very broad conclusion?*]

Biased language: Words with strong positive or negative overtones that are designed to sway opinion.

EXAMPLE   The opposition of self-indulgent hippies added to the burdens of our government during the Vietnam War. [*Does "self-indulgent hippies" accurately describe the people who objected to the war, or is it meant to evoke negative reactions?*]

Either/or fallacy: The idea that a complicated issue can be resolved by resorting to one of only two options when in reality there are additional choices.

EXAMPLE   Either the state legislature will raise taxes or our state's economy will suffer. [*Are these really the only two possibilities?*]

False analogy: The assumption that some similarities between two things indicate total similarity between the two.

EXAMPLE   If the United States negotiates with aggressive nations, we will pay for our weakness the way England did when it negotiated with Hitler before World War II. [*Is there a danger of war every time the United States negotiates with an aggressive nation?*]

Your personal feelings are not open to debate and so cannot serve as the thesis for an argument. If you write, "I feel that life in the ghetto is not very pleasant," there is nothing to debate because you are saying something about yourself rather than about the ghetto. But when William Julius Wilson writes, in his article "When Work

Disappears," that "Joblessness in the ghetto is not a result of welfare dependency," he is making a debatable claim on an issue of real concern. (*For more on theses, see Chapter 8, pp. 43–45.*)

3. Support and develop your claim with evidence.   The intelligent selection and careful documentation of evidence—facts and statistics, anecdotes, and expert opinion—will determine whether you make a credible case.

- **Facts and statistics.** Facts and statistics can be convincing support for a claim. Be aware, however, that people on different sides of an issue can interpret the same facts and statistics differently or can cite different facts and statistics to prove their point.

  In the article "When Work Disappears," Wilson argues that joblessness prevails in so many inner-city neighborhoods because jobs have disappeared from the ghetto. Wilson supports his claim that work has disappeared from the ghetto with the following facts:

  > In the neighborhood of Woodlawn, on the South Side of Chicago, there were more than 800 commercial and industrial establishments in 1950. Today, it is estimated that only 100 are left.

- **Anecdotes.** An anecdote is a brief narrative used as an illustration to support a claim. Stories appeal to the emotions as well as to the intellect and can be very effective in making an argument. Be especially careful to check anecdotes for logical fallacies (*see pp. 30–31*).

  In "When Work Disappears," for example, Wilson uses quotations from long-term residents in several different urban ghettos in metropolitan Chicago. These residents contrast life in their neighborhoods today with their memories of local employment opportunities in the 1950s.

- **Expert opinion.** The views of authorities in a given field can also be powerful support for a claim. Make sure that the expert you cite has the proper credentials to comment on the issue you are writing about. Wilson, for example, cites a former Secretary of Labor to support the claim that educational reform is part of the solution to the problem of joblessness:

  > Ray Marshall, former Secretary of Labor, points out that Japan and Germany have developed policies designed to increase the number of workers with "higher-order thinking skills."

In well-written arguments, reasoning often relies on research. As you find and read a variety of sources, you will figure out your claim and amass the evidence you need to support that claim. You will also want to demonstrate your credibility to readers by properly quoting and documenting the information you have gathered from your sources. (*See the guidelines for documenting sources in Tabs 6–8.*)

4. Appeal to your audience.   You want your readers to see you as *reasonable, ethical,* and *empathetic*—qualities that promote communication among people who have differences. You display the quality of your thought, character, and feelings—what the ancient Greeks called **logos, ethos,** and **pathos**—by the way that you argue for what you believe.

Giving reasons and supplying evidence for your position and arguing responsibly by avoiding fallacies establish your logos. (*For more on fallacies, see pp. 30–31.*) You also need to show that you are sincere (ethos) and that you care about your readers' feelings (pathos). For example, you might refer to a quality or belief you share with others, even those who disagree with you. Establishing common ground in this way will make readers more open to your argument.

- Do you share an interest in the same issue, topic, or field?
- Do you have overlapping goals or values?

When you read your argument to yourself or to peers, pay attention to how you are coming across. What would readers who have never met you think of you after reading what you have to say?

5. Consider opposing viewpoints.   Don't ignore **counterarguments**—substantiated claims that challenge or refute your thesis. Instead, think critically about them, and try to refute or accommodate them. For example, you might present at least one counterargument and then refute it, perhaps by presenting evidence that shows why it is open to question. If you are unable to refute a counterargument, you can often accommodate it by qualifying your thesis with words such as *likely, usually, most,* or *some.* Another tactic is to make a more specific statement of the conditions for or exceptions to your thesis, such as, "*If* inflation continues, X" or "*Until* cloning is perfected, Y." These kinds of qualifications often appear in the conclusion of an argument, where it is appropriate to include a more subtle version of the paper's opening thesis.

6. Check for errors in your logic.   Checking the logic of your own writing is probably the greatest challenge to your ability to read critically. It is essential to step outside yourself and assess your argument objectively for errors in reasoning. Use the chart of Common Logical

Fallacies on pages 30–31 to test your reasoning. Of course, nothing is more helpful than hearing and responding to your classmates' questions. Peer review is one of the best tools for developing critical thinking and writing skills. (*For advice on peer review, see Chapter 9, pp. 70–71.*)

7 Planning

A large part of learning in college involves writing papers that contribute to the ongoing conversation of educated people. The advice in this chapter will help you determine the kind of writing a particular assignment requires and get you started on a first draft.

7a Learn how to approach assignments.

1. Write about a question.   Whether you choose your topic or your topic is assigned, most topics must be narrowed. To arrive at a manageable topic, it helps to try to write about a question. To develop questions, play the *I wonder / They say / I think* game:

- **I wonder:** Taking the subject matter of the course or the assignment as your point of departure, list concepts and issues that you wonder about.
- **They say:** Reviewing your class notes, course reading, online postings to discussion groups, and scholarly bibliographies, check to see what topics and issues others in the field say are important. Jot down relevant information, ideas, and issues.
- **I think:** Choosing an item or two that you have listed, figure out what you think about it, and consider what purposes you might fulfill by writing about it. Give your curiosity free rein. Connect your interests to the framework of the course.

The particular course you are taking defines a range of questions that are appropriate within a given discipline. Here are examples of the way your course would help define the questions you might ask if, for example, you were writing about Thomas Jefferson:

U.S. history: How did Jefferson's ownership of slaves affect his public stance on slavery?

Political science: To what extent did Jefferson's conflict with the courts redefine the balance of power among the three branches of government?

Education: Given his beliefs about the relationship between democracy and public education, what would Jefferson think about contemporary proposals for a school voucher system?

2. Ask questions about your audience.
Who makes up your audience? Instructors are the primary readers for students' work, of course, but they represent a larger group of readers who have an interest or a stake in the paper's topic. An education professor, for example, reads and evaluates a paper as a representative of other students in the course, experts in educational policy, school board members, public school principals, and parents of school-age children, among others.

Here are some questions to answer about your audience:

- What are the demographics of this audience? What is the education level, social status, occupation, gender, and ethnicity of a typical audience member?

- What common assumptions and differences of opinion do these readers bring to the issue?

- What images do they have, what ideas do they hold, and what actions do they support?

- What is your goal in writing for this audience? Do you want to intensify, clarify, complicate, or change their assumptions and opinions?

3. Be clear about your purpose.
What kind of assignment are you doing? Think beyond the simple statement, "I have to write an essay" or "I have a paper due." Are you expected to inform, interpret, or argue?

- **Informing:** writing to transmit knowledge. Terms like *classify, illustrate, report,* and *survey* are often associated with the task of informing.

- **Interpreting:** writing to produce understanding. Terms like *analyze, compare, explain,* and *reflect* are more likely to appear when the purpose is interpreting.

- **Arguing:** writing to state and negotiate matters of public debate. *Agree, assess, defend,* and *refute* go with the task of arguing.

Some terms, such as *comment, consider,* and *discuss,* do not point to a particular purpose, but many others do. If you are not clear about the kind of work you are expected to do, ask your professor.

4. Select the appropriate genre.

Genre simply means kind of writing. Poems, stories, and plays are genres of literature, and they look and sound very differently. Different genres of writing predominate in different disciplines.

Sometimes an assignment will specify the kind of work, or genre, you are being asked to produce. For example, you may be asked to write a report (an informative genre), a comparative analysis (an interpretive genre), or a critique (an argumentative genre).

Some genres, like the case study, are common in a particular field such as sociology but not in all disciplines across the curriculum. Understanding the genre that is called for is very important in successfully fulfilling an assignment. If you are supposed to be writing a description of a snake for a field guide, you will not be successful if you write a poem—even a very good poem—about a snake. (*See Tab 3: Common Assignments across the Curriculum, pp. 75–129.*)

5. Use appropriate language.

Understanding genre helps you make decisions about language. For the description of a snake in a field guide, you would use highly specific terminology, including some Latin and Greek words, to differentiate one type of snake from another. A poem would incorporate striking images, vivid words and phrases that evoke the senses, and other forms of language commonly used in literature.

6. Choose an appropriate voice.

The concept of **voice** is difficult to grasp in a discussion of writing because we think of voice as something that we hear. But we also hear voices when we read, and we create voices when we write. The following two passages both deal with the death of a sports writer named Steve Schoenfeld. Read both passages aloud, and listen to the different voices:

> Tobin originally planned his news conference for Wednesday but postponed it out of respect for Valley sports journalist Steve Schoenfeld, who was killed Tuesday night in a hit-and-run accident in downtown Tempe.
>
> —LEE SHAPPELL, *Arizona Republic*

> Steve Schoenfeld probably would find it amusing that the NFL plans to honor him with a moment of silence in press boxes before games on Sunday and Monday. He was hardly ever quiet in the press box or anywhere else.
>
> —MARK ARMIJO and KENT SOMERS, *Arizona Republic*

The first passage is written in an even tone that emphasizes factual reporting. The second passage is written in a poignant style that quietly and movingly celebrates the sports writer's life.

Different writing situations and assignments allow you to try out different voices. As a college student, you will usually want to inspire trust in your readers by sounding informed, reasonable, and fair. Your **stance**—where you stand in relation to your audience and your subject—is seldom that of an expert. Instead, you are writing as an educated person who is sharing what you have learned and what you think about it.

Readers tend to be most comfortable with an even tone of voice, a style that values the middle and avoids the extremes of the impersonal or the intimate, the long-winded or the curt, and the stuffy or the casual.

STUFFY	The epistolary mode of literary expression has assumed numerous distinctive guises since its original manifestation more than four thousand years ago in the cuneiform inscriptions of ancient Sumer.
CASUAL	Letters have been around for a really long time.
APPROPRIATE ACADEMIC VOICE	As Kany points out, epistolary writing has flourished ever since it first emerged among the Sumerians.

Read your work aloud to yourself or to classmates so that you can literally hear your voice. Do the stance and style of your voice suit the assignment's topic, purpose, and audience? (*For more about style, see Tab 10: Editing for Clarity.*)

7b   Explore your ideas.

You usually explore ideas when you are getting started on a project, but exploration also helps when you are feeling stuck and are searching for something new to say. The following strategies will help you brainstorm and come up with ideas at any stage.

1. List.   One way to brainstorm is to start with a topic and list the words, phrases, images, and ideas that come to mind. The key to brainstorming is to turn off your internal editor and just jot things down. Later, you can review this list, underline one or more key terms, and add or delete items. Here is a list a student produced on the topic of work:

```
Work--what is it?

Skilled/unskilled

Most jobs today in service industries

Work and retirement

my dad's retired, but has he stopped working?

If you never want to retire, is your job still
considered work?

Jobs I have had: babysitter, camp counselor,
salesclerk, office worker--I'd be happy to retire
from those, especially the salesclerk job

Standing all day.

Do this, do that.

Punch the clock.

Do it over again and again

Difference between work and career

I want a career, not a job

Dress for success

High-powered lunches, late dinner.

Travel

Making presentations

Pressure

Making decisions

Big house

Fast car
```

2. Cluster.   Having something down in writing enables you to look for categories and connections. **Clustering,** sometimes called **mapping,** is a brainstorming technique that generates categories and connections from the beginning. To make an idea cluster, do the following:

- ▪ Write your topic in the center of a piece of paper, and draw a circle around it.

- Surround the topic with subtopics that interest you. Circle each, and draw a line from it to the center circle.
- Brainstorm more ideas. As you do so, connect each one to a subtopic already on the sheet, or make it a new subtopic of its own.

Working together as a group, the students in a composition course produced the following idea cluster on the topic of "Work in the U.S. today":

3. Freewrite.   When you feel blocked or unsure about what you think, try **freewriting.** Just write whatever occurs to you about a topic. If nothing comes to mind, then write "nothing comes to mind"

until something else occurs to you. The trick is to keep pushing forward without stopping. Usually, you will discover some implicit point in your seemingly random writing. The following is a student's freewriting on the topic of work:

To read more about listing, clustering, and freewriting, visit <www.mhhe.com/maimon/planning/exploring_ideas>.

```
I want to talk about the difference between a job and
work--between a job and a career. If you don't get
paid, is it work? If it is, what's the difference
between work and play? There are some things I would
only do for money--like work as a waiter. But there
are other things I would do even if I weren't paid--
garden or ride my bike or play with kids. The trick is
to find a career that would allow me to get paid for
doing those things.
```

4. Question.   Asking questions is a good way to explore a topic further. The journalist's five *w*'s and an *h* (*who? what? where? when? why?* and *how?*) can help you find specific ideas and details. For example, a student group assigned to research and write a paper about some aspect of work came up with the following questions:

- In terms of age, gender, and ethnicity, who is working in the new cyberspace infotainment industry?
- What are the working conditions, benefits, and job security of those employed in the current U.S. service economy?
- Where are all the manufacturing jobs these days?
- When is it best for people to retire from jobs?
- Why are so many U.S. businesses "downsizing"?
- How do people prepare themselves for career changes?

Other questioning techniques include the following:

- Looking at a topic dramatically, as an action (*what*) with actors (*who*), a scene (*where*), means (*how*), and purpose (*why*)
- Looking at a topic as a static thing—a particle—that has its own distinguishing features and parts, as a wave that changes over time, and as a field that operates as a system

STATIC THING   What is work? Do the words *work, job,* and *career* mean the same thing to most people?

CHARTING the TERRITORY

Different Questions Lead to Different Answers

Always consider what questions make the most sense in the context of the course you are taking. Scholars in different disciplines pose questions related to their fields.

- **Sociology:** A sociologist might ask questions about the ways management and workers interact in the high-tech workplace.
- **History:** A historian might ask how women's roles in the workplace have—or have not—changed since 1960.
- **Economics:** An economist might wonder what effect, if any, the North American Free Trade Agreement (NAFTA) has had on factory layoffs and closings in the United States.

	How do we know when someone is not doing work? What is the opposite of work?
WAVE	How has work changed over time? Over the past thirty years, have there been significant shifts in the number and kinds of jobs available in the United States? Is the computer revolution likely to make a big difference in how business will work in the twenty-first century?
FIELD	Where does work fit into our lives? To what extent does a person's self-esteem depend on the job he or she has? What does work mean for a society in which most jobs are in the service and communication areas? How will the new global economy affect the quantity and quality of work in the United States?

For other useful examples of what and how to question, take note of the problems or questions your professor poses to get class discussion going. If you are using a textbook in your course, check out the study questions.

5. Review annotated texts and journal entries.   As a critical reader (*see Chapter 6, pp. 21–24*), you have probably written notes in the margins of the texts you own. You have also made journal entries.

Reread your notes and entries. These immediate comments and reactions are your best sources for ideas. Look for patterns.

6. Browse in the library.   Your college library is filled with ideas—and it can be a great inspiration when you need to come up with your own. Sometimes it helps to take a break; leave your study carrel, stretch your legs, and browse the bookshelves containing texts that relate to a topic of interest.

7. Surf the Net.   Exploring a subject on the World Wide Web is the electronic equivalent of browsing in the library. Type keywords related to your topic into a search engine such as *Google,* and visit several sites on the list that results. (*See Tab 5: Researching, pp. 163–71.*)

8. Exchange ideas.   If you read the acknowledgments in the books on your shelves, you will see that writing is a social activity. Most authors thank family members, editors, librarians, and colleagues for help on work in progress. Likewise, you should welcome opportunities to talk about your writing with your classmates, friends, and family.

- Discuss your assignments in chat rooms and by exchanging e-mail, especially if your course has a class Web site.
- Seek out students who have taken the course in previous semesters and discuss with them their approaches to writing assignments.
- Most colleges have writing centers that welcome students for discussions of work in progress.

8   Drafting

This book offers detailed advice on planning, drafting, revising, and editing in separate chapters, but these activities are not entirely separate. You will move back and forth as you plan, draft, revise, and edit, and you may circle back and go through the entire process again as you write. But even though the parts of the writing process are interconnected, make sure to give yourself enough time not only to draft but also to revise and edit your work.

Think of drafting as an attempt to discover a beginning, a middle, and an end for what you have to say, but remember that a draft is preliminary. Avoid putting pressure on yourself to make it perfect the first time through.

8a Develop your thesis.

Your first goal in drafting is to develop a preliminary thesis—a **working thesis**—that fits your purpose, makes a difference to readers, and addresses a specific issue. A preliminary thesis is just that: preliminary. As you draft and revise your paper, you may change the thesis several times to make it stronger.

To get going quickly on a first draft, begin with the answer to a question posed by your assignment. (*For more about questions, see Chapter 7, pp. 40–41.*) For example, an assignment in a political science class might ask you to defend or critique "Healthy Inequality," an article by George Will on the increasing gap between rich and poor in the United States. The question your thesis must answer is "Is George Will's position that inequality is healthy correct or incorrect?"

To create a strong thesis, you will need to think critically, developing a point of view based on reading course materials and doing research. Writing critically, then, begins with a clear, forceful thesis statement. Not all theses can be stated in one sentence, but all strong theses are suitable, significant, and specific. (*For more on strong theses, see Chapter 6, pp. 29–32.*)

1. Make sure your thesis is suitable.   A suitable thesis fits the paper's main purpose. (*See Chapter 7, p. 35.*) If you are asked to write a report of your research on the gap between rich and poor in the United States, for example, you should not try to argue a position. An argument will not fulfill the purpose of the assignment, which is to produce an informative paper, a report. All of the following theses are on the same topic, but each is for a paper with a different purpose:

THESIS TO INFORM
: In terms of income and wealth, the gap between rich and poor has increased substantially during the past decade.

THESIS TO INTERPRET
: The economic ideas George Will expresses in "Healthy Inequality" are politically conservative.

THESIS TO ARGUE
: George Will's argument that economic inequality is healthy for the United States depends on two false analogies.

2. Make sure your thesis is significant.   A significant thesis asserts something that could potentially make a difference in what readers know, understand, or believe. Chances are that what makes a difference to you will also make a difference to your readers. When

For additional examples of theses, visit <www.mhhe.com/maimon/drafting/thesis>.

LEARNING in COLLEGE

Finding a Thesis through Questioning

It sometimes helps to think of the thesis as an answer to a question. In each of the following three examples, the topic of the thesis is in italics and the assertion about that topic is underlined.

QUESTION   What makes a photograph significant?

THESIS   *The significance of a photograph* depends on both its formal and its documentary features.

QUESTION   What did Alfred Stieglitz contribute to the art of photography?

THESIS   *Alfred Stieglitz's struggle to promote photography as an art* involved starting a journal, opening a gallery, and making common cause with avant-garde modernist artists.

QUESTION   Is Susan Sontag right that photography obstructs critical thinking?

THESIS   *Susan Sontag's critique of photography* is unconvincing, partly because it assumes that most people are visually unsophisticated and thoughtlessly voyeuristic.

you are looking for possible theses, be sure to challenge yourself to develop one that you care about.

3. Make sure your thesis is specific.   Vague theses tend to be less significant than specific ones:

TOO VAGUE   The gap between rich and poor has increased, and that's bad. [*What kind of "gap" is at issue? Who are these "rich and poor"? Why is the increase in the gap "bad"?*]

SPECIFIC   George Will's argument that economic inequality is healthy for the United States should not be accepted. His interpretation of the recent increase in income inequality is questionable. His reasoning about history is flawed. Above all, his idea of what is healthy is too narrow.

The second example thesis is sufficiently specific. It names economic inequality as the general topic, identifies George Will's argument as the particular issue, and offers three reasons for rejecting Will's argument. It also forecasts the structure of the whole paper, providing readers with a sense of direction.

8b Prepare an outline.

An informal or a formal outline often helps you clarify your ideas and move forward with a draft. An informal outline can be as simple as your working thesis followed by a list of the supporting points you plan to include. Another type of outline is an informal do/say plan. To come up with such a plan, review your notes and other relevant material. Then write down your working thesis, and list what you will say for each of the following "do" categories: introduce; support and develop; conclude. Here is an example:

Thesis: George Will is wrong about economic inequality being good for the United States.

1. **Introduce** the issue and my focus.
   - Use two examples to contrast rich and poor: "approximately 17,000 Americans declared more than $1 million of annual income on their 1985 tax returns" (Mantsios 196). Between 1979 and 1992, there was a 15% decrease in the manufacturing workforce, and in 1993, Sears eliminated 50,000 merchandising jobs (Rifkin 2).
   - Say that the issue is how to evaluate increasing economic inequality, and introduce George Will's article "Healthy Inequality." Summarize Will's argument.
   - Give Will some credit for raising issue, but then state my thesis: he's wrong about more inequality being good for the United States.

2. **Support and develop** my thesis that Will's argument is wrong.
   - Point out that Will relies on the economic interpretations of Greenwood and Yorukoglu. They see decline ("modest") in labor productivity beginning in 1974. But Rifkin says "manufacturing productivity is soaring"—up 35%.
   - Point out one thing Will and Rifkin agree on: computer revolution is affecting economy/jobs. But Will thinks the effects are like "economic turbulence" caused in 1770 by steam engine and in 1840 by electricity.
   - Show that these analogies aren't convincing. Too many differences. Use Aronowitz on "jobless future" and Rifkin for support.

- Say that Will makes fun of those who "decr[y] . . . injustice," people like Rifkin and Aronowitz. Will thinks inequality motivates people to learn new skills so that they can compete. A skilled workforce makes our society better/healthy.

- Will's idea of the healthy society is narrow. It is an economic idea only. And he thinks that an unemployed worker can just get more skilled—can learn the new technology. But who will pay for the training?

3. **Conclude** that Will doesn't ask or answer such key questions because he denies that there is any problem. Earlier he says "suffering is good." Where would he draw the line? Maybe quote from Max Weber?

In outlining his plan, this student has already begun drafting because as he works on the outline, he gets a clearer sense of what he thinks is wrong with Will's argument. He starts writing sentences that he is likely to include in the first complete draft.

Occasionally, you may find it helpful to prepare a formal outline that classifies and divides the information you have gathered. (For some assignments, your instructor might require a formal outline.) Because the process of division always results in at least two parts, in a formal outline every I must have a II; every A, a B; and so on. Also, items placed at the same level must be of the same kind; for example, if I is London, then II can be New York City but not the Bronx or Wall Street. Items at the same level should also be grammatically parallel. Here is the conventional format for a formal outline:

Topic/Thesis:

I. First subtopic or point
   A. First supporting idea
      1. First specific detail
      2. Second specific detail
   B. Second supporting idea
      1. First specific detail
      2. Second specific detail
      3. Third specific detail
         a. First part of specific detail
         b. Second part of specific detail
II. Second subtopic or point
   A. First supporting idea
      1. First specific detail
      2. Second specific detail
   B. Second supporting idea
      1. First specific detail
      2. Second specific detail
   C. Third supporting idea

8c Develop your ideas.

When you develop ideas, you move your writing forward by giving it texture and depth. The following strategies are helpful ways to develop the ideas that support your thesis into a complete draft.

1. Narration. When you narrate, you tell a story. The following paragraph comes from a personal essay on the goods that result from "a lifetime of production":

> My dad changed too. He had come to that job feeling—as I do now—that everything was still possible. He'd served his time in the air force during the Korean War. Then, while my mother worked as a secretary to support them, he earned a college degree courtesy of the GI Bill. After graduation, my father painted houses for a season until he was offered a position scheduling the production of corrugated board. He took it, though he has told me that he never planned to stay. It was not something he envisioned as his life's work. I try to imagine what it is like suddenly to look up from a stack of orders and discover that the job you started one December day has watched you age.
>
> —MICHELLE M. DUCHARME, "A Lifetime of Production"

Notice that Ducharme begins with two sentences that state the topic and point of her narration. Then using the past tense, she recounts in chronological sequence some key events that led to her father's taking a job in the box manufacturing business.

For additional examples of how to develop ideas through narration, visit <www.mhhe.com/maimon/drafting/developing_ideas>.

2. Description. To make an object, person, or activity vivid for your readers, describe it in concrete, specific words that appeal to the senses of sight, sound, taste, smell, and touch. In the following example, Ilona Bouzoukashvili describes her impression of a photograph.

> In the *Paratrooper* photograph, the rescuer's powerfully muscular arm is set firmly in the foreground and is so intensely illuminated that it appears lighter than the rest of his water-soaked body. The arm of the wounded man is also caught in the light. But it is oddly bent, as if to accentuate just how tightly—and painfully—these two bodies are intertwined. Here is a desperate yet loving embrace. Both soldiers are holding on to each other as if they were holding on to life—to the human reality of this moment with its illuminating hope. Togetherness supports that life-giving hope and ensures its life-sustaining strength.
>
> —ILONA BOUZOUKASHVILI, "On Reading Photographs," student paper, 1994

Bouzoukashvili uses words and phrases that appeal to the reader's sense of sight ("powerfully muscular arm," "oddly bent"). Emotionally charged adjectives like "desperate," "loving," and "life-giving" give readers a clear sense of the writer's feelings about the subject. So, too, do the two "as if" constructions.

3. Classification.   Classification is a useful way of grouping individual entities into identifiable categories. Classifying occurs in all academic disciplines and often appears with its complement—**division,** or breaking a whole entity into its parts.

> [M]ost of America's traditional, routinized manufacturing jobs will disappear. So will routinized service jobs that can be done from remote locations, like keypunching of data transmitted by satellite. Instead, you will be engaged in one of two broad categories of work: either complex services, some of which will be sold to the rest of the world to pay for whatever Americans want to buy from the rest of the world, or person-to-person services, which foreigners can't provide for us because (apart from new immigrants and illegal aliens) they aren't here to provide them.
>
> Complex services involve the manipulation of data and abstract symbols. Included in this category are insurance, engineering, law, finance, computer programming, and advertising. Such activities now account for almost 25 percent of our GNP, up from 13 percent in 1950. They have already surpassed manufacturing (down to about 20 percent of GNP). Even *within* the manufacturing sector, executive, managerial, and engineering positions are increasing at a rate almost three times that of total manufacturing employment. Most of these jobs, too, involve manipulating symbols.
>
> —ROBERT REICH, "The Future of Work"

To make his ideas clear, Reich first classifies future work into two broad categories: complex services and person-to-person services. Then in the next paragraph, he develops the idea of complex services in more detail, in part by dividing that category into more specific—and familiar—categories like engineering and advertising.

4. Definition.   Define any concepts that the reader needs to understand to follow your ideas. Interpretations and arguments often depend on one or two key ideas that cannot be quickly and easily defined. In the following example, John Berger defines "image," a key idea in his televised lectures on the way we see things:

> An image is a sight which has been recreated or reproduced. It is an appearance, or a set of appearances, which has been

detached from the place and time in which it first made its appearance and preserved—for a few moments or centuries. Every image embodies a way of seeing. Even a photograph. For photographs are not, as is often assumed, a mechanical record. Every time we look at a photograph, we are aware, however slightly, of the photographer selecting that sight from an infinity of other possible sights. This is true even in the most casual family snapshot. The photographer's way of seeing is reflected in his choice of subject.

—JOHN BERGER, *Ways of Seeing*

5. Illustration.   No matter what your purpose and point may be, to appeal to readers you will have to show as well as tell. Detailed examples can make abstractions more concrete and generalizations more specific, as the following paragraph shows:

> As Rubin explains, "for much of the Accord era, the ideal-typical family [. . .] was composed of a 'stay-at-home-mom,' a working father, and dependent children. He earned wages; she cooked, cleaned, cared for the home, managed the family's social life, and nurtured the family members" (97). Just such an arrangement characterized my grandmother's married life. My grandmother, who had four children, stayed at home with them, while her husband went off to work as a safety engineer. Sadly, when he died, she was left with nothing. She needed to support herself, yet had no work experience, no credit, and little education. But even though society frowned on her for seeking employment, my grandmother eventually found a clerical position—a low-level job with few perks.

—JENNIFER KOEHLER, "Response to Exercise 6," student paper for Sociology 352, 1997

6. Comparison and contrast.   *Comparison* means exploring the similarities and differences among various items. When the term *compare* is used along with the term *contrast,* then *compare* is usually defined more narrowly as "to spell out key similarities." *Contrast* always means "to itemize important differences."

In the following example, the student writer uses a **subject-by-subject** pattern to contrast the ideas of two social commentators, Jeremy Rifkin and George Will:

> Rifkin and Will have different opinions about unemployment due to downsizing and the widening income gap between rich and poor. Rifkin sees both the decrease in employment and the increase in income disparity as evils that must be immediately

dealt with lest society fall apart: "If no measures are taken to provide financial opportunities for millions of Americans in an era of diminishing jobs, then [. . .] violent crime is going to increase" (3). Will, on the other hand, seems to believe that both unemployment and income differences are necessary to the health of American society. Will writes, "A society that chafes against stratification derived from disparities of talents will be a society that discourages individual talents" (92). Apparently, the society that Rifkin wants is just the kind of society that Will rejects.

—JACOB GROSSMAN, "Dark Comes before Dawn,"
student paper, 1996

Notice that Grossman comments on Rifkin first and then turns to his second subject, George Will. To ensure paragraph unity, he begins with a topic sentence that mentions both subjects.

In the following paragraph, the student writer organizes her comparison **point by point** rather than subject by subject. Instead of saying everything about Smith's picture before commenting on the AP photo, the writer moves back and forth between the two images as she makes and supports two points: first, that the images differ in figure and scene, and second, that they are similar in theme.

Divided by an ocean, two photographers took pictures that at first glance seem absolutely different. W. Eugene Smith's well-known *Tomoko in the Bath* and the less well-known AP photo *A Paratrooper Works to Save the Life of a Buddy* portray distinctively different settings and people. Smith brings us into a darkened room where a Japanese woman is lovingly bathing her malformed child, while the AP staff photographer captures two soldiers on the battlefield, one intently performing CPR on his wounded friend. But even though the two images seem as different as women and men, peace and war, or life and death, both pictures figure something similar: a time of suffering. It is the early 1970s—a time when the hopes and dreams that modernity promoted are being exposed as deadly to human beings. Perhaps that is why the bodies in both pictures seem humbled. Grief pulls you down onto your knees. Terror impels you to crawl along the ground.

—ILONA BOUZOUKASHVILI, "On Reading Photographs,"
student paper, 1994

7. Analogy.   An analogy compares topics that at first glance seem quite different. A well-chosen analogy can make new or technical information appear more commonplace and understandable:

The human eye provides a good starting point for learning how a camera works. The lens of the eye is like the *lens* of the camera. In both instruments the lens focuses an image of the surroundings on a *light-sensitive surface*—the *retina* of the eye and the *film* in the camera. In both, the light-sensitive material is protected within a light-tight container—the *eyeball* of the eye and the *body* of the camera. Both eye and camera have a mechanism for shutting off light passing through the lens to the interior of the container—the *lid* of the eye and the *shutter* of the camera. In both, the size of the lens opening, or *aperture,* is regulated by an *iris diaphragm.*

—MARVIN ROSEN, *Introduction to Photography*

8. Process.   When you need to explain how to do something or show readers how something is done, you use process analysis, explaining each step in the process in chronological order, as in the following example:

To end our Hawan ritual of thanks, *aarti* is performed. First, my mother lights a piece of camphor in a metal plate called a *taree.* Holding the taree with her right hand, she moves the fire in a circular, clockwise movement in front of the altar. Next, she stands in front of my father and again moves the fiery *taree* in a circular, clockwise direction. After touching his feet and receiving his blessing, she attends to each of us children in turn, moving the fire in a clockwise direction before kissing us, one by one. When she is done, my father performs his *aarti* in a similar way and then my sister and I do ours. When everyone is done, we say some prayers and sit down.

—U. ROOPNARIAN, student paper, 1990

9. Cause and effect.   Use this strategy when you need to trace the causes of some event or situation, to describe its effects, or both. In the following example, Norman Cousins explains the causes of the career-ending injuries that can plague professional athletes:

Professional athletes are sometimes severely disadvantaged by trainers whose job it is to keep them in action. The more famous the athlete, the greater the risk that he or she may be subjected to extreme medical measures when injury strikes. The star baseball pitcher whose arm is sore because of a torn muscle or tissue damage may need sustained rest more than anything else. But his team is battling for a place in the World Series; so the trainer or team doctor, called upon to work his magic, reaches for a strong dose of Butazolidine or other powerful pain suppressants. Presto, the pain disappears! The pitcher takes his place on the mound and does superbly. That could be the last game, however, in which he is able to throw a ball with full strength. The drugs didn't repair the torn muscle or cause the damaged tissue to heal. What they did was to mask the pain, enabling the pitcher to throw hard, further damaging the torn muscle. Little wonder that so many star athletes are cut down in their prime, more the victims of overzealous treatment of their injuries than of the injuries themselves.

—NORMAN COUSINS, "Pain Is Not the Ultimate Enemy"

8d Write purposeful paragraphs that are unified, coherent, and well developed.

Readers expect a piece of writing to be divided into paragraphs that express a thought or point relevant to the whole piece. Introductory and concluding paragraphs have special functions in a piece of writing, but all paragraphs should have sufficient development (level of detail), unity (a single, clear focus), and coherence (internal connections).

1. Introductions and conclusions. A paper's opening and ending paragraphs are especially important. You need to hook readers at the beginning and leave them with a strong final impression at the end.

The best way to get your reader's attention is to show why the topic matters. The opening of your paper should encourage the reader to share your view of the topic's importance. Here are some opening strategies:

- Tell a brief story related to the question your thesis answers.
- Begin with a relevant and attention-getting quotation.
- Begin with a paraphrase of a commonly held view that you immediately question.
- State a working hypothesis.
- Define a key term.
- Pose an important question.

For many types of papers, especially informative reports and arguments, your opening paragraph or paragraphs will include your thesis statement, usually at the beginning or near the end of the introduction. If your purpose is analytic, however, you may either include the thesis in your introduction or build up to your thesis, which you place near the end. Some types of writing, such as narratives, may not require an explicitly stated thesis if the main idea is clear without it.

Just as the opening makes a first impression and motivates the reader to continue reading, the closing makes a final impression and motivates the reader to think further. The purpose of the conclusion is to bring your paper to an interesting close. Do not merely repeat the main idea that you introduced at the beginning of the paper. Presumably, you have developed that idea throughout the paper. Your conclusion should remind readers of the paper's significance and satisfy those who might be asking, "So what?" Here are some common strategies for concluding a paper effectively:

- Refer to the story or quotation you used in your introduction.
- Answer the question you posed in your introduction.
- Summarize your main point.
- Call for some action on your reader's part.
- Present a powerful image or forceful example.
- Suggest some implications for the future.

2. Paragraph development. As you draft and later revise your paper, ask yourself: Does each paragraph provide enough detail? Paragraphs in academic papers are usually about a hundred words long. Although sometimes you will deliberately use a one- or two-sentence paragraph for stylistic emphasis, when paragraphs are short for no apparent stylistic reason, they may need to be developed more fully. Would more information make the point clearer? Perhaps a term should be defined. Do generalizations need to be supported with examples?

Note how this writer developed one of her draft paragraphs, adding details and examples to make her argument more clearly and effectively:

FIRST DRAFT

A 1913 advertisement for Shredded Wheat illustrates Kellner's claim that advertisements sell self-images. The ad suggests that serving Shredded Wheat will give women the same sense of accomplishment as gaining the right to vote.

REVISION

According to Kellner, "advertising is as concerned with selling lifestyles and socially desirable identities [. . .] as with selling the products themselves" (193). A 1913 ad for Shredded Wheat shows how the selling of self-images works. At first glance, this ad

seems to be promoting the women's suffrage movement.
In big, bold letters, "Votes for Women" is emblazoned
across the top of the ad. But a closer look reveals
that the ad is for Shredded Wheat cereal. Holding a
piece of the cereal in her hand, a woman stands behind
a large bowlful of Shredded Wheat biscuits that is
made to look like a voting box. The text claims that
"every biscuit is a vote for health, happiness and
domestic freedom." Like the rest of the advertisement,
this claim suggests that serving Shredded Wheat will
give women the same sense of accomplishment as gaining
the right to vote.

                              --Holly Musetti, student paper, 2001

3. Paragraph unity. A unified paragraph has a single, clear focus.
To check for **unity,** identify the paragraph's topic sentence. A **topic
sentence** announces the paragraph's main point and usually appears
at its beginning or end. Everything in the paragraph should be clearly
and closely connected to the topic sentence.

Compare the first draft of the following paragraph with its revision, and note how the addition of a topic sentence (in bold in the revision) makes the paragraph more clearly focused and therefore easier for the writer to revise further. Note also that the writer deleted ideas that did not directly relate to the paragraph's main point (underlined in the first draft):

FIRST DRAFT

Germany is ranked first on worldwide production
levels. Automobiles, aircraft, and electronic equipment are among Germany's most important products for
export. As the standard of living of the citizens of
what was formerly East Germany increases due to reunification, their purchasing power and productivity will
increase. A major problem is that east Germany is not
as productive or efficient as west Germany, and so it
would be better if less money were invested in the
east. Germany is involved in most global treaties that

protect business interests, and intellectual property is well protected. A plus for potential ventures and production plans is its highly skilled workforce. Another factor that indicates that Germany will remain strong in the arena of productivity and trade is its physical location in the world. "Its terrain and geographical position have combined to make Germany an important crossroads for traffic between the North Sea, the Baltic, and the Mediterranean. International transportation routes pass through all of Germany," thus utilizing a comprehensive and efficient network of transportation, both on land and over water ("Germany," 1995, p. 185). Businesses can operate plants in Germany and have no difficulties transporting goods and services to other parts of the country. Generally, private enterprise, government, banks, and unions cooperate, making the country more amenable to negotiations for business entry or joint ventures.

REVISION

For many reasons, Germany is attractive both as a market for other nations and as a location for production. As the standard of living of the citizens of what was formerly East Germany increases due to reunification, their purchasing power and productivity increase. Intellectual property is well protected, and Germany is involved in most global treaties that protect business interests. Germany's highly skilled workforce is another plus for potential ventures and production plans. Generally, private enterprise, government, banks, and unions cooperate, making the country amenable to negotiations for business entry or joint ventures. Germany also has an excellent physical location that makes it an "important crossroads for traffic

between the North Sea, the Baltic, and the Mediterranean" ("Germany," 1995, p. 185). Equally important,
a comprehensive and efficient transportation system
allows businesses to operate plants in Germany and
easily transport their goods and services to other
parts of the country and the world.

--Jennifer Koehler, "Germany's Path
to Continuing Prosperity"

4. Paragraph coherence.   A coherent paragraph flows smoothly, with each sentence clearly related to the next. All of the sentences in a paragraph should be connected in ways that make the whole paragraph hold together. Use the following cues to strengthen **coherence:**

- Use pronouns and antecedents. In the following example, *it* refers back to *Germany* and connects the two sentences.

  Germany imports raw materials, energy sources, and food products. *It* exports a wide range of industrial products, including automobiles, aircraft, and machine tools.

- Repeat key words.

  A photograph displays a unique *moment.* To capture that *moment. . . .*

- Repeat sentence structures.

  Because the former West Germany lived through a generation of prosperity, its people developed high expectations of material comfort. Because the former East Germany lived through a generation of deprivation, its people developed disdain for material values.

- Use **synonyms,** words that are close in meaning to words or phrases that have preceded them.

  In the world of photography, critics *argue* for either a scientific or an artistic approach. This *controversy. . . .*

- Use transitional words and phrases. **Transitional expressions** link one idea with another, thereby helping readers understand your logic. (*See the list of common transitional expressions in the box on p. 58.*) Avoid mechanically sticking in transitional words and phrases. Instead, use transitions to build logical bridges between paragraphs as well as between sentences.

Compare the following two paragraphs, the first version without transitions and the second, revised version with transitions (in bold type) that connect one thought to another:

FIRST DRAFT

Glaser was in a position to powerfully affect Armstrong's career and his life. Armstrong acknowledged Glaser's importance, referring to him at one point as "the man who has guided me all through my career" (qtd. in Jones and Chilton 202). There is little evidence that the musician submitted to whatever his business manager wanted or demanded. Armstrong seemed to recognize that he gave Glaser whatever power the manager enjoyed over him. Armstrong could and did resist Glaser's control when he wanted to. That may be one reason why he liked and trusted Glaser as much as he did.

REVISION

Clearly, Glaser was in a position to affect Armstrong's career and his life powerfully. Armstrong acknowledged Glaser's importance, at one point referring to him as "the man who has guided me all through my career" (qtd. in Jones and Chilton 202). **However,** there is little evidence that the musician submitted to whatever his business manager wanted or demanded. **In fact,** Armstrong seemed to recognize that he gave Glaser whatever power the manager enjoyed over him. When he wanted to, Armstrong could and did resist Glaser's control, and that may be one reason why he liked and trusted Glaser as much as he did.

--Ester Hoffman, "Louis Armstrong and Joe Glaser"

TRANSITIONAL EXPRESSIONS

To show relationships in space: above, adjacent to, against, alongside, around, at a distance from, at the . . . , below, beside, beyond, encircling, far off, forward, from the . . . , in front of, in the rear, inside, near the back, near the end, nearby, next to, on, over, surrounding, there, through the, to the left, to the right, up front

To show relationships in time: afterward, at last, before, earlier, first, former, formerly, immediately, in the first place, in the interval, in the meantime, in the next place, in the last place, later on, latter, meanwhile, next, now, often, once, previously, second, simultaneously, sometime later, subsequently, suddenly, then, therefore, third, today, tomorrow, until now, when, years ago, yesterday

To show something added to what has come before: again, also, and, and then, besides, further, furthermore, in addition, last, likewise, moreover, next, too

To give examples that intensify points: after all, as an example, certainly, clearly, for example, for instance, indeed, in fact, in truth, it is true, of course, specifically, that is

To show similarities: alike, in the same way, like, likewise, resembling, similarly

To show contrasts: after all, although, but, conversely, differ(s) from, difference, different, dissimilar, even though, granted, however, in contrast, in spite of, nevertheless, notwithstanding, on the contrary, on the other hand, otherwise, still, though, unlike, while this may be true, yet

To indicate cause and effect: accordingly, as a result, because, consequently, hence, since, then, therefore, thus

To conclude or summarize: finally, in brief, in conclusion, in other words, in short, in summary, that is, to summarize

8e   Use online tools for drafting.

Nowadays, most writers use word processing to produce final, printed texts. Any computer you use, either at home or in your school's writing lab, probably comes equipped with a word-processing program. The two most common are Microsoft Word and WordPerfect. Get to know whatever program you have, especially the various ways of setting up and saving files.

Most programs offer more than just word processing, however. They allow you to create Web pages; embed links (called *hot links*) to sites on the World Wide Web; include graphics; use templates and wizards to design documents; and count words, check spelling, and display and print foreign language fonts. Try exploring each of the menu items of your word processor sometime to see for yourself all that the program will allow you to do.

9 Revising

Drafting and revising are interdependent. As you draft, you will often review what you write and do some revision, but most of your energy will be devoted, appropriately, to getting your words down on paper or into a computer file. Once you have a draft, you can revise in earnest. You will revise for *substance*—to clarify what you want to say—and for *style*—to say what you want to say as effectively as possible.

9a Focus on the purpose of your writing.

As you reread your paper and decide how to revise it, base your decisions on the purpose of your paper. Is your primary purpose to inform, to interpret, or to argue? (*For more on purpose, see Tab 1: Learning across the Curriculum, p. 8.*)

Clarity about your purpose is especially important when an assignment calls for interpretation. A description is not the same as an interpretation. With this principle in mind, Ilona Bouzoukashvili read over the first draft of her paper on the art of photography, a draft that included descriptions of several photographs. Here is her description of a photograph entitled *A Paratrooper Works to Save the Life of a Buddy:*

FIRST DRAFT

In *Paratrooper,* the surroundings are not entirely shown. For all we know, there could still be shelling or shooting in the area. One thing we see clearly is that the wounded soldier is lying on the muddy ground, yet his paratrooper buddy doesn't seem to mind. He leans over and tries to save his friend. Their clothes appear dirty and wet, which displays the ugliness of a war. One may even note how the paratrooper is almost crying; a part of his forehead is slightly wrinkled. His body as a whole is in a bent position.

Keeping her purpose in mind, the student asked herself which details in the paragraph were most significant—which ones could help her fulfill her interpretive purpose. She wanted to show her readers that even documentary photographs can be artistic. Her revision makes this interpretation clearer.

REVISION

Paratrooper subtly portrays the ugliness of war, not through a picture of shelling and shooting but through a close-up of war's devastating effects on the individual and on human relationships. Dirty, damp, and ugly, the photograph reflects the misery of war. The paratrooper is the rescuer, but he is bent over his wounded buddy as if he, too, is begging for help. Bodies shown in both *Tomoko* and *Paratrooper* are either squatting or lying down. Grief and terror literally knock people over.

9b   Make sure you have a strong thesis.

Understanding your purpose will help you test your thesis for clarity. Remember that a thesis makes an assertion about a topic. It links the *what* and the *why*. Is your thesis evident on the first page of your draft? Before readers get very far along, they expect an answer to the question, "What is the point of all this?" Not finding the point on the first page is a signal to revise, unless you are deliberately waiting until the end to reveal your thesis. (*For more on strong theses, see Chapter 8, pp. 43–45.*)

Most writers start with a working thesis, which often evolves into a more specific, complex assertion as they develop their ideas. One of the key challenges of revising is to compose a clear statement of this revised thesis. When she drafted the paper on Germany's economic prospects that appears in Tab 7: APA Documentation Style, pages 260–72, Jennifer Koehler stated her working thesis as follows:

WORKING THESIS

Germany is experiencing a great deal of change.

During the revision process, Koehler realized that her working thesis was too weak to serve as the thesis of her final draft. A weak thesis is predictable: readers read it, agree, and that's that. A strong thesis, on the other hand, stimulates thoughtful inquiry. Koehler's revised thesis provokes questions:

REVISED THESIS

With proper follow-through, Germany can become one of the world's primary sources of direct investment and maintain its status as one of the world's preeminent exporters.

When you need to identify or strengthen a thesis, it sometimes helps to compose a title for your paper. Koehler's title, "Germany's Path to Continuing Prosperity," which she decided on during the revising process, helped her see that her thesis needed to explain the path from Germany's economic present to its future.

Your thesis should evolve throughout the paper. Readers need to see a statement of the main idea on the first page, but they also expect a more complex or general statement near the end. After presenting much evidence to support her revised thesis, Koehler concludes her paper by stating her thesis in a more general way:

If the government efforts continue, the economy will strengthen over the next decade and Germany will reinforce its position as an integral nation in the global economy.

9c   Review the whole paper and its parts.

In a first draft, you are wise to think broadly about the different parts of your paper and how you should order them. Does the paper have a beginning, a middle, and an end, with bridges between those parts? When you revise, however, you can design a structure that supports what you want to say more effectively.

One way to review your structure is by outlining the first draft. An outline makes clear the overall pattern of your thinking. Try listing the key points of your draft in sentence form; whenever possible, use sentences that actually appear in the draft. This kind of point-by-point outlining will allow you to see the logic (or lack of it) of your draft. Ask yourself if the key points are arranged effectively or if another arrangement would work better. The following structures are typical ways of organizing papers:

- An *explanatory structure* sets out the key parts of a topic.

- An *exploratory structure* begins with a question or problem and works step-by-step to discover an answer or a solution.

- An *argumentative structure* presents a set of linked reasons plus supporting evidence.

Revising Your Draft for Content and Organization

1. **Purpose:** Is my purpose for writing clear? If not, how can I revise to make my purpose apparent?
2. **Thesis:** Is my thesis clear and specific, and do I introduce it early in my draft? (If not, do I have a good reason for withholding it or not stating it at all?)
3. **Order:** Are my key points arranged effectively? Would another order support my thesis more successfully?
4. **Paragraphs:** Is each paragraph fully developed, unified, and coherent?

The structure you choose should be appropriate to the assignment, your purpose, and your thesis, and the paper's parts should develop your ideas in an orderly way. Examine each paragraph, asking yourself what role it plays—or should play—in the paper as a whole. Keeping this role in mind, check the paragraph for development, unity, and coherence—and consider how it contributes to the paper as a whole.

9d Revise and edit sentences.

As you revise, you should consider not only the substance of what you have said but also the style—the way you have said it.

1. Use an appropriate tone. For most academic papers, your tone should reflect seriousness about the subject matter and purpose, as well as respect for your readers. You express your seriousness by stating information and interpretations fairly, presenting reasonable arguments, and citing sources for your ideas. Unless you are writing a personal essay, the topic, not yourself or your feelings, should be the center of attention. Be alert to your attitude. Writing with seriousness and authority does not mean talking down to readers. For example, the following revised sentence is informative without being condescending.

CONDESCENDING

Along with many opportunities, obstacles exist that have restricted the amount of foreign direct investment (FDI), as I already explained to you.

REVISED

Along with many opportunities, obstacles exist that have restricted the amount of foreign direct investment (FDI), as noted earlier.

2. Vary your sentences.

To capture and hold your readers attention, your writing must be both clearly focused and interestingly varied. Vary sentence openings and sentence lengths, and use different kinds of sentences to add texture to your writing. For example, a student writing a personal essay about his father for an English composition class used a variety of sentence openings:

For me, the time I spent watching my father develop and print his photographs was pure joy.

Remembering those days, I began to look through the boxes of old photos.

Shocked to discover his secret life, I felt deeply lonely, as if I didn't know my father after all.

The next day I pretended nothing had happened.

Besides varying the openings of your sentences, vary their lengths, too. A volley of short, choppy sentences will probably distract readers from what you have to say, while an unbroken stream of long, complicated sentences is likely to dull their senses. In the example that follows, notice how the revised version connects ideas for readers and, consequently, is easier to read.

CHOPPY

My father was a zealous photographer. He took pictures on every family outing. Often he spent the whole outing behind his camera. He went to his darkroom as soon as he got home. He usually developed his photos the same day he took them.

REVISED

A zealous photographer, my father took pictures on every family outing, often spending the whole afternoon behind the camera and then hurrying straight to his darkroom to develop the pictures the very same day.

Short, direct sentences are usually more powerful when they introduce or follow a set of longer, more complex sentences. Notice how the student writer emphasizes his last sentence by making it short and simple, especially in comparison to the sentences that precede it.

A few days later, I returned to college, and my dad and I didn't talk to each other for several weeks. Then one night I got a phone call from my mother, telling me, in an almost inaudible whisper and through the static of a bad connection, that she had some bad news. My father had died.

Just as too many short sentences can sound choppy, too many sentences strung together with coordinating words can make your work sound unfocused and monotonous. **Coordinating words** (*and, but, yet, or, nor, for, so*) combine equal ideas. You can often solve problems with too much coordination by subordinating one idea in your sentence to another, using **subordinating words** such as *after, although, as if, as soon as, because, even though, if, since, unless, until, when, whenever, where, wherever, while.*

UNFOCUSED

The cells were exposed to GA, but there was a lag period of eight hours, and then the enzyme was produced.

REVISED

After the cells were exposed to GA, there was a lag period of eight hours, and then the enzyme was produced.

Overuse of subordination, though, can also make it difficult for readers to see or remember your focus.

UNFOCUSED

Although both vertebral and wrist fractures cause deformity and impair movement, hip fractures, which are one of the most devastating consequences of osteoporosis, significantly increase the risk of death, since 12%–30% of patients with a hip fracture die within one year after the fracture, while the mortality rate climbs to 40% for the first two years post fracture.

REVISED

Hip fractures are one of the most devastating consequences of osteoporosis. Although vertebral and wrist fractures cause deformity and impair movement, hip fractures significantly increase the risk of death. Within one year after a hip fracture, 12%–20% of the injured die. The mortality rate climbs to 40% after two years.

Cumulative sentences—simple sentences elaborated with accumulating details—are a powerful way of providing additional

Direct vs. Indirect Sentences

Indirect sentence structures ("It was decided at the meeting that the company would not achieve its growth expectations") are standard in legal and business writing. In most humanities and social science disciplines, however, a more direct style ("The City Opera's rendition of *Don Giovanni* roars with drama.") is preferred.

details while maintaining a clear focus. Notice how the student essayist begins with a simple sentence (in italics) and then, after a comma, adds details through a succession of modifiers.

> *I was shocked,* telling myself this wasn't real, trying to discover an explanation for the photos, photos that seemed to indicate a second wife, another family, a second home in an entirely different city, willing myself to believe that the evidence could be read to mean something else entirely.

(For more on sentence variety, see Chapters 44 and 45, pp. 353–59.)

3. Write direct sentences.   More often than not, sentences beginning with *it is* or *there is* or *there are* (*it was* or *there was*)—called **expletive constructions**—are weak and indirect. Most computer style-checkers will highlight *it is* and *there is* or *there are* so that you can decide whether these phrases work. But using a clear subject and a vivid verb often makes a sentence more powerful.

WEAK   *There are stereotypes* from the days of a divided Germany that must be dealt with.

REVISED   *Stereotypes* formed in the days of a divided Germany *persist* and must be dealt with.

(Also see Chapter 38, on wordy sentences, pp. 340–42.)

4. Choose precise words.   Finding precisely the right word and putting that word in the best place is an important part of revision. In a sense, different disciplines and occupations have their own dialects that members of the community are expected to know and use. The word *significant,* for example, has a mathematical meaning for the statistician that it doesn't have for the literary critic. When taking courses in a discipline, you should use its terminology or dialect, not to impress the instructor but to be understood accurately. As you review your draft, look for general terms that might need to be made more specific.

TOO GENERAL   Foreign direct investment (FDI) in Germany will probably remain low because of several *factors.* [Factors *is so general that it should signal you to get specific and answer the question, "What factors?"*]

REVISED   Foreign direct investment (FDI) in Germany will probably remain low because of *high labor costs, high taxation, and government regulation.*

(For more on using exact language, see Chapter 48, pp. 367–71.)

A desk dictionary and a thesaurus are essential tools for choosing precise words. The dictionary gives a word's **denotations** (its exact definitions) and its **etymology** (its family history). In checking a definition in the dictionary, pay attention to the **parts of speech,** the different functions a word can have in a sentence. The same word can have a different meaning when its grammatical function changes. For example, the word *light* means one thing when it describes a "light" (noun) being turned on and something else when you note that a butterfly "lights" (verb) on a leaf. You will find both meanings in a dictionary, and you will have to choose the appropriate one. To check whether you have selected the appropriate meaning, try substituting the dictionary definition for the word. Does the sentence make sense?

A thesaurus provides synonyms, words with the same or nearly the same meaning. Just as siblings, even identical twins, differ subtly from each other, so do words differ subtly from their synonyms. Because words have different **connotations**—that is, secondary or suggested meanings—some synonyms work in one context but not in another. Synonyms can have either positive or negative connotations. For example, in describing someone's manner of speaking, the word *direct* is usually positive, but *blunt* is not.

One student used both a thesaurus and a dictionary as aids in revising the following sentence:

DRAFT   Malcolm X had a special kind of power.

Dissatisfied with the precision of the word *power,* this writer checked a thesaurus and found the word *influence* listed as a synonym for *power* and the word *charisma* given as a special kind of influence:

THESAURUS EXAMPLE

172. INFLUENCE

1. NOUNS influence, influentiality; power 157, force, clout [informal], [. . .] prestige, [. . .] esteem, [. . .] leadership, charisma, magnetism, charm [. . .]

Going back to the dictionary, she found that *charisma* means a "divinely conferred" power and has an etymological connection with *charismatic,* a term used to describe ecstatic Christian experiences like speaking in tongues. *Charisma* was exactly the word she needed to convey both the spiritual and the popular sides of Malcolm X:

DICTIONARY EXAMPLE

cha•ris•ma (kə riz′mə), *n. pl.* **–ma-ta** (-mə tə). 1. a special quality conferring extraordinary powers of leadership and the ability to inspire veneration. 2. A personal magnetism that enables an individual to attract or influence people. 3. Also, **char•ism** (kar′iz em), a divinely conferred gift or power. [1635-45; < LL < Gk., n. der. of *charízesthai* to favor, der. of *cháris* favor, grace; see –ISM]

Both the dictionary and the thesaurus sometimes list **antonyms—** words that mean the opposite or nearly the opposite of a given word. But words are opposites only within a context of similarity. *Poor* is the opposite of *rich* when the context is wealth. *Light* is the opposite of *rich* when the context is food. In word choice, as in most of the decisions you make when revising, context makes all the difference. (*For more on the dictionary and the thesaurus, see Chapter 49, pp. 371–75.*)

5. Avoid biased language.

Nonbiased language is inclusive, and achieving it requires thought as well as thoughtfulness. Because language reflects society, for good or ill, the English language has within it words and phrases that convey **stereotypes,** ideas about people that exclude, demean, ignore, or patronize them on the basis of gender, sexual preference, physical ability, race, religion, or country of origin. Effective writers are aware of language's power, and they choose to use that power to create a sense of community with readers.

■ **Use genderless nouns and pronouns.** Using masculine pronouns and nouns to refer to both women and men usually sounds biased. Whenever possible, avoid using the pronouns *he, him, his,* and *himself* unless you are referring to a specific person. Using plural forms is often a good solution; so is revising a sentence to avoid masculine pronouns altogether. You can also use *he or she* or *him or her,* as long as you do not use them excessively or more than once in a sentence.

BIASED

Every student who wrote *his* name on the class list had to pay a copying fee in advance and pledge to attend every session.

REVISED AS PLURAL

Students who wrote *their* names on the class list had to pay a copying fee in advance and pledge to attend every session.

REVISED TO AVOID PRONOUNS

Every student who signed up for the class had to pay a copying fee in advance and pledge to attend every session.

REVISED WITH *HIS OR HER*

Every student who wrote *his or her* name on the class list had to pay a copying fee in advance and pledge to attend every session.

▪ **Use parallel titles for women and men.**

BIASED   Sigmund Freud and Mrs. Brothers

REVISED   Dr. Freud and Dr. Brothers

BIASED   men and ladies

REVISED   men and women *or* gentlemen and ladies

BIASED   Jane Austen, Mrs. Gaskell, and George Eliot described life in the provinces; Dickens described life in the city.

REVISED   Austen, Gaskell, and Eliot described life in the provinces; Dickens described life in the city.
                                    or
Jane Austen, Elizabeth Gaskell, and George Eliot described life in the provinces; Charles Dickens described life in the city. [*First and last names are used for all.*]

▪ **Use terms that do not suggest gender for names of occupations and professions.**

BIASED   The salesman gave an informative presentation.

REVISED   The sales representative gave an informative presentation.

(*For more on unbiased language, see Chapter 47, pp. 364–67.*)

CHECKLIST

Revising Your Draft for Style

1. **Tone:** Is the tone I have used appropriate for my audience? Have I used any condescending language, or have I addressed the audience as equals?

2. **Sentence variety:** Are my sentences varied? Have I used too many short, choppy sentences or long, rambling ones?

3. **Direct sentences:** Are my sentences direct, or have I used too many constructions beginning with *There is (are)* or *It is*?

4. **Precise words:** Have I put the right words in the best places? Have I used any words that have the wrong connotation?

5. **Nonbiased language:** Have I used inclusive language, with parallel titles for men and women and occupation names that do not suggest gender? Have I avoided using the pronouns *he, him, his,* and *himself* to refer to anyone except a specific male?

9e Collaborate with readers online and in print.

If you check the acknowledgments section in any book, you will see evidence that writers consult with readers for comments on work in progress. Asking actual readers to comment on your draft is the best way to see your writing in a broader context. Computers may be the quintessential collaboration machines thanks to the ease with which electronic texts can move back and forth between them.

1. Write e-mail.   When you work on papers with classmates, you can use e-mail in the following ways:

- To check out your understanding of the assignment
- To try out various topics
- To ask each other useful questions about ideas
- To share your freewriting, plan, or rough draft
- To respond to each other's ideas, including requests for clarification and additional information

2. Chat with each other about ideas.   You can get together in a group to share ideas. You can also use online chats for this purpose. A great deal of collaboration and communication is possible with e-mail, but other virtual spaces for interaction abound. Your instructor may include **chat** or **MOO** activities, where you go into virtual rooms to work on assignments in small groups or visit and interact with other classes at other colleges. Some people find that chatting in such virtual rooms, or synchronous spaces, prompts them to become more creative. In the exchange that follows, for example, two students share ideas about volunteerism.

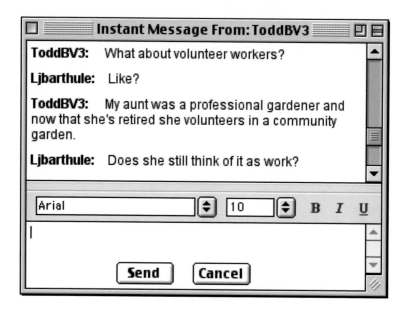

3. Try peer review. Whether it is required or optional, peer review is a process that involves reading and critiquing your classmates' work while they review yours. When you have a fairly solid draft to share, you can send it to your peer reviewers by e-mail (also print out a hard copy for yourself), or you can meet in person to exchange and read drafts. Consider including printouts of some of your peers' responses, if they arrive online, with your final draft so that your teacher knows you have taken the initiative to work with other writers. If you meet in person, you can ask your peer reviewers to write out their responses and then include these written responses with your final draft.

Most readers genuinely want to be helpful. When sharing your drafts with your peers, help them give you the assistance you need by asking them specific questions. The best compliment they can pay you is to take your work seriously enough to make constructive sug-

For MULTILINGUAL STUDENTS

Peer Review

In some cultures, only the teacher reviews a student's writing. In the United States, however, students are encouraged to reinforce and expand their own learning by identifying the strengths of their classmates' papers, pointing out problems, and working together to find solutions to these problems. As your classmates review your draft, ask them to point out problems with the substance of your paper (purpose, thesis, and organization) and not to get bogged down by focusing on problems you may have with usage or grammar. You can work on those at a later stage.

gestions. When you give them your draft, tell them the answers to the following questions:

- **What is your purpose?** Is your purpose mainly informative, interpretive, or argumentative? What do you want your readers to learn, to understand, or to believe?

- **How close is the project to being finished?** Your answer to this question helps readers understand where you are in the writing process and how best to assist you in taking the next step.

- **What steps do you plan to take to complete the project?** If readers know your plans, they can either question the direction you are taking or give you more specific advice, such as the titles of additional books or articles that you might consult.

Reading others' drafts will help you be a more objective reader of your own work, and comments from readers will help you see your own writing as others see it. As you gain more objectivity, you will become more adept at revising your work. In addition, the approaches that you see your classmates taking to the assignment will broaden your perspective and give you ideas for new directions in your own writing.

4. Use the campus writing center.   Many campuses maintain writing centers, staffed by tutors, that offer help for every stage of the writing process. Tutors in the writing center can read and comment on drafts of your work. They can also help you find and correct problems with grammar, punctuation, and mechanics.

5. Use online writing labs, or OWLs.
Most OWLs present information about writing that you can access anytime, including lists of useful online resources. Some OWLs are staffed by tutors who support students working on specific writing assignments. OWLs with tutors can be useful in the following ways:

- You can submit a draft via e-mail for feedback. OWL tutors will return your work, often within 48 hours.
- OWLs may post your paper in a public access space where you will receive feedback from more than just one or two readers.
- You can read papers online and learn how others are handling writing issues.

You can learn more about what OWLs have to offer by checking out the following Web sites:

For a list of links to additional online writing labs, click on "Links to OWLs" on the Online Learning Center for *A Writer's Resource* at <www.mhhe.com/maimon>.

- *Purdue University's Online Writing Lab*
  <http://owl.english.purdue.edu>
- *Writing Labs and Writing Centers on the Web* (visit almost 50 OWLs) <http://owl.english.purdue.edu/internet/owls/writing-labs.html>
- *Washington State University's Online Writing Lab*
  <http://owl.wsu.edu>

6. Respond to readers.
Consider and evaluate your readers' suggestions, but remember that you are under no obligation to do what they say. Sometimes you will receive contradictory advice. One reader may like a particular sentence; a second reader may suggest that you eliminate the very same sentence. Is there common ground? Yes. Both readers stopped at that sentence. Ask yourself why—and if you want readers to pause there. Remember that you are the one who is ultimately responsible for your paper, so you need to make decisions that you are comfortable with.

7. Work with experts and instructors.
In addition to sharing your work with peers in class or through e-mail or online chats, you can use e-mail to consult experts. Suppose, for example, that a friend at another college is an expert on the topic of your paper. You can use e-mail to interview that friend, and then include parts of the interview in your paper. As always, you must properly credit your source. (*See Tabs 6–8 on documentation styles.*)

You can also consult your instructor or other experts. Many students don't think to ask their instructor questions by e-mail. If your instructor is willing, you can quote from his or her response in your paper, along with a proper citation.

TextConnex

Writing Papers

The following Web sites give more information on topics presented in Tab 2.

Using Logic in Composition <http://papyr.com/hypertextbooks/ engl_101/logic.htm>: A comprehensive Web site that explains many different types of logical fallacies, as well as how to construct a logical argument.

Developing a Thesis <http://www.writing.northwestern.edu/tips/ thesis.html>: Northwestern University's tips on developing a thesis.

Paradigm Online Writing Assistant <http://www.powa.org>: A comprehensive writing site that helps with all stages of composing an essay, from brainstorming to proofreading.

Your instructor's comments on an early draft are especially valuable. He or she will raise questions and make suggestions, but remember, it is not your instructor's job to "solve" the paper for you and to tell you everything you need to do to get an "A" in the course. It is your responsibility to address the issues your instructor raises and to revise your work.

9f Use online tools for revising.

Word-processing programs can make your text look beautiful, with a pleasing format and easy-to-read typeface. Even when a first draft looks finished, however, it is still a first draft. Be sure to check below the surface for problems in content, structure, and style. Move paragraphs around, add details, and delete irrelevant sentences. The computer makes these changes almost effortless. However, it is always a good idea to print out a copy of your draft because hard copy, unlike the computer screen, allows you to see the big picture—your paper as a whole.

Your word-processing program probably offers change-tracking. Many users don't know about this feature, but it is very useful, whether you are editing your own work or collaborating with other students on writing projects. "Track Changes" or "Revisions", which may be part of the "Tools" menu, allows you to edit writing while also maintaining the original text. Usually, strike-through marks show what you have deleted or replaced. Because you can still see the original text, you can judge whether a change has improved the paper and

For specific tips on how to track changes in your paper, visit <www.mhhe. com/maimon/ revising/ revising_ online>.

whether any vital information was lost when the change was made. If you change your mind, you can restore the deleted text. When collaborating with another writer, you should keep the original text intact while suggesting changes. To do this, track changes onscreen only.

Another feature that may be included in the "File" menu is "Versions." When you are collaborating with other students on a paper, you can use the "Versions" feature to save and name various drafts of text. Too many versions can get confusing, though, so you should create versions only when your project requires it.

Whether you use special menu features or just the basic functions of a word-processing program, the computer allows you to save and compare several different versions of a piece of writing and decide which one works best. The following tips will make this process go smoothly.

1. Save your work. Always protect your creativity and hard-won drafts from power surges and other acts of technological treachery. Save often, and make backups.

2. Label revised drafts under different file names. Save successive versions of your paper under different file names: for example, Jennifer Koehler could have saved drafts of her paper as Germany1, Germany2, Germany3, and so on.

3. Print hard copies early and often. If you save and print the original, you can feel free to experiment.

Anybody who is involved in working across the disciplines is much more likely to have a lively mind and a lively life.

—MARY FIELD BELENKY

Common Assignments across the Curriculum

10. Informative Reports *77*
   a. Understanding
      the assignment *77*
   b. Selecting a topic *77*
   c. Considering what
      your readers
      already know *78*
   d. Developing an objec-
      tive stance *78*
   e. Composing a thesis *78*
   f. Providing context in
      your introduction *79*
   g. Organizing your
      paper *79*
   h. Illustrating key ideas *79*
   i. Clarifying specialized
      terms and
      abbreviations *80*
   j. Concluding by answer-
      ing "So what?" *80*
   k. Student paper: Informa-
      tive report *81*

11. Interpretive Analyses *88*
   a. Understanding the
      assignment *88*
   b. Discovering an aspect
      that is meaningful to
      you *88*
   c. Developing a thought-
      ful stance *89*
   d. Using an intellectual
      framework *89*
   e. Exploring ideas to dis-
      cover your thesis *90*
   f. Developing a focused,
      purposeful thesis *90*
   g. Writing a strong
      introduction *91*
   h. Planning your
      paper *92*
   i. Concluding by answer-
      ing "So what?" *93*
   j. Student paper: Interpre-
      tive analysis *93*

12. Arguments *97*
   a. Understanding the
      assignment *97*
   b. Figuring out what is at
      issue *98*
   c. Developing a reason-
      able stance *99*
   d. Composing a thesis
      that states your
      position *99*
   e. Using reasoning to sup-
      port and develop your
      thesis *100*
   f. Creating an
      outline *101*
   g. Using critiques
      from peers to
      understand your
      audience *102*
   h. Emphasizing common
      ground in the
      introduction *102*
   i. Concluding by
      restating and
      emphasizing your
      position *102*
   j. Reexamining your
      reasoning *103*
   k. Student paper:
      Argument *104*

13. Other Kinds of
    Assignments *111*
   a. Personal essays *111*
   b. Lab reports in the
      experimental
      sciences *113*
   c. Case studies in the
      social sciences *118*
   d. Essay exams *121*
   e. Oral
      presentations *124*
   f. Coauthored
      projects *128*
   g. Portfolios *129*

Most college courses require writing—from the lab report in chemistry to the policy proposal in economics. This section gives you tips on writing the most common kinds of college assignments and explains the distinctive features of each kind.

10 Informative Reports

10a Understand the assignment.

Imagine what the world would be like if each person had to learn everything from scratch, by trial and error, with no recipes, no encyclopedias, no textbooks, no newspapers—nothing that records what others have learned. Fortunately, we have many sources of information to draw on, including informative reports. An **informative report** passes on what someone has learned about a topic or issue; it teaches.

Because a good way for students to reinforce learning is by teaching it to others, college instructors often assign informative reports. When your instructor assigns an informative report, he or she expects you to find out what is currently known about some specific topic and to present what you discover in a clear and unbiased way.

An informative report gives you a chance to do the following:

- Read more about an issue that interests you.
- Make sense of what you have read, heard, and seen.
- Teach others what you have learned.

For online guidance as you write an informative paper, visit <www.mhhe.com/maimon/reports>.

Note: In upper-division courses, instructors sometimes assign a special kind of informative report called a *review of the literature*. Here the term *literature* refers to published research reports, not to poems and novels, and the term *review* means that you need to survey others' ideas, not evaluate them or argue for your opinion. A review presents an organized account of the current state of knowledge in a specific area, an account that you and other researchers can use to figure out new projects and directions for research.

10b Select a topic that interests you.

An informative report should be clear and reliable but not dull. The major challenge of writing informative reports is engaging the reader's interest. Selecting a topic that interests you makes it more likely that your report will interest your readers.

For tips on how to select a topic for an informative paper, visit <www.mhhe.com/maimon/reports>.

Consider connecting what you are learning in one course with a topic you are studying in another course or with your personal experience. For example, one student, Joe Smulowitz, worked part-time for a stockbroker and wanted to make a career in that area—an area significantly affected by the Internet. For his topic, he decided to investigate what online stock traders were doing and saying. (*Smulowitz's paper begins on p. 81.*)

10c Consider what your readers know about the topic.

Unless the assignment designates a different group, consider your classmates and your instructor as the audience for your report. In other words, assume that your readers have some familiarity with the topic area but that most of them do not have clear, specific knowledge of your particular topic.

10d Develop an objective stance.

When writers have an **objective stance,** they do not take sides. Instead, they present differing views fairly, without indicating a preference for one view over another. This commitment to objectivity gives an informative report its authority. Ideas and facts are presented methodically, and the emphasis is on the topic, not the writer. By contrast, when writers are **subjective,** they let readers know their view. Although a subjective stance is appropriate for other types of writing, an informative report should come across as objective rather than subjective.

10e Compose a thesis that summarizes your knowledge of the topic.

The thesis of an informative report is usually not controversial, even when the report is about a dispute. Because transmitting knowledge is the primary goal of an informative report, the thesis typically states an accepted generalization or reports the results of the writer's study.

Your thesis should also state the objective of your paper and forecast its content. Before you decide on a thesis, review the information you have collected and divide it up into categories, or subtopics. Compose a thesis statement that summarizes—either generally or by category—what the information in your paper shows. (*For more on thesis statements, see Tab 2: Writing Papers, pp. 43–45.*)

In his paper about online stock trading, Smulowitz's thesis is a generalization that he supports in the body of his paper with information he groups into categories:

> Besides honest investors with various levels of expertise, the Internet grants access to numerous investors who post false information in hopes of making a quick and sometimes large profit. [. . .] *The one hundred or so postings that I read can be divided into four categories.*

Notice how Smulowitz forecasts the body of his report. We expect to learn something about each of the four categories, and the report is structured to give us that information category by category.

10f Provide context in your introduction.

Informative reports usually begin with a relatively simple introduction to the topic and a straightforward statement of the thesis. To orient readers, the introduction may provide some relevant context or background, but writers of informative reports generally get to their topic as quickly as possible and keep it in the foreground. (*For more on introductions, see Tab 2: Writing Papers, p. 52.*)

10g Organize your paper for clarity by classifying and dividing information.

Because you are explaining something in an informative report, clarity matters. Informative writers develop their ideas in an organized way, often by classifying and dividing information into categories, subtopics, or the stages of a process. (*For more on developing your ideas, see Tab 2: Writing Papers, pp. 47–52.*)

10h Illustrate key ideas with examples.

Because clarity is so important to the success of an informative report, writers of these kinds of papers usually use specific examples to help readers understand their most important ideas. In his paper on online stock trading, Smulowitz devotes a lot of space to examples, including messages posted by various investors and an instance of gender-bending for profit. Examples make his report interesting as well as educational. (*For more on using examples, see Tab 2: Writing Papers, p. 49.*)

Informative Reports

By writing reports in college, you prepare yourself for future professional and public occasions that will require you to pass on information to others. In many professions, writing informative announcements, manuals, and reports is part of the job:

- For a music appreciation textbook, a professor of music history writes a chapter explaining three distinctive characteristics of Renaissance music.
- In a published article, an anthropologist surveys and summarizes a large body of indigenous material on warfare among the Pueblos before the arrival of the Spanish explorers.
- In a report for their colleagues, three physical therapists define what a critical pathway is, trace its development, and summarize the arguments for and against its use in patient care.
- For an encyclopedia of British women writers, a professor of literature briefly recounts the life and works of Eliza Fenwick, a recently rediscovered eighteenth-century author.
- In a journal for research biologists, two biochemists summarize the findings of more than two hundred recently published articles on defense mechanisms in plants.

10i   Define specialized terms and spell out unfamiliar abbreviations.

Most informative reports include specialized terms that will probably not be familiar to most readers, or familiar terms that are being used in a specialized or an unfamiliar way. Writers of informative reports usually explain these terms with a synonym or a brief definition. For example, Smulowitz gives a brief definition of the term *online traders* in the first paragraph of his informative report on online stock trading. (*For more on definition, see Tab 2: Writing Papers, pp. 48–49.*) Unfamiliar abbreviations like CMC (computer-mediated communication) and GNP (gross national product) are spelled out the first time they are used, with the abbreviation in parentheses.

10j   Conclude by answering "So what?"

Because informative writers want readers to remember what they have learned, they often try to conclude their reports with an image that suggests the information's value or a saying that sums it all up. The conclusion reminds readers of the topic and point that were first stated in the introduction and its straightforward thesis. It then answers the "So what?" question.

At the end of his report on online stock trading, Smulowitz answers the "So what?" question with a warning:

> Before buying any stock, investors should investigate it thoroughly. When they read what others say about a company, they should remember that if it sounds too good to be true, it probably isn't true.

(*Also see information on conclusions in Tab 2: Writing Papers, pp. 52–53.*)

For additional samples of informative papers, visit <www.mhhe.com/maimon/reports>.

10k Student paper: Informative report

In the informative paper that follows, Joe Smulowitz reports what he has learned about the people who are talking online about stocks. As you read his report, notice how Smulowitz provides a context for his topic, cites various sources, categorizes the information, and illustrates his ideas with examples, all hallmarks of a clear, carefully developed informative report. Besides being clear, informative reports are also expected to be objective. Do you think Smulowitz's report meets this requirement?

Chatting Online about Stocks

```
        The Internet has become a significant

    social laboratory for experimenting with

    the constructions and reconstructions of

    self that characterize postmodern life.

            --Sherry Turkle, Life on Screen
```

One new kind of self that the Internet has produced is the online stock market investor. Until a few years ago, the average person who wanted to invest in the stock market had to hire a professional broker at a significant cost. A stockbroker working for a reputable firm might charge $300 per trade as well as a substantial commission. Nowadays, the average person can buy

Topic introduced.

and sell stocks over the Internet at costs ranging
from $7.95 to $25 per trade. As a result, more

and more people have become online traders--
investors who use the Internet to buy and sell
stocks. According to Jupiter Communications,
of the 30 million American households with an
Internet connection, nearly a third use the World
Wide Web to research or invest in securities
(qtd. in Fluendy 48). Silicon Investor, a popular
site for chatting about stocks, receives over
12,000 posts a day from online traders (qtd. in
Lucchetti C6).

Who are these online traders, and what are
they talking about in investment-related chats?

Besides honest investors with various levels of
expertise, the Internet grants access to numerous
investors who post false information in hopes of
making a quick and sometimes large profit. According
to the Securities and Business Investments Division
of the Connecticut Department of Banking, "An
estimated four million U.S. households that
already have access to the major online services
are being exposed to hundreds of fraudulent and
abusive investment schemes, including stock
manipulations, pyramid scams, and Ponzi schemes"
(1). State securities agencies and other investment
regulators are now looking into cases in which the
price of shares in little-known stocks appears to
have been manipulated through messages posted on
Internet bulletin boards.

Many investors find out about online fraud
the hard way. Consider the case of Interlock
Consolidated Enterprises, Inc. This Canadian

company was reported to have landed a major contract to construct housing in the former USSR. When the company became the topic of online hype in early 1994, its stock jumped from 42 cents a share to $1.30 before falling back to 60 cents (Gardner and Gardner). In this type of scam, known as "pump and dump," investors spread unusually positive news about a stock, then sell it when the price gets unrealistically high. This scam is nothing new to the investment world. In fact, pump-and-dump schemes began in the 1700s (Lucchetti C1). But now the schemers can reach hundreds of thousands of people with a single posting, and that kind of reach clearly makes a difference.

To learn more about what is going on in investment-related chats, let's look at some recent online talk about a company called Chico's. The Silicon Investor Web site includes a chat room called "Miscellaneous," and it was there that I read a tip about Chico's: the company was about to release some good news, which would raise the price of its stock (Vanier). Putting aside my doubts about this tip, I decided to find out more by visiting the Yahoo! investment bulletin board that is devoted exclusively to Chico's. That bulletin board gave me access to all sorts of useful information: a brief summary of what Chico's does as a retailer of clothing and accessories for women; the company's location, phone number, number of employees, and Web address; a list of the company's recent press releases; and charts of financial data, including stock price and performance over the past year ("Chico's FAS").

Unfamiliar term defined.

Research steps explained.

Objective stance: Smulowitz uses the first person (I) to describe his research process, but his own opinions and feelings never become the center of attention.

Having learned some facts about Chico's, I
was ready to read and understand messages about
the company and its stock that were posted on the
bulletin board's discussion forum. The one hundred
or so postings that I read can be divided into
four categories. To the first category belong
postings with only positive things to say about
Chico's: "From the mouth of the president at the
conference call. CHCS [Chico's ticker name] is
expected to add 30 stores this year [. . .]. They
are expecting to grow to over 700 stores in the
near future" (mfpcpa). About 75% of the messages
I read belong to this positive-only category.
These messages appear to be posted by stockholders
trying to spread hype about Chico's so that the
stock's price will rise rather than fall. Usually,
there is no reply to this type of message. But
when there is a reply, it expresses agreement.

In the second category, I put messages that
seem to come from investors called "shorts" and
"longs." When they think a security's price is
going to decrease, shorts borrow the security from
a broker or dealer and sell it on the market. The
short investor profits if the price goes down
because he or she can replace the borrowed
security at a lower cost. Longs, on the other
hand, purchase a security because they think its
price will increase. The long investor profits if
the price goes up because he or she can sell the
security for more than it cost originally. Because
the shorts want the price to decrease and the
longs want the price to increase, these two kinds

Information about Smulowitz's classification.

Unfamiliar terms defined.

of stock traders often feud in online discussions. For example, in the following exchange about Chico's stock, a short investor's message entitled "Out of Steam" provokes a reaction entitled "Stay LONG" from cag174, a long investor:

> She can't take it Captain. The stock can't hold its new highs. It keeps closing at the bottom of the range. Shorts will live. We will see 28 again. (Startrader 1975)
>
> $38 will come before $28. $43 at year end. (cag174)

There seemed to be more long investors than short investors on the Chico's bulletin board. When a short posted a negative message aimed at lowering the stock price, usually a number of longs retaliated with messages warning that the author was misleading investors in order to sell his stock short.

In the third category are posts from sneaky investors. For example, the following post appears to be written by a woman: "Don't know much about stocks, just love the clothes and so do my daughters--31, 35, and 43. Talked hubby into buying in when I read Streisand was buying lots of sweaters [. . .]" (Katy10121). Since Chico's is a woman's clothing store, investors are likely to be interested in what women think about the store. But the person who posted this message may not be a woman. I checked the poster's online profile and discovered that it listed the poster's sex as "male." Could this investor be trying to take

Categories illustrated with examples.

advantage of other investors by engaging in gender-bending?

The last category of messages comprises posts from owners of little known and lightly traded stocks called "penny stocks." Here is an example of such messages:

> CHCS has given us a great ride, but now would be a good time to get off, while we're on top, and reinvest profits in a little soon-to-be-rediscovered gem, SNKI (Swank). Low volume right now, but check out the P/E and other stats [. . .].
> (gravytrain2030)

The price of penny stocks such as SNKI ranges from $0.01 to $5 a share. Enthusiasm from seemingly in-the-know observers like grettaship can sometimes lead to significant increases in the stock price. For that reason, Yahoo! does not offer bulletin boards for such stocks. Nevertheless, people still post their messages on other bulletin boards, just as grettaship did on the Chico's board.

Conclusion restates point and purpose.

The Internet gives the average person the opportunity to invest in the stock market without going through a broker. All the information essential to investing is available to anyone with access to a computer. But hype, manipulation, and fraud are also on the Internet. Before buying any stock, investors should investigate it thoroughly. When they read what others say about a company, they should remember that if it sounds too good to be true, it probably isn't true.

Works Cited

cag174. "Stay LONG." Online posting. 9 Nov. 1999.
    Chico's Message Board. Msg. #1001. 3 Dec.
    1999 <http://biz.yahoo.com/p/c/chcs.html>.

"Chico's FAS, Inc." 1 Dec. 1999. Yahoo! Finance. 3
    Dec. 1999 <http://biz.yahoo.com/p/c/chcs.html>.

Connecticut. Dept. of Banking. Securities and
    Business Investments Division. Investor
    Bulletin: On-line Investment Schemes.
    Connecticut: Dept. of Banking, 1998.

Fluendy, Simon. "Stock Surfin': Advice a Plenty,
    but Not Much Action on the Internet." Far
    Eastern Economic Review 24 Apr. 1997: 48+.

Lucchetti, Aaron. "Some Web Sites Getting Tough
    on Stock Chat." Wall Street Journal 28 May
    1998: C1+.

Gardner, David, and Tom Gardner. "Fairy Tale."
    The Fool's School: Buy Zeigletics. 1996-99.
    Motley Fool Inc. 8 Dec. 1999 <http://
    fool.com/School/Zeigletics/>.

gravytrain2030. "Sell CHCS, Reinvest in SNKI."
    Online posting. 3 July 1998. Chico's Message
    Board. Msg. #147. 5 Dec. 1999
    <http://biz.yahoo.com/p/c/chcs.html>.

Katy10121. "Just Love the Clothes." Online posting.
    24 June 1998. Chico's Message Board. Msg.
    #133. 3 Dec. 1999 <http://biz.yahoo.com/
    p/c/chcs.html>.

mfpcpa. "Response to Mish's Post." Online posting.
    23 Feb. 1999. Chico's Message Board. Msg.
    #502. 9 Dec. 1999 <http://biz.yahoo.com/
    p/c/chcs.html>.

"Works Cited" follows MLA style and begins a new page.

Startrader 1975. "Out of Steam." Online posting.

5 Nov. 1999. Chico's Message Board. Msg. #1000.

3 Dec. 1999 <http://biz.yahoo.com/p/c/

chcs.html>.

Turkle, Sherry. <u>Life on the Screen: Identity in

the Age of the Internet</u>. New York: Simon, 1997.

Vanier, Gary. "Time to Buy Chico's." Online

posting. 1 May 1998. Silicon Investor.

29 Nov. 1999 <http://www.siliconinvestor.com/

stocktalk/subject.gsp?subjectid=20636>.

11 Interpretive Analyses

11a Understand the assignment.

Interpretation is one of the key tasks of educated people. As the phrase "That's open to interpretation" suggests, searching for meaning does not involve looking for a single right answer. Instead, it involves figuring out a way of understanding that is meaningful to the writer and convincing to readers.

For online guidance as you write an interpretive paper, visit <www.mhhe.com/maimon/analyses_and_literature>.

In college, you will frequently get assignments that require you to explore the meaning of written documents, literary works, cultural artifacts, social situations, and natural events. When an assignment asks you to compare, explain, analyze, discuss, or do a reading of something, you are expected to study that subject closely, to figure out what it might mean.

Interpretive analyses, including comparative papers, encourage you to move beyond simple description and examine or compare particular items for a reason: to enhance your reader's understanding of peoples' conditions, actions, beliefs, or desires.

11b Discover an aspect of the subject that is meaningful to you.

Although you will not include your personal reflections in the finished version of your interpretive analysis, your interpretation will have more energy if you take time to discover why the subject is meaningful to you. Think about your own experience while you read, listen, or

CHARTING the TERRITORY

Student Analyses across the Disciplines

Students are often called upon to write interpretive analyses such as the following:

- A student in a literature course, Rajeev Bector, asserts that Flannery O'Connor's story "Everything That Rises Must Converge" can be understood as a character contest.
- A student majoring in music spells out the emotional implications of the tempo and harmonic progression in Schubert's *Der Atlas.*
- A student in an economics course demonstrates that, according to an econometric model of nine variables, deregulation has not decreased the level of airline safety.

observe. Connecting your own thoughts and experience to what you are studying can help you develop fresh interpretations.

11c Develop a thoughtful stance.

Interpretive analyses take your readers with you on an intellectual journey. You are saying, in effect, "Come, think this through with me." Consequently, your stance should be thoughtful, inquisitive, and open-minded. You are exploring the possible meaning of something. Usually it is wise to admit uncertainty, and sometimes it is good to qualify your interpretations with words like *probably, may,* and *perhaps.* Read your writing aloud, and as you listen to your words, ask yourself whether your stance sounds as exploratory as it should.

11d Use an intellectual framework.

To interpret your subject effectively, you will have to analyze it using a relevant perspective or intellectual framework. For example, the basic elements of a work of fiction, such as plot, character, and setting, are often used to analyze stories. Sigmund Freud's theory of conscious and unconscious forces in conflict has been applied to various things, including people, poems, and historical periods. In his analysis of Flannery O'Connor's story "Everything That Rises Must Converge," Rajeev Bector uses sociologist Erving Goffman's ideas about "character contests" to interpret the conflict between a son and his mother. (*Bector's analysis begins on p. 94.*)

No matter what framework you use, analysis often entails taking something apart and then putting it back together by figuring out how the parts make up a meaningful whole. Because the goal of analysis is to create a meaningful interpretation, the writer needs to treat the whole as more than the sum of its parts and recognize that meaning is a complex problem with multiple solutions.

11e   List, compare, question, and classify to discover your thesis.

To figure out a thesis, it is often useful to explore separate aspects of your subject. For example, if you are analyzing literature, you might consider the plot, the characters, the setting, and the tone before deciding to focus your thesis on how a character's personality drives the plot to its conclusion. If you are comparing two subjects, you would look for and list points of likeness and difference. Note that comparing is not just a way of presenting ideas; it is also a way of discovering ideas. What features do the items have—and not have—in common? Can you find subtle differences in aspects that at first seem alike? Subtle similarities in aspects that at first seem very different? Which do you find more interesting, the similarities or the differences? The answers to these questions might help you figure out your thesis.

As you work on discovering your thesis, try one or more of the following strategies:

- Take notes about what you see or read, and if it helps, write a summary. Look for interesting issues that emerge as you work on your summary and notes.

- Ask yourself questions about the subject you are analyzing, and write down any interesting answers. Imagine what kinds of questions your professor might ask about the artifact, document, or performance you are considering. In answering these questions, try to figure out the thesis you will present and support.

- Name the class of things to which the item you are analyzing belongs (for example, memoirs), and then identify important parts or aspects of that class (for example, scene, point of view, helpers, turning points).

11f   Make your thesis focused and purposeful.

Because the subject of an interpretative analysis is usually complex, you cannot possibly write about all of its aspects. Instead, focus your paper on one or two issues or questions that are key to understanding the subject. The whole point of an interpretive analysis is to make a point about your subject. Focusing can help you resist the temptation to describe everything you see.

EXAMPLE

In O'Connor's short story, plot, setting, and characterization work together to reinforce the impression that racism is a complex and pervasive problem.

EXAMPLE

In the first section of Shubert's *Der Atlas,* both the tempo and the harmonic progression express the sorrow of the hero's eternal plight.

Although you want your point to be clear, you also want to make sure that your thesis anticipates the "So what?" question and sets up an interesting context for your interpretation. Unless you relate your specific thesis to some more general issue, idea, or problem, your interpretive analysis may seem pointless to readers. (*For more on developing your thesis, see Tab 2: Writing Papers, pp. 43–45.*)

11g Include in your introduction the general issue, a clear thesis or question, and relevant context.

In interpretive analyses, it often takes more than one paragraph to do what an introduction needs to do:

- Identify the general issue, concept, or problem at stake. You can also present the intellectual framework that you are applying.
- Provide relevant background information.
- Name the specific item or items you will focus on in your analysis (or the items you will compare).
- State the thesis you will support and develop or the main question(s) your analysis will answer.

You need not do these things in the order listed. Sometimes it is a good idea to introduce the specific focus of your analysis before presenting either the issue or the background information. Just make sure that your introduction does the four things it needs to do, even though you may begin it with a provocative statement or a revealing example designed to capture your readers' attention. (*For more on introductions, see Tab 2: Writing Papers, p. 52.*)

For example, the following is the introductory paragraph from a paper on the development of Margaret Sanger's and Gloria Steinem's feminism that was written for a history class:

General issue: feminist struggle against oppression.

Lists items to be compared.

Thesis stated.

> In our male-dominated society, almost every woman has experienced some form of oppression. Being oppressed is like having one end of a rope fastened to a pole and the other end fastened to one's belt: it tends to hold a woman back. But a few tenacious and visionary women have fought oppression and have consequently made the lives of others easier. Two of these visionary women are Margaret Sanger and Gloria Steinem. As their autobiographical texts show, Sanger and Steinem felt compassion for women close to them, and that compassion not only shaped their lives but also empowered them to fight for changes in society.

In one relatively short paragraph, the student identifies her paper's general issue (the feminist struggle against oppression), introduces the items to be compared (two autobiographical texts), and in the last sentence, states her main point or thesis. Although she has made a good beginning, her readers need additional background information about Sanger and Steinem—information that will give them a context for the two texts that are being compared. Therefore, the student must expand on the introduction a bit more before moving on to the points she wants to make to support her thesis.

11h Plan your paper so that each point supports your thesis.

As with any paper, an interpretive analysis has three main parts: an introduction, a body, and a conclusion. After you pose a key question or state your thesis in the introduction, you need to work point by point, organizing the points to answer the question and support your interpretive thesis. From beginning to end, readers must be able to follow the train of thought in your interpretive analysis and see how each point you make is related to your thesis. (*For more on developing your ideas, see Tab 2: Writing Papers, pp. 47–52.*)

For example, if Bector had simply described the events in Flannery O'Connor's "Everything That Rises Must Converge" or presented a random list of insights, his paper would not shed any light on what the story means. Instead, Bector ends his introduction with a compelling question about one character's motives:

QUESTION But why would Julian want to hurt his mother, a woman who is already suffering from high blood pressure?

Bector answers this interpretive question in the body of his paper by pointing out and explaining three features of the character contest between mother and son.

For the paper on the roots of Margaret Sanger's and Gloria Steinem's feminism, the student used the following three points to support and develop her interpretive thesis.

Thesis: As their autobiographical texts show, Sanger and Steinem felt compassion for women close to them, and that compassion not only shaped their lives but also empowered them to fight for changes in society.

1. Steinem and Sanger are both feminists—people intent on exposing and resisting the oppression of women.

2. Each of the two women felt compassion for her mother's plight.

3. Both Sanger and Steinem saw a connection between their mothers' suffering and the condition of other women.

11i Conclude by answering "So what?"

The conclusion of an interpretive analysis needs to do more than simply repeat the paper's thesis. It needs to answer the "So what?" question by saying why your thesis—as well as the analysis that supports and develops it—is relevant to the larger issue identified in the introduction. What does your interpretation reveal about that issue? (*For information about conclusions, see Tab 2: Writing Papers, pp. 52–53.*)

For example, the student who wrote about the roots of Steinem's and Sanger's feminism concluded her paper by insisting on the continuing need for a feminist struggle rooted in love for our mothers—including, of course, such mothers of contemporary feminism as Sanger and Steinem.

11j Student paper: Interpretive analysis

In the following paper, Rajeev Bector uses Erving Goffman's ideas to analyze and interpret the actions of two characters in Flannery O'Connor's short story "Everything That Rises Must Converge." But what provoked Bector's interpretation in the first place is this question: How can we understand the mean way Julian and his mother

For an additional sample of a literary analysis, visit <www.mhhe.com/maimon/analyses_and_literature>.

WRITING CONNECTIONS

Interpretive Analyses

You can find interpretive analyses in professional journals like *PMLA* (*Publications of the Modern Language Association*) as well as popular publications like the *New Yorker* and the *Atlantic Monthly*. Take a look at some of these publications to see how your work connects with that of professional scholars and critics.

- A cultural critic contrasts the way AIDS and cancer are talked about, imagined, and therefore treated.
- Two geologists analyze photos of an arctic coastal plain taken from an airplane and infer that the effects of seismic exploration vary according to the type of vegetation.
- A professor of classics analyzes Vietnamese counterparts to U.S. memorials of the Vietnam War to understand how different cultures view war.
- A musicologist compares the revised endings of two pieces by Beethoven to figure out what makes a work complete and finished.
- A philosopher reflects on personal identity as a complex and shifting concept by investigating how the ideas of the philosophers Descartes and Hume are alike and different.
- A cultural critic explores Freud's anecdotes, showing how they are used both to control and to dramatize the uncanny.

treat each other? As he helps us better understand Julian and his mother, Bector raises the larger issue of racism. To what extent does Bector's interpretive analysis of O'Connor's story also illuminate the workings of racism in our society?

The Character Contest in Flannery O'Connor's

"Everything That Rises Must Converge"

Sociologist Erving Goffman believes that

every social interaction establishes our identity

and preserves our image, honor, and credibility in

the hearts and minds of others. Social interactions,

he says, are in essence "character contests" that

occur not only in games and sports but also

in our everyday dealings with strangers, peers,

friends, and even family members. Goffman defines
character contests as "disputes [that] are sought
out and indulged in (often with glee) as a means
of establishing where one's boundaries are" (29).
Just such a contest occurs in Flannery O'Connor's
short story "Everything That Rises Must Converge."

Key idea that
provides
intellectual
framework.

As they travel from home to the Y, Julian and
his mother, Mrs. Chestny, engage in a character
contest, a dispute we must understand in order
to figure out the story's theme. Julian is so
frustrated with his mother that he virtually
"declare[s] war on her," "allow[s] no glimmer of
sympathy to show on his face," and "imagine[s]
various unlikely ways by which he could teach her
a lesson" (O'Connor 185, 186). But why would
Julian want to hurt his mother, a woman who is
already suffering from high blood pressure?

Question
posed.

Julian's conflict with Mrs. Chestny results
from pent-up hostility and tension. As Goffman
explains, character contests are a way of living
that often leaves a "residue": "Every day in many
ways we can try to score points and every day we
can be shot down" (29). For many years, Julian has
had to live under his racist mother's authority,
and every time he protested her racist views he was
probably shot down because of his "radical ideas"
and "lack of practical experience" (O'Connor 184).
As a result, a residue of defeat and shame has
accumulated that fuels a fire of rebellion against
his mother. But even though Julian rebels against
his mother's racist views, it doesn't mean that he
isn't a racist himself. Julian doesn't realize that
in his own way, he is as prejudiced as his mother.

Interpretation
organized
point by
point—first
point.

He makes it "a point" to sit next to blacks, in contrast to his mother, who purposely sits next to whites (182). They are two extremes, each biased, for if Julian were truly fair to all, he would not care whom he sat next to.

"We" indicates thoughtful stance, not Bector's personal feelings.

Second point.

When we look at the situation from Mrs. Chestny's viewpoint, we realize that she must maintain her values and beliefs for two important reasons: to uphold her character as Julian's mother and to act out her prescribed role in society. Even if she finds Julian's arguments on race relations and integration valid and plausible, Mrs. Chestny must still refute them. If she didn't, she would lose face as Julian's mother--that image of herself as the one with authority. By preserving her self-image, Mrs. Chestny shows that she has what Goffman sees as key to "character": some quality that seems "essential and unchanging" (28).

Third point.

Besides upholding her character as Julian's mother, Mrs. Chestny wants to preserve the honor and dignity of her family tradition. Like an actor performing before an audience, she must play the role prescribed for her--the role of a white supremacist. But her situation is hopeless, for the role she must play fails to acknowledge the racial realities that have transformed her world. According to Goffman, when a "situation" is "hopeless," a character "can gamely give everything [. . .] and then go down bravely, or proudly, or insolently, or gracefully or with an ironic smile on his lips" (32). For Mrs. Chestny, being game means trying to preserve her honor and dignity as she goes down to physical defeat in the face of hopeless odds.

Given the differences between Mrs. Chestny's
and her son's values, as well as the oppressiveness
of Mrs. Chestny's racist views, we can understand
why Julian struggles to "teach" his mother "a
lesson" (185) throughout the entire bus ride.
Goffman would point out that "each individual is   Thesis.
engaged in providing evidence to establish a
definition of himself at the expense of what can
remain for the other" (29). But in the end, neither
character wins the contest. Julian's mother loses
her sense of self when she is pushed down to the   Conclusion—
ground by a "colored woman" wearing a hat identical   main point
about Julian
to hers (187). Faced with his mother's breakdown,   and his mother
Julian feels his own identity being overwhelmed by   related to
larger issue of
"the world of guilt and sorrow" (191).   racism.

....

Works Cited   "Works Cited"
list follows
Goffman, Erving. "Character Contests." <u>Text Book:</u>   MLA style and
begins on a
    <u>An Introduction to Literary Language</u>. Ed.   new page.

    Robert Scholes, Nancy Comley, and Gregory

    Ulmer. New York: St. Martin's, 1988. 27-33.

O'Connor, Flannery. "Everything That Rises Must

    Converge." <u>Fiction</u>. Ed. R. S. Gwynn. 2nd ed.

    New York: Addison, 1998. 179-91.

12 Arguments

12a Understand the assignment.

In college, reasoned positions matter more than opinions based on
personal feelings, and writing arguments is a way to form reasoned
positions. Bearing in mind that reasonable people can see things differently, always strive to write well-informed, thoughtful arguments.

For online guidance as you write an argument, visit <www.mhhe.com/maimon/arguments>.

When you write an argument paper, your purpose is not to win but to take part in a debate by stating and supporting your position on an issue. In addition to position papers, written arguments appear in various forms, including critiques, reviews, and proposals.

- **Critiques:** Critiques focus on answering the question "What is true?" Someone has taken a position on an issue, and the critique fairly summarizes that position before either refuting or defending it. Refutations use one of two basic strategies: either the presentation of contradictory evidence to show that the position is false or the exposure of inadequate reasoning to show that the position should not be considered true. Defenses make use of three strategies: clarifying a position by explaining in more detail the author's key terms and reasoning; presenting new arguments to support the position; and showing that criticisms of the position are unreasonable or unconvincing.

- **Reviews:** Reviews focus on answering the question "What is good?" In a review, the writer evaluates an event, artifact, practice, or institution. Although the evaluation may begin with an everyday gut response—"I like it" or "I don't like it"—such initial opinions must be transformed into judgments. A judge in a court case thinks through a decision in light of legal principles. Likewise, judgments in reviews should be principled; that is, they should not be determined by personal taste or the mood of the moment but by commonly accepted criteria.

- **Proposals, or policy papers:** Proposals, sometimes called policy papers, focus on answering the question "What should be done?" They are designed to cause change in the world. Readers are not only asked to see the situation in a specific way, but they are also encouraged to act on that situation in a certain way. Nicholas Buglione's argument about injuries to professional athletes (*see p. 104*) is an example of a proposal.

12b   Figure out what is at issue.

People argue about issues, not topics. Before you can take a position on a topic like air pollution or football injuries, you must figure out what is at issue. Try turning your topic into a problem by asking questions about it. Are there indications that all is not as it should be? Have things always been this way, or have they changed for the worse? From what different perspectives—economic, social, political, cultural, medical, geographic—can problems like a wide receiver's recent knee injury or a quarterback's forced retirement be under-stood? Do people interested in the topic disagree about what is true, what is good, or what should be done?

Based on your answers to such questions, identify the issues your topic raises and decide which of these issues you think is most impor-tant, interesting, and appropriate for you to write about in response to your assignment.

For tips on choosing a topic for an argument paper, visit <www.mhhe.com/maimon/arguments>.

12c Develop a reasonable stance that negotiates differences.

When writing arguments, you want your readers to respect your intelligence and trust your judgment. Conducting research on your issue can make you well informed; reading other people's views and thinking critically about them can enhance your thoughtfulness. Find out what others have to say about the issue, and make it part of your purpose to negotiate the differences between your position and theirs. Pay attention to the places where you disagree with other people's views, but also note what you have in common—topical interests, key questions, or underlying values. (*For more on appeals to your audi-ence, see Tab 2: Writing Papers, p. 33.*)

Always remember that two views on an issue can be similar yet not identical, or different yet not completely opposite. It is important to avoid language that may promote prejudice or fear. Also, misrepre-sentations of other people's ideas are as out of place in a thoughtful argument as are personal attacks on their character. You should write arguments to open minds, not slam doors shut.

Trying out different perspectives can also help you figure out where you stand on an issue. (*Also see the next section on stating your position.*) Argue with yourself. Make a list of the arguments for and against a specific position; then compare the lists and decide where you stand. Does one set of arguments seem stronger than the other? Do you want to change or qualify your initial position to make it more understandable, reasonable, or believable?

For additional information on how to develop ideas in an argument, visit <www.mhhe.com/maimon/arguments>.

12d Compose a thesis that states your position.

A strong, debatable thesis on a topic of public interest is a key ingre-dient of an effective written argument. Without debate, there can be no argument and no reason to assert your position. Personal feelings and accepted facts are not debatable and therefore cannot serve as an argument's thesis.

PERSONAL FEELING, NOT A DEBATABLE THESIS

I feel that professional football players are treated poorly.

ACCEPTED FACT, NOT A DEBATABLE THESIS

Many players in the NFL get injured.

DEBATABLE THESIS

Current NFL regulations are not enough to protect players from suffering the hardships caused by game-related injuries.

In proposals and policy papers, the thesis presents a solution in terms of the writer's definition of the problem. The logic behind a thesis for a proposal can be stated like this:

Given these key variables and their underlying cause, one solution to the problem would be . . .

Because this kind of thesis is both complex and qualified, you will often need more than one sentence to state it clearly. You will also need numerous well-supported arguments to make it creditable. Readers will finally want to know that the proposed solution will not cause worse problems than it solves; they realize that policy papers and proposals call for actions, and actions have consequences.

12e Use reasoning to support and develop your thesis.

A strong, debatable thesis needs to be supported and developed with sound reasoning. You can think of an argument as a dialogue between the writer and readers. A writer states a debatable thesis, and one reader wonders, "Why do you believe that?" Another reader wants to know, "But what about this factor?" A writer needs to anticipate questions such as these and answer them by presenting claims (reasons) that are substantiated with evidence and by refuting opposing views. (*For more on claims and evidence, see Tab 2: Writing Papers, pp. 27–29.*)

Usually, a well-developed argument paper includes more than one type of claim and one kind of evidence. Besides generalizations based on empirical data or statistics, it often includes authoritative claims based on the opinions of experts and ethical claims based on the application of principle. For example, in his proposal about reducing injuries in professional football, for example, Buglione presents facts about the number of injuries in the previous and current seasons to establish the seriousness of the problem. He also includes quotes from an expert in football safety to explain the coach's role in promoting—or failing to promote—team safety. As you conduct research for your argument, note evidence—facts, examples, and expert testimony—that can be used to support each argument for or against your position.

In developing your argument, you should also pay attention to **counterarguments,** substantiated claims that do not support your position. Think critically about such claims and consider using one of the following strategies to take the most important counterarguments into account:

- Qualify your thesis in light of the counterargument by including a word such as *most, some, usually,* and *likely*: Although many people—fans and nonfans alike—understand that football is a dangerous sport, few realize just how hard *some* NFL players have it.

- Add to the thesis a statement of the conditions for or exceptions to your position: "The NFL pension plan is unfair to the players, except for those with more than five years in the league."

- Choose one or two counterarguments and plan to refute their truth or their importance in your paper. Buglione, for example, refutes the counterargument that the NFL has a good pension plan for its players.

12f Create an outline, including a linked set of reasons.

Arguments are most effective when they present a chain—a linked set—of reasons, so it is a good idea to begin drafting by writing down your thesis and outlining the way you will support and develop it. Your outline should include the following parts:

- An introduction to the topic and the debatable issue.

- A thesis stating your position on the issue.

- A point-by-point account of the reasons for your position, including the evidence (facts, examples, authorities) you will use to substantiate each major claim.

- A fair presentation and refutation of one or two counterarguments to your thesis.

- A response to the "So what?" question. Why does your argument matter?

For MULTILINGUAL STUDENTS

Learning about Cultural Differences through Peer Review

In some cultures, writing direct and explicit arguments is discouraged, but not so in the United States. When you share your work with peers born and raised in the United States, you may learn that the way in which you have expressed certain ideas and values—the vocabulary or the style of presentation you have used—makes it difficult for them to understand and accept the point you are making. Ask your peers to suggest different words and approaches and then decide if their suggestions would really make your ideas more accessible to others.

12g Use responses from peers to help you understand your audience.

Having peers review your work is especially important when you are writing arguments about debatable issues. You cannot assume that readers will agree with your position, so asking your peers to critique the content of your draft will give you valuable clues about your readers' likely reactions. As you revise your argument, try to incorporate what you have learned from your peers. You might use a "Some say, but I think" strategy to incorporate their objections to your thesis and show, as part of your argument, that you respect your audience and value dialogue.

12h Emphasize your commitment to dialogue in the introduction.

You want your readers to listen to what you have to say, so make sure that when you present the topic and issue in your introduction, you establish some kind of common ground or shared concern with them. For example, in his essay on the NFL, Buglione begins with a vivid account of a football injury to awaken his readers' concern for injured athletes and make them receptive to his proposal about decreasing the number of injuries in professional football. If possible, you should return to that common ground at the end of your argument.

12i Conclude by restating your position and emphasizing its importance.

After presenting your reasoning in detail, conclude by restating your position. Arguments are always thesis driven, so it is appropriate to

WRITING CONNECTIONS

Arguments

Arguments are central to American democracy and its institutions of higher learning because they help create the common ground that is sometimes called public space. In this space, freedom, justice, and equality—the civic ideals set forth in such documents as the Declaration of Independence and the Constitution—are supposed to rule so that reason may prevail over prejudice. All fields of academic study value reason and welcome arguments such as the following:

- A moral philosopher argues that under certain circumstances people have the right to die and, therefore, that liberal democracies should provide them with the means to exercise their right with dignity.
- The board of a national dietetic association publishes a position statement identifying obesity as a growing health problem that dieticians should be involved in preventing and treating.
- A political scientist critiques the idea that the prospects for Russian democracy depend on the country's economy, not on the quality of its political institutions.
- An art critic praises a museum's special exhibition of modern American paintings for its diversity and its thematic coherence.
- A sociologist proposes four policies that he claims will improve the quality of life and socioeconomic prospects of people living in inner-city neighborhoods.

remind readers of your thesis. The version of your thesis that you present in your conclusion should be more complex and qualified than the thesis statement you included in your introduction, to encourage readers to appreciate both your thoughtfulness and your argument's importance. In the end, readers may not agree with you, but they should know why the issue and your argument matter.

12j Reexamine your reasoning.

After you have completed the first draft of your paper, take time to reexamine your reasoning. Ask yourself the following questions:

- **Have I given a sufficient number of reasons to support my thesis, or should I add one or two more?**
- **Have I made any mistakes in logic?** (*See the list of Common Logical Fallacies, Tab 2: Writing Papers, pp. 30–31.*)

For additional
samples of
argument papers,
visit
<www.mhhe.
com/maimon/
arguments>.

■ **Have I clearly and adequately developed each claim
presented in support of my thesis?** Is the claim clear?
Have I defined its key terms, illustrated its meaning, and
explained its implications? Is my supporting evidence sufficient? Have I quoted or paraphrased from sources accurately
and documented them properly? (*For more on quoting, paraphrasing, and documenting sources, see Tab 5: Researching,
pp. 186–92, and Tabs 6–8.*)

12k Student paper: Argument

In the following position paper, Nicholas Buglione argues that the
National Football League can and should do more to protect its players from suffering the physical and economic hardships caused by
game-related injuries. As you read Buglione's argument, notice how
he tries to get readers to sympathize with the players, how he
acknowledges what the league has already done to address the injury
problem, and why he insists that more should be done in two areas:
safety and pensions. How suitable, complex, and feasible do you think
his solutions are?

NFL:

Negligent Football League?

    It's fourth down and short on the other team's

thirty-five yard line. At this critical point in

the game, all eyes are on you, the star running

back. The ball is snapped from center into the

quarterback's hands. You sprint up into the

pocket, receive the hand-off, and race into the

hole. At that instant, a rabid 245-pound linebacker

drives his massive body into your legs. There is a

crunch, followed by excruciating pain: your career

in football is over.

Topic
introduced.

        Injuries have been a fact of life in the

National Football League (NFL) for many years. But

in 1995, leg, knee, back, and head injuries piled

up, and the NFL decided it was time to take action.

Under the auspices of Commissioner Paul Tagliabue,
league officials agreed on some basic safety
guidelines to solve pro football's woes. These
guidelines included the following: (1) making it
illegal for players to lead with their heads when
they tackle, thereby reducing helmet-to-body
contact injuries; (2) allowing the quarterback to
ground the ball intentionally in certain situations,
thereby lessening the risk of his being injured by
a lineman; (3) reducing the size of the helmet's
facemask, thereby decreasing its potential as a
weapon; and (4) levying a $10,000 to $20,000 fine
on any player who hits another player after the
play is over.

The NFL expected that these regulations would
reduce the number of injuries, but the situation
got worse, not better. The 1996 season began
with an unprecedented seven injuries to starting
quarterbacks, all within the first week. As the
season went on, more leg, rib, head, and shoulder
injuries followed, and one quarterback, Chris
Miller, was forced to retire after sustaining his
fifth head injury in less than two seasons. The
epidemic of injuries has carried over into the
1997 season. Steve Young of the San Francisco
49ers recently suffered his third concussion in
ten months, and wide receiver Jerry Rice may miss
the rest of the season due to a knee injury.

Issue introduced.

Injuries have an enormous impact on a player's
life after football. Retirees tell horror stories
about the aftermath of injuries, which too often
turn simple, everyday acts like getting out of
bed into backbreaking work. Consider the case of

Issue explained with an anecdote.

Al Toon. Toon, a wide receiver for the New York Jets, enjoyed a career filled with highlights. Unfortunately, his career was also filled with concussions. After the ninth concussion, he called it quits and tried to put the game behind him. Sadly, those nine head injuries continue to punish Toon. On sunny days, he has to wear dark sunglasses because bright light is too much for his damaged head to handle. Even worse, Toon suffers from memory loss and chronic migraine headaches. Fortunately, he has managed his finances well and can afford to live comfortably with his wife and children. Many other retired players are not so fortunate. Those injured at an early age too often find themselves without a job, without a college degree, and without physical health. Is it any wonder that a few turn to drugs and alcohol, become homeless, or end up in a morgue way before their time?

Thesis stated.

A significant problem exists in the National Football League. Much more must be done to protect players. However, little progress will be made if the league tries to rectify the problem simply by passing rules and amendments to those rules. Such attempts fail to get at the root of the problem: a coaching tradition that emphasizes aggression over safety and a pension plan that fails to support all retired players adequately.

Causes of issue identified.

First point— supported by expert testimony.

Perhaps no one is more responsible for a player's physical welfare than the coach. According to Carl Blyth, an expert on football safety, the head coach's "attitude and leadership" are the "most important" factors in "promoting" a football team's success and "safety" (94). Even though coaches should teach players to value safety, they seldom do so, especially those working with college and professional teams. Instead, coaches often encourage feelings and behavior that compromise safety. Tommy Chaikin, a former lineman for South Carolina, has pointed out that his coaches encouraged aggressive feelings and behavior during practice. Fighting was not discouraged, and players were trained to fear being ridiculed for exhibiting any compassion (87).

Because a pugnacious team is more likely to win, it is understandable that coaches want to instill a fighting spirit in their players. What coaches fail to realize, however, is that the aggressive nature of their training programs increases the incidence and severity of injuries. To disregard a player's safety for the purposes of toughening him up is unethical. It is also foolish because ensuring that players stay healthy is in the best interests of the coach and team. Nevertheless, the quarterback Steve Beuerlein contends that no one teaches players like him "to run or protect [themselves]," let alone "how to take on [the] big guys" (qtd. in Zimmerman 26). Clearly, the coaches of the National Football League do not have their players' safety in mind, and this situation must change. Their failure to teach players how to play football safely has made the NFL injury epidemic worse.

Refutes counter-argument that winning is more important than safety.

Injuries often continue to plague players even after they retire. When their football careers are finished, most players still need to

Second point—supported by statistics.

work to support themselves and their families. However, as the sportswriter Bob Glauber reports, "about 70 percent of today's current players do not get their college degree" (1: B6). Without a college degree, retired football players have little chance of obtaining white-collar jobs. The alternative, blue-collar work, is closed to many former players who suffer the lingering effects of injury. Glauber's survey of 1,425 former NFL players found that more than 50% are physically limited by previous injuries (2: A64). What compensation is there for these retired players, the ones who have essentially destroyed their bodies playing football for the league?

Refutes counter-argument that NFL pensions solve the problem.

A pension would seem to be the answer. Though the NFL does have a pension plan, it is not adequate or fair. According to Glauber, the NFL's pension plan pays retired players with five or more years of NFL service $300 a month per year of service (4: A92). The minimum pension is therefore $1,500 a month. Although players with permanent injuries certainly deserve more, the bigger problem is that the pension plan only applies to players with five or more years of NFL service. Players injured within the first five years of their career receive no pension at all.

Third point— supported by expert testimony.

Why does the NFL treat its players so poorly? One reason may be that professional sports has become big business. In The Political Economy of College Sports (1986), Hart-Nibbrig and Cottingham coined the term "corporate athleticism" to describe the business-minded attitude that has

taken over sports (1). Corporate athleticism means
that sports organizations like the NFL are
primarily concerned with increasing profits.
Winning teams make a larger profit, so coaches try
to increase the chance of winning by encouraging
anger and aggression in their players. Moreover,
it is not in the front office's financial interest
to support disabled retirees. When players cease
to be lucrative for the league's bottom line, the
NFL can simply turn to a younger group of men, all
of whom are eager to play pro football. The NFL
can then exploit this new crop of players.

Exploitation can be resisted, especially by
the Players Association of the NFL. To deal with
the injury problem, the Players Association must
take three important steps. First, it must make
the rest of the sports world aware of the
situation. Although many people--fans and nonfans
alike—understand that football is a dangerous
sport, few realize just how hard some NFL players
have it. Second, the Players Association must
pressure NFL coaches to monitor the physical well-
being of their players closely and stress the
value of staying healthy, not the ill-gotten gains
of playing through injuries.

The Players Association must also work to
ease the financial burden on injured retirees. It
should demand that the NFL amend its pension plan
so that coverage is extended to all players,
regardless of how many years they played for the
league. In the United States, workers injured on
the job are eligible for compensation. Why should

Proposed
solution.

NFL players be treated differently just because
they have been in the league less than five
years? In addition, those players who serve five
or more years in the NFL deserve more than
$1,500 a month, especially if they suffer from
debilitating injuries. Finally, young players
should receive financial counseling to make them
aware of just how short a football career can
be. On average, an "NFL career last[s] only
3.6 years," and as Commissioner Paul Tagliabue
admits, what follows that career is likely to be
both "painful and tragic" for NFL players who
have not been "well-advised and well-served"
(Glauber 1: B6, B7).

"Works Cited"
follows MLA
style and
begins a new
page.

Works Cited

Blyth, Carl S. "Tackle Football." Sports Safety.
    Ed. Charles Peter Yost. Washington: American
    Association for Health, Physical Education,
    and Recreation, 1971. 93-96.

Chaikin, Tommy. "The Nightmare of Steroids."
    Sports Illustrated Oct. 1988: 84-102.

Glauber, Bob. "Life after Football." New York
    Newsday (four-pt. series) 12 Jan. 1997:
    B6+ (Pt. 1); 14 Jan. 1997: A64+ (Pt. 2);
    15 Jan. 1997: A66+ (Pt. 3); 16 Jan. 1997:
    A92+ (Pt. 4).

Hart-Nibbrig, N., and Clement Cottingham. The
    Political Economy of College Sports.
    Lexington: Heath, 1986.

Zimmerman, Paul. "What a Downer: Why Have So Many
    NFL Quarterbacks Been Injured This Season?"
    Sports Illustrated Oct. 1988: 19+.

13 Other Kinds of Assignments

13a Personal essays

Personal writing can be found in many places, including diaries and journals, but personal writing is not the same thing as a personal essay. The personal essay is one of the most literary kinds of writing. Like a poem, it feels significant—meaningful to readers and relevant to their lives. Like a play, it speaks to readers in a distinctive voice. Like a good story, it is both compelling and memorable.

1. Make connections between your experiences and those of your readers. When you write a personal essay, you are doing much more than fulfilling an assignment; you are exploring your experiences, clarifying your values, and composing a public self. At one level, your purpose is to reveal something about who you are, how you got where you are now, and what you believe. The focus, however, does not need to be on you. You might write a personal essay about a tree in autumn or an athletic event, but whatever focus you choose, remember that your readers expect to learn more than the details of your experience. They expect to see the connections between your experience and their own.

2. Turn your essay into a conversation. Personal essayists usually use the first person (*I* and *we*) to create an interpersonal relationship—a sense that the writer and reader are engaged in the open-ended give-and-take of conversation. How you appear in this conversation—shy, belligerent, or friendly, for example—will be determined by the details you include in your essay as well as the connotations of the words you use. Consider how Meghan Daum represents herself in relation to both computer-literate and computer-phobic readers in the following excerpt from her personal essay "Virtual Love," which appeared in a 1997 issue of the *New Yorker:*

> The kindness pouring forth from my computer screen was bizarrely exhilarating, and I logged off and thought about it for a few hours before writing back to express how flattered and "touched"—this was probably the first time I had ever used that word in earnest—I was by his message.
> I am not what most people would call a computer person. I have no interest in chat rooms, news groups, or most Web sites. I derive a palpable thrill from sticking a letter in the United States mail.

Besides Daum's conversational stance, notice the emotional effect of her remark on the word *touched* and her choice of words connoting excitement: *pouring forth, exhilarating,* and *palpable thrill.*

3. Structure your essay like a story.   Typically, personal essays are centered around either actions or ideas. There are three common ways to narrate events and reflections:

- **Chronological sequence** uses an order determined by clock time; what happened first is presented first, followed by what happened second, then third, and so on.

- **Emphatic sequence** uses an order determined by the point you want to make; for emphasis, events and reflections are arranged either from least to most important or from most to least important.

- **Suspenseful sequence** uses an order determined by the emotional effect the writer wants the essay to have on the reader. To keep the reader hanging, the essay may begin in the middle of things with a puzzling event, then flash back or go forward to clear things up. Some essays may even begin with the end—with the insight achieved—and then flash back to recount how the writer came to that insight.

4. Make details tell your story.   The story of an entire election campaign can be told in one sentence: "He was nominated; he ran; he lost." It is in the details that the story takes shape. No matter what you intend your essay to accomplish, the details you emphasize, the words you choose, and the characters you create all implicitly communicate the point of your essay. Often it is not even necessary to state your thesis. You can also control the pace of your essay through details. To emphasize the importance of a particular moment or reflection, you can provide numerous details that will slow the reader down. As an alternative, you can use details sparingly, a tactic that can surprise the reader, especially when the simple and direct sentences appear in a context filled with rich detail.

5. Connect your experience to a larger issue.   To demonstrate the significance of a personal essay to its readers, writers usually connect their individual experience to a larger issue. Here, for example, are the closing lines of Daum's essay on "Virtual Love."

> The world had proved to be too cluttered and too fast for us, too polluted to allow the thing we'd attempted through technology ever to grow on the earth. PFSlider and I had joined the angry and exhausted living. Even if we met on the street, we wouldn't

Personal Essay

Nowadays it is not uncommon for people from all walks of life to use the personal essay to learn about themselves and explore their experience of the world. Doctors, social workers, nutritionists—as well as novelists—publish memoirs and personal essays based on their life's work.

- Gloria Ladson-Billings, a teacher, reflects on her own experience in the classroom to figure out what makes teachers successful.
- Carol Allen, a philosophy professor, uses Plato's allegory of the cave as a metaphor in *Tea with Demons,* her personal account of going mad and finding her way back.
- Oliver Sacks, a neurologist, writes about his experiences with people whose perceptual patterns are impaired and about what it means to be fully human.

recognize each other, our particular version of intimacy now obscured by the branches and bodies and falling debris that make up the physical world.

Notice how Daum relates the disappointment of her failed Internet romance with "PFSlider" to a larger social issue: the general contrast between cyberspace and material realities. Her point, however, is quite surprising; most people do not think of cyberspace as more "intimate"—or touching—than their everyday, earthy world of "branches and bodies."

13b Lab reports in the experimental sciences

Without writing, science would not be possible. Scientists form hypotheses and plan new experiments as they observe, read, and write. When they work in the laboratory, they keep well-organized and detailed notebooks. They also write and publish lab reports, using a format that reflects the logic of scientific argument. In this way, they share their discoveries and enable other scientists to use their work.

As a college student, you may be asked to demonstrate your scientific understanding by showing that you know how to perform and report an experiment designed to verify some well-established fact or principle. In advanced courses, you may get to design original experiments as well.

Lab reports usually include seven distinctive sections in the following order: Abstract, Introduction, Methods and Materials, Results, Discussion, Acknowledgments, and Literature Cited. Begin drafting the report, section by section, while your time in the lab is still fresh in your mind. Organize your writing as follows:

- Begin with the methods-and-materials and results sections.
- Next, draft your introduction and discussion sections, making sure your introduction includes a clearly stated hypothesis.
- Finally, prepare the literature cited section, the acknowledgments, and the abstract.

Follow the scientific conventions for abbreviations, symbols, and numbers. See if your textbook includes a list of acceptable abbreviations and symbols, or ask your professor where you might find such a list. Use numerals rather than words for dates, time, pages, figures, tables, and standard units of measurement (for example, g/ml, percentages). Spell out numbers between one and nine that do not appear in a series of larger numbers.

1. Abstract.   An abstract is a one-paragraph summary of what your lab report covers in much greater detail. Although usually written last, the abstract is the part that others will read first. Scientists often skim professional journals, reading nothing more than the titles and abstracts of articles. Abstracts generally use about 250 words to answer the following questions:

- What methods were used in the experiment?
- What variables were measured?
- What were the findings?
- What do the findings imply?

Summarizing your argument in an abstract is a good way to begin the revising process.

2. Introduction.   The introduction gives readers the information they need to understand the focus and point of your lab report. State your topic, summarize prior research, and present your hypothesis.

As in the example that follows, you should use precise scientific terminology (α-amylase), spell out the key terms that you will later abbreviate (*gibbelleric acid* [GA]), and whenever possible, prefer the active voice over the passive. (*For a discussion of active and passive voices, see Tab 10: Editing for Clarity, pp. 359–61.*) The present tense is used to state established knowledge ("the rye seed *produces*"), whereas past tense is used to summarize the work of prior researchers (e.g., "Haberlandt *reported*"). The writer cites sources using a number system.

According to studies by Yomo,[2] Paleg,[3] and others,[1,4] barley seed embryos produce a gibbelleric acid (GA) which stimulates the release of hydrolytic enzymes, especially α-amylase. It is evident that these enzymes break down the endosperm, thereby making stored energy sources available to the germinating plant. What is not evident, however, is how GA actually works on the molecular level to stimulate the production of hydrolytic enzymes. As several experiments[5–8] have documented, GA has a RNA-enhancing effect. Is this general enhancement of RNA synthesis just a side effect of GA's action, or is it directly involved in the stimulation of α-amylase?

The first sentence names both a general topic, barley seed embryos, and a specific issue, GA's stimulation of hydrolytic enzymes. The last sentence poses a question, one that prepares readers for the hypothesis by focusing their attention on the role enhanced RNA synthesis plays in barley-seed germination.

3. Methods and materials. Experiments must be repeatable. The purpose of the methods-and-materials section is to answer the *how* and *what* questions in a way that enables other scientists to replicate your work. Select the details that they will need to know to replicate the experiment. Using the past tense, recount in chronological order what was done with specific materials, as the following student did in his lab report on α-amylase production in barley seeds:

After incubating for 48 hours, the seeds were cut in half transversely. Five endosperm halves without embryos were placed in each of 14 small glass test tubes. Next, a solution with a GA_3 concentration ranging from 0 g/ml to 10^5 g/ml was added to each test tube.

Notice that the writer does not mention the time of day or the instrument used to cut the seeds. These details do not influence the results and therefore are not important variables. The student does describe the range of GA concentrations because that is the key variable.

4. Results. In this section, your purpose is to tell your reader about the results that are relevant to your hypothesis, especially those that are statistically significant. Results may be relevant to your hypothesis even if they are different from what you expected. An experiment does not need to confirm your hypothesis to be interesting.

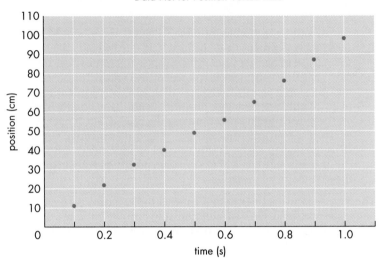

Data Plot for Position Versus Time

To report what you have learned, you might provide a summarizing table or graph. For example, the graph above, which plots the distance of a glider over a period of time, was used to summarize the results of an engineering assignment. In this instance, a paper airplane was launched and the distance it traveled in a specific period of time was measured. Each point on the graph represents the distance the glider traveled in consecutive tenths of a second from 0.1 second to 1.0 second. By reading the positions of the glider on the XY plot (X equals time; Y equals position in centimeters), we can see that the glider traveled a total distance of 98 centimeters in 1.0 second.

Every table and figure you include in a lab report must be referred to in the body of your report. Do not repeat all the information in the display, but do point out and illustrate relevant patterns. If you run statistical tests on your findings, be careful not to make the tests themselves the focus of your writing. In this section, you should emphasize the results of the tests, not the statistical procedures used to analyze the data. Refrain from interpreting why things happened the way they did. Interpretation belongs in the discussion section.

Note: Choose words carefully. Refer to an "increase," for example, as *marked* rather than as *significant*. Like the terms *correlated* and *random*, the term *significant* has a specific statistical meaning for scientists and should therefore be used in a lab report only when the appropriate statistical tests have been done.

Scientific Research

Research reports by professional scientists are published in journals such as *Science*, the *American Naturalist, Current Directions in Psychological Science,* and the *American Journal of Physics.* Take a look at one of these journals to see how your work relates to the work of professional scientists. Here are some examples of scientific research:

- A biochemist tests the hypothesis that THC (the major active ingredient in marijuana) acts as an estrogen (a female hormone).
- A mechanical engineer tests the hypothesis that 50 pounds of force is sufficient to overcome the thermal contact resistance in the coupling joint of a mechanical switch designed for use on a rocket-borne telescope.
- A social psychologist tests the hypothesis that the more open-ended a question or task is, the more likely it is that an individual will behave in conformity with the will of a group.

5. Discussion.   In your discussion section, you need to explain how and why your results do or do not confirm the hypothesis. Lab experiments produce results, not facts or laws. To transform results into accepted facts or laws, the scientific community depends on debate and consensus. In discussing your results, do the following:

- Interpret your major findings by explaining how and why each finding does or does not confirm the original hypothesis.
- Connect your research with prior scientific research. How and why do your findings and interpretations agree or disagree with the prior research summarized in your introduction?
- Look ahead to future research: where do scientists interested in this area seem to be going?

6. Acknowledgments.   You may have reason to include an acknowledgments section. In professional journals, most reports of experimental findings include a brief statement acknowledging those who assisted the author(s) during the research and writing process.

7. Literature cited.   This section of your report should include a listing of all manuals, books, and journal articles you used during your research and writing process. Do not wait until the last minute to prepare this section, or you may find that you do not have time to get some missing piece of information. Use one of the citation formats developed by the Council of Science Editors (CSE style), unless another citation format is favored by those working in the area of your research. If you are uncertain about which format to use, ask your professor for advice. (*See Tab 8: Other Documentation Styles.*)

13c Case studies in the social sciences

Social scientists are trained observers and recorders of the behavior of individuals and groups, research that depends on writing. Accurate observations are essential starting points for a case study, and writing helps observers see more clearly and precisely.

1. Choose a topic that raises a question. In doing a case study, your purpose is to connect what you see and hear with issues and concepts in the social sciences. Choose a topic and turn it into a research question. Before engaging in your field research, write down your hypothesis—a tentative answer to your research question—as well as some categories of behavior or other things to look for.

2. Assume an unbiased stance. In a case study, you are presenting empirical findings, based on careful observation. Your stance is that of an unbiased observer. Make a detailed and accurate record of what you observe, when, and how. Whenever you can, count or measure, and take down word-for-word what is said.

- **Count and measure.** Use frequency counts—the number of occurrences of specific, narrowly defined instances of behavior. If you are observing a classroom, for example, you might count the number of teacher-directed questions asked by several children. If you are observing group counseling sessions for female parolees, as sociologist Lynne Haney did for a 1996 case study, you might count the number of women who attend.

- **Include direct quotations.** What the female parolees say to each other and to their female parole officer is essential information. Here is one female parole officer's comment on the subject of tattoos, from Haney's study: "Come on, girl, you'd be better than that. I'm teachin' you better. You ain't no wall to be graffitied on. What's next, you gonna tattoo his name on your brain?"

- **Avoid value-laden terms and unsupported generalizations.** Do not use words that will evoke emotion or broad

CHARTING the TERRITORY

Case Studies

You will find case studies used in a number of social science disciplines.

- **In sociology:** You may be asked to draw on "insider" knowledge to describe and analyze a small group to which you have belonged or belong now. In this case, your study will address such issues as the group's norms and values, cultural characteristics, stratification and roles, initiation rites, and social control techniques. Your audience will be your professor, who will want to see how your observations reflect current theories on group norms.

- **In nursing:** A case study assignment may be an important part of your practicum in a local hospital. For a nursing class, you will note details of your care for a patient that corroborate or complicate what you have been taught to expect. Your audience is the supervising nurse, who is interested in your interactions with the patient.

- **In education:** As a student teacher in a classroom, you may closely observe and write about one student in the context of his or her socioeconomic and family background. Your audience will be the cooperating teacher, who seeks greater insight into the behavior of class members.

statements that you cannot support. For example, in the article "Homeboys, Babies, Men in Suits," Haney writes, "I uncovered numerous institutions in the juvenile system, most of which were staffed by women." She provides evidence that juvenile institutions are staffed by women and does not use emotionally laden adjectives to describe either the juvenile system or the women working there.

Note: Observe how Professor Haney uses *I* appropriately. The third person and the passive voice do not sound more objective or scholarly. If Haney had written that "numerous women-staffed institutions in the juvenile system were uncovered," her writing would sound stilted and unclear. Instead, she places herself, as a social scientist, in the midst of what she is studying.

3. Discover meaning in your data.   Your case study is based on the notes you made during your observations. As you review this material, try to uncover connections, identify inconsistencies, and

Case Studies

Using the data they keep in their field notebooks, social scientists write and publish their findings in such journals as the *American Sociological Review, Harvard Business Review,* and *Journal of Marriage and the Family.* Take a look at these journals to see how your work connects with that of professional social scientists like the following:

- A developmental psychologist studies conflict resolution in children by observing a group of four-year-olds in a daycare center.
- A sociologist studies the role of the state in enforcing gender stereotypes by observing and interviewing women in the juvenile justice system.
- A political scientist studies the legislative process by noting how state senators and representatives negotiate to get a bill passed.
- An anthropologist studies the function of rituals in the formation of innercity gangs by attending an initiation ceremony.

draw inferences. For example, ask yourself why a subject behaved in a specific way, and consider different explanations for the behavior.

4. Present your findings in an organized way. There are two basic ways to present your findings in the body of a case study:

- **As stages of a process:** A student studying gang initiation organized her observations chronologically into appropriate stages. If you organize your study this way, be sure to transform the minute-by-minute history of your observations into a pattern with distinctive stages.

- **In analytic categories:** A student observing the behavior of a preschool child used the following categories from the course textbook to present his findings: motor coordination, cognition, and socialization. In "Homeboys, Babies, Men in Suits," Haney uses quotes from the people she studied to organize her findings into two categories: "The Be-Your-Own Woman Rule" and "My Man Won't Do Me Like That."

Note: You will find it easier to organize the enormous amount of detail you gather for a case study if you develop stages or categories while you are making your observations. In your paper, be sure to illustrate your stages or categories with material drawn from your observations—with descriptions of people, places, and behavior, as well as with telling quotations.

5. In your introduction, include a research review, a statement of your hypothesis, and a description of your methodology.   The introduction presents the framework, background, and rationale for your study. Begin with the topic, and review related research, working your way to the specific question that your study addresses. Follow that with a statement of your hypothesis, accompanied by a description of your **methodology**—in other words, when and where you made your observations and how you kept records.

6. In the conclusion, discuss your findings.   The conclusion of your case study should answer the following three questions:

- Did you find what you expected?
- What do your findings show, or what is the bigger picture?
- Where should researchers working on your topic go now?

13d Essay exams

When you take an essay exam, you probably feel pressed for time and uninterested in the what, how, and why of the test. Still, if you spend some time thinking about what these tests expect you to do, you may feel less stress the next time you take one.

1. Understand your assignment.   Your purpose in writing an essay exam is to demonstrate informed understanding. Because essay exams are designed to test your knowledge, not just your memory, working through possible questions is one of the best ways to study. Make up some essay questions that require you to:

- **Explain** what you have learned in a clear, well-organized way. (*See question 1 on the presidency in the box on p. 122.*)
- **Connect** what you know about one topic with what you know about another topic. (*See question 2 on labor supply decisions in the box on p. 122.*)
- **Apply** what you have learned to a new situation. (*See question 3 on a hypothetical particle-scattering experiment in the box on p. 122.*)
- **Interpret** the causes, effects, meanings, value, or potential of something. (*See question 4 on* Guernica *in the box on p. 122.*)
- **Argue** for or against some controversial statement about what you have learned. (*See question 5 on Jefferson in the box on p. 122.*)

CHARTING the TERRITORY

Essay Exam Questions across the Curriculum

During finals week, you may be asked to respond to essay questions like the following:

1. Discuss the power of the contemporary presidency as well as the limits of that power. (from a political science course)

2. Compare and contrast the treatment of labor supply decisions in the economic models proposed by Greg Lewis and Gary Becker. (from an economics course)

3. Describe the observations that would be made in an a-particle scattering experiment if (a) the nucleus of an atom were negatively charged and the protons occupied the empty space outside the nucleus and (b) the electrons were embedded in a positively charged sphere. (from a chemistry course)

4. Explain two ways in which Picasso's *Guernica* evokes war's terrifying destructiveness. (from an art history course)

5. In 1800, was Thomas Jefferson a dangerous radical? Be sure to define your key terms and to support your position with evidence from specific events, documents, and so on. (from an American history course)

2. Prepare with the course and your instructor in mind. Consider the specific course as your writing context and the course's instructor as your audience. As you prepare for the exam, think about how your instructor approached and presented the course material.

- What questions or problems did your instructor explicitly or implicitly address?

- What frameworks did your instructor use to analyze topics?

- What key terms did your instructor repeatedly use during lectures and discussions?

3. Plan your time. During the exam period, time management is essential. Quickly look through the whole exam, and determine how much time you will spend on each part or question. Your instructor may give the point credit for each question or suggest the amount of time that should be spent on each part. You will want to move as quickly as possible through the short-answer questions that have lower point values so that you can spend the bulk of your time responding to the questions that are worth the greatest number of points.

4. Answer short identification questions by showing the significance of the information. The most common type of short-answer question is the identification question: Who or what is X? In answering questions of this sort, you need to present just enough information to show that you understand X's significance within the context of the course. For example, if you are asked to identify "Judith Loftus" on an American literature exam, don't just write: "character who knows Huckleberry Finn is a boy." Instead, craft a sentence or two that identify Loftus as a character Huckleberry Finn encounters while he is disguised as a girl; by telling Huck how she knows that he is not a girl, Loftus complicates the reader's understanding of gender.

5. Be tactical in responding to essay questions. When you are faced with an essay question, you may be inclined to start writing down everything you remember about the topic. Don't. Be tactical. Keep in mind that essay questions usually ask you to do something specific with a topic. Begin by determining precisely what you are being asked to do. Before you write anything, read the question—all of it—and circle key words.

EXAMPLE (Explain) (two) ways in which Picasso's *Guernica* evokes war's terrifying (destructiveness.)

To answer this question, you need to focus on two of the painting's features, such as coloring and composition, not on Picasso's life.

Sometimes you may be uncertain about what you are being asked to do, either because an essay question says too much or because it says too little. If a question includes more information or direction than necessary, try to isolate the kernel of the question—the main topic and tactic. If a question says too little, try to use the context of the course to give you clues. For example, "Discuss the power of the contemporary presidency as well as the limits of that power" can be made more specific by applying the analytic terms used in class, such as the resources, methods, and conditions of presidential power. You should also consider asking the instructor for clarification.

6. Use the essay question to structure your response. You are unlikely to have time to make a complete outline before you begin writing. Whenever possible, use the question to structure your answer. Usually, you will be able to transform the question itself into the thesis of your answer. If you are asked to agree/disagree with the

Federalists' characterization of Thomas Jefferson in the election of 1800, you might begin with the following thesis:

> In the election of 1800, the Federalists characterized Jefferson as a dangerous radical. Although Jefferson's ideas were radical for the times, they were not dangerous to the republic.

Take a minute or two to list evidence for each of your main points, and then write the essay.

7. Check your work.   Leave a few minutes to read quickly through your completed answer, looking for words you might have omitted or key sentences that make no sense. Add the missing words, and rewrite the mixed-up sentences. You can usually cross out incorrect words and sentences and make corrections neatly above the original line of text.

13e   Oral presentations

Oral presentations and written documents are quite different. When we write, we must imagine the presence of absent strangers. When we speak, the strangers are there, expecting us to connect with them right now. But thinking and working like a writer can help you prepare a speech that is appropriate, clear, and memorable.

1. Imagine the occasion and your audience.   An oral presentation should suit the occasion. Who is likely to be there to listen to your speech? How and why have these people come together as an audience? Do they have significant demographic features in common, such as age, sociocultural background, and profession? What are they expecting to hear: a business report, a sermon, an analysis of an issue, a toast to the bride and groom, or something else?

2. Decide on the purpose of your presentation.   What does the audience already think about your topic? What contribution do you most want to make? Do you want to intensify your audience's commitment to what they already think, provide new and clarifying information, provoke more analysis and understanding of the issue, or change what the audience believes about something?

3. Make the focus and organization of your presentation explicit.   Effective public speakers usually limit themselves to presenting a few clear-cut ideas. Select two or three ideas that you most want your audience to hear—and to remember. Make these ideas the focus of your presentation, and let your audience know what to expect by previewing the content of your presentation: "I intend to make three points about writing and learning."

Just as signs on the highway tell travelers where to go, signs in your presentation set the direction for your audience. In the sample preview, above, the phrase "to make three points" signals a topical organization. Of course, there are other common patterns, including chronological organization (*at first, later, in the end*), causal organization (*because of that, then this follows*), and problem-solution organization (*given the situation, then this set of proposals*). A question-answer format also works well, either as an overall strategy or as part of another organizational pattern.

4. Make your opening interesting. To get your listeners' attention, you need an interesting opener. Surprising statements, quotations, images, and anecdotes are all effective ways to begin.

5. Be direct. What your audience hears and remembers has as much to do with how you say your message as it does with what you say. For clarity, use a direct, simple style.

- Choose basic sentence structures.
- Repeat key terms.
- Pay attention to the rhythm of your speech.

Notice how applying these principles transforms the following written sentence into a group of sentences appropriate for oral presentation:

WRITTEN

Although the claim that writing increases student learning has yet to be substantiated by either an ample body or an exemplary piece of empirical research, advocates of writing across the curriculum persist in pressing the claim.

ORAL

The more students write, the more they learn. So say advocates of writing across the curriculum. But what evidence do we have that writing improves learning? Do we have lots of empirical research or even one really good study? The answer is, "Not yet."

6. Use visual aids. One way to make your focus explicit is through the use of visual aids. A computer projection of the points from your outline encourages your audience to make a few notes and discourages you from delivering—word for word—a boring, prepackaged performance. Consider using slides, posters, objects, video clips, and music.

Presentation software such as PowerPoint can help you stay focused while you are speaking. The 12 PowerPoint slides on pages 126–27 offer advice on how to design effective slides for a presentation.

For links to PowerPoint tutorials, visit <www.mhhe.com/maimon/other_assignments/oral_presentations>.

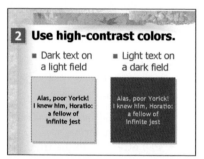

7. Make eye contact and keep your audience interested. To be an effective speaker, you need to make eye contact with your listeners to monitor their responses and adjust what you have to say accordingly. A written script can be a barrier between you and your audience. You can relate better to your audience if you speak from an outline. Write out only those parts of your presentation where precise wording counts, such as quotations. Telling a story during your oral presentation is another way to engage your listeners and keep their attention until the end.

For most occasions, it is inappropriate to write out everything you want to say and then read it word for word. In some scholarly or

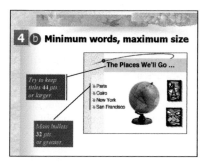

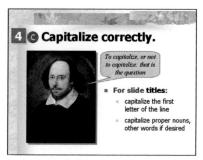

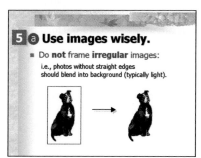

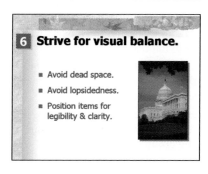

formal settings, however, precise wording may be necessary, especially if your oral presentation is to be published or if your remarks will be quoted by others, including media representatives. Sometimes the setting for your presentation may be so formal or the audience may be so large that a script feels necessary. In such instances, do the following:

- Triple-space the typescript of your text.
- Avoid carrying sentences over from one page to another.
- Mark your manuscript for pauses, emphasis, and the pronunciation of proper names.

- Practice your delivery. It should take about seventy-five seconds to deliver one triple-spaced page of text.

8. Conclude in a memorable way.   Your final comments will be the part of your speech that most members of your audience remember. Try to make your ending truly memorable: return to that surprising opener, play with the words of your opening quotation, look at the initial image from another angle, or reflect on the story you told.

For additional samples of visual aids, visit <www.mhhe.com/maimon/other_assignments/oral_presentations>.

9. Rehearse.   Whether you are using an outline or a script, it takes a practiced performer to deliver a memorable oral presentation. Practice with a clock, but be sure to leave yourself time to insert conversational gambits every now and then during the actual performance.

13f   Coauthored projects

A project is coauthored when more than one person is responsible for producing it. In many fields, working collaboratively is essential. Here are some suggestions to help you make the most of this challenge:

- Working with your partners, decide on some ground rules, including meeting times, deadlines, and ways of reconciling differences. Will the majority rule, or will some other principle prevail? Is there an interested and respected third party who can be consulted if the group's dynamics break down?
- Divide the work fairly so that everyone has a part to contribute to the project. Keep in mind that each group member should do some researching, drafting, revising, and editing.
- In your personal journal, record, analyze, and evaluate the intellectual and interpersonal workings of the group as you see and experience them. If the group's dynamics begin to break down, seek the assistance of a third party.

Tips   LEARNING in COLLEGE

For Coauthoring Online

Computer networks make it easier for two or more writers to coauthor texts. With e-mail, you can preserve your individual contributions to the final paper and, if need be, share them with your instructor. You will also have a record of how the piece developed and how well you and your coauthor actually worked as a team.

TextConnex

Common Assignments

The following Web sites can provide you with additional information about and help with the assignments presented in Tab 3.

The Argument Clinic <http://www.unco.edu/philosophy/clinic.html>: Visitors can submit arguments via e-mail and get a response that tells them whether their arguments are logical. The site includes a link to the *Arguments and Their Evaluation* site, which defines what constitutes a sound argument.

Writing Papers of Literary Analysis <http://unix.cc.wmich.edu/cooneys/tchg/lit/adv/lit.papers.html>: This site displays helpful tips for students from a professor at Western Michigan University.

Virtual Presentation Assistant <http://www.ukans.edu/cwis/units/coms2/vpa/vpa.htm>: An online tutorial for improving public speaking skills, this site includes tips for selecting and researching a topic, audience analysis, using visual aids, and presenting your speech.

- After each group member has completed his or her assigned part or subtopic, the whole group should weave the parts together to create a focused piece of writing with a consistent voice. This is the point where group members usually need to negotiate with one another. Tact is essential. Keep the excellence of the project in the forefront, and all should go well.

13g Portfolios

A **portfolio** is an ordered selection of your work. The principles that guide selection and order depend on the occasion, purpose, and intended audience. Your first experience with portfolios is likely to be in a composition course. In your writing course, your instructor is likely to give you the principles for selecting and ordering your writing.

As soon as you select a major, you should consider keeping an organized folder of your work in that area. The folder can be organized chronologically, by field or subfield, or by issue. In your senior year, it is a good idea to create a portfolio that reflects what you have learned and how you learned it during your college career. Successful job candidates often prepare well-organized portfolios of carefully selected materials to take with them to job interviews.

4

The aim of education must be the
training of independently acting and
thinking individuals, who, however, see
in the service of the community their
highest life problem.

—ALBERT EINSTEIN

Writing
Connections

College, Community, Career

4 Writing Connections

14. Service Learning and
    Community-Service
    Writing *133*

15. Letters to Get Action:
    Protest and Praise *134*

16. Writing to Get
    and Keep a Job *138*
    a. Exploring internship
       possibilities *138*

b. Keeping an up-to-date
   résumé *139*
c. Writing an application
   letter *141*
d. Applying college
   writing to writing on
   the job *144*

Although college may be unfamiliar territory to the newcomer, it is part of the larger world. Like an access road, writing is a way of connecting classroom, workplace, and community.

14 Service Learning and Community-Service Writing

Your ability to research and write can be of great value to organizations that serve the community. Courses at every level of the university, as well as extracurricular activities, offer opportunities to work with organizations such as homeless shelters, tutoring centers, and environmental groups. Your work with groups like these may involve writing newsletters, press releases, or funding proposals. When you are writing for a community group, ask yourself these questions:

- What do community members talk about?
- How do they talk about these issues, and why?
- Who is an outsider (member of the community), and who is an insider (member of the organization)?
- How can I best write from the inside to the outside?

Your answers will help you shape your writing so that it reaches its intended audience and moves the members of that audience to action.

Writing on behalf of a community organization almost always involves negotiation and collaboration. When you write on behalf of others, the concept of individual authorship becomes problematic. A community organization may revise your draft to fit its needs, and you will have to live with those revisions. In these situations, having a cooperative attitude is as important as having strong writing skills.

Even if you are not writing on behalf of a group, you can still do community-service writing. You can write in your own name to raise an issue of concern to the community in a public forum; for example, you might write a newspaper editorial or a letter to a public official. Any time you address readers as fellow citizens with the purpose of educating them or making a change for the better, you are doing community-service writing.

A Writer at Work

When Laura Amabisca entered Glendale Community College, she volunteered to be a tutor in the writing center. Upon transferring to Arizona State University West, she joined the Writing Tutors Club, continuing her service to the campus community. In addition, she became a mentor for other Glendale Community College students who were trying to build the confidence to transfer to the university.

In a course in advanced expository writing, she was able to draw on these experiences for an essay on the special needs of community college transfer students. She also wrote a letter on the same theme to the student newspaper.

The satisfaction and sense of involvement she felt about her on-campus service motivated her to visit the ASU West Volunteer Office for ideas about off-campus service. She then became a volunteer for America Reads, joining students from ASU West and from various community colleges who tutor in this national literacy project.

The Phoenix office of America Reads asked Laura to help design a public relations campaign to explain the value of America Reads. After writing reflectively in her journal, Laura volunteered to draft a brochure to convince other college students to join the project. In this way, Laura moved from involvement in her own campus to service in the wider community.

15 Letters to Get Action: Protest and Praise

Your ability to write can influence how you are treated as an employee, a client, or a customer by large and seemingly faceless organizations. For example, suppose that the customer service representatives for an airline have bumped you from a flight without offering you any consideration or compensation, leaving you angry and frustrated. You want action. Compose yourself, and then compose a letter of protest. Your task is to present yourself as a polite and reasonable person who has experienced rude and unfair treatment by representatives of the company.

TEXTCONNEX

Writing Connections

The New York Times on the Web: Editorial Op-Ed <http://www.nytimes.com/yr/mo/day/oped>: The op-ed page of the *New York Times,* including letters to the editor. Most major daily newspapers include a similar section on their Web sites.

Guidelines for writing a letter of protest

- Address the letter to the person in charge by name. (If you do not know the correct name and title to use, call the corporate headquarters.)

- Use the format for a business letter. (*See the example of a business letter in block form on pp. 136–37.*)

- In the first paragraph, concisely state the problem and the action you request.

- In the following paragraphs, narrate clearly and objectively what happened, referring to details such as the date and time of the incident so that the person you are writing to can follow up.

- Recognize those who tried to help you as well as those who did not.

- Mention previous positive experiences with the organization, if you can. Your protest will have more credibility if you come across as a person who does not usually complain but is forced to do so in this instance.

- Increase your credibility by proposing reasonable recompense and enclosing receipts, if appropriate.

- Conclude by thanking the person you are writing to for his or her time and expressing the hope that you will be able to continue as a customer.

- Send copies to the people whom you mention.

Consider, for example, the letter on pages 136–37 by Jonathan Corrigan. Notice how Corrigan's letter adheres to the guidelines just presented.

↕ 1"

Return address
and date.

10653 North 53rd Drive
Glendale, AZ 85308-9100
August 12, 2002

Double space.

Inside address.

Mr. Thomas Stern
Chief Executive Officer
Europe Atlantic Airways
PO Box 43
London, England

Double space.

Salutation.

Dear Mr. Stern:

Double space.

Because Europe Atlantic Airways (EA) strives to
provide the best international service possible,
my fiancée and I chose to fly EA on our recent
trip to Berlin. The service for most of the trip
was excellent, but unfortunately, on the final
leg of our journey, EA failed to transfer our
luggage, leaving us stranded without our clothing
for several days. When we finally did receive
our luggage, it was damaged and items were
missing. I am writing to request compensation
for the expenses we incurred because of this
problem.

1" ↔   1" ↔

Body—
paragraphs
single spaced,
double spaced
between
paragraphs.

Service was excellent on our flights from
Phoenix to Berlin. On Wednesday, August 2, we
flew EA 642 from Berlin to London and EA 2146
from London to Phoenix. The crew of flight
2146 from London to Phoenix, in particular,
was exceptional.

After arriving in Phoenix, we were told that our
luggage had not been transferred from Heathrow
Airport to flight 2146 at Gatwick Airport. When
we requested that our luggage be sent to Denver
once it arrived in Phoenix, EA representative
Jane Franklin informed us, rather impolitely,
that EA would not transfer our luggage because
we were flying on a different carrier from

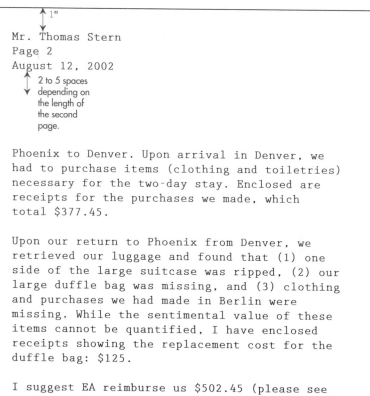

Mr. Thomas Stern
Page 2
August 12, 2002

2 to 5 spaces
depending on
the length of
the second
page.

Phoenix to Denver. Upon arrival in Denver, we had to purchase items (clothing and toiletries) necessary for the two-day stay. Enclosed are receipts for the purchases we made, which total $377.45.

Upon our return to Phoenix from Denver, we retrieved our luggage and found that (1) one side of the large suitcase was ripped, (2) our large duffle bag was missing, and (3) clothing and purchases we had made in Berlin were missing. While the sentimental value of these items cannot be quantified, I have enclosed receipts showing the replacement cost for the duffle bag: $125.

I suggest EA reimburse us $502.45 (please see enclosures). Your doing so would go a long way toward restoring our confidence in EA. Review of this matter would be greatly appreciated.

I look forward to hearing from you.

Sincerely,

Jonathan Corrigan

Jonathan Corrigan

cc: Ms. Jane Franklin

Close.

Signature.

Name of
person to
whom a copy
will be sent.

On the other hand, suppose that an airline employee has been exceptionally helpful to you when you missed a connecting flight, and you are grateful. Express your gratitude by writing a letter of praise. Like letters of protest, letters of praise are intended to shape future action. The writing techniques are very similar.

Guidelines for writing a letter of praise

- Address the letter to the person in charge by name. (If you do not know the correct name and title to use, call the corporate headquarters.)
- Use the format for a business letter.
- In the first paragraph, concisely state the situation and the help that was provided.
- In following paragraphs, narrate what happened, referring to details such as the date and time of the incident so that the person you are writing to can follow up with the person who helped you.
- Conclude by thanking the person you are writing to for his or her time and expressing your intention to continue doing business with the company.
- Send copies to the people whom you mention.

16 Writing to Get and Keep a Job

Like many students, you may already have a job on or off campus, or you may be serving an internship or volunteering for a community-based organization. Writing is one way to connect your work, your other activities, and your studies. Strong writing skills will also help you find a good job once you leave college and advance in your chosen career.

16a Explore internship possibilities, and keep a portfolio of career-related writing.

An internship, in which you do actual work in your chosen field, is a vital connection between the classroom and the workplace. You gain academic credit, not for the hours you spend on the job, but for what you learn from the job. Writing and learning go together. During your internship, keep a journal to record and analyze your experiences, as well as a file of any writing you do on the job. Your final project for the internship credit may require you to analyze the file of writing that you have produced.

Files of writing from internships, clippings of articles and editorials you have written for the student newspaper, writing you have done for a community organization—these and other documents demonstrate your ability to apply intellectual concepts to real-world demands. Organized into a portfolio, this material displays your marketable skills. Use a tabbed loose-leaf notebook or an actual portfolio with compartments for different categories of work. Arrange your writing samples by project or by kind of writing. Within each category, use reverse chronological order so that your most recent work will appear first.

16b Keep your résumé up-to-date and available on a computer disk.

A **résumé** is an informative piece of writing, a brief summary of your education and your work experience that you send to prospective employers. It is never finished. As you continue to learn, work, and write, you should be rethinking and reorganizing your résumé. You will want to emphasize different accomplishments and talents for different employers. Some employers—for example, banks and accounting firms—expect a résumé from a college student or recent graduate to be no longer than one page. Some public relations firms and other organizations with more informal cultures want to see more detail, especially about a future employee's special skills and interests. Saving your résumé as a computer file allows you to tailor it to the needs and requirements of its readers.

Your résumé should be designed for quick reading. Expect the person reviewing it to give it no more than sixty seconds at first glance. Make that first impression count. Design a document that is easy to read, attractively formatted, and flawlessly spelled. Few things will lose you a job quicker than a messy résumé with misspelled words.

Guidelines for writing a résumé. Always include the following *necessary* categories in a résumé:

- Heading (name, address, phone number, e-mail address)
- Education (in reverse chronological order; do not include high school)
- Work experience (in reverse chronological order)
- References (often included on a separate sheet; for many situations, you can add the line "References available on request" instead)

Laura Amabisca
20650 North 58th Avenue, Apt. 15A
Glendale, AZ 85308
(602) 555-7310
lamabisca@peoplelink.com

EDUCATION
B.A., Arizona State University West, Phoenix (May 2000)
    Major: History
    Minor: Global Management
    Senior Thesis: Picturing the Hopi, 1920-1940:
    A Historical Analysis
Glendale Community College, Glendale, AZ (1996-97)

HONORS AND AWARDS
Westmarc Writing Prize (2000)
Arizona Regents Scholarship (1997-2000)

WORK EXPERIENCE
Sears, Bell Road, Phoenix, AZ
    Assistant Manager, Sporting Goods Department (1999-present)
    Sales Associate, Sporting Goods Department (1997-99)
    Stock Clerk, Sporting Goods Department (1994-97)

INTERNSHIP
Public Relations Office, Arizona State University West
(Summer 1998)

ACTIVITIES AND SERVICE
Tutor, Public-Relations Consultant, America Reads (2000)
Student Coordinator, Multicultural Festival, ASU West (1999)
Tutor, Writing Center, Glendale Community College (1996-97)

SPECIAL SKILLS
Bilingual: Spanish/English
Skill and experience with Windows, WordPerfect, Word (IBM
and Mac), and HTML authoring

REFERENCES
Ms. Carol Martinez
Director, Public Relations
Arizona State University West
PO Box 371000
Phoenix, AZ 85069-7100

Mr. James Corrothers
Sales Manager
Sporting Goods Department
Sears
302 N. Central Avenue
Phoenix, AZ 85043-6011

A file of confidential references is available upon request
to Career Services, Arizona State University West

Include the following *optional* categories in your résumé as appropriate:

- Honors and awards
- Internships
- Activities and service
- Special skills

Laura Amabisca has organized the information in her résumé (*see p. 140*) by time and by categories. Within each category, she has listed items from the most to least recent. This reverse chronological order gives appropriate emphasis to what she has just done and is doing now. At the time Amabisca prepared this résumé, she had just graduated from Arizona State University West (May 2000) and was continuing to work as a department manager at Sears (1999–present).

Because Amabisca is applying for jobs in public relations, she has highlighted her internship in that field by giving it its own category. People who have been working for a while often divide their work experience into separate categories, emphasizing experience pertinent to their career goal and listing other jobs separately. For example, Amabisca might have used the categories "Public Relations Experience" and "Other Work Experience" instead of "Work Experience" and "Internship."

Sometimes career counselors recommend that you list a career objective right under the heading of your résumé. There is a delicate balance between presenting yourself as someone with clear goals and as someone who can be flexible, however. Unless you have done enough research to know exactly what a particular company is looking for, it is usually best to leave your career objective out of your résumé. Deal with this issue in your application letter instead.

Note that Amabisca's résumé does not include bold or italic type, and it is not formatted in columns. It could, therefore, be scanned or sent electronically if Amabisca were replying to an online employment advertisement. She also uses clear, specific words for her work experience and skills (*Assistant Manager, Bilingual*). Some employers may conduct keyword searches of the résumés they have on file, so using clear, unambiguous terms is always a smart strategy.

16c Write an application letter that highlights the information on your résumé and demonstrates that your skills match the job you are seeking.

A clear and concise **application letter** should always accompany a résumé. Before drafting a job application letter, do some research about the organization you are writing to. For example, even though

20650 North 58th Avenue, Apt. 15A
Glendale, AZ 85308
August 17, 2002

Ms. Jaclyn Abel
Director of Public Relations
Heard Museum
2301 North Central Avenue
Phoenix, AZ 85004

Dear Ms. Abel:

I am writing to apply for the position of Public Relations
Assistant that you recently advertised in the *Arizona
Republic*. I believe that my experience and qualifications
fit well with your needs at the Heard, a museum that I have
visited and loved all my life.

As the enclosed résumé indicates, I have experience in the
public relations field. While at Arizona State University
West, I worked as an intern in the Public Relations Office,
where I was responsible for analyzing and reporting on the
image projected by the university's external publications.
I also had a hand in creating the brochure for the University-
College Center and participated in planning ASU West's "Dream
Big" campaign. I also assisted in organizing an opening
convocation attended by 800 people. This work in the not-for-
profit sector has prepared me well for employment at the Heard.

Additionally, my undergraduate major in American history has
helped me understand the rich heritage of Native Americans. In
my senior thesis, which received the Westmarc Writing Award, I
studied the history of the relationship between the Hopis and
the Anglo population as reflected in photographs taken from
1920 to 1940. Although my thesis focuses on a specific tribe,
I have been interested for many years in Native-American
culture and have often made use of resources in the Heard. I
think that I would do a superior job of presenting the Heard
as the premier museum of Native-American culture.

Confidential reference letters are available from ASU West
Career Services. I sincerely hope that we will have an
opportunity to talk further about the Heard Museum and its
outstanding cultural contributions to the Phoenix metropolitan
area. Please contact me at 623-555-7310.

Sincerely,

Laura Amabisca

Laura Amabisca

Enc.

Laura Amabisca was already familiar with the Heard Museum when she applied for a position there, she took time to find out the name of the Director of Public Relations instead of mailing her letter and résumé to an unnamed recipient. (*Amabisca's application letter appears on p. 142.*) If the want ad you are answering does not include a name, call the organization and find out the name of the person responsible for your area of interest. If you try but are unable to identify an appropriate name, or if the want ad does not include the name of the organization, it is better to direct the letter to "Dear Director of Public Relations" than to "Dear Sir or Madam."

Here are some additional guidelines for composing a letter of application:

- **Use business style:** Use the block form shown on pages 136–37. Type your address flush at the top of the page, with each line starting at the left margin; place the date at the left margin two lines above the recipient's name and address; use a colon (:) after the greeting; double space between single-spaced paragraphs; use a traditional closing (*Sincerely, Sincerely yours, Yours truly*); make sure that the inside address and the address on the envelope match exactly.

- **Limit your letter to three or four paragraphs:** Many prospective employers will not bother to turn to page two of an application letter. Focus clearly and concisely on what the employer needs to know. In the first paragraph, identify the position you are applying for, mention how you heard about it, and briefly state that you are qualified. In the following one or two paragraphs, explain your qualifications, elaborating on the most pertinent items in your résumé. Because Amabisca was applying for a public relations job at a museum of Native American culture, she chose to highlight her internship and her thesis. In another application letter, however, this time for a management position at American Express, she made different choices; in that letter, she emphasized her work experience at Sears, including the fact that she had moved up in the organization through positions of increasing responsibility.

- **State your expectation for future contact:** Conclude with a one- or two-sentence paragraph informing the reader that you are anticipating a follow-up to your letter.

- **Use *Enc.* if you are enclosing additional materials.** Decide whether it is appropriate to enclose supporting materials other than your résumé, such as samples of your writing. Amabisca decided to do so because she was applying for her ideal job and had highly relevant materials to send.

For MULTILINGUAL STUDENTS

Applying for a Job

Different cultures approach the job application process differently. Whatever your experiences may have been, keep the following guidelines in mind as you search for a job in the United States:

- A form letter accompanied by a generic résumé is not an effective way of getting a job interview. Before writing an application letter or preparing a résumé, you need to have a sense of exactly what the employer is looking for. You can then tailor your documents to those exact requirements.
- The main purpose of the application letter is to motivate the employer to read your résumé carefully and to arrange for an interview. It is a brief introduction, not the place to present your qualifications and work experience in detail.
- Time is of the essence when you send in application materials and when you arrive at the interview. American culture is notoriously time-conscious; a last-minute application or a late appearance at an interview can count heavily against you.

16d Apply what you learn in college to your on-the-job writing.

Once you get a job, writing is a way to establish and maintain lines of communication with your colleagues and other contacts. You will probably be writing much of the time, to internal and external audiences, both on- and off-line. Much of what you have learned in college about writing for different purposes, occasions, and audiences will come in handy. When you write in the workplace, you should imagine a reader who is pressed for time and wants you to get to the point immediately.

1. Writing e-mail and memos in the workplace. In the workplace you will do much of your writing online, in the form of e-mail. Most e-mail programs set up messages in memo format, with "To," "From," "Date," and "Subject" lines, as in the example on page 145.

Whether you are writing an e-mail message or a conventional memo, you need to consider not only what your workplace document says but also the way it looks. Various strategies can make your doc-

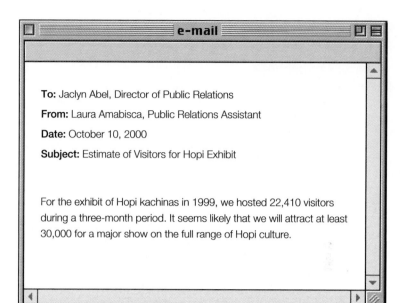

ument easier to read. For example, presenting your information as a numbered or bulleted list surrounded by white space aids readability and allows you to highlight important points and to emphasize crucial ideas. (*For more help with document design, see Tab 9: Document and Web Design, pp. 313–19.*)

2. Other business genres. Conventional forms such as the following also increase readability because readers have built-in expectations for the genre and therefore know what to look for. Besides the memo, there are a number of common business genres:

- **Business letters:** Use business letters to communicate formally with people outside an organization. Typically, letters in business format have single-spaced block paragraphs with double spacing between the paragraphs. (*See the examples on pp. 136–37 and 142.*)

- **Business reports and proposals:** Like college research papers, business reports and proposals can be used to inform, analyze, and interpret. An abstract, sometimes called an *executive summary,* is almost always required, as

TextConnex

Writing Connections

Job Central <http://jobstar.org/tools/resume/samples.cfm>: This site provides samples of résumés for many different situations, as well as sample cover letters.

Career Collection: Write a Résumé <http://college.library.wisc.edu/collections/career/careerrésumé.html>: This site provides help with preparing cover letters and writing résumés.

are tables and graphs. (*For more on these visual elements, see Tab 9: Document and Web Design, pp. 319–25.*)

- **Evaluations and recommendations:** You might need to evaluate a person, or you might be called on to evaluate a product or a procedure and recommend whether the company should buy or use it. Like the reviews and critiques that college writers compose, workplace evaluations are supposed to be reasonable as well as convincing. It is important to be fair, so you should always support your account of both strengths and weaknesses with specific illustrations or examples.

For all knowledge and wonder
(which is the seed of knowledge) is
an impression of pleasure in itself.

—FRANCIS BACON

Researching

5 Researching

17. Understanding Research *149*
    a. Understanding primary and secondary research *149*
    b. Recognizing the connection between research and college writing *150*
    c. Choosing an interesting research question *150*
    d. Creating a research plan *153*

18. Finding Print and Online Sources *153*
    a. Consulting various kinds of sources *154*
    b. Using the library *155*
    c. Searching the Internet *163*

19. Evaluating Sources *171*
    a. Questioning print sources *171*
    b. Questioning Internet sources *173*
    c. Evaluating a source's arguments *174*

20. Doing Research in the Archive, Field, and Lab *175*
    a. Adhering to ethical principles *175*
    b. Preparing yourself for archival research *176*
    c. Planning your field research carefully *176*
    d. Keeping a notebook when doing lab research *179*

21. Working with Sources *180*
    a. Maintaining a working bibliography *180*
    b. Taking notes on your sources *181*
    c. Taking stock of what you have learned *183*

22. Writing the Paper *184*
    a. Planning and drafting your paper *184*
    b. Quoting and paraphrasing properly and effectively *186*
    c. Avoiding plagiarism and copyright infringement *188*
    d. Documenting your sources *189*

23. Discipline-Specific Resources in the Library and on the Internet *192*

17 Understanding Research

You do research all the time. When you shop for a car, you talk with friends about their cars, read *Consumer's Digest,* interview car dealers, and take a number of test drives. When your doctor says that you have a particular medical condition, you find out as much as possible about the condition and the conventional and latest treatments for it.

College faculty in all fields are researchers. Besides searching out existing information about a particular subject in their specialty, they do research to create new knowledge about that topic.

17a Understand the purpose of primary and secondary research.

Primary research means working in a laboratory, in the field, or with an archive of raw data, original documents, and authentic artifacts to make firsthand discoveries.

Secondary research means looking to see what other people have learned and written. Knowing how to identify facts, interpretations, and evaluations is key to good secondary research:

- **Facts** are objective. Like your body weight, facts can be measured, observed, or independently verified in some way.

- **Interpretations** spell out the implications of facts. Are you as thin as you are because of your genes—or because you exercise every day? The answer to this question is an interpretation.

- **Evaluations** are debatable judgments about a set of facts or a situation. Attributing a person's thinness to genes is an interpretation, but the assertion that "one can never be too rich or too thin" is an evaluation.

Once you are up-to-date on the facts, interpretations, and evaluations in a particular area, you will be able to design a research project that adds to this knowledge. Usually, what you will add is your *perspective* on the sources you found and read:

- Given all that you have learned about the topic, what strikes you as important or interesting?

- What patterns do you see, or what connections can you make between one person's work and another's?

- Where is the research going, and what problems still need to be explored?

17b Recognize the connection between research and college writing.

In one way or another, research informs all college writing. To get material for a personal essay, you have to search through your memory; reflect on events that have happened to you; and select a person, event, place, or other topic to write about. When you write essay exams, you rely on what you have read in college textbooks and learned from lectures.

But some assignments require more rigorous and systematic research than others. These **research project** assignments offer you a chance to go beyond your course texts—to find and read both classic and current material on a specific issue.

CLASSIC and CURRENT SOURCES

Classic sources are well known and respected older works that made such an important contribution to a discipline or a particular area of research that contemporary researchers use them as touchstones for further research in that area. In many fields, sources published within the past five years are considered current.

A paper based on research is not just a step-by-step account of your "search and find" mission. Nor is it a string of quotes from other writers or a set of summaries based on your sources. A researched paper constitutes your contribution to the ongoing conversation about a specific issue.

When you are assigned to write a research paper for any of your college courses, the project may seem overwhelming at first. If you break it down into phases, however, and allow an adequate amount of time for each phase, you should be able to manage your work and write a paper that will become your contribution to the academic community. This chapter and the five that follow it offer advice on completing each phase.

17c Choose an interesting research question to guide your critical inquiry.

If you choose an interesting question to inquire about critically, your research is likely to be more meaningful.

1. Choose a question with personal significance. Even though you are writing for a college assignment, you can still get personally involved in your work. Begin with the wording of the assignment, ana-

LEARNING in COLLEGE

For Scheduling Your Research

Project Planning (three days for an assignment due in one month): Activities include the following:

- Analyzing the assignment
- Deciding on a topic and a question
- Outlining a research plan

Research Phase I (five days for an assignment due in one month): Get a general overview of your topic by doing the following:

- Reading **reference works**
- Making a list of relevant **keywords**
- Compiling a **working bibliography** of print and online sources
- Sampling some of the items in your bibliography

Research Phase II (twelve days for an assignment due in one month): Most likely you will spend twice as much time in the second phase as you did in the first phase. Activities include the following:

- Locating, reading, and evaluating selected sources
- Taking notes
- Doing primary research

Research Phase III (ten days for an assignment due in one month): Count on spending one third to one half of the available time working on the paper that grows out of your research:

- Drafting your paper
- Revising and editing your paper

lyzing the project's required scope, purpose, and audience (*see Tab 1: Learning across the Curriculum, pp. 8–9*). Then browse through the course texts and your class notes, looking for a match between your interests and topics, issues, or problems in the subject area.

For example, suppose you have been assigned to write a seven- to ten-page report on some country's global economic prospects for a business course. If you have recently visited Mexico, you might find it interesting to explore that country's prospects.

2. Make your question specific. The more specific your question, the more your research will have direction and focus. To make a question more specific, use the "five *w*'s and an *h*" strategy by asking about the *who, what, why, when, where,* and *how* of a topic (*see Tab 2: Writing Papers, pp. 40–41*).

CHARTING the TERRITORY

Typical Lines of Inquiry in Different Disciplines

Research topics and questions differ from one discipline to another, as the following examples show:

- **History:** Explain the meaning of the events leading up to the fall of the Berlin Wall in 1989.
- **Education:** How do textbooks used in German schools deal with the Nazi period?
- **Political science:** What is the German concept of citizenship, and how does this concept apply to people born in Germany who are not of German ethnicity?
- **Sociology:** What factors determine social class in twenty-first-century Germany?

After you have compiled a list of possible research questions, look through the list and choose one that is relatively specific or rewrite a broad one to make it more specific and therefore answerable. For example, a student could rewrite the following broad question about Germany to make it answerable:

TOO BROAD — What are the prospects of the recently reunified Germany?

ANSWERABLE — In terms of international trade and capital investment, what are Germany's current economic prospects?

3. Find a challenging question.
To be interesting to you and to your readers, a research question must be challenging. If a question can be answered with a simple yes or no, a dictionary-like definition, or a textbook presentation of information, you should choose another question or rework the simple one to make it more challenging.

NOT CHALLENGING — Have Germany's capital investment inflows increased since reunification?

CHALLENGING — How likely is it that the current trends in Germany's capital investment inflows will continue in the same direction?

4. Speculate about answers.
Sometimes it can be useful to speculate on the answer to your research question so that you have a **hypothesis** to work with during the research process. But don't forget that a

Tips LEARNING in COLLEGE

Creating Specific Questions

If the assignment is stated in general terms, review your course notes and texts for relevant issues, subtopics, and terms that can help you make it more specific. You might also check out an encyclopedia like the *New Encyclopædia Britannica* (15th edition). In volume 30, the *Britannica* presents an "outline of knowledge" that can help you narrow a broad topic; volumes 31 and 32 contain an index that lists numerous subdivisions for big topics.

hypothesis is not the truth; it is a speculation, or guess, that must be tested and revised through research. Keep an open mind as you work, and be aware of the assumptions embedded in your research question or hypothesis. Consider, for example, the following hypothesis:

> HYPOTHESIS With the problems caused by reunification behind it, Germany should enjoy a strong economy during the coming decade.

This hypothesis assumes that the worst is over for the German economy. But assumptions are always open to question. Researchers must be willing to adjust their ideas as they learn more about a topic.

17d Create a research plan.

Your research will be more productive if you take some time at the beginning to outline a plan for it. Even though you will probably modify your plan as you work through each phase of the research process, your work will go more smoothly if you have definite goals from the beginning. As a starting point, use the box on page 151, which outlines the steps in a research project, as a starting point, adjusting the time allotments based on the amount of time that you have to complete the assignment.

18 Finding Print and Online Sources

Your research process will take place both in the library and on the Internet. The amount of information available in the library and on the Internet is vast. Usually, a search for useful sources entails three activities:

Researching a Full Range of Sources

If English is your second language, you may be tempted to start your research by consulting sources written in your first language. Although you may find reading research in English challenging, it is important to broaden the scope of your search as soon as you can to include the full range of print and Internet resources written in English. Relying on what is available in your first language will severely limit the range of materials you have to choose from and may cause you to miss out on important sources of information on your topic.

- Collecting keywords from reference works
- Using library databases
- Finding material in the library and on the World Wide Web

18a Consult various kinds of sources.

The number and kinds of sources you use will vary from one research project to another. It is always necessary, however, to consult more than one source and usually important to check out more than one kind of source. These are some of the kinds of sources available to you:

- **General Reference Works**
  Encyclopedias, annuals, almanacs
  Computer databases, bibliographies, abstracts
- **Specialized Reference Works**
  Discipline-specific encyclopedias, almanacs, and dictionaries
- **Books and Electronic Texts**
- **Periodical Articles**
  In newspapers
  In magazines
  In scholarly and technical journals
  On the World Wide Web
- **Web Sites**
- **News Groups, ListServs, and E-mail**

Tips LEARNING in COLLEGE

Who's Talking, Anyway?

Some sources are written for the general public and are classified as **popular sources.** Such publications include magazines like *Time* or *Newsweek* and books like Elizabeth Wurtzel's *Prozac Nation* (Boston: Houghton Mifflin, 1994), an account of Wurtzel's battle with depression. Other sources report research findings and are classified as **scholarly sources.** They include journals like the *New England Journal of Medicine* or the *Oxford Review of Economic Policy* and books like R. S. Lazarus's *Emotion and Adaption* (New York: Oxford UP, 1991), a work by an expert in psychology.

- **Virtual Communities**
  MUDs (multiuser dimensions)
  MOOs (multiuser dimensions, object oriented)
- **Pamphlets, Government Documents, Census Data**
- **Primary Sources**
  Original documents like literary works, art objects, performances, manuscripts, letters, and personal journals
  Museum collections; maps; photo, film, sound, and music archives
  Field notes, surveys, interviews
  Results of observation and lab experiments

18b Use the library.

Consider your college librarians as consultants in your research. They know what is available at your library and how to get material on loan from other libraries. They can also show you how to access the library's computerized book catalog, periodical databases, and electronic resources or how to use the Internet to find information relevant to your research project. Most college libraries list their reference works, books, and periodical holdings online, as shown in the example on page 156. Your library's Web site may also have links to important reference works available on the Internet.

In addition, **help sheets** can be found at most college libraries. These discipline-specific documents list the location of relevant periodicals and noncirculating reference books, along with information about special databases, indexes, and sources of information on the

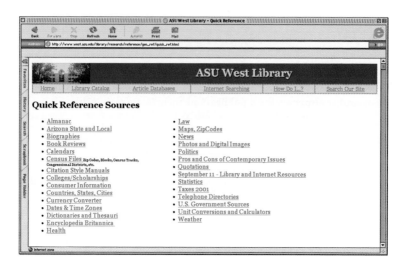

Internet. Invaluable time-savers, help sheets are a good way to get your investigation of a topic underway. You may be able to access your library's help sheets online from the library's Web site or its online catalog.

1. Reference works. Reference works provide an overview of a subject area. The information contained in general encyclopedias like *Encyclopædia Britannica, Collier's Encyclopedia,* and *Encyclopedia Americana* is less authoritative than the specialized knowledge found in discipline-specific encyclopedias, academic journals, and scholarly books. There is nothing wrong with starting your research by consulting a general encyclopedia for your own information, but for college research you will need to explore your topic in more scholarly resources. Often, the list of references at the end of an encyclopedia article can lead you to useful sources on your topic.

Reference books do not circulate, so plan to take notes or make photocopies of the pages you may need to consult later. Many college libraries subscribe to services that provide access to online encyclopedias. Check your college library's home page for a link to reference materials like online encyclopedias.

Here is a list of some other kinds of reference materials available in print, on the Internet, or both. Depending on your topic, you may want to consult one or more of these for information related to your topic:

ALMANACS	Almanac of American Politics
	Information Please Almanac
	World Almanac

BIBLIOGRAPHIES   *Bibliographic Index*
Bibliography of Asian Studies
MLA Bibliography

BIOGRAPHIES   *African American Biographies*
American Men and Women of Science
Chicano Scholars and Writers Biographical Dictionary
Dictionary of American Biography
Dictionary of National Biography
Dictionary of Philosophy
Webster's New Biographical Dictionary
Who's Who

DICTIONARIES   *American Heritage Dictionary of the English Language*
Dictionary of American History
Dictionary of Literary Terms
Dictionary of the Social Sciences
Oxford English Dictionary (OED)

2. Books. A search of the library's catalog will provide you with a list composed mostly of books. Be sure to jot down the **call number** of each book that might prove useful so that you will know where to look for the book on the shelves. Most college libraries use the Library of Congress (LOC) classification system for shelving books, but a few use the Dewey Decimal system, which classifies knowledge in divisions of 10 from 000 to 990. In the LOC system, books are arranged alphabetically and numerically by the call number printed on their spine. Books on the same topic have similar call numbers and are shelved together.

Usually, online library catalogs can be searched by author, by title, by keyword, or by a subject term listed in the *Library of Congress Subject Headings (LCSH)*. The *LCSH* shows you how your research topic is classified and provides you with a set of key terms that can be used in your search for sources. Under boldfaced headings, you will also find the call number most college libraries use for books on that subject. Here are the results of a search using the subject term "Armstrong Louis."

Results of a search by LCSH subject

Search Request: S=ARMSTRONG LOUIS   Queens Catalog

Search Results: 40 Entries Found   Subject Index

   ARMSTRONG LOUIS 1901-1971

1 HORN OF PLENTY THE STORY OF LOUIS ARMSTRONG <1947>

2 HORN OF PLENTY THE STORY OF LOUIS ARMSTRONG <1977>

3 LOUIS ARMSTRONG <1961>

4 LOUIS ARMSTRONG <1969>

5 LOUIS ARMSTRONG <1971>

6 LOUIS ARMSTRONG AN AMERICAN GENIUS <1983>

7 LOUIS ARMSTRONG AN EXTRAVAGANT LIFE <1997>

8 LOUIS ARMSTRONG COMPANION EIGHT DECADES OF COMMENTARY <1999>

9 LOUIS ARMSTRONG HIS LIFE TIMES <1987>

10 LOUIS ARMSTRONG IN HIS OWN WORDS SELECTED WRITINGS <1999>

11 LOUIS ARMSTRONG ODYSSEY FROM JANE ALLEY TO AMERICA'S JAZZ
      AMBASSADOR <1997>

12 LOUIS THE LOUIS ARMSTRONG STORY 1900 1971 <1971>

--CONTINUED on next page -----

STArt over   Type number to display record   <F8> FORward

HELp   MARk

OTHer options CHOose

NEXT COMMAND:

Library databases may also be searched by keyword. As you consult reference works, spend some time collecting ten or more key terms associated with your topic and learning how those terms are related conceptually. If you only have one or two keywords on hand, you may not get what you really need: a reasonable number of relevant sources. For example, notice how experimenting with different keywords on the topic of Louis Armstrong yields very different results, as shown on pages 159–61.

Search by keywords

TOO MANY RESULTS

Search Request: K=JAZZ   Queens Catalog

Search Results: 4943 Entries Found   Keyword Index

    DATE TITLE: AUTHOR:

1 2000 History of the Airmen of Note, the premier Mittelstadt, Rich

2 2000 Once upon a time in New York : Jimmy Walke Mitgang, Herbert

3 2000 Schwann inside jazz & classical <serial>

4 2000 Sir Roland Hanna collection <music>   Hanna, Roland

5 2000 The United States Air Force Airmen of Note

6 1999 At the Octoroon balls A fiddler's <sound> Marsalis, Wynton

7 1999 The biographical encyclopedia of jazz   Feather, Leonard G

8 1999 The biographical encyclopedia of jazz   Feather, Leonard G

9 1999 Drifting on a read : jazz as a model for w Jarrett, Michael

10 1999 Drifting on a read jazz as a model for wri Jarrett, Michael

11 1999 Evolution <sound>   Lewis, John

12 1999 Fancy fretwork : the great jazz guitarists Gourse, Leslie

13 1999 The Gershwin style : new looks at the music

14 1999 A history of US   Hakim, Joy

-------------------------------------- CONTINUED on next page --------

STArt over   Type number to display record   <F8> FORward page

HELp   MARk

OTHer options   CHOose

NEXT COMMAND:

TOO FEW RESULTS

Search Request: K=ARMSTRONG AND GLASER   Queens Catalog

Search Results: 0 Entries Found   No Keyword Entries Found

                    No Keyword Matches Found

Possible reasons for this message are:

1. The keyword search term(s) are incorrectly spelled.

2. A numeric '1' is used instead of an alphabetic 'l'.

3. There is punctuation used in the search.

4. A term from the stopword list is used in the search.

5. No records in the online system contain the search term(s) used.

Try the following techniques:

--Change the boolean operator to one that is broader. For example, use

    OR instead of AND, or add terms to the search with the OR operator

--Truncate your search term(s) using a question mark ?

--Delete field codes which have been used as qualifiers

-- Page 1 of 1 ----------------

STArt over   REView prior searches

OTHer options   CHOose

NEXT COMMAND:

If your college's library is part of a regional consortium, its online catalog may list books available in affiliated libraries. A librarian can also get you books that are not in your college's library through an interlibrary loan process. This process can take time, however. Your librarian can tell you how many days to allow for delivery of the requested material.

A REASONABLE NUMBER OF RESULTS

Search Request: K=LOUIS ARMSTRONG   Queens Catalog

Search Results: 68 Entries Found   Keyword Index

DATE TITLE: AUTHOR:

1 1999 The Louis Armstrong companion : eight deca

2 1999 Louis Armstrong, in his own words : select Armstrong, Louis

3 1999 The roaring 20s <sound>   Windscape (Musical)

4 1998 Louis Armstrong : king of jazz   Old, Wendie C

5 1997 If I only had a horn : young Louis Armstro Orgill, Roxane

6 1997 Louis Armstrong : an extravagant life   Bergreen, Laurence

7 1997 The Louis Armstrong odyssey : from Jane Al Travis, Dempsey

8 1996 Satchmo's blues   Schroeder, Alan

9 1995 Louis Armstrong   Woog, Adam

10 1994 Louis Armstrong : a cultural legacy

11 1992 The California concerts <sound>   Armstrong, Louis

12 1991 Louis Rhythm saved the world <sound>   Armstrong, Louis

13 1991 and his orchestra <sound> Armstrong, Louis

--------------------------------- CONTINUED on next page --------

STArt over   Type number to display record   <F8> FORward page

HELp   MARk

OTHer options   CHOose

NEXT COMMAND:

3. Periodicals.   Newspapers, magazines, and scholarly journals that are published at regular intervals, be it daily, weekly, monthly, or quarterly, are classified as **periodicals.** Scholarly and technical journals, which publish articles written by experts and based on up-to-date research and information, are generally more reliable than

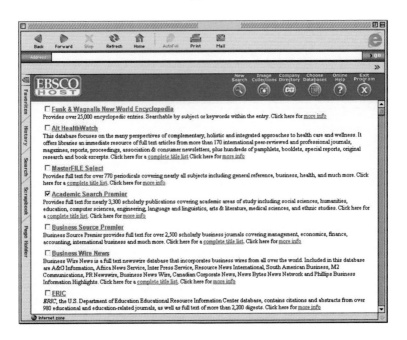

articles written by journalists for popular newspapers and magazines. Although newspapers and magazines can provide useful background information, the journalists who write for them are often not specialists in the field they are writing about, and occasionally they depend on sensationalism to attract attention. If you do not know which periodicals are considered important in a discipline you are studying, ask your instructor or librarian.

For information on interpreting periodical index entries, visit <www.mhhe.com/maimon/finding_sources>.

Indexes. Articles published in periodicals are cataloged in general and specialized indexes, many of which are available in electronic formats, known as **databases**, as well as in print volumes shelved in the library's reference section. Many databases provide abstracts— short summaries of the works they list. Abstracts should not be mistaken for the full-text articles offered by such online subscription services as *InfoTrac* and *EBSCOhost* (sample *EBSCOhost* screens are shown above and on page 163). If you are searching for articles that are more than twenty years old, you should use printed indexes. Otherwise, see what your library has available on CD-ROM or through an online subscription service. (*For help with search terms, see pp. 157–58 and 166–69.*) The list in the box on pages 164–65 includes many of the most popular online indexes to periodical articles.

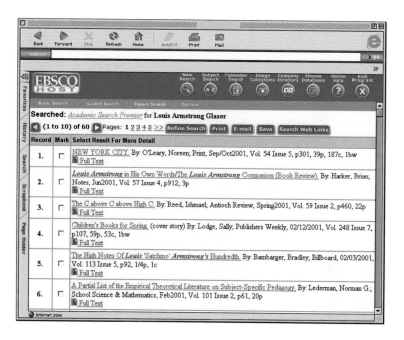

18c Search the Internet.

The **Internet** is a global network of computers; it connects businesses, academic institutions, and individuals electronically. The easiest and most familiar way to gain access to the Internet is through the **World Wide Web,** which connects information through the use of hypertext links. Besides providing access to online databases, reference works, and periodicals, the Internet can bring you closer to primary materials that were once difficult to examine firsthand. It can also put you in touch with a research community through e-mail, chat rooms, online class discussions, MOOs (multiuser dimensions, object-oriented), MUDs (multiuser dimensions), discussion lists, and news groups. Most often the people you meet on the Web will not be experts, but they might be able to lead you to material that is relevant for your research topic.

As with any type of source you use, resources that you find on the Web must be critically evaluated for their reliability. This step is especially important for information you find on the Web, however, because anyone can publish on the Web, and unlike most books and articles, Web sites do not need to go through a rigorous process of peer review and evaluation before publication. (*For help with evaluating Web sources critically, see the box on pp. 173–74.*)

TextConnex

Some Online Databases

- **ABC-CLIO:** This Web-based service offers one interface for searching two indexes: *American History and Life* and *Historical Abstracts.*
- **Academic Universe (Lexis-Nexis):** Updated daily, this online service provides full-text access to around 6,000 newspapers, professional publications, legal references, and congressional sources.
- **EBSCOhost:** The Academic Search Premier service provides full-text coverage for more than 3,000 scholarly publications and indexes articles in all academic subject areas.
- **ERIC:** This database lists publications in the area of education.
- **FirstSearch:** Offering a common interface for access to general databases such as NetFirst and WorldCat, this service also permits searches of such subject-specific bibliographic databases as ERIC, *Medline,* and the *MLA Bibliography.*
- **General Science Index:** As its name indicates, this index is general rather than specialized and is therefore most appropriate for beginning science students. It lists articles by biologists, chemists, and other scientists.
- **GDCS:** Updated monthly, the Government Documents Catalog Service (GDCS) contains records of all publications printed by the United States Government Printing Office since 1976.
- **Humanities Index:** This index lists articles from journals in language and literature, history, philosophy, and similar areas.
- **InfoTrac SearchBank:** This Web-based service searches bibliographic and other databases such as the General Reference Center Gold, General Business File ASAP, and Health Reference Center.
- **JSTOR:** This electronic archive provides full-text access to scholarly journals in the humanities and social sciences.
- **MLA Bibliography:** Covering from 1963 to the present, the *MLA Bibliography* indexes more than 3,400 journals, essay collections,

To get the most out of your Internet research, you need to learn how to use search engines and keywords to find useful Web sites, as well as how to gain access to and use other Internet resources such as discussion groups (ListServs), Usenet news groups, MOOs, and MUDs.

1. Search engines.   To search for sources on the World Wide Web, you type a keyword or phrase into a **search engine,** a software program that searches for Web sites that include your keyword and

proceedings, and series published worldwide in the fields of modern languages, literature, literary criticism, linguistics, and folklore. Coverage includes all modern national literatures.

- *New York Times Index:* This index lists major articles published by the *Times* since 1913.
- *Newspaper Abstracts:* This database provides an index to 25 national and regional newspapers.
- *PAIS International:* Produced by the Public Affairs Information Service, this database indexes literature on public policy, social policy, and the general social sciences from 1972 to the present, with subject areas including political science, government, international relations, law, economics, business, finance, and other social sciences.
- *Periodical Abstracts:* This database indexes more than 1,500 general and academic journals covering business, current affairs, economics, literature, religion, psychology, and women's studies from 1986 to the present.
- *PsycInfo:* Sponsored by the American Psychological Association (APA), this database indexes and abstracts books, scholarly articles, technical reports, and dissertations in the area of psychology and related disciplines such as psychiatry, medicine, nursing, and education.
- *PubMed:* The National Library of Medicine publishes this database, which indexes and abstracts nine million journal articles in biomedicine and provides links to related databases.
- *Sociological Abstracts:* For researchers in the area of sociology and related disciplines, this database indexes and abstracts articles from more than 2,600 journals, as well as books, conference papers, and dissertations.
- *Social Science Index:* This index lists articles from journals in such fields as economics, psychology, political science, and sociology.

returns a list of potentially relevant sites. There are many search engines available, and because each covers a different group of Web sites and searches them in its own way, most researchers find it necessary to use more than one. (*See the box on p. 167 for a list of popular search engines.*)

Each search engine's home page provides a link to advice on using the search engine efficiently to get targeted results. Look for a link labeled "search help," "about us," or something similar, and click on it to learn how a specific search engine can best serve your needs.

TEXTCONNEX

Good Starting Points for Web-Based Research

The following sites list online academic resources by subject or field of research:

- *Academic Info* <http://www.academicinfo.net>
- *Infomine: Scholarly Internet Resource Collections* <http://infomine.ucr.edu>
- *Voice of the Shuttle General Humanities Page* <http://vos.ucsb.edu/index.asp>
- *World Wide Web Virtual Library* <http://www.vlib.org>

2. Keyword Internet searches.   Besides learning more about the search engines you use, you need to know how to fine-tune your search process by adjusting your keyword or phrase. For example, a search of *AltaVista* using the keyword *Louis Armstrong* yields a list of more than 119,000 Web sites, a staggering number of links, or **hits.**

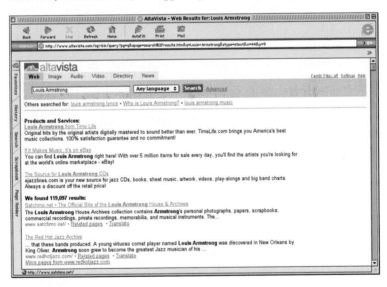

Altering the keyword to make it more specific narrows the results significantly. The box on page 168 offers suggestions for refining keywords, and the sample searches of *AltaVista* that follow it illustrate two approaches.

TEXTCONNEX

Popular Search Engines

Simple search engines, or *directories,* use hierarchical indexes created by people who have been trained to categorize information. These directories are a good way to start your Internet research because they are easy to use and selective in the results they return.

- *Yahoo!* <http://www.yahoo.com>
- *Galaxy* <http://www.galaxy.com>

Standard search engines send "robots" or "spiders" to all points on the Web to return results. Using mathematical calculations, they inform you about the relevancy of each site to your search, putting the most relevant items at the top of the list.

- *AltaVista* <http://www.altavista.com>
- *Go.com* <http://infoseek.go.com>
- *All the Web* <http://www.alltheweb.com>
- *HotBot* <http://hotbot.lycos.com>

Meta search engines return results by searching other search engines. They provide more sites than a simple search engine, but they are not as selective.

- *Dogpile* <http://www.dogpile.com>
- *MetaCrawler* <http://www.metacrawler.com>

Alternative search engines allow users to ask for information in different ways.

- *Northern Light* <http://www.northernlight.com>: Supports Boolean searching (*see p. 168*), natural language searching (by question), and fielded searching.

- *Ask Jeeves* <http://www.ask.com>: Supports natural language searching. Type a question and click on "ask."

- *Google* <http://www.google.com>: Responds to a query in a way that ranks relevant Web sites based on the link structure of the Internet itself.

Tips

Refining Keyword Searches

Although search engines vary, the following advice should work for many of the search engines you will use.

Group words together. Put quotation marks or parentheses around the phrase you are looking for—for example, "Dixieland Jazz."

Use Boolean operators.

AND (+)   Use AND or + when words must appear together in a document: Germany + Economy.

OR   Use OR if one of two or more terms must appear in your results: jazz OR "musical improvisation."

NOT (–)   Use NOT or – in front of words that you do not want to appear together in your results: Germany NOT west.

Add a wildcard. For more results, combine part of a keyword with an asterisk (*) used as a wildcard: German* AND econom* or +German* +econom*.

Search the fields. Some search engines enable searching within fields, such as the title field of Web pages. You will find Web pages that are about your topic by doing a title search: TITLE: +Louis +Armstrong will give you pages about Louis Armstrong.

KEYWORD REFINED

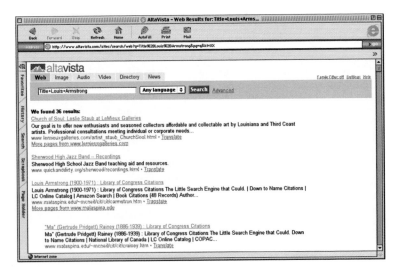

KEYWORD REFINED FURTHER

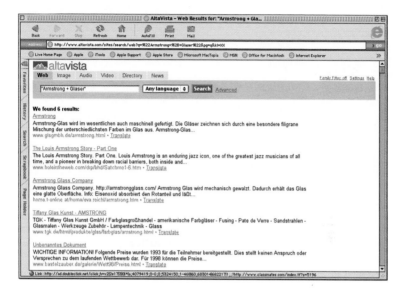

3. Online communication. In addition to providing information, the Internet also provides access to communities with common interests and varying levels of expertise on different subjects. Discussion lists (electronic mailing lists), Usenet news groups, MOOs, and MUDs are the most common communities that can provide help with your research topics. They can help you in the following ways:

- You can get an idea for a paper by finding out what topics interest and concern people.
- You can learn what people think about almost any topic from food to pop culture to sports to science.
- You can zero in on a very specific topic, such as sushi, a comic book character, a vintage TV show, a singer, or a scientific theory.

Discussion lists (electronic mailing lists) are networked e-mail conversations on particular topics that may be relevant to your research topic. Lists can be open (anyone can join) or closed (only certain people, such as members of a particular class or group, can join). If the list is open, you can subscribe by sending a message to a computer that has list-processing software installed on it.

TEXTCONNEX

Discussion Lists

Check out the following Web sites for more information about discussion lists:

Harness E-mail: Mailing Lists <http://www.learnthenet.com/english/html/24mlists.htm>: Explains how discussion lists work.

Topica <http://www.topica.com>: Contains a searchable directory of 90,095 discussion lists.

Tile.net: The Reference to Internet Discussion and Information Lists <http://tile.net/lists>: Allows you to search for discussion lists by name, description, or domain.

Usenet news groups are one of the oldest features of the Internet. Like lists, news groups may exist on topics relevant to your research. You must subscribe to read postings. Unlike lists, news groups are posted to a *news server,* a computer that hosts the news group and distributes postings to participating servers. Postings are not automatically distributed by e-mail.

TEXTCONNEX

News Groups

For more information about news groups, refer to these resources online:

Newsreaders.com <http://www.newsreaders.com/guide/news.html>: Explains why you would want a newsreader and how to use one.

Tile.net.news <http://tile.net/news>: A complete index to Internet Usenet news groups. Browse by subject, hierarchy, or search. Provides links to news group FAQs and use statistics.

Harley Hahn's Master List of Usenet Newsgroups <http://www.harley.com/usenet>: A master list of Usenet news groups with descriptions. Search by category or keyword.

Multiuser dimensions, known as **MUDs,** or **multiuser dimensions, object oriented,** known as **MOOs,** exist in many disciplines, including biology (BioMOO) and French (MOOFrancais). Participants interested in a topic meet and interact with each other in a virtual space, where they use writing to create a world of objects and actions and feelings. To join a MUD or MOO, you need to apply to the managers for a password and character.

TEXTCONNEX

MOOs

For more information about MOOs, visit the following sites:

MOO Resources <www.english.upenn.edu/PennMOO/resources.html>

More about MOOs <www.itp.berkeley.edu/~thorne/MOO.html>

19 Evaluating Sources

When someone insults you or expresses an outrageous idea, your friends may advise you to "consider the source." In other words, *who* is speaking affects the credibility of what is said. In the same way, when you are doing research, you must evaluate the reliability of your sources.

Even when a source is reliable, however, it may have little to do with your research questions. One of the most important tasks for any researcher is to assess the relevance as well as the reliability of his or her sources.

19a Question print sources.

Just because something is in print does not make it true or relevant. How can you determine if a print source is likely to be both reliable and useful? Here are some questions to ask about any source you are considering:

Reliability

- **What information can you find about the writer's credentials?** Is the writer affiliated with a research institution dedicated to contributing to knowledge about an issue?

- **Who is the publisher?** University presses and academic publishers are considered more scholarly than the popular

TextConnex

Evaluating Sources

Primary or Secondary? Popular or Scholarly?
<http://www.sport.ussa.edu/library/primary.htm>: Discusses the difference between primary and secondary research sources, as well as the difference between popular and scholarly sources.

Evaluating Sources of Information
<http://owl.english.purdue.edu/workshops/hypertext/EvalSrcW/internet.html>: From the Purdue Online Writing Lab, this page provides guidelines for evaluating sources.

press because work published by them is usually based on research and subjected to rigorous peer review.

▪ **Does the work include a bibliography of works consulted or cited?** Reliable research is always part of a conversation among specialists. To show familiarity with what other researchers have said about a topic, trustworthy writers cite a variety of sources and document their citations properly. Does this source do so? Does the source include a variety of citations?

▪ **Is there any indication that the writer has a particular point of view on your topic or that the writer is biased?** What kind of tone does the author use? Is the text objective or subjective? (*For more on evaluating a source's argument, see Tab 2: Writing Papers, pp. 24–29.*)

Relevance

▪ **Do the source's title and subtitle indicate that it addresses your specific research question?**

▪ **What is the publication date?** Is the material up-to-date (published within the past five years)? Or if you have a reason for working with older sources, is the publication date appropriate for your research?

▪ **Does the table of contents indicate that the source covers useful information?**

▪ **If the source is an article, does it have an abstract at the beginning? Is there a summary at the end?** An abstract or a summary presents the main points made in an article and can help you decide if a source is likely to be useful.

▪ **Does the work contain subheadings?** Skim the headings to see if they indicate that the source covers useful information.

▪ **If the source is a book, does it have an index?** Scan the index for keywords related to your topic to see how useful the book might be.

In college research, relevance can be a tricky matter. Your sociology instructor will expect you to give special preference to sociological sources in a project on the organization of the workplace. Your business management instructor will expect you to use material from that field in a project on the same topic. Be prepared to find that some promising sources turn out to be less relevant than you first thought.

19b Question Internet sources.

With print sources, you can have at least some confidence that the material has been filtered through editors and publishers. But the Internet is unfiltered. Anyone can design an attractive Web page that looks authoritative but contains utter nonsense. The Internet is a free-for-all. You will find highly valuable, up-to-the-minute material there, but you must closely question every source you find on the Internet.

For a list of questions to ask when evaluating Internet sources, visit <www.mhhe.com/maimon/evaluating_sources>.

 LEARNING in COLLEGE

Critically Evaluating Web Resources

When you use sources from the Internet for a paper or a presentation, one of your most important responsibilities is to analyze their reliability carefully and critically. Here are some points to keep in mind and guidelines to follow.

Authority and credibility. Are the author and producer of the Web site identifiable? Does the author include biographical information? Is there any indication that the author has relevant expertise on the subject? Look for information about the individual or organization sponsoring the site; that can be an important indication of its reliability. The following extensions in the Web address, or uniform resource locator (URL), can help you determine the type of site (which often tells you something about its purpose):

.com	commercial (business)	**.edu**	educational	**.mil**	military
.org	nonprofit organization	**.gov**	U.S. government	**.net**	network

A tilde (~) followed by a name in a URL usually means the site is a personal home page not affiliated with any organization.

(continued)

LEARNING in COLLEGE *(continued)*

Purpose. A site's purpose influences its presentation of information and its reliability. Is the site's main purpose to advocate a cause, advertise a product or service, provide factual information, present research results, provide news, share personal information, or offer entertainment?

Objectivity and reasonableness (bias). Don't take the information that the site presents at face value. Look carefully at the purpose and tone of the text. Is there evidence of obvious bias? Clues that indicate a lack of reasonableness or bias include an intemperate tone, broad claims, exaggerated statements of significance, conflicts of interest, no recognition of opposing views, and strident attacks on opposing views. (*For more on evaluating a source's argument, see Tab 2: Writing Papers, pp. 24–29.*)

Relevance. Is the information appropriate for your research? Consider the intended audience of the site, based on its purpose, content, tone, and style. Carefully consider the site's subject matter and the depth of its coverage of the subject.

Timeliness. Is the information current enough for your needs, or is it outdated? Reliable sites usually post the date an item was published or loaded onto the Web or tell you when the information was last updated.

Context. Finally, keep in mind that search engines retrieve individual Web pages *out of context*. Always try to return to the site's home page to determine the source of the information and to complete your citation.

Adapted with the permission of Lisa Kammerlocher and Dennis Isbell, Arizona State University West.

19c Evaluate a source's arguments.

As you read the sources you have selected, you should continue to assess their reliability. Does the writer of a piece appeal to your emotions, to your reason, or to both in a balanced way? Regardless of where a source comes from, always ask yourself whether a particular writer is objective and fair-minded. Look for arguments that are qualified, supported with evidence, and well documented. Avoid relying on biased sources that appeal to emotions instead of rational thought or promote one-sided political or religious agendas instead of inquiry and discussion.

The extended debate surrounding the 2000 presidential election is an excellent example of the need to evaluate arguments for possible bias. Editorials in Democratic-leaning newspapers or Web sites are more likely to cite statistics and refer to documents favorable to Al Gore's position on the Florida vote count, whereas editorials in Republican-leaning print or online publications are going to present information that supports their conclusions about a George W. Bush victory in Florida. A fair-minded researcher needs to read and evaluate sources on both sides of this and other issues, including the relevant primary sources that are available, such as the testimony in the Florida court cases and the Supreme Court arguments. (*For more guidance on reading critically, see Chapter 6, pp. 21–24.*)

20 Doing Research in the Archive, Field, and Lab

Often research involves more than finding answers to questions in books and other printed material (secondary research). When you conduct primary research—examining authentic documents and original records, observing the world, and experimenting in the laboratory—you participate in the discovery of knowledge.

The Internet is transforming primary research. In meteorology, for example, weather databases housed in Colorado are now available on the Internet in a format that students as well as specialists can understand. As for lab research, it too is being transformed by the development of dry labs—computer-based experimental arenas in which research is conducted through simulations. Also, researchers can now use e-mail to carry out surveys and interviews.

20a Adhere to ethical principles when doing primary research.

In the archive, field, or lab, you are working directly with something precious and immediate: an original record, a group of people, or special materials. Sometimes you will be the first person to see the significance of a document, to observe a particular pattern of behavior, or to perform a new test in the lab. An ethical researcher shows respect for materials, experimental subjects, fellow researchers, and readers. Here are some guidelines to follow:

- Handle original documents and materials with great care, always leaving sources and data available for other researchers.

- Accurately report your sources and results.

- Follow the procedures mandated by your college and your field when working with human participants.

Research with human participants that you do as an undergraduate should also adhere to the following basic principles:

- **Confidentiality:** People who fill out surveys, participate in focus groups, or respond to interviews should be assured that their names will not be used without their permission.

- **Informed consent:** Before participating in an experiment, all particpants must sign a statement affirming that they understand the general purpose of the research. Researchers agree that observations of crowds in a shopping mall or children in a classroom do not require informed consent, unless your observations intrude on the lives of the people you are observing.

- **Minimal risk:** Researchers must design experiments so that participants do not incur any risks greater than they do in everyday life.

- **Protection of vulnerable groups:** Researchers must be held strictly accountable for research done with participants in the following categories: the physically disabled, prisoners, those who are mentally incompetent, minors, the elderly, and pregnant women.

Be fair when you refute the primary research or the views of others. Even if your purpose is to prove fellow researchers wrong, review their work and state their viewpoints in words that they themselves would recognize as accurate.

20b   Prepare yourself before undertaking archival research.

Archives are collections of specialized or rare books, manuscripts, and documents. They are accessible in libraries, other institutions, private collections, and on video- and audiotape. Your own attic may contain family archives—letters, diaries, and photograph collections that could have value to a researcher.

The more you know about your area of study, the more likely you will be to see the significance of an item in an archival collection. Reading about your topic in books, journals, and Internet documents will provide a framework for discovery and lead you to questions that can be answered only by consulting original materials in an archive.

Some archival collections are accessible through audio- and videotape as well as the Internet; others you must visit in person. (*See the box on p. 177.*) If you intend to do research in a rare-books library, you will need a letter of introduction, usually from your professor or your college librarian.

20c   Plan your field research carefully.

Field research involves recording observations, conducting interviews, or administering surveys. For the best results, you will need a strong research design and a plan for keeping accurate records.

TEXTCONNEX

Online Information about Archives

Here are some Internet sites that will help you find and understand a wide range of archival sources:

- *American Memory* <http://memory.loc.gov>: This site offers access to more than seven million digital items from over 100 collections of material on U.S. history and culture.
- *ArchivesUSA* <http://archives.chadwyck.com>: This subscription service is available via ProQuest. It provides information about 80,000 manuscript collections, more than 50,000 document collections, and more than 5,000 other archival repositories.
- *U.S. National Archives and Record Administration (NARA)* <http://www.nara.gov>: Learn how to use the National Archives in this site's research room, and then search the site for the documents you want.
- *Radio Program Archive* <http://www.people.memphis.edu/~mbensman>: This site lists radio archives available from the University of Memphis and explains how to obtain cassettes of significant radio programs.
- *Repositories of Primary Sources* <www.uidaho.edu/special-collections/OtherRepositories.html>: This site lists more than 4,800 Web sites describing holdings of manuscripts, rare books, historical photographs, and other archival materials.
- *Television News Archive* <http://tvnews.vanderbilt.edu>: This site provides summaries of television news broadcasts and information on how to order videocassettes.
- *Virtual Library Museums Page* <http://www.icom.org/vlmp>: This site lists online museums throughout the world.
- *Women Writers Project* <http://wwp.stg.brown.edu>: This site lists archived texts by pre-Victorian women writers that are available through the project.

1. Observing and writing field notes.

When you use direct observation, you need to keep careful records in order to gather the information you require. Here are some guidelines to follow:

- Be systematic and purposeful in your observations, but be alert to unexpected behavior.
- Record what you see and hear as objectively as possible.
- Take more notes than you think you will ever need.
- When appropriate, categorize the types of behavior you are looking for, and devise a system for counting instances of each type.

- When you have recorded data over a significant period of time, group your observations into categories for more careful study and discussion.

(For advice on conducting direct observations for a case study, see Tab 3: Common Assignments across the Curriculum, pp. 118–20.)

2. Conducting interviews.
Asking relevant questions of experts or people who are members of a population you are studying is a powerful research tool. Group interviews, called *focus groups,* are used in a number of fields, including marketing, education, and psychology. Interviews should be conducted in a relaxed atmosphere, but they are not simply conversations. To be useful as research tools, interviews require systematic preparation and implementation.

- Identify appropriate people for your interviews.
- Do background research, and plan your questions.
- Take careful notes, and if possible, tape-record the interview. (Be sure to obtain your subject's permission if you use audiotape.)
- Follow up on vague responses with questions that get at specific information.
- Politely probe inconsistencies and contradictions.
- Write thank-you notes to interviewees, and later send them copies of your report.

3. Taking surveys.
Conducted either orally from a script or in writing, **surveys** are made up of structured questions. Written surveys are called **questionnaires.** Survey research is much more complex than it looks. In fact, students in advanced social science courses spend a great deal of time studying the design and analysis of surveys. The following suggestions will help you prepare informal surveys, which you should use only after checking with your instructor:

- **Define your purpose.** Are you trying to gauge attitudes, learn about typical behaviors, or both?
- **Write clear directions and questions.** For example, if you are asking multiple-choice questions, make sure that you cover all possible options and that none of your options overlap.
- **Make sure that your questions are neutral,** that they do not suggest a preference for one answer over another.
- **Make the survey brief and easy to complete.** Most informal surveys should be no longer than one page (front and back).

20d Keep a notebook when doing lab research.

All experimenters, from undergraduates to professional scientists, are required to keep careful records of their laboratory work in a notebook. The purpose of this research notebook is to provide a complete and accurate account of the testing of a hypothesis in the controlled environment of the laboratory. In many courses, you will be required to use a lab manual for your notes. Whether or not you are using such a manual, the following guidelines will help you take accurate notes on your research.

1. Record immediate, on-the-spot, accurate notes on what happens in the lab. Write down as much detail as possible. Measure precisely; do not estimate. Identify major pieces of apparatus, unusual chemicals, and laboratory animals in enough detail so that, for example, a reader can determine the size or type of equipment you used (instead of "physiograph," write "physiograph, Grass model 7B"). Use drawings, when appropriate, to illustrate complicated equipment setups. Include tables, when useful, to present results.

2. Follow a basic format. If you are working without a lab manual or if no standard format is provided, you will be expected to present your results in a format that allows you to communicate all the major features of an experiment. The five basic sections that must be included are title, purpose, materials and methods, results, and conclusions. (*For more advice on preparing a lab report, see Tab 3: Common Assignments across the Curriculum, pp. 113–18.*)

3. Write in complete sentences, even if you are filling in answers to questions in a lab manual. Resist using shorthand to record your notes. Writing in complete sentences will ensure that you understand the concepts in the experiment. Later, when you study your lab notebook, the complete sentences will provide a clear, unambiguous record of your procedures and results. Notice the difference between the following two responses to a typical question in a lab manual:

Why is water readily polluted?

INCOMPLETE ANSWER   universal solvent

COMPLETE ANSWER   Water is a universal solvent. Consequently, many compounds, including pollutants, dissolve in water.

Highlight connections in your sentences by using the following transitions: *then, next, consequently, because,* and *therefore.* Cause-effect relationships are important to working scientists and should have similar importance in your lab notebook.

4. When necessary, revise and correct your laboratory notebook in visible ways.   If you make a mistake in recording laboratory results, correct them as clearly as possible, either by erasing or by crossing out and rewriting on the original sheet. If you make an uncorrectable mistake in your lab notebook, do not tear the sheet out. Simply fold the sheet lengthwise and mark *omit* on the face side.

If you need to add sheets to your notebook, paste them permanently to the appropriate pages. No matter how much preparation you do, unanticipated results often occur in the lab, and you may find yourself jotting down notes on a convenient piece of scrap paper or even a paper towel. Attach these notes to your laboratory notebook.

21 Working with Sources

For three basic rules on when to cite sources, visit <www.mhhe.com/maimon/working_with_sources>.

Once you have a research question to answer, an idea about what the library and Internet have to offer, and some sense of the kinds of materials you need, you are ready to begin selecting and using sources.

21a   Maintain a working bibliography.

As you research, compile a **working bibliography**—a list of those books, articles, pamphlets, Web sites, and other sources that seem most likely to help you answer your research question. It is essential to maintain an accurate and complete record of all sources you consult. For each source, record the following bibliographic information:

- Call number of book, reference work, or other print source; URL of each Web site
- All authors, editors, and translators
- Title of chapter, article, or Web page
- Title of book, periodical, or Web site in which the chapter, article, or page appears
- For books, date of publication, place, and publisher as well as edition or volume numbers, if applicable
- For periodical articles, the date and edition or volume number, issue, and page numbers if applicable
- For a Web source, the date you consulted it

You can record bibliographic information on 3" × 5" cards, printouts, or directly on photocopies of source material.

1. 3" × 5" cards.   Before computers became widely available, most researchers used 3" × 5" cards to compile the working bibliography, with each potential source getting a separate card. This method is still useful. Besides including all the information you need to document the source, you can also use the cards to record brief quotations from or comments on those sources you decide to read and use. Today, however, some researchers prefer to use printouts as records of bibliographic information.

2. Printouts. When you conduct online searches, the screen may offer you the option of printing out the results or saving them on a disk. On the printout or disk, be sure to note all relevant bibliographic information, including the database you used. If you rely on printouts to compile your working bibliography, you may want to use a highlighter to indicate those sources you actually plan to consult.

If your college's library makes it possible for you to compile a list of sources and e-mail it to yourself, you can keep your working bibliography in electronic form, printing out specific entries as you need them.

3. Photocopies. If you photocopy articles, essays, or pages of reference works from a print or a microform source, take time to note the bibliographic information on the photocopy. Spending a few extra minutes now can save you lots of time later.

21b Take notes on your sources.

Taking notes increases learning and helps you to think through the answer to your research question. As you work, you can take notes on the information you glean from your sources by annotating photocopies of your source material or by noting useful quotations and ideas on paper, on cards, or in a computer file.

1. Annotation. One way to take notes is to annotate photocopied articles and printouts from online information services or Web sites. As you read, write the following notes directly on the page:

- On the first page, write down complete bibliographic information for the source (*see p. 180*).
- As you read, record your questions, reactions, and ideas in the margins.
- Comment in the margin on ideas that agree with or differ from those you have already learned about.
- Put important and difficult passages into your own words by paraphrasing or summarizing them in the margin. (*For help with paraphrasing and summarizing, see pp. 182–83.*)
- Use a highlighter to mark statements that you may want to quote because they are key to gaining an understanding of the issue or are especially well expressed.

For information on using direct quotations, summaries, and paraphrases while taking notes, visit <www.mhhe.com/maimon/working_with_sources>.

When you are finished annotating the article or printout, use a research notebook to explore some of the comments, connections, and questions you recorded in the margins.

2. Separate notes.   If you do not have photocopies to annotate, take notes on paper, index cards, or a computer. Using a separate card or page for each idea you write down will make it easier to organize the material. Whatever method you use, be sure to record the source's bibliographic information as well as the specific page number for each idea.

It is important to enclose in quotation marks any exact words from a source. If you think that you may forget that the phrasing, as well as the idea, came from someone else, label the passage a "quote," as the student writing about Louis Armstrong did in the following excerpt from her research notebook:

> Notes on Dan Morgenstern. "Louis Armstrong and the Development and Diffusion of Jazz." Louis Armstrong: A Cultural Legacy. Ed. Marc H. Miller. Seattle: U of Washington P and Queens Museum of Art, 1994. 95-145.
>
> ■ Armstrong having trouble with managers. Fires Johnny Collins in London, 1933. Collins blocks Armstrong from playing with Chick Webb's band (pp. 124-5).
>
> ■ Armstrong turned to Glaser, an old Chicago acquaintance. Quote: "Joe Glaser [. . .] proved to be the right man at the right time" (p. 128).

Unless you think you might use a particular quotation in your paper, it is usually better to express the author's ideas in your own words by using a paraphrase or a summary.

When you **paraphrase,** you put someone else's statements into other words. Keep in mind that a paraphrase is not a word-for-word translation. Instead, you need to express the source's ideas *in your own way,* a way that will usually be shorter and less detailed than the original. Even though the sentences are yours, you must still give credit for the ideas to the original writer by citing his or her work properly. And if your paraphrase includes any exact phrasing from the source, put quotation marks around those phrases.

In the first, unacceptable paraphrase that follows, the writer has done a word-for-word translation, using synonyms for some terms but retaining the phrasing of the original. The writer also failed to enclose all borrowed expressions in quotation marks ("nonsense syllables," "it is more likely that"). The acceptable paraphrase, by contrast, is more concise that the original and although it quotes a few words from the source, the writer has expressed the definition in a new and different way.

SOURCE

Scat singing. A technique of jazz singing in which onomatopoeic or nonsense syllables are sung to improvised melodies. Some writers have traced scat singing back to the practice, common in West African musics, of translating percussion patterns into vocal lines by assigning syllables to characteristic rhythms. However, since this allows little scope for melodic improvisation and the earliest recorded examples of jazz scat singing involved the free invention of rhythm, melody, and syllables, it is more likely that the technique began in the USA as singers imitated the sounds of jazz instrumentalists.

—J. BRADFORD ROBINSON, *The New Grove Dictionary of Jazz*

UNACCEPTABLE PARAPHRASE: PLAGIARISM

Scat is a way of singing that uses nonsense syllables and extemporaneous melodies. Some people think that scat goes back to the custom in West African music of turning drum rhythms into vocal lines. But that doesn't explain the "free invention of rhythm, melody, and syllables" of the first recorded instances of scat singing. It is more likely that scat was started in the U.S. by singers imitating the way instrumental jazz sounded (Robinson 425).

ACCEPTABLE PARAPHRASE

Scat, a highly inventive type of jazz singing, combines "nonsense syllables [with] improvised melodies." Although syllabic singing of drum rhythms occurs in West Africa, scat probably owes more to the early attempts of American singers to mimic both the sound and the inventive musical style of instrumental jazz (Robinson 425).

When you **summarize,** you state the main point of a piece, condensing a few paragraphs into one sentence or a few pages into one paragraph. (*For guidelines on writing a summary, see Tab 2: Writing Papers, p. 23.*) Here is a summary of Robinson on scat singing:

Scat singing probably originated in the United States when singers tried to mimic the sound of instrumental jazz.

21c Take stock of what you have learned.

When you take stock, you assess the research you have done and synthesize what you have learned.

In college writing, the credibility of your work depends on the relevance and reliability of your sources as well as the scope and depth of your reading and observation. A paper on Louis Armstrong, for example, is unlikely to be credible if it relies on only one source of information. For lab reports, detailed observations are likely to be most important because they are the main kind of source that experimenters use when writing up their work.

As the context and kind of writing change, so too will the requirements for particular types and numbers of sources. As a general rule, however, you should consult more than two sources and use only sources that are both reliable and respected by people working in the field. Ask yourself the following questions about the sources you have consulted:

- Are your sources trustworthy? (*See Chapter 19, pp. 171–75, for more on evaluating sources.*)

- If you have started to develop a tentative answer to your research question, have your sources provided you with a sufficient number of facts, examples, and ideas to support that answer?

- Have you used sources that examine issues from several different perspectives?

It is also important to think about how the sources you have read relate to one another. Ask yourself when, how, and why your sources agree or disagree, and consider where you stand on the issues they raise. Did anything you read surprise or disturb you? Writing down your responses to such questions can help you clarify what you have learned from working with sources.

22 Writing the Paper

You have chosen a challenging research question and have located, read, and evaluated a variety of relevant sources. Now you need to come up with a thesis that will allow you to share what you have learned as well as your perspective on the issue.

22a Plan and draft your paper.

Begin planning by recalling the context and the purpose of your paper. If you have an assignment sheet, review it to see if the paper is supposed to be primarily informative, interpretive, or argumentative. Keep your purpose and context in mind as you decide on a thesis to support and develop.

1. Decide on a thesis.   Consider the question that guided your research as well as others provoked by what you have learned during your research. Revise the wording of your question to make it intriguing as well as suitable (*see Chapter 17, pp. 151–52*). After you write down this question, compose an answer that you can use as your tentative thesis, as Esther Hoffman does in the following example:

HOFFMAN'S FOCAL QUESTION

What kind of relationship did Louis Armstrong and Joe Glaser actually have?

HOFFMAN'S TENTATIVE ANSWER

Armstrong and Glaser enjoyed not only a successful business partnership but also a complex friendship based on mutual respect and caring.

(*For more on devising a thesis, see Tab 2: Writing Papers, pp. 43–45.*)

2. Outline a plan for supporting and developing your thesis.

Guided by your tentative thesis, outline a plan that uses your sources in a purposeful way. Decide on the kind of structure you will use to support your thesis—explanatory, exploratory, or argumentative—and develop your support by choosing facts, examples, and ideas drawn from a variety of sources. (*See Chapters 10–12 in Tab 3 for more on explanatory, exploratory, and argumentative structures.*)

For her interpretive paper on Armstrong and Glaser, Hoffman decided on an exploratory structure, an approach organized around raising and answering a central question:

- Introduce Armstrong as a great musician who was once a poor waif.
- Introduce Glaser, Armstrong's manager for thirty-four years.
- State the question: What kind of relationship did these two actually have? Did Glaser dominate Armstrong?
- Glaser as Armstrong's business manager: support for idea that it was Glaser who made Armstrong a star.
- Armstrong's resistance to being controlled by Glaser.
- Conclude: Armstrong and Glaser worked well together as friends who respected and cared for each other.

To develop this outline, Hoffman would need to list supporting facts, examples, or ideas for each point. (*For more on developing an outline, see Tab 2: Writing Papers, pp. 45–46.*)

3. Write a draft that you can revise and edit.

When you have a tentative thesis and a plan, you are ready to write a draft. As her outline shows, Hoffman planned to use a few pages to set up the context for her issue, but many writers find that they can present their thesis or focal question at the end of an introductory paragraph or two.

As you write beyond the introduction, be prepared to reexamine and refine your thesis. Discovering interesting connections as well as new ways to express your ideas makes writing exciting. Such discoveries often occur when writers use what they have read in various sources to support and develop their ideas. When you draw on ideas from your sources, be sure to quote and paraphrase effectively and properly. (*For advice on quoting and paraphrasing, see Chapter 21, pp. 182–83 and the next section.*)

Make your conclusion as memorable as possible. In the final version of Hoffman's paper, on page 239, note how she uses a visual and a play on words—"more than meets the eye"—to end her paper. In doing so, she enhances her concluding point—that the two men were different, yet complementary, and that their relationship was complex.

Hoffman did not come up with the last line of her paper until she revised and edited her first draft. Often writers will come up with fresh ideas for their introduction, body paragraphs, or conclusion at this stage, one reason it is important to spend time revising and editing your paper. (*For more on revising, see Tab 2, pp. 59–74. For help with editing, see Tabs 10–13.*)

22b Quote and paraphrase both properly and effectively.

To support and develop your ideas, use quoted, paraphrased, or summarized material from sources. To do so properly and effectively, follow these guidelines.

1. Integrating quotations. Use quotations when a source's exact words are important to your point and make your writing more memorable, fair, or authoritative. Quotes should be short, enclosed in quotation marks, and well integrated into your sentence structure, as in the following example from Esther Hoffman's paper on Louis Armstrong and Joe Glaser:

> In his dedication to the unpublished manuscript "Louis Armstrong and the Jewish Family in New Orleans," Armstrong calls Glaser "the best friend that I ever had," while in a letter to Max Jones, he writes, "I did not get really happy until I got with my man—my dearest friend—Joe Glaser" (qtd. in Jones and Chilton 16).

2. Using brackets within quotations. Sentences that include quotations must make sense grammatically. Sometimes you may have to adjust a quotation to make it fit properly into your sentence. Use brackets to indicate any minor adjustments you have made. For example, *my* has been changed to *his* to make the quotation fit in the following sentence:

> Armstrong confided to a friend that Glaser's death "broke [his] heart" (Bergreen 490).

Tips LEARNING in COLLEGE

Varying Signal Phrases

When a writer relies on the same signal phrase throughout a paper, readers quickly become bored. To keep things interesting, vary your signal phrases. Instead of using the verbs *says* and *writes* again and again, consider using *acknowledges, asserts, claims, concludes, emphasizes, explains, expresses, notes, points out, proves, reports, responds, shows,* or *suggests.*

3. Using ellipses within quotations.   Use ellipses to indicate that words have been omitted from the body of a quotation, but be sure that what you omit does not significantly alter the source's meaning. If you are using MLA style, place the ellipsis points within square brackets. (*For more on using ellipses, see Tab 12: Editing for Correctness, pp. 472–73.*)

> As Morgenstern put it, "Joe Glaser [. . .] proved to be the right man at the right time" (128).

5. Using block format for longer quotations.   Quotations longer than four lines should be used rarely. When they are used too frequently, long quotations tend to break up your text and make your reader impatient. If you include a longer quotation, put it in block format (*see Tab 12: Editing for Correctness, pp. 458–60*) and be especially careful to integrate it into your paper. Tell your readers why you want them to read the block quotation, and afterwards, comment on it.

6. Using signal phrases to introduce quotations and paraphrases.   When you are integrating someone else's thoughts or words into your writing, use a **signal phrase** that indicates whom you are quoting. Besides crediting others for their work, signal phrases can make ideas more interesting by giving them a human face. Here are two examples, the first from Esther Hoffman's paper on Louis Armstrong and Joe Glaser (*see Tab 6, pp. 230–42*) and the second from Jennifer Koehler's paper on Germany's economy (*see Tab 7, pp. 261–72*):

> *As Bergreen points out,* Armstrong easily reached difficult high notes, the F's and G's that stymied other trumpeters (248).

> *According to Agarwal* (1997), "privatization-related FDI often leads to reinvestments, and improves the climate for more FDI, reassuring investors about the continuation of liberal policies in the future."

CHARTING the TERRITORY

Using Data

Statistics—numerical data and methods of interpreting those data—are a critical part of research in many disciplines, particularly the social sciences. When providing statistics, always cite the source of the information, as Jennifer Koehler does in this example:

> In 1993, 11.7% of Germany's exports went to France, while 11.3% of its imports came from France (CIA, 1996).

22c Avoid plagiarism and copyright infringement.

As they use secondary research, writers need to remember that knowledge develops socially in a give-and-take process akin to conversation. In this kind of social situation, it is a matter of both personal integrity and academic honesty to acknowledge others, especially when you use their words or ideas. Writers who fail to acknowledge their sources correctly—either intentionally or inadvertently—commit **plagiarism.** And writers who unfairly use copyrighted material found on the World Wide Web or in print are legally liable for their acts.

1. Avoiding plagiarism. To avoid plagiarism, adhere to these guidelines:

- Do not rely too much on one source, or you may easily slip into using that person's thoughts as your own.
- Keep accurate records while doing research and taking notes, or you may lose track of where an idea came from. If you do not know where you got an idea or a piece of information, do not use it in your paper until you find out.
- When you take notes, be sure to put quotation marks around words, phrases, or sentences taken verbatim from a source. If you use any of those words, phrases, or sentences when summarizing or paraphrasing the source, make sure to put them in quotation marks. Keep in mind that changing a word here and there while keeping a source's sentence structure or phrasing constitutes plagiarism, even if you credit the source for the ideas. (*See p. 183 for an example.*)
- Cite the source of all ideas, opinions, facts, and statistics that are not common knowledge.
- Choose an appropriate documentation style, and use it consistently and properly.

To learn more about plagiarism and how to avoid it, visit <www.mhhe.com/maimon/writing_the_paper>.

Tips LEARNING in COLLEGE

Determining What Is "Common Knowledge"

Information that readers in a field would know about from a wide range of general resources is considered common knowledge. For example, in biology, the structure of DNA and the process of cell division or photosynthesis are considered common knowledge. A recent scientific discovery about genetics, however, would not be common knowledge, so you would need to cite the source of this information. The sequence of major historical events is considered common knowledge, but one historian's thoughts about the causes or impact of an event would need to be cited.

2. Using copyrighted materials fairly.   All written materials, including student papers, letters, and e-mail, are covered by copyright, even if they do not bear an official copyright symbol. A copyright grants its owner exclusive rights to the use of a protected work, including reproducing, distributing, and displaying the work. The popularity of the World Wide Web has led to increased concerns about the fair use of copyrighted material. Before you post your paper on the Web or produce a multimedia presentation that includes audio, video, and graphic elements copied from a Web site, make sure that you have used copyrighted material fairly.

The following four criteria are used to determine if copyrighted material has been used fairly:

- **What is the purpose of the use?** Educational, nonprofit, and personal use are more likely to be considered fair than commercial use.

- **What is the nature of the work being used?** In most cases, imaginative and unpublished materials can be used only if you have the permission of the copyright holder.

- **How much of the copyrighted work is being used?** If a writer uses a small portion of a text for academic purposes, this use is more likely to be considered fair than if he or she uses a whole work for commercial purposes.

- **What effect would this use have on the market for the original?** The use of a work is usually considered unfair if it would hurt sales of the original.

22d Document your sources.

Whenever you use information, ideas, or words from someone else's work, you must acknowledge that person. As noted in the box on

TEXTCONNEX

Using Sources Properly

Plagiarism: What It Is and How to Recognize and Avoid It
<http://www.indiana.edu/~wts/wts/plagiarism.html> is filled with tips
from educators at Indiana University on how to recognize and avoid
plagiarism.

Copyright and Fair Use
For in-depth information and discussion of fair use, check out *Copyright
and Fair Use* <http://fairuse.stanford.edu>, *Copyright* <http://www.
benedict.com>, or *the U.S. Copyright Office* <www.loc.gov/copyright>.

CHARTING the TERRITORY

Documentation Styles Covered in This Text

TYPE OF COURSE	DOCUMENTATION STYLE MOST COMMONLY USED	WHERE TO FIND THIS STYLE IN THE HANDBOOK
Humanities (English, religion, music, art, philosophy)	MLA (Modern Language Association) or *Chicago* (*Chicago Manual of Style*) and COS (Columbia Online Style)	MLA: pp. 201–42; *Chicago:* pp. 276–95; COS: pp. 303–9
Social sciences (anthropology, psychology, sociology, education, and business)	APA (American Psychological Association) and COS	APA: pp. 243–71; COS: pp. 303–9
Sciences (mathematics, natural sciences, engineering, physical therapy, computer science)	CSE (Council of Science Editors) and COS	CSE: pp. 296–303; COS: pp. 303–9

page 189, the only exception to this principle is when you use information that is common knowledge, such as the chemical composition
of water or the names of the thirteen original states. When you tell

CHARTING the TERRITORY

Style Manuals for Specific Disciplines

SPECIFIC DISCIPLINE	POSSIBLE STYLE MANUAL
Chemistry	Dodd, Janet S., ed. *The ACS Style Guide: A Manual for Authors and Editors.* 2nd ed. Washington: American Chemical Society, 1997.
Geology	Bates, Robert L., Rex Buchanan, and Marla Adkins-Heljeson, eds. *Geowriting: A Guide to Writing, Editing, and Printing in Earth Science.* 5th ed. Alexandria: American Geological Institute, 1995.
Government and Law	Garner, Diane L., and Diane H. Smith, eds. *The Complete Guide to Citing Government Information Resources: A Manual for Writers and Librarians.* Rev. ed. Bethesda: Congressional Information Service, 1993.
	The Bluebook: A Uniform System of Citation. 17th ed. Cambridge: Harvard Law Review Assn., 2000.
Journalism	Goldstein, Norm, ed. *Associated Press Stylebook and Libel Manual.* 35th ed. New York: Associated Press, 2000.
Linguistics	Linguistic Society of America. "LSA Style Sheet." *LSA Bulletin.* Published annually in the December issue.
Mathematics	American Mathematical Society. *AMS Author Handbook: General Instructions for Preparing Manuscripts.* Providence: AMS, 1997.
Medicine	Iverson, Cheryl, ed. *American Medical Association Manual of Style: A Guide for Authors and Editors.* 9th ed. Chicago: AMA, 1997.
Physics	American Institute of Physics. *Style Manual for Guidance in the Preparation of Papers.* 4th ed. New York: American Institute of Physics, 1990.
Political Science	Lane, Michael K. *Style Manual for Political Science Papers.* Rev. ed. Washington: American Political Science Assn., 1993.

readers what sources you have consulted, they can more readily understand your paper as well as the conversation you are participating in by writing it.

To find links to many of these style guides, visit <www.mhhe. com/maimon/ writing_the_ paper>.

How sources are documented varies by field and discipline. Choose a documentation style that is appropriate for the particular course you are taking, and use it properly and consistently.

If you are not sure which of the five styles covered in this handbook to use, ask your instructor. If you are required to use an alternative, discipline-specific documentation style, consult the list of manuals on page 191.

23 Discipline-Specific Resources in the Library and on the Internet

The list that follows will help you get started doing research in specific disciplines. You will find both print and electronic resources listed because you should use both types in your research. (Print entries precede electronic entries.) Most major academic disciplines have computerized bibliographies, databases, and indexes that you can access through your college's library. (*For a list of online databases, see pp. 164–65.*)

For an online list of discipline-specific resources, visit <www.mhhe. com/maimon/ discipline-specific>.

Note: Remember that Web addresses change frequently, so if you get the 4040 (File not found) message, try doing a search for the page using a search engine, or look for the URL on this handbook's Web site, which is updated frequently.

Anthropology
Abstracts in Anthropology
Annual Review of Anthropology
Dictionary of Anthroplogy
Encyclopedia of World Cultures
American Anthropology Association
   <http://www.aaanet.org>
WWW Virtual Library: Anthropology
   <http://vlib.anthrotech.com>

Art and Architecture
Art Abstracts
Art Index
BHA: Bibliography of the History of Art
Encyclopedia of World Art
McGraw-Hill Dictionary of Art
Academic Info: Art and Art History
   <http://www.academicinfo.net/art.html>
The Louvre
   <http://www.louvre.fr/anglais/title.htm>

The Metropolitan Museum of Art (New York)
   <http://www.metmuseum.org>
The National Gallery (Washington, D.C.)
   <http://www.nga.gov>
Voice of the Shuttle Art History and Architecture
   <http://vos.ucsb.edu/index.asp>

Biology

Biological Abstracts
Biological and Agricultural Index
Encyclopedia of the Biological Sciences
Henderson's Dictionary of Biological Terms
Zoological Record
Biochem Links
   <http://www.biochemlinks.com>
BioView
   <http://www.bioview.com>
National Science Foundation: Biology
   <http://www.nsf.gov/home/bio>
Harvard University Biology Links
   <http://mcb.harvard.edu/BioLinks.html>

Business

Accounting and Tax Index
Blackwell Encyclopedia of Management
Encyclopedia of Business Information Sources
ABI/Inform
Business Index
Scout Report for Business and Economics
   <http://www.scout.cs.wisc.edu/report/bus-econ/current/index.html>

Chemistry

Chemical Abstracts (CASEARCH)
Dictionary of Chemistry
Van Nostrand Reinhold Encyclopedia of Chemistry
American Chemical Society
   <http://www.acs.org/portal/Chemistry>
Sheffield ChemDex
   <http://www.chemdex.org>
WWW Virtual Library: Chemistry
   <http://www.chem.ucla.edu/chempointers.html>

Classics

Illustrated Encyclopedia of the Classical World
Oxford Classical Dictionary
Princeton Encyclopedia of Classical Sites

Ancient World Web
   <http://www.julen.net/ancient>
Internet Classics Archive
   <http://classics.mit.edu>
Perseus Digital Library
   <http://www.perseus.tufts.edu>

Communications and Journalism

Annotated Media Bibliography
Communication Abstracts
International Encyclopedia of Communications
Journalism Abstracts
American Communication Association
   <http://www.americancomm.org>
Communication Institute for Online Scholarship
   <http://www.cios.org>
FAIR: Fairness and Accuracy in Reporting
   <http://www.fair.org>
Journalism Resources on the Web
   <http://library.austin.cc.tx.us/research/w3/
   humanities/jrn/jrn.htm>

Computer Science and Technology

Computer Abstracts
Dictionary of Computing
Encyclopedia of Computer Science
McGraw-Hill Encyclopedia of Science and Technology
FOLDOC (Free Online Dictionary of Computing)
   <http://wombat.doc.ic.ac.uk/foldoc/index.html>
MIT Laboratory for Computer Science
   <http://www.lcs.mit.edu>
Information Technology Resource Central
   <http://www.utexas.edu/computer>

Cultural Studies, American and Ethnic Studies

Encyclopedia of World Cultures
Dictionary of American Negro Biography
Gale Encyclopedia of Multicultural America
Mexican American Biographies
American Studies Web
   <http://www.georgetown.edu/crossroads/asw>
Center for Folklife and Cultural Heritage
   <http://www.si.edu/folklife>
Ethnic and Cultural Studies Resources
   <http://www.educationindex.com/culture>

National Museum of the American Indian
   <http://www.nmai.si.edu>

Economics

EconLit
PAIS: Public Affairs Information Service
American Economic Association
   <http://www.aeaweb.org>
Resources for Economists on the Internet
   <http://rfe.wustl.edu>
Securities and Exchange Commission
   <http://www.sec.gov>

Education

Dictionary of Education
Education Index
Encyclopedia of Educational Research
International Encyclopedia of Education
Resources in Education
Ask ERIC
   <http://ericir.sunsite.syr.edu>
EdWeb
   <http://edwebproject.org>
U.S. Department of Education
   <http://www.ed.gov>

Engineering

Applied Science and Technology Index
Engineering Index
McGraw-Hill Encyclopedia of Engineering
IEEE Spectrum
   <http://www.spectrum.ieee.org>
WWW Virtual Library: Engineering
   <http://www.eevl.ac.uk/wwwvl.html>

Environmental Sciences

Dictionary of the Environment
Encyclopedia of Energy, Technology, and the Environment
Encyclopedia of the Environment
Environment Abstracts
Environment Index
Envirolink
   <http://envirolink.org>
Environmental Protection Agency
   <http://www.epa.gov>

WWW Virtual Library: Earth Science
    <http://www.vlib.org/EarthScience.html>

Film

Dictionary of Film Terms
The Film Encyclopedia
Film Index International
Film Literature Index
Cinema Sites
    <http://www.cinema-sites.com>
Internet Movie Database
    <http://us.imdb.com>
Movie Web
    <http://www.movieweb.com>

Geography

Geographical Abstracts
Longman Dictionary of Geography
Modern Geography: An Encyclopedic Survey
Atlapedia Online
    <http://www.atlapedia.com/index.html>
Resources for Geographers
    <http://www.Colorado.EDU/geography/virtdept/resources/
    contents.htm>

Geology

Bibliography and Index of Geology
Challinor's Dictionary of Geology
The Encyclopedia of Field and General Geology
American Geological Institute
    <http://www.agiweb.org>
U.S. Geological Survey
    <http://www.usgs.gov>

Health and Medicine

American Medical Association Encyclopedia of Medicine
Cumulated Index Medicus
Medical and Health Information Directory
Nutrition Abstracts and Reviews
Martindale's Health Science Guide
    <http://www-sci.lib.uci.edu/~martindale/HSGuide.html>
U.S. National Library of Medicine
    <http://www.nlm.nih.gov>
World Health Organization
    <http://www.who.int>
Yale Medical Library
    <http://www.med.yale.edu/library>

History

America: History and Life
Dictionary of Historical Terms
Encyclopedia of American History
An Encyclopedia of World History
Historical Abstracts
Electronic Documents in History
    <http://www.tntech.edu/history/edocs.html>
The History Net
    <http://www.thehistorynet.com>
WWW Virtual Library: History
    <http://www.ukans.edu/history/VL>

Languages and Linguistics

Cambridge Encyclopedia of Language
An Encyclopedic Dictionary of Language and Languages
International Encyclopedia of Linguistics
LLBA: Linguistics and Language Behavior Abstracts
MLA International Bibliography
Center for Applied Linguistics
    <http://www.cal.org>
Linguistics in SIL
    <http://www.sil.org/linguistics>

Literature

Concise Oxford Dictionary of Literary Terms
MLA International Bibliography
The New Princeton Encyclopedia of Poetry and Poetics
Literary Resources on the Net
    <http://andromeda.rutgers.edu/~jlynch/Lit>
Project Gutenberg
    <http://promo.net/pg>
Voice of the Shuttle
    <http://vos.ucsb.edu/index.asp>

Mathematics

American Statistics Index
Dictionary of Mathematics
International Dictionary of Applied Mathematics
Mathematical Reviews (MathSciNet)
American Mathematical Society
    <http://www.ams.org>
Math Forum
    <http://mathforum.com>
WWW Virtual Library: Mathematics
    <http://web.math.fsu.edu/Science/math.html>

Music

Music Index
New Grove Dictionary of Music and Musicians
New Oxford Companion to Music
RILM Abstracts of Musical Literature
Classical Music on the Web
   <http://classicalusa.com>
MusicLink
   <http://www.lib.utk.edu:90/~music/songwizard/
   musicbrief.html>
Worldwide Internet Music Resources
   <http://www.music.indiana.edu/music_resources>

Philosophy

Dictionary of Philosophy
Philosopher's Index
Routledge Encyclopedia of Philosophy
American Philosophical Association
   <http://www.apa.udel.edu/apa/index.html>
Guide to Philosophy on the Internet
   <http://www.earlham.edu/~peters/philinks.htm>
Philosophy in Cyberspace
   <http://www-personal.monash.edu.au/~dey/phil>

Physics

Dictionary of Physics
McGraw-Hill Encyclopedia of Physics
Physics Abstracts
American Institute of Physics
   <http://www.aip.org>
American Physical Society
   <http://www.aps.org>
Physics: An Annotated List of Key Resources on the Internet
   <http://www.ala.org/acrl/resmar00.html>
PhysicsWeb
   <http://physicsweb.org/TIPTOP>

Political Science

Almanac of American Politics
Congressional Quarterly Almanac
Encyclopedia of Government and Politics
International Political Science Abstracts
Public Affairs Information Service (PAIS)

National Political Index
  <http://www.politicalindex.com>
Thomas: Legislative Information on the Internet
  <http://thomas.loc.gov>
United Nations
  <http://www.un.org>

Psychology

International Dictionary of Psychology
International Encyclopedia of Psychiatry, Psychology,
  Psychoanalysis, and Neurology
Psychological Abstracts
American Psychological Association
  <http://www.apa.org>
American Psychological Society
  <http://www.psychologicalscience.org>
PsychWeb
  <http://www.psywww.com>

Religion

Dictionary of Bible and Religion
Encyclopedia of Religion
Religion Index
Religion Gateway
  <http://www.academicinfo.net/religindex.html>
Religions and Scriptures
  <http://www.wam.umd.edu/~stwright/rel>
Religious and Sacred Texts
  <http://davidwiley.com/religion.html>

Sociology

Annual Review of Sociology
Encyclopedia of Social Work
Encyclopedia of Sociology
Sociological Abstracts
Academic Info Sociology: Databases and Centers
  <http://www.academicinfo.net/socdata.html>
American Sociological Association
  <http://asanet.org>
The SocioWeb
  <http://www.socioweb.com/~markbl/socioweb/indexes>

Theater and Dance

International Index to the Performing Arts
International Encyclopedia of the Dance

McGraw-Hill Encyclopedia of World Drama
Brief Guide to Internet Resources in Theatre and Performance
   Studies
   <http://www.stetson.edu/departments/csata/thr_guid.html>
Theatre-link.com
   <http://www.theatre-link.com>

Women's Studies

Women's Studies Abstracts
Women's Studies: A Guide to Information Sources
Women's Studies Encyclopedia
National Women's History Project
   <http://www.nwhp.org>
Women's Resources on the Internet
   <http://ibiblio.org/cheryb/women/wresources.html>

6

Next to the originator of a good
sentence is the first quoter of it.

—RALPH WALDO EMERSON

MLA
Documentation
Style

6 MLA Documentation Style

24. MLA Style: In-Text
    Citations *204*

25. MLA Style: List of Works
    Cited *212*

26. MLA Style: Explanatory
    Notes *227*

27. MLA Style: Paper
    Format *228*

28. Student Paper in MLA Style
    229

MLA IN-TEXT CITATIONS: DIRECTORY TO SAMPLE TYPES (CHAPTER 24)

(See pp. 212–27 for works-cited examples.)

1. Author named in sentence *206*
2. Author named in parentheses *206*
3. Two or more works by the same author *206*
4. Two or more authors *207*
5. Authors with the same last name *207*
6. Organization as author *208*
7. Unknown author *208*
8. Entire work *208*
9. Web site or other online electronic source *209*
10. Work with numbered paragraphs or screens instead of pages *209*
11. Work with no page or paragraph numbers *209*
12. Multivolume work *209*
13. Literary works *210*
14. The Bible *210*
15. Indirect source *211*
16. Two or more sources in one citation *211*
17. Work in an anthology *211*
18. E-mail, letter, personal interview *211*

MLA WORKS-CITED ENTRIES: DIRECTORY TO SAMPLE TYPES (CHAPTER 25)

(See pp. 204–11 for examples of in-text citations.)

Books

1. Book with one author *212*
2. Two or more works by the same author(s) *212*
3. Book with two or more authors *212*
4. Organization as author *213*
5. Book by an editor or editors *214*

6. Book with an author and an editor *214*
7. Work in an anthology or chapter in an edited book *214*
8. Two or more items from one anthology *214*
9. Article in a reference work *214*
10. Preface, foreword, introduction, or afterword *215*
11. Translation *215*
12. Edition other than the first *215*
13. The Bible *215*
14. Multivolume work *215*
15. Book in a series *216*
16. Republished book *216*
17. Title in a title *216*
18. Unknown author *216*

Periodicals
19. Article in a journal paginated by volume *217*
20. Article in a journal paginated by issue *217*
21. Article in a monthly magazine *217*
22. Article in a weekly magazine *217*
23. Article in a newspaper *217*
24. Unsigned article *218*
25. Review *218*
26. Editorial *218*

Other Print Sources
27. Government document *218*
28. Pamphlet *219*
29. Conference proceedings *219*
30. Published dissertation *219*
31. Unpublished dissertation *219*
32. Abstract of a dissertation *219*
33. Published or broadcast interview *220*
34. Map or chart *220*
35. Cartoon *220*
36. Advertisement *220*
37. Published letter *220*
38. Personal letter *221*
39. Manuscripts, typescripts, and material in archives *221*

Electronic Sources
40. Online database or scholarly project *221*
41. Professional or personal Web site *222*
42. Online book *223*
43. Article in an online periodical *223*
44. CD-ROM *224*
45. Work from an online service *224*
46. Online posting *224*
47. Synchronous communication *225*

203

48. E-mail *225*
49. Online graphic, audio, or video file *225*
50. Computer software *225*

Audiovisual and Other Nonprint Sources
51. Film or videotape *226*
52. TV or radio program *226*
53. Sound recording *226*
54. Musical composition *226*
55. Artwork *227*
56. Unpublished interview *227*
57. Lecture or speech *227*
58. Performance *227*

For links to Web sites for documentation styles used in various disciplines, visit <www.mhhe.com/maimon/mla_documentation>.

College papers include information, ideas, and quotations from sources that must be accurately documented. Documentation allows others to see the path you have taken in researching and writing your paper, be it informative, interpretive, or argumentative. (*For more on what to document, see Tab 5: Researching, pp. 189–92.*)

The documentation style developed by the Modern Language Association (MLA) is used by many researchers in the arts and humanities, especially those who write about language and literature. The guidelines presented here are based on the fifth edition of Joseph Gibaldi's *MLA Handbook for Writers of Research Papers,* (New York: MLA, 1999).

MLA documentation style has three parts:

- In-text citations
- List of works cited
- Explanatory notes

In-text citations and a list of works cited are mandatory; explanatory notes are optional.

24 MLA Style: In-Text Citations

MLA in-text citation format requires that you do the following:

- **Name the author,** either in a signal phrase such as *Bergreen maintains* or in a parenthetical citation.

CHARTING the TERRITORY

Documentation across the Curriculum

How sources are documented varies by discipline, so you should choose a documentation style that is appropriate to the particular course you are taking.

- **MLA (Modern Language Association) style** is often used for course papers in the arts and humanities, although some professors of music, religion, and philosophy prefer the *Chicago Manual of Style (Chicago)* format (*see below*), as do many historians. (*For MLA style, see the guidelines in this Tab.*)

- **APA (American Psychological Association) style** is often used for written work in such social sciences as anthropology, psychology, and sociology as well as for course papers in such professional fields as education and business. (*See pp. 243–72.*)

- ***Chicago (Chicago Manual of Style)* style** is often used for course papers in history, communications, and business. (*See pp. 276–95.*)

- **CSE (Council of Science Editors) style** is typically used for written work in the natural sciences, math, and such technical fields as engineering, physical therapy, and computer science. (*See pp. 296–304.*)

- **COS (Columbia Online Style)** provides the most in-depth guidance for documenting online sources and can be used with all types of documentation styles, including MLA, APA, *Chicago,* and CSE. (*See pp. 304–9.*)

If your instructor asks you to use a documentation style other than MLA, APA, *Chicago,* or CSE, consult the appropriate discipline-specific manual. (*See p. 191.*)

- **Include a page reference** in parentheses. No "p." precedes the page number, and if the author is named in the parentheses, there is no punctuation between the author's name and the page number.

- **Place the citation as close to the material being cited as possible** and before any punctuation marks that divide or end the sentence, such as commas, semicolons, or periods— except in a block quotation, where the citation comes after the period.

TEXTCONNEX

FAQs on MLA

For updates and responses to frequently asked questions (FAQs)
about MLA documentation style, check out the MLA Web site at
<http://www.mla.org>.

1. Author named in sentence: You can use the last name
only, unless two or more of your sources have the same last name.

> As Hennessey explains, record deals were usually
>
> negotiated by "white middlemen" (127).

Note that the parenthetical page citation comes after the closing quotation mark but before the period.

2. Author named in parentheses: If you do not name the
source's author in your sentence, then you must provide the name in
the parentheses.

> Armstrong easily reached difficult high notes, the F's
>
> and G's that stymied other trumpeters (Bergreen 248).

Note that there is no comma between the author's name and the page
number. If you cite two or more distinct pages, however, separate the
numbers with a comma: (Bergreen 450, 457).

3. Two or more works by the same author: If you use two or
more works by the same author, you must identify which work you
are citing, either in your sentence or in an abbreviated form in
parentheses.

> In Louis Armstrong, an American Genius, Collier
>
> reports that Glaser paid Armstrong's mortgage, taxes,
>
> and basic living expenses (330).

> During those years, Glaser paid Armstrong's mortgage,
>
> taxes, and basic living expenses (Collier, Louis
>
> Armstrong 330).

Tips LEARNING in COLLEGE

What Is the Modern Language Association?

The Modern Language Association (MLA) is a professional organization of language teachers that was founded in the United States in 1883. Its purpose is to support the study and teaching of languages. The MLA published its first handbook in 1977, and since then the book has become a widely accepted guide to rules for writing research papers in the United States. The *MLA Handbook* focuses on the mechanics of academic writing, including punctuation, quotation, and documentation of sources. In addition, the MLA guidelines are used outside the classroom by academic journals, newsletters, magazines, and university presses in both the United States and Canada. Recently, translated versions have also appeared in Japan and China. Following the MLA guidelines will help you document your research and write a clear and credible research paper.

4. Two or more authors of the same work: If a source has up to three authors, you should name them all either in your text, as shown below, or in parentheses: (Jones and Chilton 160, 220).

TWO AUTHORS

```
According to Jones and Chilton, Glaser's
responsibilities included booking appearances,
making travel arrangements, and paying the band
members' salaries (160, 220).
```

If the source has more than three authors, either list all the authors or give the first author's last name followed by "et al.," the abbreviation for the Latin phrase meaning "and others."

MORE THAN THREE AUTHORS

```
Changes in social regulations are bound to produce new
forms of subjectivity (Henriques et al. 275).
```

5. Authors with the same last name: If two or more of your sources have the same last name, include the first initial of the author you are citing; if the first initial is also shared, use the full first name, as shown below.

> In the late nineteenth century, the sale of
> sheet music spread rapidly in a Manhattan area
> along Broadway known as Tin Pan Alley (Richard
> Campbell 63).

6. Organization as author: To cite works by organized groups, government agencies, commissions, associations, or corporations, treat the organization as the author. If the organization's name is long, either put it in a signal phrase or use an abbreviated version of the name in the parentheses.

> The Centre for Contemporary Cultural Studies
> claims that "there is nothing inherently
> concrete about historiography" (10).
>
> Historiography deals with abstract issues
> (Centre 10).

7. Unknown author: When no author is given, you can cite a work by its title, using either the full title in a signal phrase or an abbreviated version in the parentheses.

> "Squaresville, U.S.A. vs. Beatsville" makes the
> Midwestern small-town home seem boring compared
> with the West Coast artist's "pad" (31).
>
> The Midwestern small-town home seems boring
> compared with the West Coast artist's "pad"
> ("Squaresville" 31).

8. Entire work: When you want to acknowledge an entire work, such as a film, a concert, or a book, it is usually better to do so in your text, not in a parenthetical citation. Be sure to include the work in your list of works cited.

> Sidney J. Furie's film <u>Lady Sings the Blues</u>
> presents Billie Holiday as a beautiful woman in
> pain rather than as the great jazz artist she was.

9. Web site or other online electronic source: For online sources such as Web sites, MLA recommends using the author and page guidelines already established for print sources. A title in parentheses can be abbreviated, but be sure to do so in a way that points clearly to the corresponding entry in your list of works cited. If you cannot find the author of an online source, then identify the source by title, either in your text or in a parenthetical citation. Because most online sources do not have set page, section, or paragraph numbers, they must usually be cited as entire works. (*Also see COS and MLA documentation style, pp. 305–6.*)

```
In the 1920s, many young black musicians from New

Orleans migrated north to Chicago, hoping for a

chance to perform with the best ("Chicago").
```

10. Work with numbered paragraphs or screens instead of pages: Give the paragraph or screen number(s) after the author's name and a comma. To distinguish them from page numbers, use the abbreviation *"par(s)."* or the word *"screen(s)."*

```
Goodman understood how to balance the public's demand

for pop with his own desire to push his players

(Edgers, screen 1).
```

11. Work with no page or paragraph numbers: When citing an online or print source without page, paragraph, or other reference numbers, try to work the author's name into your text or put it in a parenthetical citation.

```
Armstrong remains a driving force in present-day

music, from country and western music to the chanted

doggerel of rap (Crouch).
```

12. Multivolume work: When using and citing more than one volume of a multivolume source, include the volume number, followed by a colon, a space, and the page number.

```
Schuller argues that even though jazz's

traditional framework appears European, its

musical essence is African (1: 62).
```

However, if you consulted only one volume of a multivolume work, it is unnecessary to cite the volume number in the parenthetical reference. You should include it as part of the works-cited entry (*see pp. 215–16*).

13. Literary works:

Novels and literary nonfiction books: Include the relevant page number, followed by a semicolon, a space, and the chapter number.

```
Louis Armstrong figures throughout Ellison's
Invisible Man, including in the narrator's
penultimate decision to become a "yes" man who
"undermine[s] them with grins" (384; ch. 23).
```

If the author is not named in your sentence, add the name in front of the page number: (Ellison 384; ch. 23).

Poems: Use line numbers, not page numbers.

```
In "Trumpet Player," Hughes says that the music "Is
honey / Mixed with liquid fire" (lines 19-20). This
image returns at the end of the poem, when Hughes
concludes that "Trouble / Mellows to a golden note"
(43-44).
```

Note: The word *lines* (not *l.* or *ll.*) is used in the first citation to establish what the numbers in parentheses refer to; subsequent citations need not use the word *lines*. (*See pp. 458–60 and 473–74 for more information about quoting poetry.*)

Plays and long, multisection poems: Use division (act, scene, canto, book, part) and lines, not page numbers. In the following example, notice that arabic numerals are used for a ct and scene divisions as well as for line numbers: (*Hamlet* 2.3.22–27). The same is true for citation of canto, verse, and lines in the following citation of Byron's *Don Juan*: (*DJ* 1.37.4–8).

14. The Bible: Cite material in the Bible by book, chapter, and verse, using an appropriate abbreviation when the name of the book is in the parentheses rather than in your sentence.

> As the Bible says, "The wise man knows there will
>
> be a time of judgment" (Eccles. 8.5).

Note that titles of biblical books are not underlined.

15. Indirect source: When you quote or paraphrase a quotation you found in someone else's work, put *qtd. in* (meaning "quoted in") before the name of your source.

> Armstrong confided to a friend that Glaser's death
>
> "broke [his] heart" (qtd. in Bergreen 490).

In your list of works cited, list only the work you consulted, in this case the indirect source by Bergreen.

16. Two or more sources in one citation: When you need to credit two or more sources for an idea, use a semicolon to separate the citations.

> Giving up his other business ventures, Glaser now
>
> became Armstrong's exclusive agent (Bergreen 376-78;
>
> Collier 273-76; Morgenstern 124-28).

17. Work in an anthology: When citing a work in a collection, give the name of the specific work's author, not the name of the editor of the whole collection.

> When Dexter Gordon threatened to quit, Armstrong
>
> offered him a raise--without consulting with Glaser
>
> (Morgenstern 132).

Here, Morgenstern is cited as the source even though his work appears in a collection edited by Marc Miller. Note that the list of works cited must include an entry for Morgenstern (*see p. 242*).

18. E-mail, letter, personal interview: Cite by name the person you communicated with, using either a signal phrase or parentheses.

> Much to Glaser's surprise, both "Hello, Dolly" and
>
> "What a Wonderful World" became big hits after the
>
> rights had been sold (Jacobs).

In the works-cited list, you will need to identify the kind of communication and its date (*see pp. 221, 225, and 227*).

25   MLA Style: List of Works Cited

Besides in-text citations, MLA documentation style requires a works-cited page, where readers can find full bibliographic information about the sources you have used. The list of works cited should appear at the end of your paper, beginning on a new page entitled "Works Cited." Include only those sources you cite in your paper, unless your instructor tells you to prepare a "Works Consulted" list.

Books

1. Book with one author: Underline the book's title. Only the city, not the state, is included in the publication data. Notice that in the example the publisher's name, *Wayne State University Press,* is abbreviated to *Wayne State UP.*

> Hennessey, Thomas J. From Jazz to Swing: African-
>
>   Americans and Their Music 1890-1935. Detroit:
>
>   Wayne State UP, 1984.

2. Two or more works by the same author(s):   When you list more than one work by the same author, give the author's name in the first entry only. For subsequent works authored by that person, replace the name with three hyphens and a period. Multiple works by one author are alphabetized by title.

> Collier, James Lincoln. Jazz: The American Theme Song.
>
>   New York: Oxford UP, 1993.
>
> ---. Louis Armstrong, an American Genius. New York:
>
>   Oxford UP, 1983.

3. Book with two or more authors: Name the two or three authors in the order in which they appear on the title page, putting the last name first for the first author only. When a work has more than three authors, use the abbreviation *et al.* (meaning "and others") to replace the names of all authors except the first.

> Davis, Miles, and Quincy Troupe. Miles: The
>
>   Autobiography. New York: Simon, 1989.

1. Begin on a new page.
2. Begin with the centered title "Works Cited."
3. Include an entry for every in-text citation.
4. Include author, title, and publication data for each entry, if available. Use a period to set off each of these elements from the others. Leave one space after the periods.
5. Do not number the entries.
6. Put entries in alphabetical order by author's or editor's last name. (If the author is unknown, use the first word of the title, excluding the articles *a, an,* or *the*).
7. Underline titles of books and periodicals.
8. Capitalize the first and last and all important words in all titles and subtitles. Do not capitalize articles, prepositions, coordinating conjunctions, and the *to* in infinitives.
9. In the publication data, abbreviate publishers' names and months (*Dec.* rather than *December; Oxford UP* instead of *Oxford University Press*), and include the name of the city in which the publisher is located but not the state: *Danbury: Grolier.*
10. Do not use *p., pp.,* or *page(s).* Numbers alone will do. When page spans over 100 have the same first digit, use only the last two digits of the second number: 243–47.
11. Use a hanging indent: Start the first line of each entry at the left margin, and indent all subsequent lines of the entry five spaces (or one-half inch on the computer).
12. Double-space within entries and between them.

Henriques, Julian, et al. Changing the Subject: Psychology, Social Regulation, and Subjectivity. New York: Methuen, 1984.

4. Organization as author: Consider as an organization any group, commission, association, or corporation whose members are not identified on the title page.

Centre for Contemporary Cultural Studies. Making Histories: Studies in History Writing and Politics. London: Hutchinson, 1982.

5. Book by an editor or editors: If the title page lists an editor instead of an author, treat the editor as an author but put the abbreviation *ed.* after the name. Use the plural *eds.* when more than one editor is listed, and put only the first editor's name in reverse order.

> Miller, Paul Eduard, ed. Esquire's Jazz Book. New
>
> York: Smith, 1944.

6. Book with an author and an editor: Put the author and title first, followed by *Ed.* (meaning "edited by") and the name of the editor. However, if you cited something written by the editor rather than the author, see #10.

> Armstrong, Louis. Louis Armstrong--A Self-Portrait.
>
> Ed. Richard Meryman. New York: Eakins, 1971.

7. Work in an anthology or chapter in an edited book: List the author and title of the selection, followed by the title of the anthology, the abbreviation *Ed.* for "edited by," the editor's name, publication data, and page numbers of the selection.

> Smith, Hale. "Here I Stand." Readings in Black
>
> American Music. Ed. Eileen Southern. New York:
>
> Norton, 1971. 286-89.

8. Two or more items from one anthology: Include a complete entry for the anthology, beginning with the name of the editor(s). Each selection from the anthology that you are citing should have its own entry in the alphabetical list that includes only the author, title of the selection, editor, and page numbers.

> Southern, Eileen, ed. Readings in Black American
>
> Music. New York: Norton, 1971.
>
> Johnson, Hall. "Notes on the Negro Spiritual."
>
> Southern 268-75.
>
> Still, William Grant. "The Structure of Music."
>
> Southern 276-79.

9. Article in a reference work: If an entry in an encyclopedia or dictionary is signed, cite the author's name, title of the entry (in quotation marks), title of the reference work (underlined), and publication information. If the entry is not signed, start with the title. If the work arranges articles alphabetically, do not include the volume or page numbers. (For well-known reference works, such as the *Ency-clopædia Britannica,* the place and publisher can also be omitted.)

Robinson, J. Bradford. "Scat Singing." The New Grove

Dictionary of Jazz. London: Macmillan, 1988.

10. Preface, foreword, introduction, or afterword: When the writer of the part is different from the author of the book, use the word *By* after the book's title and cite the author's full name. If the writer of the part is the same as the book's author, use only the author's last name after the word *By.*

Crawford, Richard. Foreword. The Jazz Tradition. By

Martin Williams. New York: Oxford UP, 1993. v-xiii.

Fowles, John. Preface. Islands. By Fowles. Boston:

Little, 1978. 1-2.

11. Translation: Cite the work under the author's, not the translator's. The translator's name goes after the title, with the abbreviation *Trans.* (meaning "translated by").

Goffin, Robert. Horn of Plenty: The Story of Louis

Armstrong. Trans. James F. Bezov. New York: Da

Capo, 1977.

12. Edition other than the first: If you are citing an edition other than the first, include the number of the edition: *2nd ed., 3rd ed.,* and so on. Place the number after the title, or if there is an editor, after that person's name.

Panassie, Hugues. Louis Armstrong. 2nd ed. New York:

Da Capo, 1980.

13. The Bible: Give the version, underlined; the editor's name (if any); and the publication information.

New American Standard Bible. La Habra: Lockman

Foundation, 1995.

14. Multivolume work: Your citation should indicate whether you used more than one volume of a multivolume work. The first example indicates that the researcher used more than one volume of a three-volume work; the second shows that only the second volume of the work was used.

> Lissauer, Robert. Lissauer's Encyclopedia of Popular
> Music in America. 3 vols. New York: Facts on
> File, 1996.

> Lissauer, Robert. Lissauer's Encyclopedia of Popular
> Music in America. Vol. 2. New York: Facts on
> File, 1996.

15. Book in a series: After the title of the book, put the name of the series and, if available on the title page, the number of the work.

> Floyd, Samuel A., Jr., ed. Black Music in the Harlem
> Renaissance. Contributions in Afro-American
> and African Studies 128. New York: Greenwood,
> 1990.

16. Republished book: Put the original date of publication, followed by a period, before the current publication data. In the following example, the writer cites a 1974 republication of a book that originally appeared in 1936.

> Cuney-Hare, Maud. Negro Musicians and Their Music.
> 1936. New York: Da Capo, 1974.

17. Title in a title: When a book's title contains the title of another book, do not underline the second title. In the following example, the novel *Invisible Man* is not underlined.

> O'Meally, Robert, ed. New Essays on Invisible Man.
> Cambridge: Cambridge UP, 1988.

18. Unknown author: The citation begins with the title. In the list of works cited, alphabetize the citation by the first important word, not by articles like *A, An,* or *The.*

> Webster's College Dictionary. New York: Random; New
> York: McGraw, 1991.

Note that this entry includes both of the publishers listed on the dictionary's title page; they are separated by a semicolon.

Periodicals   Periodicals are published at set intervals, usually four times a year for scholarly journals, monthly or weekly for magazines, and daily or weekly for newspapers. Between the author and the publication data are two titles: the title of the article, in quotation marks, and the title of the periodical, underlined.

19. Article in a journal paginated by volume: Many scholarly journals are published a handful of times each year and are then bound together by libraries into yearly volumes. When these journals are paginated by yearly volume, not individual issue, put the volume number after the title. Give the year of publication in parentheses, followed by a colon, a space, and the page numbers of the article.

> Tirro, Frank. "Constructive Elements in Jazz
>
>   Improvisation." Journal of the American
>
>   Musicological Society 27 (1974): 285-305.

20. Article in a journal paginated by issue: For scholarly journals paginated by issue, not volume, you must also indicate the issue number. Place a period after the volume number and follow it with the issue number. In the example, the volume is 25 and the issue is number 4.

> Aguiar, Sarah Appleton. "'Everywhere and Nowhere':
>
>   Beloved's 'Wild' Legacy in Toni Morrison's Jazz."
>
>   Notes on Contemporary Literature 25.4 (1995):
>
>   11-12.

21. Article in a monthly magazine: Provide the month and year, abbreviating the names of all months except May, June, and July.

> Walker, Malcolm. "Discography: Bill Evans." Jazz
>
>   Monthly June 1965: 20-22.

22. Article in a weekly magazine: Include the complete date of publication: day, month, and year.

> Taylor, J. R. "Jazz History: The Incompleted Past."
>
>   Village Voice 3 July 1978: 65-67.

23. Article in a newspaper: Provide the day, month, and year. If an edition is named on the masthead, specify the edition (*natl. ed.* or *late ed.,* for example) after the date and use a comma between the date and the edition. Whenever possible, give a section designation (*E* in the example) along with the page number. If the article appears on nonconsecutive pages, put a plus (+) beside the first page number.

> Blumenthal, Ralph. "Satchmo with His Tape Recorder
> Running." New York Times 3 Aug. 1999: E1+.

24. Unsigned article: The citation begins with the title and is alphabetized by the first word other than an article like *A, An,* or *The.*

> "Squaresville, U.S.A. vs. Beatsville." Life 21 Sept.
> 1959: 31.

25. Review: Begin with the name of the reviewer and, if there is one, the title of the review. Add *Rev. of* (meaning "review of") and the title plus the author of the work being reviewed. Notice that the word *by* precedes the author's name.

> Ostwald, David. "All That Jazz." Rev. of Louis
> Armstrong: An Extravagant Life, by Laurence
> Bergreen. Commentary Nov. 1997: 68-72.

26. Editorial: Treat editorials as articles, but add the word *Editorial* after the title. If the editorial is unsigned, begin with the title.

> Shaw, Theodore M. "The Debate over Race Needs Minority
> Students' Voices." Editorial. Chronicle of Higher
> Education 25 Feb. 2000: A72.

Other Print Sources

27. Government document: Either the name of the government and agency or the document's author's name comes first. If the government and agency name come first, follow the title of the document with the word *By* for a writer, *Ed.* for an editor, or *Comp.* for a compiler. Publication information, abbreviated, comes last.

> United States. Bureau of National Affairs. The Civil
> Rights Act of 1964: Text, Analysis, Legislative
> History; What It Means to Employers, Businessmen,
> Unions, Employees, Minority Groups. Washington:
> BNA, 1964.

28. Pamphlet: Treat as you would a book. If the pamphlet has an author, list his or her name first; otherwise, begin with the title.

> All Music Guide to Jazz. 2nd ed. San Francisco: Miller
>
>   Freeman, 1996.

29. Conference proceedings: Cite as you would a book, but include information about the conference if it is not in the title.

> American Musicological Society. Papers Read at the
>
>   International Congress of Musicology. New York:
>
>   Music Educators' Natl. Conf. for the Amer.
>
>   Musicological Soc.

30. Published dissertation: Cite as you would a book, underlining the title and giving the place of publication, the publisher, and the year of publication. After the title, add *Diss.* for "dissertation," the name of the institution, and the year the dissertation was written.

> Fraser, Wilmot Alfred. Jazzology: A Study of the
>
>   Tradition in Which Jazz Musicians Learn to
>
>   Improvise. Diss. U of Pennsylvania, 1983. Ann
>
>   Arbor: UMI, 1987.

31. Unpublished dissertation: Begin with the author's name, followed by the dissertation title in quotation marks, the abbreviation *Diss.,* the name of the institution, and the year the dissertation was written.

> Reyes-Schramm, Adelaida. "The Role of Music in the
>
>   Interaction of Black Americans and Hispanos in New
>
>   York City's East Harlem." Diss. Columbia U, 1975.

32. Abstract of a dissertation: Use the format for an unpublished dissertation. After the dissertation date, give the abbreviation *DA* or *DAI* (for *Dissertation Abstracts* or *Dissertation Abstracts International*), then the volume number, the date of publication, and the page number.

> Quinn, Richard Allen. "Playing Together: Improvisation
>
>   in Postwar American Literature and Culture."
>
>   Diss. U of Iowa, 2000. DAI 61 (2001): 2305A.

33. Published or broadcast interview: Name the person interviewed and give the title of the interview or the descriptive term *Interview,* the name of the interviewer (if known and relevant), and the publication information.

> Armstrong, Louis. "Authentic American Genius."
>
> Interview with Richard Meryman. Life 15 Apr.
>
> 1966: 92-102.

34. Map or chart: Cite as you would a book with an unknown author. Underline the title of the map or chart, and add the word *Map* or *Chart* following the title.

> Let's Go Map Guide to New Orleans. Map. New York: St.
>
> Martin's, 1997.

35. Cartoon: Include the cartoonist's name, the title of the cartoon (if any) in quotation marks, the word *Cartoon,* and the publication information.

> Myller, Jorgen. "Louis Armstrong's First Lesson."
>
> Cartoon. Melody Maker Mar. 1931: 12.

36. Advertisement: Name the item or organization being advertised, include the word *Advertisement,* and indicate where the ad appeared.

> Hartwick College Summer Music Festival and Institute.
>
> Advertisement. New York Times Magazine 3 Jan.
>
> 1999: 54.

37. Published letter: Treat like a work in an anthology, but include the date. Include the number, if one was assigned by the editor. If you use more than one letter from a published collection, follow the instructions for cross-referencing in #8.

> Hughes, Langston. "To Arna Bontemps." 17 Jan. 1938.
>
> Arna Bontemps--Langston Hughes Letters 1925-
>
> 1967. Ed. Charles H. Nichols. New York: Dodd,
>
> 1980. 27-28.

38. Personal letter: To cite a letter you received, start with the writer's name, followed by the descriptive phrase *Letter to the author* and then the date.

> Cogswell, Michael. Letter to the author. 15 Mar. 1998.

To cite someone else's unpublished personal letter, see the guidelines in #39.

39. Manuscripts, typescripts, and material in archives: Give the author, a title or description of the material (*Letter, Notebook*), the form (*ms.* if manuscript, *ts.* if typescript), any identifying number, and the name and location of the institution housing the material.

> Glaser, Joe. Letter to Lucille Armstrong. 28 Sept.
>
>   1960. Box 3. Armstrong Archives. Queens College
>
>   CUNY, Flushing, NY.

Electronic Sources The examples that follow are based on the well-developed guidelines for the citation of electronic sources in the fifth edition of the *MLA Handbook for Writers of Research Papers* (1999). (*See also COS and MLA documentation style, pp. 305–6.*)

Note: The Internet address for an electronic source is its uniform resource locator, or URL. If you are providing a URL in your citation and need to divide it between lines, divide the URL after a slash. Do not insert a hyphen.

TEXTCONNEX

URL Addresses

Some popular word-processing programs like Word 97 and Word 2000 automatically turn all URLs into hyperlinks. The MLA recommends disabling this automatic hyperlinking before you print your document. To turn off automatic hyperlinking, go to "AutoFormat as You Type" in the "AutoCorrect" part of the "Tools" menu and remove the check mark next to "Internet and network paths with hyperlinks."

40. Online database or scholarly project:

> **Entire database:** Begin with the title (underlined) of the source, followed by the name of the editor (if any) and the

electronic publication data, which includes, if relevant, the version number, the date of publication or update, and the name of the sponsoring institution (if any). End with the date you used the database or project and, in angle brackets (< >), the source's complete URL.

New York Times on the Web. 21 June 2000. The New
        York Times Company. 21 June 2000 <http://
        www.nytimes.com>.

William Ransom Hogan Archive of New Orleans Jazz.
        Ed. Bruce Boyd Raeburn. 30 May 2000. Tulane.
        6 June 2000 <http://www.tulane.edu/~1miller/
        jazzHome.html>.

Part of a database: When citing one part, document, or page of a database, add the author (if known) and the title of the part in quotation marks. If the author is unknown, start with the title of the part in quotation marks.

Raeburn, Bruce Boyd. "An Introduction to New
        Orleans Jazz." William Ransom Hogan Archive of
        New Orleans Jazz. Ed. Bruce Boyd Raeburn. 29
        May 2000. Tulane U. 21 June 2000 <http://
        www.tulane.edu/~1miller/BeginnersIntro.html>.

"Biography." Satchmo.Net: The Official Site for
        the Louis Armstrong House and Archives.
        2000. Queens College CUNY. 21 June 2000
        <http://independentmusician.com/louis/
        biography.php3>.

41. Professional or personal Web site: Name the person responsible for the site, the title of the site (underlined), the name of the associated institution or organization (if any), date of access, and URL. If no title is available, use a descriptive term such as "Home page" (without underlining or quotation marks).

Henson, Keith. Jazzpage. 11 Feb. 1998 <http://
        www.accessone.com/~khenson>.

```
Wildman, Joan. The World of Jazz Improvisation.
    U of Wisconsin, Madison. 19 Apr. 2000 <http://
    hum.lss.wisc.edu/jazz>.
```

42. Online book:

Entire book: Cite as for print books, including author; title (underlined); editor, translator, or compiler (if any); and publication data for the print version. Add, if available, the name of the database or project, date of electronic publication, sponsoring organization, date of access, and URL.

```
Sandburg, Carl. Chicago Poems. New York: Holt,
    1916. Bartleby. Aug. 1999. 14 June 2000
    <http:// www.bartleby.com/165/index.html>.
```

Work in an online book: If you use part of an online book, add the title of the part after the author and put it in quotation marks, unless the part cited is an introduction, foreword, preface, or afterword.

```
Sandburg, Carl. "Chicago." Chicago Poems. New York:
    Holt, 1916. Bartleby. Aug. 1999. 14 June 2000.
    <http://www.bartleby.com/165/1.html>.
```

43. Article in an online periodical:

Many newspapers, magazines, and scholarly journals are now available online. When citing a work from an online periodical, provide as much of the following information as is available: the writer's name; title of the work in quotation marks or a descriptive term (for example, *Editorial*); the name of the periodical, underlined; volume, issue, or other identifying number; publication date; total pages, paragraphs, or sections, if numbered; date of access; and URL.

```
Ross, Michael E. "The New Sultans of Swing." Salon.
    18 Apr. 1996. 6 Mar. 1998 <http://www.salon.com/
    weekly/music1.html>.
```

```
Schmalfeldt, Janet. "On Keeping the Score." Music
    Theory Online 4.2 (1998). 20 pars. 2 May 1998
    <http://smt.ucsb.edu/mto/issues/mto.98.4.2/
    mto.98.4.2.schmalfeldt.html>.
```

44. CD-ROM: Works on CD-ROM are usually cited like books or parts of books, but the term *CD-ROM* and the name of the vendor, if different from the publisher, are added before the publication data.

> "Armstrong, (Daniel) Louis 'Satchmo.'" Microsoft
>
>   Encarta Multimedia Encyclopedia CD-ROM. Redmond:
>
>   Microsoft, 1994.

45. Work from an online service: Sometimes online services such as *Lexis-Nexis, InfoTrac,* and *America Online* do not supply a network address (URL) for material. If you accessed such material from a library, include the following in your citation: the name of the database (underlined); the name of the online service used; the library's name; the date of access; and, if known, the URL of the online service's home page.

> Hardack, Richard. "'A Music Seeking Its Words':
>
>   Double-Timing and Double Consciousness in Toni
>
>   Morrison's Jazz." Callaloo 18 (1995): 451-72.
>
>   Expanded Academic ASAP. InfoTrac. Rosenthal Lib.,
>
>   Queens College CUNY. 18 Jul. 2000 <http://
>
>   web7.infotrac.galegroup.com>.

If you used a keyword or a topic path to get a source from a service you subscribe to, identify the title of the source, the online service, the date accessed, and either the keyword used (for example, "Keyword: Compton's") or the path taken.

> "Jazz." Concise Columbia Electronic Encyclopedia. 3rd
>
>   ed. 1994. America Online. 21 Apr. 2000. Path:
>
>   Research and Learn; Encyclopedia; Columbia
>
>   Concise; Louis Armstrong; Jazz.

46. Online posting: Begin with the author and (in quotation marks) the title or subject line; the words *Online posting,* without quotation marks or underlining, follow. End with the posting date, the list or group name, the date of access, and the URL of the list. Include the e-mail address of the list's moderator if no URL is available.

> Mopsick, Don. "Favorite Jazz Quotes." Online
>
>   posting. 17 Mar. 2000. Big Band-Music Fans. 17

June 2000 <http://www.remarq.com/list/

4755?nav+FIRST&rf+1&si+grou>.

47. Synchronous communication: Include a description and the date of the event, the title of the forum, the date of access, and the URL. If relevant, the speaker's name can begin the citation.

Curran, Stuart, and Harry Rusche. Discussion:

Plenary Log 6. Third Annual Graduate Student

Conference in Romanticism. 20 Apr. 1996. Prometheus

Unplugged: Emory MOO. 4 Jan. 1999 <http://

prometheus.cc.emory.edu/plen/plenary6.txt>.

48. E-mail: Include the author; the subject line (if any), in quotation marks; the descriptive term *E-mail* plus the name of the recipient; and the date of the message.

Hoffman, Esther. "Re: My Louis Armstrong Paper."

E-mail to J. Peritz. 14 Jan. 1999.

49. Online graphic, audio, or video file: Base the form of your citation on the most closely related print or nonprint model. When possible, include the creator's name, the title or description of the source, the title of the larger work in which the source appears (underlined), the publication data, the date of access, and the URL.

Adderley, Nat. Interview with Jimmy Owens. Video

clip. Louis Armstrong Jazz Oral History Project.

2 Apr. 1993. Schomburg Center for Research in

Black Culture. 6 June 2001 <http://www.nypl.org/

research/sc/scl/MULTIMED/JAZZHIST/jazzhist.html>.

50. Computer software: Provide the author's or editor's name, if available, the medium, title (underlined), the version number, and the publication information, including place of publication, publisher, and date. If you downloaded the software from the Internet, replace the publication information with the date of access and the Internet address.

AllWrite! 3.0 with Online Handbook. CD-ROM. Vers. 3.0.

New York: McGraw, 2003.

Audiovisual and Other Nonprint Sources

51. Film or videotape: Begin with the title (underlined). For a film, cite the director and the lead actors or narrator (*Perf.* or *Narr.*), followed by the distributor and year. For a videotape or DVD, add the medium (*Videocassette or DVD*) before the name of the distributor.

> Artists and Models. Dir. Raoul Walsh. Perf. Louis
>
>   Armstrong, Martha Raye, and Connie Boswell.
>
>   Paramount Pictures, 1937.

52. TV or radio program: Start with the episode title (in quotation marks), followed by the program title (underlined), the name of the series (if any), the name of the network, the city, and the broadcast date.

> "The Music of Charlie Parker." Jazz Set. WBGO-FM,
>
>   New York. 2 Dec. 1998.

53. Sound recording: The entry starts with the composer, conductor, or performer, depending on your focus. Include the following information: the work's title (underlined); the medium (*LP* below), unless it is a compact disc; the artist(s), if not already mentioned; the manufacturer; and the date of release.

> Armstrong, Louis. Town Hall Concert Plus. LP. RCA
>
>   Victor, 1957.

54. Musical composition: Include only the composer and title, unless you are referring to a published score. Published scores are treated like books except that the date of composition appears after the title. Note that the titles of instrumental pieces are underlined only when they are known by name, not just by form and number, or when the reference is to a published score.

> Ellington, Duke. Satin Doll.
>
> Haydn, Franz Josef. Symphony no. 94 in G Major.
>
> Haydn, Franz Josef. Symphony No. 94 in G Major. 1791.
>
>   Ed. H. C. Robbins Landon. Salzburg: Haydn-Mozart,
>
>   1965.

55. Artwork: Provide the artist's name, the title of the artwork (underlined), and the institution and city in which the artwork can be found.

> Leonard, Herman. <u>Louis Armstrong: Birdland</u>. Barbara
>
>   Gillman Gallery, Miami.

If you used a photograph of a work of art from a book, treat it like a work in an anthology (#7), but underline the titles of both the work and the book.

56. Unpublished interview: Begin with the person interviewed, followed by *Personal interview* (if you conducted the interview personally) and the date of the interview. (*See #33 for a published interview.*)

> Jacobs, Phoebe. Personal interview. 12 Nov. 1997.

57. Lecture or speech: To cite an oral presentation, give the speaker's name, the title (in quotation marks) or a descriptive label such as *Address* or *Lecture,* the name of the forum or sponsor, the location, and the date.

> Taylor, Billy. "What Is Jazz?" John F. Kennedy Center
>
>   for the Performing Arts, Washington. 14 Feb. 1995.

58. Performance. To cite a play, opera, ballet, or concert, begin with the title; followed by the authors (*By*); pertinent information about the live performance, such as the director (*Dir.*) and major performers; the site; the city; and the performance date.

> <u>Ragtime</u>. By Terrence McNally, Lynn Athrens, and
>
>   Stephen Flaherty. Dir. Frank Galati. Ford
>
>   Performing Arts Center, New York. 11 Nov. 1998.

---

26   MLA Style: Explanatory Notes

Explanatory notes are used to cite multiple sources for borrowed material or to give readers supplemental information. Their purpose is to avoid distracting readers with an overly long parenthetical citation or an interesting but not directly relevant idea. You can also use explanatory notes to acknowledge people who helped you with research and writing. Explanatory notes can be formatted either as footnotes at the bottom of a manuscript page or as endnotes on a separate page (titled "Notes") before the works-cited list. Identify each note with a raised arabic number in the text.

TEXT

```
As a young man during Prohibition, Glaser got caught
up in the Chicago underworld.¹
```

NOTE

```
     ¹Bergreen 372-76. Even though Ostwald points out
a few mistakes in Bergreen's Louis Armstrong: An
Extravagant Life, I think the book's new information
about Glaser is useful and trustworthy.
```

27   MLA Style: Paper Format

The following guidelines will help you prepare your research paper in the format recommended by the fifth edition of the *MLA Handbook for Writers of Research Papers*. For an example of a research paper that has been prepared using MLA style, see pages 230–42.

Materials.   Before printing your paper, make sure that you have stored your final draft on a backup disk. Use a high-quality printer and good, white 8½-by-11-inch paper. Choose a standard 10- or 12-point font such as Courier, Times, or Bookman. Put the printed pages together with a paper clip, not a staple, and do not use a binder unless you have been told to do so by your instructor.

Heading and title.   No separate title page is needed. In the upper left-hand corner of the first page, one inch from the top and side, type on separate lines your name, your instructor's name, the course name and number, and the date. Double-space between the date and the paper's title and the title and the first line of text, as well as throughout your paper. The title should be centered and properly capitalized (*see p. 230*). Do not underline the title or put it in quotation marks or bold type.

Margins and spacing.   Use one-inch margins all around, except for the right-hand top corner, where the page number goes. Your right margin should be ragged (not "justified," or even).

TEXTCONNEX

Electronic Submission of Papers

If you are asked to submit your work electronically, find out which format your instructor prefers. If you are submitting your paper in a format that lacks page numbers, you may want to number your paragraphs: at the beginning of each paragraph, include the appropriate number in brackets, followed by a space and the text.

Double-space lines throughout the paper, including in quotations, notes, and the works-cited list. Indent the first word of each paragraph one-half inch (or five spaces) from the left margin. For block quotations, indent one inch (or ten spaces) from the left.

Page numbers.   Put your last name and the page number in the upper right-hand corner of the page, one-half inch from the top and flush with the right margin.

Visuals.   Place visuals (tables, charts, graphs, and images) close to the place in your text where you refer to them. Label and number tables consecutively (*Table 1, Table 2*) and give each one an explanatory caption; put this information above the table. The term *Figure* (abbreviated *Fig.*) is used to label all other kinds of visuals, except for musical illustrations, which are labeled *Example* (abbreviated *Ex.*). Place figure or example captions below the visual. Below all visuals, cite the source of the material and provide explanatory notes as needed. *(For more on using visuals effectively, see Tab 9: Document and Web Design, pp. 319–25.)*

28 Student Paper in MLA Style

As a first-year college student, Esther Hoffman wrote the following paper for her composition course. Esther knew little about Louis Armstrong and jazz before her instructor took the class to visit the Louis Armstrong Archives. For this paper, Esther did archival research based on what she had learned from consulting online and print sources.

For another sample of a student paper in MLA style, visit <www.mhhe.com/maimon/mla_paper_format>.

1"

Esther Hoffman

1"

Professor Tucker

English 120

5 May 1998

Louis Armstrong and Joe Glaser:

More Than Meets the Eye

In the 1920s, jazz music was at its height in 1"

creativity and popularity. Chicago had become one

of the jazz capitals of America, and its clubs

showcased the premier talents of the time,

performers like Jelly Roll Morton and Joe Oliver.

It has always been difficult to break into the

music business, and the jazz scene of the twenties

was no exception. Eager for fame and fortune,

though many young black musicians who had honed

their craft in New Orleans migrated north to

Chicago, hoping for a chance to perform with the

best ("Chicago").

Among these émigres was Louis Armstrong, a

gifted musician who developed into the "first

true virtuoso soloist of jazz" ("Armstrong").

Armstrong played the trumpet and sang with unusual

improvisational ability as well as technical

mastery. As Bergreen points out, he easily reached

difficult high notes, the F's and G's that stymied

other trumpeters (248). His innovative singing

style also featured "scat," a technique that

combines "nonsense syllables [with] improvised

melodies" (Robinson 425). Eventually Armstrong's

Margin notes (left column):

On every page: writer's last name and page number.

Title: centered, no underline.

Double-spaced throughout.

Background scene sketched.

Web source cited by title.

Paragraph indent 5 spaces or ½".

Topic introduced.

MLA in-text citation: author named in signal phrase.

MLA in-text citation: author named in parentheses.

Hoffman 2

innovations became the standard, as more and more jazz musicians took their cue from his style.

Armstrong's beginnings give no hint of the greatness that he would achieve. In New Orleans, he was born into poverty and received little formal education. As a youngster, Armstrong had to take odd jobs like delivering coal and selling newspapers so that he could earn money to help his family. At the age of twelve, Armstrong was placed in the Colored Waifs' Home to serve an eighteen-month sentence for firing a gun in a public place. There "Captain" Peter Davis gave him "basic musical training on the cornet" ("Satchmo!"). Older, more established musicians soon noticed Armstrong's talent and offered him opportunities to play with them. In 1922, Joe Oliver invited Armstrong to join his band in Chicago, and the twenty-one-year-old trumpeter headed north.

It was in Chicago that Armstrong met Joe Glaser, the man who eventually became his longtime manager. According to Bergreen, Glaser had a reputation for being a tough but trustworthy guy who could handle any situation. He was raised in a middle-class home by parents who were Jewish immigrants from Russia. As a young man, Glaser got caught up in the Chicago underworld and soon had a rap sheet that included indictments for running a brothel as well as for statutory rape.[1] Glaser's mob

Development by narration (*see p. 47*).

Focus introduced.

Superscript number indicating an explanatory note.

connections also led to his involvement in Chicago's club scene, a business almost completely controlled by gangsters like Al Capone. During the era of Prohibition, Glaser managed the Sunset Cafe, a club where Armstrong often performed:

Block quotation indented 10 spaces or 1".

> There was a pronounced gangster element at the Sunset, but Louis, accustomed to being employed and protected by mobsters, didn't think twice about that. Mr. Capone's men ensured the flow of alcohol, and their presence reassured many whites. (Bergreen 279)

By the early thirties, Armstrong had become one of the most popular musicians in the world. He attracted thousands of fans during his 1930 European tour, and his "Hot Five" and "Hot Seven"

Summary of material from a number of sources.

recordings were considered some of the best jazz ever played. Financially, Armstrong should have been doing very well, but instead he was having business difficulties. He owed money to Johnny Collins, his former manager, and Lil' Hardin, his ex-wife, was suing him for a share of the royalties on the song "Struttin' with Some Barbecue." At this point, Armstrong asked Glaser to be his business manager. Glaser quickly paid off Collins and settled with Lil' Hardin. Giving up his other business ventures, Glaser now became

Citation of multiple sources.

Armstrong's exclusive agent (Morgenstern 124-28; Collier 273-76; Bergreen 376-78). For the next thirty-four years, his responsibilities included

booking appearances, organizing the bands, making
travel arrangements, and paying the band members'
salaries (Jones and Chilton 160, 220).

    Under Glaser's management, Armstrong reached
the pinnacle of his fame, an achievement for which
he was profoundly grateful. Once, while discussing
the creation of the All-Star bands, Armstrong even
credited his musical accomplishments to Glaser,
saying, "Anything that I have done musically since
I signed up with Joe Glaser at the Sunset, it was
his suggestions" (qtd. in Jones and Chilton 175).
Was Glaser really as central to Armstrong's
work and life as this comment makes him seem? To
what extent did Glaser create and control the star
known nowadays as a "King of Jazz"? What kind of
relationship did Joe Glaser and Louis Armstrong
actually have?

    One answer to these questions is suggested by
a large (24-by-36-inch) oil painting discovered
in Armstrong's house.[2] Joe Glaser is pictured in
the middle of the canvas. Four black-and-white
quadrants surround the central image of Glaser.
One quadrant depicts a city scene, the scene in
which Glaser thrived. The bottom two quadrants
picture dogs, a reminder that Glaser raised show
dogs. The remaining quadrant presents an image of
Louis Armstrong. By placing Glaser in the center
and Armstrong off in a corner, the unknown artist
seems to suggest that even though Armstrong was
the star, it was Glaser who made him one.

Use of
information
from two
separate
pages in one
source.

Indirect
source.

Poses key
questions that
thesis will
answer.

Development
by descrip-
tion (see pp.
47–48).

In fact, Glaser did advance Armstrong's

Presents a
claim plus
supporting
evidence.
career in numerous important ways. In 1935, he
negotiated the lucrative record contract with
Decca that led to the production of hits like "I'm
in the Mood for Love" and "You Are My Lucky Star"
(Bergreen 380). Glaser also decided when to sell
the rights to Armstrong's songs. Determined to
make as much money as possible, he sometimes sold
the rights to a song as soon as it was released,
especially when he thought the song might not turn
out to be a big hit. However, in at least two
instances, this money-making strategy backfired:
much to Glaser's surprise, both "Hello, Dolly" and
"What a Wonderful World" became big hits after the
rights had been sold (Jacobs).

To expand Armstrong's popularity, Glaser
increased his exposure to white audiences in the
United States. In 1935, articles on Armstrong

Development
by illustration
(see p. 49).
appeared in Vanity Fair and Esquire, two magazines
with a predominantly white readership (Bergreen
385). Glaser also promoted Armstrong's movie
career. At a time when only a handful of black
performers were accepted in Hollywood, Armstrong
had roles in a number of films, including Pennies

Note use of
transitional
expressions
(see pp.
56–58).
from Heaven (1936) with Bing Crosby. Moreover,
"Jeepers Creepers," a song Armstrong sang in
Going Places (1938), received an Academy Award
nomination (Bogle 149, 157). Of course, more
exposure sometimes meant more discomfort, if not
danger, especially when Armstrong and his band

Hoffman 6

members were touring in the South. There, where
blacks were prohibited from entering many stores,
Glaser sometimes had to shop for the band's food
and other supplies (Bergreen 378, 381).

As Armstrong's manager, Glaser also exerted
some control over the musician's personal finances
and habits. According to Dave Gold, an accountant
who worked for Associated Booking, it was Glaser
who paid Armstrong's mortgage, taxes, and basic
living expenses (Collier 330). A 1960 letter
from Glaser to Lucille Armstrong corroborates
Gold's account; it shows that Glaser assumed
responsibility for buying the musician and his
wife a new car as well as for filing the paperwork
needed to retain the old license plate number.
More personal were Glaser's attempts to control
Armstrong's habitual use of marijuana. In 1931,
Armstrong received a suspended sentence after his
arrest for marijuana possession. He continued
to use the drug, however, especially during
performances, and told Glaser that he wanted to
write a book about marijuana's positive effects.
Glaser flatly rejected the book idea and, fearful
of a scandal, also forbade Armstrong's smoking any
marijuana while on tour in Europe (Pollack).

Clearly, Glaser was in a position to affect
powerfully Armstrong's career and his life.
Armstrong acknowledged Glaser's importance, at one
point referring to him as "the man who has guided
me all through my career" (qtd. in Jones and

Support by
expert opinion
(*see p. 32*).

Support by
key fact (*see
p. 32*).

Support by
anecdote (*see
p. 32*).

Thesis
paragraph.

Chilton 175). However, there is little evidence
that the musician submitted to whatever his
business manager wanted or demanded. In fact,
Armstrong seemed to recognize that he gave Glaser
whatever power over him the manager enjoyed. When
he wanted to, Armstrong could and did resist
Glaser's control, and that may be one reason why
he liked and trusted Glaser as much as he did.

After Glaser became his manager, Armstrong no
longer had to worry about the behind-the-scenes
details of his career. He was free to concentrate
on creating music and making the most of the
opportunities his manager worked out for him.
Glaser booked Armstrong into engagements with
legendary performers like Benny Goodman, Ella
Fitzgerald, and Duke Ellington. He also worked
with the record companies to ensure that Armstrong
would make the best and most profitable recordings
possible (Bergreen 457). During the thirty-four
years they worked together, both Armstrong and
Glaser made lots of money. More important, their
relationship freed Armstrong to make extraordinary
music.

If Armstrong acquiesced to most of Glaser's
business decisions, it may be because he had no
reason to resist them. However, when he deemed it
necessary, Armstrong acted on his own. For example,
in 1944 a talented band member named Dexter Gordon
threatened to quit, so Armstrong offered him a
raise--without consulting first with Glaser
(Morgenstern 132). In 1957, when Armstrong wanted

Hoffman 8

to put a stop to backstage crowding, he not only
directed Glaser to make a sign prohibiting guests
from going backstage but also told him exactly
what to say on the sign (Armstrong, Backstage
Instructions). As these incidents suggest, when
Armstrong was displeased with the way his career
was being handled, he acted to amend the situation.

Armstrong also knew how to resist Glaser's
attempts to control the more personal aspects of
his life. In a recent interview, Phoebe Jacobs,
formerly one of Glaser's employees, shed new light
on the relationship between the manager and the
musician. Armstrong's legendary generosity was
tough on his pocketbook. It was well known that if
someone needed money, Armstrong would readily hand
over some bills. At one point, Glaser asked Jacobs
to give Armstrong smaller denominations so that he
would not give away so much money. The trumpeter
soon figured out what was going on and admonished
Jacobs for following Glaser's orders about money
that belonged to him, not Glaser. On another
occasion, Armstrong declined an invitation to join
Glaser for dinner at a Chinese restaurant, saying,
"I want to eat what I want to eat" (Jacobs).

Even though he sometimes pushed Glaser away,
though, Armstrong obviously loved and trusted his
manager. In all the years of their association,
the two men signed only one contract and, in the
musician's words, "after that we didn't bother"
(qtd. in Jones and Chilton 240). A picture of Joe
Glaser in one of Armstrong's scrapbooks bears the

Source cited: archival material.

Source cited: personal interview.

Authoritative quotation (see p. 32).

Hoffman 9

following label in the star's handwriting: "the
greatest." In his dedication to the unpublished
manuscript "Louis Armstrong and the Jewish Family
in New Orleans," Armstrong calls Glaser "the best
friend that I ever had," while in a letter to Max
Jones, he writes, "I did not get really happy until
I got with my man--my dearest friend--Joe Glaser"
(qtd. in Jones and Chilton 16). In 1969, Joe Glaser
died. Referring to him again as "the greatest,"
Armstrong confided to a friend that Glaser's death
"broke [his] heart" (qtd. in Bergreen 490).

Although there are hints of a struggle for
the upper hand, the relationship between Louis
Armstrong and Joe Glaser seems to have been
genuinely friendly and trusting. Armstrong gave
Glaser a good deal of authority over his career,
and Glaser used that authority to make Armstrong a
musical and monetary success. Armstrong was happy
to take the opportunities that Glaser provided for
him, but he was not submissive. This equitable and
friendly relationship is depicted by another picture
found in Armstrong's house. The 25-by-21-inch
picture, shown in Fig. 1, is a caricature of
Armstrong and Glaser. The pair stand side by side,
and Glaser has his hand on Armstrong's shoulder.
Armstrong, who is dressed for a performance, looks
and smiles at us as if he were facing an audience.
But Glaser looks only at Armstrong, the musician
who was his main concern from 1935 to the day he
died. In appearance alone, the men are clearly

Memorable
quotation
(see p. 186).

Wording of
quote adjusted
(see
pp. 470–71).

Concludes
with a
qualified
version of the
thesis.

Memorable
illustration.

Hoffman 10

Effective visual
(*pp. 323–25*).

Fig. 1. An anonymous watercolor caricature of
Armstrong with his manager, Joe Glaser, c. 1950.
Louis Armstrong Archives, Queens College, City
University of New York, Flushing.

different. But seen in their longstanding
partnership, the two make up a whole--one picture
that offers us more than meets the eye.

Hoffman 11

Notes

¹Bergreen 372-76. Even though Ostwald points out a few mistakes in Bergreen's <u>Louis Armstrong: An Extravagant Life</u>, I think the book's new information about Glaser is useful and trustworthy.

²I want to thank George Arevalo of the Louis Armstrong Archives for his help on this project. When I was low on inspiration and in search of some direction, George showed me the two pictures I describe in this paper. Seeing those pictures helped me figure out what I wanted to say--and why I wanted to say it. For introducing me to archival research and to the art of Louis Armstrong, I also want to thank the head of the Louis Armstrong Archives, Michael Cogswell, and my English teacher, Professor Amy Tucker.

Gives supplemental information about key source.

Indent first line 5 spaces or ½".

Acknowledges others who helped.

Hoffman 12

Works Cited

"Armstrong, (Daniel) Louis 'Satchmo.'" Microsoft
    Encarta Multimedia Encyclopedia. CD-ROM.
    Redmond: Microsoft, 1994.

Armstrong, Louis. Backstage instructions to
    Glaser. April 1957. Accessions 1997-26. Louis
    Armstrong Archives. Queens College CUNY,
    Flushing, NY.

---. "Louis Armstrong and the Jewish Family in New
    Orleans." Unpublished ms. 31 March 1969.
    Louis Armstrong Archives. Queens College
    CUNY, Flushing, NY.

Bergreen, Laurence. Louis Armstrong: An
    Extravagant Life. New York: Broadway, 1997.

Bogle, Donald. "Louis Armstrong: The Films." Louis
    Armstrong: A Cultural Legacy. Ed. Marc H.
    Miller. Seattle: U of Washington P and Queens
    Museum of Art, 1994. 147-79.

"Chicago: Early 1920s." Wolverine Antique Music
    Society. Ed. R. D. Frederick. 1998.
    26 Feb. 1998 <http://www.shellac.org/wams/
    wchicag1.html>.

Collier, James Lincoln. Louis Armstrong, an
    American Genius. New York: Oxford UP, 1983.

Glaser, Joe. Letter to Lucille Armstrong. 28 Sept.
    1960. Box 3. Armstrong Archives. Queens
    College CUNY, Flushing, NY.

Jacobs, Phoebe. Personal interview. 12 Nov. 1997.

New page,
title centered.

Entries in
alphabetical
order.

Source:
archival
material.

3 hyphens
used instead
of repeating
author's
name.

Hanging
indent
5 spaces
or
½".

Source:
whole book.

Source: Web
site document.

Source:
personal
interview.

Hoffman 13

Jones, Max, and John Chilton. <u>Louis: The Louis
Armstrong Story, 1900-1971</u>. Boston: Little,
1971.

Morgenstern, Dan. "Louis Armstrong and the
Development and Diffusion of Jazz." <u>Louis
Armstrong: A Cultural Legacy</u>. Ed. Marc H.
Miller. Seattle: U of Washington P and Queens
Museum of Art, 1994. 95-145.

Ostwald, David. "All That Jazz." Rev. of <u>Louis
Armstrong: An Extravagant Life</u>, by Laurence
Bergreen. <u>Commentary</u> Nov. 1997: 68-72.

Pollack, Bracha. "A Man ahead of His Time."
Unpublished essay, 1997.

Robinson, J. Bradford. "Scat Singing." <u>The New
Grove Dictionary of Jazz</u>. London: Macmillan,
1988.

"Satchmo!" <u>New Orleans Online</u>. 1998. New Orleans
Tourism Marketing Corporation. 26 Feb. 1998
<http://neworleansonline.com/sno9.htm>.

Source:
selection in an
edited book.

Source: review
in a monthly
magazine.

Source: a
classmate's
paper.

Take the whole range of imaginative
literature, and we are all wholesale
borrowers. In every matter that relates
to invention, to use, or beauty or form,
we are borrowers.

—WENDELL PHILLIPS

APA
Documentation
Style

7 APA Documentation Style

29. APA Style: In-Text
Citations *245*

30. APA Style:
References *250*

31. APA Style:
Paper Format *259*

32. Student Paper
in APA Style *260*

APA IN-TEXT CITATIONS: DIRECTORY TO SAMPLE TYPES (CHAPTER 29)

(See pp. 250–58 for examples of references.)

1. Author named in your sentence *246*
2. Author named in parentheses *246*
3. Two to five authors *247*
4. Six or more authors *247*
5. Organization as author *248*
6. Unknown author *248*
7. Two or more authors with the same last name *248*
8. Two or more sources cited at one time *248*
9. E-mail, letters, conversations *249*
10. Indirect source *249*
11. Electronic source *249*

APA REFERENCE ENTRIES: DIRECTORY TO SAMPLE TYPES (CHAPTER 30)

(See pp. 245–50 for examples of in-text citations.)

Books

1. Book with one author *250*
2. Book with two or more authors *250*
3. Organization as author *250*
4. Two or more works by the same author *250*
5. Book with editor(s) *251*
6. Selection in an edited book or anthology *252*
7. Translation *252*
8. Article in a reference work *252*
9. Unknown author or editor *252*
10. Edition other than the first *252*
11. One volume of a multivolume work *253*
12. Republished book *253*

Periodicals

13. Article in a journal paginated by volume *253*
14. Article in a journal paginated by issue *253*
15. Two or more works in one year by same author *253*
16. Article in a magazine *254*

17. Article in a newspaper   *254*
18. Editorial or letter to the editor   *254*
19. Unsigned article   *254*
20. Review   *255*

Other Print and Audiovisual Sources
21. Government document   *255*
22. Report or working paper   *255*
23. Conference presentation   *255*
24. Unpublished dissertation or dissertation abstract   *256*
25. Film, videotape, recording   *256*
26. Television program   *256*

Electronic Sources
27. Online article or abstract from a database   *257*
28. Internet article   *257*
29. Document in a Web site   *258*
30. Online posting   *258*
31. Computer software   *258*

Instructors of social science and professional courses in psychology, sociology, political science, communications, education, and business usually prefer a documentation style that emphasizes the author and the year of publication, in part because the style makes it easy to tell if the sources cited are current.

The American Psychological Association (APA) has developed a widely used version of the author-year style; the information in Chapters 29–31 is based on the fifth edition of its *Publication Manual* (Washington: APA, 2001).

APA documentation style has two mandatory parts:

- In-text citations
- List of references

For links to Web sites for documentation styles used in various disciplines, visit <www.mhhe.com/maimon/mla_documentation>.

29   APA Style: In-Text Citations

When you use ideas, information, or words from a source, APA in-text citation format requires that you do the following:

- **Identify the author(s) of the source,** either in the sentence or in a parenthetical citation.

245

TEXTCONNEX

FAQs on APA Style

For updates to the APA documentation system, check the APA-sponsored Web site at <http://www.apastyle.org>.

- **Indicate the year of publication of the source** following the author's name, either in parentheses if the author's name is part of the sentence or if the author is not named in the sentence, after the author's name and a comma in a parenthetical citation.

- **Include a page reference for a quotation or a specific piece of information.** Put a *p.* before the page number. If the author is named in the text, the page number appears in the parenthetical citation following the borrowed material. Page numbers are not necessary when you are summarizing the source as a whole or paraphrasing an idea found throughout a work. (*For more on summary, paraphrase, and quotation, see Tab 5: Researching, pp. 186–87.*)

1. Author named in your sentence: When the author is named in a signal phrase, follow the name with the year of publication (in parentheses).

```
According to Eidson (1992), several political parties
vie for power at every level during regularly
scheduled elections.
```

2. Author named in parentheses: If you do not name the source's author in your sentence, then you must include the name in the parentheses, followed by the date and, if you are giving a quotation or a specific piece of information, the page number. The name, date, and page number are separated by commas.

```
This safety net plus the free market comprise what
Germany calls a "social market" economy (Eidson, 1992,
p. 122).
```

Tips LEARNING in COLLEGE

What Is the American Psychological Association?

The American Psychological Association (APA) is the largest psychological organization in the world. This scientific and professional group has more than 155,000 members and supports advances in psychological research and in the practice of psychology. Now in its fifth edition, the *Publication Manual of the American Psychological Association* has become an accepted guide for writers in many areas of science, not just psychology. Like the *MLA Handbook* (*see p. 204*), the *Publication Manual* is concerned with the mechanics of academic writing. The manual is especially useful in helping students prepare and present scientific facts and figures, and it contains special sections on how to construct tables, how to present statistics, and how to cite scientific references.

3. Two to five authors: If a source has five or fewer authors, name all of them the first time you cite the source.

```
As Calhoun, Light, and Keller (1997) point out,

"Income-based rankings are not necessarily a measure

of development" (p. 468).
```

If you put the names of the authors in parentheses, use an ampersand (&) instead of *and*.

```
Although income-based rankings are important, they

"are not necessarily a measure of development"

(Calhoun, Light, & Keller, 1997, p. 468).
```

After the first time you cite a work by three or more authors, use the first author's name plus *et al.* Always use both names when citing a work by two authors.

```
Another key factor is income distribution within

countries (Calhoun et al., 1997, p. 470).
```

4. Six or more authors: In all in-text citations of a work by six or more authors, give the first author's name plus *et al.* In the reference list, however, list the first six authors' names, followed by *et al.* for all others.

```
As Barbre et al. (1989) have argued, using personal
narratives enables researchers to connect the
individual and the social.
```

5. Organization as author: Treat the organization as the author and spell out its name the first time the source is cited. If the organization is well known, you may use an abbreviation thereafter.

```
The Deutsche Bank's Economics Department (1991)
identified a handful of key problems raised by
efforts to rebuild eastern Europe.
```

```
Public service announcements were used to inform
parents of these findings (National Institute of
Mental Health [NIMH], 1991).
```

In subsequent citations, as long as you are sure that readers will know what the abbreviation stands for, only the abbreviation and the date need to be given: (*NIMH, 1991*).

6. Unknown author: When no author or editor is listed for a work, use the first one or two important words of the title. Use quotation marks for titles of articles or chapters and italics for titles of books or reports.

```
The transformation of women's lives has been hailed as
"the single most important change of the past 1,000
years" ("Reflections," 1999, p. 77).
```

7. Two or more authors with the same last name: If the authors of two or more sources have the same last name, always include the appropriate first initial, even when the year of publication differs.

```
M. Smith (1988) showed how globalization has
restructured both cities and states.
```

8. Two or more sources cited at one time: When you are indebted to two or more sources for an idea, cite the authors in the order in which they appear in the list of references. Separate the two sources with a semicolon.

During World War II, the Nazi regime developed an
agrarian ideology while accelerating the pace of
industrial growth (Eidson, 1992; "Germany," 1995).

9. E-mail, letters, conversations: To cite information received from unpublished forms of personal communication, such as conversations, letters, notes, and e-mail messages, give the source's initials and last name, and provide as precise a date as possible.

According to A. Tapolcai (personal communication,
April 3, 1996), college-educated Hungarians had long
expected this kind of change.

Note: Because readers do not have access to them, you should not include personal communications—e-mail, notes, and letters—in your reference list.

10. Indirect source: When referring to a source that you know only from reading another source, use the phrase *as cited in,* followed by the author of the source you actually read and its year of publication.

A study by Passell (as cited in Calhoun et al., 1997,
p. 469) found that investments in education and
technology were lower for countries that exported
natural resources.

Note: The work by Passell would not be included in the reference list, but the work by Calhoun et al. would.

11. Electronic source: Cite an electronic source the same way you would a print source, with the author's last name and the publication date. If the document is a pdf (portable document format) file with stable page numbers, cite the page number as you would a print source. If the source has paragraph numbers instead of page numbers, use *para.* or ¶ instead of *p.* when citing a specific part of the source.

According to Gordeeva (2000), by the time the Truehand
was disbanded, it had privatized around 14,000
enterprises (para. 2).

Note: If the specific part lacks any kind of page or paragraph numbering, cite the heading and the number of the paragraph under that heading where the information can be found. If you cannot find the name of the author, or if the author is an organization, follow the appropriate guidelines for print sources (*see #5 and #6*). If you cannot determine the date, use the abbreviation "n.d." in its place: (*Wilson, n.d.*).

30 APA Style: References

APA documentation style requires a list of references where readers can find complete bibliographical information about the sources referred to in your paper. The list of references should appear at the end of your paper, beginning on a new page entitled "References."

Books

1. Book with one author:

```
Brown, J. F. (1991). Surge to freedom: The end of
     communist rule in eastern Europe. Durham, NC:
     Duke University Press.
```

2. Book with two or more authors:

```
Brown, L., Lenssen, N., & Kane, H. (1995). Vital signs
     1995: The trends that are shaping our future. New
     York: Norton.
```

```
Zelikow, P., & Rice, C. (1995). Germany unified and
     Europe transformed: A study in statecraft.
     Cambridge, MA: Harvard University Press.
```

3. Organization as author: To credit a subdivision like "Economics Department," put its name after the name of the parent organization. When the publisher is the same as the author, use the word "Author" instead of repeating the organization's name as the publisher.

```
Deutsche Bank, Economics Department. (1991). Rebuilding
     eastern Europe. Frankfurt, Germany: Author.
```

4. Two or more works by the same author: List the works in publication order, the earliest one first.

1. Begin on a new page.
2. Begin with the centered title "References."
3. Include a reference for every in-text citation.
4. Put references in alphabetical order by author's last name.
5. Give the last name and first or both initials for each author.
6. Put the publication year in parentheses following the author or authors' names.
7. Capitalize only the first word and proper nouns in titles. Also capitalize the first word following the semicolon in a subtitle.
8. Use italics for titles of books but not articles. Do not enclose titles of articles in quotation marks.
9. Include the city and publisher for books. If the city is not well known, include the state, using its two-letter postal abbreviation.
10. Include the periodical name and volume number (both in italics) as well as the page numbers for a periodical article.
11. Separate the author's or authors' names, date (in parentheses), title, and publication information with periods.
12. Use a hanging indent: Begin the first line of each entry flush left, and indent all subsequent lines of an entry one-half inch (five spaces).
13. Double-space within and between entries.

Brown, J. F. (1988). *Eastern Europe and communist rule.* Durham, NC: Duke University Press.

Brown, J. F. (1991). *Surge to freedom: The end of communist rule in eastern Europe.* Durham, NC: Duke University Press.

If the works were published in the same year, put them in alphabetical order by title and add a letter (*a, b, c*) to the year so that you can distinguish each entry in your in-text citations; see #15 for an example related to periodicals.

5. Book with editor(s):   Add (*Ed.*) or (*Eds.*) after the name. If a book lists an author and an editor, treat the editor like a translator (*see* #7).

```
Stares, P. B. (Ed.). (1992). The new Germany and the
    new Europe. Washington, DC: Brookings Institution.
```

6. Selection in an edited book or anthology:
The selection's author, year of publication, and title come first, followed by the word *In* and information about the edited book. Note that the page numbers of the selection go in parentheses after the book's title.

```
Kreile, M. (1992). The political economy of the new
    Germany. In P. B. Stares (Ed.), The new Germany
    and the new Europe (pp. 55–92). Washington, DC:
    Brookings Institution.
```

7. Translation:
After the title of the translation, put the name(s) of the translator(s) in parentheses, followed by the abbreviation *Trans.*

```
Jarausch, K. H., & Gransow, V. (1994). Uniting
    Germany: Documents and debates, 1944–1993 (A.
    Brown & B. Cooper, Trans.). Providence, RI: Berg.
```

8. Article in a reference work:
Some encyclopedias and similar reference works name the authors of individual selections. Begin with the author's name, if given. If no author is given, begin with the title of the selection.

```
Eidson, J. R. (1992). Germans. In Encyclopedia of
    world cultures (Vol. 4, pp. 121–124). Boston:
    G. K. Hall.
```

9. Unknown author or editor:
Start with the title. When alphabetizing, use the first important word of the title (excluding articles such as *The, A,* or *An*).

```
Give me liberty. (1969). New York: World.
```

10. Edition other than the first:
After the title, put the edition number in parentheses, followed by a period.

```
Smyser, W. R. (1993). The German economy: Colossus at
    crossroads (2nd ed.). New York: St. Martin's
    Press.
```

11. One volume of a multivolume work: If the specific volume used has its own title, put it before the title of the whole work. Note that no period separates the parenthetical volume number and the title that precedes it.

> Kintner, E. W. (Ed.). (1978). The Clayton Act and
>
> amendments. In *The legislative history of the*
>
> *federal antitrust laws and related statutes:*
>
> *The antitrust laws* (Vol. 2). New York: Chelsea
>
> House.

12. Republished book:

> Le Bon, G. (1960). *The crowd: A study of the popular*
>
> *mind.* New York: Viking. (Original work published
>
> 1895).

Note: In-text citations should give both years: "As Le Bon (1895/1960) pointed out. . . ."

Periodicals

13. Article in a journal paginated by volume: Do not put the article title in quotation marks, and do not use *pp.* before the page numbers. Italicize the title of the periodical and the volume number.

> Arnold, E. (1991). German foreign policy and
>
> unification. *International Affairs, 67,* 483–491.

14. Article in a journal paginated by issue: Include the issue number (in parentheses). Notice that the issue number is not italicized as part of the journal's title.

> Lowe, J. H., & Bargas, S. E. (1996). Direct investment
>
> positions and historical-cost basis. *Survey of*
>
> *Current Business, 76*(7), 45–60.

15. Two or more works in one year by the same author: Alphabetize the works by title, and attach a letter to each entry's year of publication, beginning with *a,* then *b,* and so on. In-text citations must use the letter as well as the year so that readers know exactly which work is being cited.

> Agarwal, J. P. (1996a). *Does foreign direct investment contribute to unemployment in home countries?— An empirical survey* (Discussion Paper No. 765). Kiel, Germany: Institute of World Economics.

> Agarwal, J. P. (1996b). Impact of Europe agreements on FDI in developing countries. *International Journal of Social Economics, 23*(10/11), 150–163.

Note: Also see #22, which explains the format for a report or working paper.

16. Article in a magazine: After the year, add the month for magazines published monthly or the month and day for magazines published weekly. Note that the volume number is also included, as it is for journals.

> Klee, K. (1999, December 13). The siege of Seattle. *Newsweek, 134*, 30–35.

17. Article in a newspaper: Use *p.* or *pp.* with the section and page number. List all page numbers, separated by commas, if the article appears on discontinuous pages: *pp. C1, C4, C6.* If there is no identified author, begin with the title of the article.

> Andrews, E. L. (1999, February 7). With German craft rules it's hard just to get work. *The New York Times*, p. A16.

18. Editorial or letter to the editor: In brackets, add to the title a phrase describing the form of the source.

> Krugman, P. (2000, July 16). Who's acquiring whom? [Editorial]. *The New York Times*, Sec. 4, p. 15.

19. Unsigned article: Begin the entry with the title, and alphabetize it by the first important word (excluding articles such as *The, A,* or *An*).

> Reflection on a thousand years: Introduction. (1999, April 18). *The New York Times Magazine*, p.77.

20. Review:

Bontolft, G. J. (1992). Culture shock in east Germany.
[Review of the book *Freedom was never like this:
A winter's journey in east Germany*]. *Contemporary
Review, 260,* 49–50.

Note: If the review is untitled, use the bracketed description in place of a title.

Other Print and Audiovisual Sources

21. Government document: When no author is listed, use the government agency as the author.

U.S. House Committee on Small Business. (1990). *East
Germany's time of crisis.* Washington, D.C.: U.S.
Government Printing Office.

22. Report or working paper: If the issuing agency numbered the report, include that number in parentheses after the title.

Agarwal, J. P. (1996a). *Does foreign direct investment
contribute to unemployment in home countries?—An
empirical survey* (Discussion Paper No. 765).
Kiel, Germany: Institute of World Economics.

Note: For reports from a deposit service like the *Educational Resources Information Center (ERIC)*, put the document number in parentheses at the end of the entry.

23. Conference presentation: Treat published conference presentations as a selection in a book (#6), as a periodical article (#13 or #14), or as a report (#22), whichever applies. For unpublished conference presentations, including poster sessions, provide the author, the year and month of the conference, the title of the presentation, and information on the presentation's form, forum, and place.

Markusen, J. (1998, June). *The role of multinationals
in global economic analysis.* Paper presented at
the First Annual Conference in Global Economic
Analysis, West Lafayette, IN.

Desantis, R. (1998, June). *Optimal export taxes,*
welfare, industry concentration and firm size:
A general equilibrium analysis. Poster session
presented at the First Annual Conference in
Global Economic Analysis, West Lafayette, IN.

24. Unpublished dissertation or dissertation abstract:

Weinbaum, A. E. (1998). Genealogies of "race" and
reproduction in transatlantic modern thought
(Doctoral dissertation, Columbia University,
1998). *Dissertation Abstracts International,*
58, 229.

If you used the abstract but not the actual dissertation, treat the
entry like a periodical article, with *Dissertation Abstracts Interna-*
tional as the periodical.

Weinbaum, A. E. (1998). Genealogies of "race" and
reproduction in transatlantic modern thought.
Dissertation Abstracts International, 58, 229.

25. Film, videotape, recording: Begin with the cited person's name and, if appropriate, a parenthetical notation of his or her role. After the title, identify the medium in brackets, followed by the country and name of the distributor.

Towner, R. (1989). *City of eyes* [Record]. Munich: ECM.

Wenders, W. (Director). (1989). *Wings of desire*
[Videotape]. Germany: Orion Home Video.

26. Television program: When citing a single episode, treat the script writer as the author and the producer as the editor of the series.

Weissman, G. (Writer). (2000). Mississippi: River out
of control [Television series episode]. In J.
Towers (Producer), *Wrath of God.* New York: The
History Channel.

When citing a whole series or a specific news broadcast, name the producer as author.

> Towers, J. (Producer). (2000). *Wrath of God*. New York:
>   The History Channel.

> Crystal, L. (Executive Producer). (2000, July 18).*The*
>   *NewsHour with Jim Lehrer* [Television broadcast].
>   Washington, D.C.: Public Broadcasting Service.

Electronic Sources

27. Online article or abstract from a database: When you use material from databases such as *PsycInfo, Sociological Abstracts, General BusinessFile ASAP,* and *Lexis-Nexis,* include a retrieval date and the name of the database in addition to the standard information about author, year, title, and publisher.

> Waelde, T. W. (1996). International energy investment.
>   *Energy Law Journal, 17,* 191–223. Retrieved May
>   10, 2000, from Lexis-Nexis database.

> Haas, R. (1994). Eastern Europe: A subsidy strategy
>   for ecological recovery. *Global Energy Issues*
>   *6*(3), 133–138. Abstract retrieved April 22, 2001,
>   from Lexis-Nexis database.

Note: When citing an abstract instead of the article, add the word *abstract* to the retrieval statement.

28. Internet article: When citing an article from a journal that appears only online, include a retrieval date and the URL.

> Leydesdorff, L., & Etzkowitz, H. (2001). The
>   transformation of university-industry-government
>   relations. *Electronic Journal of Sociology 5.*
>   Retrieved December 10, 2001, from http://
>   www.sociology.org/content/vol005.004/th.html

Note: To cite an electronic version of an article from a print journal, use the standard format for a periodical article (*see #13*) and add [*Electronic version*] after the article title.

Tips

APA EXPLANATORY NOTES

APA discourages the use of explanatory content notes to supplement the ideas in your paper, but they *are* an option. If you decide it is necessary to include a few content notes, put superscript numbers at appropriate points in your text. Type the notes, double spaced, on a separate page with the centered title "Footnotes." Indent the first line of each note five spaces, and type the appropriate superscript number followed by the note, with all lines after the first flush with the left margin.

29. Document in a Web site:

Fisher, B. (1995). *U.S. global trade outlook: Germany* (Office of European Union and Regional Affairs Report). Retrieved November 7, 1997, from http://tradeport.org/ts/ntdb/usgto/selcoun.html

U.S. Department of State. (1997). *Germany: Economic policy and trade practices, 1996.* Retrieved November 7, 1997, from http://tradeport.org/ts/countries/germany.html

30. Online posting to news group, discussion forum, or mailing list:
Messages posted to archived online electronic mailing lists, discussion forums, or news groups can be retrieved and should therefore be included in the reference list when you use them as sources. Provide the message's author, its date, and the subject line as the title. After the phrase *Message posted to,* give the name of the discussion forum or news group, followed by the address of the message.

Red Wave. (2000, April 8). Pareto/allocative efficiency of gift economy. Message posted to alt.society.economic-dev message board, archived at http://www.remarq.com/read/9755/qAyjNymZ61SoC-vwH#LR

31. Computer software:

AllWrite! 3.0 with Online Handbook. (2003). [Computer software]. New York: McGraw-Hill.

31 APA Style: Paper Format

The following guidelines will help you prepare your research paper in the format recommended by the *Publication Manual of the American Psychological Association,* fifth edition. For an example of a research paper that has been prepared using APA style, see pages 261–72.

Materials. Before printing your paper, make sure that you have stored your final draft on a backup disk. Use a high-quality printer and good white $8\frac{1}{2}$-by-11-inch paper. Choose a standard 10- or 12-point font such as Courier, Times, or Bookman. Do not justify your text or hyphenate words at the right margin; it should be ragged.

Title page. The first page of your paper should be a title page. Center the title between the left and right margins in the upper half of the page, and put your name a few lines below the title. Most instructors will also want you to include the course number and title, the instructor's name, and the date. (*See p. 261 for an example.*)

Margins and spacing. Use one-inch margins all around, except for the right-hand top corner, where the page number goes.

Double-space lines throughout the paper, including in the abstract, within any notes, and in the list of references. Indent the first word of each paragraph one-half inch (or five spaces).

For quotations of more than 40 words, use block format and indent five spaces from the left margin. Double-space the quoted lines.

Page numbers and abbreviated titles. All pages, including the title page, should have a number preceded by a short (one- or two-word) version of your title. Put this information in the upper right-hand corner of each page, about one-half inch from the top.

Abstract. Instructors sometimes require an abstract—a 75- to 100-word summary of your paper's thesis, major points or lines of development, and conclusions. The abstract appears on its own numbered page, entitled "Abstract," and is placed right after the title page. (*For more on abstracts, see Tab 3: Common Assignments across the Curriculum, p. 114.*)

Headings. Although headings are not required, most instructors of social science and professional courses welcome them. The primary headings should be centered, and all key words in the heading should be capitalized.

You can also use secondary headings if you need them; they should be italicized and should appear flush against the left-hand margin. Do not use a heading for your introduction, however. (*For more on headings, see Tab 9: Document and Web Design, pp. 318–19.*)

Visuals. Place visuals (tables, charts, graphs, and images) close to the place in your text where you refer to them. Label each visual as a table or a figure, and number each kind consecutively (Table 1, Table 2). You will also need to provide an informative caption for each visual. Cite the source of the material, preceded by the word *Note* and a period, and provide explanatory notes as needed. (*For more on using visuals effectively, see Tab 9: Document and Web Design, pp. 319–25.*)

32 Student Paper in APA Style

To view another sample student paper written in APA style, visit <www.mhhe.com/maimon/apa_paper_format>.

Jennifer Koehler researched and wrote the following report on Germany for a course entitled *Business in the Global Environment.* Because the most up-to-date business information was available on the World Wide Web, Jennifer consulted a number of online sources in addition to print sources.

All pages:
short title and
page number.

Germany's Path to Continuing Prosperity

Jennifer L. Koehler

GLB301 Country Report

Business in the Global Environment

Professor Meznar

November 14, 1997

Full title,
centered.

Abstract

With reunification, Germany faces a major economic challenge. With proper follow through, it can become one of the world's primary sources of direct investment and maintain its status as one of the world's preeminent exporters. The eastern area needs to be brought up to the western area's standards. Germany is as attractive a market for other nations and as a location for production because of its position at the crossroads of Europe. If government efforts continue, the economy will strengthen, and Germany will reinforce its position as a nation integral to the global economy.

First line is not indented.

Abstract summarizes main points of paper.

Paragraph should be no longer than 120 words.

1"   ½"

Germany's Path   3

Germany's Path to Continuing Prosperity

With reunification, Germany faces a major economic challenge. How might a society succeed in combining two completely different economies and cultures bound only by a common language? The German government stepped in to ease the reunification process, but the result was unfortunate: an expensive and intrusive bureaucracy drained Germany's resources and reduced its appeal for corporate investors. A sagging economy followed. Recognizing that its original approaches were not working, Germany decided to pursue a course that would make it more attractive economically. With proper follow-through, the nation can become one of the world's primary sources of direct investment and maintain its status as one of the world's preeminent exporters.

1"

Economic Realities

The German economy is the third largest in the world. Despite this strength, the nation faces a unique problem: how to bring its eastern area up to the western area's standards after forty-five years of Communist rule in the east. According to the *World Factbook*, western Germany accounts for 90% of overall German GDP and has three times the per capita income of eastern Germany (Central Intelligence Agency [CIA], 1996).

German citizens have a secure social safety net with substantial unemployment, health, and

Full title repeated on first page only.

Introduces topic and key question.

Short thesis, answers question.

Primary heading, centered, helps readers follow the argument.

Citation of source for all the information in this paragraph.

educational benefits. This safety net plus the
free market comprise what Germany calls a "social
market" economy (Eidson, 1992, p. 122). The west's
generous social welfare system was extended to
eastern Germany at reunification. Since 1990,
government transfers to eastern Germany have meant
ballooning public-sector deficits and borrowing.
To deal with these problems, the German government
decided to work on narrowing the federal budget
deficit for 1997. These efforts included cutting
back parts of the state's role in the economy
through privatization of formerly government-run
enterprises.

APA in-text citation: author, date, and, for specific information, page number.

Currency Issues

The deutschemark (DM) is Germany's exchange
currency until January 2002, when the euro will
be introduced. According to the U.S. State
Department's country report (1997), Germany
participates in the exchange rate mechanism of
the European Monetary System (EMS). Against
non-EMS currencies, the value of its freely
convertible currency floats and has done so for
the past ten years. How the euro will affect
exchange rates remains to be seen. However,
exchange rate movements over a five-year period
indicate that the DM is strengthening against the
dollar (CIA, 1996). As shown in Figure 1, the
DM strengthened from about DM1.66/\$ in 1991 to
DM1.53/\$ in 1995.

Point of figure is stated before figure is presented; figure is placed close to where it is discussed in the text.

Germany's Path   5

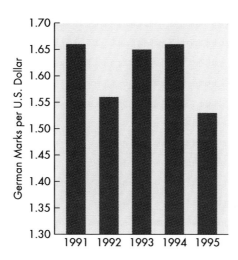

Figure 1 Direct exchange rate, 1991–1995: German marks per U.S. dollar. *Note*. The data are from *The World Factbook*, by the Central Intelligence Agency, 1996, retrieved November 1, 1997, from http://www. odci.gov/cia/publications/factbook/gm.htm

Foreign Direct Investment and International Trade

German foreign direct investment (FDI), as represented by the purchase of real business capital in other countries, has been primarily influenced by German integration into the European Union (EU). Also, trade between Germany and Central Europe has increased, partly because transaction costs are significantly lower for countries that are geographically close as well as for those within the EU.

Caption indicates source of data: a government publication.

Paragraph indent 5 spaces or ½".

But even though Germany's industrial/technical focus attracts foreign firms, FDI inflows have been lower than expected overall. As Agarwal (1997) points out, some factors that account for the low inflows include Germany's stringent environmental regulations, high corporate income taxes as well as wage costs, and rigid labor laws regulating hiring and firing. Germany's outflow, on the other hand, is quite high. Germany is the fourth most important global investor and is by far the biggest investor in such Central European countries as Hungary, the Czech Republic, and Slovenia (Agarwal, 1997).

Given its $1.9 trillion economy, the largest in Europe, Germany has an important role to play in trade relations with other countries, industrialized and developing (Fisher, 1995). Figures 2 and 3 show that Germany imports goods from its primary export recipients and that the countries of the EU are Germany's primary trading partners.

Germany's trade balance (surplus of merchandise exports over imports) has been somewhat more predictable than the economy as a whole. Trade balances have consistently increased over the years and reflect Germany's export-oriented economy. The increase was more dramatic in some years than in others, as data tabulated by Redman (1996) indicate. Between 1992 and 1993, for example, the trade balance increased by almost

Support by key facts (see p. 32).

Figures introduced and commented on.

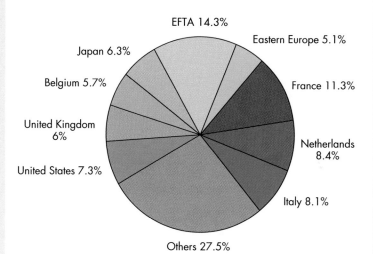

Imports and Exports

Figure 2 Germany: Percentages of total imports from European countries, the United States, Japan, and other countries (1993). *Note.* From *The World Factbook,* by the Central Intelligence Agency, 1996, retrieved November 1, 1997, from http://www.odci. gov/cia/publications/factbook/gm.htm

DM30 billion. Between 1993 and 1994, it increased by only DM10 billion.

Economic Prospects

Many factors make Germany attractive both as a market for other nations and as a location for production. As the former east German citizens' standard of living increases due to reunification, their purchasing power and productivity increase. Intellectual property is well protected, and

Development by reasoning (*see pp. 25–26*).

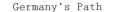

Germany's Path   8

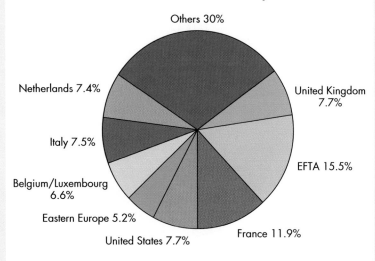

Exports

Figure 3 Germany: Percentages of total exports to European countries, the United States, Japan, and other countries (1993). EFTA stands for European Free Trade Association. *Note.* From *The World Factbook,* by the Central Intelligence Agency, 1996, retrieved November 1, 1997, from http://www.odci.gov/cia/publications/factbook/gm.htm

Germany is involved in most global treaties that protect business interests. Germany's highly skilled workforce is another plus for potential ventures and production plans. Generally, private enterprise, government, banks, and unions cooperate, making the country more amenable to negotiations for business entry or joint ventures.

Germany also has an excellent physical location that makes it an "important crossroads for traffic between the North Sea, the Baltic, and the Mediterranean" ("Germany," 1996, p. 185). Equally important, a comprehensive and efficient transportation system allows businesses operating plants in Germany to transport their goods and services easily to other parts of the country and the world.

However, for the next few years, FDI will probably remain low because of high labor costs, high taxation, and government regulation. Recent government efforts to lower the tax burden on companies and consumers will help, as will the privatization of many publicly owned industries. According to Agarwal (1997), "privatisation related FDI often leads to reinvestments, and improves the climate for more FDI, reassuring investors about the continuation of liberal policies in the future."

During this period of restructuring, the DM might decline in value as foreign investors wait for change. But as Bindenagel (1997) points out, devaluation of the DM compared with the dollar and most other currencies should lead to a boost in exports and to accelerated economic growth:

> [E]xport growth will be an even stronger engine for growth in the next two years than expected, while growth in domestic demand

Quotation of more than 40 words indented 5 spaces.

remains moderate. Export orders remained
strong throughout December 1996, the trade
weighted DM dropped 3.9 percent . . . from the
middle of last year to February of this year,
and the prospects for growth in Germany's main
trading partners remain optimistic. (para. 16)
Continued export strength combined with the
eventual increase in inflows will result in
stronger economies in both east and west Germany
(Fisher, 1995).

Paragraph
cited because
no page
numbers are
available and
paragraphs
are numbered
in the
document.

Conclusion

All in all, Germany is experiencing a great
deal of change. In fact, it is remarkable that
just eight years after the fall of the Berlin
Wall, the German economy is working so well. If
the government efforts continue, the economy will
strengthen over the next decade, and Germany will
reinforce its position in the global economy. High
unemployment, high wages, high taxes, and the high
cost of doing business, especially in the east,
will continue to challenge economists and
government planners. Germany's path to continuing
prosperity depends on a national will to encourage
foreign investment. Economic advancement will not
occur without obstacles, but given Germany's
position at the crossroads of Europe, we can have
confidence in the nation's economic progress.

Thesis
restated and
qualified.

Germany's Path   11

References

Agarwal, J. P. (1997, April). European integration and German FDI: Implications for domestic investment and central European economies. *National Institute Economic Review.* No. 160. Retrieved November 1, 1997, from InfoTrac (General BusinessFile ASAP) database.

Bindenagel, J. D. (1997). *Germany—Economic trends.* U.S. Department of Commerce, International Trade Administration. Retrieved November 5, 1997, from DIALOG database. (IT Market IMI970409)

Central Intelligence Agency. (1996). Germany. In *The world factbook.* Retrieved November 1, 1997, from http://www.odci.gov/cia/publications/factbook/gm.htm

Eidson, J. R. (1992). Germans. In *Encyclopedia of world cultures* (Vol. 4, pp. 121–124). Boston: G. K. Hall.

Fisher, B. (1995). *U.S. global trade outlook: Germany* (Office of European Union and Regional Affairs Report). Retrieved November 7, 1997, from http://tradeport.org/ts/ntdb/usgto/selcoun.html

Germany. (1995). In S. P. Parker (Ed.), *World geographical encyclopedia* (Vol. 4, pp. 180-187). New York: McGraw-Hill.

New page, heading centered.

Entries in alphabetical order and double-spaced.

Hanging indent, 5 spaces or ½".

Redman. (1996). *Germany—Balance of payment
    statistics.* U.S. Department of Commerce,
    International Trade Administration. Retrieved
    November 5, 1997, from DIALOG database. (IT
    Market IM960611.008)

U.S. Department of State. (1997). *Germany: Economic
    policy and trade practices, 1996.* Retrieved
    November 7, 1997, from http://tradeport.org/
    ts/countries/germany.html

Nothing gives an author so much
pleasure as to find his works respectfully quoted by other learned authors.

—BENJAMIN FRANKLIN

Other
Documentation
Styles

Chicago, CSE, and COS

8   Other Documentation Styles

33. *Chicago* Documentation Style *276*
   a. *Chicago* style: In-text citations and notes *277*
   b. *Chicago* style: Bibliography *278*
   c. Sample *Chicago*-style notes and bibliography entries *279*
   d. Sample from a student paper in *Chicago* style *291*

34. CSE Documentation Styles *296*
   a. CSE name-year style *296*
   b. CSE number style *299*

35. Columbia Online Style (COS) *304*
   a. COS: Required information *304*
   b. COS and common documentation styles *305*

DIRECTORY TO *CHICAGO* STYLE (CHAPTER 33)

Books
1. Book with one author *279*
2. Multiple works by the same author *279*
3. Book with two or more authors *280*
4. Book with an author and an editor or a translator *281*
5. Book with editor(s) *281*
6. Organization as author *281*
7. Work in an anthology or part of an edited book *282*
8. Article in an encyclopedia or a dictionary *282*
9. The Bible *283*
10. Edition other than the first *283*
11. Multivolume work *283*
12. Work in a series *283*
13. Unknown author *284*

Periodicals
14. Article in a journal paginated by volume *284*
15. Article in a journal paginated by issue *285*
16. Article in a magazine *285*
17. Article in a newspaper *286*

Other Sources
18. Review *286*
19. Interview *287*
20. Government document *287*
21. Unpublished dissertation or document *287*
22. Musical score or composition *287*
23. Film or videotape *288*
24. Sound recording *288*
25. Artwork *289*

26. Performance   *289*
27. CD-ROM   *289*

Online Sources
28. Online book or periodical article   *290*
29. Online database, Web site, or discussion group   *290*

DIRECTORY TO CSE STYLES (CHAPTER 34)

CSE Name-Year Style
(See pp. 299–303 for examples of CSE number style.)

In-text citations   *296*
Reference list entries   *296*

Books
1. One author   *297*
2. Two or more authors   *297*
3. Selection in an edited book   *297*
4. Online book   *297*
5. Organization as author   *298*
6. Book with editor(s)   *298*

Periodicals
7. Article in a journal paginated by volume   *298*
8. Article in a journal paginated by issue   *298*
9. Article available online   *298*
10. Article in a supplement to a journal   *299*
11. Article in a magazine   *299*

CSE Number Style
(See pp. 296–99 for examples of CSE name-year style.)

In-text citations   *299*
Reference list entries   *300*

Books and Reports
1. One author   *300*
2. Two or more authors   *300*
3. Organization as author   *301*
4. Chapter in a book   *301*
5. Book with editor(s)   *301*
6. Selection in an edited book   *301*
7. Technical report or government document   *301*

Periodicals
8. Article in a journal paginated by volume   *302*
9. Article in a journal paginated by issue   *302*
10. Article in a magazine or newspaper   *302*

Online Sources

11. Online journal article   *303*
12. Online book   *303*
13. Online database or Web site   *303*

DIRECTORY TO COS STYLE (CHAPTER 35)

COS and Common Documentation Styles

1. COS and MLA style   *305*
2. COS and APA style   *306*
3. COS and *Chicago* style   *307*
4. COS and CSE name-year style   *308*
5. COS and CSE number style   *309*

For links to Web sites for documentation styles used in various disciplines, visit <www.mhhe.com/maimon/mla_documentation>.

There are many documentation styles besides those developed by the Modern Language Association (*see Tab 6*) and the American Psychological Association (*see Tab 7*). In this section, we cover four additional documentation styles: the *Chicago Manual* style, the two styles developed by the Council of Science Editors, and the Columbia Online Style. To find out where you can learn about other style types, consult the list of style manuals on page 191. If you are not sure which style to use, ask your instructor.

33 *Chicago* Documentation Style

The note and bibliography documentation style presented in the fourteenth edition of *The Chicago Manual of Style* (Chicago: University of Chicago Press, 1993) is used in many disciplines, including history, art, philosophy, business, and communications. The *Chicago* style has three parts:

- Numbered in-text citations
- Numbered footnotes or endnotes
- A bibliography of works consulted

The first two parts are necessary; the third is optional, unless your instructor requires it. (*Chicago* also has an alternative author-date system that is similar to APA style.) For more information on *Chicago*

For MULTILINGUAL STUDENTS

Deciding Which Documentation Style to Use

Always check with your instructor if you are not sure which documentation style you should use for a particular paper. Each of the styles presented in this book is academically sound, and it is quite possible that any one of several styles could provide the guidance you need to write the paper and document the information you have used. The choice of which style to use is often guided by the personal preference of the professor.

TEXTCONNEX

FAQs on Chicago *Style*

For updates and answers to frequently asked questions (FAQs), go to the *Chicago Manual*'s Web site at <http://www.Press.uchicago.edu> and click on "Chicago Manual of Style FAQ."

style, consult the *Manual of Style* or *A Manual for Writers of Term Papers, Theses, and Dissertations,* sixth edition, by Kate L. Turabian (Chicago: University of Chicago Press, 1996).

 Use numbered in-text citations and notes.

Whenever you use information or ideas from a source, you need to indicate what you have borrowed by putting a superscript number in the text ([1]) at the end of the borrowed material. These superscript numbers are placed after all punctuation marks except for the dash.

As Bergreen points out, Armstrong easily reached
difficult high notes, the F's and G's that stymied
other trumpeters.[3] And his innovative singing style
featured "scat," a technique that combines "nonsense
syllables [with] improvised melodies."[4]

TextConnex

Superscript Numbers

To find the superscript option in your computer's word-processing program, click on "Format" on your tool bar and then choose "Font." Superscript is one of many font options.

Each in-text superscript number must have a corresponding note either at the foot of the page or at the end of the text. Footnotes begin with the number and are single-spaced, with a double space between notes.

If you are using endnotes instead of footnotes, they should begin after the last page of your text on a new numbered page entitled "Notes." Double-space within and between endnotes.

The first time a source is cited in either a footnote or an endnote, include a full citation. Subsequent citations require only the author's name and a page number.

FIRST REFERENCE TO A SOURCE

    3. Laurence Bergreen, *Louis Armstrong:*
An Extravagant Life (New York: Broadway Books,
1997), 248.

ENTRY FOR A SOURCE ALREADY CITED

    6. Bergreen, 370.

33b Prepare a separate bibliography if your instructor requires one.

Some instructors require a separate list of works cited or of works consulted. If you are asked to provide a works-cited list, then do so on a separate, numbered page that has the title "Works Cited." If the list is supposed to include works consulted as well as cited, then title it "Bibliography."

    Bergreen, Laurence. *Louis Armstrong: An Extravagant*
        Life. New York: Broadway Books, 1997.

GENERAL GUIDELINES for a
BIBLIOGRAPHY or a WORKS-CITED
LIST in *CHICAGO* STYLE

1. Begin on a new page.
2. Begin with the centered title "Works Cited" if you are including only works referred to in your paper. Use the title "Bibliography" if you are including every work you consulted.
3. List sources alphabetically by author's (or editor's) last name.
4. Capitalize the first and last words in titles as well as all important words and words that follow colons.
5. Use a hanging indent: Indent all lines except the first of each entry five spaces (or one-half inch).
6. Use periods between author and title as well as between title and publication data.
7. Single-space each entry; double-space between entries.

33c Use the correct *Chicago* style for notes and bibliography entries.

Books

1. Book with one author:

NOTE

1. James Lincoln Collier, *Louis Armstrong, an American Genius* (New York: Oxford University Press, 1983), 82.

BIBLIOGRAPHY

Collier, James Lincoln. *Louis Armstrong, an American Genius.* New York: Oxford University Press, 1983.

2. Multiple works by the same author: After providing complete information in the first footnote, include only a shortened version of the title with the author's last name and the page number in any subsequent footnote. In the bibliography, list entries in either alphabetical order by title or chronological order from earliest to latest. After the first listing, replace the author's name with a long underline (hit the underscore key eight times).

NOTE

>   7. Collier, *Jazz*, 154.

>   12. Collier, *Louis Armstrong*, 32.

BIBLIOGRAPHY

Collier, James Lincoln. *Jazz: The American Theme Song.*
>   New York: Oxford University Press, 1993.

_____. *Louis Armstrong, An American Genius.* New
>   York: Oxford University Press, 1983.

3. Book with two or more authors: In notes, you can name up to three authors. When there are three authors, put a comma after the first name and a comma plus *and* after the second.

NOTE

>   2. Miles Davis and Quincy Troupe, *Miles: The Autobiography* (New York: Simon & Schuster, 1989), 15.

BIBLIOGRAPHY

Davis, Miles, and Quincy Troupe. *Miles: The
>   Autobiography.* New York: Simon & Schuster, 1989.

When more than three authors are listed on the title page, use *et al.* after the first author's name in the note.

NOTE

>   3. Julian Henriques et al., *Changing the Subject: Psychology Social Regulation, and Subjectivity* (New York: Methuen, 1984), 275.

BIBLIOGRAPHY

Henriques, Julian, Wendy Holloway, Cathy Urwin, Couze
>   Venn, and Valerie Walkerdine. *Changing the
>   Subject: Psychology, Social Regulation, and
>   Subjectivity.* New York: Methuen, 1984.

Notice that *et al.* is not used in bibliography entries, even when a book has more than three authors.

4. Book with an author and an editor or a translator: Put the author's name first and add the editor's (*ed.*) or translator's (*trans.*) name after the title.

NOTE

4. Louis Armstrong, *Louis Armstrong--A Self-Portrait*, ed. Richard Meryman (New York: Eakins Press, 1971), 54.

BIBLIOGRAPHY

Armstrong, Louis. *Louis Armstrong--A Self-Portrait*. Edited by Richard Meryman. New York: Eakins Press, 1971.

BIBLIOGRAPHY

Goffin, Robert. *Horn of Plenty: The Story of Louis Armstrong.* Translated by James F. Bezov. New York: Da Capo Press, 1977.

5. Book with editor(s):

NOTE

5. Paul Eduard Miller, ed., *Esquire's Jazz Book* (New York: Smith & Durrell, 1944), 31.

BIBLIOGRAPHY

Miller, Paul Eduard, ed. *Esquire's Jazz Book.* New York: Smith & Durrell, 1944.

6. Organization as author:

NOTE

6. Centre for Contemporary Cultural Studies, *Making Histories: Studies in History Writing and Politics* (London: Hutchinson, 1982), 10.

BIBLIOGRAPHY

Centre for Contemporary Cultural Studies. *Making Histories: Studies in History Writing and Politics.* London: Hutchinson, 1982.

7. Work in an anthology or part of an edited book: Begin with the author and title of the specific work or part.

NOTE

> 7. Hale Smith, "Here I Stand," in *Readings in Black American Music*, ed. Eileen Southern (New York: Norton, 1971), 287.

NOTE

> 8. Richard Crawford, foreword to *The Jazz Tradition*, by Martin Williams (New York: Oxford University Press, 1993), xii.

BIBLIOGRAPHY

> Smith, Hale. "Here I Stand." *Readings in Black American Music*, ed. Eileen Southern, 286-89. New York: W. W. Norton, 1971.

BIBLIOGRAPHY

> Crawford, Richard. Foreword to *The Jazz Tradition*, by Martin Williams. New York: Oxford University Press, 1993.

In notes, the descriptive terms *foreword, introduction, preface,* and *afterword* are not capitalized. In bibliography entries, these descriptive terms are capitalized.

8. Article in an encyclopedia or a dictionary: For well-known reference works, publication data can be omitted from a note, but the edition or copyright date should be included. There is no need to include page numbers for entries in reference works that are arranged alphabetically; the abbreviation *s.v.* (meaning "under the word") plus the entry's title can be used instead.

NOTE

> 9. J. Bradford Robinson, "Scat Singing," in *The New Grove Dictionary of Jazz* (1988).

NOTE

> 10. *Encyclopedia Britannica*, 15th ed., s.v. "Jazz."

Reference works are not listed in the bibliography unless they are unusual or crucial to your paper.

BIBLIOGRAPHY

Robinson, J. Bradford. "Scat Singing." In *The New Grove Dictionary of Jazz.* London: Macmillan, 1988.

9. The Bible: Abbreviate the name of the book, and use arabic numbers for chapter and verse. Name the version of the Bible cited only if it matters, and do not include the Bible in your bibliography.

NOTE

11. Eccles. 8.5 Jerusalem Bible.

10. Edition other than the first: Include the number of the edition after the title or, if there is an editor, after that person's name.

NOTE

12. Hugues Panassie, *Louis Armstrong,* 2d ed. (New York: Da Capo Press, 1980), 12.

BIBLIOGRAPHY

Panassie, Hugues. *Louis Armstrong.* 2d ed. New York: Da Capo Press, 1980.

11. Multivolume work: Put the volume number, followed by a colon, before the page number.

NOTE

13. Robert Lissauer, *Lissauer's Encyclopedia of Popular Music in America* (New York: Facts on File, 1996), 2:33-34.

BIBLIOGRAPHY

Lissauer, Robert. *Lissauer's Encyclopedia of Popular Music in America.* Vol. 2. New York: Facts on File, 1996.

12. Work in a series: Include the name of the series as well as the book's series number.

NOTE

    14. Samuel A. Floyd, ed., *Black Music in the Harlem Renaissance*, Contributions in Afro-American and African Studies, no. 128 (New York: Greenwood Press, 1990), 2.

BIBLIOGRAPHY

Floyd, Samuel A., ed. *Black Music in the Harlem Renaissance*. Contributions in Afro-American and African Studies, no. 128. New York: Greenwood Press, 1990.

13. Unknown author: Cite anonymous works by title and alphabetize them by the first word, ignoring *A, An,* or *The.*

NOTE

    15. *The British Album* (London: John Bell, 1790), 2:43-47.

BIBLIOGRAPHY

The British Album. Vol. 2. London: John Bell, 1790.

Periodicals

14. Article in a journal paginated by volume: Many scholarly journals are issued a handful of times each year, and the issues are bound together by libraries to make yearly volumes. When journals are paginated by yearly volume, your citation should include the following: author, title of article in quotation marks, title of journal, volume number and year, page number(s).

NOTE

    16. Frank Tirro, "Constructive Elements in Jazz Improvisation," *Journal of the American Musicological Society* 27 (1974): 300.

BIBLIOGRAPHY

Tirro, Frank. "Constructive Elements in Jazz Improvisation." *Journal of the American Musicological Society* 27 (1974): 285-305.

15. Article in a journal paginated by issue: If the periodical is paginated by issue rather than by volume, add the issue number, preceded by the abbreviation *no.*

NOTE

    17. Sarah Appleton Aguiar, "'Everywhere and Nowhere': *Beloved*'s 'Wild' Legacy in Toni Morrison's *Jazz*," *Notes on Contemporary Literature* 25, no. 4 (1995): 11.

BIBLIOGRAPHY

Aguiar, Sarah Appleton. "'Everywhere and Nowhere': *Beloved*'s 'Wild' Legacy in Toni Morrison's *Jazz*." *Notes on Contemporary Literature* 25, no. 4 (1995): 11-12.

16. Article in a magazine: Identify magazines by week (if available) and month of publication.

NOTE

    18. Malcolm Walker, "Discography: Bill Evans," *Jazz Monthly*, June 1965, 22.

BIBLIOGRAPHY

Walker, Malcolm. "Discography: Bill Evans." *Jazz Monthly*, June 1965, 20-22.

If the article cited does not appear on consecutive pages, do not put any page numbers in the bibliography entry. You can, however, give specific pages in the note.

NOTE

    19. J. R. Taylor, "Jazz History: The Incompleted Past," *Village Voice*, 3 July 1978, 65, 67.

BIBLIOGRAPHY

Taylor, J. R. "Jazz History: The Incompleted Past." *Village Voice*, 3 July 1978.

17. Article in a newspaper:

NOTE

20. Ralph Blumenthal, "Satchmo with His Tape Recorder Running," *New York Times*, 3 August 1999, sec. E, p. 1.

BIBLIOGRAPHY

Blumenthal, Ralph. "Satchmo with His Tape Recorder Running." *New York Times*, 3 August 1999, sec. E, p. 1.

Other Sources

18. Review:

NOTE

21. David Ostwald, "All That Jazz," review of *Louis Armstrong: An Extravagant Life*, by Laurence Bergreen, *Commentary*, November 1997, 72.

BIBLIOGRAPHY

Ostwald, David. "All That Jazz." Review of *Louis Armstrong: An Extravagant Life*, by Laurence Bergreen. *Commentary*, November 1997, 68-72.

19. Interview: Start with the name of the person interviewed, and note the nonprint medium (tape recording, video). Only interviews accessible to your readers are listed in the bibliography.

NOTE

22. Louis Armstrong, "Authentic American Genius," interview by Richard Meryman, *Life*, 15 April 1966, 92.

NOTE

23. Michael Cogswell, interview by author, tape recording, Louis Armstrong Archives, Queens College CUNY, Flushing, N.Y., 11 March 1998.

BIBLIOGRAPHY

Armstrong, Louis. "Authentic American Genius." Interview by Richard Meryman. *Life*, 15 April 1966, 92-102.

20. Government document: If it is not already obvious in your text, name the country first.

NOTE

24. Bureau of National Affairs, *The Civil Rights Act of 1964: Text, Analysis, Legislative History; What It Means to Employers, Businessmen, Unions, Employees, Minority Groups* (Washington, D.C.: BNA, 1964), 22-23.

BIBLIOGRAPHY

U.S. Bureau of National Affairs. *The Civil Rights Act of 1964: Text, Analysis, Legislative History; What It Means to Employers, Businessmen, Unions, Employees, Minority Groups.* Washington, D. C.: BNA, 1964.

21. Unpublished dissertation or document: Include a description of the document as well as information about where it is available.

NOTE

25. Adelaida Reyes-Schramm, "The Role of Music in the Interaction of Black Americans and Hispanos in New York City's East Harlem" (Ph.D. diss., Columbia University, 1975), 34-37.

NOTE

26. Joe Glaser to Lucille Armstrong, 28 September 1960, handwritten letter, Louis Armstrong Archives, Rosenthal Library, Queens College CUNY, Flushing, N.Y.

BIBLIOGRAPHY

Reyes-Schramm, Adelaida. "The Role of Music in the Interaction of Black Americans and Hispanos in New York City's East Harlem." Ph.D. diss., Columbia University, 1975.

BIBLIOGRAPHY

Glaser, Joe, to Lucille Armstrong, 28 September 1960. Handwritten letter. Louis Armstrong Archives, Rosenthal Library, Queens College CUNY, Flushing, N.Y.

22. Musical score or composition: Treat a published score as a book, and include it in the bibliography.

NOTE

27. Franz Josef Haydn, *Symphony No. 94 in G Major,* ed. H. C. Robbins Landon (Salzburg: Haydn-Mozart Press, 1965), 22.

BIBLIOGRAPHY

Haydn, Franz Josef. *Symphony No. 94 in G Major.* Edited by H. C. Robbins Landon. Salzburg: Haydn-Mozart Press, 1965.

For a musical composition, give the composer's name, followed by the title of the work. Put the title in italics unless it names an instrumental work known only by its form, number, and key.

NOTE

28. Duke Ellington, *Satin Doll.*

NOTE

29. Franz Josef Haydn, Symphony no. 94 in G Major.

23. Film or videotape:

NOTE

30. *Artists and Models,* dir. Raoul Walsh with performance by Louis Armstrong (Hollywood: Paramount Pictures, 1937), feature film.

BIBLIOGRAPHY

Artists and Models. Directed by Raoul Walsh. Performance by Louis Armstrong. Hollywood: Paramount Pictures, 1937.

24. Sound recording: Begin with the composer or other person responsible for the content.

NOTE

31. Louis Armstrong, *Town Hall Concert Plus,* RCA INTS 5070, 1957.

BIBLIOGRAPHY

Armstrong, Louis. *Town Hall Concert Plus.* RCA INTS 5070, 1957.

25. Artwork: Begin with the artist's name, and include both the name and location of the institution holding the work. Works of art are usually not included in the bibliography.

NOTE

32. Herman Leonard, *Louis Armstrong: Birdland,* black-and-white photograph, 1956, Barbara Gillman Gallery, Miami.

26. Performance: Begin with the author, director, or performer—whoever is most relevant to your study.

NOTE

33. Terrence McNally, Lynn Athrens, and Stephen Flaherty, *Ragtime,* dir. Frank Galati, Ford Performing Arts Center, New York, 11 November 1998.

BIBLIOGRAPHY

McNally, Terrence, Lynn Athrens, and Stephen Flaherty. *Ragtime.* Directed by Frank Galati. Ford Performing Arts Center, New York, 11 November 1998.

27. CD-ROM:

NOTE

34. *Microsoft Encarta Multimedia Encyclopedia,* s.v. "Armstrong, (Daniel) Louis 'Satchmo'" [CD-ROM] (Redmond, Wash.: Microsoft, 1994).

BIBLIOGRAPHY

Microsoft Encarta Multimedia Encyclopedia. "Armstrong, (Daniel) Louis 'Satchmo.'" CD-ROM. Redmond, Wash.: Microsoft, 1994.

Online Sources   *Chicago* style does not yet have a developed set of guidelines for citing online sources. Writers are advised not to substitute URL addresses for authors, titles, or publishers and to use angle brackets around URLs. When necessary, break Internet addresses after a slash or before a period.

28. Online book or periodical article:

NOTE

35. Carl Sandburg, *Chicago Poems* [book online]
(New York: Henry Holt, 1916), available from Bartleby
at ⟨http://www.bartleby.com/165/index.html⟩; accessed
14 June 2000.

NOTE

36. Janet Schmalfeldt, "On Keeping the Score,"
Music Theory Online 4, no. 2 (1998): pars. 4-7 [journal
online]; available from ⟨http://smt.ucsb.edu/mto/issues/
mto.98.4.2.schmalfeldt.html⟩; accessed 2 May 1998.

BIBLIOGRAPHY

Sandburg, Carl. *Chicago Poems* [book online]. New York:
    Henry Holt, 1916. Available from Bartleby at
    ⟨http://www.bartleby.com/165/index.html⟩.
    Accessed 14 June 2000.

BIBLIOGRAPHY

Schmalfeldt, Janet. "On Keeping the Score" *Music Theory
    Online* 4, no. 2 (1998) [journal online]. Available
    from ⟨http://smt.ucsb.edu/mto/issues/
    mto.98.4.2.schmalfeldt.html⟩. Accessed 2 May 1998.

29. Online database, Web site, or discussion group: Identify as many of the following items as you can: author, title, kind of source (in brackets), publication data, URL, and date of access.

NOTE

37. Bruce Boyd Raeburn, "An Introduction to New
Orleans Jazz," in *William Ransom Hogan Archive of New
Orleans Jazz* [Web site and database] (Tulane University,
30 May 2000); available from ⟨http://www.tulane.edu/
~lmiller/BeginnersIntro.html⟩; accessed 21 June 2000.

NOTE

38. Don Mopsick, "Favorite Jazz Quotes" in Big Band Music Fans, 17 March 2000 [online discussion group]; available from <http://www.remarq.com/list/4755?nav+FIRST&rf+1&si+grou>; accessed 17 June 2000.

BIBLIOGRAPHY

Raeburn, Bruce Boyd. "An Introduction to New Orleans Jazz." In *William Ransom Hogan Archive of New Orleans Jazz* [Web site and database]. Tulane University, 30 May 2000. Available from <http://www.tulane.edu/~lmiller/BeginnersIntro.html>. Accessed 21 June 2000.

BIBLIOGRAPHY

Mopsick, Don. "Favorite Jazz Quotes." Big Band Music Fans, 17 March 2000 [online discussion group]. Available from <http://www.remarq.com/list/4755?nav+FIRST&rf+1&si+grou>. Accessed 17 June 2000.

33d Sample from a student paper in *Chicago* style

The following excerpt from Esther Hoffman's paper on Louis Armstrong has been put into *Chicago* style so that you can see how citation numbers, endnotes, and bibliography work together. (Esther's entire paper, in MLA style, can be found on pages 230–42.)

Chicago style allows you the option of including a title page. If you do provide a title page, count it as page 1, but do not include the number on the page. Put page numbers in the upper right-hand corner of the remaining pages, except for the pages with the titles "Notes" and "Bibliography" or "Works Cited"; on these pages, the number should be centered at the bottom of the page.

To view a full student paper in *Chicago* style, visit <www.mhhe.com/maimon/cms>.

2

In the 1920s, jazz music was at its height in creativity and popularity. Chicago had become one of the jazz capitals of America, and its clubs showcased the premier talents of the time, performers like Jelly Roll Morton and Joe Oliver. It has always been difficult to break into the music business, and the jazz scene of the twenties was no exception. Eager for fame and fortune, though many young black musicians who had honed their craft in New Orleans migrated north to Chicago, hoping for a chance to perform with the best.[1]

Among these emigres was Louis Armstrong, a gifted musician who developed into the "first true virtuoso soloist of jazz." Armstrong played the trumpet and sang with unusual improvisational ability as well as technical mastery. As Bergreen points out, he easily reached difficult high notes, the F's and G's that stymied other trumpeters.[3] And his innovative singing style featured "scat," a technique that combines "nonsense syllables [with] improvised melodies."[4] Eventually, Armstrong's innovations innovations became the standard, as more and more jazz musicians took their cue from his style.

Armstrong's beginnings give no hint of the greatness that he would achieve. In New Orleans, he was born into poverty and received little

3

formal education. As a youngster, Armstrong had to take odd jobs like delivering coal and selling newspapers so that he could earn money to help his family. At the age of twelve, Armstrong was placed in the Colored Waifs' Home to serve an eighteen-month sentence for firing a gun in a public place. There "Captain" Peter Davis gave him "basic musical training on the cornet."[5] Older, more established musicians soon noticed Armstrong's talent and offered him opportunities to play with them. In 1922, Joe Oliver invited Armstrong to join his band in Chicago, and the twenty-one-year-old trumpeter headed north.

It was in Chicago that Armstrong met Joe Glaser, the man who eventually became his longtime manager. According to Bergreen, Glaser had a reputation for being a tough but trustworthy guy who could handle any situation. He was raised in a middle-class home by parents who were Jewish immigrants from Russia. As a young man, Glaser got caught up in the Chicago underworld and soon had a rap sheet that included indictments for running a brothel as well as for statutory rape.[6] Glaser's mob connections also led to his involvement in Chicago's club scene, a business almost completely controlled by gangsters like Al Capone. During the era of Prohibition, Glaser managed the Sunset

Notes

1. R. D. Frederick, ed., "Chicago; Early 1920s," Wolverine Antique Music Society [Web site]; available from <http://www.shellac.org/wams/wchicag1.html>; accessed 26 February 1998.

2. *Microsoft Encarta Multimedia Encyclopedia,* s.v. "Armstrong, (Daniel) Louis 'Satchmo'" [CD-ROM] (Redmond, Wash.: Microsoft, 1994).

3. Laurence Bergreen, *Louis Armstrong: An Extravagant Life* (New York: Broadway Books, 1997), 248.

4. J. Bradford Robinson, "Scat Singing," in *The New Grove Dictionary of Jazz* (1988).

5. "Satchmo!" *New Orleans Online* [Web site] (New Orleans Tourism Marketing Corporation, 1998); available from <http://neworleansonline.com/sno9.htm>; accessed 28 Feb. 1998.

6. Bergreen, 372-76.

Bibliography

Armstrong, Louis. "Authentic American Genius."
Interview by Richard Meryman. *Life,* 15 April
1966, 92-102.

_____. Backstage Instructions to Glaser. April
1957. Handwritten note. Accessions 1997-26.
Louis Armstrong Archives, Rosenthal Library,
Queens College CUNY, Flushing, N.Y.

_____. "Louis Armstrong and the Jewish Family in
New Orleans." Unpublished manuscript, 31 March
1969. Louis Armstrong Archives, Rosenthal
Library, Queens College CUNY, Flushing, N.Y.

_____. *Town Hall Concert Plus.* RCA INTS 5070,
1957.

Bergreen, Laurence. *Louis Armstrong: An Extravagant
Life.* New York: Broadway Books, 1997.

Bogle, Donald. "Louis Armstrong: The Films." In *Louis
Armstrong: A Cultural Legacy,* ed. Marc H.
Miller, 147-79. Seattle: University of
Washington Press and Queens Museum of Art, 1994.

Collier, James Lincoln. *Jazz: The American Theme
Song.* New York: Oxford University Press, 1993.

_____. *Louis Armstrong, an American Genius.* New
York: Oxford University Press, 1983.

Crawford, Richard. Foreword to *The Jazz Tradition,*
by Martin Williams. New York: Oxford
University Press, 1993.

Davis, Miles, and Quincy Troupe. *Miles: The
Autobiography.* New York: Simon & Schuster,
1989.

Frederick, R. D., ed. "Chicago; Early 1920s."
Wolverine Antique Music Society [Web site].
Available from <http://www.shellac.org/wams/
wchicag1.html>. Accessed 26 February 1998.

Writer
includes *all*
sources she
consulted,
not just those
she cited in
the body of
her paper.

34 CSE Documentation Styles

The Council of Science Editors (CSE), formerly known as the Council of Biology Editors (CBE), endorses two documentation styles in the sixth edition of *Scientific Style and Format: The CBE Manual for Authors, Editors, and Publishers* (New York: Cambridge University Press, 1994):

- **A name-year style** that includes the last name of the author and year of publication in the text. (This system resembles APA style; *for APA style, see pp. 243–72.*)
- **A number style** that includes a superscript number ([1]) in the text and a list of references in citation sequence. (This system is distinctive to the natural and applied sciences.)

These two styles cannot be mixed within a paper. Consult your instructor for the preferred style, and use it consistently.

34a CSE name-year style

CSE name-year style: In-text citations.   Include the source's author, the publication date, and if you are citing a particular passage, the page number(s).

> According to Gleason (1993), a woman loses 35% of cortical bone and 50% of trabecular bone during her lifetime.

> Osteoporosis has been defined as "a disease characterized by low bone mass, micro-architectural deterioration of bone tissue, leading to enhanced bone fragility and a consequent increase in fracture risk" (Johnston 1996, p 30S).

Note: When a page number is cited, no period follows the *p*.

CSE name-year style: List of references.   Every source cited in your paper must correspond to an entry in your list of references, which should be prepared according to the guidelines in the box on page 297.

1. Begin the list on a new page after your text but before any appendixes, tables, and figures.
2. Use the centered title "References."
3. Include only references that are cited in your paper.
4. Indent all lines except the first in each entry.
5. Arrange the entries alphabetically by author's last name.
6. Do not underline or italicize titles.
7. Capitalize only the first word and proper nouns in titles.

Books Include the author(s), last name first; publication year; title; place and publisher; and number of pages.

1. One author:

Bailey C. 1991. The new fit or fat. Boston: Houghton
Mifflin. 167 p.

2. Two or more authors:

Begon M, Harper JL, Townsend CR. 1990. Ecology:
Individuals, populations, and communities. 2nd
ed. Boston: Blackwell. 945 p.

3. Selection in an edited book:

Bohus B, Koolhaas JM. 1993. Psychoimmunology of
social factors in rodents and other subprimate
vertebrates. In: Ader R, Felten DL, Cohen N,
editors. Psychoneuroimmunology. San Diego (CA):
Academic Pr. p 807-30.

4. Online book:

Kohn LT, Corrigan JM, Donaldson MS. 2000. To err is
human: building a safer health system [online
book]. Washington, DC: National Academy Pr.

312 p. Available from: National Academy Pr at
http://www.nap.edu/books/0309068371/html.
Accessed 2000 Jul 6.

5. Organization as author:

[NIH] National Institutes of Health. 1993. Clinical
trials supported by the National Eye Institute:
celebrating vision research. Bethesda (MD): US
Dept. of Health and Human Services. 112 p.

6. Book with editor(s):

Wilder E, editor. 1988. Obstetric and gynecologic
physical therapy. New York: Churchill
Livingstone. 225 p.

Periodicals　When listing periodical articles, include the following information: author(s); year; title of article; title of journal; number of the volume and if needed, of the issue; page numbers.

Note: Up to ten authors can be listed by name; periodical titles are abbreviated; an issue number is needed only when a journal is not paginated by volume; year, month, and day are listed for magazines.

7. Article in a journal paginated by volume:

Devine A, Prince RL, Bell R. 1996. Nutritional effect
of calcium supplementation by skim milk powder or
calcium tablets on total nutrient intake in
postmenopausal women. Am J Clin Nutr 64: 731-7.

8. Article in a journal paginated by issue:

Hummel-Berry K. 1990. Obstetric low back pain, a
comprehensive review, part 2: evaluation and
treatment. J Ob Gyn PT 14(2):9-11.

9. Article available online:

Krieger D, Onodipe S, Charles PJ, Sclabassi RJ. 1998.
Real time signal processing in the clinical
setting. Ann Biomed Engn 26(3):462-72. Available

from: Online Journal Publishing Service of the
American Institute of Physics via the INTERNET.
Accessed 2000 Jul 6.

10. Article in a supplement to a journal:

Seeman E, Tsalamandris C, Bass S, Pearce G. 1995.
Present and future of osteoporosis therapy. Bone
17(2 Suppl):23S-29S.

11. Article in a magazine:

Sternfeld P. 1997 Jan 1. Physical activity and
pregnancy outcome review and recommendations.
Sports Med:33-47.

34b CSE number style

CSE number style: In-text citations. To cite a source, insert a
superscript number immediately after the relevant name, word, or
phrase.

As a group, American women over 45 years of age
sustain approximately 1 million fractures each year,
70% of which are due to osteoporosis.[1]

That number now belongs to that source, and it should be used if you
refer to that source again later in your paper.

A BMD value more than 1 SD but less than 2.5 SD below
the young adult mean is considered as osteopenia,[4]
while osteoporosis is defined as a BMD 2.5 SD below
the young adult mean.[1]

You can credit more than one source at a time by referring to each
source's number. If the numbers are not in sequence, separate them
with a comma.

According to studies by Yomo,[2] Paleg,[3] and others,[1,4]
barley seed embryos produce a substance which
stimulates the release of hydrolytic enzymes.

If the numbers are in sequence, separate them with a hyphen.

As several others[1-4] have documented, GA has a RNA-
enhancing effect.

CSE number style: List of references.   Every source cited in
your paper must correspond to an entry in your list of references,
which should be prepared according to the following guidelines:

GUIDELINES for the CSE LIST of REFERENCES: NUMBER STYLE

1. Assign numbers to the sources cited in your paper, in the order in which you cite them.
2. In the list of references (titled "References"), list sources in the numerical order of their citation, not in alphabetical order.
3. Align the second and subsequent lines of the entry with the first word of the first line, not with the number.
4. Single-space within each entry, and double-space between entries.
5. Do not underline or italicize titles.
6. Capitalize only the first word and proper nouns in titles.

Books and Reports

1. One author:

1. Bailey C. The new fit or fat. Boston: Houghton
   Mifflin; 1991. 167 p.

2. Two or more authors: Up to ten authors can be individually listed; if there are more than ten, use the first author's name with the phrase *and others*.

2. Begon M, Harper JL, Townsend CR. Ecology:
   Individuals, populations, and communities. 2nd ed.
   Boston: Blackwell; 1990. 945 p.

3. Organization as author:

> 3. National Institutes of Health. Clinical trials
>   supported by the National Eye Institute:
>   celebrating vision research. Bethesda (MD):
>   US Dept. of Health and Human Services;
>   1993. 112 p.

4. Chapter in a book: Note that the author of the chapter and the book are the same. Consult #6 below when the authors are not the same person.

> 4. Castro J. The American way of health: how medicine
>   is changing and what it means to you. Boston:
>   Little, Brown; 1994. Chapter 9, Why doctors,
>   hospitals, and drugs cost so much; p 131-53.

5. Book with editor(s):

> 5. Ader R, Felten DL, Cohen N, editors.
>   Psychoneuroimmunology. San Diego (CA):
>   Academic Pr; 1993. 1218 p.

6. Selection in an edited book:

> 6. Bohus B, Koolhaas JM. Psychoimmunology of
>   social factors in rodents and other subprimate
>   vertebrates. In: Ader R, Felten DL, Cohen N,
>   editors. Psychoneuroimmunology. San Diego (CA):
>   Academic Pr; 1993. p 807-30.

7. Technical report or government document: For purposes of identification, include the name of the sponsoring organization or agency as well as any report or contract number.

> 7. Gleeson P. Osteoporosis. Rockville (MD): Public
>   Health Service of US Dept. of Health and Human
>   Services; 1993 Mar. Agency for Health Care Policy
>   Research [AHCPR] Publication nr 92-0038. 27 p.

Periodicals

8. Article in a journal paginated by volume: There is no need to designate issue number and month for journals paginated by yearly volume rather than issue. Note that titles of journals are abbreviated.

```
8. Devine A, Prince RL, Bell R. Nutritional effect
   of calcium supplementation by skim milk powder
   or calcium tablets on total nutrient intake in
   postmenopausal women. Am J Clin Nutr 1996;
   64:731-7.
```

9. Article in a journal or supplement paginated by issue: Include the year, the month, the volume number, and the issue number (in parentheses). Be sure to indicate when the article is in a supplement rather than in the issue itself. Note that semicolons are used to separate the month from the volume number.

```
9. Hummel-Berry K. Obstetric low back pain, a
   comprehensive review, part 2: evaluation and
   treatment. J Ob Gyn PT 1990 Jun;14(2):9-11.

10. Seeman E, Tsalamandris C, Bass S, Pearce G.
    Present and future of osteoporosis therapy. Bone
    1995 Aug;17(2 Suppl):23S-29S.
```

10. Article in a magazine or newspaper: Instead of issue and volume number, indicate the year, month, and day of publication. For newspapers, identify the section before the page number: *NY Times 2000 Jul 9;Sect C:2.*

```
11. Sternfeld P. Physical activity and pregnancy
    outcome review and recommendations. Sports Med
    1997 Jan 1:33-47.
```

Online Sources   The *CSE Manual* offers only general guidelines for citing online sources. In addition to the information that is normally required, it recommends adding the following data: type of document, availability information, and date of access.

11. Online journal article:

12. Krieger D, Onodipe S, Charles PJ, Sclabassi RJ.
    Real time signal processing in the clinical
    setting. Ann Biomed Engn 1998;26(3):462-72.
    Available from: Online Journal Publishing Service
    of the American Institute of Physics via the
    INTERNET. Accessed 2000 Jul 6.

12. Online book:

13. Kohn LT, Corrigan JM, Donaldson MS. To err is
    human: building a safer health system [online
    book]. Washington, DC: National Academy Pr; 2000.
    Available from: National Academy Pr at http://www.
    nap.edu/books/0309068371/html. Accessed 2000 Jul 6.

13. Online database or Web site:

14. National Osteoporosis Foundation. Osteoporosis and
    related bone diseases--national resource center
    [www site]. Sponsored by National Institutes of
    Health [NIH] at http://www.osteo.org/osteo.html.
    Accessed 2000 Jul 6.

SAMPLE REFERENCE LIST: CSE NUMBER SYSTEM

References

1. American Association of Clinical Endocrinologists.
   Clinical practice guidelines for the prevention and
   treatment of postmenopausal osteoporosis. J Fla Med
   Assoc 1991;83:552-66.

2. Johnston CC. Development of clinical practice
   guidelines for prevention and treatment of
   osteoporosis. Calci Tiss Int 1996;59(1 Suppl):30S-33S.

(continued)

SAMPLE REFERENCE LIST:
CSE NUMBER SYSTEM *(continued)*

3. Caldwell JR. Epidemiologic and economic considerations of osteoporosis. J Fla Med Assoc 1996;83:548-51.

4. Seeman E, Tsalamandris C, Bass S, Pearce G. Present and future of osteoporosis therapy. Bone 1995 Aug;17(2 Suppl):23S-29S.

5. Roberts MM. Osteoporosis: update on prevention and treatment [lecture handout]. Pennsylvania Physical Therapy Assn [PPTA] Conference. 1997 Oct. Harrisburg.

6. Gleeson P. Osteoporosis. Rockville (MD): Public Health Service of US Dept. of Health and Human Services; 1993 Mar. AHCPR Publication nr 92-0038. 27 p.

35 Columbia Online Style (COS)

The Internet has transformed research and, at the same time, has increased the challenge of source documentation. Janice Walker and Todd Taylor have published *The Columbia Guide to Online Style* (New York: Columbia University Press, 1998) to address online documentation issues. Because Columbia Online Style (COS) is designed to supplement already established types of documentation (such as MLA, APA, *Chicago,* and CSE), it requires certain pieces of information but does not prescribe their format.

35a Information required by COS

COS requires the inclusion of as many of the following pieces of information as are applicable and available:

- Author's name
- Title of the particular piece, article, or file

FAQs on COS

For updates and more information about Columbia Online Style (COS), check out the online version of the *Columbia Guide to Online Style* at <http://www.columbia.edu/cu/cup/cgos/update.html>.

- Title of the complete work
- Publication data for a print version
- Publication data for the online version
- Date of last update and date of access
- Electronic address, usually the uniform resource locator (URL)

The specific form and punctuation of these pieces of information vary according to the documentation style that you are using.

35b COS and common documentation styles

The examples that follow show how COS works with the MLA, APA, *Chicago,* and CSE documentation styles that are presented in detail elsewhere in this book.

1. COS and MLA documentation style

In-text citation.   If an author's real name is unavailable, use the screen name or an abbreviated version of the document's title. Never put a URL in an in-text citation.

```
One person responded that SNKI was "due for a swift
lift" (gravytrain2030).
```

Works-cited list.   As the following examples illustrate, COS entries in a works-cited list differ from MLA style in the following ways:

- COS does not use angle brackets around the URL.
- COS places the access date after the URL.
- COS puts the access date in parentheses.
- COS recommends using italics instead of underlining for titles. However, you should follow your instructor's preference.

Document from an online database:

Hardack, Richard. "'A Music Seeking Its Words':
Double-timing and Double Consciousness in Toni
Morrison's *Jazz*." *Callaloo* 18 (1995): 451-72.
Expanded Academic ASAP. InfoTrac. File #A18253789
(18 July 2000).

Material from a Web site:

"Biography." *Satchmo.Net: The Official Site for the
Louis Armstrong House and Archives.* 2000.
http://independentmusician.com/louis/biography
.php3 (21 June 2000).

Online periodical article:

Schmalfeldt, Janet. "On Keeping the Score." *Music
Theory Online* 4.2 (1998). http://smt.ucsb.edu/
mto/issues/to.98.4.2/mto.98.4.2.schmalfeldt.html
(2 May 1998).

Online posting to electronic mailing list or news group:

Burstein, Miriam. "Re: Feminist and Gender Criticism."
NASSR-L@WVNVM.WVNET.EDU (5 July 2000).

Personal e-mail:

Hoffman, Esther. "Re: My Louis Armstrong Paper."
Personal e-mail (14 Jan. 1999).

Note: Do not include personal e-mail addresses; use the descriptive
term *Personal e-mail* instead.

2. COS and APA documentation style

In-text citation. If you cannot find an author—either some individual(s) or an organization—use the title of the site or item on the
site, suitably abbreviated. To find the publication year for a Web site,
check the home page, especially the last few lines.

In the 1920s, many young black musicians from New
Orleans migrated north to Chicago ("Chicago," 1998).

List of references.   As the following examples illustrate, COS entries in the list of references differ from APA style in two main ways:

- COS uses access dates instead of retrieval statements.
- COS puts the access date at the end of the entry.

Online article from a database:

Waelde, T. W. (1996). International energy investment.

  Energy Law Journal, 17, 191-223. *Lexis-Nexis*

  database (10 May 2000).

Document in a Web site:

Fisher, B. (1995). U.S. global trade outlook: Germany.

  TradePort. http://tradeport.org/ts/ntdb/usgto/

  selcoun.html (7 Nov. 1997).

Note: Include the title of the site as well as the specific document. If there is no known author, begin with the title of the document.

Online book:

Suler, J. (2000). *The psychology of cyberspace* (Rev.

  July 2000). *http://www.rider.edu/users/*suler/

  psycyber/psycyber.html (22 Aug. 2000).

Note: The publication year is the same as the most recent update, and the update information goes in parentheses after the title. For online books published previously in print, provide the print publication information before the electronic information.

3. COS and *Chicago* style.

As the examples in this section illustrate, COS format differs from *Chicago* style in the following ways:

- COS puts the access date in parentheses.
- COS does not use availability statements, bracketed descriptions, or angle brackets around URLs.

The COS examples in this section are endnotes, but you can easily turn an endnote into an entry for a bibliography. Here is an example:

Document in a Web site:

ENDNOTE

  1. Bruce Boyd Raeburn, "An Introduction to New Orleans Jazz," *William Ransom Hogan Archive of New Orleans Jazz* (30 May 2000), http://www.tulane.edu/ ~lmiller/BeginnersIntro.html (21 June 2000).

BIBLIOGRAPHY ENTRY

Raeburn, Bruce Boyd. "An Introduction to New Orleans Jazz." *William Ransom Hogan Archive of New Orleans Jazz* (30 May 2000). http://www.tulane .edu/~1miller/BeginnersIntro.html (21 June 2000).

Note: If no author is listed, begin with the document's title.

Document from an online service or a database:
2. Richard Hardack, "'A Music Seeking Its Words': Double-timing and Double Consciousness in Toni Morrison's *Jazz*," *Callaloo* 18 (1995): 451-72. *Expanded Academic ASAP, InfoTrac,* File #A18253789 (18 July 2000).

Online book:
3. Carl Sandburg, *Chicago Poems* (New York: Henry Holt, 1916). Aug. 1999, *Bartleby,* http://www.bartleby .com/165/index.html (14 June 2000).

Online periodical article:
4. Janet Schmalfeldt, "On Keeping the Score," *Music Theory Online* 4, no. 2 (1998), http://smt.ucsb .edu/mto/issues/mto.98.4.2/mto.98.4.2.schmalfeldt.html (2 May 1998).

Online posting:
12. Don Mopsick, "Favorite Jazz Quotes," (17 Mar. 2000), Big Band-Music Fans, http://www.remarq.com/ list/4755?nav+FIRST&rf+1&si+grou (17 June 2000).

Note: Use the subject line as the title, and include the date of the message when it differs from the access date.

4. COS and CSE name-year style. Although CSE endorses two documentation styles, you must use only one or the other in a paper. This section provides examples for using COS with the CSE name-year style. (*If you are using the CSE number style, see #5.*)

Document from an online service or database:

Krieger D, Onodipe S, Charles PJ, Sclabassi RJ. 1998. Real time signal processing in the clinical setting. Ann Biomed Engn 26:462-72. Online Journal Publishing Service of the American Institute of Physics. http://ojps .aip.org/abme (2000 Jul 6).

Document in a Web site:

National Osteoporosis Foundation. 2000. Osteoporosis
overview. Osteoporosis and Related Bone Diseases--
National Resource Center, National Institutes
of Health. http://www.osteo.org/osteo.html (2000
Jul 6).

Online posting:

Ghost. 2000 Jul 20. Broken bone--fifth metacarpal in
hand, msg 5. sci.med. http://www.deja.com/
group/sci.med (2000 Jul 22).

Note: If the author's real name is unknown, use the screen name.

5. COS and CSE number style.
Although CSE endorses two documentation styles, you must use only one or the other in a paper. This section provides examples for using COS with the CSE number style. (*If you are using the CSE name-year style, see #4.*)

Document from an online service or database:

1. Krieger D, Onodipe S, Charles PJ, Sclabassi RJ.
   Real time signal processing in the clinical setting.
   Ann Biomed Engn 1998;26:462-72. Online Journal
   Publishing Service of the American Institute of
   Physics. http://ojps.aip.org/abme (2000 Jul 6).

Document in a Web site:

2. National Osteoporosis Foundation. Osteoporosis
   overview. Osteoporosis and Related Bone Diseases:
   National Resource Center. Rev. June 2000.
   http://www.osteo.org/osteo.html (2000 Jul 6).

Online posting:

3. Ghost. Broken bone--fifth metacarpal in hand, msg
   5. 2000 Jul 20; sci.med. http://www.deja.com/group/
   sci.med (2000 Jul 22).

Note: If the author's real name is unknown, use the screen name.

We come to see ourselves differently
as we catch sight of our images in the
mirror of the machine.

—SHERRY TURKLE

Document
and Web Design

9 Document and Web Design

36. Document Design *313*
    a. Getting margins, spacing, type, and page numbers right *313*
    b. Thinking intentionally about design *314*
    c. Emphasizing text effectively *318*
    d. Organizing long papers with headings *318*
    e. Using visuals to clarify and explain a point *319*
    f. Integrating visuals into documents effectively *323*
    g. Designing brochures and newsletters *325*

37. Writing for the World Wide Web *328*
    a. Designing Web pages to hold interest *329*
    b. Designing a Web site with a unified look *331*
    c. Including your name and e-mail address on each page *332*
    d. Providing a navigation bar on each page *332*
    e. Using links to make connections *333*
    f. Using graphics that load quickly *333*
    g. Using peer feedback to revise your Web site *334*

One of the final tasks you will face as a writer is assembling your text in a format that enables your readers to "see" your ideas clearly. In this section, we discuss formatting and designing the academic paper and other documents. We also suggest ways to think about design when you are making your knowledge visible in nonprint forms, such as on the World Wide Web.

36 Document Design

Like writing decisions, design decisions must be purposeful to be effective. As you plan your document, consider your purpose for writing, as well as the needs of your audience. If you are writing an informative paper for a psychology class, ask your instructor—your primary audience—which format he or she prefers and then follow that format. If you are writing a newsletter intended to persuade the citizens of your town to support a community project, use design to draw attention to your most important points. Your goal is to enhance the content of your text, not just decorate it.

Whatever the purpose of your document, good design decisions should make it more understandable and informative.

36a Get the basics right: margins, spacing, type, and page numbers.

The way you format a document determines how your text appears on the page—and how it affects readers. Here are a few basic guidelines for formatting academic papers:

- **First page:** The first page of your paper is often different from the other pages. In a short paper, less than five pages, page 1 contains a header with your name, your professor's name, your course and section number, and the date. If your paper exceeds five pages, page 1 is usually a title page. (*For an example of a title page, see the first page of the student paper by Koehler, p. 261.*)

- **Type:** Select a common typeface, or **font,** such as Courier, Times, or Bookman, and choose a 10- or 12-point size. Typefaces such as Arial and Eras Book are sometimes used for headings because of their simplicity.

Many typefaces available on your computer are display fonts—Antique, Calligrapher, 𝕺𝕝𝕕 𝕰𝕟𝕘𝕝𝕚𝕤𝕙, and others—and should be used rarely, if ever, in papers, on the screen, or in presentations.

▪ **Margins:** Use one-inch margins on all four sides of your text.

▪ **Margin justification:** Line up, or **justify,** the lines of your document along the left margin but not along the right margin. This procedure gives you a "ragged-right" margin, with lines ending unevenly on the right side, and enables you to avoid odd spacing between words.

▪ **Line spacing:** Double-space your paper unless you are instructed to do otherwise.

▪ **Page numbers:** Page numbers typically appear in the upper right-hand corner of all pages after the first.

36b Think intentionally about design.

From straightforward academic papers to more elaborate documents such as reports, newsletters, or brochures, the same design principles apply.

1. Get to know your computer toolbar. The toolbars on your computer give you a range of options for editing, designing, and sharing your documents. There are a variety of toolbars available in the most widely used word-processing program, Microsoft Word; you can find them by looking at the pulldown menu under "View." You will not want to have more than three toolbars showing at any one time, however. Displaying more than three reduces your working screen area. In the following example, three toolbars are open: the standard, drawing, and reviewing toolbars. The standard toolbar allows

CHARTING the TERRITORY

Style Guides

The Modern Language Association (MLA) and the American Psychological Association (APA) have developed widely used guidelines for documentation and manuscript format. For more about the basic document styles recommended by MLA and by APA, see pages 204–28 and pages 245–58, respectively. For style guides in math, biology, chemistry, and other fields, see page 191.

you to choose different typefaces; bold, italic, or underlined type; numbered or bulleted lists; and so on. (*See p. 318 for more help with these design options.*) The drawing toolbar allows you to insert boxes, drawings, and clip art into your text; and the reviewing toolbar enables you to mark changes, add comments, and even send your document to a reader.

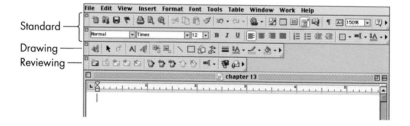

Standard

Drawing

Reviewing

If you are using a word-processing program other than Microsoft Word, take some time to learn the different toolbars and formatting options that are available to you.

2. Use design to organize information.   You can organize information visually and topically by grouping related items as closely together as your space allows. To help readers grasp the importance of each piece of information, use graphic accents such as boxes or indents, headings, spacing, and lists. For example, in this book headings help group information, and italics and bold type draw readers' attention to particular words and phrases. These variations in text appearance help readers scan, locate information, and dive in when they need to know more about a topic.

Decisions about typeface and type size can improve the readability of both print and online documents (or make them more difficult to read), as the following example illustrates:

AviationNow.com Insider—June 18
Headlines Direct from Paris Air Show

Updated News and Features from Global Aviation Event Available on AviationNow.com

New York, N.Y., June 19, 2001—*Aviation Week*'s AviationNow.com Insider—Daily Paris Extra newsletter announced the following headlines for June 18, 2001. The full text of the articles plus additional news items and features are available at AviationNow.com (www.AviationNow.com), a leading Internet portal serving the global aviation and aerospace industry. The Insider is written and produced onsite at the Paris Air Show by *Aviation Week*'s multinational team of editors and reporters.

The first lines are in 12-point type, large enough to set the heading apart but not so large that it overwhelms the rest of the text. After a space, the next two lines are in a 10-point font, in bold italic type. The spacing and italics differentiate these lines, helping readers see that they explain the heading above. After the date line, in bold type, the title *Aviation Week* is italicized because it is the name of a periodical publication. Finally, the URL for *AviationNow* is underlined, a visual cue that this is a link to another Web site.

In the following example, visual cues are used to bring items together into a group as well as to highlight their singularity. A heading in capital letters and 12-point type labels the group of headlines. Each headline then gets its own **bullet,** the ▪ symbol.

TOP STORIES
- Murder at Midnight
- Taxes and Congress
- Lightning Bugs: Unexpected Discovery
- Bird Brains: What Do They Tell Us about People

3. Use design elements consistently. In design, simplicity, contrast, and consistency matter. If you emphasize an item by putting it in italic or bold type or in color, or if you use a graphic accent such as a box to set it off, consider repeating this effect for similar items to give your document a unified look. Even a simple horizontal line can be a purposeful element in a long document when used consistently to help organize information.

For example, in the following text describing Washington State University, the headings appear in crimson, one of the university's colors, reminding readers that each item is another example of the high-quality education the university provides.

A world-class education. At Washington State University you can work side by side with nationally and internationally renowned scholars. Get hands-on experience in your field of study through internships, fieldwork, community service, and in-depth labs. Take part in faculty research–or even conduct your own.

- Ranked among the top research universities in America according to the Carnegie Foundation for the Advancement of Teaching.
- One of just two Northwest universities ranked among the top 50 public universities in America by . . .

One of the nation's top Honors Colleges. In the University's nationally ranked Honors College, you'll find yourself in small classes, engaging in one-on-one discussions with renowned professors. You'll take enriched courses . . .

A vibrant college town. Here you won't find smog or traffic jams. You will find a relaxed, friendly atmosphere with people who are happy to lend a . . .

Note: For the second item, the writer used gray shading, thereby calling even more attention to the Honors College.

4. Use restraint. If you use too many graphics, headings, bullets, boxes, or other elements in a document, you risk making it as "noisy" as a loud radio. Standard fonts have become standard because they are easy on the eye. Variations from these standard fonts jar the eye. Unusual typefaces are attention getting, but they lose their force when overused. Bold or italic type, underlining, or any other graphic effect should not continue for more than one sentence at a time.

Refrain from relying on bold and italics to emphasize ideas. Instead, use the structure of your text and your choice of words to let your readers know what is important. You should also be aware of certain conventions that govern the use of bold and italic type, especially in academic documents. Boldfaced words often signal that a glossary with key words and their definitions accompanies the text. Italics can be used instead of quotation marks to indicate that a word is being referred to as a word. They are also used for the titles of books and periodicals. (*See pp. 485–87.*)

36c Emphasize text by varying your type style and using lists.

1. Bold, *italics,* and <u>underlining.</u> You can emphasize a word or phrase in your text by selecting it and clicking on a button on your toolbar to make it **bold,** *italicized,* or <u>underlined</u>.

2. ALL CAPS/SMALL CAPS. In general you should avoid capitalizing entire words or phrases in your academic papers. This option should be used only for headlines in newsletters, brochures, and other nonacademic documents. The "Caps Lock" key on your keyboard allows you to type words or phrases in capital letters. You can change your text to small caps by choosing "Font" in the "Format" menu and then clicking next to "Small Caps" (a checkmark will appear in the box). To turn small caps off, click on the "Small Caps" box a second time to remove the checkmark.

3. Lists. Numbered or bulleted lists help you cluster ideas. Because they stand out from your text visually, lists help readers see that ideas are related. For example, you can use a numbered list to display steps in a sequence, present checklists, or suggest recommendations for action.

Format your text as a numbered or bulleted list by choosing the option you want from the standard toolbar. Use parallel structure in your list, introduce it with a complete sentence followed by a colon, and put a period at the end of each entry if the entries are complete sentences. If they are not complete sentences, no punctuation is necessary.

36d Organize long papers visually through the use of headings.

Headings interrupt the text in short papers. In longer papers, though, they help you organize complex information.

Effective headings are short, descriptive, and, like lists, consistent in emphasis and parallel in grammatical structure. All of your headings in a paper might be in the form of questions, declarative or imperative

Tips LEARNING in COLLEGE

Template Designs

Templates, preformatted styles, establish the structure and settings for a document and apply them automatically. Having a template can save you time when you need to design documents such as presentations, flyers, brochures, newsletters, announcements, memos, and reports. If you know you will need to produce a certain kind of document that requires a specific kind of formatting—such as a lab report—on a regular basis, you might want to create a template.

sentences, or phrases beginning with *-ing* verbs. Note, for example, that each heading in this chapter starts with a verb telling you what to do: *get, think, emphasize, organize, use,* and so on. This is parallel structure. *(For more on parallel structure, see Tab 10: Editing for Clarity, pp. 349–50.)*

Place and highlight headings consistently throughout your paper. For example, you might center all first-level headings—which are like the main points in an outline—and put them in bold type. If you have second-level headings—your supporting points—you might align them at the left margin and underline them.

First-Level Heading

<u>Second-Level Heading</u>

36e Use visuals to clarify and explain a point.

Used judiciously, visuals such as tables, charts, and graphs provide clarity. Effective visuals are used for a specific purpose, not for decoration, and each type of visual illustrates some kinds of material better than others. For example, compare the table on page 320 and the line graph on page 322. Both present similar types of data, but do both have the same effect on you? Does one strike you as clearer or more powerful than the other?

Make your visuals simple and clear. If a chart is overloaded with information, separate it into several charts instead.

Because the inclusion of visual elements in papers is more accepted in some fields than in others, you may want to ask your instructor for advice before including a visual in your paper.

1. Tables.   Tables are the easiest visuals to prepare. They are made up of rows and columns of cells; each cell presents an element of textual, numeric, or graphic information. Tables organize data for readers.

TEXTCONNEX

Preparing Tables

You can usually create and edit tables in your word-processing program. If you use Microsoft Word, for example, the program allows you to size columns proportionally to avoid distorting their contents and to make them fit your text. Under the "Table" pulldown menu, select "Insert," then click on "Table." You will see a dialogue box. Choose "Autofit to content" instead of "Fixed column width." As you create the table, the borders will automatically increase.

You can also create tables using database, spreadsheet, presentation, and Web-site-construction software.

Consider this example taken from the Web site of the Environmental Protection Agency:

TABLE 34. U.S. Emissions of Criteria Pollutants, 1989–1996 (million metric tons of gas)

SOURCE	1989	1990	1991	1992	1993	1994	1995	1996
Carbon monoxide	93.5	91.3	88.3	85.3	85.4	89.6	83.5	NA
Nitrogen oxides	21.1	20.9	20.6	20.7	21.1	21.5	19.7	NA
Nonmethane VOCs	21.7	21.4	20.8	20.3	20.5	21.1	20.7	NA

NA = not available.

Note: Data in this table are revised from the data contained in the previous EIA report, *Emissions of Greenhouse Gases in the United States 1995*, DOE/EIA-0573(95) (Washington, DC, October 1996).

Source: U.S. Environmental Protection Agency, Office of Air Quality Planning and Standards, *National Air Pollutant Emission Trends*, 1900–1995, EPA-454/R-96-007 (Research Triangle Park, NC, October 1996), pp. A-5, A-9, and A-16.

2. Bar graphs. Perhaps because they are relatively easy to prepare and to read, bar graphs are quite common. These graphs show relationships and highlight comparisons between two or more variables, such as the exchange rate of the German mark per U.S. dollar in different years (*see Figure 1 in Jennifer Koehler's paper, p. 265*). The following example compares the frequency of three kinds of activities during certain periods of the year.

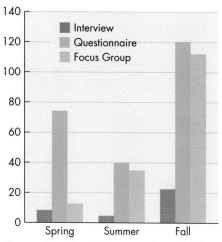

Figure 1.   Market research activities.

3. Pie charts.   Good for showing differences between parts in relation to a whole, pie charts are circles divided into segments, with each segment representing a piece of the whole. The segments must add up to approximately 100 percent of something, such as the countries where Germany imports and exports goods (*see Figure 2 in Koehler's paper, p. 267*). For another example, see the pie chart that follows:

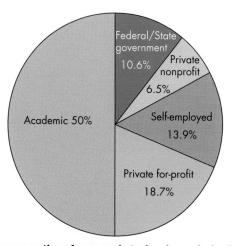

Figure 1.   Career paths of research-trained psychologists.
Source: American Psychological Association (APA) Web site at <http://www.apa.org/science/nonacad.html>.

4. Line graphs. Line graphs or charts are used to show changes over time or to show the relationship between two variables, such as U.S. emissions of nitrous oxide over a sixteen-year period:

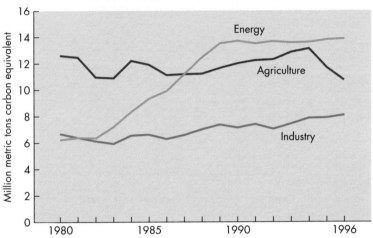

Figure ES5. U.S. Nitrous Oxide Emissions by Source, 1980–1996.
Source: Energy Information Administration, U.S. Department of Energy, *Emissions of Greenhouse Gases in the United States 1996*, Oct. 1997, <http://www.eia.doe.gov/oiaf/1605/gg97rpt/execsum.html#figes5>.

5. Diagrams. Used to show concepts or structures visually, diagrams are often included in scientific or technical writing. The following diagram, for example, shows the factors involved in the decision to commit a burglary.

Figure 1. Event model for a burglary.
Source: Adapted from Ronald V. Clarke and Derek B. Cornish, "Modeling Offenders' Decisions: A Framework for Research and Policy," *Crime and Justice*, vol. 6, ed. Michael Tonry and Norval Morris (Chicago: University of Chicago, 1985), p. 169.

Decision to commit burglary

Selected (Middle-Class) Area
Easily accessible; few police patrols; low-security housing; larger gardens

Rejected (Middle-Class) Area
Unfamiliar; distant; neighborhood watch; no public transport

Burgled Home
No one at home; especially affluent; detached; patio doors; bushes and other cover; corner site

Not Burgled
Nosy neighbors; burglar alarm; no rear access; visible from street; window locks; dog

6. Photographs and illustrations.   Photographs and illustrations can reinforce a point you are making in your text in ways that words cannot, showing readers what your subject actually looks like or how it has been affected or changed. For example, the illustration reproduced in Esther Hoffman's paper on Louis Armstrong and his manager (*see Tab 6: MLA Style Documentation, p. 239*), provides further evidence of the relationship Hoffman is describing. When you use photographs or illustrations, always credit your source, and be aware that most photographs and illustrations are protected by copyright. If you plan to use a photograph as part of a Web page, for example, you will usually need to obtain permission from the copyright holder.

7. Clip art.   Computer clip art, readily available on the World Wide Web and also in newer versions of word-processing software, should be used only when a piece of art will help clarify or reinforce your point. Do not use clip art like the examples that follow just to fill space or make your document "look nice."

36f   Integrate visuals into documents effectively.

If you decide to use a table, chart, diagram, or clip art, keep this general advice in mind:

1. **Number tables and other figures** consecutively throughout your paper, and label them appropriately: Table 1, Table 2, and so on. Do not abbreviate *Table*. *Figure* may be abbreviated as *Fig.*

Reporting Data

If you are writing a lab report or any other report for which you have gathered data, consider including graphic representations of your data in your final report. (*See Tab 3: Common Assignments across the Curriculum, pp. 113–18.*) Using a chart or graph to display the data lets you show rather than just tell your reader about your findings. The bar chart on page 321, for example, was created using the PowerPoint software program, which provides templates that allow you to create visual reports from "live" spreadsheets or databases.

To create a pie chart, just open a "blank presentation" in PowerPoint. A group of different slide layouts will appear. Click on the pie chart, and you will see a premade slide with numbers already in the chart. Replace those numbers with your own by deleting the text in the little spreadsheet that is displayed along with the pie chart and typing in your own numbers. Relabel the categories, and you have your own spreadsheet graphic. A simple print screen of the full slide then allows you to paste that graphic into your text.

2. **Refer to the visual element in your text** before it appears, placing the visual as close as possible to the text in which you state why you are including it. If your project contains many or complex tables or other visuals, however, you may want to group them in an appendix. Always refer to a visual by its label: for example, "See Figure 1."

3. **Give each visual a title and caption** that clearly explains what the visual shows. A visual with its caption should be clear without the discussion in the text, and the discussion of the visual in the text should be clear without the visual itself. For an example, see page 239.

4. **Include explanatory notes below the visuals,** and use the word *Note* followed by a colon to introduce explanations of the visual as a whole. If you want to explain a specific element within the visual, use a superscript *letter* (not a number) both after the specific element and before the note. This is essentially a footnote, but the explanation should appear directly beneath the graphic, not at the foot of the page or at the end of your paper. Do not use your word

processor's "Insert/Footnote" commands to create the footnote because the program will put the note in one of those two places.

5. **Credit sources for visuals.** If you use a visual element from a source, you need to credit the source. Use the word *Source,* followed by a colon and complete documentation of the source, including the author, title, publication information, and page number if applicable.

Note: The Modern Language Association (MLA) and the American Psychological Association (APA) provide guidelines for figure captions and crediting sources of visuals that differ from the previous guidelines. (*See Tab 6: MLA Documentation Style, p. 229, and Tab 7: APA Documentation Style, p. 260.*)

36g Design brochures and newsletters with an eye to purpose and audience.

If you are participating in a service learning program or an internship, you may have opportunities to design brochures and newsletters for wide distribution. You may also need to design brochures as part of your job, to promote your company or one of its products. To create an effective brochure or newsletter, you will need to integrate your skills in document design with what you have learned about purpose and audience.

Here are a few tips that will help you design effective brochures and newsletters, whatever your audience and purpose may be:

1. Before you begin, consider how your reader will gain access to and review the pages of the brochure or newsletter. How will it be mailed or distributed? What are the implications for the overall design?

2. Sketch the design in pencil before you immerse yourself in the high tech capacities of the computer. Use the computer to solve design problems, not to create them.

3. In making decisions about photographs, illustrations, type fonts, and the design in general, think about the overall image that should be conveyed about the organization sponsoring the brochure or newsletter.

4. If the organization has a logo, include it; if not, suggest designing one.

5. Create a template for the brochure or newsletter so that you can create future editions.

For example, notice how the brochure for the PSFS Building in Philadelphia, Pennsylvania, shown on page 327, purposefully connects the history and importance of an architectural landmark with the prestige of Loews Hotel, into which "the world's first Modernist skyscraper" has been renovated. The brochure has an informative and also a subtly persuasive purpose. Readers are meant to feel that by staying at the Loews Philadelphia Hotel they are participating in a great tradition. The front cover is divided in half, with a striking photo of the building on the left side and an account of its history on the right. The name of the hotel appears in white letters near the bottom of the page. The interior page places a vintage photo of the revered banking establishment next to an image of hotel comfort. On both pages, quotations running vertically beside the photographs reinforce the building's architectural significance.

The newsletter from the Harvard Medical School entitled, "Women's Health Watch," shown on page 328, has a much simpler design than the PSFS/Loews brochure. But in a similar way, the designer keeps in mind the purpose and audience, which are explicitly stated in the title and the headline below the title. The shaded area on the right lists the topics that are covered on the interior pages so that readers can get to the information they need quickly and easily. The Web address is prominently displayed in blue so that readers can find further information. The lead article, "Does Excess Vitamin A Cause Hip Fracture?" is simply designed in two columns, with the headline in bold type, subheadings in blue, a readable typeface, and a graphic strategically placed to break up the text and add visual interest. In all of these ways, the design supports the Harvard Medical School's purpose of helping the general public get reliable information about the latest advances in medical research.

The PSFS Building:
A 20th Century Masterpiece

As the world's first Modernist skyscraper, the landmark PSFS Building revolutionized the form and functionality of the urban landscape and is considered among the most significant buildings of the 20th century. The building was completed in 1932 as the bold new headquarters for the Philadelphia Saving Fund Society, the first savings bank in the United States, established in 1813 at an earlier location.

The PSFS Building was a dramatic, visual departure from the ornate structures that preceded it. The skyscraper represents the single moment when classical expression first gave way to Modernist design on a grand architectural scale.

Erected 36-stories high, the PSFS Building was developed as a technological marvel and was the world's second skyscraper with central air conditioning, which the public dubbed "weather in a box."

Architects George Howe and William Lescaze were meticulous in every detail, lavishing on the building an abundance of marble, polished granite and rare woods. Art Deco clocks by Cartier adorn the elevator lobbies on each floor and three larger and more dramatic Cartiers adorn the former banking floor, the escalator entrance and the 12th Street elevator lobby.

The building's materials and features would be virtually impossible to afford today. The cost in 1932 of $8 million was a staggering sum for the Depression Era. The building contains 625,000 square feet of space within 36 stories, two basements and three partial mezzanine floors. The street level façade is a polished granite base, which supports the dramatic expanse of polished, gray granite and clear glass of the banking hall exterior.

The PSFS Building is one of the top architectural treasures of the 20th century.

"It (the PSFS Building) is a superbly crafted object, refined in its every detail... PSFS is the rarest of phenomenon in our time, a working monument." – Robert M. Stern, 1976

An Architectural Icon Meets A Legend In Hospitality

Loews Hotels is proud to have restored the landmark PSFS Building to its original grandeur, while transforming it into a hotel that people from all over the world will experience and enjoy.

The new design, created by Daroff Design and the architectural firm of Bower Lewis Thrower, takes full advantage of the building's historical features. The three-story former banking room has been preserved as Millennium Hall, a dramatic banquet space. The historic, rooftop boardroom has been converted to a spectacular setting for catered events. Today, the Loews Philadelphia Hotel is a 583-room luxury convention property housed in one of the most beautiful and historic buildings in the country.

The 33rd Floor features the Howe and Lescaze meeting rooms, named for the PSFS architects, and the Roberts Boardroom, named for the savings bank's first depositor in 1813, an African American laborer named Curtis Roberts. The Terrace, a 1,334 square-foot, glass solarium offers sweeping views of the city, up to a visibility of 20 miles.

The PSFS Building, as the Loews Philadelphia Hotel stands as a testament to the enduring value of the world's great landmark buildings.

L O E W S
PHILADELPHIA HOTEL
P E N N S Y L V A N I A

327

HARVARD

Women's Health Watch

INFORMATION FOR ENLIGHTENED CHOICES FROM HARVARD MEDICAL SCHOOL

Does Excess Vitamin A Cause Hip Fracture?

Hip fracture is one of the most dreaded risks of aging. More than 350,000 hip fractures occur annually in the United States, mostly in women over 65. Half of these women never regain the ability to live independently. About 20% die within a year. Many others suffer chronic pain, anxiety, and depression. The consequences are so grim that many older women contacted in surveys on this subject say they'd rather die than suffer a hip fracture that would send them to a nursing home.

Current recommendations on reducing fracture risk advise women to exercise, make sure they get enough calcium and vitamin D, and, if necessary, take medications that help preserve bone strength. Some women also learn strategies for preventing falls or take classes such as tai chi to improve their balance. Now, a new study suggests that we should also pay attention to vitamin A. At high levels, this essential nutrient may actually increase our risk for hip fracture.

NEW STUDY FINDS LINK

Researchers at Harvard Medical School reported in the Jan. 2, 2002, *Journal of the American Medical Association* on the relationship between postmenopausal hip fracture and vitamin A intake. The data came from 72,337 women enrolled in the Nurses' Health Study. The women were divided into five groups according to their average daily consumption, over an 18-year period, of vitamin A from food and supplements.

Researchers then correlated vitamin A intake with hip fracture incidence. They found that women with the highest intake—3,000 micrograms (mcg) or more per day—had a 48% greater risk for hip fractures, compared to women with the lowest intake (1,250 mcg or less per day).

The increased risk was mainly due to *retinol*, a particular form of vitamin A. In fact, women consuming 2,000 mcg of retinol or more daily had a hip fracture risk almost *double* that of women whose daily intake was under 500 mcg. In contrast, consuming high levels of *beta-carotene*, also a source of vitamin A, had a negligible impact on hip fracture risk. Participants taking hormone replacement therapy (HRT) were somewhat protected from the effects of too much retinol.

ABOUT VITAMIN A

Vitamin A is important for vision, the immune system, and the growth of bone, hair, and skin cells. Retinol, also called "preformed vitamin A," is the active form of the vitamin. It occurs naturally in animal products such as eggs, whole milk, cheese, and liver. Other food sources of vitamin A are *carotenoids*, which are found in green leafy vegetables and in dark yellow or orange fruits and vegetables. The body can convert these plant compounds to retinol. Beta-carotene is the most plentiful carotenoid and it converts most efficiently. Even so, you need about 12 times as much beta-carotene as retinol to get the same amount of vitamin A.

Because vitamin A is lost in the process of removing fat, many fat-free dairy products are fortified with retinol. So are some margarines and ready-to-eat cereals. The vitamin A in supplements and multivitamins may come from retinol, beta-carotene, or both. Beta-carotene is preferable because it's also an antioxidant.

Although vitamin A deficiency is a leading cause of blindness in developing countries, it's not a major problem in the United States. The main concern here is excess vitamin A, which can produce birth defects, liver damage, and reduced bone mineral density (BMD).

15% of women age 50 will suffer a hip fracture before age 80.

Source: Genant, D., et al. Annals int. Med. 1962; 117: 1016-37

Volume IX Number 7
March 2002

In Brief
HRT and Dry Eyes
page 3

❖

Mental Health
When Anxiety Is Overwhelming
pages 4–6

❖

Research Brief
The Genetics of Lactose Intolerance
page 6

❖

Massage
Massage Is More Than an Indulgence
page 7

❖

By the Way, Doctor
Should I Still Get Mammograms?
page 8

www.health.harvard.edu

---

37 Writing for the World Wide Web

The best known part of the Internet, the World Wide Web is a gigantic intertwined network of information. It is also a publishing network. A personal Web page gives you a space for presenting yourself,

TEXTCONNEX

Understanding Web Jargon

Browser: Software that allows you to view and access material on the World Wide Web. When you identify a site you want to see on the Web by typing in a URL (see below), your browser (Netscape Navigator or Microsoft Internet Explorer, for example) tells a distant computer (a **server**) to send that site to you.

Home page: The opening page of a Web site. A home page typically includes general information about the site as well as links to various parts of it.

HTML/XML: Hypertext markup language/eXtensible markup language. These languages tag or code text so that your browser can rebuild a document from the compressed files that are sent through the Internet. When your browser retrieves a page, you end up with an "original copy" of the document, usually in a matter of seconds. Not too long ago, writers who wanted to publish their ideas on the World Wide Web had to learn to write in HTML or XML code and to stay current with new versions of these codes as they evolved, but now programs such as FrontPage, PageMill, and Netscape Composer provide a WYSIWYG (what you see is what you get) interface for creating Web pages.

Protocol: A set of rules controlling data exchange between computers. **HTTP** (hypertext transfer protocol) is a way of breaking down and then reconstructing a document when it is sent over the Internet. The protocol uses a set of "tags" or codes (such as those used in HTML or XML) to transfer and receive data.

URL: Uniform resource locator or Web address. When you type or paste a URL into your Web browser, you are sending a request through your browser to another computer, asking it to transfer data to your computer.

your interests, and your ideas. Project Web sites for class assignments are a good way to work with others to share the knowledge you have produced collaboratively.

37a Design Web pages to hold interest.

Visitors to a Web page decide in ten to twenty seconds whether to stay. On good Web sites, you will find such easy-to-follow links as "what you'll find here," FAQs (frequently asked questions), or "list of those involved." Readers do not want lengthy text explanations. Instead,

Designing a Web Site Collaboratively

If you are asked to create a Web site as part of a class assignment, try to make arrangements to work with a partner or a small group. The kind of interaction involved in writing the content and designing the site will provide you with beneficial language support. Periodically, you can invite peers to check over the writing you contribute and make suggestions. At the same time, you will be able to provide the project with the benefit of your unique multicultural viewpoint.

they want to find the button they are looking for within a few seconds. For example, notice how easy it is for readers to find what they need on the *Ask Jeeves* Web site:

As you surf the Internet, observe how the different Web sites you visit address various audiences and have different purposes. As you design your own Web page, ask yourself the following questions: Who is my audience? What is my purpose in publishing on the Web? Remember that if your visitors do not find your site engaging, they can easily hop to another one.

37b Design a Web site with a unified look.

Because the Web is a visual medium, readers appreciate a site with a unified look. "Sets" or "themes" are readily available at free graphics sites offering banners, navigation buttons, and other design elements. Design your home page to complement your other pages, or your readers may lose track of where they are in the site—as well as their interest in staying.

- Consider including a site map, a Web page that serves as a table of contents for your entire site.
- Select elements such as buttons, signs, animations, sounds, and backgrounds with a consistent design.
- Use colors that provide adequate contrast and fonts that make text easy to read. Pages that are too busy are not visually compelling.

For example, here is the table of contents and site navigation page from the Web site of Habitat for Humanity International:

37c Include your name, a date, and your e-mail address on each page.

Remember that people will not always enter your Web site through the front door. Therefore, your name should appear on each page in your Web site. Every time you change the content of your Web page, change the date as well so that your visitors will know you have updated it. Include an e-mail link so visitors can contact you with questions or comments.

On the following Web site for Janice Walker, a professor at Georgia Southern University, note the name of the site and her e-mail address in the top left-hand corner of the page. This information appears in the same place on each page of her site.

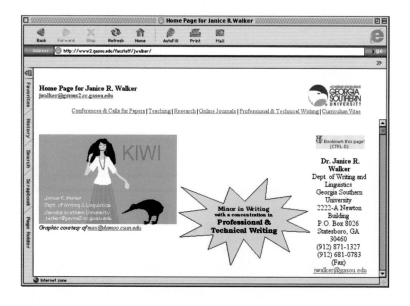

37d Provide a navigation bar on each page.

A **navigation bar** can be a simple line of links that you copy and paste at the top or bottom of each page. Provide a navigation bar on each page to make it easy for visitors to move from the site's home page to other pages. For example, on the following Web page from ASU West, visitors can choose from seven links in the navigation bar under the title.

37e Use links to make connections.

When you move your mouse over a Web page link, the arrow turns into a pointing index finger to indicate that clicking on the link will take you to a new location on the Web. These "hot links" are anchored to specific text that, when activated, opens another Web page.

Avoid using the command "Click here" on your Web site. Instead, make links part of your text. Web writers use these hypertextual links to connect their interests with those of others and to provide extra sources of information. Hypertext links also give readers and writers ways to create their own reading and writing paths.

37f Use graphics that load quickly.

Be considerate of viewers who have older computers that can't handle huge graphics files. Minimize the size of your images so that they will load faster.

TEXTCONNEX

JPEG and GIF

When adding graphics to your Web site, you should use photographs saved in JPEG (pronounced "*jay-peg*") format, which stands for Joint Photographic Experts Group. The file extension is .jpg or .jpeg. Use clip art saved as GIF files (Graphics Interchange Format, pronounced like *gift* without the *t*.)

For links to sites that provide more Web design tips, visit <www.mhhe.com/maimon/writing_for_the_web>.

Even though a picture may be worth a thousand words, your Web site should not depend on graphics alone to make its message clear and interesting. Graphics should be used to reinforce your message. For example, the designers of the Library of Congress Web site use graphics to help visitors navigate the site:

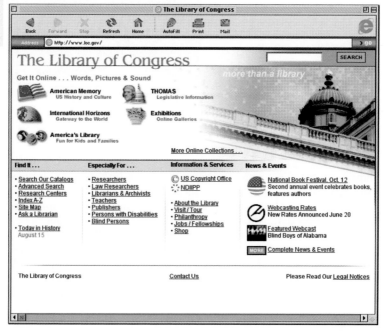

37g Use peer feedback to revise your Web site.

Before publishing your site on the Web, proofread your text carefully, and ask a couple of friends to look at your site and share their

TEXTCONNEX

Web Resources for Site Design and Construction

- *www.teach.science's Surf and Master the Web: Writing Web Pages*
  <http://www2.ncsu.edu/ncsu/pams/science_house/workshops/web/writing.html>
- *Web Guide: Designing a Web Page*
  <http://people.depauw.edu/djp/webguide/designwebpage.html>
- *Designing Accessible Web Pages*—information about creating Web pages for people with disabilities <http://nadc.ucla.edu/dawpi.htm>

responses with you. It is understood that Web pages are dynamic and will change over time, so usually it is best to avoid using "under construction" signs on your Web site. When you publish on the Web, you offer your work to be read by anyone in the world. Make sure your site reflects favorably on your abilities.

I . . . believe that words *can* help us move or keep us paralyzed, and that our choices of language and verbal tone have something—a great deal—to do with how we live our lives and whom we end up speaking with and hearing. . . .

—ADRIENNE RICH

Editing for Clarity

10 Editing for Clarity

38. Wordy Sentences 340
    a. Eliminating redundancies 340
    b. Avoiding unnecessary repetition 340
    c. Finding concise alternatives 341
    d. Making sentences straightforward 341
    e. Reducing clauses and phrases 342

39. Missing Words 342
    a. Adding words needed in compound structures 342
    b. Including *that* when it is needed for clarity 343
    c. Making comparisons clear 343
    d. Adding articles (*a, an, the*) where necessary 344

40. Mixed Constructions 344
    a. Untangling mixed-up sentence structures 344
    b. Making sure predicates fit subjects 345

41. Confusing Shifts 347
    a. Making your point of view consistent in person and number 347
    b. Keeping verb tenses consistent 347
    c. Avoiding unnecessary shifts in mood and voice 348

42. Faulty Parallelism 349
    a. Making items in a series parallel 349
    b. Making paired ideas parallel 350

43. Misplaced and Dangling Modifiers 350
    a. Putting modifiers close to the words they modify 350
    b. Clarifying ambiguous modifiers 351
    c. Moving disruptive modifiers 351
    d. Avoiding split infinitives 352
    e. Fixing dangling modifiers 352

44. Coordination and Subordination 353
    a. Combining short, choppy sentences 354
    b. Using subordination for ideas of unequal importance 355
    c. Avoiding subordination of major ideas 355
    d. Avoiding excessive subordination 355

45. Sentence Variety 356
    a. Varying sentence openings 356
    b. Varying sentence length and structure 356
    c. Including cumulative and periodic sentences 357
    d. Trying inversions, rhetorical questions, or exclamations 358

46. Active Verbs 359
    a. Considering alternatives to some *be* verbs 359
    b. Preferring the active voice 360

47. Appropriate
    Language *361*
    a. Avoiding slang,
       regionalisms, and
       nonstandard
       English *361*
    b. Using an appropriate
       level of formality *362*
    c. Avoiding jargon *362*
    d. Avoiding euphemisms
       and doublespeak *363*
    e. Removing biased or sexist
       language *364*

48. Exact Language *367*
    a. Choosing words
       with suitable
       connotations *368*

    b. Including specific,
       concrete words *368*
    c. Using standard
       idioms *369*
    d. Avoiding clichés *369*
    e. Creating suitable
       figures of speech *369*
    f. Avoiding misuse of
       words *371*

49. The Dictionary and the
    Thesaurus *371*
    a. Using the dictionary
       as a habit *371*
    b. Consulting a
       thesaurus *375*

50. Glossary of Usage *375*

Like drafting and revising, editing can be a creative process, especially when your goal is to make your sentences both clear and forceful. Sometimes being creative means focusing on the sentence as a whole and asking whether the parts fit together well. At other times, it means assessing your word choice. To start editing, ask yourself the following questions:

- Are all sentences concise and straightforward? Are any overloaded in ways that make them difficult to read and understand? (*See Chapter 38, Wordy Sentences, p. 340.*)

- Are all sentences complete? Are any necessary words missing from compounds or comparisons? (*See Chapter 39, Missing Words, p. 342.*)

- Do the parts of each sentence fit together in a way that makes sense, or is the sentence mixed up? (*See Chapter 40, Mixed Constructions, p. 344.*)

- Do the key parts of each sentence fit together well, or are there disturbing mismatches in person, number, or grammatical structure? (*See Chapters 41 and 42, Confusing Shifts, p. 347, and Faulty Parallelism, p. 349.*)

- Are the parts of each sentence clearly and closely connected, or are some modifiers separated from what they modify? (*See Chapter 43, Misplaced and Dangling Modifiers, p. 350.*)

- Are the focus, flow, and voice of the sentences clear, or do some sentences have ineffective coordination, subordination, sentence patterning, and verb choice? (*See Chapters 44–46, Coordination and Subordination, p. 353, Sentence Variety, p. 356, and Active Verbs, p. 359.*)

▪ Are the words used in each sentence appropriate and accurate, or are some biased, overspecialized, vague, or clichéd? (*See Chapters 47–50, Appropriate Language, p. 361, Exact Language, p. 367, The Dictionary and the Thesaurus, p. 371, and Glossary of Usage, p. 375.*)

38 Wordy Sentences

A sentence does not have to be short and simple to be concise. Instead, every word in it must count, especially when the subject matter is complex or technical.

38a Eliminate redundancies.

Redundancies are meaningless repetitions that result in wordiness. Be on the lookout for such commonplace redundancies as *first and foremost, full and complete, final result, past history, mix together, join together, round in shape, blue in color,* and *refer back.*

For more information on and practice eliminating redundancies, visit <www.mhhe.com/maimon/wordy_sentences>.

➤ **Students living in close proximity in the dorms need to cooperate together if they want to live in harmony.**

Sometimes, modifiers such as *very, rather,* and *really* and intensifiers such as *absolutely, definitely,* and *incredibly* do not add meaning to a sentence but are simply redundant and can be deleted.

➤ **The ending definitely shocked us very much.**

38b Do not repeat words unnecessarily.

Although repetition is sometimes used for emphasis, unnecessary repetitions weaken sentences and should be removed.

➤ **The children enjoyed watching television more than they enjoyed reading books.**

38c Replace wordy phrases with concise alternatives.

Make your sentences more concise by replacing wordy phrases with appropriate one-word alternatives.

> ➤ ~~It is necessary at this point in time~~ that ~~tests~~ be run ~~for the~~
> Tests must now
> to measure
> ~~purposes of measuring~~ the switch's strength.

Wordy Phrases	Concise Alternatives
at this point in time	now
in this day and age	nowadays, today
at that point in time	then
in the not-too-distant future	soon
in close proximity to	near
is necessary that	must
is able to	can
has the ability to	can
has the capacity to	can
due to the fact that	because
for the reason that	because
in spite of the fact that	although
in the event that	if
in order to	to
for the purpose(s) of	to

38d Make your sentences straightforward.

Concise sentences are straightforward; they get to the point quickly instead of in a roundabout way. To make a roundabout sentence more direct, eliminate expletive constructions like *there is, there are,* and *it is* and replace the static verbs *to be* and *to have* with active verbs. To find the action in a sentence, ask yourself what the subject does.

ROUNDABOUT

There are stylistic similarities between "This Lime-Tree Bower" and "Tintern Abbey," which are indications of the influence that Coleridge had on Wordsworth.

STRAIGHTFORWARD

The stylistic similarities between "This Lime-Tree Bower" and "Tintern Abbey" indicate that Coleridge influenced Wordsworth.

Eliminating the expletive *there are* makes the main subject of the sentence—*similarities*—clearer. To find the action in the sentence, ask what *similarities* do here; they *indicate*. Do the same for the sentence's other subject, *Coleridge,* by asking what he did: *Coleridge . . . influenced.*

38e Reduce clauses and phrases.

For conciseness and clarity, simplify your sentence structure by turning modifying clauses into phrases.

➤ **The film *JFK*, ~~which was~~ directed by Oliver Stone, revived interest in the conspiracy theory.**

Also look for opportunities to reduce phrases to single words.

➤ **Stone's film *JFK* revived interest in the conspiracy theory.**

39 Missing Words

When editing, make sure you have not omitted any words the reader needs to understand the meaning of your sentence.

39a Add words needed to make compound structures complete and clear.

For conciseness, words can sometimes be omitted from compound structures. In the following example, the second *is* can be omitted because the verb in the first part of the compound structure is also *is: His anger is extreme and his behavior violent.*

Do not leave out part of a compound structure unless both parts of the compound are the same, however.

> *with*
> The gang members neither cooperated ^ nor listened to the
>
> authorities.

39b Include *that* when it is needed for clarity.

The subordinator *that* should be omitted only when the clause it introduces is short and the sentence's meaning is clear: *Faith Hill sings the
kind of songs many women love.* Usually, *that* should be included.

> *that*
> The attorney argued ^ men and women should receive equal pay
>
> for equal work.

39c Make comparisons clear.

To be clear, comparisons must be complete. If you have just said "Peanut
butter sandwiches are boring," you can say immediately afterward
"Curried chicken sandwiches are more interesting," but you cannot say
in isolation "Curried chicken sandwiches are more interesting." You
need to name who or what completes of the comparison.

  Check comparisons to make sure your meaning is clear. In the
following example, does the writer mean that she loved her grand-
mother more than her sister did—or more than she loved her sister?
To clarify, add the missing words.

> *did*
> I loved my grandmother more than my sister. ^
> *I loved*
> I loved my grandmother more than ^ my sister.

When you use *as* to compare people or things, be sure to use it twice:

> *as*
> Napoleon's temper was ^ volatile as a volcano.

Include *other* or *else* to indicate that people or things belong to
the group with which the subject is being compared.

> *Gone with the Wind* won more awards than any *other* film in
>
> Hollywood history.

> Professor Koonig wrote more books than anyone *else* in the
>
> department.

Use a possessive form when comparing attributes or possessions.

WEAK   Plato's philosophy is easier to read than *that of Aristotle*.

BETTER   Plato's philosophy is easier to read than *Aristotle's*.

Keep in mind that complex comparisons may require more than one addition to be completely clear.

➤ Smith's book is longer, but his account of the war is more _{*than Jones's book*}

interesting than ~~Jones's.~~ _{*Jones's account.*}

39d Add articles (*a*, *an*, *the*) where necessary.

In English, omitting an article usually makes an expression sound odd, unless the omission occurs in a series of nouns.

➤ A dog that bites should be kept on *a* leash.

➤ He gave me *the* books he liked best.

➤ The classroom contained a fish tank, birdcage, and rabbit hutch.

Note: If the articles in a series are not the same, each one must be included.

➤ The classroom contained an aquarium, *a* birdcage, and *a* rabbit hutch.

(*For more information about the use of articles, multilingual writers should consult Tab 13: Basic Grammar Review, pp. 506–7.*)

40 Mixed Constructions

When a sentence's parts do not fit together either grammatically or logically, a mixed construction results. Mixed constructions confuse readers and must be revised to make meaning clear.

40a Untangle mixed-up sentence structures.

Mixed-up sentences occur when writers start a sentence one way and then, midway through, change grammatical direction. The following sentence begins with a prepositional phrase (a phrase introduced by a preposition such as *at, by, for, in,* or *of*) and then, midway through, tries to make that phrase into the subject. A prepositional phrase cannot be the subject of a sentence, however.

MIXED-UP SENTENCE   For family members who enjoy one another's company often decide on a vacation spot together.

Eliminating the preposition *for* makes it clear that *family members* is the subject of the verb *decide.*

REVISED SENTENCE   Family members who enjoy one another's company often decide on a vacation spot together.

In the following sentence, the dependent clause *when a Curanderos is consulted* cannot serve as the subject of the sentence.

MIXED-UP SENTENCE   In Mexican culture, when a Curanderos is consulted can address spiritual or physical illness.

The revision transforms the dependent clause into an independent clause with a subject and predicate (a complete verb) that make sense together.

REVISED SENTENCE   In Mexican culture, a Curanderos can be consulted for spiritual or physical illness.

Sometimes you may have to separate your ideas into more than one sentence to clarify the point you are trying to make.

MIXED-UP SENTENCE   In an oligarchy like England was in 1805, a few people had the power rather than a dictatorship like France, which was ruled by Napoleon.

This writer is trying to do two things at one time: to contrast England and France in 1805 and to define the difference between an oligarchy and a dictatorship. By using two sentences instead of one, the writer makes both ideas clear.

REVISED SENTENCE   In 1805, England was an oligarchy, a state ruled by the few. In contrast, France was a dictatorship, a state ruled by one man: Napoleon.

40b Make sure predicates fit their subjects.

A **predicate** is the complete verb along with any words that modify it, any objects or complements, and any words that modify them.

A predicate must match a sentence's subject both logically and grammatically. When it does not, the result is faulty predication.

FAULTY PREDICATION

The best kind of education for me would be a university with both a school of music and a school of government.

A university is an institution, not a type of education, so the sentence needs revision.

REVISED SENTENCE

A university with both a school of music and a school of government would be best for me.

Avoid using the phrases *is where, is when,* and *the reason is . . . because.* These phrases may sound logical, but they usually result in faulty predication.

FAULTY PREDICATION

Photosynthesis is where carbon dioxide, water, and chlorophyll interact in the presence of sunlight to form carbohydrates.

Photosynthesis is not a place, so *is where* is illogical. Also, to be grammatically correct, the linking verb *is* needs to be followed by a **subject complement**—a word or word group that specifies or describes the subject.

REVISED SENTENCE

Photosynthesis is the production of carbohydrates from the interaction of carbon dioxide, water, and chlorophyll in the presence of sunlight.

Although *is because* may seem logical, it creates an adverb clause following the linking verb rather than the required subject complement.

FAULTY PREDICATION

The reason the joint did not hold is because the coupling bolt broke.

To fix this kind of faulty predication, turn the adverb clause into a noun clause by changing *because* to *that,* or change the subject of the sentence.

REVISED SENTENCES

➤ The reason the joint did not hold is ~~because~~ *that* the coupling bolt broke.

or

➤ ~~The reason~~ The joint did not hold ~~is because~~ the coupling bolt broke.

41 Confusing Shifts

When you are editing, look for jarring shifts in point of view, tense, mood, or voice that may confuse readers.

41a Make your point of view consistent in person and number.

A writer has three points of view to choose from. First person (*I* or *we*) emphasizes the writer and is used in personal writing. Second person (*you*) focuses attention on the readers and is used to give them orders, directions, or advice. Third person (*he, she, it, one,* or *they*) is topic oriented and therefore prevalent in academic writing. Once you choose a point of view, you should use it consistently.

Writers sometimes make jarring shifts in person when they compose generalizations. For example, the writer of the following sentence initially shifted from the third person (*students*) to the second person (*you*), a common kind of confusing shift.

> **Students will have no trouble getting access to a computer if**
> *they*
> **~~you~~ arrive at the lab before noon.**

Note: When making a general statement about what people should or should not do, use the third person, not the second person.

Confusing shifts in number occur when writers switch from singular to plural or plural to singular for no apparent reason. When you correct such shifts, you should usually choose the plural to avoid using *his or her* or introducing gender bias. (*See Tab 11: Editing for Grammar Conventions, pp. 419–20.*)

> *People are*
> **~~A person is~~ often assumed to be dumb if they are attractive and**
>
> **smart if they are unattractive.**

41b Keep your verb tenses consistent.

Verb tenses show the time of an action in relation to other actions. Writers are expected to choose a time frame for their work—present, past, or future—and use it consistently, changing tense only when the meaning requires it.

CHARTING the TERRITORY

Present Tense and Literary Works

By convention, the present tense is used to write about the content of literary works. When you write about literary characters and events, be careful not to shift out of the present tense as you move from one sentence to another.

➤ **David Copperfield observes other people with a fine**

   and sympathetic eye. He describes villains such as

   Mr. Murdstone and heroes such as Mr. Micawber in

                                               is

   unforgettable detail. But Copperfield ~~was~~ not himself

   an especially interesting person.

Confusing shifts in time from past to present may occur when you are narrating events that are still vivid in your mind.

➤ **The wind was blowing a hundred miles an hour when suddenly**

      was   *fell*

   there ~~is~~ a big crash, and a tree ~~falls~~ into the living room.

You may also introduce inconsistencies when you are using the present perfect tense, perhaps because the past participle causes you to slip from present tense to past tense.

➤ **She has admired many strange buildings at the university but**

     thinks   *looks*

   ~~thought~~ that the new Science Center ~~looked~~ completely out of

   place.

For more information on shifts in verb tense and voice, visit <www.mhhe.com/maimon/confusing_shifts>.

41c Avoid unnecessary shifts in mood and voice.

Besides tense, verbs in a sentence also have a mood and a voice. There are three basic moods: the **indicative,** used to state or question facts, acts, and opinions; the **imperative,** used to give commands or advice; and the **subjunctive,** used to express wishes, conjectures, and hypothetical conditions. Unnecessary shifts in mood can confuse and distract your readers. Be on the lookout for shifts between the indicative and the subjunctive.

could go
➤ If he ~~goes~~ to night school, he would take a course in accounting.

Most verbs have two voices. In the **active voice** the subject does the acting; in the **passive voice** the subject is acted upon. Do not shift abruptly from one voice to the other, especially when the subject remains the same.

They favored violet,
➤ The Impressionist painters hated black. ~~Violet,~~ green, blue,

pink, and red. ~~were favored by them.~~

42 Faulty Parallelism

Parallel constructions enhance clarity by presenting equally important ideas in the same grammatical form.

➤ At Gettysburg in 1863, Lincoln said that the Civil War was being

fought to make sure that government *of the people, by the people*,

and *for the people* might not perish from the earth.

For information and exercises on parallelism, visit <www.mhne. com/maimon/ faulty_ parallelism>.

When you notice that items in a series or paired ideas do not have the same grammatical form, correct them by making them parallel.

42a Make items in a series parallel.

A list or series of equally important items should be parallel in grammatical structure. To make the series in the following sentence parallel, the writer changed *working* to *work* so that it matches *receive* and *are*.

➤ The Census Bureau classifies people as employed if they receive

payment for any kind of labor, are temporarily absent from their

work
jobs, or ~~working~~ at least fifteen hours as unpaid laborers in a

family business.

In the next example, the writer changed a noun to an adjective. Notice that the writer also decided to repeat the word *too* to make the sentence more forceful and memorable.

➤ My sister obviously thought that I was too young, ~~*too*~~ ignorant, and
~~*too troublesome.*~~
~~a troublemaker.~~

42b Make paired ideas parallel.

Paired ideas are connected with a coordinating conjunction (*and, but, or, nor, for, so, yet*), a correlative conjunction (*not only . . . but also, both . . . and, either . . . or, neither . . . nor*), or a comparative expression (*as much as, more than, less than*). Paired ideas must have parallel grammatical form.

➤ Successful teachers must *both* inspire students and ~~challenging them~~ *challenge their students.*
~~is also important.~~

➤ I dreamed not only of getting the girl but also of *winning* the gold medal.

➤ The junta preferred to fight rather than ~~compromising.~~ *to compromise.*

43 Misplaced and Dangling Modifiers

For a sentence to make sense, its parts must be arranged appropriately. When a modifying word, phrase, or clause is misplaced or dangling, readers get confused.

43a Put modifiers close to the words they modify.

For clarity, modifiers should come immediately before or after the words they modify. In the following sentence, the clause *after the police arrested them* modifies *protesters,* not *property.* Putting the clause before the word it modifies makes it clear that if any property destruction occurred, it occurred before—not after—the arrest.

➤ *After the police arrested them, the* ~~The~~ protesters were charged with destroying college property.
~~after the police had arrested them.~~

Like adverbial clauses, prepositional phrases used as adverbs are easy to misplace. The following sentence was revised to make it clear that the hikers were watching the storm from the porch:

> *From the cabin's porch, the*
> ➤ ~~The~~ hikers watched the storm gathering force. ~~from the~~
> ^
>
> ~~cabin's porch.~~

43b   Clarify ambiguous modifiers.

Because adverbs can modify what precedes or what follows them, it is important to make sure that the adverbs you use are not ambiguously placed. In the following sentence, what is vehement, the objection or the argument? Changing the position of *vehemently* eliminates this ambiguity.

> *vehemently*
> ➤ Historians who object to this account ~~vehemently~~ argue that the
> ^
>
> presidency was never endangered.

Problems often occur with limiting modifiers such as *only, even, almost, nearly,* and *just.* When you edit, check every sentence that includes one of these modifiers. In the following sentence, does the writer mean that vegetarian dishes are the only dishes served at dinner or that dinner is the only time when vegetarian dishes are available? Editing clears up the ambiguity.

AMBIGUOUS   The restaurant *only offers* vegetarian dishes for dinner.

REVISED   The restaurant *offers only* vegetarian dishes for dinner.

or

The restaurant *offers* vegetarian dishes *only* at dinner.

43c   Move disruptive modifiers.

When you separate grammatical elements that belong together with a lengthy modifying phrase or clause, the resulting sentence can be difficult to read. In the following sentence, the phrase beginning with *despite* initially came between the subject and verb, disrupting the flow of the sentence. With the modifying phrase at the beginning of the sentence, the edited version restores the connection between subject and verb.

> *Despite their similar conceptions of the self,*
> ➤ Descartes and Hume, ~~despite their similar conceptions of the self,~~
> ^
>
> deal with the issue of personal identity in different ways.

43d Avoid splitting infinitives.

An **infinitive** couples the word *to* with the present tense of a verb. In a **split infinitive,** one or more words intervene between *to* and the verb form. Avoid separating the parts of an infinitive with a modifier unless keeping them together results in an awkward or ambiguous construction.

In the following example, the modifier *successfully* should be moved. The modifier *carefully* should probably stay where it is, however, even though it splits the infinitive *to assess. Carefully* needs to be close to the verb it modifies, and putting it after *assess* would cause ambiguity because readers might think it modifies *projected economic benefits.*

➤   To ~~successfully~~ complete this assignment _{successfully,} students have to

carefully assess projected economic benefits in relation to

potential social problems.

43e Fix dangling modifiers.

For information and exercises on dangling modifiers, visit <www.mhhe.com/maimon/modifiers>.

A **dangling modifier** is a descriptive phrase that implies an actor different from the sentence's subject. When readers try to connect the modifying phrase with the subject, the results may be humorous as well as confusing. The following sentence, for example, describes a *crowded beach* as *swimming.*

> DANGLING MODIFIER   *Swimming toward the boat on the horizon,* the crowded beach felt as if it were miles away.

To fix a dangling modifier, its implied actor must be explicitly named, either as the subject of the sentence or in the modifier itself.

> REVISED   Swimming toward the boat on the horizon, *I* felt as if the crowded beach were miles away.
>
> *or*
>
> As *I swam* toward the boat on the horizon, the crowded beach seemed miles away.

Note that simply moving a dangling modifier won't fix the problem. To make the meaning clear, the implied actor in the modifying phrase must be made explicit.

> DANGLING MODIFIER   *After struggling for weeks in the wilderness,* the town pleased them mightily.

Moving the dangling modifier to the end of the sentence won't change its unintended meaning, which is that the town had been struggling in the wilderness for weeks.

REVISED   After struggling for weeks in the wilderness, *they were pleased to come upon the town.*

or

After *they had struggled* for weeks in the wilderness, the town was a pleasing sight.

44 Coordination and Subordination

Coordination and subordination allow you to combine and develop your ideas in ways that readers can easily follow and understand, but coordination and subordination frequently cause problems for writers. If you do not fix these problems, your readers will have difficulty following your train of thought.

Use coordination to express equal ideas. **Coordination** gives two or more ideas equal weight. To coordinate parts within a sentence, join them with a coordinating conjunction (*and, but, or, for, nor, yet,* or *so*). To coordinate two or more sentences, use a comma plus a coordinating conjunction, or insert a semicolon.

➤ **The auditorium was huge,** *and* **the acoustics were terrible.**

➤ **The tenor bellowed loudly,** *but* **no one in the back could hear him.**

➤ **Jones did not agree with her position on health care;**

   nevertheless, **he supported her campaign for office.**

Note: When a semicolon is used to coordinate two sentences, it is often followed by a conjunctive adverb such as *moreover, nevertheless, however, therefore,* or *subsequently.* (*For more on conjunctive adverbs, see Tab 13: Basic Grammar Review, p. 520.*)

Use subordination to express unequal ideas. **Subordination** makes one idea depend on another and is therefore used to combine ideas that are not of equal importance. The main idea is expressed in an independent clause, and the secondary ideas are expressed in subordinate clauses or phrases. Subordinate clauses start with a relative pronoun (*who, whom, that, which, whoever, whomever, whose*) or a subordinating conjunction such as *after, although, because, if, since, when,* and *where.*

➤ The blue liquid, *which will be added to the beaker later,* must be

kept at room temperature.

➤ Christopher Columbus discovered the New World in 1492,

although he never understood just what he had found.

➤ *After writing the opening four sections,* Wordsworth put the work

aside for two years.

Note: Commas often set off subordinate ideas, especially when the subordinate clause or phrase opens the sentence. (*For more on using commas, see Tab 12: Editing for Correctness, pp. 434–47.*)

44a Combine short, choppy sentences.

Short sentences are easy to read, but several of them in a row can become so monotonous that meaning gets lost.

CHOPPY   My cousin Jim is not an accountant. But he does my taxes every year. He suggests various deductions. These deductions reduce my tax bill considerably.

You can use subordination to combine a series of short, choppy sentences such as these to form a longer, more meaningful sentence. Put the idea you want to emphasize in the main clause, and use subordinate clauses and phrases to include the other ideas. In the following revision, the main clause is underlined.

REVISED   Even though he is not an accountant, <u>my cousin Jim does my taxes every year</u>, suggesting various deductions that reduce my tax bill considerably.

If a series of short sentences includes two major ideas of equal importance, use coordination for the two major ideas and subordinate the secondary information. The following revision shows that Smith's and Johnson's opinions are equally important. The information about bilingual education is of secondary interest.

CHOPPY   Bilingual education is designed for children. The native language of these children is not English. Smith supports expanding bilingual education. Johnson does not support expanding bilingual education.

REVISED   Smith supports bilingual education for children whose native language is not English; Johnson, however, does not support bilingual education.

44b Use subordination for ideas of unequal importance.

Coordination should be used only when two or more ideas deserve equal emphasis: *Smith supports bilingual education, but Johnson does not.* Subordination, not coordination, should be used to indicate that information is of secondary importance and to show its logical relation to the main idea.

> When the
> ~~The~~ police arrived, ~~and~~ the burglars ran away.
> ^

> The fourth set of needs to be met, ~~are~~ esteem needs, ~~and they~~
> ^
> includes
> ~~include~~ the need for success, self-respect, and prestige.
> ^

44c Do not subordinate major ideas.

Major ideas belong in main clauses, not in subordinate clauses or phrases where readers are unlikely to give them the attention they deserve. The writer revised the following sentence because the subject of the paper was definitions of literacy, not who values literacy.

INEFFECTIVE SUBORDINATION	Literacy, which has been defined as the abillity to talk intelligently about many topics, is highly valued by businesspeople as well as academics.
REVISION	Highly valued by businesspeople as well as academics, literacy has been defined as the ability to talk intelligently about many topics.

44d Avoid excessive subordination.

When a sentence seems overloaded, try separating it into two or more sentences.

OVERLOADED	Big-city mayors, who are supported by public funds, should be cautious about spending tax-payers' money for personal needs, such as home furnishings, especially when municipal budget shortfalls have caused extensive job layoffs, angering city workers and the general public.
REVISED	Big-city mayors should be cautious about spending taxpayers' money for personal needs, especially when municipal budget shortfalls have caused extensive job layoffs. They risk angering city workers and the general public by using public funds for home furnishings.

45 Sentence Variety

Writers can enliven their prose while maintaining their focus by using a variety of sentence patterns. Varying your sentence structure helps you keep your readers interested.

45a Vary your sentence openings.

When all the sentences in a passage begin with the subject, you risk losing your readers' attention. To open some of your sentences in a different way, try moving a modifier to the beginning. The modifier may be a single word, a phrase, or a clause.

> *Eventually,*
> ➤ Armstrong's innovations ~~eventually~~ became the standard.
>   ^

> *In at least two instances, this*
> ➤ ~~This~~ money-making strategy backfired. ~~in at least two instances.~~
>   ^   ^

> *After Glaser became his manager,*
> ➤ Armstrong no longer had to worry about business. ~~after Glaser~~
>   ^   ^
>
> ~~became his manager.~~

A **participial phrase** begins with an *-ing* verb (*driving*) or a past participle (*moved, driven*) and is used as an adjective. You can often move it to the beginning of a sentence for variety, but if you move it, make sure that the phrase describes the explicit subject of the sentence or you will end up with a dangling modifier. (*See pp. 352–53.*)

> *Pushing the other children aside,*
> ➤ Joseph~~, pushing the other children aside,~~ demanded that the
>   ^
>
> teacher give him a cookie first.

> *Stunned by the stock market crash, many*
> ➤ ~~Many~~ brokers~~, stunned by the stock market crash,~~ committed
>   ^
>
> suicide.

45b Vary the length and structure of your sentences.

Short, simple sentences will keep your readers alert, but only if they occur in a context that also includes longer, complex sentences. Variety is the spice of life—and of writing.

As you edit your work, check to see if you have overused one kind of sentence structure. Are all or most of the sentences in a passage short and simple? If so, use subordination to combine some of the short sentences into longer, complex sentences. (*See p. 354.*) But if all or most of your sentences are long and complex, put at least one of your ideas into a short, simple sentence. Your goal is to achieve a good mix, as the following writer tried to do when revising this paragraph from a personal essay.

DRAFT   I dived quickly into the sea. I peered through my mask at the watery world. It turned darker. A school of fish went by. The distant light glittered on their bodies and I stopped swimming. I waited to see if the fish might be chased by a shark. I was satisfied that there was no shark and continued down.

REVISED   I dived quickly into the sea, peering through my mask at a watery world that turned darker as I descended. A school of fish went by, the distant light glittering on their bodies. I stopped swimming and waited. Perhaps the fish were being chased by a shark? Satisfied that there was no shark, I continued down.

(*For more information on sentence types, see Tab 13: Basic Grammar Review, pp. 530–31. For more on sentence variety, see Tab 2: Writing Papers, p. 63.*)

45c Include a few cumulative and periodic sentences.

Cumulative sentences add a series of descriptive participial or absolute phrases to the basic subject-plus-verb pattern, making your writing more forceful and detailed. (*See Tab 13: Basic Grammar Review, pp. 526–27 for more on participial and absolute phrases.*) The following example, with the participial phrases underlined, illustrates the force a cumulative sentence can have.

➤ **The motorcycle spun out of control, <u>plunging down the ravine,</u>**

   <u>crashing through a fence,</u> and <u>coming to rest at last on its side.</u>

Besides making your writing more forceful, cumulative sentences can also be used to add details, as the following example shows.

➤ **Wollstonecraft headed for France, <u>her soul determined to be</u>**

   <u>free, her mind committed to reason, her heart longing for love.</u>

Another way to increase the force of your writing is to use a few periodic sentences. In a **periodic sentence,** the key word, phrase, or idea appears at the end, precisely where readers are most likely to remember it.

WEAK   Young people fell in love with the jukebox in 1946 and 1947 and turned away from the horrors of World War II.

FORCEFUL   In 1946 and 1947, young people turned away from the horrors of World War II and fell in love—with the jukebox.

45d Try an occasional inversion, rhetorical question, or exclamation.

Most of the sentences you write will be declarative in purpose, designed to make statements. Most of the time, those statements will follow the normal sentence pattern of subject plus verb plus object. Occasionally, though, you might try using an inverted sentence pattern or another sentence type, such as a rhetorical question or an exclamation. (*For more on sentence types, see Tab 13: Basic Grammar Review, pp. 530–31.*)

1. Inversions. You can create an **inversion** by putting the verb before the subject. In a passage on the qualities of various contemporary artists, the following inversion makes sense and adds interest.

➤ **Characteristic of Smith's work are bold design and original**

    thinking.

Because many inversions sound odd, they should be used infrequently and carefully.

2. Rhetorical questions. To get your readers to participate more actively in your work, you can ask a question. Because you do not expect your audience to answer you, this kind of question is called a **rhetorical question.**

➤ **Players injured at an early age too often find themselves without**

    a job, without a college degree, and without physical health. Is it

    any wonder that a few turn to drugs and alcohol, become

    homeless, or end up in a morgue long before their time?

Rhetorical questions are attention-getting devices that work best in the middle or at the end of a long, complicated passage. Sometimes they can also help you make a transition from one topic to another. Avoid using them more than a few times in a paper, however, and never begin an essay with a broad rhetorical question, such as "Why should we study *Huckleberry Finn*?" or "How did the Peace Corps begin?" Such openings sound canned and may lead readers to suspect that the writer could not be bothered to think of something better.

3. Exclamations.   In academic writing, exclamations are rare, per-haps because they seem adolescent rather than adult. If you decide to use one for special effect, be sure that you want to express strong emotion about the idea and can do so without losing credibility with your readers.

➤ **Wordsworth completed the twelve-book *Prelude* in 1805, after seven years of hard work. Instead of publishing his masterpiece, however, he devoted himself to revising it—for 45 years! The poem, in a thirteen-book version, was finally published in 1850, after he had died.**

46 Active Verbs

Active verbs such as *run, shout, write,* and *think* are more direct and forceful than forms of the *be* verb (*am, are, is, was, were, been, being*) or passive-voice constructions. As you edit your work for clarity, pay attention to verb choice. The more active verbs you use, the stronger and clearer your writing will be.

46a Consider alternatives to some *be* verbs.

Although it is not a strong verb, *be* does a lot of work in English. As a linking verb, a form of *be* can connect a subject with an informative adjective or noun complement.

➤ **Germany *is* relatively poor in natural resources.**

➤ **Decent health care *is* a necessity, not a luxury.**

As a helping verb, a form of *be* can work with a present participle to indicate an ongoing action.

➤ **Macbeth *was* returning from battle when he met the three witches.**

Be verbs are so useful, in fact, that they can easily get overworked. Watch for weak, roundabout sentences containing *be* verbs, and consider replacing those verbs with active verbs.

➤ **The mayor's refusal to meet with our representatives**

    demonstrates
    ~~is a demonstration of~~ **his lack of respect for us, as well as for the**
        ^

environment.

46b Prefer the active voice.

Verbs can be in the active or passive voice. In the **active voice,** the subject of the sentence acts; in the **passive voice,** the subject is acted upon.

    ACTIVE   The Senate finally passed the bill.

    PASSIVE   The bill was finally passed by the Senate.

The passive voice downplays the actors as well as the action, so much so that the actors are often left out of the sentence.

    PASSIVE   The bill was finally passed.

CHARTING the TERRITORY

Passive Voice

The passive voice is often used in scientific reports to keep the focus on the experiment and its results rather than on the experimenters:

➤ **After the bacteria were isolated, they were treated**

   carefully with nicotine and were observed to stop

   reproducing.

The passive voice also appears in some forms of business writing, such as memos, when it is important to deliver information impersonally and objectively.

Unless you have a good reason to use the passive voice, prefer the active voice. It is more forceful, and readers usually want to know who or what does the acting.

PASSIVE Polluting chemicals were dumped into the river.

ACTIVE Industrial Products Corporation dumped polluting chemicals into the river.

When the recipient of the action is more important than the doer of the action, however, the passive voice is the more appropriate choice.

➤ **After her heart attack, my mother was taken to the hospital.**

Mother and the fact that she was taken to the hospital are more important than who took her to the hospital.

47 Appropriate Language

Language is appropriate when it fits your topic, purpose, and audience. But how do you know what is fitting? One way you can develop a sense of audience is through reading. Whether you are preparing to write about literature or natural science or history, take some time to read how writers in the field have handled your topic.

47a In college writing, avoid slang, regional expressions, and nonstandard English.

Slang, regional sayings, and nonstandard English appear often in conversation but rarely in college writing—unless that writing is reporting conversation.

Slang words change frequently. (Remember *awesome*?). They are popular mostly with the young, even though some American journalists may occasionally use such terms as *homey*—slang for "a close friend or fellow gang member," according to *Webster's College Dictionary*. In college papers, slang terms and the hip tone that goes with them should be avoided.

SLANG In *Heart of Darkness,* we hear a lot about a *dude* named Kurtz, but we don't see the *guy* much.

REVISED In *Heart of Darkness,* Marlow, the narrator, talks almost continually about Kurtz, but we meet Kurtz himself only at the end.

Like slang, regional and nonstandard expressions such as *y'all,* *hisself,* and *don't be doing that* work fine in conversation but do not translate well into formal college writing. In American colleges, professions, and businesses, the dominant dialect is standard written English, the language this book focuses on. Most of your instructors will expect you to write in this dialect, unless you have a good reason not to.

47b Use an appropriate level of formality.

College writing assignments usually call for a style that avoids the extremes of the stuffy and the casual, the pretentious and the chatty. Some people consider this middle style formal, perhaps because it adheres to the grammatical and mechanical rules of standard written English more than the style of a personal letter or a journal does. Others, however, think that the middle style is informal, perhaps because it is more direct than formal treatises and scholarly papers usually are. Both perspectives are probably true; the point is that as a college writer, you will need to find and revise passages that veer to one extreme or the other.

PRETENTIOUS Romantic lovers are characterized by a preoccupation with a deliberately restricted set of qualities in the love object that are viewed as means to some ideal end.

REVISED People in love see what they want to see, usually by idealizing the beloved.

47c Avoid jargon.

When specialists communicate with each other, they often use technical language that can sound incomprehensible to nonspecialists. Such language is appropriate in many contexts and has a place in college writing. Without it, no one could write a lab report, an economic analysis, or a philosophical argument. Technical language becomes a problem, however, when it is used as jargon.

Jargon is the inappropriate use of specialized or technical language. Technical language becomes jargon when it does not fit a writer's purpose and audience. If you want to be understood, you should not use discourse that is appropriate for specialists when you are writing for a general audience. Jargon puts people off, making them feel like outsiders.

CHARTING the TERRITORY

Discourse Communities

People who share certain interests, knowledge, and customary ways of communicating constitute a **discourse community.** Members of the discourse community of baseball fans, for example, talk and write about *switch-hitters, batting averages,* and *earned-run averages*— terms that are probably unfamiliar to people outside the community. Each of us belongs to several discourse communities, in and out of school. Historians, literary critics, economists, astronomers, pilots, surgeons, lovers of fishing, and thousands of others have their own discourse communities. The more familiar you are with a discourse community, the more you will know about the language that is appropriate in that community.

As you edit, look for jargon and revise any you find.

JARGON   An *opposition education theory* holds that children learn Spanish best *under strict discipline conditions.*

REVISED   An *alternative theory of education* holds that children learn Spanish best *when strict discipline is enforced.*

If you need to use a few technical terms when writing for nonspecialists, be sure to define them.

➤ **Armstrong's innovative singing style featured "scat," a technique**

that combines "nonsense syllables [with] improvised melodies"

(Robinson 425).

For more information on and practice avoiding jargon, euphemisms, and doublespeak, visit <www.mhhe.com/maimon/exact_language>.

47d Avoid most euphemisms and all doublespeak.

Although most writers strive to be clear and direct, euphemisms and doublespeak have another goal: to cover up the truth. **Euphemisms** substitute nice-sounding words like *correctional facility* and *passing away* for such harsh realities as *prison* and *death.* On some occasions, a euphemism like *passing away* may serve a useful purpose; for example, you may wish to avoid upsetting a grieving person. Usually, however, words should not be used to evade or deceive.

Doublespeak is another word for deceit. Its purpose is not to prevent hurt feelings but to confuse or mislead readers. As the following example shows, bureaucrats sometimes use doublespeak to obscure facts and evade responsibility.

➤ **Pursuant to the environmental protection regulations**

  enforcement policy of the Bureau of Natural Resources, special

  management area land use permit issuance procedures have

  been instituted.

Although it is difficult to figure out what is being said here, we can surmise that the bureau is issuing permits for the use of lands designated as "special management areas." What are these "special management areas"? In reality, they are ecologically fragile lands that the government had decided to protect against development. Now the bureau is telling firms that want to develop those lands to go ahead and do so but to secure a permit first. In other words, the bureau's "policy" is to ignore regulations established to protect the environment.

47e Do not use biased or sexist language.

1. Recognizing biased language. Words can wound. Ethnic and religious groups, people with disabilities, gay men and lesbians, and workers in some occupations often object to the way people talk and write about them. Always review your writing to see if it is unintentionally biased. Be on the lookout for subtle stereotypes that demean, ignore, or patronize people on the basis of gender, race, religion, national origin, ethnicity, physical ability, sexual orientation, occupation, or any other human condition. Revise for inclusiveness.

For example, do not assume that Irish Catholics have large families.

➤ ~~Although the~~ *The* Browns are Irish ~~Catholics, there are only~~ *an Catholic family with* two

  children. ~~in the family.~~

In addition, remember that a positive stereotype is still a stereotype.

➤ ~~Because Asian students are whizzes at math, we~~ *We* all wanted

  math whizzes
  them in our study group.

Biased Language

When writing on topics in history and the social sciences, take special care not to use terms like *underprivileged* or *culturally deprived.* The American Psychological Association recommends this test: substitute your own group for the group you are discussing. If you are offended by the resulting statement, revise your comments to eliminate bias.

2. Recognizing sexist language   Sexist language demeans or stereotypes women and men, but women are usually the explicit targets. For example, many labels and clichés imply that women are not as able or as mature as men. Consider the meaning of words and phrases like *the weaker sex, the fair sex, the little woman, [acting like a] girl, gal, broad, dame, my better half, working mother, housewife, poetess,* and *coed.*

3. Avoiding stereotypes.   Avoiding bias means more than simply not using derogatory words and slurs. It also means avoiding subtle stereotypes.

For example, not all heads of state are or have to be men. Secretaries can be either women or men.

BIASED   Wives of heads of state typically choose to promote a charity that benefits a cause they care about.

REVISED   Spouses of heads of state typically choose to promote a charity that benefits a cause they care about.

BIASED   We advertised for a new secretary because we needed another girl in the office.

REVISED   We advertised for a new secretary because we had too much work for the staff on hand.

(For additional examples, see Tab 2: Writing Papers, pp. 67–68.)

4. Avoiding the generic *he.*   Traditionally, the pronoun *he* has been used to represent either gender. Today, however, unless a group consists only of men, the use of *he* to represent everyone in the group offends many people.

BIASED   Everybody had his way.

REVISED   We all had our way.

Avoiding Biased Language

The first time you read the examples of stereotyped and biased language in this section, you may wonder whether some of them are worth worrying about. You may find it hard to believe that people really take the use of these words all that seriously. You may also discover that it can sometimes be quite difficult to eliminate biased language from your writing, particularly when you need to refer to people in general. However, the use of unbiased language is a cornerstone of solid academic writing. By eliminating bias, not only do you avoid offending others, but you also demonstrate that you are capable of thinking and expressing yourself in a thoughtful and impartial manner.

5. Revising sexist language.   Review your writing to see if it is unintentionally biased. As you revise, follow these simple principles.

- Replace terms that indicate gender with their genderless equivalents:

No	Yes
chairman	chair, chairperson
congressman	representative, member of Congress
forefathers	ancestors
man, mankind	people, humans
man-made	artificial
policeman	police officer
spokesman	spokesperson

- Do not make unnecessary references to or overemphasize a woman's marital status, relationship to children, or appearance. Refer to men and women in parallel ways: *ladies and gentlemen* [not *ladies and men*], *men and women, husband and wife.*

  BIASED   D. H. Lawrence and Mrs. Woolf met each other, but Lawrence did not like the Bloomsbury circle that revolved around Virginia.

  REVISED   D. H. Lawrence and Virginia Woolf met each other, but Lawrence did not like the Bloomsbury circle that revolved around Woolf.

- Whenever possible, replace the masculine pronouns *he, him, his,* and *himself* when they are being used generically to refer to both women and men. One satisfactory way to replace masculine pronouns is to use the plural.

BIASED It's every man for himself.

REVISED All of us have to save ourselves.

Some writers alternate *he* and *she, him* and *her.* This strategy may be effective in some writing situations, but switching back and forth can also be distracting. The constructions *his or her* and *he or she* are acceptable, as long as they are not used excessively or more than once in a sentence.

AWKWARD Each student in the psychology class was to choose a different book according to *his or her* interests, to read the book overnight, to do without *his or her* normal sleep, to write a short summary of what *he or she* had read, and then to see if *he or she* dreamed about the book the following night.

REVISED Every student was to choose a book, read it overnight, do without sleep, write a short summary of the book the next morning, and then see if *he or she* dreamed about the book the following night.

The construction *his/her* and the unpronounceable *s/he* are not acceptable in academic writing.

Note: Using the neuter impersonal pronoun *one* can sometimes help you avoid masculine pronouns. *One* can make your writing sound stuffy, though, so it is usually better to try another option.

STUFFY The American creed holds that if *one* works hard, *one* will succeed in life.

REVISED The American creed holds that those who work hard will succeed in life.

(*For more on editing to avoid the generic use of* he, him, his, *or* himself, *see Tab 11: Editing for Grammar Conventions, pp. 419–20.*)

---

48 Exact Language

To convey your meaning clearly, you need to put words in the right order, but you also need to choose the right words. As you revise, be on the lookout for problems with diction: is your choice of words as precise as it should be?

48a Choose words with suitable connotations.

Words have primary (or explicit) meanings, called **denotations,** and secondary (or implicit) meanings, called **connotations.** Connotations come from the feelings and images people associate with a word, so they influence what readers understand a writer to be saying.

Consider, for example, the following three statements:

Murdock *ignored* the no-smoking rule.

Murdock *disobeyed* the no-smoking rule.

Murdock *flouted* the no-smoking rule.

Even though the three sentences depict the same event, each sentence describes Murdock's action somewhat differently. If Murdock *ignored* the rule, it may simply have been because he did not know or care about it. If he *disobeyed* the rule, he must have known about it and consciously decided not to follow it, but what if he *flouted* the rule? Well, then there was probably a look of disdain on his face as he made sure that others would see him ostentatiously puffing away at a cigarette.

As you revise, consider replacing any word whose connotations do not exactly fit what you want to say.

➤ The players' union should ~~request~~ that the NFL amend its
                            demand

pension plan.

If you cannot think of a more suitable word, consult a print or an online thesaurus (*see p. 375*) for **synonyms,** words with similar meanings. Keep in mind, however, that most words have connotations that allow them to work in some contexts but not in others. To find out more about a synonym's connotations, look the word up in a dictionary.

48b Include specific and concrete words.

In addition to general and abstract terms, clear writers use specific and concrete words.

General words name broad categories of things, such as *trees, books, politicians,* or *students.* **Specific words** name particular kinds of things or items, such as *pines, Victorian novels, Republicans,* or *college sophomores.*

Abstract words name qualities and ideas that do not have physical properties, such as *charity, beauty, hope,* or *radical.* **Concrete words** name things we can sense by touch, taste, smell, hearing, and sight, such as *velvet, vinegar, smoke, screech,* or *sweater.*

By creating images that appeal to the senses, specific and concrete words can help make your writing more precise.

VAGUE   The trees were affected by the bad weather.

PRECISE   The small pines shook in the gale.

As you edit, make sure that you have developed your ideas with specific and concrete details. Also check for overused, vague terms—such as *factor, thing, good, nice,* and *interesting*—and replace them with more specific and concrete alternatives.

> The protesters were charged with ~~things~~ they never ~~did.~~
crimes committed.

48c Use standard idioms.

Idioms are habitual ways of expressing ideas, and they usually cannot be translated from one language to another. In fact, sometimes they cannot be transferred from one region to another within a country. If you ask a southerner in the United States for a "poke," he or she will hand you a paper bag; if you ask a New Yorker, he or she may hit you in the mouth.

As customary forms of expression, idioms are not always logical. Often they involve selecting the right preposition. We are not capable *to* but capable *of;* we do not go *with* the car but *in* the car or simply *by* car; we do not abide *with* a rule but *by* a rule. If you are not sure which preposition to use, look up the main word in a dictionary.

Some verbs, called **phrasal verbs,** include a preposition to make their meaning complete. These verbs often have an idiomatic meaning that changes significantly when the attached preposition changes.

Henry *made up* with Gloria.

Henry *made off* with Gloria.

Henry *made out* with Gloria.

(*For more on phrasal verbs, see p. 517.*)

48d Avoid clichés.

A **cliché** is an overworked expression. The moment we read the first word or two of a cliché, we know how it will end. If someone says, "She was as mad as a ___," we expect the next word to be *hornet.* We have heard this expression so often that it no longer creates a vivid picture in our imagination. It is usually best to rephrase a cliché as simply as you can in plain language.

For more information on and practice avoiding clichés, visit <www.mhhe.com/maimon/exact_language>.

CLICHÉ   When John turned his papers in three weeks late, he had to *face the music*.

BETTER   When John turned his papers in three weeks late, he had to *accept the consequences*.

The list that follows gives some common clichés to avoid.

Common Clichés

acid test	flat as a pancake	quick as a flash
agony of suspense	gild the lily	quiet as a church mouse
beat a hasty retreat	give 110 percent	
beyond the shadow of a doubt	green with envy	rise and shine
	heave a sigh of relief	rise to the occasion
blind as a bat		sadder but wiser
blue as the sky	hit the nail on the head	shoulder to the wheel
brave as a lion		
brutal murder	in this day and age	sink or swim
bustling cities	ladder of success	smart as a whip
calm, cool, and collected	last but not least	sneaking suspicion
	live from hand to mouth	sober as a judge
cold, hard facts		straight and narrow
cool as a cucumber	livid with rage	
crazy as a loon	the other side of the coin	tempest in a teapot
dead as a doornail		tired but happy
deep, dark secret	paint the town red	tried and true
depths of despair	pale as a ghost	ugly as sin
doomed to disappointment	pass the buck	untimely death
	pick and choose	walking the line
every dog has his day	poor but honest	wax eloquent
	poor but proud	white as a ghost
face the music	pretty as a picture	white as a sheet
few and far between	primrose path	worth its weight in gold
	proud possessor	

48e   Create suitable figures of speech.

Figures of speech make writing vivid, most often by using a comparison to supplement the literal meaning of words. A **simile** is a comparison that contains the word *like* or *as*.

➤ **His smile was like the sun peeking through after a rainstorm.**

A **metaphor** is an implied comparison. It treats one thing or action, such as a critic's review, as if it were something else, in this case, an extreme method of clearing land.

➤ **The critic's slash-and-burn review devastated the cast.**

Because it is compressed, a metaphor is often more forceful than a simile.

Comparisons can make your prose more vivid, but only if they suit your subject and purpose. Be especially careful not to mix metaphors; if you use two or more comparisons together, make sure they are compatible. Not only does the following sentence mix three incompatible figures (a mineral, running, and a ship), but two of the three are also unsuitable (running a race, boarding a ship).

MIXED   His presentation of the plan was so *crystal clear* that in a *burst of speed* we decided *to come aboard.*

REVISED   His clear presentation immediately convinced us to support the plan.

48f Avoid misusing words.

In college, your vocabulary will grow as you learn more about various subjects and ways of talking about them. You can expect some growing pains, however, including mistakes in your use of new terms and unfamiliar words. You can reduce such mistakes by consulting a dictionary whenever you include an unfamiliar word in your writing.

➤ The aristocracy ~~exuded~~ *exhibited* numerous vices, including greed *licentiousness.* and ~~license.~~

Also, check your course textbooks for glossaries that can help you use new terms properly.

49 The Dictionary and the Thesaurus

A desk dictionary and a thesaurus are essential tools for all writers. You should also find out about specialized dictionaries for the subject area of your major.

49a Make using the dictionary a habit.

A standard desk dictionary—such as the *Random House Webster's College Dictionary,* the *Webster's New World Dictionary,* or the *American*

Heritage College Dictionary—contains 140,000 to 180,000 entries. Along with words and their definitions, most dictionaries provide additional information such as the correct spellings of important place names, the official names of countries with their areas and populations, and the names of capital cities. Biographical entries give birth and death years and enough information to explain each person's importance to society. Many dictionaries also include lists of abbreviations and symbols, names and locations of colleges and universities, titles and correct forms of address, and conversion tables for weights and measures.

All dictionaries include guides to their use, usually in the front. The guides explain the terms and abbreviations that appear in the entries as well as special notations such as *slang, nonstandard,* and *vulgar.*

An entry from the *Random House Webster's College Dictionary* follows. The labels point to the kinds of information discussed in the following sections.

Phonetic symbols showing pronunciation.

Word endings and grammatical abbreviations.

Dictionary entry.

com•pare (kəm pâr´), *v.,* **-pared, -par • ing,** *n.* —*v.t.* **1.** to examine (two or more objects, ideas, people, etc.) in order to note similarities and differences. **2.** to consider or describe as similar; liken: *"Shall I compare thee to a summer's day?"* **3.** to form or display the degrees of comparison of (an adjective or adverb). — *v.i.* **4.** to be worthy of comparison: *Whose plays can compare with Shakespeare's?* **5.** to be in similar standing; be alike: *This recital compares with the one he gave last year.* **6.** to appear in quality, progress, etc., as specified: *Their development compares poorly with that of neighbor nations.* **7.** to make comparisons. —*n.* **8.** comparison: *a beauty beyond compare.* —*Idiom.* **9. compare notes,** to exchange views, ideas, or impressions. [1375–1425; late ME < OF *comperer* < L *comparāre* to place together, match, v. der. of *compar* alike, matching (see COM-, PAR)] —**com•par´er,** *n.* —**Usage.** A traditional rule states that COMPARE should be followed by *to* when it points out likenesses between unlike persons or things: *she compared his handwriting to knotted string.* It should be followed by *with,* the rule says, when it examines two entities of the same general class for similarities or differences: *She compared his handwriting with mine.* This rule, though sensible, is not always followed, even in formal speech and writing. Common practice is to use *to* for likeness between members of different classes: *to compare a language to a living organism.* Between members of the same category, both *to* and *with* are used: *Compare the Chicago of today with* (or *to*) *the Chicago of the 1890s.* After the past participle COMPARED, either *to* or *with* is used regardless of the type of comparison.

Definitions as a transitive verb (*v.t.*).

Definitions as an intransitive verb (*v.i.*).

Definition as a noun (*n.*).

Etymology.

Special meaning.

Usage note.

1. Spelling, word division, and pronunciation.

Entries in a dictionary are listed in alphabetical order according to their standard spelling. In the *Random House Webster's College Dictionary,* the verb *compare* is entered as **com•pare.** The dot separates the word into its two syllables. If you had to divide the word *compare* at the end of a line, you would place the hyphen where the dot appears.

Phonetic symbols in parentheses following the entry show its correct pronunciation; explanations of these symbols appear on the bottom of each right-hand page in some dictionaries. The second syllable

CHARTING the TERRITORY

Dictionaries

In the library's reference section, you can usually find numerous specialized dictionaries such as biographical and geographical dictionaries; foreign language dictionaries; dictionaries of first lines of poems and of famous quotations; dictionaries of legal and medical terms; and dictionaries of philosophy, sociology, engineering, and other disciplines. These dictionaries can help you write an essay or simply expand your knowledge of various subjects. Ask the reference librarian to help you locate a useful specialized dictionary for your topic or field.

of *compare* receives the greater stress when you pronounce the word correctly: you say "comPARE." In this dictionary, an accent mark (´) appears after the syllable that receives the primary stress.

Plurals of nouns are usually not given if they are formed by adding an *s*, unless the word is foreign (*gondolas, dashikis*). Irregular plurals—such as *children* for *child*—are noted.

Note: Some dictionaries list alternate spellings, always giving the preferred spelling first or placing the full entry under the preferred spelling only.

2. Word endings and grammatical labels.   The abbreviation *v.* immediately after the pronunciation tells you that *compare* is most frequently used as a verb. The *-pared* shows the simple past and past participle form of the verb; the present participle form, *-paring,* follows, indicating that *compare* drops the final *e* when *-ing* is added. The next abbreviation, *n.,* indicates that *compare* can sometimes function as a noun, as in the phrase *beyond compare.*

Here is a list of common abbreviations for grammatical terms:

adj.	adjective	*prep.*	preposition
adv.	adverb	*pron.*	pronoun
conj.	conjunction	*sing.*	singular
interj.	interjection	*v.*	verb
n.	noun	*v.i.*	intransitive verb
pl.	plural	*v.t.*	transitive verb
poss.	possessive		

3. Definitions and word origins.   In the sample entry, the definitions begin after the abbreviation *v.t.,* which indicates that the first three meanings relate to *compare* as a transitive verb. A little further

Tips LEARNING in COLLEGE

Using a Dictionary

- **Use the guide words.** At the top of each dictionary page are guide words (usually in bold type) that tell you the first and last words on the page. Because all the entries are in alphabetical order, you can locate the word you are seeking by looking for guide words that would appear before and after your word in an alphabetical listing.

- **Try alternate spellings.** If you cannot find a word on the first try, think of another way to spell it.

- **Use the pronunciation key.** The letters and symbols that indicate each word's pronunciation are explained in a separate section at the front or back of a dictionary. In some dictionaries, they are also summarized at the bottom of each right-hand page of entries. Pronouncing new words aloud will help you learn them.

- **Pay attention to the parts of speech in a definition.** The same word can have different meanings depending on how it is used in a sentence—that is, its part of speech.

- **Always test the meaning you find.** To check whether you have selected the correct word, substitute the meaning for the word in your sentence and see if the sentence makes sense.

down in the entry, *v.i.* introduces definitions of *compare* as an intransitive verb. Next, after *n.* comes the definition of *compare* as a noun. Finally, the word *Idiom* signals a special meaning not included in the previous definitions. As an idiom, *compare notes* means "to exchange views, ideas, or impressions," not to sit down and see how two sets of notes are alike and different.

Included in most dictionary entries is an etymology—a brief history of the word—set off in brackets. There we see the date of the first known use of the word in English together with the earlier words from which it is derived. *Compare* came into English between 1375 and 1425 and was derived from the Old French word *comperer,* which came from Latin. Etymological information can be useful to writers who need to define a word for their readers.

For a list of links to online dictionaries and thesauruses, visit <www.mhhe.com/maimon/dictionary_and_thesaurus>.

4. Usage. A usage note concludes some main entries in the dictionary. In the sample entry, the usage note gives the traditional rule for using *compare to* or *compare with* as well as some examples of and comments about common practice.

Using a Thesaurus

- Use a thesaurus to find a more precise word, not a fancier one.
- Know how the words in your thesaurus are arranged. In *Roget's International Thesaurus,* the words are listed in numbered categories, and you need to use the index in the back to find the word whose synonyms you seek. In other thesauruses, the words are arranged in simple alphabetical order like a dictionary. Usually, an online thesaurus will provide synonyms for words that you highlight in your text.
- Never use an unfamiliar synonym that you pick up from a thesaurus without first looking it up in the dictionary. Otherwise, your sentence may be unintentionally humorous or incomprehensible.
- Treat the replacement word carefully in your sentence. Make sure that your replacement has appropriate connotations as well as the correct denotation.

49b Consult a thesaurus for words that have similar meanings.

The word *thesaurus* in Latin means "treasury" or "collection." A thesaurus is a dictionary of synonyms. Several kinds of thesauruses are available, many called *Roget's* after Peter Mark Roget (pronounced roZHAY), who published the first one in 1852. Today, thesauruses are included in most word-processing software packages.

Most writers find a thesaurus a pleasure to use, but you need to be cautious when using one. Consider the connotations as well as the denotations of the words you find in the thesaurus. Do not choose a word just because you think it sounds smart or fancy.

50 Glossary of Usage

Although the meanings of some words change over time, clear communication is enhanced when change takes place slowly and meanings remain relatively constant. The following words and expressions are often confused (such as *advice* and *advise*), misused (such as *etc.*), or considered nonstandard (such as *could of*). Consulting this list will help you use words more precisely.

a, an   Use *a* with a word that begins with a consonant sound: *a cat, a dog, a one-sided argument, a house.* Use *an* with a word that begins with a vowel sound: *an apple, an X ray, an honor.*

accept, except   *Accept* is a verb meaning "to receive willingly": *Please accept my apologies. Except* is a preposition meaning "but": *Everyone except Julie saw the film.*

adapt, adopt   *Adapt* means "to adjust or become accustomed to": *They adapted to the customs of their new country. Adopt* means "to take as one's own": *We adopted a puppy.*

advice, advise   *Advice* is a noun; *advise* is a verb: *I took his advice and deeply regretted it. I advise you to disregard it, too.*

affect, effect   As a verb, *affect* means "to influence": *Inflation affects our sense of security.* As a noun, *affect* means "a feeling or an emotion:": *To study affect, psychologists probe the unconscious.* As a noun, *effect* means "result": *Inflation is one of the many effects of war.* As a verb, *effect* means "to make or accomplish": *Inflation has effected many changes in the way we spend money.*

agree to, agree with   *Agree to* means "consent to"; *agree with* means "be in accord with": *They will agree to a peace treaty, even though they do not agree with each other on all points.*

ain't   A slang contraction for *is not, am not,* or *are not, ain't* should not be used in formal writing or speech.

all/all of, more/more of, some/some of   Except before some pronouns, the "of" in these constructions can usually be eliminated. *All France rejoiced. Some students cut class.* But: *All of us wish you well.*

all ready, already   *All ready* means "fully prepared." *Already* means "previously." *We were all ready to go out when we discovered that Jack had already ordered a pizza.*

all right, alright   The spelling *alright* is an alternate, but many educated readers still think it is incorrect in standard written English. *He told me it was all right to miss class tomorrow.*

all together, altogether   *All together* expresses unity or common location. *Altogether* means "completely," often in a tone of ironic understatement. *At the NRA convention, it was altogether startling to see so many guns set out all together on one table.*

allude, elude, refer to   *Allude* means "to refer indirectly": *He alluded to his miserable adolescence. Elude* means "to avoid" or "to escape from": *She eluded the police for nearly two days.* Do not use *allude* to mean "to refer directly": *The teacher referred* [not *alluded*] *to page 468 in the text.*

almost, most   *Almost* means "nearly." *Most* means "the greater part of." Do not use *most* when you mean *almost. He wrote to me about almost* [not *most*] *everything he did. He told his mother about most things he did.*

a lot   *A lot* is always two words. Do not use *alot.*

A.M., AM, a.m.   These abbreviations mean "before noon" when used with numbers: 6 A.M., 6 a.m. Be consistent in the form you choose, and do not use the abbreviations as a synonym for *morning: In the morning* [not *a.m.*]*, the train is full.*

among, between   Generally, use *among* with three or more nouns, *between* with two. *The distance between Boston and Knoxville is a thousand miles. The desire to quit smoking is common among those who have smoked for a long time.*

amoral, immoral   *Amoral* means "neither moral nor immoral" and "not caring about moral judgments." *Immoral* means "morally wrong." *Unlike such amoral natural disasters as earthquakes and hurricanes, war is intentionally violent and therefore immoral.*

amount, number   Use *amount* for quantities you cannot count; use *number* for quantities you can count. *The amount of oil left underground in the United States is a matter of dispute, but the number of oil companies losing money is tiny.*

an   *See* a, an.

anxious, eager   *Anxious* means "fearful": *I am anxious before a test. Eager* signals strong interest or desire: *I am eager to be done with that exam.*

anymore, any more   *Anymore* means "no longer." *Any more* means "no more." Both are used in negative contexts. *I do not enjoy dancing anymore. I do not want any more peanut butter.*

anyone/any one, anybody/any body, everyone/every one, everybody/every body   *Anyone, anybody, everyone,* and *everybody* are indefinite pronouns: *Anybody can make a mistake.* When the pronoun *one* or the noun *body* is modified by the adjective *any* or *every,* the words should be separated by a space: *A good mystery writer accounts for every body that turns up in the story.*

as   Do not use *as* as a synonym for *since, when,* or *because. I told him he should visit Alcatraz since* [not *as*] *he was going to San Francisco. When* [not *as*] *I complained about the meal, the cook said he did not like to eat there himself. Because* [not *as*] *we asked her nicely, our teacher decided to cancel the exam.*

as, like   In formal writing, avoid the use of *like* as a conjunction: *He sneezed as if* [not *like*] *he had a cold. Like* is perfectly acceptable as a preposition that introduces a comparison: *She handled the reins like an expert.*

at   Avoid the use of *at* to complete the notion of *where:* not *Where is Michael at?* but *Where is Michael?*

awful, awfully   Use *awful* and *awfully* to convey the emotion of terror or wonder (awe-full): *The vampire flew out the window with an awful shriek.* In writing, do not use *awful* to mean "bad" or *awfully* to mean "very" or "extremely."

awhile, a while   *Awhile* is an adverb: *Stay awhile with me. A while* is an article and a noun. Always use *a while* after a preposition: *Many authors are unable to write anything else for a while after they publish their first novel.*

being as, being that   Do not use *being as* or *being that* as synonyms for *since* or *because. Because* [not *being as*] *the mountain was there, we had to climb it.*

belief, believe   *Belief* is a noun meaning "conviction"; *believe* is a verb meaning "to have confidence in the truth of." *Her belief that lying was often justified made it hard for us to believe her story.*

beside, besides   *Beside* is a preposition meaning "next to" or "apart from": *The ski slope was beside the lodge. She was beside herself with joy. Besides* is both a preposition and an adverb meaning "in addition to" or "except for": *Besides a bicycle, he will need a tent and a pack.*

between, among   *See* among, between.

better   Avoid using *better* in expressions of quantity: *Crossing the continent by train took more than* [not *better than*] *four days.*

bring, take   Use *bring* when an object is being moved toward you, *take* when it is being moved away: *Please bring me a new disk and take the old one home with you.*

but that, but what   In expressions of doubt, avoid writing *but that* or *but what* when you mean *that: I have no doubt that* [not *but that*] *you can learn to write well.*

can, may   *Can* refers to ability; *may* refers to possibility or permission. *I see that you can rollerblade without crashing into people, but nevertheless you may not rollerblade on the promenade.*

can't hardly   This double negative is ungrammatical and self-contradictory. *I can* [not *can't*] *hardly understand algebra. I can't understand algebra.*

capital, capitol   *Capital* refers to a city; *capitol* refers to a building where lawmakers meet. *Protesters traveled to the state capital to converge on the capitol steps. Capital* also refers to wealth or resources.

censor, censure   *Censor* means "to remove or suppress material." *Censure* means "to reprimand formally." *The Chinese government has been censured by the U.S. Congress for censoring newspapers.*

cite, sight, site   The verb *cite* means "to quote or mention": *Be sure to cite all your sources in your bibliography.* As a noun, the word *sight* means "view": *It was love at first sight. Site* is a noun meaning "a particular place": locations on the Internet are referred to as *sites.*

compare to, compare with   Use *compare to* to point out similarities between two unlike things: *She compared his singing to the croaking of a wounded frog.* Use *compare with* for differences or likenesses between two similar things: *Compare Shakespeare's* Antony and Cleopatra *with Dryden's* All For Love.

complement, compliment   *Complement* means "to go well with": *I consider sauerkraut the perfect complement to sausages. Compliment* means "praise": *She received many compliments on her thesis.*

conscience, conscious   The noun *conscience* means "a sense of right and wrong": *His conscience bothered him.* The adjective *conscious* means "awake" or "aware": *I was conscious of a presence in the room.*

continual, continuous   *Continual* means "repeated regularly and frequently": *She continually checked her computer for new e-mail. Continuous* means "extended or prolonged without interruption": *The car alarm made a continuous wail in the night.*

could of, should of, would of   Avoid these ungrammatical forms of *could have, should have,* and *would have.*

criteria, criterion   *Criteria* is the plural form of the Latin word *criterion,* meaning "standard of judgment." *The criteria are not very strict. The most important criterion is whether you can do the work.*

data *Data* is the plural form of the Latin word *datum,* meaning "fact." Although *data* is often used informally as a singular noun, in writing, treat *data* as a plural noun: *The data indicate that recycling has gained popularity.*

differ from, differ with *Differ from* expresses a lack of similarity; *differ with* expresses disagreement. *The ancient Greeks differed less from the Persians than we often think. Aristotle differed with Plato on some important issues.*

different from, different than The correct idiom is *different from.* Avoid *different than. The east coast of Florida is very different from the west coast.*

discreet, discrete *Discreet* means "tactful" or "prudent." *Discrete* means "separate" or "distinct." *What's a discreet way of telling them that these are two discrete issues?*

disinterested, uninterested *Disinterested* means "impartial": *We expect members of a jury to be disinterested. Uninterested* means "indifferent" or "unconcerned": *Most people today are uninterested in alchemy.*

don't, doesn't *Don't* is the contraction for *do not* and is used with *I, you, we, they,* and plural nouns. *Doesn't* is the contraction for *does not* and is used with *he, she, it,* and singular nouns. *You don't know what you're talking about. He doesn't know what you're talking about either.*

due to, because of *Due to* is an overworked and often confusing expression when it is used for *because of.* Use *due to* only in expressions of time in infinitive constructions or in other contexts where the meaning is "scheduled." *The plane is due to arrive in one hour. He is due to receive a promotion this year.*

each and every Use one of these words or the other but not both. *Every cow came in at feeding time. Each one had to be watered.*

each other, one another Use *each other* in sentences involving two subjects and *one another* in sentences involving more than two. *Husbands and wives should help each other. Classmates should share ideas with one another.*

eager, anxious *See* anxious, eager.

effect, affect *See* affect, effect.

e.g., i.e. The abbreviation *e.g.* stands for the Latin words meaning "for example." The abbreviation *i.e.* stands for the Latin for "that is." *Come as soon as you can, i.e., today or tomorrow. Bring fruit with you, e.g., apples and peaches.* In formal writing, replace the abbreviations with the English words: *Keats wrote many different kinds of lyrics, for example, odes, sonnets, and songs.*

either, neither Both *either* and *neither* are singular: *Neither of the two boys has played the game. Either of the two girls is willing to show you the way home. Either* has an intensive use that *neither* does not, and when it is used as an intensive, *either* is always negative: *She told him she would not go either.* (For *either . . . or* and *neither . . . nor* constructions, see pages 399–400.)

elicit, illicit The verb *elicit* means "to draw out." The adjective *illicit* means "unlawful." *The detective was unable to elicit any information about other illicit activity.*

elude, allude *See* allude, elude, refer to.

emigrate, immigrate *Emigrate* means "to move away from one's country": *My grandfather emigrated from Greece in 1905. Immigrate* means "to move to another country and settle there": *Grandpa immigrated to the United States.*

eminent, imminent, immanent   *Eminent* means "celebrated" or "well known": *Many eminent Victorians were melancholy and disturbed. Imminent* means "about to happen" or "about to come": *In August 1939, many Europeans sensed that war was imminent. Immanent* refers to something invisible but dwelling throughout the world: *Medieval Christians believed that God's power was immanent through the universe.*

etc.   The abbreviation *etc.* stands for the Latin *et cetera,* meaning "and others" or "and other things." Because *and* is included in the abbreviation, do not write *and etc.* In a series, a comma comes before *etc.*, just as it would before the coordinating conjunction that closes a series: *He brought string, wax, paper, etc.* In most college writing, it is better to end a series of examples with a final example or the words *and so on.*

everybody/every body, everyone/every one   *See* anyone/any one . . .

except, accept   *See* accept, except.

expect, suppose   *Expect* means "to hope" or "to anticipate": *I expect a good grade on my final paper. Suppose* means "to presume": *I suppose you did not win the lottery on Saturday.*

explicit, implicit   *Explicit* means "stated outright." *Implicit* means "implied, unstated." *Her explicit instructions were to go to the party without her, but the implicit message she conveyed was disapproval.*

farther, further   *Farther* describes geographical distances: *Ten miles farther on is a hotel. Further* means "in addition" when geography is not involved: *He said further that he didn't like my attitude.*

fewer, less   *Fewer* refers to items that can be counted individually; *less* refers to general amounts. *Fewer people signed up for indoor soccer this year than last. Your argument has less substance than you think.*

first, firstly   *Firstly* is common in British English but not in the United States. *First, second, third* are the accepted forms.

flaunt, flout   *Flaunt* means "to wave" or "to show publicly" with a delight tinged with pride and even arrogance: *He flaunted his wealth by wearing overalls lined with mink. Flout* means "to scorn" or "to defy," especially in a public way, seemingly without concern for the consequences: *She flouted the traffic laws by running through red lights.*

former, latter   *Former* refers to the first and *latter* to the second of two things mentioned previously: *Mario and Alice are both good cooks; the former is fonder of Chinese cooking, the latter of Mexican.*

further, farther   *See* farther, further.

get   In formal writing, avoid colloquial uses of *get,* as in *get with it, get it all together, get-up-and-go, get it,* and *that gets me.*

good, well   *Good* is an adjective and should not be used in place of the adverb *well. He felt good about doing well on the exam.*

half, a half, half a   Write *half, a half,* or *half a* but not *half of, a half a,* or *a half of. Half the clerical staff went out on strike. I want a half-dozen eggs to throw at the actors. Half a loaf is better than none, unless you are on a diet.*

hanged, hung   People are *hanged* by the neck until dead. Pictures and all other things that can be suspended are *hung.*

hopefully *Hopefully* means "with hope." It is often misused to mean "it is hoped." *We waited hopefully for our ship to come in* [not *Hopefully, our ship will come in*].

i.e., e.g. *See* e.g., i.e.

if . . . then Avoid using these words in tandem. Redundant: *If I get my license, then I can drive a cab.* Better: *If I get my license, I can drive a cab. Once I get my license, I can drive a cab.*

illicit, elicit *See* elicit, illicit.

imminent, immanent *See* eminent, imminent, immanent.

immigrate, emigrate *See* emigrate, immigrate.

immoral, amoral *See* amoral, immoral.

implicit, explicit *See* explicit, implicit.

imply, infer *Imply* means "to suggest something without stating it directly": *By putting his fingers in his ears, he implied that she should stop singing. Infer* means "to draw a conclusion from evidence": *When she dozed off in the middle of his declaration of eternal love, he inferred that she did not feel the same way about him.*

in, in to, into *In* refers to a location inside something: *Charles kept a snake in his room. In to* refers to motion with a purpose: *The resident manager came in to capture it. Into* refers to movement from outside to inside or from separation to contact: *The snake escaped by crawling into a drain. The manager ran into the wall, and Charles got into big trouble.*

incredible, incredulous The *incredible* cannot be believed; the *incredulous* do not believe. Stories and events may be *incredible*; people are *incredulous. Nancy told an incredible story of being abducted by a UFO over the weekend. We were all incredulous.*

infer, imply *See* imply, infer.

inside of, outside of The "of" is unnecessary in these phrases: *He was outside the house.*

ironically *Ironically* means "contrary to what was or might have been expected." It should not be confused with *surprisingly,* which means "unexpected," or with *coincidentally,* which means "occurring at the same time or place." *Ironically, his fast ball lost speed after his arm healed.*

irregardless This construction is a double negative because both the prefix *ir-* and the suffix *-less* are negatives. Use *regardless* instead.

it's, its *It's* is a contraction, usually for *it is* but sometimes for *it has: It's often been said that English is a difficult language to learn. Its* is a possessive pronoun: *The dog sat down and scratched its fleas.*

kind, kinds *Kind* is singular: *This kind of house is easy to build. Kinds* is plural and should be used only to indicate more than one kind: *These three kinds of toys are better than those two kinds.*

lay, lie *Lay* means "to place." Its main forms are *lay, laid,* and *laid.* It generally has a direct object, specifying what has been placed: *She laid her book on the steps and left it there. Lie* means "to recline" and does not take a direct object. Its main forms are *lie, lay,* and *lain: She often lay awake at night.*

less, fewer *See* fewer, less.

like, as *See* as, like.

literally *Literally* means "actually" or "exactly as written": *Literally thousands gathered along the parade route.* Do not use *literally* as an intensive adverb when it can be misleading or even ridiculous, as here: *His blood literally boiled.*

loose, lose *Loose* is an adjective that means "not securely attached." *Lose* is a verb that means "to misplace." *Better tighten that loose screw before you lose the whole structure.*

may, can *See* can, may.

maybe, may be *Maybe* is an adverb meaning "perhaps": *Maybe he can get a summer job as a lifeguard. May be* is a verb phrase meaning "is possible": *It may be that I can get a job as a lifeguard, too.*

moral, morale *Moral* means "lesson," especially a lesson about standards of behavior or the nature of life: *The moral of the story is do not drink and drive. Morale* means "attitude" or "mental condition": *Office morale dropped sharply after the dean was arrested.*

more/more of *See* all/all of. . . .

more important, more importantly The correct idiom is *more important*, not *more importantly*.

most, almost *See* almost, most.

myself (himself, herself, etc.) Pronouns ending with *-self* refer to or intensify other words: *Jack hurt himself. Standing in the doorway was the man himself.* When you are unsure whether to use *I* or *me, she* or *her, he* or *him* in a compound subject or object, you may be tempted to substitute one of the *-self* pronouns. Don't do it. *The quarrel was between her and me* [not *myself*]. (*Also see Problems with Pronouns beginning on p. 417 in Tab 11.*)

neither, either *See* either, neither

nohow, nowheres These words are nonstandard for *anyway, in no way, in any way, in any place,* and *in no place.* Do not use them in formal writing.

number, amount *See* amount, number.

off of Omit the *of: She took the painting off the wall.*

one another, each other *See* each other, one another.

outside of, inside of *See* inside of, outside of.

plus Avoid using *plus* as a substitute for *and: He had to walk the dog, do the dishes, empty the garbage, and* [not *plus*] *write a term paper.*

practicable, practical *Practicable* is an adjective applied to things that can be done: *A space program that would land human beings on Mars is now practicable. Practical* means "sensible": *Many people do not think such a journey is practical.*

precede, proceed *Precede* means "come before;" *proceed* means "go forward." *Despite the heavy snows that preceded us, we managed to proceed up the hiking trail.*

previous to, prior to Avoid these wordy and somewhat pompous substitutions for *before*.

principal, principle   *Principal* is an adjective meaning "most important" or a noun meaning "the head of an organization" or "a sum of money": *Our principal objections to the school's principal are that he is a liar and a cheat. Principle* is a noun meaning "a basic standard or law": *We believe in the principles of honesty and fair play.*

proceed, precede   *See* precede, proceed.

raise, rise   *Raise* means "to lift or cause to move upward." It takes a direct object—someone raises something: *I raised the windows in the classroom. Rise* means "to go upward." It does not take a direct object—something rises by itself: *We watched the balloon rise to the ceiling.*

real, really   Do not use the word *real* when you mean *very: The cake was very* [not *real*] *good.*

reason is because   This is a redundant expression. Use either *the reason is that* or *because: The reason he fell on the ice is that he cannot skate. He fell on the ice because he cannot skate.*

refer to   *See* allude, elude, refer to.

relation, relationship   *Relation* describes a connection between things: *There is a relation between smoking and lung cancer. Relationship* describes a connection between people: *The brothers have always had a close relationship.*

respectfully, respectively   *Respectfully* means "with respect": *Treat your partners respectfully. Respectively* means "in the given order": *The three Williams she referred to were Shakespeare, Wordsworth, and Yeats, respectively.*

rise, raise   *See* raise, rise.

set, sit   *Set* is usually a transitive verb meaning "to establish" or "to place." It takes a direct object, and its principal parts are *set, set,* and *set: DiMaggio set the standard of excellence in fielding. She set the box down in the corner. Sit* is usually intransitive, meaning "to place oneself in a sitting position." Its principal parts are *sit, sat,* and *sat: The dog sat on command.*

shall, will   *Shall* was once the standard first-person future form of the verb *to be* when a simple statement of fact was intended: *I shall be twenty-one on my next birthday.* Today, most writers use *will* in the ordinary future tense for the first person: *I will celebrate my birthday by throwing a big party. Shall* is still used in questions. *Shall we dance?*

should of, could of   *See* could of, should of, would of.

site, sight, cite   *See* cite, sight, site.

some   Avoid using the adjective *some* in place of the adverb *somewhat: He felt somewhat* [not *some*] *better after a good night's sleep.*

some of   *See* all/all of. . . .

somewheres   Use *somewhere* or *someplace* instead.

stationary, stationery   *Stationary* means "standing still": *I worked out on my stationary bicycle. Stationery* is writing paper: *That stationery smells like a rose garden.*

suppose, expect   *See* expect, suppose.

sure   Avoid confusing the adjective *sure* with the adverb *surely: The dress she wore to the party was surely bizarre.*

sure and, sure to *Sure and* is often used colloquially. In formal writing, *sure to* is preferred: *Be sure to* [not *be sure and*] *get to the wedding on time.*

take, bring *See* bring, take.

that, which Many writers use *that* for restrictive (i.e., essential) clauses and *which* for nonrestrictive (i.e., nonessential) clauses. *The bull that escaped from the ring ran through my china shop, which was located in the square.* (*Also see Commas, pp. 438–39, in Tab 12.*)

their, there, they're *Their* is a possessive pronoun: *They gave their lives. There* is an adverb of place: *She was standing there. They're* is a contraction of *they are: They're reading more poetry this semester.*

this here, these here, that there, them there When writing, avoid these nonstandard forms.

to, too, two *To* is a preposition; *too* is an adverb; *two* is a number. *The two of us got lost too many times on our way to his house.*

try and, try to *Try to* is the standard form: *Try to* [not *try and*] *understand.*

uninterested, disinterested *See* disinterested, uninterested.

use, utilize *Utilize* seldom says more than *use,* and the simpler term is almost always better: *We must learn how to use the computer's zip drive.*

verbally, orally To say something *orally* is to say it aloud: *We agreed orally to share credit for the work, but when I asked her to confirm it in writing, she refused.* To say something *verbally* is to use words: *His eyes flashed anger, but he did not express his feelings verbally.*

wait for, wait on People *wait for* those who are late; they *wait on* tables.

weather, whether The noun *weather* refers to the atmosphere: *She worried that the weather would not clear up in time for the victory celebration. Whether* is a conjunction referring to a choice between alternatives: *I can't decide whether to go now or next week.*

well, good *See* good, well.

which, who, whose *Which* is used for things, *who* and *whose* for people. *My fountain pen, which I had lost last week, was found by a child who had never seen one before, whose whole life had been spent with ballpoints.*

whether, weather *See* weather, whether.

will, shall *See* shall, will.

would of *See* could of, should of, would of.

your, you're *Your* is a possessive pronoun: *Is that your new car? You're* is a contraction of *you are: You're a lucky guy.*

There is a core simplicity to the English
language and its American variant, but
it's a slippery core.

—STEPHEN KING

Editing
for Grammar
Conventions

11 Grammar Conventions

51. Sentence Fragments *388*
    a. Dependent clauses as fragments *389*
    b. Phrases as fragments *390*
    c. Other types of fragments *391*

52. Comma Splices and Run-on Sentences *392*
    a. Repairing with a comma and a coordinating conjunction *394*
    b. Repairing with a semicolon *395*
    c. Repairing by separating into two sentences *396*
    d. Repairing by making one clause dependent *396*
    e. Repairing by reworking the sentence *397*

53. Subject-Verb Agreement *397*
    a. Standard subject-verb combinations *398*
    b. A word group between subject and verb *399*
    c. Compound subjects connected by conjunctions (*and, but, either . . . or*) *399*
    d. Collective subjects (*committee, jury*) *400*
    e. Indefinite subjects (*everybody, no one*) *401*
    f. Subject following verb *403*
    g. Subject complements *403*

h. Relative pronouns (*who, which, that*) *403*
i. *-ing* phrases (gerund phrases) as subjects *404*

54. Problems with Verbs *404*
    a. Principal forms of regular and irregular verbs *404*
    b. *Lay* and *lie, sit* and *set, rise* and *raise* *408*
    c. *-s* or *-es* endings *409*
    d. *-d* or *-ed* endings *410*
    e. Verb tenses *410*
    f. Past perfect tense *412*
    g. Special uses of the present tense *413*
    h. Tense with infinitives and participles *414*
    i. Complete verbs *415*
    j. Mood *416*
    k. Voice *417*

55. Problems with Pronouns *417*
    a. Pronoun-antecedent agreement *418*
    b. Pronoun reference *421*
    c. Pronoun case (for example, *I* vs. *me*). *422*
    d. *Who* vs. *whom* *425*

56. Problems with Adjectives and Adverbs *426*
    a. Adverbs *426*
    b. Adjectives *427*
    c. Positive, comparative, and superlative adjectives and adverbs *428*
    d. Double negatives *429*

Sections of Special Interest to Multilingual Students

Using correct grammar involves more than just making sure that the mechanics of the language are correct. Even sentences that are grammatically correct can sometimes confuse or even offend readers. With this caution in mind, you may wish to pay special attention to the following sections:

- **54e:** Use verb tenses accurately.
- **54k:** Use the active voice most of the time.
- **55a:** Avoid bias when using generic nouns.
- **55b:** Make pronoun references clear.

(*For help with areas that are especially troublesome for multilingual writers, see Tab 13.*)

When you edit, your purpose is to make the sentences in your text both clear and strong. The previous section focused on editing for clarity. This section of the handbook focuses on editing for common grammatical problems. How can you tell if one of your sentences has a grammatical problem that needs to be fixed? Focusing on each sentence in turn, look for problems that may confuse or distract readers. Ask yourself the following questions:

- Is each sentence grammatically complete, or is some necessary part missing? Does each sentence include a subject, a complete verb, and an independent clause? (*See Chapter 51, Sentence Fragments, p. 388.*)

- Does any sentence seem like two or more sentences jammed together without a break? If a sentence has more than one independent clause, are those clauses joined in an acceptable way? (*See Chapter 52, Comma Splices and Run-on Sentences, p. 392.*)

- Do the key parts of each sentence fit together well, or are the subjects and verbs mismatched in person and number? (*See Chapter 53, Subject-Verb Agreement, p. 397.*)

- Is the time frame of events represented accurately, conventionally, and consistently, or are there problems with verb form, tense, and sequence? (*See Chapter 54, Problems with Verbs, p. 404.*)

- Do the pronouns in every sentence clearly refer to a specific noun or pronoun and agree with the nouns or pronoun they replace? (*See Chapter 55, Problems with Pronouns, p. 417.*)

▪ Does the form of each modifier match its function in the sentence? (*See Chapter 56, Problems with Adjectives and Adverbs, p. 426.*)

51 Sentence Fragments

A word group that begins with a capital letter and ends with a period may not actually be a complete sentence. As you edit, look for unintentional sentence fragments.

For more information on and practice avoiding sentence fragments, visit <www.mhhe.com/maimon/frag>.

Learn how to identify sentence fragments.   Does the following example contain two complete sentences?

> **POSSIBLE FRAGMENT**   Pool hustlers deceive their opponents in many ways. For example, deliberately putting so much spin on the ball that it jumps out of the intended pocket.

A complete sentence meets all three of the following requirements:

▪ **A sentence names a *subject*,** the who or what that the sentence is about. To locate a sentence's subject, find the verb and ask the *who* or *what* question about it. In the first word group in the example above, *who* or *what deceive*s opponents? The answer is *Pool hustlers,* the subject of the first sentence. In the second word group in the example, *who* or *what* is *putting spin on the ball*? The word group does not provide an answer, but it does provide an answer to the question *who or what jumps*? The answer is *it* (the ball).

▪ **A sentence has a complete *verb* that indicates tense, person, and number.** In the first word group, *deceive* is the third-person plural form of the verb in the present tense and is a complete verb. In the second word group, however, *putting* is not a complete verb; instead, it is a verbal, a word derived from a verb. (*For more on verbals, see pp. 390–91.*) *Jumps* is a complete verb, however.

▪ **A sentence includes at least one independent *clause*.** An independent clause has a subject and a complete verb and does not begin with a subordinating word such as *although, because, since, that, unless, which,* or *while*. In the example, the first word group, which has a subject and a complete verb, does not begin with a subordinating word; it is an independent clause. Even though the second word group includes the subject-plus-verb combination *it jumps,* the combination is preceded by the subordinating word *that,* so the clause it appears in can-

Intentional Fragments

Advertisers often use attention-getting fragments: "Got Milk?" "Nothing but Net." "Because you're worth it." Occasionally, you may want to use a sentence fragment for stylistic reasons. Keep in mind, however, that advertising and college writing have different contexts and purposes. In formal writing, use deliberate sentence fragments sparingly.

not be considered an independent clause. The words that precede it, *deliberately putting so much spin on the ball,* do not include a subject and a complete verb.

In the example, the first word group meets all three requirements and is a complete sentence. Although the second word group has a subject and a complete verb, they are part of a dependent clause that begins with the subordinating word *that.* Because the second word group does not have an independent clause with a subject and a complete verb, it is not a complete sentence.

Repair sentence fragments in one of two ways. You can fix unintentional fragments in one of two ways: either transform them into sentences or attach them to a nearby independent clause. Consider the following examples. Do you prefer one way of fixing the fragment over the other approach?

➤ **Pool hustlers deceive their opponents in many ways.**
                    they
   For example, deliberately putting so much spin on
                    ^

   the ball that it jumps out of the intended pocket.

➤ **Pool hustlers deceive their opponents in many ways./,**
                                                          ^
   for example, by
   ~~For example,~~ deliberately putting so much spin on
    ^

   the ball that it jumps out of the intended pocket.

51a Connect a dependent-clause fragment to another sentence, or eliminate the subordinating word.

Fragments often begin with a subordinating word such as *although, because, even though, since, so that, whenever,* or *whereas.* Usually, a fragment that begins with a subordinating word can be attached to a nearby independent clause.

➤ **On the questionnaire, none of the thirty-three subjects**

indicated any concern about the amount or kind of fruit the

even
institution served., ~~Even~~ though all of them identified diet
                    ^

as an important issue for those with diabetes.

As the next example shows, however, it is sometimes better to transform such a fragment into a complete sentence by deleting the subordinating word.

➤ **The solidarity of our group was undermined in two ways.**
Participants
~~When participants~~ either disagreed about priorities or advocated
   ^

significantly different political strategies.

51b Connect a phrase fragment to another sentence, or add the missing elements.

Unintentional fragments come in a variety of shapes and sizes. Often they are **phrases,** word groups that lack a subject or a complete verb or both and usually function as modifiers or nouns. Phrase fragments frequently begin with **verbals**—words derived from verbs, such as *putting* or *to put.* Here is an example of a phrase fragment that begins with an *-ing* verbal.

FRAGMENT That summer, we had the time of our lives. *Fishing in the early morning hours, splashing in the lake after lunch, exploring the woods before dinner, and playing Scrabble until it was time for bed.*

One way to fix this fragment is to transform it into an independent clause with its own subject and verb:

                                                We fished
➤ **That summer, we had the time of our lives. ~~Fishing~~ in the early**
                                                        ^
     splashed   *explored*
morning hours, ~~splashing~~ in the lake after lunch, ~~exploring~~
                     ^   ^
                              played
the woods before dinner, and ~~playing~~ Scrabble until it was
                                 ^

time for bed.

Notice that all of the *-ing* verbals in the fragment need to be changed to keep the phrases in the new sentence parallel. (*For more on parallelism, see Tab 10: Editing for Clarity, p. 349–50.*)

Another way to fix the problem is to attach the fragment to the part of the previous sentence that it modifies (in this case, *the time of our lives*):

➤ That summer, we had the time of our lives./, ~~Fishing~~ in the early
   fishing

   morning hours, splashing in the lake after lunch, exploring the

   woods before dinner, and playing Scrabble until it was time for bed.

Phrase fragments can also begin with one-word prepositions such as *as, at, by, for, from, in, of, on,* or *to.* To correct these types of fragments, it is usually easiest to attach them to a nearby sentence.

➤ Impressionist painters often depicted their subjects in everyday
   at
   situations./, ~~At~~ a restaurant, perhaps, or by the seashore.

51c Connect other types of fragments to another sentence, or add the missing elements.

Phrase fragments don't always begin with subordinating words, verbals, or one-word prepositions. Other word groups that can also cause problems include word groups that start with transitions or with words that introduce examples, appositives, lists, and compound predicates.

1. Watch for word groups that start with transitions. As the following example shows, some fragments start with two- or three-word prepositions that function as transitions, such as *as well as, as compared with, except for, in addition to, in contrast with, in spite of,* and *instead of.*

➤ For the past sixty-five years, the growth in consumer spending
   as
   has been both steep and steady./, ~~As~~ compared with the growth

   in gross domestic product (GDP), which fluctuated significantly

   between 1929 and 1950.

2. Watch for words and phrases that introduce examples. It is always a good idea to check word groups beginning with *for example,* *like, specifically,* or *such as.* When you spot one of these words or phrases, make sure that the word group it introduces is a complete sentence.

➤ **Elizabeth I of England faced many dangers as a princess. For**
she fell
example, ~~falling~~ out of favor with her sister, Queen Mary, and
          ^
was
~~being~~ imprisoned in the Tower of London.
^

3. Watch for appositives. An **appositive** is a noun or noun phrase that renames a noun or pronoun.

➤ **In 1965, Lyndon Johnson increased the number of troops in**
a
Vietnam./, A former French colony in southeast Asia.
    ^

4. Watch for fragments that consist of lists. Usually, you can connect a list to the preceding sentence using a colon. If you want to emphasize the list, consider using a dash instead.

➤ **In the 1930s, three great band leaders helped popularize**

jazz./: Louis Armstrong, Benny Goodman, and Duke Ellington.
  ^

5. Watch for fragments that are parts of compound predicates. A **compound predicate** is made up of at least two verbs as well as their objects and modifiers, connected by a coordinating conjunction such as *and, but,* or *or.* The parts of a compound predicate have the same subject and should be together in one sentence.

                                   and
➤ **The group gathered at dawn at the base of the mountain./~~And~~**
                                               ^

assembled their gear in preparation for the morning's climb.

52   Comma Splices and Run-on Sentences

A frequent error in college writing, a **comma splice** is a sentence with at least two independent clauses joined by only a comma.

COMMA   Dogs that compete in the annual Westminster Dog Show
SPLICE   are already champions, they have each won at least one
               dog show before arriving at Madison Square Garden.

A **run-on sentence,** sometimes called a **fused sentence,** does not even have a comma between the independent clauses, making it difficult for readers to tell where one clause ends and the next clause begins.

RUN-ON From time to time, new breeds enter the ring the Border Collie is a recent addition to the show.

Learn how to identify comma splices and run-on sentences.

Comma splices and run-ons often occur when clauses are linked with a transitional expression such as *as a result, for example, in addition, in other words, on the contrary* or a conjunctive adverb such as *however, consequently, moreover, nevertheless.(See p. 395 for a list of familiar conjunctive adverbs and transitional expressions.)*

For more information on and practice avoiding comma splices, visit <www.mhhe.com/maimon/cs>.

COMMA SPLICE Rare books can be extremely valuable, for example, an original edition of Audubon's *Birds of America* is worth thousands of dollars.

RUN-ON Most students complied with the new policy however a few refused to do so.

(For help punctuating a sentence that links clauses with a transitional expression or conjunctive adverb, see Tab 12: Editing for Correctness, pp. 448–49.)

Run-ons may also occur when a sentence's second clause either specifies or explains its first clause.

For more information on and practice avoiding run-on sentences, visit <www.mhhe.com/maimon/run-ons>.

RUN-ON The economy changed in 1991 corporate bankruptcies increased by 40 percent.

To find comma splices and run-ons, begin by checking those sentences that include transitional expressions or conjunctive adverbs. If a comma precedes one of these words or phrases, you may have found a comma splice. If no punctuation precedes one of them, you may have found a run-on sentence. Check the word groups that precede and follow the conjunctive adverb or transitional expression. Can they both stand alone as sentences? If so, you have found a comma splice or a run-on sentence.

A second method for locating comma splices is to check sentences that contain commas. Can the word groups that appear on both sides of the comma stand alone as sentences? If so, you have found a comma splice.

Repair comma splices and run-on sentences in one of five ways.

1. Join the two clauses with a comma and a coordinating conjunction (*and, but, or, nor, for, so, yet*).

   ➤ **Dogs that compete in the annual Westminster Dog Show**
   for
   are already champions, they have each won at least

   one dog show before arriving at Madison Square Garden.

2. Join the two clauses with a semicolon.

   ➤ **From time to time, new breeds enter the ring; the Border**

   Collie is a recent addition to the show.

   You can also add an appropriate conjunctive adverb or transitional expression, followed by a comma.

   ; for instance,
   ➤ **From time to time, new breeds enter the ring the Border**

   Collie is a recent addition to the show.

3. Separate the clauses into two sentences.

   . Therefore,
   ➤ **Salt air corrodes metal easily therefore automobiles**

   in coastal regions require frequent washing.

4. Turn one of the independent clauses into a dependent clause.

   ➤ **Treasure hunters shopping in thrift stores and at garage**
   because
   sales should be realistic, valuable finds are extremely rare.

5. Transform the two clauses into a single independent clause.

   or
   ➤ **Some collectors favor old cookie jars, ~~some even like~~**

   antique stoves.

52a Join the two clauses with a comma and a coordinating conjunction such as *and, but, or, nor, for, so,* or *yet.*

If you decide to correct a comma splice or run-on by joining the two clauses, be sure to choose the coordinating conjunction that most clearly expresses the logical relationship between the clauses. In the example below, the logical coordinating conjunction is *so*.

➤ John is a very stubborn person, I had a hard time convincing

so

him to let me take the wheel.

52b Join the two clauses with a semicolon.

Like a coordinating conjunction, a semicolon tells your reader that two clauses are logically connected. However, a semicolon does not spell out the logic of the connection.

➤ Most students complied with the new policy; a few refused

to do so.

To make the logic of the connection clear, you can add an appropriate conjunctive adverb or transitional expression.

➤ Most students complied with the new policy; a few refused

; however,

to do so.

Familiar Conjunctive Adverbs and Transitional Expressions

also	incidentally	now
as a result	indeed	nonetheless
besides	in fact	of course
certainly	in other words	on the contrary
consequently	instead	otherwise
finally	in the meantime	similarly
for example	likewise	still
for instance	meanwhile	then
furthermore	moreover	therefore
however	nevertheless	thus
in addition	next	undoubtedly

Note: The conjunctive adverb or transitional expression is usually followed by a comma when it appears at the beginning of the second clause. It can also appear in the middle of a clause, set off by two commas, or at the end, preceded by a comma.

➤ Most students complied with the new policy,/; a few refused *, however,*

to do so.

➤ Most students complied with the new policy,/; a few refused
, however
to do so.

Often the first independent clause introduces the second one. In this situation, you can add a colon instead of a semicolon. A colon is also appropriate if the second clause expands on the first one in some way. (*See Tab 12: Editing for Correctness, pp. 450–52.*)

➤ Professor Johnson then revealed his most important point: the

paper would count for half of my grade.

52c Separate the clauses into two sentences.

The simplest way to correct comma splices and run-on sentences is to turn the clauses into separate sentences. The simplest solution is not always the best solution, however, especially if the result is one short, simple sentence followed by another. The simplest solution works well in this example because the second sentence is a compound sentence.

➤ I realized that it was time to choose,/ either I had to learn how *. Either*

to drive, or I had to move back to the city.

When the two independent clauses are part of a quote, with a phrase such as *he said* or *she noted* between them, each clause should be a separate sentence.

➤ "This was the longest day of my life," she said,/ "unfortunately, *. "Unfortunately,*

it's not over yet."

52d Turn one of the independent clauses into a dependent clause.

In editing the following sentence, the writer chose to make the clause about *a few* her main point and the clause about *most students* a subordinate idea. Because she made this choice, readers will expect subsequent sentences to tell them more about those few students who refused to comply.

> *Although most*
> M̶o̶s̶t̶ students complied with the new policy, ~~however~~ a few
> ^   ^
>
> refused to do so.

52e Transform the two clauses into one independent clause.

It is sometimes possible—but seldom easy—to transform the two clauses into one clear and correct independent clause. This kind of transformation is often worth the work, however.

> I realized that it was time t̶o̶ ̶c̶h̶o̶o̶s̶e̶,̶ either I̶ ̶h̶a̶d̶ to learn how to
>
> drive or I̶ ̶h̶a̶d̶ to move back to the city.

Often you can change one of the clauses to a phrase and place it next to the word it modifies.

>   *, first printed in the nineteenth century,*
> Baseball cards are an obsession among some collectors╱. the
>   ^   ^
>
> c̶a̶r̶d̶s̶ ̶w̶e̶r̶e̶ ̶f̶i̶r̶s̶t̶ ̶p̶r̶i̶n̶t̶e̶d̶ ̶i̶n̶ ̶t̶h̶e̶ ̶n̶i̶n̶e̶t̶e̶e̶n̶t̶h̶ ̶c̶e̶n̶t̶u̶r̶y̶.̶

53 Subject-Verb Agreement

All verbs must agree with their subjects in person (first, second, or third—*I, we; you; he, she, it, they*) and number (singular or plural).

> A *bear lives* in the woods near my home.

Bear is a third-person singular noun, and *lives* is the third-person singular form of the verb.

> Many North American *mammals hibernate* in the winter.

Mammals is a third-person plural noun, and *hibernate* is the third-person plural form of the verb.

For a summary of standard verb forms as well as the forms of the irregular verbs *be, have,* and *do,* see page 398.

Problems with subject-verb agreement tend to occur when writers do the following:

- Lose sight of the subject (*53b, p. 399*)
- Use compound, collective, or indefinite subjects (*53c–e, pp. 399–402*)

For more information on and practice in subject-verb agreement, visit <www.mhhe.com/maimon/subj/vb_agreement>.

- Have a subject that follows the verb (*53f, p. 403*)
- Confuse a subject complement with the subject (*53g, p. 403*)
- Use a relative pronoun as the subject of a dependent clause (*53h, pp. 403–4*)
- Use a phrase beginning with an *-ing* verb as the subject (*53i, p. 404*)

53a Learn the standard subject-verb combinations.

For regular verbs, the present tense *-s* or *-es* ending is added to the verb if its subject is third-person singular; otherwise, the verb has no ending.

Present Tense Forms of a Regular Verb: *Read*

	SINGULAR	PLURAL
First Person	I *read.*	We *read.*
Second Person	You *read.*	You *read.*
Third Person	He, she, it *reads.*	They *read.*

Note, however, that the verb *be* has irregular forms in both the present and the past tense.

Present Tense and Past Tense Forms of the Irregular Verb *Be*

	SINGULAR	PLURAL
First Person	I *am/was* here.	We *are/were* here.
Second Person	You *are/were* here.	You *are/were* here.
Third Person	He, she, it *is/was* here.	They *are/were* here.

The verbs *have* and *do* have the following forms in the present tense.

Present Tense Forms of the Verb *Have*

	SINGULAR	PLURAL
First Person	I *have.*	We *have.*
Second Person	You *have.*	You *have.*
Third Person	He, she, it *has.*	They *have.*

Present Tense Forms of the Verb *Do* and Its Negative *Don't*

	SINGULAR	PLURAL
First Person	I *do/don't.*	We *do/don't.*
Second Person	You *do/don't.*	You *do/don't.*
Third Person	He, she, it *does/doesn't.*	They *do/don't.*

53b Do not lose sight of the subject when a word group separates it from the verb.

When you are checking for subject-verb agreement, begin by locating the subject. A word group often separates the subject and the verb.

To locate the subject of a sentence, find the verb (for example, *is*), and then ask the *who* or *what* question about it ("Who is?" "What is?"). Does that subject match the verb in number?

➤ **The leaders of the trade union ~~opposes~~ the new law.**
                                      oppose

    The answer to the question "Who opposes?" is *leaders,* a plural noun, so the verb should be in the plural form: *oppose.*

Note: If a word group beginning with *as well as, along with,* or *in addition to* follows a singular subject, the subject does not become plural.

➤ **My teacher, as well as other faculty members, ~~oppose~~ the new**
                                              opposes

    school policy.

53c Treat most compound subjects—subjects connected by *and, or, nor, both . . . and, either . . . or, neither . . . nor*—as plural.

Compound subjects are made up of two or more parts joined by either a coordinating conjunction (*and, or, nor*) or a correlative conjunction (*both . . . and, either . . . or, neither . . . nor*).

1. Most compound subjects are plural. Most subjects that are joined by *and* should be treated as plural.

PLURAL   *The king and his advisers were shocked by this turn*

            of events.

PLURAL   This poem's *first line and last word have* a powerful

effect on the reader.

2. Some compound subjects are singular. There are exceptions to the rule that subjects joined by *and* are plural. Compound subjects should be treated as singular in the following circumstances:

▪ When they refer to the same entity:

➤ *My best girlfriend and most dependable advisor is* my mother.

▪ When they are considered as a single unit:

➤ In some ways, *forty acres and a mule continues* to be what is

needed.

▪ When they are preceded by the word *each* or *every:*

➤ *Each* man, woman, and child *deserves* respect.

3. Some compound subjects can be either plural or singular.
Compound subjects connected by *or, nor, either . . . or,* or *neither . . . nor* can take either a singular or a plural verb, depending on the subject that is closest to the verb.

SINGULAR   Either the children or *their mother is* to blame.

PLURAL   Neither the experimenter nor *her subjects were*

aware of the takeover.

53d Treat most collective subjects—subjects like
audience, family, and *committee*—as singular.

A **collective noun** names a unit made up of many persons or things, treating it as an entity. Some familiar examples are *audience, family, group,* and *team.*

1. Most often, collective nouns are singular. Collective nouns such as *audience, family, group, crowd, team, committee, chorus, herd,* and *tribe* are usually treated as singular. *News* is usually singular as well, despite its *-s* ending, because it functions as a collective subject, representing a collective unit. Units of measurement used collectively, such as *six inches* or *20%,* are also treated as singular.

➤ The *audience is* restless.

➤ That *news leaves* me speechless.

➤ *One-fourth* of the liquid *was* poured into test tube 1.

Note: Titles of works or names of companies are singular.

➤ Ernest Hemingway's *For Whom the Bell Tolls is* arguably his

darkest work.

2. Some collective subjects are plural. When the members of a group are acting as individuals, the collective subject can be considered plural.

➤ The *group were* passing around a bottle of beer.

You may want to add a modifying phrase that contains a plural noun to make the sentence clearer and avoid awkwardness.

➤ The *group of troublemakers were* passing around a bottle of beer.

The modifying phrase *of troublemakers* makes the sentence less awkward.

When units of measurement refer to people or things, they are plural.

➤ *One-fourth* of the students in the class *are* failing the course.

53e Treat most indefinite subjects—subjects like *everybody, no one, each, all,* and *none*—as singular.

Indefinite pronouns such as *everybody* and *no one* do not refer to a specific person or item.

1. Most indefinite pronouns are singular. The following indefinite pronouns are always singular: *all, anybody, anyone, anything, each, either, everybody, everyone, everything, neither, nobody, no one, none, nothing, one, somebody, someone,* and *something.*

➤ *Everyone* in my hiking club *is* an experienced climber.

None and *neither* are singular when they appear by themselves.

➤ In the movie, five men set out on an expedition, but *none returns*.

➤ *Neither sees* a way out of this predicament.

If a prepositional phrase that includes a plural noun or pronoun follows *none* or *neither,* the indefinite pronoun seems to have a plural meaning. Although some writers treat *none* or *neither* as plural in such situations, other authorities on language maintain that these two pronouns are always singular. It is a safe bet to consider them singular.

SINGULAR   In the movie, five men set out on an expedition,

but *none* of them *returns*.

SINGULAR   *Neither* of the hikers *sees* a way out of this

predicament.

2. Some indefinite pronouns are always plural.
A handful of indefinite pronouns (*both, few, many, several*) are always plural because they mean more than one by definition. *Both,* for example, always indicates two.

➤ *Both* of us *want* to go to the rally for the environment.

➤ *Several* of my friends *were* very happy about the outcome of

the election.

3. Some indefinite pronouns can be either plural or singular.
Some indefinite pronouns (*some, any, all, most*) may be either plural or singular. To decide, consider the context of the sentence, especially noting any noun or pronoun that the indefinite pronoun refers to.

➤ *Some* of the *book is* missing, but *all* of the *papers are* here.

53f Make sure the subject and verb agree when the subject comes after the verb.

In most English sentences, the verb comes after the subject. Sometimes, however, a writer will switch this order. In the following sentence, you can locate the subject by asking, "Who or what stand?" The answer is the sentence's subject: *an oak and a weeping willow.* Because the subject is a compound subject (two subjects joined by *and*), the verb must be plural.

➤ Out back behind the lean-to *stand an old oak tree and a*

weeping willow.

In sentences that begin with *there is* or *there are,* the subject always follows the verb.

➤ There *is* a worn wooden *bench* in the shade of the two trees.

53g Make sure the verb agrees with its subject, not the subject complement.

A **subject complement** renames and specifies the sentence's subject. It follows a **linking verb**—a verb, often a form of *be,* that joins the subject to its description or definition: *children <u>are</u> innocent.* In the sentence below, the singular noun *gift* is the subject. *Books* is the subject complement. Therefore, *are* has been changed to *is* to agree in number with *gift.*

is
➤ One gift that gives her pleasure ~~are~~ books.
     ^

53h *Who, which,* and *that* (relative pronouns) take verbs that agree with the subject they replace.

When a relative pronoun such as *who, which,* or *that* is the subject of a dependent clause, the pronoun is taking the place of a noun that appears earlier in the sentence—its **antecedent.** Therefore, the verb that goes with *who, which,* or *that* needs to agree with this antecedent. In the following sentence, the relative pronoun *that* is the subject of the dependent clause *that has a number of dangerous side effects.* Disease, a singular noun, is the antecedent of *that;* therefore, the verb in the dependent clause is singular.

➤ Measles is a childhood *disease that has* dangerous side effects.

The phrases *one of the* and *only one of the* imply number.
When *one of the* or *only one of the* precedes the antecedent in a sentence, writers can become confused about which form of the verb to use. The phrase *one of the* implies more than one and is, therefore, plural. *Only one of the* implies just one, however, and is singular. Generally, use the plural form of the verb when the phrase *one of the* comes before the antecedent. Use the singular form of the verb when *only one of the* comes before the antecedent.

PLURAL   Tuberculosis is *one of the* diseases *that have* long,

tragic histories in many parts of the world.

SINGULAR   Barbara is the *only one of the* scientists *who has* a

degree in physics.

53i Phrases beginning with *-ing* verbs take the singular form of the verb when they are subjects.

A **gerund phrase** is an *-ing* verb form followed by objects, complements, or modifiers. When a gerund phrase is the subject in a sentence, it is singular.

➤   *Experimenting with drugs is* a dangerous rave practice.

54   Problems with Verbs

Verbs provide a great deal of information. They report action (*run, write*) and show time (*going, gone*). They change form to indicate person (first, second, or third—*I, we; you; he, she, it, they*) and number (singular or plural). They also change to indicate voice and mood.

54a Learn the principal forms of regular and irregular verbs.

All English verbs have five main forms, except for the *be* verb, which has eight.

- The **base form** is the form you find if you look up the verb in a dictionary. (*For irregular verbs, other forms are given as well. See pp. 405–7 for a list.*)
- The **present tense** form is used to indicate an action occurring at the moment or habitually, as well as to introduce quotations,

literary events, and scientific facts (*54e, pp. 410–12 and 54g, pp. 413–14*).

- The **past tense** is used to indicate an action completed at a specific time in the past (*54e, pp. 410–12*).

- The **past participle** is used with *have, has,* or *had* to form the perfect tenses (*54e, pp. 410–12*); with a form of the *be* verb to form the passive voice (*54k, p. 417*); and as an adjective (the *polished* silver).

- The **present participle** is used with a form of the *be* verb to form the progressive tenses (*54e, pp. 410–12*). It can also be used as a noun (the *writing* is finished) and as an adjective (the *smiling* man).

Regular verbs always add *-d* or *-ed* to the base verb to form the past tense and past participle. **Irregular verbs,** by contrast, do not form the past tense or past participle in a consistent way. Here are the five principal forms of the regular verb *walk* and the irregular verb *begin* as well as the eight forms of the verb *be*.

Principal Forms of *Walk* and *Begin*

BASE	PRESENT TENSE (THIRD PERSON)	PAST TENSE	PAST PARTICIPLE	PRESENT PARTICIPLE
walk	*walk<u>s</u>*	*walk<u>ed</u>*	*walk<u>ed</u>*	*walk<u>ing</u>*
begin	*begin<u>s</u>*	*beg<u>an</u>*	*beg<u>un</u>*	*begin<u>ning</u>*

Principal Forms of *Be*

BASE	PRESENT TENSE	PAST TENSE	PAST PARTICIPLE	PRESENT PARTICIPLE
be	I *am.*	I *was.*	I have *been.*	I am *being.*
	He, she, it *is.*	He, she, it *was.*		
	We, you, they *are.*	We, you, they *were.*		

1. Refer to the list of common irregular verbs.

If you are not sure which form of an irregular verb is called for in a sentence, consult the list of common irregular verbs that follows. You can also find the past tense and past participle forms of irregular verbs by looking up the base form in a standard dictionary.

Forms of Common Irregular Verbs

BASE	PAST TENSE	PAST PARTICIPLE
awake	awoke	awoke/awakened
arise	arose	arisen

BASE	PAST TENSE	PAST PARTICIPLE
be	was/were	been
beat	beat	beaten
become	became	become
begin	began	begun
blow	blew	blown
break	broke	broken
bring	brought	brought
buy	bought	bought
catch	caught	caught
choose	chose	chosen
cling	clung	clung
come	came	come
do	did	done
draw	drew	drawn
drink	drank	drunk
drive	drove	driven
eat	ate	eaten
fall	fell	fallen
fight	fought	fought
fly	flew	flown
forget	forgot	forgotten/forgot
forgive	forgave	forgiven
freeze	froze	frozen
get	got	gotten/got
give	gave	given
go	went	gone
grow	grew	grown
hang	hung	hung (for things)
hang	hanged	hanged (for people)
have	had	had
hear	heard	heard
know	knew	known
lose	lost	lost
pay	paid	paid
raise	raised	raised
ride	rode	ridden

BASE	PAST TENSE	PAST PARTICIPLE
ring	rang	rung
rise	rose	risen
say	said	said
see	saw	seen
set	set	set
shake	shook	shaken
sit	sat	sat
spin	spun	spun
steal	stole	stolen
spend	spent	spent
strive	strove/strived	striven/strived
swear	swore	sworn
swim	swam	swum
swing	swung	swung
take	took	taken
tear	tore	torn
tread	trod	trod/trodden
wear	wore	worn
weave	wove	woven
wring	wrung	wrung
write	wrote	written

 LEARNING in COLLEGE

Finding a Verb's Principal Forms

If you are unsure of a verb's principal forms, check a dictionary. If the verb is regular, the dictionary will list only the present form and you will know that you should form the verb's past tense and past participle by adding *-ed* or *-d*. If the verb is irregular, the dictionary will give its principal forms.

Dictionary entry for an irregular verb:

Preferred past tense form given first

sing (sing) *v.*, sang or, often, sung; sung; singing

part of speech (v, verb)   past participle   present participle

2. Use the correct forms of irregular verbs that end in *-en* (*rode/ridden*).
The forms of irregular verbs with past tenses that end in *-e* and past participles that end in *-n* or *-en,* such as *ate/eaten, rode/ridden, wore/worn, stole/stolen,* and *swore/sworn,* are sometimes confused.

eaten
➤ He had ate the apple.
    ^
    ridden
➤ They had rode the whole way on the bus.
      ^
      sworn
➤ I could have swore the necklace was here.
         ^

3. Use the correct forms of *went* and *gone, saw* and *seen.*
Went and *saw* are the past tense forms of the irregular verbs *go* and *see. Gone* and *seen* are the past participle forms. These verb forms are commonly confused. Check carefully to make sure that you are using the correct form as you edit your writing.

gone
➤ I had went there yesterday.
      ^
  saw
➤ We seen the rabid dog and called for help.
    ^

4. Use the correct forms of irregular verbs such as *drink* (*drank/drunk*).
For a few irregular verbs, such as *swim (swam/ swum), drink (drank/drunk),* and *ring (rang/rung),* the difference between the past tense form and the past participle is only one letter. Be careful not to mix up these forms in your writing.

drunk
➤ I had drank more than eight bottles of water that day.
    ^

54b Distinguish between *lay* and *lie, sit* and *set,* and *rise* and *raise.*

Even the most experienced writers commonly confuse the verbs *lay* and *lie, sit* and *set,* and *rise* and *raise.* The correct forms are given below.

Often-Confused Verb Pairs and Their Principal Forms

BASE	PAST	PAST PARTICIPLE	PRESENT PARTICIPLE
lay (to place)	laid	laid	laying
lie (to recline)	lay	lain	lying
sit (to be seated)	sat	sat	sitting
set (to put on a surface)	set	set	setting

Tips LEARNING in COLLEGE

Using Lay *and* Lie *Correctly*

Lay (to place) and *lie* (to recline) are also confusing because the past tense of the irregular verb *lie* is *lay* (*lie, lay, lain*). To avoid using the wrong form, always double-check the verb *lay* when it appears in your writing.

> *laid*
> ➤ He washed the dishes carefully, then ~~lay~~ them on a clean towel.

Often-Confused Verb Pairs and Their Principal Forms (*continued*)

BASE	PAST	PAST PARTICIPLE	PRESENT PARTICIPLE
rise (to go/get up)	rose	risen	rising
raise (to lift up)	raised	raised	raising

One verb in each of these pairs (*lay, set, raise*) is **transitive,** which means that an object receives the action of the verb. The other verb (*lie, sit, rise*) is **intransitive** and cannot take an object. You should use a form of *lay, set,* or *raise* if you can replace the verb with *place* or *put.* (*See Tab 13: Basic Grammar Review, pp. 523–25 for more on transitive and intransitive verbs.*)

> direct object
> ➤ The dog *lays a bone* at your feet, then *lies* down and closes his eyes.

> direct object
> ➤ The technician *sits* down at the table and *sets the samples* in
>
> front of her.

> direct object
> ➤ As the flames *rise* from the fire, the heat *raises the temperature*
>
> of the room.

54c Do not forget to add an *-s* or *-es* ending to the verb when it is necessary.

In the present tense, almost all verbs add an *-s* or *-es* ending if the subject is third-person singular. (*See pp. 398–99, for more on standard subject-verb combinations.*) Third-person singular subjects can be nouns (*woman, Benjamin, desk*), pronouns (*he, she, it*), or indefinite pronouns (*everyone*).

> *rises*
> The stock market ~~rise~~ when economic news is good.
>   ^

If the subject is in the first person (*I*), the second person (*you*), or the third-person plural (*people, they*), the verb does *not* add an -s or -es ending.

> You invest~~s~~ your money wisely.

> People need~~s~~ to learn about companies before buying their stock.

54d Do not forget to add a -d or an -ed ending to the verb when it is necessary.

When they are speaking, people sometimes leave the -*d* or -*ed* ending off certain verbs such as *asked, fixed, mixed, supposed to,* and *used to,* but in writing the endings should be included on all regular verbs in the past tense and all past participles of regular verbs.

> *asked*
> The driving instructor ask the student driver to pull
>   ^
>
> over to the curb.

> *mixed*
> After we had mix the formula, we let it cool.
>   ^

Also check for missing -*d* or -*ed* endings on past participles used as adjectives.

> *concerned*
> The concern parents met with the school board.
>   ^

54e Use verb tenses accurately.

For more information on and practice with verbs, visit <www.mhhe.com/maimon/verbs>.

Tenses show the time of a verb's action. English has three basic time frames: present, past, and future, and each tense has simple, perfect, and progressive verb forms to indicate the time span of the actions that are taking place. (*For a review of the present tense forms of a typical verb and of the verbs* be, have, *and* do, *see 53a, Standard Subject-Verb Combinations, pp. 398–99; for a review of the principal forms of regular and irregular verbs, which are used to form tenses, see 54a, pp. 404–8.*)

1. The simple present and past tenses use only the verb itself, without a helping verb or verbs. The **simple present tense** is used for actions occurring at the moment or habitually. The **simple past tense** is used for actions completed at a specific time in the past.

Tips LEARNING in COLLEGE

Checking Verb Tenses

Is the time frame of your paper predominantly present, past, or future? Keep this time frame in mind as you edit, and you will be better able to see and solve problems with the accuracy and consistency of your verb tenses.

SIMPLE PRESENT

Every May, she *plans* next year's marketing strategy.

SIMPLE PAST

In the early morning hours before the office opened, she *planned* her marketing strategy.

2. The simple future tense takes *will* plus the verb. The **simple future tense** is used for actions that have not yet begun.

SIMPLE FUTURE

In May, I *will plan* next year's marketing strategy.

3. Perfect tenses take a form of *have* (*has, had*) plus the past participle. The **perfect tenses** are used to indicate actions that were or will be completed by the time of another action or a specific time.

PRESENT PERFECT

She *has* already *planned* next year's marketing strategy.

PAST PERFECT

By the time she resigned, Mary *had* already *planned* next year's marketing strategy.

FUTURE PERFECT

By the end of May, she *will have planned* next year's marketing strategy.

When the verb in the past perfect is irregular, be sure to use the proper form of the past participle.

➤ By the time the fight was over, both children had ~~forgot~~ *forgotten* what

started it.

4. Progressive tenses take a form of *be* (*am, are, were*) plus the present participle. The progressive forms of the simple and perfect tenses are used to indicate ongoing action.

PRESENT PROGRESSIVE

She *is planning* next year's marketing strategy now.

PAST PROGRESSIVE

She *was planning* next year's marketing strategy when she started to look for another job.

FUTURE PROGRESSIVE

During the month of May, she *will be planning* next year's marketing strategy.

5. Perfect progressive tenses take *have* plus *be* plus the verb. Perfect progressive tenses indicate an action that takes place over a specific period of time. The present perfect progressive tense is used for actions that start in the past and continue to the present; the past and future perfect progressive tenses are used for actions that ended or will end at a specified time or before another action.

PRESENT PERFECT PROGRESSIVE

She *has been planning* next year's marketing strategy since the beginning of May.

PAST PERFECT PROGRESSIVE

She *had been planning* next year's marketing strategy when she was offered another job.

FUTURE PERFECT PROGRESSIVE

By May 18, she *will have been planning* next year's marketing strategy for more than two weeks.

54f Use the past perfect tense to indicate an action completed at a specific time or before another event.

When a past event was ongoing but ended before a particular time or another past event, use the past perfect rather than the simple past.

➤ **Before the Johnstown Flood occurred in 1889, people in the**
　　had
area expressed their concern about the safety of the dam
　　^

on the Conemaugh River.

People expressed their concern before the flood occurred.

Reporting Research Findings

Although a written work may be seen as always present, research findings are thought of as having been collected at one time in the past. Use the past or present perfect tense to report the results of research:

responded

➤ **Three of the compounds (nos. 2, 3, and 6) respond positively**

by turning purple.

has reviewed

➤ **Clegg (1990) reviews studies of workplace organization**

focused on struggles for control of the labor process.

If two past events happened simultaneously, however, use the simple past, not the past perfect.

➤ **When the Conemaugh flooded, many people in the area had lost**

their lives.

54g Use the present tense for literary events, scientific facts, and introductions to quotations.

If the conventions of a discipline require you to state what your paper does, do so in the present, not the future, tense.

➤ **In this paper, I *describe* the effects of increasing NaCl**

concentrations on the germination of radish seeds.

Here are some other special uses of the present tense.

▪ By convention, events in a novel, short story, poem, or other literary work are described in the present tense.

is

➤ **Even though Huck's journey down the river was an escape from**

is

society, his relationship with Jim was a form of community.

▪ Like events in a literary work, scientific facts are considered to be perpetually present, even though they were discovered in the past.

have
➤ **Mendel discovered that genes ~~had~~ different forms, or alleles.**
^

▪ The present tense is also used to introduce a quote, paraphrase, or summary of someone else's writing.

writes
➤ **William Julius Wilson ~~wrote~~ that "the disappearance of work has**
^

become a characteristic feature of the inner-city ghetto" (31).

54h Make sure infinitives and participles fit with the tense of the main verb.

Infinitives and participles are **verbals,** words formed from verbs that have various functions within a sentence. Because they are derived from verbs and can express time, verbals need to fit with the main verb in a sentence. Verbals can also form phrases by taking objects, modifiers, or complements.

1. Use the correct tense for infinitives. An **infinitive** is *to* plus the base verb (*to breathe, to sing, to dance*). The perfect form of the infinitive is *to have* plus the past participle (*to have breathed, to have sung, to have danced*). The tense of an infinitive needs to fit with the tense of the main verb. If the action of the infinitive happens at the same time as or after the action of the main verb, use the present tense (*to* plus the base form). If the action of the infinitive happened before the action of the main verb, use the perfect form.

➤ **I hope *to sing and dance* on Broadway next summer.**

The infinitive expresses an action (*to sing and dance*) that will occur later than the action of the sentence (*hope*), so the infinitive needs to be in the present tense.

➤ **My talented mother would like *to have sung and danced* on**

Broadway as a young woman, but she never had the chance.

The action of the main verb (*would like*) is in the present, but the missed opportunity is in the past, so the infinitive needs to be in the perfect tense.

2. Use the correct tense for participles that are part of phrases. Participial phrases can begin with the present participle (*breathing, dancing, singing*), the present perfect participle (*having breathed, having danced, having sung*), or the past participle (*breathed, danced, sung*). If the action of the participle happens simultaneously with the action of the sentence's verb, use the present participle. If the action of the participle happened before the action of the main verb, use the present perfect or past participle form.

➤ ***Singing one hour a day together***, **the chorus developed perfect harmony.**

The chorus developed harmony as they sang together, so the present participle (*singing*) is appropriate.

➤ ***Having breathed*** **the air of New York, I exulted in the possibilities for my life in the city.**

The breathing took place before the exulting, so the present perfect (*having breathed*) is appropriate.

➤ ***Tinted*** **with a strange green light, the western sky looked threatening.**

The green light had to appear before the sky started to look threatening, so the past participle (*tinted*) is the right choice.

54i Make sure your verbs are complete.

With only a few exceptions, all English sentences must contain complete verbs. A **complete verb** consists of the main verb along with any helping verbs that are needed to express the tense (*see pp. 410–12*) or voice (*see p. 417*). **Helping verbs** include forms of *be, have,* and *do* and the modal verbs *can, could, may, might, shall, should,* and *will.* Helping verbs can be part of contractions (*He's running, we'd better go*), but they cannot be left out of the sentence entirely.

        will
➤ **They be going on a field trip next week.**
     ^

Linking verbs are another type of verb that writers sometimes accidentally omit. A **linking verb,** often a form of *be,* connects the subject to a description or definition of it: *Children <u>are</u> innocent.* Linking verbs can be part of contractions (*She's a student*), but they should not be left out entirely.

       is
➤ **Montreal a major Canadian city.**
     ^

54j Use the subjunctive mood for wishes, requests, and conjecture.

The **mood** of a verb indicates the writer's attitude. Use the **indicative mood** to state or to question facts, acts, and opinions (*Our collection is on display. Did you see it?*). Use the **imperative mood** for commands, directions, and entreaties. The subject of an imperative sentence is always *you*, but the *you* is usually understood, not written out (*Shut the door!*). Use the **subjunctive mood** to express a wish or a demand or to make a statement contrary to fact (*I wish I were a millionaire*). The mood that writers have the most trouble with is the subjunctive.

Verbs in the subjunctive mood may be in the present tense, the past tense, or the perfect tense. Present tense subjunctive verbs do not change form to signal person or number. The only form used is the verb's base form: *accompany* or *be*, not *accompanies* or *am, are, is*. Also, the verb *be* has only one past tense form in the subjunctive mood: *were*.

1. Use the subjunctive mood to express a wish.

WISH

If only I *were* more prepared for this test.

Note: In everyday conversation, most speakers use the indicative rather than the subjunctive when expressing wishes (*If only I was more prepared for this test*).

2. Use the subjunctive mood for requests, recommendations, and demands.
Because requests, recommendations, and demands have not yet happened, they—like wishes—are expressed in the subjunctive mood. Words such as *ask, insist, recommend, request,* and *suggest* indicate the subjunctive mood; the verb in the *that* clause that follows should be in the subjunctive.

DEMAND

I insist that all applicants *find* their seats by 8:00 a.m.

3. Use the subjunctive in statements that are contrary to fact.
Often such statements contain a subordinate clause that begins with *if:* the verb in the *if* clause should be in the subjunctive mood.

CONTRARY-TO-FACT STATEMENT

He would not be so irresponsible if his father *were* [not *was*] still alive.

Note: Some common expressions of conjecture are in the subjunctive mood, including *as it were, come rain or shine, far be it from me,* and *be that as it may.*

CHARTING the TERRITORY

Passive Voice in Scientific Writing

To keep the focus on objects and actions, scientists writing about the results of their research regularly use the passive voice in their laboratory reports.

PASSIVE A sample of 20 radish seeds *was germinated* on filter paper soaked in a 10% sodium chloride solution.

54k Choose the active voice unless a special situation calls for the passive.

A verb is in the **active voice** when the subject of the sentence does the acting; it is in the **passive voice** when the subject is acted upon by an agent that is implied or that is expressed in a prepositional phrase. To make a verb passive, use the appropriate form of the *be* verb plus the past participle. Only transitive verbs—verbs that take objects—can be passive.

ACTIVE Professor Jones *solved* the problem.

PASSIVE The problem *was solved*.

PASSIVE The problem *was solved* by Professor Jones.

Whenever possible, choose the active voice. The passive voice emphasizes the recipient rather than the doer of the action. Use it only when the doer is not known or is not important.

PASSIVE My car *was stolen* last night.

55 Problems with Pronouns

A **pronoun** (*he / him, it / its, they / their*) takes the place of a noun. The noun that the pronoun replaces is called its **antecedent.** In the following sentence, *snow* is the antecedent of the pronoun *it*:

➤ The *snow* fell all day long, and by nightfall *it* was three feet deep.

For more information on and practice with using pronouns, visit <www.mhhe.com/maimon/pronouns>.

Like nouns, pronouns are singular or plural.

SINGULAR

The *house* was dark and gloomy, and *it* sat in a grove of tall cedars.

PLURAL

The *cars* swept by on the highway, all of *them* doing more than

sixty-five miles per hour.

A pronoun needs a specific and explicit antecedent to refer to and agree with, and a pronoun must match its antecedent in number (*plural/singular*) and gender (*he/his, she/her, it/its*). A pronoun must also be in a form, or case, that matches its function in the sentence.

55a Make pronouns agree with their antecedents.

Problems with pronoun-antecedent agreement tend to occur when a pronoun's antecedent is an indefinite pronoun, a collective noun, or a compound noun. Problems may also occur when writers are trying to avoid the generic use of *he*.

1. Avoid bias when you use indefinite pronouns. **Indefinite pronouns** such as *someone, anybody,* and *nothing* refer to nonspecific people or things. They sometimes function as antecedents for other pronouns. Most indefinite pronouns are singular (*anybody, anyone, anything, each, either, everybody, everyone, everything, much, neither, nobody, none, no one, nothing, one, somebody, something*).

ALWAYS SINGULAR   Did *either* of the boys lose *his* bicycle?

A few indefinite pronouns—*both, few, many,* and *several*—are plural.

ALWAYS PLURAL   *Both* of the boys lost *their* bicycles.

The indefinite pronouns *all, any, more, most,* and *some* can be either singular or plural depending on the noun to which the pronoun refers.

PLURAL   The students debated, *some* arguing that *their*

assumptions about the issue were more credible

than the teacher's.

SINGULAR   The bread is on the counter, but *some* of it has

already been eaten.

Problems arise when writers attempt to make indefinite pronouns agree with their antecedents without introducing gender bias. In the following sentence, for example, the writer chose to change the indefinite pronoun *none* to *all* instead of changing the plural pronoun *their* to a singular form. Why?

All
➤ ~~None~~ of the great Romantic writers believed that their
      fell short of
achievements ~~equaled~~ their aspirations.

Replacing *their* in the original sentence with *his* would have made the sentence probably untrue and certainly biased: many women were writing and publishing during the Romantic Age. The writer could have changed *their* to *his or her* to avoid bias but thought *his or her* sounded awkward. The writer solved the problem by choosing an indefinite pronoun that can have a plural meaning (*all*) and revising the sentence. An alternative would be to eliminate the indefinite pronoun altogether:

➤ The great Romantic writers believed that their achievements fell

short of their aspirations.

To summarize, here are the three ways to avoid gender bias when an indefinite pronoun is the antecedent in a sentence:

▪ If possible, change a singular indefinite pronoun to a plural pronoun.

▪ Reword the sentence to eliminate the indefinite pronoun.

▪ Substitute *he or she* or *his or her* (but never *his/her*) for the singular pronoun to maintain pronoun-antecedent agreement.

2. Avoid bias when you use generic nouns.   A **generic noun** represents anyone and everyone in a group—a typical doctor, the average voter. Because most groups consist of both males and females,

using male pronouns to refer to generic nouns is usually sexist. To fix agreement problems with generic nouns, use one of the three options suggested above.

INCORRECT

A college *student* should have a mind of *their* own.

CHANGE TO PLURAL

College *students* should have minds of *their* own.

REWORD TO AVOID PRONOUN

A college student should have an independent point of view.

USE *HIS OR HER*

A college *student* should have a mind of *his or her* own.

3. Treat most collective nouns as singular.

Collective nouns such as *team, family, jury, committee,* and *crowd* are treated as singular unless the people in the group are acting as individuals.

➤ **All together, the crowd surged through the palace gates,**

 its
trampling over everything in ~~their~~ path.
                              ^

The phrase *all together* indicates that this writer does not see—and does not want readers to see—the crowd as a collection of distinct individuals. Therefore, the plural *their* has been changed to the singular *its.*

 their
➤ **The committee left the conference room and returned to ~~its~~ offices.**
                                                            ^

In this case, the writer sees—and wants readers to see—the members of the committee as individuals.

If you are using a collective noun that has a plural meaning, consider adding a plural noun to clarify the meaning.

➤ **The *committee members* left the conference room and returned**

to *their* offices.

4. Choose the right pronoun for a compound antecedent.

Compound antecedents joined by *and* are almost always plural.

➤ **To remove all traces of the crime, James put the book and the**

 their
magnifying glass back in ~~its~~ place.
                          ^

When a compound antecedent is joined by *or* or *nor,* the pronoun should agree with the closest part of the compound antecedent. If one part is singular and the other is plural, the sentence will be smoother and more effective if the plural antecedent is closest to the pronoun.

PLURAL   Neither *the child nor the parents* shared *their* food.

Note: When the two parts of the compound antecedent refer to the same person, or when the word *each* or *every* precedes the compound antecedent, use a singular pronoun.

SINGULAR   Being *a teacher and a mother* keeps *her* busy.

SINGULAR   *Every* poem and letter by Keats has *its* own special

          power.

55b Make pronoun references clear.

If a pronoun does not clearly refer to a specific antecedent, readers can become confused. Two common problems are ambiguous references and implied references.

1. Avoid ambiguous pronoun references.   If a pronoun can refer to more than one noun in a sentence, the reference is ambiguous. In the following unedited sentence, who is the antecedent of *him* and *his*—Hamlet or Horatio?

VAGUE   The friendly banter between Hamlet and Horatio
            eventually provokes him to declare that his world
            view has changed.

To clear up the ambiguity, the writer decided to eliminate the pronoun and use the appropriate noun.

CLEAR   The friendly banter between Hamlet and Horatio
            eventually provokes Hamlet to declare that his
            world view has changed.

Sometimes the ambiguous reference can be cleared up by rewriting the sentence.

VAGUE   Jane Austen and Cassandra corresponded regularly
            when she was in London.

CLEAR   When Jane Austen was in London, she
            corresponded regularly with Cassandra.

2. Watch out for implied pronoun references.   The antecedent that a pronoun refers to must be present in the sentence, and it must be a noun or another pronoun, not a word that modifies a noun. Possessives and verbs cannot be antecedents.

➤ In ~~Wilson's~~ *his* essay "When Work Disappears," ~~he~~ *Wilson* proposes a four-

point plan for the revitalization of blighted inner-city communities.

Replacing *he* with *Wilson* gives the pronoun *his* an antecedent that is stated explicitly, not just implied. Note that in the revised sentence the antecedent follows the pronoun.

➤ Every weekday afternoon, my brothers skateboard home
from school, and then they leave ~~them~~ *their skateboards* in the driveway.

In the original sentence, *skateboard* is a verb, not a noun, and cannot act as a pronoun antecedent.

3. Use clear references for *this, that,* and *which.*   The pronouns *this, that,* and *which* are often used to refer to ideas expressed in preceding sentences. To make the sentence containing the pronoun clearer, either change the pronoun to a specific noun or add a specific antecedent or clarifying noun.

VAGUE   As government funding for higher education decreases, tuition increases. Are we students supposed to accept *this* without protest?

CLEAR   As government funding for higher education decreases, tuition increases. Are we students supposed to accept *these higher costs* without protest?

CLEAR   As government funding for higher education decreases, tuition increases. Are we students supposed to accept *this situation* without protest?

4. Use clear references for *you, they,* and *it.*   The pronouns *you, they,* and *it* should refer to definite, explicitly stated antecedents. If their antecedents are unclear, they should be replaced with appropriately specific nouns, or the sentence should be rewritten to eliminate the pronoun.

➤ In some countries such as Canada, ~~they pay~~ *the government pays* for such medical

procedures.

➤ According to college policy, ~~you~~ *students* must have a permit to park a

car on campus.

The
> ~~In the textbook/~~ it states that borrowing to fund the purchase
      ^

of financial assets results in a double-counting of debt.

55c Make pronoun cases match their function (for example, *I* vs. *me*).

When a pronoun's form, or **case,** does not match its function in a sentence, readers will feel that something is wrong. Most problems with pronoun case involve the subjective and objective forms.

- Pronouns in the subjective case are used as subjects or subject complements in sentences: *I, you, he, she, it, we, they, who, whoever.*

- Pronouns in the objective case are used as objects of verbs or prepositions: *me, you, him, her, it, us, them, whom, whomever.*

1. Use the correct pronouns in compound structures.
Compound structures (words or phrases joined by *and, or,* or *nor*) can appear as subjects or objects. If you are not sure which form of a pronoun to use in a compound structure, treat the pronoun as the only subject or object, and note how the sentence sounds.

SUBJECT   Angela and ~~me~~ were cleaning up the kitchen.
                                 I
                                      ^

If you treat the pronoun as the only subject, the sentence is clearly wrong: *Me [was] cleaning up the kitchen.* The correct form is the subjective pronoun *I.*

OBJECT   My parents waited for an explanation from John
                         me
                     and ~~I~~.
                       ^

If you treat the pronoun as the only object, the sentence is clearly wrong: *My parents waited for an explanation from I.* The correct form is the objective pronoun *me.*

2. Use the correct pronoun in subject complements
A **subject complement** renames and specifies the sentence's subject. It follows a **linking verb,** which is a verb, often a form of *be,* that links the subject to its description or definition: *Children are innocent.*

SUBJECT   Mark's best friends are Jane and ~~me~~.
COMPLEMENT   *I*
                                      ^

If you think the edited sentence sounds too awkward or formal, try switching the order to make the pronoun into the subject: *Jane and I are Mark's best friends.*

3. Use the correct pronoun in appositives.
Appositives are nouns or noun phrases that rename nouns or pronouns. They appear right after the word they rename and have the same function in the sentence that the word has.

➤ The two weary travelers, Ramon and ~~me~~ *I*, found shelter in an

old cabin.

> The appositive renames the subject, *two weary travelers,* so the pronoun should be in the subjective case: *I.*

➤ The police arrested two protesters, Jane and ~~I~~ *me*.

> The appositive renames the direct object, *protesters,* so the pronoun should be in the objective case: *me.*

4. Use either *we* or *us* before a noun, depending on the noun's function.
When *we* or *us* comes before a noun, it has the same function in the sentence as the noun it precedes.

➤ ~~Us~~ *We* students never get to decide such things.

> *We* renames the subject: *students.*

➤ Things were looking desperate for ~~we~~ *us* campers.

> *Us* renames the object of the preposition *for: campers.*

5. Use the correct pronoun in comparisons with *than* or *as.*
In comparisons, words are often left out of the sentence because the reader can guess what they would be. When a pronoun follows *than* or *as,* make sure you are using the correct form by mentally adding the missing word or words.

➤ Meg is quicker than she [is].

➤ We find ourselves remembering Maria as often as [we remember]

her.

If a sentence with a comparison sounds too awkward or formal, add the missing words: *Meg is quicker than she is.*

6. Use the correct form when the pronoun is the subject or the object of an infinitive.
An **infinitive** is *to* plus the base verb (*to breathe, to sing, to dance*). Whether a pronoun functions as the subject or the object of an infinitive, it should be in the objective case.

subject   object

➤ **We wanted our lawyer and *her* to defend *us* against this**

unfair charge.

Both the subject of the infinitive (*her*) and its object (*us*) are in the objective case.

7. Use the possessive case in front of an *-ing* noun (a gerund).

When a noun or pronoun appears before a **gerund** (an *-ing* verb form functioning as a noun), it should usually be treated as a possessive. Possessive nouns are formed by adding *'s* to singular nouns (*the teacher's desk*) or an apostrophe only (*'*) to plural nouns (*three teachers' rooms*). (*See Tab 12: Editing for Correctness, pp. 452–57.*) The possessive pronouns are *my, your, his/her/its, our, their.*

      animals'
➤ **The ~~animals~~ fighting disturbed the entire neighborhood.**
        ^

        their
➤ **Because of ~~them~~ screeching, no one could get any sleep.**
          ^

55d Distinguish between *who* and *whom.*

The relative pronouns *who, whom, whoever,* and *whomever* are used to introduce dependent clauses and in questions. Their case depends on their function in the dependent clause or question.

- **Subjective:** *who, whoever*
- **Objective:** *whom, whomever*

1. Determine how the pronoun functions in a dependent clause.

If the pronoun is functioning as a subject and is performing an action, use *who* or *whoever.* If the pronoun is the object of a verb or preposition, use *whom* or *whomever.*

➤ **Henry Ford, *who* started the Ford Motor Company, was**

autocratic and stubborn.

Who, which refers to *Henry Ford,* is performing an action in the dependent clause: starting a company.

➤ **Ford's son Edsel, *whom* the auto magnate treated cruelly, was a**

brilliant automobile designer.

Whom, which refers to *Edsel,* is the object of the verb *treated.* You can check the pronoun by changing the order within the clause: *The auto magnate treated whom [him] cruelly.*

2. Determine how the pronoun functions in a question. To choose the correct form for the pronoun, answer the question with a personal pronoun.

➤ **_Who_ founded the General Motors Corporation?**

The answer could be _He founded it. He_ is in the subjective case, so _who_ is correct.

➤ **_Whom_ did the Chrysler Corporation turn to for leadership in the 1980s?**

The answer could be _It turned to him. Him_ is in the objective case, so _whom_ is correct.

56   Problems with Adjectives and Adverbs

For more information on and practice with adjectives and adverbs, visit <www.mhhe.com/maimon/adj_and_adv>.

Adjectives and **adverbs** are words that describe. Because they qualify the meanings of other words—for example, telling which, how many, what kind, or where—we say that they _modify_ them. Adjectives modify nouns and pronouns. Adverbs modify verbs, adjectives, and other adverbs. When they are used with care, they add flavor and precision to writing.

56a   Use adverbs to modify verbs, adjectives, and other adverbs.

Adverbs modify verbs, adjectives, other adverbs, and even whole clauses. They tell where, when, why, how, how often, how much, or to what degree.

➤ The authenticity of the document is _hotly_ contested.

➤ The water was _brilliant_ blue and _icy_ cold.

➤ Dickens mixed humor and pathos _better_ than any other English writer after Shakespeare.

➤ _Consequently,_ Dickens is still read by millions.

Distinguish between _bad_ and _badly, real_ and _really, good_ and _well._ In casual speech, the adjectives _bad, good,_ and _real_ sometimes substitute for the adverbs _badly, well,_ and _really;_ in formal writing, however, it is not acceptable to substitute an adjective for an adverb.

badly
➤ He plays the role so ~~bad~~ that it is an insult to Shakespeare.

really ^
➤ At times, he gets ~~real~~ close to the edge of the stage.
    ^

well
➤ I've seen other actors play the role good, but they were
                                        ^

classically trained.

56b Use adjectives to modify nouns or as subject complements.

Adjectives modify nouns and pronouns; they do not modify any other kind of word. Adjectives tell what kind or how many and may come before or after the noun or pronoun they modify.

➤ *Ominous gray* clouds loomed over the lake.

➤ The *looming* clouds, *ominous* and *gray,* frightened the children.

Some proper nouns have adjective forms. Proper adjectives, like the proper nouns they are derived from, are capitalized: *Victoria / Victorian, Britain / British, America / American, Shakespeare / Shakespearean.*

In some cases, a noun is used as an adjective without a change in form:

➤ *Cigarette* smoking harms the lungs and is banned in offices.

Occasionally, descriptive adjectives function as if they were nouns:

➤ The *unemployed* should not be equated with the *lazy*.

1. Do not use an adjective when an adverb is needed. In common speech, we sometimes treat adjectives as adverbs. In writing, this informal usage should be avoided.

NONSTANDARD   He hit that ball *real good.*

REVISED   He hit that ball *really well.*

Both *real* and *good* are adjectives, but they are used here as adverbs, *real* modifying *good* and *good* modifying the verb *hit.*

NONSTANDARD   She *sure* made me work hard for my grade.

REVISED   She *certainly* made me work hard for my grade.

Here the adjective *sure* tries to do the work of an adverb modifying the verb *made.*

2. Use adjectives after linking verbs to describe the subject.
Linking verbs connect the subject of a sentence to its description. The most common linking verb is *be*. Descriptive adjectives that modify a sentence's subject but appear after a linking verb are called **subject complements**.

➤ During the winter, both Emily and Anne *were sick*.

➤ The road *is long, winding,* and *dangerous*.

Other linking verbs are related to states of being and the five senses: *appear, become, feel, grow, look, smell, sound,* and *taste*. Verbs related to the senses can be either linking or action verbs, depending on the meaning of the sentence.

ADJECTIVE The dog smelled *bad*.

Bad modifies the noun *dog,* which is connected to the adjective by the linking verb *smelled*. The sentence indicates that the dog needed a bath.

ADVERB The dog smelled *badly*.

Badly modifies the verb *smelled,* an action verb in this sentence. The sentence indicates that the dog had lost its sense of smell and could not track anything.

3. Be aware that some adjectives and adverbs are spelled alike.
In most instances, *-ly* endings indicate adverbs; however, words with *-ly* endings can sometimes be adjectives (*the lovely girl*). In standard English, many adverbs do not require the *-ly* ending, and some words are both adjectives and adverbs: *fast, only, hard, right,* and *straight*. Note that *right* also has an *-ly* form as an adverb: *rightly*. When you are in doubt, consult a dictionary.

56c Use positive, comparative, and superlative adjectives and adverbs correctly.

Most adjectives and adverbs have three forms: positive (*dumb*), comparative (*dumber*), and superlative (*dumbest*). The simplest form of the adjective is the positive form.

1. Distinguish between comparatives and superlatives.
Use the comparative form to compare two things and the superlative form to compare three or more things.

➤ In total area, New York is a *larger* state than Pennsylvania.

➤ Texas is the *largest* state in the Southwest.

2. Learn when to use -er/-est endings *(bigger/biggest)* and when to use *more/most (more friendly/most friendly).* To form comparatives and superlatives of short adjectives, add the suffixes *-er* and *-est (brighter / brightest)*. With longer adjectives (three or more syllables), use *more* or *less* and *most* or *least (more dangerous / most dangerous)*.

nearest
➤ Mercury is the ~~most near~~ planet to the sun.
      ^

A few short adverbs have *-er* and *-est* endings in their comparative and superlative forms *(harder / hardest)*. Most adverbs, however, including all adverbs that end in *-ly,* use *more* and *most* in their comparative and superlative forms *(more loudly / most loudly)*.

➤ She sings *more loudly* than we expected.

Two common adjectives—*good* and *bad*—form the comparative and superlative in an irregular way: *good, better, best* and *bad, worse, worst.*

worse
➤ He felt ~~badder~~ as his illness progressed.
      ^

3. Watch out for double comparatives and superlatives. Use either an *-er* or an *-est* ending or *more / most* to form the comparative or superlative, as appropriate; do not use both.

➤ Since World War II, Britain has been the ~~most~~ closest ally of the

   United States.

4. Be aware of concepts that cannot be compared. Do not use comparative or superlative forms with adjectives such as *unique, infinite, impossible, perfect, round, square,* and *destroyed*. These concepts are *absolutes.* If something is unique, for example, it is the only one of its kind, making comparison impossible.

another   *like*
➤ You will never find ~~a more~~ unique restaurant ~~than~~ this one.
                    ^   ^

56d Avoid double negatives.

The words *no, not,* and *never* can modify the meaning of nouns and pronouns as well as other sentence elements.

NOUN   You are *no* friend of mine.

ADJECTIVE   The red house was *not* large.

VERB   He *never* ran in a marathon.

However, it takes only one negative word to change the meaning of a sentence from positive to negative. When two negatives are used together, they cancel each other out, resulting in a positive meaning. Unless you want your sentence to have a positive meaning *(I am not unaware of your feelings in this matter),* edit by changing or eliminating one of the negative words.

any
➤ They don't have ~~no~~ reason to go there.

can
➤ He ~~can't~~ hardly do that assignment.

Note that *hardly* has a negative meaning and cannot be used with *no, not,* or *never.*

It wasn't a matter of rewriting but
simply of tightening up all the bolts.

—MARGUERITE YOURCENAR

Editing
for Correctness

Punctuation, Mechanics, and Spelling

57. Commas   434

COMMON USES OF THE COMMA   434

a. Introductory word groups   435
b. Items in a series   436
c. Independent clauses joined by a coordinating conjunction   437
d. Series of adjectives   437
e. Nonessential additions to a sentence   438
f. Transitional and parenthetical expressions, contrasting comments, absolute phrases   440
g. Words of direct address, *yes* and *no*, mild interjections, tag questions   441
h. Direct quotations   441
i. Parts of dates, addresses, people's titles, and numbers   442
j. Omitted words or phrases, confusing combinations   443

COMMON MISUSES OF THE COMMA   443

k. To separate major elements in an independent clause   444
l. In front of the first or following the final item in a series   444
m. To separate compound word groups that are not independent clauses   444
n. To set off restrictive modifiers, appositives, or slightly parenthetical elements   445
o. Other common errors   446

58. Semicolons   447

a. Independent clauses   447
b. Independent clauses with transitional expressions   448
c. Items in a series that contain commas   448
d. Common errors   449

59. Colons   450

a. With lists, appositives, or quotations   450
b. With a second independent clause that elaborates on the first one   451
c. Other conventional uses   451
d. Common errors   452

60. Apostrophes   452

a. To indicate possession   452
b. With indefinite pronouns   454
c. For missing letters in contractions and for missing numbers   454
d. To form plural numbers, letters, abbreviations, words used as words   455
e. Incorrect use with some proper names   456
f. Incorrect use with some plural nouns   456
g. Distinguishing between possessive pronouns and contractions   456

61. Quotation Marks   457

a. Exact words of a speaker or writer   457
b. Long quotations in indented blocks   458
c. A quotation within a quotation   460
d. Titles of short works   460
e. A word or phrase used in a special way   461
f. Other punctuation marks with quotation marks   462
g. Integrating quotations into sentences   463

h. Common
errors *465*

62. Other Punctuation
Marks *466*
a. Periods *466*
b. Question marks *467*
c. Exclamation points *467*
d. A dash or dashes *468*
e. Parentheses *469*
f. Brackets *470*
g. Ellipses *472*
h. Slashes *473*

63. Capitalization *474*
a. Names of people and
derived names, includ-
ing brand names, cer-
tain abbreviations *475*
b. Titles of persons *476*
c. Titles of creative
works, documents,
courses *477*
d. Names of areas and
regions *478*
e. Names of races, ethnic
groups, and sacred
things *478*
f. First word of a quoted
sentence *478*
g. First word of a
sentence *480*
h. First word of an
independent clause
after a colon *480*

64. Abbreviations and
Symbols *481*
a. Titles that precede
or follow a person's
name *481*
b. Familiar vs. unfamiliar
abbreviations *482*
c. Words typically used
with times, dates, and
numerals; units of mea-
surement in charts and
graphs *482*
d. Latin abbreviations *483*

e. Inappropriate
abbreviations and
symbols *484*

65. Numbers *484*
a. Numbers up to
one hundred and
round numbers over
one hundred *484*
b. Numbers that begin a
sentence *484*
c. Numbers in technical
and business
writing *485*
d. Dates, times of day,
addresses *485*

66. Italics (Underlining) *485*
a. Titles of lengthy
works or separate
publications *486*
b. Names of ships,
trains, aircraft, and
spaceships *487*
c. Foreign terms *487*
d. Scientific names *487*
e. Words, letters, and
numbers referred to as
themselves *488*
f. Overuse *488*

67. Hyphens *488*
a. Compound words *488*
b. Compound adjective
or noun forms *489*
c. Fractions and com-
pound numbers *490*
d. With some prefixes
and suffixes *490*
e. To divide words at the
ends of lines *491*

68. Spelling *491*
a. Spelling rules and
exceptions *492*
b. Words pronounced
alike but spelled
differently *494*
c. Commonly misspelled
words *495*

433

CHARTING the TERRITORY

Styles within Disciplines

The rules for capitalizing, abbreviating, and italicizing terms, as well as conventions for using numbers and hyphens, vary sometimes from one course or discipline to another. If you are not sure about the conventions for a discipline, see what rules your course textbook follows. In particular, look for answers to these questions:

- Does the text use numerals or words for numbers under one hundred? Under ten?
- What abbreviations appear throughout the text?
- Does the book include a list of abbreviations for technical terms, as many books in the natural and applied sciences do?

If you cannot figure out what the accepted practice is from your texts, ask your instructor for help, or consult one of the following style manuals:

- *The Chicago Manual of Style,* fourteenth edition (used in history and in the humanities)
- *MLA Handbook for Writers of Research Papers,* fifth edition (used for literature, composition, and other humanities disciplines)
- *Publication Manual of the American Psychological Association,* fifth edition (used for the social sciences, such as psychology and sociology)
- *Scientific Style and Format: The CBE Manual for Authors, Editors, and Publishers,* sixth edition (used for the natural sciences, such as biology)

Punctuation is a set of signals intended to help readers. Imagine what would happen if we could not smile, point with our fingers, nod our heads, or roll our eyes? We would still be able to communicate, but our words would not be quite as meaningful and interesting as they are when we use these signals with them. Like physical gestures in spoken communication, correct punctuation and mechanics matter.

57 Commas

COMMON USES OF THE COMMA

You may have been told that commas are used to mark pauses, but that is not an accurate general principle. To clarify meaning, commas are used in the following situations:

- Following introductory elements (*pp. 435–36*)
- After each item in a series and between coordinate adjectives (*pp. 436 and 437*)
- Between coordinated independent clauses (*pp. 437–38*)
- To set off nonessential elements and phrases that interrupt or interject something in a sentence (*pp. 438–39*)
- To set off direct quotations (*pp. 441–42*)
- In dates, addresses, people's titles, and numbers (*pp. 442–43*)
- To take the place of an omitted word or phrase or to prevent misreading (*p. 443*)

For more information on and practice using commas, visit <www.mhhe.com/maimon/commas>.

For MULTILINGUAL STUDENTS

Dealing with Punctuation, Mechanics, and Spelling

If English is your second language, it is probably a challenge to write a thoughtful, well-organized paper and at the same time make sure you are following every rule of punctuation, mechanics, and spelling. To improve the accuracy of your paper, try going through an extra draft or two.

When you write your first draft, pay close attention to the content and organization of your paper, but do not focus on problems with punctuation, mechanics, and misspellings. When you have revised your paper and are satisfied that the content is sound, the writing is clear (*see Tab 10*), and your sentences are grammatically correct (*see Tab 11*), edit the revised draft for correct punctuation, mechanics, and spelling, keeping in mind the problem areas mentioned in this tab.

Next, show your edited draft to a native speaker of English and ask that person to read it and circle anything that does not seem right. When you get the paper back, try making the corrections yourself. If you do not understand why something has been circled, ask the reader to explain what is wrong and suggest possible solutions, or ask for help from a tutor in your campus's writing center. Then prepare the final copy, and review it one more time before handing it in.

57a Use a comma after an introductory word group that is *not* the subject of the sentence.

Like an overture, an introductory word group must be distinct from, yet clearly attached to, what follows. A comma both attaches an introductory word, phrase, or clause to and distinguishes it from the rest of the sentence.

➤ **Finally, the car careened to the right, endangering passers-by.**

➤ **Reflecting on her life experiences, Washburn attributed her successes to her own efforts.**

➤ **Until he noticed the handprint on the wall, the detective was frustrated by the lack of clues.**

Do not add a comma after a word group that functions as the subject of the sentence, however.

➤ **Persuading his or her constituents/ is one of a politician's most important tasks.**

Note: When the introductory phrase is less than five words long and there is no danger of confusion without a comma, the comma can be omitted.

➤ **For several hours we rode on in silence.**

CHARTING the TERRITORY

Commas in Journalism

If you are writing for a journalism course, you may be required to leave out the final comma that precedes *and* in a series, just as magazines and newspapers usually do. Follow the convention that your instructor prefers.

57b Use commas between items in a series.

A comma should appear after each item in a series.

➤ **Three industries that have been important to New England are shipbuilding, tourism, and commercial fishing.**

Commas clarify which items are part of the series. In the following example, the third comma clarifies that the hikers are packing lunch *and* snacks, not chocolate and trail mix for lunch.

CONFUSING   For the hiking trip, we needed to pack lunch, chocolate and trail mix.

CLEAR   For the hiking trip, we needed to pack lunch, chocolate, and trail mix.

57c Use a comma in front of a coordinating conjunction (such as *and* or *but*) that joins two independent clauses.

When a coordinating conjunction (*and, but, for, nor, or, so, yet*) is used to join clauses that could each stand alone as a sentence, put a comma before the coordinating conjunction.

➤ **Injuries were so frequent that he began to worry, and his style**

of play became more cautious.

If the word groups you are joining are not independent clauses, do not add a comma. See 57m on page 444.

Note: If you are joining two short clauses, you may leave out the comma unless it is needed for clarity.

➤ **The running back caught the ball and the fans cheered.**

57d Add a comma between coordinate adjectives, unless they are joined by *and*, but do not separate cumulative adjectives with a comma.

When a series of adjectives comes before a noun or pronoun, each may modify the noun independently (*a brave, intelligent, persistent woman*), or each adjective may modify the ones that follow it (*the world-famous Italian tenor*). Use a comma between adjectives only if they are the first type, or **coordinate adjectives**—that is, if they could be joined by *and* (brave *and* intelligent *and* persistent) or if their order could be changed (*a persistent, brave, intelligent woman*).

➤ **This brave, intelligent, persistent woman was the first female to**

earn a Ph.D. in psychology.

If you cannot add *and* between the adjectives or change their order, they are **cumulative adjectives** and should not be separated with a comma or commas.

➤ **Andrea Boccelli, the world-famous Italian tenor, has performed**

in concerts and operas.

World-famous modifies *Italian tenor,* not just the noun *tenor.* You could not add *and* between the adjectives (world-famous *and* Italian tenor) or change their order (*Italian world-famous tenor*).

57e Use commas to set off nonessential additions to a sentence, but do not set off essential words or word groups with commas.

Nonessential, or **nonrestrictive,** words, phrases, and clauses add information to a sentence but are not required for its basic meaning to be understood. Nonrestrictive additions are set off with commas.

NONRESTRICTIVE

Mary Shelley's best-known novel, *Frankenstein or the Modern*
                    ^

***Prometheus,* was first published in 1818.**
      ^

The sentence would have the same basic meaning without the title (*Mary Shelley's best-known novel was first published in 1818*).

Restrictive words, phrases, and clauses are essential to a sentence because they identify exactly who or what the writer is talking about. Restrictive additions are not set off with commas.

RESTRICTIVE

Mary Shelley's novel *Frankenstein or the Modern Prometheus* was

first published in 1818.

Without the title, the reader would not know which novel the sentence is referring to, so *Frankenstein or the Modern Prometheus* is a restrictive.

Three types of additions to sentences often cause problems for writers: adjective clauses, adjective phrases, and appositives.

1. Adjective clauses. Adjective clauses include a subject and verb, but they do not function independently. They begin with a relative pronoun or an adverb—*who, whom, whose, which, that, where,* or *when*—and modify a noun or pronoun within the sentence by telling *how many, what kind,* or *which one.* The relative pronoun or adverb at the beginning of the clause connects it to the noun or pronoun it modifies and usually appears right after the modified word.

NONRESTRICTIVE

With his tale of Odysseus, *whose journey, which can be traced on modern maps,* Homer brought accounts of alien and strange creatures to the ancient Greeks.

RESTRICTIVE

The contestant *whom he most wanted to beat* was his father.

Note: Use *that* only with restrictive clauses. W*hich* can introduce either restrictive or nonrestrictive clauses. Some writers prefer to use *which* only with nonrestrictive clauses.

2. Adjective phrases. Like an adjective clause, an adjective phrase also modifies a noun or pronoun in a sentence by answering the question *how many? what kind?* or *which one?* Adjective phrases begin with a preposition (for example, *with, by, at,* or *for*) or a verbal (a word formed from a verb that can have various functions within a sentence). Adjective phrases can be either restrictive or nonrestrictive.

NONRESTRICTIVE

Some people, *by their faith in human nature or their general good will,* bring out the best in others.

The phrase that begins with the preposition *by* is nonessential because it does not specify which people are being discussed. The sentence would have the same basic meaning without it (*Some people bring out the best in others*).

RESTRICTIVE

People *fighting passionately for their rights* can inspire others to join a cause.

The phrase *fighting passionately for their rights,* which begins with the verbal *fighting,* indicates which people the writer is talking about and therefore is restrictive. It is not set off with commas.

3. Appositives. Appositives are nouns or noun phrases that rename nouns or pronouns and appear right after the word they rename.

NONRESTRICTIVE APPOSITIVE

One researcher, *the widely respected R. S. Smith,* has shown that a child's performance on IQ tests can be very inconsistent.

Because the word *one* already restricts the word *researcher,* the researcher's name is not essential to the meaning of the sentence, and the appositive phrase is nonrestrictive.

RESTRICTIVE APPOSITIVE

The researcher *R. S. Smith* has shown that a child's performance on IQ tests is not reliable.

The name *R. S. Smith* tells readers which researcher is meant.

57f   Use a comma or commas with transitional expressions, parenthetical expressions, contrasting comments, and absolute phrases.

1. Transitional expressions.   Transitional expressions show the relationship between ideas in a sentence and make the sentence clearer. Conjunctive adverbs (*however, therefore, moreover*) and other transitional phrases (*for example, on the other hand*) are usually set off by commas when used at the beginning, in the middle, or at the end of a sentence. (*For a list of transitional expressions, see Tab 11: Editing for Grammar Conventions, p. 395.*)

➤   Brian Wilson, for example, was unable to cope with the

   pressures of touring with the Beach Boys.

➤   As a matter of fact, he had a nervous breakdown shortly after a tour.

➤   He is still considered one of the most important figures in rock

   and roll, however.

When a transitional expression connects two independent clauses, use a semicolon before and a comma after it.

➤   The Beatles were a phenomenon when they toured the United

   States in 1964; subsequently, they became the most successful

   rock band of all time.

Note: Short expressions such as *also, at least, certainly, instead, of course, then, perhaps,* and *therefore* do not always need to be set off with commas.

➤   I found my notes and *also* got my story in on time.

2. Parenthetical expressions.   Parenthetical expressions are like whispered asides or a shrug in a conversation. The information they provide is relatively insignificant and could easily be left out. Therefore, they are set off with a comma or commas.

➤   Human cloning, so they say, will be possible within a decade.

➤   The experiments would take a couple of weeks, more or less.

3. Contrasting comments.   Contrasting comments beginning with words such as *not, unlike,* or *in contrast to* should be set off with commas.

➤   **As an actor, Adam Sandler is a talented comedian, not a tragedian.**

4. Absolute phrases.   Absolute phrases usually include a noun (*sunlight*) followed by a participle (*shining*) and are used to modify whole sentences.

➤   **The snake slithered through the tall grass, the sunlight shining now and then on its green skin.**

57g Use a comma or commas to set off words of direct address, *yes* and *no,* mild interjections, and tag questions.

Like nonrestrictive phrases and clauses, words that interrupt a sentence are set off by commas because they are not essential to the sentence's meaning.

➤   **We have finished this project, Mr. Smith, without any help from your foundation.**

➤   **Yes, I will meet you at noon.**

➤   **Of course, if you think that's what we should do, then we'll do it.**

➤   **We can do better, don't you think?**

57h Use a comma or commas to separate a direct quotation from the rest of the sentence.

Commas are used with quotation marks to set off what the source of the quotation says from the words identifying the source, such as *she said* or *Robert Rubin maintains.* (*See Chapter 61, pp. 457–65, for more on quotation marks.*)

➤   **Irving Howe declares, "Whitman is quite realistic about the place of the self in an urban world" (261).**

➤   **"Whitman is quite realistic about the place of the self in an urban world," declares Irving Howe (261).**

Note: A comma is not needed to separate an indirect quotation or a paraphrase from the words that identify its source.

➤ **Irving Howe notes/ that Whitman realistically depicts the urban**

self as free to wander (261).

57i Use commas to distinguish parts of dates and addresses, with people's titles, and in numbers.

1. Dates.   Use paired commas in dates when the month, day, and year are included. Do not use commas when the day of the month is omitted or when the day appears before the month.

➤ **On March 4, 1931, she traveled to New York.**

➤ **She traveled to New York in March 1931.**

➤ **She traveled to New York on 4 March 1931.**

2. Addresses.   Use commas to set off the parts of an address or the name of a state, but do not use a comma preceding a zip code.

➤ **He lived at 1400 Crabgrass Lane, Garrison, New York.**

➤ **At Cleveland, Ohio, the river changes direction.**

➤ **Here is my address for the summer: 63 Oceanside Drive,**

Apt. 2A, Surf City, New Jersey 06106.

3. People's titles.   Put a comma between the person's name and the title. If the title appears in the middle of a sentence, put a comma after the title as well.

➤ **Luis Mendez, MD, gave her the green light to resume her**

exercise regimen.

4. Numbers.   When a number has more than four digits, use commas to mark off the numerals by hundreds—that is, by groups of three beginning at the right.

➤ **Andrew Jackson received 647,276 votes in the 1828 presidential**

election.

If the number is four digits long, the comma is not required.

➤ **The survey had 1856 [or 1,856] respondents.**

Exceptions: Street numbers, zip codes, telephone numbers, page numbers (p. 2304), and years (1828) do not include commas.

57j Use a comma to take the place of an omitted word or phrase or to prevent misreading.

When a writer omits one or more words from a sentence to create an effect, a comma is often needed to make the meaning of the sentence clear for readers.

➤ **Under the tree he found his puppy, and under the car, his cat.**

The second comma substitutes for the phrase *he found.*

Commas are also used to keep readers from misunderstanding a writer's meaning when words are repeated or might be misread.

➤ **Many birds that sing, sing first thing in the morning.**

➤ **Any offbeat items that can be, are sold at auction sites on the**

World Wide Web.

COMMON MISUSES OF THE COMMA

Just as a comma used correctly can clarify the meaning of a sentence, a comma used incorrectly can confuse readers. Commas should *not* be used in the following situations:

- To separate major elements in an independent clause (*p. 444*)
- In front of the first or following the last item in a series (*p. 444*)
- To join compound word groups that are not independent clauses (*p. 444*)
- To set off restrictive modifiers or appositives (*pp. 445–46*)
- To set off very slight asides (*p. 446*)

57k Do not use commas to separate major elements in an independent clause.

Do not use a comma to separate a subject from a verb or a verb from its object.

➤ **Reflecting on one's life,/ is necessary for emotional growth.**

The subject, *reflecting,* should not be separated from the verb, *is.*

➤ **Washburn decided,/ that her own efforts were responsible for**

her successes.

The verb *decided* should not be separated from its direct object, the subordinate clause *that her own efforts were responsible for her successes.*

57l Do not add a comma before the first or after the final item in a series.

Use commas to separate items in a series but never before or after the series.

➤ **Americans work longer hours than,/ German, French, or British**

workers,/ are expected to work.

Note: Commas should never be used after *such as* or *like.* (*See p. 447.*)

57m Do not use commas to separate compound word groups unless they are independent clauses.

A comma should not be used between word groups joined with a coordinating conjunction such as *and* unless they are both full sentences.

➤ **Injuries were so frequent that he became worried,/ and started**

to play more cautiously.

Here, *and* joins two verbs (*became* and *started*), not two independent clauses.

➤ **He is worried that injuries are more frequent,/ and that he will**

have to play more cautiously to avoid them.

Here, *and* joins two subordinate clauses—both beginning with the word *that*—not two independent clauses.

57n Do not use commas to set off restrictive modifiers, appositives, or slightly parenthetical words or phrases.

If a word, phrase, or clause in a sentence is necessary to identify the noun or pronoun that precedes it, it is **restrictive** and should not be set off with commas. (*For more on restrictive and nonrestrictive elements, see pp. 438–39.*)

➤ The applicants *who had studied for the admissions test* were

restless and eager for the exam to begin.

Because only those applicants who had studied were eager for the test to begin, the clause *who had studied for the admissions test* is restrictive and should not be set off with commas.

1. Appositives identifying nouns and pronouns should not be set off with commas.
An **appositive** is a noun or noun phrase that renames a noun or pronoun and appears right after the word it renames.

➤ The director,/ Michael Curtiz,/ was responsible for many great

films in the 1930s and 1940s, including *Casablanca.*

The name *Michael Curtiz* identifies the director for readers.

2. Concluding adverb clauses that are necessary to the meaning of the sentence should not be set off with commas.
Adverb clauses beginning with *after, as soon as, before, because, if, since, unless, until,* and *when* are usually essential to a sentence's meaning and therefore are not usually set off with commas when they appear at the end of a sentence.

RESTRICTIVE I am eager to test the children's IQ again *because significant variations in a child's test score indicate that the test itself may be flawed.*

Clauses beginning with *although, even though, though,* and *whereas* present a contrasting thought and are usually nonrestrictive.

NONRESTRICTIVE IQ tests can be useful indicators of a child's abilities, *although they should not be taken as the definitive measurement of a child's intelligence.*

Note: An adverb clause that appears at the beginning of a sentence is an introductory element and is usually followed by a comma: *Until we meet, I'm continuing my work on the budget.* (See pp. 435–36.)

3. Words and phrases that are slightly parenthetical should not be set off with commas.   Commas should be used for most parenthetical expressions. (*See p. 440.*) However, if setting off a brief parenthetical remark with commas would draw too much attention to the remark and interrupt the flow of the sentence, the commas can be left out.

➤   Science is *basically* the last frontier.

57o Watch out for and correct other common errors in using the comma.

▪ **Between cumulative adjectives:** Do not use a comma with **cumulative adjectives,** adjectives that modify each other and therefore are dependent on each other for their meaning to be clear. (*For more on cumulative adjectives, see pp. 437–38.*)

➤   Three⁄ well-known⁄ American writers visited the artist's

   studio.

   The three are well-known American writers, not just well-known writers and not just American writers; you would not write *three American well-known writers.*

▪ **Between adjectives and nouns:** A comma should not separate a noun from the adjective or adjectives that modify it.

➤   An art review by a celebrated, powerful⁄ writer would be

   guaranteed publication.

▪ **Between adverbs and adjectives:** A comma should not separate an adjective from the adverb that modifies it.

➤   The artist's studio was a delightfully⁄ chaotic environment, with

   canvases on every surface and paints spilled out in a fiesta of

   color.

▪ **After coordinating conjunctions** (*and, but, or, nor, for, so, yet*):

➤ The *duomo* in Siena was begun in the thirteenth century, and⁄ it was used as a model for other Italian cathedrals.

▪ After *although, such as,* or *like*:

➤ Puppets were used in the stage version of *The Lion King* to represent many different animals, although⁄ human actors were still needed to convey the characters' emotions.

➤ Stage designers can achieve many unusual effects, such as⁄ the helicopter that landed in *Miss Saigon.*

▪ Before an opening parenthesis:

➤ When they occupy an office cubicle⁄ (a relatively recent invention), workers need to be especially considerate of their neighbors.

▪ With a question mark or an exclamation point that ends a quotation (*Also see Chapter 61, p. 463*):

➤ "Where are my glasses?⁄" she asked in a panic.

58 Semicolons

Semicolons are used to join ideas that are closely related and grammatically equivalent. Usually, there must be a full sentence (independent clause) on each side of the semicolon.

58a Use a semicolon to join independent clauses.

A semicolon should be used to join closely related independent clauses when they are not joined by a comma and a coordinating conjunction (*and, but, or, nor, for, so, yet*). A semicolon is an effective way to link two clauses if readers are able to see the relationship between the two without the help of a coordinating conjunction.

For more information on and practice using semicolons, visit <www.mhhe.com/maimon/semicolons>.

➤ **Before 8000 BC wheat was not the luxuriant plant it is today; it**

was merely one of many wild grasses that spread throughout

the Middle East.

The writer could have separated the clauses with a period but chose a semicolon to mark the close relationship between the ideas in the two clauses.

Sometimes, the close relationship is a contrast.

➤ **Philip had completed the assignment; Lucy had not.**

Note: If a comma is used between two clauses without a coordinating conjunction, the sentence is a comma splice, a serious error. One way to correct a comma splice is by changing the comma to a semicolon.

➤ **Tracy Kidder wanted to write about architecture/; *House* is**

the result.

If no punctuation appears between the two clauses, the sentence is a run-on. One way to correct a run-on sentence is to add a semicolon between the two clauses.

➤ **Magnolias bloom in the early spring; daffodils blossom at the**

same time.

(*For more on comma splices and run-on sentences, see Tab 11: Editing for Grammar Conventions, pp. 392–97.*)

58b Use semicolons with transitional expressions that connect independent clauses.

Transitional expressions, including transitional phrases (*after all, even so, for example, in addition, on the contrary*) and conjunctive adverbs (*consequently, however, moreover, nevertheless, then, therefore*), indicate the way that two clauses are related to each other. When a transitional expression appears between two clauses, it is preceded by a semicolon and usually followed by a comma. (*For a list of transitional expressions, see Tab 11, Editing for Grammar Conventions, p. 395.*)

➤ **Sheila had to wait until the plumber arrived; consequently, she**

was late for the exam.

Note: The semicolon always appears between the two clauses, even when the transitional expression appears in another position within the second clause. Wherever it appears, the transitional expression is usually set off with a comma or commas.

➤ **My friends are all taking golf lessons; my roommate and I,**

⌃

however, are more interested in tennis.

Coordinating conjunctions (*and, but, or, nor, for, so, yet*) also indicate the way clauses are related. Unlike transitional expressions, however, they are preceded by a comma, not a semicolon, when they join two independent clauses. (*For more on comma splices and run-on sentences, see Tab 11: Editing for Grammar Conventions, pp. 392–97.*)

58c Use a semicolon to separate items in a series when the items contain commas.

Because the following sentence contains so many elements, the semicolons are needed for clarity.

➤ **The committee included Dr. Curtis Youngblood, the county medical**

examiner; Roberta Collingwood, the director of the bureau's

⌃

criminal division; and Darcy Coolidge, the chief of police.

Note: This rule is an exception to the general principle that there should be a full sentence (independent clause) on each side of a semicolon.

58d Watch out for and correct common errors in using the semicolon.

▪ **To join a dependent clause to an independent clause:** A semicolon can join two independent clauses because they are grammatically equivalent, but a dependent clause is never equivalent to an independent clause.

➤ **Professional writers need to devote time every day to their**

writing; because otherwise they can lose momentum.

➤ **Although housecats seem tame and lovable; they can be**

⌃

fierce hunters.

- **To join independent clauses linked by a coordinating conjunction (*and, but, or, nor, for, so, yet*):** A comma, not a semicolon, should precede the coordinating conjunction.

➤ Women in the nineteenth century wore colorful clothes⁄, but their

  clothes often look drab in the black-and-white photographs.

- **To introduce a series or an explanation:** A colon should usually be used for this purpose.

➤ My day was planned⁄: a morning walk, an afternoon in the

  library, dinner with friends, and a great horror movie.

➤ The doctor finally diagnosed the problem⁄: a severe sinus infection.

---

59 Colons

For more information on and practice using colons, visit <www.mhhe.com/maimon/colons>.

Like an announcer on a television show, a colon draws the reader's attention to what it is introducing. It also has other conventional uses.

59a Use colons to introduce lists, appositives, or quotations.

In sentences, colons are most often used to introduce lists, appositives (nouns or noun phrases that rename nouns or pronouns and appear right after the word they rename), and quotations. They are almost always preceded by complete sentences (independent clauses). (*For more on quotations, see Chapter 61, pp. 456–65.*)

LIST **The novel deals with three kinds of futility: perva-**

  sive poverty, unrequited love, and inescapable

  aging.

APPOSITIVE **In October 1954, the Northeast was devastated by**

  a ferocious storm: Hurricane Hazel.

Biblical Citations

Colons are often used to separate biblical chapters and verses
(John 3:16), but the Modern Language Association (MLA)
recommends using a period instead (John 3.16).

QUOTATION   **He took my hand and said the words I had been**

dreading: "I really want us to be just friends."
          ^

59b Use a colon when a second closely related independent clause elaborates on the first one.

The colon can be used to link independent clauses when the second
clause restates or elaborates on the first. Use it when you want to
emphasize the second clause.

➤   **I can predict tonight's sequence of events: My brother will arrive**
                                            ^
    late, talk loudly, and eat too much.

Note: When a complete sentence follows a colon, the first word may
begin with either a capital or a lowercase letter. Whatever you decide to
do, though, you should use the same style throughout your document.

59c Use colons in business letters, to indicate ratios, to indicate times of day, for city and publisher citations in bibliographies, and to separate titles and subtitles.

➤   **Dear Mr. Worth:**

➤   **The ratio of armed to unarmed members of the gang was 3:1.**

➤   **He woke up at 6:30 in the morning.**

➤   **New York: McGraw-Hill, 2003**

➤   *Possible Lives:* **The Promise of Public Education in America**

59d Watch out for and correct common errors in using the colon.

- **Between a verb and its object or complement:**

➤ The critical elements in a good smoothie are:/ yogurt, fresh fruit,

and honey.

- **Between a preposition and its object or objects:**

➤ The novel deals with:/ pervasive poverty.

➤ Many feel that cancer can be prevented by a diet of:/ fruit, nuts,

and vegetables.

- **After** *such as, for example,* **or** *including:*

➤ I am ready for a change, such as:/ a trip to the Bahamas or a

move to another town.

60 Apostrophes

For more information on and practice using apostrophes, visit <www.mhhe.com/maimon/apostrophes>.

Apostrophes show possession (*the dog's bone*) and indicate omitted letters in contractions (*don't*). They are also used to express concepts of duration (*an hour's wait*) and of monetary value (*five dollars' worth*). Apostrophes are used in such a wide variety of ways that they can be confusing. The most common confusion is between plurals and possessives.

   Note: If you are wondering whether a particular noun should be in the possessive form, reword the sentence using the word *of* (*the bone of the dog*) to make sure that the noun is not plural.

60a Use apostrophes to indicate possession.

For a noun to be possessive, two elements are usually required: someone or something is the possessor; and someone, something, or some attribute or quality is possessed.

POSSESSION	POSSESSOR	PERSON, THING, ATTRIBUTE, QUALITY, VALUE, OR FEATURE POSSESSED
the woman's son	woman	son
Juanita's shovel	Juanita	shovel
a child's bright smile	child	bright smile

Sometimes the thing possessed precedes the possessor.

➤ **The motorcycle is the student's.**

Sometimes the sentence may not name the thing possessed, but its identity (in this case, *house*) is clearly understood by the reader.

➤ **I saw your cousin at Nick's.**

1. Forming possessives with -'s.
To form the possessive of all singular nouns, as well as plural nouns that do not end in -s, add an apostrophe plus -s to the noun.

NOUN/PRONOUN	NUMBER	AS A POSSESSIVE
baby	singular	a baby's smile
hour	singular	an hour's time
men	plural	the men's club
children	plural	the children's papers

Even singular nouns that end in -s form the possessive by adding -'s.

➤ **James's adventure, Ross's flag, Elvis's songs**

Note: If a singular noun with more than two syllables ends in -s and adding -'s would make the word sound awkward, it is acceptable to use only an apostrophe to form the possessive.

➤ **Socrates' students remained loyal to him.**

2. Forming possessives with only an apostrophe.
Plural nouns that end in -s take only an apostrophe to form the possessive.

NOUN/PRONOUN	NUMBER	AS A POSSESSIVE
babies	plural	the babies' smiles
companies	plural	the companies' employees
robbers	plural	the robbers' clever plan

3. Showing joint possession. To express joint ownership by two or more people, use the possessive form for the last name only; to express individual ownership, use the possessive form for each name.

➤ Felicia and Elias's report

➤ The city's and the state's finances

4. Forming the possessive of compound nouns. For compound words, add an apostrophe plus -*s* to the last word in the compound to form the possessive.

➤ My father-in-law's job

➤ The editor-in-chief's responsibilities

60b Use an apostrophe and -*s* with indefinite pronouns.

Indefinite pronouns such as *no one, everyone, everything,* and *something* do not refer to a specific person or a specific item. They are generic references to people and things. (*See Tab 11: Editing for Grammar Conventions, pp. 401–2.*)

➤ Well, it is *anybody's* guess.

60c Use apostrophes for missing letters in contractions and for missing numbers.

A contraction is a shortened word or group of words formed when some letters or sounds are omitted. In a contraction, the apostrophe serves as a substitute for the omitted letters.

it's	for *it is* or *it has*
weren't	for *were not*
here's	for *here is*

CHARTING the TERRITORY

Plurals of Numbers, Letters, and Abbreviations

Style guides differ in their rules for making numbers, letters, and abbreviations plural. For example, the Modern Language Association (MLA) recommends adding an *-s* without an apostrophe to form the plurals of abbreviations and numbers: *DVDs, 3s and 4s.*

In informal writing, apostrophes can also substitute for omitted numbers in a decade. It is usually better to spell out the name of the decade in formal writing, however:

INFORMAL   In the twentieth century, the *'50s* were relatively calm; the *'60s* were much more turbulent.

MORE FORMAL   In the twentieth century, the *fifties* were relatively calm; the *sixties* were much more turbulent.

60d Use an apostrophe with *-s* to form plural numbers, letters, abbreviations, and words used as words.

An apostrophe plus *-s* (*'s*) can be used to show the plural of a number, a letter, or an abbreviation. Underline or italicize single letters but not the apostrophe or the *-s.*

➤ He makes his 2's look like 5's.

➤ Committee has two *m*'s, two *t*'s, and two *e*'s.

➤ Professor Morris has two Ph.D.'s.

Exceptions: If an abbreviation does not have periods, the apostrophe is not necessary (*RPMs*). The apostrophe is also not necessary to form the plural of dates (*1990s*).

If a word is used as a word rather than as a symbol of the meaning it conveys, it can be made plural by adding an apostrophe plus *-s.* The word should be italicized or underlined but not the *-s.*

➤ There are twelve *no*'s in the first paragraph.

60e Do not use apostrophes with some proper names of geographical locations and organizations.

If you are not sure whether to add an apostrophe to a place name or leave it out, look up the name in a dictionary or an atlas. If you need to verify the spelling of an organization's name, try searching for its Web site.

➤ **Kings Point**

➤ **Department of Veterans Affairs**

60f Do not use an apostrophe with a plural noun.

Most often, writers misuse the apostrophe by adding it to a plural noun that is not possessive. The plurals of most nouns are formed by adding *-s: boy/boys; girl/girls; teacher/teachers*. Possessives are formed by adding an apostrophe plus *-s ('s): boy/boy's; girl/girl's; teacher/teacher's*. The possessive form and the plural form are not interchangeable.

➤   *teachers*   *girls*   *boys*
    The teacher's asked the girl's and boy's for their attention.

60g Distinguish between possessive pronouns and contractions.

Be careful not to use a contraction when a possessive is called for, and vice versa. Personal pronouns and the relative pronoun *who* have special possessive forms, which never require apostrophes (*my/mine, your/yours, his, her/hers, it/its, our/ours, their/theirs,* and *whose*). When an apostrophe appears with a pronoun, the apostrophe usually marks omissions in a contraction, unless the pronoun is indefinite. (*See pp. 454–55.*)

The following pairs or groups of words often cause problems for writers.

Its/it's: *Its* is a possessive pronoun. *It's* is a contraction for *it is* or *it has: It's [It + is] too hot.*

➤ **The dog sat down and scratched *its* fleas.**

➤ ***It's* often been said that English is a difficult language to learn.**

Their/there/they're: *Their* is a possessive pronoun. *There* is an adverb of place. *They're* is a contraction of *they are*.

➤ **They gave *their* lives.**

> She was standing *there*.

> *They're* reading more poetry this semester.

Whose/who's: *Whose* is the possessive form of *who; who's* is a contraction of *who is.*

> Harry, *whose* dream had always been to own a 1969 Camaro,

> searched the used car lot in vain.

> *Who's* there?

Your/you're: *Your* is a possessive pronoun; *you're* is a contraction of *you are.*

> Is that *your* new car?

> *You're* a lucky guy.

61 Quotation Marks

Quotation marks always appear in pairs. They are used to enclose words, phrases, and sentences that are quoted directly; titles of short works such as poems, articles, songs, and short stories; and words and phrases used in a special sense.

For more information on and practice working with quotation marks, visit <www.mhhe.com/maimon/quotation_marks>.

61a Use quotation marks to indicate the exact words of a speaker or writer.

Direct quotations from written material may include whole sentences or only a few words or phrases.

> In *Angela's Ashes,* Frank McCourt writes, "Worse than the ordinary

> miserable childhood is the miserable Irish childhood" (11).

> Frank McCourt believes that being Irish worsens what is all too

> "ordinary"—a "miserable childhood" (11).

Use quotation marks to enclose everything a speaker says in written dialogue. If the quoted sentence is interrupted by a phrase like *he said,* enclose the rest of the quotation in quotation marks.

When another person begins to speak, begin a new paragraph to indicate a change in speaker.

> "I don't know what you're talking about," he said. "I did listen to everything you told me."
> "If you had been listening, you would know what I was talking about."

If a speaker continues for a more than a paragraph, begin each subsequent paragraph with quotation marks, but do not insert a closing quotation mark until the end of the quotation.

Note: Do not use quotation marks to set off an indirect quotation, which reports what a speaker said but does not use the exact words.

➤ **He said that "he didn't know what I was talking about."**

Two or three lines of poetry may be run in to your text, much like any other *short* quotation. Line breaks are shown with a slash. Leave a space before and after the slash. (*For more on slashes, see Chapter 62, pp. 473–74.*)

➤ **In the nineteenth century, Wordsworth wrote of the weary**

acquisitiveness of our modern age: "The world is too much

with us; late and soon, / Getting and spending, we lay waste

our powers" (lines 1–2).

Note: In the style of the Modern Language Association (MLA), line numbers should appear in parentheses following the quotation. The word *lines* should precede the numbers the first time the poem is quoted.

61b Set off long quotations in indented blocks.

If you are using a quotation that is longer than four typed lines, set it off from the text as a block quotation. Start a new line for the quotation, type it double-spaced, and indent every line of the quotation one inch (ten spaces) from the left margin. Double-space above and below the quotation. Be sure that you indent every line in a block quotation.

A block quotation is *not* surrounded by quotation marks. If the text you are quoting includes a direct quotation, however, use quotation marks to set that off. If your quotation is more than one paragraph long, indent the first line of each new paragraph an extra quarter inch (three spaces). A block quotation is usually introduced by a sentence that ends with a colon.

As Carl Schorske points out, the young Freud was
passionately interested in classical archeology:

> He cultivated a new friendship in the
> Viennese professional elite--especially rare
> in those days of withdrawal--with Emanuel
> Loewy, a professor of archeology. "He keeps
> me up till three o'clock in the morning,"
> Freud wrote appreciatively to Fliess. "He
> tells me about Rome." (273)

CHARTING the TERRITORY

Documentation Styles

Providing the page number in parentheses after the quotation is a
convention of the Modern Language Association (MLA), explained in
the *MLA Handbook for Writers of Research Papers.* The American
Psychological Association (APA), a system widely used in the social
sciences, employs a different documentation convention: ". . . Rome"
(p. 273). The APA also has different rules for setting off long quotations. (*For more on the differences among documentation styles, see
Tabs 6–8.*)

Longer verse quotations (four lines or more) are indented block-
style, like long prose quotations. (*For short quotations of poetry, see
pp. 458 and 473–74.*) If you cannot fit an entire line of poetry on a
single line of your typescript, you may indent the turned line an extra
quarter inch (three spaces).

In the following lines from "Crossing Brooklyn Ferry,"
Walt Whitman celebrates the beauty of the Manhattan
skyline, and his love for that city:

> Ah, what can ever be more stately and
>   admirable to me than mast-hemm'd
>   Manhattan?
> River and sunset and scallop-edg'd waves of
>   flood-tide?

```
        The sea-gulls oscillating their bodies, the
        hay-boat in the twilight, and the belated
        lighter?
    What gods can exceed these that clasp me by
        the hand, and with voices I love call me
        promptly and loudly by my nighest name as
        I approach? (lines 92-95)
```

Note: Because they interrupt your text and decrease its readability, you should use block quotations sparingly. (*For more on when to use quotations, see Tab 5: Researching, pp. 186–87.*)

61c Enclose a quotation within a quotation with single quotation marks.

Unless you are using a block quotation, set off a quotation within a quotation with a pair of single quotation marks.

➤ **What happened when the faculty demanded an investigation of dishonest recruiting practices in the athletic department? The president of the university said, "I know you're saying to me, 'We want an honest football team.' But I'm telling you this: 'I want a winning football team.'"**

61d Use quotation marks to enclose titles of short works such as articles, poems, and stories.

The titles of long works, such as books, are usually underlined or put in italics. (*See Chapter 66, pp. 486–87.*) The titles of book chapters, essays, most poems, and other short works are usually put in quotation marks. Quotation marks are also used for titles of unpublished works, including student papers, theses, and dissertations.

▪ **Book chapters or sections**

"The Girl in Conflict" (Chapter 11 of *Coming of Age in Samoa*)

"Science and Technology" (Part 4 of *The Universal Almanac*)

- **Essays**
    "A Hanging"
    "Once More to the Lake"
- **Songs**
    "Every Morning"
    "I Will Remember You"
- **Short poems**
    "Daffodils"
    "Love Song"
- **Articles in periodicals**
    "Post-Soviet Baltic Republic: Still Stunted and Struggling" (from the *New York Times*)
    "Scotland Yard of the Wild" (from *American Way*)
- **Short stories**
    "A Wagner Matinee"
    "The Tell Tale Heart"
- **Episodes of radio and television programs**
    "I Can't Remember" (on *48 Hours*)
    "The Final Problem" (on *Sherlock Holmes Mysteries*)

Note: If quotation marks are needed within the title of a short work, use single quotation marks: "The 'Animal Rights' War on Medicine."

61e Use quotation marks to indicate that a word or phrase is being used in a special way.

Put quotation marks around a word or phrase that someone else has used in a way that you or your readers may not agree with. Quotation marks used in this way function as raised eyebrows do in conversation and should be used sparingly.

➤ The **"worker's paradise"** of Stalinist Russia included slave-labor

camps.

Words cited as words can also be put in quotation marks, although the more common practice is to italicize them.

➤ The words **"compliment"** and **"complement"** sound alike but

have different meanings.

61f Place punctuation marks within or outside quotation marks, as convention and your meaning require.

As you edit, check all closing quotation marks and the marks of punctuation that appear next to them to make sure that you have placed them in the right order.

- Periods (.) always belong inside quotation marks.
- Commas (,) always belong inside quotation marks.
- Semicolons (;) always belong outside quotation marks.
- Colons (:) always belong outside quotation marks.
- Exclamation points (!) belong inside quotation marks if they are part of the statement or title being quoted but outside quotation marks if they are the end mark for the entire sentence.
- Question marks (?) belong inside quotation marks if they are part of the question or title being quoted but outside quotation marks if they are the end mark for the entire sentence.
- Dashes (—) belong inside quotation marks if they are part of the quotation but outside quotations marks if they are part of the sentence that introduces or surrounds the quotation.

1. Periods and commas.   Place the period or comma before the final quotation mark even when the quotation is only one or two words long.

➤ In *The Atlantic,* **Katha Pollitt writes, "The first thing that strikes one about Plath's journals is what they leave out."**

➤ **"The first thing that strikes one about Plath's journals is what they leave out," writes Katha Pollitt in *The Atlantic.***

Note: In British punctuation, the comma and period are placed outside the quotation mark; American usage places these punctuation marks inside the quotation marks, except in some specific instances in documenting sources.

2. Colons and semicolons.   Place colons and semicolons after the final quotation mark.

➤ **Dean Wilcox cited the items he called his "daily delights": a free parking space for his scooter at the faculty club, a special table in the club itself, and friends to laugh with after a day's work.**

3. Question marks and exclamation points.

Place a question mark or an exclamation point after the final quotation mark if the quoted material is not itself a question or an exclamation.

➤ **Why did she name her car "Buck"?**

Place a question mark or an exclamation point inside the final quotation mark when it is part of the quotation. No additional punctuation is needed after the closing quotation.

➤ **He had many questions, such as "Can you really do unto others**

as you would have them do unto you?"

4. Dashes.

Place a dash outside either an opening or a closing quotation mark, or both, if it precedes or follows the quotation or if two dashes are used to set off the quotation.

➤ **One phrase—"time is running out"—haunted me throughout**

my dream.

Place a dash inside either an opening or a closing quotation mark if it is part of the quotation.

➤ **"Where is the—" she called. "Oh, here it is. Never mind."**

61g Integrate quotations smoothly into your sentences, using the correct punctuation.

1. Formal introductions.

If you introduce a quotation with a complete sentence, you can use a colon before it.

➤ **He was better than anyone else at the job, but he didn't want it:**

"I don't know what to do," he said.

2. *She said* and similar expressions.

If you introduce a direct quotation with *he said, she noted,* or a similar expression, add a comma after the expression and use a capital letter to begin the quotation. If the expression follows the quotation, add a comma at the end of the quotation, before the closing quotation mark.

➤ **He said, "She believed I could do it."**

➤ **"She believed I could do it," he said.**

Note: Do not use a comma after such expressions as *he said* or *the researchers note* if an indirect quotation or a paraphrase follows.

➤ He said,/ that he believed he could do it.

3. Quotations that are integrated into a sentence.

When a quotation is integrated into a sentence's structure, treat the quotation as you would any other sentence element, adding a comma or not as appropriate.

➤ Telling me that she wanted to "play hooky from her life," she set

off on a three-week vacation.

➤ He said he had his "special reasons."

4. Quotations that begin a sentence.

If your quotation begins a sentence, capitalize the first letter after the quotation mark even if the first word does not begin a sentence in the original source.

➤ "The only white people who came to our house were welfare

workers and bill collectors," James Baldwin wrote.

5. Interrupted quotations.

If the sentence you are quoting is interrupted by an expression such as *she said,* begin the sentence with a quotation mark and a capital letter, end the first part of the quotation with a comma and a quotation mark, insert the interrupting words followed by another comma, and then resume the quotation with a lowercase letter.

➤ "The first thing that strikes one about Plath's journals," writes

Katha Pollitt in *The Atlantic,* "is what they leave out."

If you end one quoted sentence and insert an expression such as *he said* before beginning the next quoted sentence, place a comma at the end of the first quoted sentence and a period after the interruption.

➤ "There are at least four kinds of doublespeak," William Lutz

observes. "The first is the euphemism, an inoffensive or

positive word or phrase used to avoid a harsh, unpleasant, or

distasteful reality."

61h Watch out for and correct common errors in using quotation marks.

▪ **To distance yourself from slang, clichés, or trite expressions:** It is best to avoid overused or slang expressions altogether in college writing. If your writing situation permits slang, however, do not enclose it in quotation marks.

WEAK   Californians are so "laid back."

REVISED   Many Californians have a relaxed, carefree style.

▪ **For indirect quotations:** Do not use quotation marks for indirect quotations. Watch out for errors in pronoun reference as well. (*See Tab 11: Editing for Grammar Conventions, pp. 421–22.*)

INCORRECT   He wanted to tell his boss that "he needed a vacation."

CORRECT   He told his boss that his boss needed a vacation.

CORRECT   He said to his boss, "You need a vacation."

▪ **In quotations that end with a question:** Only the question mark that ends the quoted sentence is needed, even when the entire sentence that includes the quotation is also a question.

➤ **What did Juliet mean when she cried, "O Romeo, Romeo!**

     Wherefore art thou Romeo?"̸?

If a question is quoted before the end of a sentence that makes a statement, place a question mark before the last quotation mark and put a period at the end of the sentence.

➤ **"What was Henry Ford's greatest contribution to the**

     Industrial Revolution?" he asked.

▪ **To enclose the title of your own paper:**

➤ **̸"Edgar Allan Poe and the Paradox of the Gothic̸"**

If you use a quotation or a title of a short work in your title, though, put quotation marks around it.

➤ **Edgar Allan Poe's "The Raven" and the Paradox of the Gothic**

62 Other Punctuation Marks: Periods, Question Marks, Exclamation Points, Dashes, Parentheses, Brackets, Ellipses, and Slashes

62a Use a period after most statements, polite requests, and indirect questions. Use it in abbreviations according to convention.

1. Use a period to end most statements. Most English sentences are statements.

➤ **Soap melts in the bathtub.**

Polite requests that do not ask a question also end in a period.

➤ **Please go with me to the lecture.**

Statements that ask questions indirectly end in a period.

➤ **She asked me where I had gone to college.**

2. Use periods in abbreviations when convention requires them. A period or periods are used with the following common abbreviations, which end in lowercase letters.

Mr.	Dr.	Mass.
Ms.	i.e.	Jan.
Mrs.	e.g.	

If the abbreviation is made up of capital letters, however, the periods are optional.

RN (or R.N.)	BA (or B.A.)
MD (or M.D.)	PhD (or Ph.D.)

Periods are omitted in abbreviations for organizations, famous people, states in mailing addresses, and acronyms (words made up of initials).

FBI	JFK	MA	NATO
CIA	LBJ	TX	NAFTA
NASA			

When in doubt, consult a dictionary.

When an abbreviation ends a sentence, the period at the end of the abbreviation serves as the period for the sentence. If a question mark or an exclamation point ends the sentence, place it *after* the period in the abbreviation.

➤ **When he was in the seventh grade, we called him "Stinky," but**

now he is William Percival Abernathy, Ph.D.!

62b Use a question mark after a direct question.

➤ **Who wrote *The Old Man and the Sea*?**

Occasionally, a question mark changes a statement into a question.

➤ **You expect me to believe a story like that?**

When questions follow one another in a series, each one can be followed by a question mark even if the questions are not complete sentences, as long as the meaning is understood.

➤ **What will you contribute? Your time? Your talent? Your money?**

Use a question mark in parentheses to indicate a questionable date, number, or word, but do not use it to convey an ironic meaning.

➤ **Chaucer was born in 1340 (?) and lived until 1400.**

➤ **His yapping dog had recently graduated from obedience ~~(?)~~**

training.

Note: Do not use a question mark after an indirect quotation, even if the words being indirectly quoted were originally a question.

➤ **He asked her if she would be at home later~~?~~.**

62c Use exclamation points sparingly to convey shock, surprise, or some other strong emotion.

➤ **Stolen! The money was stolen! Right before our eyes, somebody**

snatched my purse and ran off with it.

Note: Using numerous exclamation points throughout a document actually weakens their force. As much as possible, try to convey emotion with your choice of words and your sentence structure instead of with an exclamation point.

➤ **Jefferson and Adams both died on the same day in 1826, exactly fifty years after the signing of the Declaration of Independence!.**

The fact that the sentence reports is surprising enough without the addition of an exclamation point.

62d Use a dash or dashes to set off words, phrases, or sentences that deserve special attention.

Think of the dash as a very strong pause intended to emphasize what follows—and sometimes to emphasize what comes immediately before. A typeset dash, sometimes called an *em dash*, is a single, unbroken line about as wide as a capital M. Most word-processing programs provide the em dash as a special character. Otherwise, the dash can be made on the keyboard with two hyphens in a row. Do not put a space before or after the dash.

1. Use a dash or dashes to set off parenthetical material.

➤ **All finite creations—including humans—are incomplete and contradictory.**

➤ **I think the Mets have a chance to win the pennant—if they can just get through this next series with the Dodgers.**

2. Use a dash or dashes to set off a series or an explanation. Sometimes a dash will set off a series of nouns placed for special emphasis at the beginning of a sentence and then summarized by a pronoun after the dash.

➤ **Coca-Cola, potato chips, and brevity—these are the marks of a good study session in the dorm.**

A dash can also be used to set off a series or an explanation that appears at the end of a sentence.

➤ **A surprising number of people have taken up birdwatching—a peaceful, relatively inexpensive hobby.**

3. Use a dash or dashes to add, and emphasize, a nonessential independent clause.   Sometimes a dash is used to set off an independent clause within a sentence. In such sentences, the set-off clause provides interesting information but is not essential to the main assertion.

➤ **The first rotary gasoline engine—it was made by Mazda—burned**

   15% more fuel than conventional engines.

4. Use a dash or dashes to indicate a sudden change in tone or idea.

➤ **Breathing heavily, the archaeologist opened the old chest in wild**

   anticipation and found—an old pair of socks and an empty soda can.

5. Do not overuse dashes.   Used sparingly, the dash can be an effective mark of punctuation, but if it is overused, it can make your writing disjointed.

CHOPPY   After we found the puppy—shivering under the
             porch—we brought her into the house—into the
             entryway, actually—and wrapped her in an old
             towel—to warm her up.

SMOOTHER   After we found the puppy shivering under the
             porch, we brought her into the house—into the
             entryway, actually—and wrapped her in an old
             towel to warm her up.

62e Use parentheses to set off relatively unimportant information.

Parentheses should be used infrequently and only to set off supplementary information, a digression, or a comment that interrupts the flow of thought within a sentence or paragraph. Parentheses enclose material that is useful or interesting but not important enough to receive any emphasis, unlike material set off by commas or dashes.

➤ **The tickets (ranging in price from $10 to $50) go on sale Monday**

   morning.

   When parentheses enclose a whole sentence by itself, the sentence begins with a capital letter and ends with a period before the final parenthesis. A sentence that appears inside parentheses *within a sentence* should neither begin with a capital letter nor end with a period.

➤ **Folktales and urban legends often reflect the concerns of a**

particular era. (The familiar tale of a cat accidentally caught in

a microwave oven is an example of this phenomenon.)

➤ **John Henry (he was the man with the forty-pound hammer) was**

a hero to miners fearing the loss of their jobs to machines.

If the material in parentheses is at the end of an introductory or nonessential word group that is followed by a comma, the comma should be placed after the closing parenthesis. A comma should never appear before the opening parenthesis.

➤ **As he walked past/ (dressed, as always, in his Sunday best),**

I got ready to throw the spitball.

Parentheses are used to enclose numbers or letters that label items in a list.

➤ **He says the argument is nonsense because (1) university presi-**

dents don't work as well as machines, (2) university presidents

don't do any real work at all, and (3) universities would be better

off if they were run by faculty committees.

Parentheses also enclose in-text citations in many systems of documenting sources. (*For more on documenting sources, see Tabs 6–8.*)

Note: Too many parentheses are distracting to readers. If you find that you have used a large number of parentheses in a draft, go over it carefully to see if any of the material within parentheses really deserves more emphasis.

62f When quoting, use brackets to set off material that is not part of the original quotation.

Brackets set off information you add to a quotation that is not part of the quotation itself. Use brackets to add significant information that is needed to make the quote clear.

➤ **Samuel Eliot Morison has written, "This passage has attracted a good deal of scorn to the Florentine mariner [Verrazzano], but without justice."**

In this sentence, a writer is quoting Morison, but Morison's sentence does not include the name of the "Florentine mariner." The writer places the name—Verrazzano—in brackets so that readers will know the identity of the mariner Morison is talking about.

Information that explains or corrects something in a quotation is also bracketed.

➤ **Vasco da Gama's man wrote in 1487, "The body of the church [it was not a church but a Hindu shrine] is as large as a monastery."**

Brackets are also used around words that you insert within a quotation to make it fit the grammar or style of your own sentence. If you replace a word with your own word in brackets, ellipses are not needed.

➤ **At the end of *Pygmalion,* Henry Higgins confesses to Eliza Doolittle that he has "grown accustomed to [her] voice and appearance."**

To make the quote fit properly into the sentence, the bracketed word *her* is inserted in place of *your.*

If you are using the style of the Modern Language Association (MLA), you should also use brackets with ellipses to indicate that the ellipses did not appear in the original. (*See the following section on ellipses.*)

Note: Brackets may be used to enclose the word *sic* (Latin for "thus") after a word in a quotation that was incorrect in the original. The word *sic* should not be underlined or italicized when it appears in brackets.

➤ **The critic noted that "the battle scenes in *The Patriot* are realistic, but the rest of the film is historically inaccurate [sic] and overly melodramatic."**

Sic should be used sparingly because it can appear pretentious and condescending, and it should not be used to make fun of what someone has said or written.

62g Use ellipses to indicate that words have been omitted.

If you wish to shorten a passage you are quoting, you may omit words, phrases, or even entire sentences. To show readers that you have done so, use three spaced periods, called ellipses or an ellipsis mark. If you are following the style of the Modern Language Association (MLA), used in English and in other disciplines in the humanities, you should use brackets to enclose any ellipses that you add, as shown in the second and fourth examples below. Other punctuation either precedes or follows the brackets, depending on what you have left out.

FULL QUOTATIONS FROM A WORK BY WILKINS

In the nineteenth century, railroads, lacing their way across continents, reaching into the heart of every major city in Europe and America, and bringing a new romance to travel, added to the unity of nations and fueled the nationalist fires already set burning by the French Revolution and the wars of Napoleon.

EDITED QUOTATION

In his account of nineteenth-century society, Wilkins argued that "railroads . . . added to the unity of nations and fueled the nationalist fires already set burning by the French Revolution and the wars of Napoleon."

EDITED QUOTATION (MLA STYLE)

In his account of nineteenth-century society, Wilkins argued that "railroads [. . .] added to the unity of nations and fueled the nationalist fires already set burning by the French Revolution and the wars of Napoleon."

If you are leaving out the end of a quoted sentence, the three ellipsis points are preceded by a period to end the sentence. If you are using MLA style, however, the ellipsis points, enclosed in brackets, precede the period.

EDITED QUOTATION

In describing the growth of railroads, Wilkins pictures them "lacing their way across continents, reaching into the heart of every major city in Europe and America. . . ."

EDITED QUOTATION (MLA STYLE)

In describing the growth of railroads, Wilkins pictures them "lacing their way across continents, reaching into the heart of every major city in Europe and America [. . .]."

When you need to add a parenthetical reference after the ellipses at the end of a sentence, place it after the quotation mark but before the final period: [. . .]" (253).

Ellipses are usually not needed to indicate an omission when only a word or phrase is being quoted.

➤ **Railroads brought "a new romance to travel," according to Wilkins.**

To indicate the omission of an entire line or more from the middle of a poem, insert a line of spaced periods enclosed in brackets.

```
Shelley seems to be describing nature, but what's
really at issue is the seductive nature of desire:
          See the mountains kiss high Heaven,
          And the waves clasp one another;
          [. . . . . . . . . . . . . . . . .]
          And the sunlight clasps the earth,
          And the moonbeams kiss the sea:
          What is all this sweet work worth
          If thou kiss not me? (1-2, 5-8)
```

Ellipses should be used only as a means of shortening a quotation, never as a device for changing its fundamental meaning or for creating emphasis where none exists in the original.

Ellipses may be used at the end of a sentence if you mean to leave a thought hanging. In the following passage, Dick Gregory uses an ellipsis to suggest that there was no end to his worries.

➤ **Oh God, I'm scared. I wish I could die right now with the feeling I have because I know Momma's gonna make me mad and I'm going to make her mad, and me and Presley's gonna fight . . . "Richard, you get in here and put your coat on. Get in here or I'll whip you."**

62h Use slashes to mark line divisions for poetry quotations that are less than four lines long, to separate options or combinations, and in electronic addresses.

The slash has only a few uses. As a rule, use the slash to show divisions between lines of poetry when you quote more than one line of a poem as part of a sentence. Add a space on either side of the slash.

When you are quoting four or more lines of poetry, use a block quotation instead. (*See pp. 458–60 and 473.*)

➤ **In "The Tower," Yeats makes his peace with "All those things**

whereof / Man makes a superhuman / Mirror-resembling dream"

(163–165).

The slash is sometimes used between two words that represent choices or combinations. Do not add a space on either side of the slash when it is used in this way.

➤ **The college offers three credit/noncredit courses.**

➤ **He is the owner/operator of that business.**

Slashes are also used to mark divisions in online addresses (URLs): *http://www.georgetown.edu/crossroads/navigate.html*

Some writers use the slash as a marker between the words *and* and *or* or between *he* and *she* or *his* and *her* to avoid sexism. Most writers, however, consider such usage awkward. It is usually better to rephrase the sentence. (*See also Tab 11: Editing for Grammar Conventions, pp. 418–21.*)

➤ **A bill can originate in the House of Representatives, and/or** *in*

, or both

the Senate.

➤ **Everyone should be acquainted with his/her neighbors.** *his or her*

Note: Occasionally, the slash is used to show that an event happened over a span of two calendar years.

➤ **The book sold well in 1998/99.**

It is usually better to use *and* or to show inclusive dates with a hyphen, however.

➤ **The book sold well in 1996 and 1997.**

➤ **The book sold well in 1996–97.**

63 Capitalization

Many rules for the use of capital letters have been fixed by custom, such as the convention of beginning each sentence with a capital letter, but the rules change all the time. A recent dictionary is a good guide to capitalization. As you revise your drafts, check to make sure you are using capital letters appropriately in the following types of words:

- Proper nouns (names), words derived from proper nouns, brand names, and certain abbreviations (*below*)
- People's titles (*p. 476*)
- Titles of works of literature, art, and music; documents; and courses (*p. 477*)
- Names of areas and regions (*p. 478*)
- Names of races, ethnic groups, and sacred things (*p. 478*)
- The first word of a quotation (*p. 478*)
- The first word of a sentence (*p. 480*)
- The first word of an independent clause after a colon (*p. 480*)

For more information on and practice using capitalization, visit <www.mhhe.com/maimon/capital_letters>.

63a Capitalize proper nouns (names), words derived from them, brand names, certain abbreviations, and call letters.

Proper nouns are the names of specific people, places, or things, names that set off the individual from the group, such as the name *Jane* instead of the common noun *person*. Capitalize proper nouns, words derived from proper nouns, brand names, abbreviations of capitalized words, and call letters at radio and television stations.

PROPER NOUNS

Ronald Reagan
the Sears Tower

WORDS DERIVED FROM PROPER NOUNS

Reaganomics
Siamese cat

BRAND NAMES

Apple computer
Kleenex

ABBREVIATIONS

FBI (government agency)
A&E (cable television station)

CALL LETTERS

WNBC (television)
WMMR (radio)

1. **People:** John F. Kennedy, Ruth Bader Ginsburg, Albert Einstein
2. **Nationalities, ethnic groups, and languages:** English, Swiss, African Americans, Arabs, Chinese, Turkish
3. **Places:** the United States of America, Tennessee, the Irunia Restaurant, the Great Lakes
4. **Organizations and institutions:** Phi Beta Kappa, Republican Party (Republicans), Department of Defense, Cumberland College, the North Carolina Tarheels
5. **Religious bodies, books, and figures:** Jews, Christians, Baptists, Hindus, Roman Catholic Church, the Bible, the Koran, the Torah, God, Holy Spirit, Allah
6. **The genus in scientific names:** *Homo sapiens, H. sapiens, Acer rubrum, A. rubrum*
7. **Days and months:** Monday, Veterans Day, August, the Fourth of July
8. **Historical events, movements, and periods:** World War II, Impressionism, the Renaissance, the Jazz Age

Note: Although holidays and the names of months and days of the week are capitalized, seasons, such as *summer,* are not. Neither are the days of the month when they are spelled out.

➤ **Why would *Valentine's Day,* the day representing love and romance, fall in *winter*—and in the coldest month of the year at that.**

➤ **She'll be available to meet with you on Sunday, the *seventh* of March.**

63b Capitalize titles when they appear before a proper name but not when they are used alone.

Capitalize titles when they come before a proper name, but do not capitalize them when they appear alone or after the name.

TITLE USED BEFORE A NAME

Every Sunday, *Aunt Lou* tells fantastic stories.

TITLE USED BEFORE A NAME

Everyone knew that *Governor Grover Cleveland* of New York was the most likely candidate for the Democratic nomination.

TITLE USED ALONE

My *aunt* is arriving this afternoon.

TITLE USED AFTER A NAME

The most likely candidate for the Democratic nomination was Grover Cleveland, *governor* of New York.

Exceptions: If the name for a family relationship is used alone (without a possessive such as *my* before it), it should be capitalized.

➤ **I saw *Father* infrequently during the summer months.**

President of the United States or the *President* (meaning the chief executive of the United States) is frequently but not always capitalized. Most writers do not capitalize the title *president* unless they are referring to the President of the United States: "The *president* of this university has seventeen honorary degrees." Although usage varies, you should be consistent. If you write "the President of the University," you should also write "the Chair of the History Department."

63c Capitalize titles of works of literature, works of art, musical compositions, documents, and courses.

Capitalize the important words in titles and subtitles. Do not capitalize articles (*a, an,* and *the*), the *to* in infinitives, or prepositions and conjunctions unless they begin or end the title or subtitle. Capitalize both words in a hyphenated word. Capitalize the first word after a colon or semicolon in a title.

Book: *Two Years before the Mast*
Play: *The Taming of the Shrew*
Building: the Eiffel Tower
Ship or aircraft: the *Titanic* or the *Concorde*
Painting: the *Mona Lisa*
Article or essay: "On Old Age"
Poem: "Ode on a Grecian Urn"
Music: "The Star-Spangled Banner"
Document: the Bill of Rights
Course: Economics 206: Macro-Economic Analysis

63d Capitalize names of areas and regions.

Names of geographical regions are generally capitalized if they are well established, like *the Midwest* and *Central Europe*. Names of directions, as in the sentence *Turn south,* are not capitalized.

CORRECT   *East* meets *West* at the summit.

CORRECT   You will need to go *west* on Sunset.

Note: The word *western,* when used as a general direction or the name of a genre, is not capitalized. It is capitalized when it is part of the name of a specific region.

➤ The ~~Western~~ *High Noon* is one of my favorites movies.
    western

➤ I visited ~~western~~ Europe last year.
    Western

63e Follow standard practice for capitalizing names of races, ethnic groups, and sacred things.

The words *black* and *white* are usually not capitalized when they are used to refer to members of racial groups because they are adjectives that substitute for the implied common nouns *black person* and *white person*. However, names of ethnic groups and races are capitalized: *African Americans, Italians, Asians, Caucasians*.

    Note: In accordance with current APA guidelines, most social scientists capitalize the terms *Black* and *White,* treating them as proper nouns.

    Many religious terms, such as *sacrament, altar,* and *rabbi,* are not capitalized. The word *Bible* is capitalized (though *biblical* is not), but it is never capitalized when it is used as a metaphor for an essential book.

➤ His book *Winning at Stud Poker* used to be the *bible* of gamblers.

63f Capitalize the first word of a quoted sentence but not the first word of an indirect quotation.

➤ She cried, "Help!"

➤ He said that jazz was one of America's major art forms.

    The first word of a quotation from a printed source is capitalized if the quotation is introduced with a phrase such as *she notes* or *he concludes*.

TEXTCONNEX

Emphasis in E-Mail

When you are writing an e-mail message, you may be tempted to use all capital letters for emphasis when italics are not available. Although capital letters are sometimes used this way in print documents, they are not always welcome in online chat rooms and electronic mailing list postings, where participants may feel that they are equivalent to shouting. Also, strings of words or sentences in capital letters can be difficult to read. If you want to emphasize a word or phrase in an online communication, put an asterisk before and after it instead:

➤ *I *totally* disagree with what you just wrote.*

➤ **Jim, the narrator of *My Ántonia*, concludes, "Whatever we had missed, we possessed together the precious, the incommunicable past" (324).**

When a quotation from a printed source is treated as an element in your sentence, not a sentence on its own, the first word is not capitalized.

➤ **Jim took comfort in sharing with Ántonia "the precious, the incommunicable past" (324).**

If you need to change the first letter of a quotation to fit your sentence, enclose the letter in brackets.

➤ **The lawyer noted that "[t]he man seen leaving the area after the blast was not the same height as the defendant."**

If you interrupt the sentence you are quoting with an expression such as *he said,* the first word of the rest of the quotation should not be capitalized.

➤ **"When I come home an hour later," she explained, "the trains are usually less crowded."**

Many authors in earlier centuries and some writers today—especially poets—use capital letters in obsolete or eccentric ways. When quoting a text directly, reproduce the capitalization used in the original source, whether or not it is correct by today's standards.

➤ **Blake's marginalia include the following comment: "Paine is either a Devil or an Inspired Man" (603).**

63g Capitalize the first word of a sentence.

A capital letter is used to signal the beginning of a new sentence.

➤ **Robots reduce human error, so they produce uniform products.**

Sentences in parentheses also begin with a capital letter unless they are embedded within another sentence:

➤ **Although the week began with the news that he was hit by a car, by Thursday we knew he was going to be all right. (It was a terrible way to begin the week, though.)**

➤ **Although the week began with the news that he was hit by a car (it was a terrible way to begin the week), by Thursday we knew he was going to be all right.**

63h Capitalizing the first word of an independent clause after a colon is optional.

If the word group that follows a colon is not a complete sentence, do not capitalize it. If it is a complete sentence, you can capitalize it or not, but be consistent throughout your document.

➤ **The question is serious: do you think the peace process has a chance?**

or

➤ **The question is serious: Do you think the peace process has a chance?**

Scientific Abbreviations

Most abbreviations used in scientific or technical writing, such as those related to measurement, should be given without periods: *mph, lb, dc, rpm.* If an abbreviation looks like an actual word, however, you can use a period to prevent confusion: *in., Fig.*

64 Abbreviations and Symbols

Unless you are writing a scientific or technical report, spell out most terms and titles, except in the following cases.

64a Abbreviate familiar titles that always precede or follow a person's name.

Some abbreviations appear before a person's name (*Mr., Mrs., Dr.*). and some follow a proper name (*Jr., Sr., MD, Esq., PhD*). Abbreviations that follow a person's name often indicate academic or professional degrees or honors. When an abbreviation follows a person's name, a comma is placed between the name and the abbreviation.

TITLES BEFORE NAMES
Mrs. Jean Bascom
Dr. Epstein

TITLES AFTER NAMES
Robert Robinson, Jr.
Elaine Less, CPA, LL.D.

Do not use two abbreviations that represent the same thing: *Dr. Peter Joyce, MD.* Use either *Dr. Peter Joyce* or *Peter Joyce, MD.*
Spell out titles used without proper names.

doctor.
➤ Mr. Carew asked if she had seen the dr.
        ^

CHARTING the TERRITORY

Latin Abbreviations

In some types of scholarly writing, the use of Latin abbreviations is acceptable. When Latin abbreviations are used in scholarly work, they generally appear in parenthetical statements.

64b Use abbreviations only when you know your readers will understand them.

If you use a technical term or the name of an organization in a report, you may abbreviate it as long as your readers are likely to be familiar with the abbreviation. Abbreviations of three or more capital letters generally do not use periods: *CBS, CIA, EPA, FBI, IRS, NAACP, NASA, USA, YMCA*

FAMILIAR ABBREVIATION	The EPA has had a lasting impact on the air quality in this country.
UNFAMILIAR ABBREVIATION	**After you have completed them, take these** *the Human Resources and Education Center.* **forms to ~~HREC.~~**

Write out an unfamiliar term or name the first time you use it, and give the abbreviation in parentheses.

➤ **The Student Nonviolent Coordinating Committee (SNCC) was**

far to the left of other civil rights organizations, and its leaders

often mocked the "conservatism" of Dr. Martin Luther King, Jr.

SNCC quickly burned itself out and disappeared.

64c Abbreviate words typically used with times, dates, and numerals, as well as units of measurement in charts and graphs.

Abbreviations or symbols associated with numbers should be used only when accompanying a number: *3 p.m.,* not *in the p.m.; $500,* not *How many $ do you have?* The abbreviation *B.C.* ("Before Christ") follows a date; *A.D.* ("in the year of our Lord") precedes the date. The

CHARTING the TERRITORY

Abbreviations and Symbols

Some abbreviations and symbols may be acceptable in certain contexts, as long as readers will know what they stand for. For example, a medical writer might use *PT* (*physical therapy*) in a medical report or professional newsletter.

alternative abbreviations B.C.E. ("Before the Common Era") and C.E. ("Common Era") can be used instead of B.C. or A.D., respectively.

> 6:00 p.m. or 6:00 P.M.
>
> 9:45 a.m. or 9:45 A.M.
>
> 498 B.C. (or 498 B.C.E.)
>
> A.D. 275 (or 275 C.E.)
>
> 6,000 rpm
>
> 271 cm

Note: Be consistent. If you use *a.m.* in one sentence, do not switch to *A.M.* in the next sentence. If an abbreviation is made up of capital letters, the periods are optional: *B.C. or BC. (For more on using periods with abbreviations, see Chapter 62, pp. 466–67.)*

In charts and graphs, abbreviations and symbols such as = for *equals, in.* for *inches,* % for *percent,* and *$* with numbers are acceptable because they save space.

64d Avoid Latin abbreviations in formal writing.

Latin abbreviations can be used in notes or works-cited lists, but in formal writing it is usually a good idea to avoid even common Latin abbreviations (*e.g., et al., etc.,* and *i.e.*). Instead of *e.g.,* use *such as* or *for example.*

cf.	compare (*confer*)
e.g.	for example, such as (*exempli gratia*)
et al.	and others (*et alii*)
etc.	and so forth, and so on (*et cetera*)
i.e.	that is (*id est*)
N.B.	note well (*nota bene*)
viz.	namely (*videlicet*)

64e Avoid inappropriate abbreviations and symbols.

Days of the week (*Sat.*), places (*TX* or *Tex.*), the word *company* (*Co.*), people's names (*Wm.*), disciplines and professions (*econ.*), parts of speech (*v.*), parts of written works (*ch., p.*), symbols (@), and units of measurement (*lb.*) are all spelled out in formal writing.

➤ The *environmental* (not *env.*) engineers from the Paramus Water

Company (not *Co.*) are arriving in *New York City* (not *NYC*) this

Thursday (not *Thurs.*) to correct the problems in the *physical*

education (not *phys. ed.*) building in time for *Christmas* (not *Xmas*).

Exceptions: If an abbreviation such as *Inc., Co.,* or *Corp.* is part of a company's official name, then it can be included in formal writing: *Time Inc. announced these changes in late December.* The ampersand symbol (&) can also be used but only if it is part of an official name: *Church & Dwight.*

65 Numbers

For more information on and practice working with numbers, visit <www.mhhe.com/maimon/numbers>.

65a In nontechnical writing, spell out numbers up to one hundred and round numbers greater than one hundred.

➤ Approximately *twenty-five* students failed the exam, but more

than *two hundred and fifty* passed.

When you are using a great many numbers or when a spelled-out number would require more than three or four words, use numerals.

➤ This regulation affects nearly *10,500* taxpayers, substantially more

than the *200* originally projected. Of those affected, *2,325* filled out

the papers incorrectly and another *743* called the office for help.

65b Spell out a number that begins a sentence.

If a numeral begins a sentence, reword the sentence or spell out the numeral.

➤ *Twenty-five* children are in each elementary class.

65c In technical and business writing, use numerals for exact measurements and all numbers greater than ten.

➤ **Five endosperm halves were placed in each of 14 small glass test tubes.**

➤ **A solution with a GA$_3$ concentration ranging from 0 g/ml to 10^5 g/ml was added to each test tube.**

➤ **With its $1.9 trillion economy, Germany has an important trade role to play.**

65d Use numerals for dates, times of day, addresses, and similar kinds of conventional quantitative information.

Dates: October 9, 2002; A.D. 1066 (*or* AD 1066)

Time of day: 6 A.M. (*or* AM *or* a.m.), a quarter past eight in the evening, three o'clock in the morning

Addresses: 21 Meadow Road, Apt. 6J

Percentages: 73 percent, 73%

Fractions and decimals: 21.84, 6½

Measurements: 100 mph, 9 kg

Volume, page, chapter: volume 4, chapter 8, page 44

Scenes in a play: *Hamlet,* act 2, scene 1

Scores and statistics: 0 to 3, 98–92, an average age of 35

Amounts of money: $125, $2.25, $2.8 million

66 Italics (Underlining)

To set off certain words and phrases, printers have traditionally used *italics,* a typeface in which the characters slant to the right. Now any word-processor program can produce italics. If italics are not available, however, you can <u>underline</u> words that would be typeset in italics. Your instructor may prefer that you use underlining rather than italics, especially if you are following the MLA style of documentation. (*See Tab 6: MLA Documentation Style.*)

For more information on and practice using italics, visit <www.mhhe.com/maimon/italics>.

➤ Tom Hanks gives one of his best performances in *Saving Private Ryan.*

➤ Tom Hanks gives one of his best performances in <u>Saving Private Ryan.</u>

TEXTCONNEX

Italics and Underlining

Depending on the software you are using, italics or underlining may not be available for your e-mail messages. To indicate underlining, put an underscore mark or an asterisk before and after what you would italicize or underline in a manuscript: Tom Hanks gives one of his best performances in _Saving Private Ryan_.

To create Web sites, many people use hypertext markup language (HTML). In HTML, underlining indicates a hypertext link. If your work is going to be posted on the World Wide Web, use italics for titles instead of underlining to avoid confusion.

66a Italicize (underline) titles of lengthy works or separate publications.

Italicize (or underline) titles of books, magazines, journals, newspapers, comic strips, plays, films, musical compositions, choreographic works, artworks, Web sites, software, long poems, pamphlets, and other long works. In titles of lengthy works, *a, an,* or *the* is capitalized and italicized (underlined) if it is the first word, but *the* is not generally treated as part of the title in names of newspapers and periodicals: the *New York Times.*

➤ Picasso's *Guernica* captures the anguish and despair of violence.

➤ Plays by Shakespeare provide details and story lines for Verdi's opera *Falstaff,* Cole Porter's musical comedy *Kiss Me, Kate,* and Franco Zeffirelli's film *Romeo and Juliet.*

Court cases may also be italicized or underlined.

➤ **In *Brown v. Board of Education of Topeka* (1954), the U.S.**

Supreme Court ruled that segregation in public schools is

unconstitutional.

Exceptions: Do not use italics or underlining when referring to the Bible and other sacred books.

Quotation marks are used for the titles of short works—essays, newspaper and magazine articles and columns, short stories, individual episodes of television and radio programs, short poems, songs, and chapters or other book subdivisions. Quotation marks are also used for titles of unpublished works, including student papers, theses, and dissertations. (*See Chapter 61, pp. 460–61, for more on quotation marks with titles.*)

66b Italicize (underline) the names of ships, trains, aircraft, and spaceships.

➤ **The commentators were stunned into silence when the**

***Challenger* exploded.**

66c Italicize (underline) foreign terms.

➤ **In the Paris airport, we recognized the familiar no smoking**

sign: *Défense de fumer*.

Many foreign words have become so common in English that everyone accepts them as part of the language and they require no italics or underlining: rigor mortis, pasta, and sombrero, for example.

66d Italicize (underline) scientific names.

The scientific (Latin) names of organisms are always italicized.

➤ **Most chicks are infected with *Cryptosporidium baileyi*, a**

parasite typical of young animals.

Note: Although the whole name is italicized, only the genus part of the name is capitalized.

66e Italicize (underline) words, letters, and numbers referred to as themselves.

For clarity, italicize words or phrases used as words rather than for the meaning they convey. (You may also use quotation marks for this purpose.)

➤ The term *romantic* does not mean the same thing to the Shelley

scholar as it does to the fan of Danielle Steele's novels.

Letters and numbers used alone should also be italicized.

➤ The word *bookkeeper* has three sets of double letters: double *o*,

double *k*, and double *e*.

➤ Add a *3* to that column.

66f Use italics (underlining) sparingly for emphasis.

Sometimes writers are tempted to italicize words to show the kind of emphasis they would give the word in speaking. An occasional word in italics helps you make a point. Too much emphasis, however, may mean no emphasis at all.

WEAK   You don't *mean* that your *teacher* told the whole *class* that *he* did not know the answer *himself*?

REVISED Your teacher admitted that he did not know the answer? That is amazing.

Note: If you add italics or underlining to a quotation, indicate the change in parentheses following the quotation.

➤ Instead of promising that no harm will come to us, Blake only

assures us that we "need not *fear* harm" (emphasis added).

For more information on and practice in using hyphens, visit <www.mhhe.com/maimon/hyphens>.

67 Hyphens

67a Use hyphens to form compound words and to avoid confusion.

Think of hyphens as bridges. A hyphen joins two nouns to make one compound word. Scientists speak of a *kilogram-meter* as a measure of force, and professors of literature talk about the *scholar-poet.* The hyphen lets us know that the two nouns work together as one. As compound nouns come into general use, the hyphens between them tend to disappear: *firefighter, thundershower.*

A dictionary is the best resource when you are unsure about whether to use a hyphen. The dictionary sometimes gives writers several options, however. For example, you could write *life-style* or *life style* or *lifestyle* and be correct in each case, according to the *Random House Webster's College Dictionary.* If you cannot find a compound word in the dictionary, spell it as two separate words. Whatever spelling you choose, be consistent throughout your document.

67b Use hyphens to join two or more words to create compound adjective or noun forms.

A noun can also be linked with an adjective, an adverb, or another part of speech to form a compound adjective.

> accident-prone
>
> quick-witted

Hyphens are also used in nouns designating family relationships and compounds of more than two words:

> brother-in-law
>
> stay-at-home
>
> stick-in-the-mud

Note: Compound nouns with hyphens generally form plurals by adding *-s* or *-es* to the most important word.

> attorney general/attorney<u>s</u> general
>
> mother-in-law/mother<u>s</u>-in-law
>
> court-martial/court<u>s</u>-martial

Some proper nouns that are joined to make an adjective are hyphenated.

> the Franco-Prussian war
>
> of Mexican-American heritage
>
> the Sino-Japanese agreement

Hyphens often help clarify adjectives that come before the word they modify. If you say "She was a quick thinking person," you might mean that she was quick and that she was also a thinking person. If you say "She was a quick-thinking person," though, your meaning is unmistakable: she thought rapidly. Modifiers that are hyphenated when they are placed *before* the word they modify are usually not hyphenated when they are placed *after* the word they modify.

➤ It was a *bad-mannered* reply.

➤ The reply was *bad mannered.*

Do not use a hyphen to connect *-ly* adverbs to the words they modify.

➤ They explored the newly⁄discovered territories.

In a pair or series of compound nouns or adjectives, add suspended hyphens after the first word of each item.

➤ The child care center accepted three-, four-, and five-year-olds.

67c Use hyphens to spell out fractions and compound numbers.

Use a hyphen when writing out fractions or compound numbers from twenty-one to ninety-nine.

three-fourths of a gallon

thirty-two

twenty-five thousand

Note: Use a hyphen to show inclusive numbers: *pages 100–140.*

67d Use a hyphen to attach some prefixes and suffixes.

Use a hyphen to join a prefix and a capitalized word.

➤ Skipping the parade on the Fourth of July is positively

un-American!

A hyphen is sometimes used to join a capital letter and a word: *T-shirt, V-six engine.*

The prefixes *ex-, self-,* and *all-* and the suffixes *-elect* and *-odd* (or *-something*) generally take hyphens. However, most prefixes are not attached by hyphens, unless a hyphen is needed to show pronunciation or to reveal a special meaning that distinguishes the word from the same word without a hyphen: *recreate* vs. *re-create.* Check a dictionary to be certain you are using the standard spelling.

➤ Because he was an *ex-convict,* he was a *nonjudgmental coworker.*

➤ The *president-elect* of the *extracurricular* support group suffers

from *post-traumatic* stress syndrome.

➤ They were *self-sufficient, antisocial* neighbors.

67e Use hyphens to divide words at the ends of lines.

When you must divide words, do so between syllables, but pronunciation alone cannot always tell you where to divide a word. If you are unsure about how to break a word into syllables, consult your dictionary.

➤ My writing group had a very fruitful *collab-*

oration. [not *colla-boration*]

Never leave just one or two letters on a line.

He seemed so sad and vulnerable and so *discon-*

nected from his family. [not *disconnect-ed*]

Compound words such as *hardworking, rattlesnake,* and *book-case* should be broken only between the words that form them: *hard-working, rattle-snake, book-case.* Compound words that already have hyphens, like *brother-in-law,* are broken after the hyphens only.

Note: Never hyphenate an acronym (CIA) or a one-syllable word.

TEXTCONNEX

Dividing Internet Addresses

If you need to divide an Internet address between lines, divide it after a slash. Do not divide a word within the address with a hyphen; readers may assume the hyphen is part of the address.

68 Spelling

Frequent or even occasional misspellings can make people believe that you are careless or ignorant, and you will then have to work twice as hard to convince them to take your ideas seriously. Proofread your writing carefully. Misspellings creep into the prose of even the best writers. Here are some suggestions to help you improve your spelling.

For more information on and practice in spelling, visit <www.mhhe.com/maimon/spelling>.

- Use your computer software's spell checker. Remember, though, that a spell checker cannot tell how you are using a particular word. If you write *their* when you should write *there,* the spell checker cannot point out your mistake. Keep a dictionary nearby to check words you are unsure of.
- Become familiar with major spelling rules and commonly misspelled words, and use your dictionary whenever you are unsure about the spelling of a specific word.
- Learn to distinguish *homophones*—words pronounced alike but with different meanings and spellings. (*See pp. 494–95.*)

68a Learn the rules that generally hold for spelling, as well as their exceptions.

1. *i* before e. Use *i* before *e* except after *c* or when sounded like *a,* as in *neighbor* and *weigh.*

I BEFORE *E*	believe, relieve, chief, grief, wield, yield
EXCEPT AFTER *C*	receive, deceive, ceiling, conceit
EXCEPTIONS	seize, caffeine, codeine, weird, height

2. Adding suffixes.

- **Final silent -*e*:** When adding a suffix that begins with a vowel, drop the final silent -*e* from the root word. Keep the final -*e* if the suffix begins with a consonant.

    force/forcing

    surprise/surprising

    remove/removable

    care/careful

    achieve/achievement

Exceptions: argue/argument, true/truly, change/changeable, judge/judgment, acknowledge/acknowledgment

Exception: Keep the silent -*e* if it is needed to clarify the pronunciation or if the word would be confused with another word without the -*e.*

    dye/dyeing (to avoid confusion with *dying*)

    hoe/hoeing (to avoid mispronunciation)

- **Final -y:** When adding the suffix -ing to a word ending in -y, retain the -y.

    enjoy/enjoying

    cry/crying

    Change the y to i or ie when the final y follows a consonant but not when it follows a vowel.

    happy/happier

    defray/defrayed

- **Final consonants:** When adding a suffix to a word that ends in a consonant preceded by a vowel, double the final consonant if the root word has only one syllable or an accent on the last syllable.

grip/gripping	refer/referred
stun/stunning	transmit/transmitted

    Exceptions: bus/busing, focus/focused

3. Forming plurals

- **-s or -es:** Add a final -s to make most nouns plural. Add a final -es to form a plural when the singular form of a noun ends in -s, -x, -ch, or -sh.

cobra/cobras	kiss/kisses
scientist/scientists	box/boxes

    Exception: The plural of a few nouns ending in -is is formed by changing -is to -es.

analysis/analyses	basis/bases
crisis/crises	thesis/theses

- **Other Plurals:** If a noun ends in -y preceded by a consonant, change the -y to -i and add -es to form the plural; if the final -y is preceded by a vowel, keep the -y and add -s to make the plural.

beauty/beauties	boy/boys
city/cities	obey/obeys

    Exceptions: Always keep the final -y when forming the plural of a person's name.

    Joe and Mary Kirby/the Kirbys

    When a noun ends in a consonant and an -o in the singular, form the plural by adding -es. If the -o is preceded by a vowel, add an -s.

hero/heroes	folio/folios
tomato/tomatoes	

    Exception: solo/solos

American and British Spelling

Standard British spelling differs from American spelling for some words—among them, *color/colour, canceled/cancelled, theater/theatre, realize/realise,* and *judgment/judgement.*

- **Irregular plurals:** Most plurals follow standard rules, but some have irregular forms (*child/children, tooth/teeth),* and some words with foreign roots create plurals in the pattern of the original language, as do these words derived from Latin and Greek.

  addendum/addenda   datum/data

  alumna/alumnae   medium/media

  alumnus/alumni   phenomenon/phenomena

  criterion/criteria   stimulus/stimuli

Note: Some writers now treat *data* as though it were singular, but the preferred practice is still to recognize that *data* is plural and takes a plural verb.

➤ **The *data are* clear on this point: the pass/fail course has**

   become outdated by events.

Compound nouns with hyphens generally form plurals by adding *-s* or *-es* to the most important word.

  attorney general/attorneys general

  mother-in-law/mothers-in-law

  court-martial/courts-martial

68b Learn to distinguish words pronounced alike but spelled differently.

Homophones are words that sound alike but have different meanings and different spellings. Many are commonly confused. (*See Tab 10: Editing for Clarity, pp. 375–84.*) The words in the following box should be checked every time you proofread your work.

SOME COMMONLY CONFUSED HOMOPHONES

AFFECT, EFFECT
affect: "to influence" (verb); "a feeling or an emotion" (noun)
effect: "to make or accomplish" (verb); "result" (noun)

DISCREET, DISCRETE
discreet: "tactful" or "prudent"
discrete: "separate" or "distinct"

ITS, IT'S
it's: the contraction for *it is* or *it has*
its: a possessive pronoun

LOOSE, LOSE
loose: "not tight"
lose: "to misplace"

PRECEDE, PROCEED
precede: "to come before"
proceed: "to go forward"

PRINCIPAL, PRINCIPLE
principal: "most important" (adjective); "the head of an organization" or "a sum of money" (noun)
principle: "a basic standard or law" (noun)

THEIR, THERE, THEY'RE
their: a possessive pronoun
there: an adverb of place
they're: the contraction for *they are*

YOUR, YOU'RE
your: a possessive pronoun
you're: the contraction for *you are*

68c Check for commonly misspelled words.

Words that are exceptions to standard spelling rules are commonly misspelled. In a list or spelling log, write down words you often misspell. Try to group your errors. Misspellings often fall into patterns—errors with suffixes or plurals, for example. (*See p. 496 for a sampling of commonly misspelled words.*)

A Sampling of Commonly Misspelled Words

accommodate	kindergarten	questionnaire
already		quizzes
	license	
conscience	lieutenant	recommend
conscious	livelihood	reminisce
	luxury	restaurant
eighth		rhyme
embarrass	meant	rhythm
exaggerate	misspelled	
exercise	mortgage	sacrilegious
	muscle	separate
fascinate		sophomore
February	nuclear	supersede
foreign	nuisance	
fulfill		tomatoes
	occasion	tomorrow
gauge	occurrence	twelfth
guard	omission	
		vacuum
innocuous	parliament	vengeance
inoculate	personnel	
irrelevant	playwright	wholly
	pronunciation	
jealousy		
judgment		

> Grammar and rhetoric are complementary. . . . Grammar maps out the possible; rhetoric narrows the possible down to the desirable or effective.
>
> —FRANCIS CHRISTENSEN

Basic Grammar Review

with Tips for Multilingual Writers

13 Basic Grammar Review

69. Parts of Speech *499*
    a. Verbs *500*
    b. Nouns *504*
    c. Pronouns *507*
    d. Adjectives *511*
    e. Adverbs *513*
    f. Prepositions *514*
    g. Conjunctions *518*
    h. Interjections *520*

70. Parts of Sentences *521*
    a. Subjects *521*
    b. Verbs, objects, and complements *522*

71. Phrases and Dependent Clauses *526*
    a. Noun phrases *526*
    b. Verb phrases and verbals *526*
    c. Appositive phrases *527*
    d. Absolute phrases *527*
    e. Dependent clauses *528*

72. Types of Sentences *530*
    a. Sentence structures *530*
    b. Sentence purposes *531*

Tips for Multilingual Writers:

Recognizing language differences *499*

Using verbs followed by gerunds and infinitives *501*

Matching helping verbs (*do, have, be*) with the appropriate form of the main verb *502*

Understanding the form and meaning of modal verbs *503*

Using quantifiers with count and noncount nouns *505*

Using articles (*a, an, the*) appropriately *506*

Putting adjectives in the correct order *512*

Using present and past participles as adjectives to describe feelings *512*

Using prepositions *515*

Using coordination and subordination appropriately *519*

Putting sentence parts in the correct order for English *521*

Including a subject (but not two) *522*

Including a complete verb *523*

Including only one direct object *524*

Understanding the purposes and constructions of *if* clauses *529*

What Was the Language of Your Ancestors?

Your native language or even the language of your ancestors may influence the way you use English. Even if English is your first language, you may be part of a group that immigrated generations ago but has retained traces of other grammatical structures. For example, the slang contraction *ain't,* brought here by Scottish settlers, may have meant *am not* at one time. Take note of the Tips for Multilingual Writers in this section. Some might help native speakers as well.

When we speak in our native language or dialect, we usually do not worry too much about grammar. The order and endings of our words seem to come naturally. Written language, although based on the grammar of spoken language, has a logic and rules of its own, however. The chapters that follow explain the basic rules of standard written English.

 Tip for Multilingual Writers: *Recognizing language differences*

The standard structures of sentences in languages other than English can be very different from those in English. In other languages, the way verbs are conjugated can indicate their grammatical function more powerfully than can their placement in the sentence. Also, in languages other than English, adjectives may take on the function that articles (*a, an,* or *the*) perform, or articles can be absent entirely.

If your first language is not English, try to pinpoint the areas of difficulty you have in English. See whether you are attempting to *translate* the structures of your native language into English, which has a different structure. If so, you will need to learn more about English sentence structure.

69 Parts of Speech

Grammar gives us a way of talking about how sentences are put together to make sense. Although *The toves gimbled in the wabe*—from Lewis Carroll's poem "Jabberwocky"—is a group of words that in and of themselves do not make sense, the sentence does make grammatical sense. Because what makes a sentence meaningful is not just the individual words but also the pattern or ordering of its parts, you can answer questions like *What gimbled in the wabe?* (*the toves*), *What did the toves do in the wabe?* (*they gimbled*), and *Where did the toves gimble?* (*in the wabe*).

English has eight primary grammatical categories, or parts of speech: *verbs, nouns, pronouns, adjectives, adverbs, prepositions, conjunctions,* and *interjections.* All English words belong to one or more of these categories. Particular words can belong in different categories, depending on the role they play in a sentence. For example, the word *button* can be a noun (*the button on a coat*) or a verb (*he will button his jacket now*).

69a Verbs

Verbs carry a lot of information. They report action (*run, write*), condition (*bloom, sit*), or state of being (*be, seem*). Verbs also change form to indicate person, number, tense, voice, and mood. To do all this, a **main verb** is sometimes accompanied by one or more **helping verbs,** thereby becoming a **verb phrase.** Helping verbs precede the main verb in a verb phrase.

➤   The play *begins*^{mv} at eight.

➤   I *may*^{hv} *change*^{mv} seats after the play *has*^{hv} *begun.*^{mv}

1. Main verbs. Main verbs change form (**tense**) to indicate when something has happened. If a word does not indicate tense, it is not a main verb. All main verbs have five forms, except for *be,* which has eight.

BASE FORM	(*talk, sing*)
PAST TENSE	Yesterday I (*talked, sang*).
PAST PARTICIPLE	In the past, I have (*talked, sung*).
PRESENT PARTICIPLE	Right now I am (*talking, singing*).
-*S* FORM	Usually he/she/it (*talks, sings*).

Whether or not English is your first language, verb forms—especially irregular verb forms—can be troublesome. (*For more on subject-verb agreement and verb tense, see Tab 11: Editing for Grammar Conventions, pp. 397–98 and 404–5, and the list of common irregular verbs on pp. 405–7.*)

Tip for Multilingual Writers: *Using verbs followed by gerunds or infinitives*

When verbs are followed by other verbs to make a verb chain, some can be followed only by a gerund (the *-ing* form of the verb used as a noun) and some are usually followed by an infinitive (*to* plus the base form of the verb).

Gerunds. The following verbs can only be followed by a gerund. The gerund usually names an action occurring before the action of the main verb: *admit, appreciate, avoid, complete, deny, discuss, dislike, enjoy, finish, imagine, keep, miss, postpone, practice, put off, quit, recall, recommend, resist, risk, suggest, tolerate.*

VERB + GERUND

She admits *wanting* the best seat.

The wanting occurs before the admission.

Infinitives. Some verbs are typically followed by an infinitive that names an action occurring after the action of the main verb. Verbs that are followed by an infinitive include the following: *afford, agree, arrange, ask, beg, choose, claim, decide, deserve, expect, fail, hope, manage, need, offer, plan, pretend, promise, refuse, want, wish.*

VERB + INFINITIVE

She wants *to win.*

The winning would happen after the wanting.

Sometimes a noun or pronoun comes between the verb and the infinitive. Verbs that are followed by a noun or pronoun plus an infinitive include the following: *advise, allow, ask, cause, command, convince, encourage, expect, force, need, order, persuade, remind, require, tell, urge, want, warn.*

VERB + NOUN/PRONOUN+ INFINITIVE

She wants *her friend* to win.

Note: *Make, let,* and *have* are followed by a noun or pronoun plus the base form without *to: Make that boy come home on time.*

2. Helping verbs that show time.

Some helping verbs—mostly forms of *be, have,* and *do*—function to signify time (*will have been playing, has played*) or emphasis (*does play*). Forms of *do* are also used to ask questions (*Do you play?*). Here is a fuller list of such helping (or **auxiliary**) verbs.

be, am, is	being, been	do, does, did
are, was, were	have, has, had	

Tip for Multilingual Writers: *Matching helping verbs (do, have, be) with the appropriate form of the main verb*

Do, Does, Did. The helping verb *do* and its forms *does* and *did* combine with the base form of a verb to ask a question or to emphasize something. It can also combine with the word *not* to create an emphatic negative statement.

QUESTION	*Do* you hear those dogs barking?
EMPHATIC STATEMENT	I *do* hear them barking.
EMPHATIC NEGATIVE	I *do not* want to have to call the police about those dogs.

Have, Has, Had. The helping verb *have* and its forms *has* and *had* combine with a past participle (usually ending in *-d, -t,* or *-n*) to form the *perfect tenses*. Do not confuse the simple past tense with the present perfect tense (formed with *have* or *has*), which is distinct from the simple past because the action can continue in the present. (*For a review of perfect tense forms, see Tab 11: Editing for Grammar Conventions, pp. 411–13.*)

SIMPLE PAST	Those dogs *barked* all day.
PRESENT PERFECT	Those dogs *have barked* all day.
PAST PERFECT	Those dogs *had barked* all day.

Be. Forms of *be* combine with a present participle (ending in *-ing*) to form the *progressive tenses,* which express continuing action. Do not confuse the simple present tense or the present perfect with these progressive forms. Unlike the simple present, which indicates an action that occurs frequently and might include the present moment, the present progressive form indicates an action that is going on right now. In its past form, the progressive tense indicates actions that are going on simultaneously. (*For a review of progressive tense forms, see Tab 11: Editing for Grammar Conventions, p. 412.*)

SIMPLE PRESENT	Those dogs *bark* all the time.
PRESENT PROGRESSIVE	Those dogs *are barking* all the time.
PAST PROGRESSIVE	Those dogs *were barking* all day while I *was trying* to study.

Forms of *be* combine with the past participle (which usually ends in *-d, -t,* or *-n*) to form the passive voice, which is often used to express a state of being instead of an action.

BE + PAST PARTICIPLE

PASSIVE   The dogs *were scolded* by their owner.

PASSIVE   I was satisfied by her answer. ═══════════════

3. Modals.   Other helping verbs, called **modals,** signify the manner, or mode, of an action. Unlike the auxiliaries *be, have,* and *do,* one-word modals such as *may, must,* and *will* are almost never used alone as main verbs, nor do they change form to show person, or number. Modals do not add -*s* endings, two modals are never used together (such as *might could*), and modals are always followed by the base form of the verb without *to* (*He could be nicer*).

The one-word modals are: *can, could, may, might, will, would, shall, should, must.*

➤   hv   mv
   Contrary to press reports, she *will* not *run* for political office.

Note that a negative word such as *not* may come between the helping and the main verb.

Phrasal modals, however, do change form to show time, person, and number. Here are some phrasal modals: *have to, have got to, used to, be supposed to, be going to, be allowed to, be able to.*

➤   hv   mv
   Yesterday, I *was going to study* for three hours.

➤   hv   mv
   Next week, *I am going to study* three hours a day.

     Tip for Multilingual Writers: *Understanding the form and meaning of modal verbs*

To indicate intention: *will, shall; would* + *have* + past participle

   I *will* (*shall*) go today. I *would have gone* yesterday.

To indicate ability: *can, am/is/are able to; would, was/were able to*

   I *can* (*am able to*) take one piece of luggage.

   I *would have taken* (*was able to take*) one piece of luggage.

To ask for permission: *may, might, can, could*

   May (*Might/Can/Could*) I come at five o'clock?

To pose a polite question: *would*

   Would you please open the door?

To speculate: *would (could, might)* or *would (could, might)* + *have* + past participle

> She *would* be there if the weather were nice.
>
> She *could (might)* still come.
>
> He *would have been* pleased by this outcome.
>
> He *could (might) have known* yesterday.

To indicate advisability: *should* or *should* + *have* + past participle

> You *should* wear a coat.
>
> You *should have worn* a coat.

To indicate necessity: *must (have to)*; *had to*

> I *must (have to)* pass this test.
>
> I *had to* find a new apartment.

To prohibit: *must* + *not*

> You *must not* go there.

To indicate expectation: *should* or *should* + *have* + past participle

> I *should* finish my project today.
>
> I *should have finished* my project yesterday.

To indicate possibility: *may (might)* or *might* + *have* + past participle

> She *may (might)* return this afternoon.
>
> She *might have been* delayed.

To indicate logical assumption: *must* or *must* + *have* + past participle

> He *must* be there by now.
>
> He *must have been* pleased with your success.

To indicate repeated past action: *would (used to)* + base form

> I *would (used to)* always take the early train.

69b Nouns

Nouns name people (*Shakespeare, actors, Englishman*), places (*Manhattan, city, island*), things (*Kleenex, handkerchief, sneeze, cats*), and ideas (*Marxism, justice, democracy, clarity*).

➤ *Shakespeare* lived in *England* and wrote *plays* about the human

condition.

1. Proper and common nouns. **Proper nouns** name specific people, places, and things and are always capitalized: *Aretha Franklin, Hinduism, Albany, Microsoft.* All other nouns are **common nouns:** *singer, religion, capital, corporation.*

2. Count and noncount nouns. A common noun that refers to something specific that can be counted is a **count noun.** Count nouns can be singular or plural, like *cup* or *suggestion* (*four cups, several suggestions*). **Noncount nouns** are nonspecific; these common nouns refer to categories of people, places, or things and cannot be counted. They do not have a plural form. (*The pottery is beautiful. His advice was useful.*)

Count and Noncount Nouns

COUNT NOUNS	NONCOUNT NOUNS
cars	transportation
computers	Internet
facts	information
clouds	rain
stars	sunshine
tools	equipment
machines	machinery
suggestions	advice
earrings	jewelry
tables	furniture
smiles	happiness

 Tip for Multilingual Writers: *Using quantifiers with count and noncount nouns*

Ideas about what is countable vary across cultures. *Furniture* might be a count noun in some languages, but in English it is a noncount noun. Consult an ESL dictionary if you have trouble determining whether a word is a count or noncount noun. If a word is a noncount noun, it will not have a plural form.

Count and noncount nouns are often preceded by **quantifiers,** words that tell how much or how many. Use the following quantifiers:

- **With count nouns only:** *several, many, a couple of, a few*
- **With noncount nouns only:** *a good deal of, not much, a little, less*
- **With either count or noncount nouns:** *some, a lot of, plenty of, a lack of, most of the*

(For help using articles with count and noncount nouns, see the section below.)

3. Concrete and abstract nouns.

Nouns that name things that can be perceived by the senses are called **concrete nouns:** *boy, wind, book, song.* **Abstract nouns** name qualities and concepts that do not have physical properties: *charity, patience, beauty, hope.* (*For more on using concrete and abstract nouns, see Tab 10: Editing for Clarity, pp. 368–69.*)

4. Singular and plural nouns.

Most nouns name things that can be counted and are *singular* or *plural.* Singular nouns typically become plural by adding *-s* or *-es: boy/boys, ocean/oceans, church/churches, agency/agencies.* Some have irregular plurals, such as *man/men, child/children,* and *tooth/teeth.* Noncount nouns like *intelligence,* and *electricity* do not form plurals.

5. Collective nouns.

Collective nouns such as *team, family, herd,* and *orchestra* are treated as singular. They are not noncount nouns, however, because collective nouns can be counted and can be made plural: *teams, families.* (*Also see Tab 11: Editing for Grammar Conventions, pp. 400–401 and 420–21.*)

6. Possessive nouns.

When nouns are used in the **possessive case** to indicate ownership, they change their form. To form the possessive case, singular nouns add apostrophe plus *-s* (*'s*), whereas plural nouns ending in *-s* just add an apostrophe (*'*). (*Also see Tab 12: Editing for Correctness, pp. 452–57.*)

SINGULAR	insect	insect's sting
PLURAL	neighbors	neighbors' car

 Tip for Multilingual Writers: *Using articles* (**a, an, the**) *appropriately*

Some languages such as Russian, Chinese, Japanese, Farsi, and Swahili do not use articles at all, and most languages do not use articles in the same way as English. Therefore, articles often cause prob-

lems for multilingual writers. In English, there are only three articles: *a, an,* and *the.* When an article identifies a noun, it functions as
an adjective. (*For more on adjectives, see pp. 511–12.*)

A or *an* refers to one nonspecific person, place, or thing. Count
nouns that are singular and refer to a nonspecific person, place, or
thing take *a* or *an* (*A girl is here; I have an apple*). Noncount nouns
and plural nouns do not take *a* or *an.*

Note that *a* is used before words that begin with consonant sounds,
whether or not the first letter is a vowel (*a European vacation, a country*), and *an* is used before words that begin with vowel sounds, whether
or not the first letter is a consonant (*an hour, an opener*).

The, on the other hand, refers to a specific person, place, or thing
and can be used with singular or plural nouns. It means "this (these)
and no other (none others)." (*The girl you have been waiting for is
here; the girls you have been waiting for are here.*)

Common nouns that refer to a specific person, place, or thing take
the article *the.* Most proper nouns do not use articles unless they are
plural, in which case they take the article *the.* There are some exceptions, however:

- Proper nouns that include a common noun and *of* as part of
  the title (*the Museum of Modern Art, the Fourth of July, the
  Statue of Liberty*)

- Names of highways (*the Santa Monica Freeway*)

- Landmark buildings (*the Eiffel Tower*)

- Hotels (*the Marriott Hotel*)

- Cultural and political institutions (*the Metropolitan Opera,
  the Pentagon*)

- Parts of the globe, names of oceans and seas, deserts, land
  and water formations (*the West, the Equator, the North Pole,
  the Mediterranean, the Sahara, the Bering Strait*)

- Countries with more than one word in their names (*the
  Dominican Republic*)

69c Pronouns

A pronoun takes the place of a noun. The noun that the pronoun
replaces is called its **antecedent.** (*For more on pronoun-antecedent
agreement, see Tab 11: Editing for Grammar Conventions, pp. 418–21.*)

➤ The *snow* fell all day long, and by nightfall *it* was three feet deep.

The box on pages 508–9 summarizes the different kinds of pronouns.

PRONOUNS

PERSONAL (INCLUDING POSSESSIVE)

SINGULAR	PLURAL
I, me, my, mine	we, us, our, ours
you, your, yours	you, your, yours
he, him, his	they, them, their, theirs
she, her, hers	
it, its	

REFLEXIVE AND INTENSIVE

SINGULAR	PLURAL
myself	ourselves
yourself	yourselves
himself, herself, itself	themselves
oneself	

RELATIVE

who	whoever	what	whatever	that
whom	whomever	whose	whichever	which

DEMONSTRATIVE

this, that, these, those

1. Personal pronouns.   The personal pronouns *I, me, you, he, his, she, her, it, we, us, they* and *them* refer to specific people or things and vary in form to indicate person, number, gender, and case. (*For more on pronoun reference and case, such as distinguishing between* I *and* me, *see Tab 11: Editing for Grammar Conventions, pp. 421–25.*)

➤ *You* told *us* that *he* gave Jane a lock of *his* hair.

2. Possessive pronouns.   Like possessive nouns, possessive pronouns indicate ownership. However, unlike possessive nouns, posses-

INTERROGATIVE

who	what	which
whoever	whatever	whichever
whom	whomever	whose

INDEFINITE

SINGULAR		PLURAL	SINGULAR/PLURAL
anybody	nobody	both	all
anyone	no one	few	any
anything	none	many	either
each	nothing	several	more
everybody	one		most
everyone	somebody		some
everything	someone		
much	something		
neither			

RECIPROCAL

each other

any other

sive pronouns do not add apostrophes: *my/mine, your/yours, her/hers, his, its, our/ours, their/theirs.*

➤ **Brunch is at *her* place this Saturday.**

3. Reflexive and intensive pronouns.   Pronouns ending in *-self* or *-selves* are either reflexive or intensive. **Reflexive pronouns** refer back to the subject and are necessary for sentence sense.

➤ **Many of the women blamed *themselves* for the problem.**

Intensive pronouns add emphasis to the nouns or pronouns they follow and are grammatically optional.

➤ **President Harding** *himself* **drank whiskey during Prohibition.**

4. Relative pronouns.

Who, whom, whose, that, and *which* are relative pronouns. A **relative pronoun** relates a dependent clause— a word group containing a subject and verb and a subordinating word—to an antecedent noun or pronoun in the sentence.

dependent clause

➤ **In Kipling's story, Dravot is the man** *who* **would be king.**

The form of a relative pronoun varies according to its case—the grammatical role it plays in the sentence. (*For more on pronoun case, particularly distinguishing between* who *and* whom, *see Tab 11: Editing for Grammar Conventions, pp. 425–26.*)

5. Demonstrative pronouns.

The **demonstrative pronouns** *this, that, these,* and *those* point out nouns and pronouns that come later.

➤ *This* **is the book literary critics have been waiting for.**

Sometimes these pronouns function as adjectives: *This* book won the Pulitzer. Sometimes they are noun equivalents: *This* is my book.

6. Interrogative pronouns.

Interrogative pronouns such as *who, whatever,* and *whom* are used to ask questions.

➤ *Whatever* **happened to you?**

The form of the interrogative pronouns *who, whom, whoever* and *whomever* indicates the grammatical role they play in a sentence. (*See Tab 11: Editing for Grammar Conventions, pp. 425–26.*)

7. Indefinite pronouns.

Indefinite pronouns such as *someone, anybody, nothing,* and *few* refer to a nonspecific person or thing and do not change form to indicate person, number, or gender.

➤ *Anybody* **who cares enough to come and help may take** *some* **home.**

Most indefinite pronouns are always singular (*anybody, everyone*). Some are always plural (*many, few*), and a handful can be singular or plural (*any, most*). (*See Tab 11, pp. 401–2 and Tab 12, p. 454.*)

8. Reciprocal pronouns.

Reciprocal pronouns such as *each other* and *one another* refer to the separate parts of their plural antecedent.

➤ **My sister and I are close because we live near** *each other.*

69d Adjectives

Adjectives modify nouns and pronouns by answering questions like *Which one? What kind? How many? What size? What color? What condition?* and *Whose?* They can describe, enumerate, identify, define, and limit (*one person, that person*). When articles (*a, an,* and *the*) identify nouns, they function as adjectives.

Sometimes proper nouns are treated as adjectives; the proper adjectives that result are capitalized: *Britain/British*. Pronouns can also function as adjectives (*his green car*), and adjectives often have forms that allow you to make comparisons (*great, greater, greatest*).

➤ The *decisive* and *diligent* king regularly attended meetings of

the council. [What kind of king?]

➤ *These four artistic* qualities affect how an advertisement is

received. [Which, how many, what kind of qualities?]

➤ *My little blue* Volkswagen died *one icy winter* morning.

[Whose, what size, what color car? Which, what kind of

morning?]

Like all modifiers, adjectives should be close to the words they modify. Most often, adjectives appear before the noun they modify, but **descriptive adjectives**—adjectives that designate qualities or attributes—may come before or after the noun or pronoun they modify for stylistic reasons. Adjectives that describe the subject and follow linking verbs (*be, am, is, are, was, being, been, appear, become, feel, grow, look, make, prove, taste*) are called **subject complements.**

BEFORE THE SUBJECT

The *sick* and *destitute* poet no longer believed that love would save him.

AFTER THE SUBJECT

The poet, *sick* and *destitute,* no longer believed that love would save him.

AFTER A LINKING VERB

No longer believing that love would save him, the poet was *sick* and *destitute.*

Tip for Multilingual Writers: *Putting adjectives in the correct order*

When several single-word adjectives precede a noun, each modifying the words that follow (*the beautiful new baby*), they are **cumulative adjectives** and do not have commas between them. Cumulative adjectives usually appear in the following order:

➤ *Two priceless small old round handmade blue Swedish wine*

glasses were displayed in the cabinet.

Order of Cumulative Adjectives
1. **Limiting adjective:** *Two*
2. **Quality:** *priceless*
3. **Size:** *small*
4. **Age:** *old*
5. **Shape:** *round*
6. **Participle:** *handmade*
7. **Color:** *blue*
8. **Origin:** *Swedish*
9. **Type:** *wine*
10. **Noun:** *glasses*

 Tip for Multilingual Writers: *Using present and past participles as adjectives to describe feelings*

The present and past participle forms of verbs that refer to feelings can also be used as adjectives. Use the past participle to describe having a feeling:

➤ *The disappointed man felt let down by his friends.*

Use the present participle to describe what is causing the feeling:

➤ *The disappointing friends let the man down.*

Other past and present participle forms that often cause problems include the following:

bored/boring	*interested/interesting*
confused/confusing	*pleased/pleasing*
excited/exciting	*satisfied/satisfying*
frightened/frightening	*surprised/surprising*

69e Adverbs

Adverbs often end in *-ly* (*beautifully, gracefully, quietly*) and usually answer such questions as *When? Where? How? How often? How much? To what degree?* and *Why?*

➤ **The authenticity of the document is *hotly* contested. [How is it**

contested?]

Adverbs modify verbs, other adverbs, and adjectives. Like adjectives, adverbs can be used to compare (*less, lesser, least*). In addition to modifying individual words, they can be used to modify whole clauses. Adverbs can be placed at the beginning or end of a sentence or before the verb they modify, but they should not be placed between the verb and its direct object.

➤ **The water was *brilliant* blue and *icy* cold. [The adverbs intensify**

the adjectives *blue* and *cold*.]

➤ **Dickens mixed humor and pathos *better* than any other English**

writer after Shakespeare. [The adverb compares Dickens with

other writers.]

➤ *Consequently,* **he is still read by millions.**

Consequently is a conjunctive adverb that modifies the independent clause that follows it and shows how the sentence is related to the preceding sentence. (*For more on conjunctive adverbs, see the material on conjunctions, pp. 518–20.*)

The negators *no, not,* and *never* are among the most common adverbs.

SAY *NO* ONLY ONCE

In English, it only takes one negator (*no/not/never*) to change the meaning of a sentence from positive to negative. In fact, when two negatives are used together, they may seem to cancel each other out.

➤ **They don't have _^ no reason to go there.** *any*

69f Prepositions

Prepositions (*on, in, at, by*) usually appear as part of a **prepositional phrase.** Their main function is to allow the noun or pronoun in the phrase to modify another word in the sentence. Prepositional phrases always begin with a preposition and end with a noun, pronoun, or other word group that functions as the **object of the preposition** (in *time,* on the *table*).

A preposition can be one word (*about, despite, on*) or a word group (*according to, as well as, in spite of*). Place prepositional phrases as close as possible to the words they modify. Adjectival prepositional phrases usually appear right after the noun or pronoun they modify and answer questions like *Which one?* and *What kind of?* Adverbial phrases can appear anywhere in a sentence and answer questions like *When? Where? How?* and *Why?*

AS ADJECTIVE	Many species *of birds* nest there.
AS ADVERB	The younger children stared *out the window.*

COMMON PREPOSITIONS

about	by	near
above	by means of	of
according to	by way of	on
across	down	on account of
after	during	over
against	except	since
along	except for	through
along with	excluding	to
among	following	toward
apart from	from	under
as	in	underneath
as to	in addition to	until
as well as	in case of	up
at	in front of	up to
because of	in place of	upon
before	in regard to	via
behind	including	with
below	inside	with reference to
beside	instead of	with respect to
between	into	within
beyond	like	without

Tip for Multilingual Writers: *Using prepositions*

Every language uses prepositions idiomatically in ways that do not match their literal meaning, which is why prepositional phrases can be difficult for multilingual writers. In English, prepositions combine with other words in such a variety of ways that the combinations can only be learned with repetition and over time (*see pp. 516–17*).

Idiomatic uses of prepositions indicating time and location.
The prepositions that indicate time and location are often the most idiosyncratic in a language. In English, the prepositions *at, by, in,* and *on* all have different uses, depending on context. The following are some common ways in which these words are used.

Time

AT   The wedding ceremony starts *at two o'clock.* [a specific clock time]

BY   Our honeymoon plans should be ready *by next week.* [a particular time]

IN   The reception will start *in the evening.* [a portion of the day]

ON   The wedding will take place *on May 1.* The rehearsal is *on Tuesday.* [a particular date or day of the week]

Location

AT   I will meet you *at the zoo.* [a particular place]

You need to turn right *at the light.* [a corner or an intersection]

We took a seat *at the table.* [near a piece of furniture]

BY   Meet me *by the fountain.* [a familiar place]

IN   Park your car *in the parking lot* and give the money to the attendant *in the booth.* [on a space of some kind or inside a structure]

I enjoyed the bratwurst *in Chicago.* [a city, state, or other geographic location]

I found that article *in this book.* [a print medium]

ON   An excellent restaurant is located *on Mulberry Street.* [a street, avenue, or other thoroughfare]

I spilled milk *on the floor.* [a surface]

I watched the report *on television.* [an electronic medium]

Prepositions plus gerunds (*-ing*).
A gerund is the *-ing* form of a verb acting as a noun. A gerund can occur after a preposition (*thanks for coming*), but when the preposition is *to,* be careful not to confuse it with the infinitive form of a verb.

INFINITIVE   I want to win at Jeopardy.

I used to win at Jeopardy.

PREPOSITION + GERUND   I look forward to winning at Jeopardy again.

I am used to winning at Jeopardy.

COMMON ADJECTIVE + PREPOSITION COMBINATIONS

afraid of: fearing someone or something

anxious about: worried

ashamed of: embarrassed by someone or something

aware of: know about

content with: having no complaints about; happy about

fond of: having positive feelings for

full of: filled with

grateful to (someone) (for something): thankful; appreciative

interested in: curious; wanting to know more about

jealous of: feeling envy toward

proud/suspicious of: pleased about/distrustful of

tired of: had enough of; bored with

responsible to (someone) (for something): accountable; in charge

satisfied with: having no complaints about

COMMON VERB + PREPOSITION COMBINATIONS

apologize to: express regret for actions

arrive in (a place): come to a city/country (*I arrived in Paris.*)

arrive at (an event at a specific location): come to a building or a house
  (*I arrived at the Louvre at ten.*)

blame for: hold responsible; accuse

complain about: find fault; criticize

concentrate on: focus; pay attention

consist of: contain; be made of

congratulate on: offer good wishes for success

depend on: trust

explain to: make something clear to someone

insist on: be firm

laugh at: express amusement

look up: visit

rely on: trust

smile at: act friendly toward

take care of: look after; tend

thank for: express appreciation

throw to: toss something to someone to catch

COMMON VERB + PREPOSITION COMBINATIONS

throw at: toss an object toward someone or something without the intention that the object will be caught

throw (something) away: discard

throw (something) out: discard; present an idea for consideration

worry about: feel concern; fear for someone's safety or well-being

COMMON PARTICLES (verb + preposition combinations that create *verb phrasals,* expressions with meanings that are different from the meaning of the verb itself)

break down: stop functioning

bring up: mention in conversation; raise a child

call off: cancel

call up: contact by telephone

catch up with: reach the same place as

catch up on: get up-to-date information on

drop in on: visit unexpectedly

drop off: deliver

fill out: complete

find out: discover

get away with: avoid discovery

get off (your chest): tell a long-concealed secret or problem

get off (the couch): stand up

get over: recover

give up: surrender; stop work on

leave out: omit

look down on: despise

look forward to: anticipate

look into: research

look up: check a fact

look up to: admire

put up with: endure

run across: meet unexpectedly

run out: use up

send off: say goodbye to

stand up for: defend

take after: resemble

take off: leave the airport (a plane); miss time from work

turn down: reject

69g   Conjunctions

Conjunctions join words, phrases, or clauses and indicate their relation to each other.

1. Coordinating conjunctions.   The common **coordinating conjunctions** (or **coordinators**) are *and, but, or, for, nor, yet,* and *so.* Coordinating conjunctions join elements of equal weight or function.

➤   She was strong *and* healthy.

➤   The war was short *but* devastating.

➤   They must have been tired, *for* they had been climbing all

    day long.

2. Correlative conjunctions.   The **correlative conjunctions** also link sentence elements of equal value, but they always come in pairs: *both . . . and, either . . . or, neither . . . nor,* and *not only . . . but also.*

➤   *Neither* the doctor *nor* the police believe his story.

3. Subordinating conjunctions.   Common **subordinating conjunctions** (or **subordinators**) link sentence elements that are not of equal importance. They include the following words and phrases:

Subordinating Words

after	once	until
although	since	when
as	that	whenever
because	though	where
before	till	wherever
if	unless	while

Subordinating Phrases

as if	even though	in that
as soon as	even when	rather than
as though	for as much as	so that
even after	in order that	sooner than
even if	in order to	

Because subordinating conjunctions join unequal sentence parts, they are used to introduce dependent, or subordinate, clauses in a sentence.

➤ **The software will not run properly *if* the computer lacks**

sufficient memory.

 Tip for Multilingual Writers: *Using coordination and subordination appropriately*

Some languages (such as Arabic, for example) favor coordination over the inclusion of subordinate clauses. In English, however, writers who rely too much on coordination tend to use *and* and *so* excessively, which becomes tiresome for readers. In other languages (such as Chinese), conjunctions occur in pairs. Be careful not to include double conjunctions, such as *although . . . but* or *because . . . so* or *even . . . also,* in the same sentence, unless you are using a standard correlative conjunction such as *either . . . or.*

INCORRECT

Although I was happy, *but* I could not smile.

CORRECT

Although I was happy, I could not smile.

When you use a coordinating conjunction (*and, but, or, for, nor, yet,* and *so*), make sure that you use the conjunction that expresses the relationship between the two clauses that you want to show.

NOT PRECISE

My daughter's school is close to my house, and my office is far away.

PRECISE

My daughter's school is close to my house, but my office is far away.

In the revised version, *but* shows the contrast the writer is describing.

When you use a subordinating conjunction, make sure you attach it to the clause that you want to subordinate and not to the main idea in the sentence. For example, if the main point is that commuting to work takes too much time, then the following sentence is unclear.

MAIN POINT OBSCURED	Although commuting to work takes two hours out of every day, I use the time to catch up on my reading.
MAIN POINT CLEAR	Commuting to work takes two hours out of every workday, although I use the time to catch up on my reading.

(For help in punctuating sentences with conjunctions, see Tab 12: Editing for Correctness, pp. 435, 437 and 444.)

4. Conjunctive adverbs. **Conjunctive adverbs** indicate the relation between one clause and another, but unlike conjunctions (*and, but*), they are not grammatically strong enough on their own to hold the two clauses together. A period or semicolon is also needed.

➤ **Swimming is an excellent exercise for the heart and for the muscles; *however,* swimming does not help a person control weight as well as jogging does.**

The most common conjunctive adverbs include the following:

accordingly	however	now
also	incidentally	otherwise
anyway	indeed	similarly
as a result	instead	specifically
besides	likewise	still
certainly	meanwhile	subsequently
consequently	moreover	suddenly
finally	nevertheless	then
furthermore	next	therefore
hence	nonetheless	thus

69h Interjections

Interjections are forceful expressions, usually written with an exclamation point. They are not often used in academic writing except in quotations of dialogue.

➤ *"Wow!"* Davis said. "Are you telling me that there's a former

presidential adviser who hasn't written a book?"

➤ Tell-all books are, *alas,* the biggest sellers.

70 Parts of Sentences

Every complete sentence contains at least one **subject** (a noun and its modifiers) and one **predicate** (a verb and its objects, complements, and modifiers) that fit together to make a statement, ask a question, or give a command.

subject   predicate

➤ The *children solved* the puzzle.

 Tip for Multilingual Writers: *Putting sentence parts in the correct order for English*

In some languages (such as Spanish), it is acceptable to omit subjects; in others (such as Arabic), to omit certain kinds of verbs. Other languages (such as Japanese) place verbs last; and still others (such as Hebrew) allow verbs to precede the subject. English, however, has its own distinct order for sentence parts that most sentences follow.

MODIFIERS + SUBJECT → VERB + OBJECTS, COMPLEMENTS, MODIFIERS

mod   subj   v   mod   obj   obj comp
The playful kitten batted the crystal glasses on the shelf.

70a Subjects

The **simple subject** is the word or words that name the topic of the sentence; it is always a noun or pronoun. To find the subject, ask who or what the sentence is about. The **complete subject** is the simple subject plus its modifiers.

simple subject

➤ Did *Sir Walter Raleigh* give Queen Elizabeth I the requisite

obedience? [Who gave the queen obedience?]

complete subject
simple subject

➤ *Three six-year-old children* solved the puzzle in less than five

minutes. [Who solved the puzzle?]

A **compound subject** contains two or more simple subjects connected with a conjunction such as *and, but, or,* or *neither . . . nor.*

compound

simple   simple
➤ *Original thinking* and *bold design* **are characteristic of**

her work.

In **imperative sentences,** which give directions or commands, the subject *you* is usually implied, not stated. A helping verb is needed to transform an imperative sentence into a question.

➤ **[*You*] Keep this advice in mind.**

➤ ***Would* you keep this advice in mind?**

In sentences beginning with *there* or *here* followed by some form of *be,* the subject comes after the verb.

simple subject
➤ **Here are the *remnants* of an infamous empire.**

Tip for Multilingual Writers: *Including a subject (but not two)*

Every clause in English has a subject, even if it is only a stand-in subject like *there* or *it.* Check your clauses to make sure that each one has a subject.

                                         it
NO SUBJECT   **No one thought the party could end, but** ^

                      ended abruptly when the stock market

                      crashed.

However, do not repeat your subject.

TOO MANY   **The celebrity he signed my playbill.**
SUBJECTS

70b   Verbs and their objects or complements

In a sentence, the **predicate** says something about the subject. The verb constitutes the **simple predicate.** All the words (the verb plus its object or complement) in a predicate make up the **complete predicate.**

Tip for Multilingual Writers: *Including a complete verb*

Verb structure, as well as where the verb is placed within a sentence, varies dramatically across languages, but in English each sentence needs to include at least one complete verb. (*See Chapter 69, pp. 500–504.*) The verb cannot be an infinitive—the *to* form of the verb—or an *-ing* form without a helping verb.

NOT COMPLETE	The caterer *to bring* dinner.
COMPLETE VERBS	The caterer *brings* dinner.
	The caterer *will bring* dinner.
	The caterer *is bringing* dinner.
NOT COMPLETE	Children *running* in the park.
COMPLETE VERBS	Children *are running* in the park.
	Children *have been running* in the park.
	Children *will be running* in the park.

Verb functions in sentences. Based on how they function in sentences, verbs are *linking, transitive,* or *intransitive.* The kind of verb determines what elements the complete predicate must include and therefore determines the correct order of sentence parts. Most meaningful English sentences use one of five basic sentence patterns.

1. SUBJECT + LINKING VERB + SUBJECT COMPLEMENT

   New Yorkers are busy people.

2. SUBJECT + TRANSITIVE VERB + DIRECT OBJECT

   The police officer caught the jaywalker.

3. SUBJECT + TRANSITIVE VERB + INDIRECT OBJECT + DIRECT OBJECT

   The officer gave the jaywalker a ticket.

4. SUBJECT + TRANSITIVE VERB + DIRECT OBJECT + OBJECT COMPLEMENT

   The ticket made the jaywalker unhappy.

5. SUBJECT + INTRANSITIVE VERB

   She sighed.

1. Linking verbs and subject complements. A **linking verb** joins a subject to a piece of further information about the subject that is located on the other side of the verb. That piece of information is called the **subject complement.** The subject complement may be a noun, a pronoun, or an adjective.

subj   lv   comp

➤ **Ann Yearsley was** *a milkmaid.*

The most frequently used linking verb is the *be* verb (*is, are, was, were*), but verbs such as *seem, look, appear, feel, become, smell, sound,* and *taste* can also function as links between a sentence's subject and its complement.

subj   lv   comp

➤ **That new hairstyle** *looks* **beautiful.**

2. Transitive verbs and direct objects. A **transitive verb** identifies an action that the subject performs or does to somebody or something else—the receiver of the action, or **direct object.** To complete its meaning, a transitive verb needs a direct object in the predicate. Direct objects are usually nouns, pronouns, or word groups that act like nouns or pronouns.

NOUN   I threw *the ball.*

PRONOUN   I threw *it* over a fence.

WORD GROUP I put *what I needed* into my backpack.

Most often, the subject is doing the action, the direct object is being acted upon, and the transitive verb is in the **active voice.**

subj   tv   dir obj

ACTIVE   **Parents sometimes consider their** *children* **unreasonable.**

If the verb in a sentence can be in the active voice, it can be in the **passive voice** as well. In the following revised sentence, the direct object (*children*) has become the subject; the original subject (*parents*) is introduced with the preposition *by* and is now part of a prepositional phrase.

PASSIVE Children are considered unreasonable by their parents.

 Tip for Multilingual Writers: *Including only one direct object*

In English, a transitive verb takes a direct object, which must be explicit. For example, *Take it!* is a complete sentence but *Take!* is not, even if *it* is clearly implied. Be careful not to repeat the object, especially if the object includes a relative adverb (*where, when, how*) or a relative pronoun (*which, who, what*), even if the relative pronoun does not appear in the sentence but is only implied.

➤ **Our dog guards the house** *where* **we live ~~there~~.** ─────

3. Transitive verbs, indirect objects, and direct objects.   **Indirect objects** name to whom an action was done or for whom it was completed and are most commonly used with verbs such as *give, ask, tell, sing,* and *write.*

> subj   v   ind obj   dir obj
> **Coleridge wrote *Sara* a heartrending letter.**

Note that indirect objects appear after the verb but before the direct object.

4. Transitive verbs, direct objects, and object complements.   In addition to a direct object and an indirect object, a transitive verb can take another element in its predicate: an **object complement.** An object complement describes or renames the direct object it follows.

>   dir obj   obj comp
> **His investment in a plantation made Johnson *a rich man.***

5. Intransitive verbs.   An **intransitive verb** describes an action by a subject, but it is not an action that is done directly to anything or anyone else. Therefore, an intransitive verb cannot take an object or a complement. However, adverbs and adverb phrases often appear in predicates built around intransitive verbs. In the sentence that follows, the complete predicate is in italics and the intransitive verb is underlined.

> **As a recruit, I *<u>complied</u> with the order mandating short hair.***

Some verbs, such as *cooperate, assent, disappear,* and *insist,* are always intransitive. Others, such as *increase, grow, roll,* and *work,* can be either transitive or intransitive.

TRANSITIVE	I *grow* carrots and celery in my victory garden.
INTRANSITIVE	My son *grows* taller every week.

(tv above "grow"; iv above "grows")

iTips LEARNING in COLLEGE

Using the Dictionary to Determine Prepositions, Transitive and Intransitive Verbs

Your dictionary will note if a verb is *v.i.* (intransitive), *v.t.* (transitive), or both. It will also tell you—or show by example—the appropriate preposition to use when you are modifying an intransitive verb with an adverbial phrase. For example, we may *accede to* a rule, but if and when we *comply*, it has to be *with* something or someone.

71 Phrases and Dependent Clauses

A **phrase** is a group of related words that lacks either a subject or a predicate or both. Phrases function within sentences but not on their own. A **dependent clause** has a subject and a predicate but cannot function as a complete sentence because it begins with a subordinating word.

71a Noun phrases

A **noun phrase** consists of a noun or noun substitute plus all of its modifiers. Noun phrases can function as a sentence's subject, object, or subject complement.

SUBJECT	*The old, dark, ramshackle house* collapsed.
OBJECT	Greg cooked *an authentic, delicious haggis* for the Robert Burns dinner.
SUBJECT COMPLEMENT	Tom became *an accomplished and well-known cook.*

71b Verb phrases and verbals

A **verb phrase** is a verb plus its helping verbs. It functions as the predicate in a sentence: *Mary should have photographed me.* **Verbals** are words derived from verbs. They function as nouns, adjectives, or adverbs, not as verbs.

VERBAL AS NOUN	*Crawling* comes before walking.
VERBAL AS ADJECTIVE	Chris tripped over the *crawling* child.
VERBAL AS ADVERB	The child began *to crawl.*

Verbals may take modifiers, objects, and complements to form **verbal phrases.** There are three kinds of verbal phrases: participial, gerund, and infinitive.

1. Participial phrases. A **participial phrase** begins with either a present participle (the *-ing* form of a verb) or a past participle (the *-ed* or *-en* form of a verb). Participial phrases always function as adjectives.

➤ *Working in groups,* the children solved the problem.

➤ *Insulted by his remark,* Elizabeth refused to dance.

➤ His pitching arm, *broken in two places by the fall,* would never

be the same again.

2. Gerund phrases.   A **gerund phrase** uses the *-ing* form of the verb, just as some participial phrases do. But gerund phrases always function as nouns, not adjectives.

subj
➤ *Walking one hour a day* will keep you fit.

dir obj
➤ The instructor praised *my acting in both scenes.*

3. Infinitive phrases.   An **infinitive phrase** is formed using the infinitive, or *to* form, of a verb: *to be, to do, to live.* It can function as an adverb, an adjective, or a noun and can be the subject, subject or object complement, or direct object in a sentence.

noun/subj
➤ *To finish his novel* was his greatest ambition.

adj/obj comp
➤ He made many efforts *to finish his novel* for his publisher.

adv/dir obj
➤ He rushed *to finish his novel.*

71c Appositive phrases

Appositives rename nouns or pronouns and appear right after the word they rename.

noun   appositive
➤ One researcher, *the widely respected R. S. Smith,* has shown

that a child's performance on such tests can be very consistent.

71d Absolute phrases

Absolute phrases modify an entire sentence. They include a noun or pronoun, a participle, and their related modifiers, objects, or complements.

➤ The sheriff strode into the bar, *his hands hovering over his pistols.*

71e   Dependent clauses

Although **dependent clauses** (also known as **subordinate clauses**) have a subject and predicate, they cannot stand alone as complete sentences. They are introduced by subordinators—either by a subordinating conjunction such as *after, in order to, since (for a more complete listing, see p. 519)* or by a relative pronoun such as *who, which,* or *that (for more, see box on p. 508)*. They function in sentences as adjectives, adverbs, or nouns.

1. Adjective clauses. An **adjective clause** modifies a noun or pronoun. Relative pronouns (*who, whom, whose, which,* or *that*) or relative adverbs (*where, when*) are used to connect adjective clauses to the nouns or pronouns they modify. The relative pronoun usually follows the word that is being modified and also serves to point back to the noun or pronoun. (*For help with punctuating restrictive and nonrestrictive clauses, see Tab 12, pp. 438–39 and 445–46.*)

➤   Odysseus' journey, *which can be traced on modern maps,* has

inspired many works or literature.

In adjective clauses, the direct object sometimes comes before rather than after the verb.

dir obj   subj   v
➤   The contestant *whom he most wanted to beat* was his father.

2. Adverb clauses. An **adverb clause** modifies a verb, an adjective, or an adverb and answers the questions adverbs answer: *When? Where? What? Why?* and *How?* Adverb clauses are often introduced by subordinators (*after, when, before, because, although, if, though, whenever, where, wherever*).

➤   *After we had talked for an hour,* he began to get nervous.

➤   He reacted *as if he already knew.*

3. Noun clauses. A **noun clause** is a dependent clause that functions as a noun. Often the noun clause is so essential that without it, the independent clause would be incomplete. In a sentence, a noun clause may serve as the subject, object, or complement and is usually introduced by a relative pronoun (*who, which, that*) or a relative adverb (*how, what, where, when, why*).

SUBJECT   *What he saw* shocked him.

OBJECT   The instructor found out *who had skipped class.*

COMPLEMENT   The book was *where I had left it.*

As in an adjective clause, in a noun clause the direct object or subject complement can come first, violating the typical sentence order.

dir obj   subj

➤ **The doctor wondered *to whom he* should send the bill.**

 Tip for Multilingual Writers: *Understanding the purposes and constructions of* **If** *clauses*

If clauses (also called **conditional clauses**) state facts, make predictions, and speculate about unlikely or impossible events. These conditional constructions most often employ *if,* but *when, unless,* or other words can introduce conditional constructions as well.

■ Use the present tense for facts. When the relationship you are describing is usually true, the verbs in both clauses should have the same tense.

STATES FACTS

If people *practice* doing good consistently, they *have* a sense of satisfaction.

When Meg *found* a new cause, she always *talked* about it incessantly.

■ In a sentence that predicts, the verb in the *if* clause is in the present tense. The verb in the independent clause is a modal plus the base form of the verb.

PREDICTS POSSIBILITIES

If you *practice* doing good through politics, you *will have* a greater effect on your community.

■ If you are speculating about something that is unlikely to happen, use the past tense in the *if* clause and *could, should,* or *would* plus the base verb in the independent clause.

SPECULATES ON THE UNLIKELY

If you *were* a better person, you *would practice* doing good every day.

▪ Use the past perfect tense in the *if* clause if you are speculating about an event that did not happen. In the independent clause, use *could have, might have,* or *would have* plus the past participle.

SPECULATES ON SOMETHING THAT DID NOT HAPPEN

If you *had practiced* doing good when you were young, you *would have been* a different person today.

▪ Use *were* in the *if* clause and *could, might,* or *would* plus the base form in the main clause if you are speculating about something that could never happen.

SPECULATES ABOUT THE IMPOSSIBLE

If Lincoln *were* alive today, he *would fight* for equal protection under the law.

72 Types of Sentences

Sentences can be classified by the number of clauses they contain and how those clauses are joined. This method of classification results in four types of sentences: simple, compound, complex, and compound-complex. Sentences can also be classified by the purpose they fulfill: declarative, interrogative, imperative, and exclamatory.

72a Sentence structures

A clause is a group of related words that includes a subject and a predicate. Some clauses are independent; others are dependent, or subordinate. **Independent clauses** can stand on their own as complete sentences. **Dependent,** or **subordinate, clauses** cannot stand alone. They function in sentences as adjectives, adverbs, or nouns. The presence of one or both of these two types of clauses, and their relation to each other, determines whether the sentence is simple, compound, complex, or compound-complex.

1. Simple sentences. A simple sentence is composed of only one independent clause. Simple does not necessarily mean short, however. Although a simple sentence does not include any dependent clauses, it may have several embedded phrases, a compound subject, and a compound predicate. No matter how long it is, however, a sentence that has only one independent clause is, grammatically speaking, a simple sentence.

INDEPENDENT CLAUSE

The bloodhound is the oldest known breed of dog.

INDEPENDENT CLAUSE: COMPOUND SUBJ + COMPOUND PRED

Historians, novelists, short-story writers, and playwrights write about characters, design plots, and usually seek the dramatic resolution of a problem.

2. Compound sentences. A compound sentence contains two or more coordinated independent clauses but no dependent clause. The independent clauses may be joined by a comma and a coordinating conjunction or by a semicolon with or without a conjunctive adverb.

➤ **The police arrested him for drunk driving, *so* he lost his car.**

➤ **The sun blasted the earth; *therefore*, the plants withered and died.**

3. Complex sentences. A complex sentence contains one independent clause and one or more dependent clauses.

independent clause   dependent clause

➤ **He consulted the dictionary *because he did not know how to***

pronounce the word.

4. Compound-complex sentences. A compound-complex sentence contains two or more coordinated independent clauses and at least one dependent clause (italicized in the example).

➤ **She discovered a new world of international finance, but she**

worked so hard investing other people's money *that she had no*

time to invest any of her own.

72b   Sentence purposes

When you write a sentence, your purpose helps you decide which sentence type to use. If you want to provide information, you usually use a declarative sentence. If you want to ask a question, you usually use an interrogative sentence. To make a request or give an order (a command), you use the imperative. An exclamatory sentence emphasizes a point or expresses strong emotion.

DECLARATIVE   He watches *Seinfeld* reruns.

INTERROGATIVE   Does he watch *Seinfeld* reruns?

IMPERATIVE   Do not watch reruns of *Seinfeld*.

EXCLAMATORY   I'm really looking forward to watching *Seinfeld* reruns with you!

Further Resources
for Learning

Selected Terms from across the Curriculum

Your professors will explain the vocabulary and concepts that are specific to the study of particular disciplines, but they might assume you understand certain terms that commonly appear in academic **discourse.** *As you look at the sampling that follows, feel free to jump around among the words printed in bold, each of which has its own entry.*

alienation (from the Latin *alius,* "other") Being estranged from one's society or even from oneself. First used in psychology, the term was adapted by Karl **Marx** (1818–1883) in his writings on the relationship of workers to the products of their labor. In the twentieth century, **existentialist** philosophers used the word to mean an individual's loss of a sense of self, his or her *authenticity,* amid the pressures of modern society. *See also* **Marxism.**

Apollonian From *Apollo,* Greek god of prophecy, music, medicine, and poetry, often identified with the sun. Today *Apollonian* describes works of art or other cultural products characterized by clarity, harmony, and restraint. *See also* **Dionysian.**

archetype A model after which other things are patterned. The psychoanalyst Carl Jung (1875–1961) used the term to denote a number of universal symbols—such as the Mother or the universal Creator—that inhabit the **collective unconscious.**

Aristotelian Relating to the writings of Aristotle (384–322 BCE), Greek philosopher and author of works on logic, ethics, rhetoric, and the natural sciences. Aristotle established a tradition that values **empirical** observation, **deductive reasoning,** and science. This tradition can be contrasted with **Platonic idealism.**

arithmetic progression *See* **geometric progression.**

bell curve In statistics and science, a graph showing a normal distribution of results—in other words, a distribution in which the greatest number of results are grouped in the middle. If a math test is graded on a bell curve, for instance, most students will receive B's and C's, whereas only a few will receive A's or F's. Plotted on a graph, the curve will evoke the shape of a bell.

Big Bang Theory A **hypothesis** about the origins of the universe: some 14 billion years ago, all the matter in the universe was concentrated in one almost infinitely dense point, which then exploded, dispersing matter in all directions at tremendous velocity. The Big Bang Theory implies a universe of finite size and age.

binary oppositions Paired terms conventionally treated as stable and logical opposites, such as *light / dark* and *man / woman.* Certain **postmodern** trends in philosophy and literary theory, notably **deconstruction,** seek to expose the "artificiality" of these and other **constructs** that shape the way we see the world. *See also* **structuralism.**

black hole From astronomy, a region in space-time where matter is infinitely dense and dimensionless and where the gravitational field is so strong that nothing can escape from it. The term is often used metaphorically to indicate something that is limitless or unresolvable.

Boolean logic (after the English mathematician George Boole, 1815–1864) A specialized algebra developed for the analysis of logical statements, used extensively in the development of the modern computer. A computer performs everything from simple math to Internet searches by means of Boolean logic, which uses **variables** and operators such as AND, OR, NOT, IF, THEN, and EXCEPT.

bourgeois Of or relating to the middle **class.** Although it originally referred to the artisans and craftsmen of medieval French towns, the term came into wide use with the Industrial Revolution, which created the modern middle class, and it is used in **Marxist** analysis to represent the capitalist class. *Bourgeois* commonly connotes an excessive concern with respectability and material goods.

canon Originally referring to a code of laws established by the church, the *canon* now typically refers to a collection of books deemed necessary for a complete education. What works are *canonical* is often debated and has changed over time. Current debate tends to focus on the exclusion from the canon of works by and about women and people of color. *See also* **multiculturalism.**

capitalism An economic system that emerged during the Industrial Revolution of the nineteenth century and offered private individuals the ownership of industry as well as unregulated market freedom. Today capitalism includes **Keynesian economic** models that allow government to regulate industry, particularly regarding such concerns as the minimum wage, tariffs, and taxes.

case study An intensive investigation and analysis of a person or group; often the object of study is proposed as the model of a certain phenomenon. Originally used in medicine, the term is now also common in psychology and business. Among the most famous and widely imitated case studies are those of Sigmund **Freud** (1856–1939), who used them to expound his theory of psychoanalysis. In business, a case study denotes a detailed examination of a corporation or enterprise with a view to determining the causes of its success or failure.

chaos theory A branch of mathematics used to describe highly complex phenomena such as weather or the flow of blood through the body. Chaos theory starts with the recognition that minute changes in a system can have large and unpredictable results. The *butterfly effect,* for instance, states that the flap of a butterfly's wings in China could theoretically cause a hurricane in New York. *See also* **iteration.**

class A term denoting social and/or economic standing in society (*upper class, lower class, middle class; working class, professional class, leisure class*). Karl **Marx** (1818–1883) argued that class conflict is economically based and so necessarily occurs between the working class and the capitalist class (those who control the means of production). Many have argued that economic standing alone does not determine class and that factors such as family, cultural background, and education play significant roles. *See also* **bourgeois, proletariat.**

classical Originally used to describe the artistic and literary conventions of ancient Greece and Rome. *Classical* (or *classicism / neoclassicism*) is also used for periods and products in the sciences, social sciences, philosophy, and music marked by straightforwardly rational models that describe the workings of the universe and human society as logical and ultimately harmonious. *See also* **modernism, postmodernism.**

coefficient In mathematics, a number or symbol multiplying a **variable** in an algebraic term, such as the 4 in 4*x*. In the physical sciences, a coefficient is the numerical measure of a physical or chemical **constant.** In general usage, *coefficient* can denote factors working together to produce a result, as in "Jobs and longer prison terms are *coefficients* in the prevention of crime."

collective unconscious In the psychology of Carl Jung (1875–1961), the elements of the **unconscious** that are common to all humans. In the same way that each human body shares many features with others while at the same time being unique, the collective unconscious represents the general framework of the human unconscious, within which each individual's unconscious mind presents a unique pattern. *See also* **archetype.**

colonialism A policy by which a nation extends and maintains political and military control over a territory, often reducing it to a state of dependence. Begun as a way of acquiring resources such as spices, precious metals, and slaves, later instances of colonialism—such as the United States's occupation of the Philippines from 1898 to 1946—have served mostly political or strategic purposes. *Postcolonial* refers to a state (or a cultural product or even a state of mind) that reflects former colonial occupation. *See also* **imperialism.**

constant In mathematics, science, and general usage, a factor that does not change. A mathematical or scientific constant is a quantity assumed to have a fixed value within a specific context. In physics, for example, the speed of light in a vacuum is 186,000 miles per second and is denoted by the constant c. Thus, in Einstein's famous equation $E = mc^2$, c is a constant and m, standing for any mass, is a **variable.**

construct (*noun*) Something that is shaped by culture ("constructed") but sometimes assumed to be "natural." For example, some might hold that the idea of gender ("maleness" and "femaleness") is a *construct* rather than the essential or inborn quality that past generations have assumed it to be.

contingent In logic, that which is true only under certain circumstances. In common usage, *contingent* often connotes that which has happened or can happen only as a result of a long, perhaps improbable sequence of events. Whenever you think, "It could easily have been different," you are feeling a sense of *contingency.*

correlation In statistics, a number that describes the relationship between two variables. In a *positive correlation,* the variables increase in tandem—for example, the higher a student's IQ, the better his or her scholastic performance. In a *negative correlation,* one variable increases while the other decreases—for example, the more green tea consumed, the lower the incidence of cancer.

counterculture See **culture.**

cross section A sample meant to be representative of a whole population. *See also* **longitudinal.**

culture Knowledge, beliefs, behavior, arts, institutions, and other products of work and thought that characterize a society. Within a dominant *culture* there may exist many *subcultures:* groups of particular ethnicity, age, education, employment, inclination, or other factors. A *counterculture* is a form of subculture whose values and lifestyle reject those of the dominant culture. *See also* **relativism.**

Darwinism British naturalist Charles Darwin's (1809–1882) theory of the historical evolution of species based on *natural selection,* or "the survival of the fittest." Where insects living within the bark of trees constitute a major food source, for instance, birds with longer, more pointed beaks tend to survive longer and produce more offspring, who then pass on longer, sharper beaks to ensuing generations. Although Darwin felt his theories had little relevance to human societies, they have given rise to the concept of *social Darwinism,* in which those who fail to get ahead are deemed less "fit" for survival. This application of the principles of natural selection to social groups has often served as justification for racist doctrines.

deconstruction A method of literary criticism whose best known theorist, Jacques Derrida (b. 1930), has postulated that texts rest on **binary oppositions** such as nature/culture, subject/object, and spirit/matter that have been incorrectly assumed to be "true"; in exposing this fallacy, Derrida reveals the illogic of texts thought to be logical and coherent. Although often associated with **postmodernism** and the debate about the **canon,** deconstruction is in a philosophical sense a radical form of skepticism. In more common usage, to *deconstruct* something is to analyze it intensively, exposing it as (perhaps) something unexpected.

deductive reasoning Reasoning to a conclusion based on a previously held principle. *Inductive reasoning,* on the other hand, is the process of deriving a conclusion based on data. **Empiricism** holds that all knowledge is derived from sense experience by induction, whereas *rationalism* claims that knowledge can be deduced from certain a priori (presumptive) claims.

demographics (from the Greek *demos,* "people," and *graphia,* "writing") The quantitative study of human populations. A *demographic* study of a city might include how fast its population is growing, the size and distribution of its middle **class,** or the number of its families who have access to the Internet.

determinism In philosophy and science, the doctrine that every event is *determined,* or entirely shaped by earlier events, and that given complete knowledge of prior events and the laws that govern them, all future events can be predicted. Something described as *overdetermined* is thought to be shaped by more than one equally significant cause. Usually contrasted with **free will,** determinism is a feature of eighteenth- and nineteenth-century **classical** thought. In science, determinism has come to be opposed by the *indeterminism* of **quantum physics.**

dialectic In philosophy, history, and the humanities, the use of logical oppositions as a means of arriving at conclusions about ideas or events. *Dialectical reasoning* is most often associated with the philosophies of Georg Hegel (1770–1831) and Karl **Marx** (1818–1883). According to Hegel, any human idea or *thesis* (for example, the sun circles the earth) naturally gives rise to an opposing idea or *antithesis* (the earth circles the sun), and these ideas resolve into a new idea or *synthesis* (the earth revolves around the sun but in an ellipse). Hegel's famous *master/slave dialectic* describes a seeming paradox: a slave holds power over his master because the master could not hold power without the slave. Marx extended dialectical reasoning in his theory of *dialectical materialism,* which analyzes not opposing ideas but contradictory **class** interests.

Dionysian That which embodies creativity, intuition, and by extension, ecstasy, orgiastic release, and the irrational. The term is most often associated with the philosophy of Friedrich **Nietzsche** (1844–1900), where it opposes the **Apollonian.**

discourse (from the French *discours,* "speech" or "talk") *Discourse* is most often used in English to denote verbal expression in general, without distinguishing between writing and speech. *Discourse* can also refer to habits of expression characteristic of a particular community or to the content of that expression ("The *discourse* of experimental science does not often allow the use of the personal pronoun *I*").

disenfranchise Literally, to deprive of the right to vote; more loosely, to *disenfranchise* means to deny rights or exclude from privileges, most often those associated with citizenship: "The rioters in Oklahoma felt themselves to have been effectively *disenfranchised* by post–World War I economic and political change."

ecosystem A principal unit of study in ecology, the science of the relationships between organisms and their environments. All parts of an ecosystem are interdependent, and even small perturbations of one part (such as might be caused by pollution) can have profound effects on all of the other parts—a phenomenon often studied in **chaos theory.**

ego **Freudian** term for the "I" of mental functioning—that is, the capacity for realistic assessment of the needs of the self and the means of fulfilling these needs. *See also* **id, superego, repression, projection, unconscious.**

empiricism (from the Greek *empierikos,* "experienced") A philosophical trend, developed in large part by the philosophers John Locke (1632–1704) and David Hume (1711–1776), that **privileges** data derived from experience or the senses over knowledge derived from reason, tradition, or authority. *Empirical* data are data gained through observation or experiment. Especially in medicine and psychology, *empirical* is often contrasted with *theoretical.* In its emphasis on observation and experience, empiricism is a conceptual cousin of **inductive reasoning** and **Aristotelianism.**

Enlightenment An intellectual movement committed to secular views based on reason that established itself in Europe in the eighteenth century (ca. 1688–1790).

epistemology The study of the nature of knowledge, its foundations and limits.

ethos (Greek for "character, a person's nature or disposition") The spirit or code of behavior peculiar to a specific person or group of people. "Part of the college student *ethos* is to stay up late drinking cola and eating Captain Crunch." Ethos is one of the parts of Aristotle's **rhetorical triangle** (**ethos-logos-pathos**): in order to argue effectively, a speaker or writer must communicate a persuasive ethos, that is, a credible **persona** and a coherent perspective.

existentialism A strain in philosophy that emphasizes the isolation of the individual in an indifferent universe and stresses the individual's freedom (and responsibility) to determine his or her own existence. Having roots in the philosophies of Friedrich **Nietzsche** (1844–1900) and Martin Heidegger (1889–1976), existentialism was extremely influential in France after World War II, where French intellectuals like Jean-Paul Sartre (1905–1980) and Albert Camus (1913–1960) argued that by making conscious choices and taking responsibility for one's acts, one could overcome the otherwise absurd nature of the universe.

extrapolation In mathematics and computer science, the estimation of an unknown value using projections based on known information. For example, one might *extrapolate* the total number of votes cast for a political candidate nationwide based on a representative **sample.** *Interpolation,* on the other hand, is the estimation of an unknown value made by comparing known values that are closely related or nearby. The size of a colony of ants in June, for example, might be *interpolated* based on the numbers for May and July.

fascism (from the Italian *fascio,* "group") A name for the form of government established by Benito Mussolini (1883–1945) in Italy and Adolf Hitler (1889–1945) in Germany. Arising in response to economic and political upheaval in Europe after World War I, both governments centralized authority under a dictator, exerted strong economic controls, suppressed opposition through censorship and terror, and implemented belligerent nationalist and racist policies. The term is sometimes used today to describe governments and individuals acting in an authoritarian manner.

formalism (also sometimes called *New Criticism*) In literary criticism, a school whose principles include *close reading*—rigorous attention to the structural elements and artistic techniques of a text—and deemphasis of the historical or social context in which the text was written and its relationship to other texts. *See also* **structuralism.**

Freudian Relating to the theories of *Sigmund Freud* (1856–1939), the Viennese neurologist who invented psychoanalysis. A *Freudian* interpretation focuses on the unconscious emotional dynamics that are played out in a particular situation; in the study of literature, a *Freudian* interpretation focuses on such dynamics as they are represented in the **text.** *See also* **ego, id, super-ego, repression, projection, unconscious.**

game theory (also sometimes called *decision theory*) A mathematical method for analyzing situations of conflict or competition so as to determine a winning strategy. *Game theory* is useful not only in *true games* such as poker but also in business management, economics, and military strategy. *See also* **zero sum game.**

geometric progression A sequence of numbers determined by multiplying or dividing each number in succession by a **constant.** For example, *1, 4, 16, 64, 256* is a geometric progression with a constant multiplier, or **coefficient,** of 4. *Arithmetic progressions* proceed more slowly by adding or subtracting a constant: for example, *1, 4, 7, 10, 13* is an arithmetic progression with a constant *addend* of 3.

gestalt (German for "form" or "structure") The recognition of the whole of something that precedes the notice of any of its parts. In psychology, *Gestalt theory* asserts that psychological phenomena are irreducible and cannot be derived from the simple total of sensations a person experiences.

globalization The process by which communications and transportation technologies have made the world seem smaller as well as more interconnected. In economics, *globalization* refers to the way these advances have made national borders far less relevant in determining markets. The *anti-globalization* movement aims to protect workers from exploitation by multinational corporations, to prevent job loss among domestic workers, and to counter cultural homogenization. The presence of a McDonald's in Beijing is a good example of the effects of globalization.

hegemony Generally, the dominance of one nation or state over its neighbors. The Italian Marxist Antonio Gramsci (1891–1937) and his followers often used the term to refer to the dominance of the capitalists over the working **class.** *Hegemony* is now also used to describe a theory that has dominance in a particular field of study: "Dualism has long exercised *hegemony* in Western thought."

humanism (also *secular humanism*) A movement traditionally associated with Renaissance philosophers who deemphasized the role of religion or God in society while celebrating the achievements of human beings. There are *humanistic* branches of psychology, theology, and other disciplines that move the role of the human individual to the forefront of their studies.

hypothesis A statement that can be shown to be true or false either experimentally (in science) or through the use of logic (in other disciplines). For example, a simple *hypothesis* is that light is necessary for the survival of a certain plant. This hypothesis could be proved or disproved by the simple experiment of trying to grow the plant in a dark closet.

icon In **semiotics,** a **sign** that looks like what it refers to. A picture of the globe used to signify the earth or a line drawing of a suitcase indicating where to go to get your luggage at an airport are *icons*. Historically, an icon was a small picture of a religious figure, usually Jesus or the Virgin Mary. *See also* **sign, semiotics.**

id In **Freud**'s model of mental functioning, the "id," or the raw desires and instincts of the individual, whose impulses are mediated both by the reality-testing capacities of the **ego** and the socializing function of the **superego.** *See also* **unconscious, projection, repression.**

idealism In philosophy and psychology, the notion that the mind determines ultimate reality, an idea that can be traced to **Plato** (428–347 BCE).

ideology A set of beliefs about the world (and often how it can be changed) espoused by an individual, a group, or an organization; a systematized worldview. **Capitalism,** for example, is an ideology. In the work of the Marxist critic Louis Althusser (1918–90), an *ideology* is that which allows the individual to find his or her place and sense of self-worth within a given society.

imperialism One country's imposition of political and economic rule upon other countries. The British annexation of several countries in Africa in the nineteenth century is an example of this brand of *imperialism*. Today the term has been broadened to include the exportation of dominant cultural products and values; for example, some people in Europe and other parts of the world see the influx of American films into their markets as a form of *cultural imperialism*. *See also* **colonialism.**

inductive reasoning *See* **deductive reasoning.**

interpolation *See* **extrapolation.**

iteration Generally, the process of repeating steps over and over. In computer science, *iteration* refers to a computer's repeated looping through a set of programming instructions until it reaches the program's goal. In **chaos theory,** *iteration* involves getting data from an equation and repeatedly plugging the results back into the equation.

Keynesian economics The theory of economics developed by John Maynard Keynes (1883–1946), distinguished by the belief that government must intervene in the marketplace in order to promote stability and growth, specifically by increasing the money supply during economic downturns. *See* **laissez-faire.**

laissez-faire (French for "allow to act") Generally, noninterference in the affairs or conduct of others. In economic and political theory, the idea that governments should not intervene in markets. The concept is based on the **classical** economic theory developed by Adam Smith (1723–90) and others, which argues that an "invisible hand"—supply and demand and competition—is sufficient to guide economic markets. *See* **Keynesian economics.**

logos (Greek for "word") In Aristotle's **rhetorical triangle,** the topic of the argument or argument itself.

longitudinal A study in which the same group of subjects is examined over a long period of time. A *longitudinal study* could, for example, be conducted to test the onset of obesity over time among a certain group of school children.

Marxism Economic and political doctrine put forth by *Karl Marx* (1818–83) and Friedrich Engels (1820–95). Its basic teachings center around the **class** struggle between the **proletariat** (the working class) and the **bourgeoisie** (capitalists, those who own the *means of production*). *Marxism* predicts that in time the working class will inevitably revolt, wresting the means of production from the bourgeoisie and ceding them to the state, which will distribute goods equitably. A classless society would result.

materialism In philosophy, the belief that physical matter is all that exists and that so-called higher phenomena—for example, thought, feeling, mind, will—are wholly dependent on and **determined** by physical processes. Since the **Enlightenment,** almost all scientists have been materialists. In history and economics, the *dialectical* materialism of Karl **Marx** (1818–83) held that **cultural** phenomena are determined wholly by economic conditions.

mean (also *average*) The sum of a set of numbers divided by the number of terms in the set. For example, the *mean* of the set (1, 2, 3) is 2 because its sum (6) divided by the number of terms (3) equals 2.

median The middle term in an ordered set of numbers. For example, the *median* of the ordered set (2, 6, 10, 12, 15) is 10 because there are two numbers (2 and 6) below 10 and two (12 and 15) above 10.

meta- A prefix often used to suggest "moving beyond," "going up a level," or "transcending." Thus, *metaphysics* is the branch of philosophy that deals with questions that cannot be resolved by physical observation, such as whether God exists. Similarly, *metapsychology* deals not with perception, emotion, or cognition per se, but rather with how such things are discussed and defined.

Freud's division of the psyche into **id, ego,** and **superego** is an example of metapsychology.

modernism Often used in opposition to *classicism* or *neoclassicism* when denoting periods in the sciences, social sciences, philosophy, and music, *modernism* as a trend in thought represents a break with the certainties of the past, among them a confidence that everything can be known. *Modern* science has been characterized by highly counterintuitive theories such as **relativity**—where there is no absolute way to measure time—and **quantum physics**—where you can know the speed or position of a subatomic particle but never both. In literature, the **stream of consciousness** and/or *free association* style of *modernist* writers like Virginia Woolf (1882–1941) and James Joyce (1882–1941) broke decisively with the storytelling conventions of the late-nineteenth-century, or Victorian, novel. Thus, some critics believe that **postmodernism** is really only the development of a trend begun in the modernist era.

multiculturalism An educational and social approach advocating that many cultures, not just the dominant one, should be given attention in the classroom and in broader society. The debate on multiculturalism is related to the debate on the **canon.**

nature-nurture A debate about whether genetic (*nature*) or environmental (*nurture*) factors have the upper hand in determining human behavior. Experimental studies involving fraternal and identical twins raised together and apart have been undertaken to investigate the issue, but fundamental questions about method and the small **samples** involved have left the question unresolved. This issue pervades countless topics studied in the social sciences, among them questions of gender difference, intelligence, poverty, crime, and childhood development.

Nietzschean Following the ideas of *Friedrich Nietzsche* (1844–1900), a pioneering **existentialist** philosopher. Nietzsche believed that overemphasis on the Christian belief in the afterlife had led people away from what is real in the world. Nietzsche used the term *superman* (*Übermensch* in German) to apply to those who found the strength to cast aside these traditional social and moral values, using their **will to power.** *See also* **Apollonian, Dionysian.**

object/subject In philosophy and psychology, the *subject* does the observing or experiencing, while the *object* is that which is observed or experienced. Throughout history, this philosophical dualism has been studied, refined, and debated extensively. In **Freudian** and post-Freudian psychology, an *object* is an external person or thing that gratifies an infant and is therefore loved.

objective Pertaining to that which is independent of perception or observation, as opposed to *subjective,* which pertains to that which is determined by perception or observation. The old philosophical puzzle—If a tree falls in the woods, and no one is there to hear it, does it make a sound?—plays upon the notions of philosophical *objectivity* and *subjectivity.*

Oedipus complex The psychological notion expounded by Sigmund **Freud** (1856–1939) that describes the unconscious sexual longing of a son for his mother and his unconscious wish to kill his father, his rival for possession of the mother. The name is a reference to Sophocles's play *Oedipus Rex.* Freud also wrote of the *Electra* complex, which describes the similar sexual longing of a daughter for her father.

ontology Generally, the study of being and human consciousness.

paradigm A theoretical framework that serves as a foundation for a field of study or branch of knowledge. Darwinian evolution, Newtonian physics, and Aristotle's chemistry are all examples of scientific paradigms. *Paradigm shifts* designate the transition from one paradigm to another, usually with a profoundly transformative effect. For example, the shift from Newtonian physics to quantum physics might be termed a *paradigm shift.*

pathos (Greek for "suffering, experience, emotion") In Aristotle's **rhetorical triangle,** the feelings evoked in the audience by an argument.

persona (Latin for "mask") An assumed or public identity (as distinct from the *inner self*); a character adopted for a particular purpose; in literature, the voice or character of the speaker.

placebo effect A psychological process wherein subjects in medical research respond to an inactive compound, often a sugar pill, as if it contained active ingredients intended to treat a disease or condition.

Platonic Following the teachings of the Greek philosopher Plato (428–347 BCE), *Platonic* **idealism** is a system that attempts to show a rational relationship between the individual, the state, and the universe, governed by what is good, true, and beautiful. Basic tenets of this seminal branch of philosophy are that only a reflection of the truth can be perceived and that the gap between the ideal and its reflection motivates human consciousness. It can be contrasted with the **Aristotelian** tradition, which values empirical observation and scientific reasoning. In common usage, a *platonic relationship* is a close friendship that does not have a sexual component.

pluralism In everyday language, a condition of society in which multiple religions, ethnicities, and subcultures coexist peacefully. *Pluralism* can also refer to any philosophical system that proposes that reality is made up of a number of distinct entities. The pragmatist William James (1842–1910) and the analytic philosopher Bertrand Russell (1872–1970) were prominent *pluralist* thinkers.

postcolonial *See* **colonialism.**

postmodernism A cultural trend that seeks to expose the artificiality of the **constructs** that defined earlier periods of cultural production while confessing—indeed, even in some cases boasting of—an inability to replace them with an authentic substitute. One of the hallmarks of *postmodern* cultural products is *pastiche,* or *collage,* a form that borrows from other trends and emphasizes the disjuncture between disparate elements. *See also* **modernism.**

praxis Often used as a substitute for *practice* in ordinary usage, and opposed to **theory.** In the work of Antonio Gramsci (1891–1937), the "philosophy of praxis" outlined the refinements to Marxism that were necessary to make it relevant in the twentieth century.

privilege (*verb*) To value more highly than other things; to prefer; to champion: "Feeling that Enlightenment thought had been too doggedly rational, the Romantics *privileged* the imagination."

projection In **Freudian** psychology, a mechanism by which the individual, unable to come to terms with his or her own fears and desires, imagines that these unwelcome impulses exist outside of him- or herself. *See also* **id, ego, superego, repression, unconscious.**

proletariat In **Marxism,** the *proletariat* is the downtrodden working **class,** who will revolt against the **bourgeois,** or capitalist, class, seizing from its members the means of production (factories and other industrial concerns).

quantum physics A theoretical branch of physics that deals with the behavior of atoms and subatomic particles. The work of such pioneers as Max Planck (1858–1947), Niels Bohr (1885–1962), and later Werner Heisenberg (1901–76) has had a profound impact on the way we understand such things as the relationships between matter and energy. *See also* **relativity.**

relativism The belief that the meaning and value of all things are determined by their *context*—their relationship to other things in that time and place—rather than that things have inherent or absolute meaning or worth. *Moral relativism* is the idea that different people, groups, nations, or cultures have differing ideas about what constitutes good and evil and that those differences must be respected. *Cultural relativism* is the position that there is no absolute point of view from which one set of cultural values or beliefs can be deemed intrinsically superior to any other. *See also* **culture, humanism.**

relativity In physics, the theory expounded by Albert Einstein (1879–1955), which states that all motion is relative and that energy and matter are convertible. The famous formulation $E = mc^2$ equates energy (E) with matter (m) multiplied by the speed of light (c) squared. Einstein's work directly challenged two cornerstones of **classical** physics—that motion is an absolute and that energy and matter are two completely different entities.

repression In **Freudian** psychology, the process that keeps unacceptable desires, fears, and other troubling material (such as memories of traumatic experiences) from reaching (or returning to) consciousness. *See also* **unconscious, projection.**

rhetoric In classical times, the art of public speaking. Currently, the term more broadly encompasses *language* or *speech,* often in a derogatory context (as in "The mayor's speech was so much empty *rhetoric*"), as well as the study of writing and the effective use of language.

rhetorical triangle Aristotle's description of the context of argument, consisting of **ethos** (roughly, the character of the speaker), **logos** (the topic of the argument or the argument itself), and **pathos** (the feelings evoked in the audience).

sample A subset or selection of a group from a population. In a *random sample,* each subject is chosen in ways that replicate pure chance, and all members of the population have an equal chance of being selected for the sample.

scientific method A process involving observations of phenomena and the conducting of experiments to test ideas suggested by those observations. The development of the scientific method, a specialized form of trial and error, ushered in the scientific revolution of the seventeenth century. Francis Bacon (1561–1626), René Descartes (1596–1650), and especially Galileo Galilei (1564–1642) are most often credited with developing its constituent procedures: (1) choosing a question or problem (for example, what causes yellow fever); (2) developing a **hypothesis** (the disease is caused by a bacteria or virus transmitted by mosquitoes); (3) conducting observations and experiments (noting **correlations** between mosquito populations and incidence of yellow fever); (4) examining and interpreting the data (high correlations exist between incidence of yellow fever and that of the *A. aegypti* mosquito); (5) affirming, revising, or rejecting the hypothesis; and (6) deriving further experiments and hypotheses from it (microscopically examining the bodies of *A. aegypti* and yellow fever victims to try to find a virus or bacteria present in both).

secular Not having to do with religion or the church; deriving its authority from nonreligious sources. *See also* **humanism.**

semiotics The theory and study of **signs** and symbols. According to semiotics, meaning is never inherent but is always a product of social conventions, and **culture** can be analyzed as a series of **sign** systems. *See also* **structuralism.**

sign In **semiotics,** a constituent of a text—that is, any cultural product, including but not limited to language and human behavior—that derives its meaning only by means of its differentiation from surrounding signs. A recurring word in a poem can function as a sign, as can a wink or a nod; the meaning of each of these signs can be derived only from the study of their context.

skepticism The belief that nothing can be held true until grounds are established for believing it to be true. Rene Descartes (1596–1650), one of the founders of modern philosophy, expressed this attitude in his famous statement "Cogito, ergo sum" (I think, therefore I am).

sociobiology The study of human behavior within an evolutionary/ biological context. E. O. Wilson's *Sociobiology: The New Synthesis* (1975) provoked a controversial debate over whether social behavior has a biological basis. *See also* **Darwinism.**

Socratic method Repeated questioning to arrive at implicit truths, a teaching method used by the Greek philosopher Socrates (470?–399? BCE), who influenced **Plato.**

solipsism Philosophical theory that the self is the only thing that can be known and verified and therefore is the only reality.

somatic (from the Greek for "body") Relating to the body. A *psychosomatic* illness is a physical condition that has a psychological origin.

standard deviation A measure of the degree to which data diverge from the **mean.** A high *standard deviation* means a greater range of results. Thus, in a **bell curve,** a tall, skinny curve represents a smaller standard deviation than does a wide, flat one.

statistical significance A value assigned to a research result as a measure of how likely it is that the result reflects mere chance. The higher the *statistical significance,* the less likely it is that chance determined the outcome. The results of studies employing large numbers of subjects typically have a higher statistical significance than do those from studies of a small number of subjects.

stream of consciousness A **modernist** literary technique in which the writer renders the moment-by-moment progress of a character's or narrator's thoughts. Among those writers who have used the technique are James Joyce (1882–1941) in *Ulysses,* Virginia Woolf (1882–1941) in *Mrs Dalloway,* and Marcel Proust (1871–1922) in *Remembrance of Things Past.*

structuralism An analytical method, today often subsumed under **semiotics,** that is used in the social sciences, the humanities, and the arts to examine underlying deep structures in a **text** by close investigation of its constituent parts (often termed **signs**). For example, in *narratology* (the study of narratives), myths, folktales, novels, paintings, and even comic books are reduced to their essential structures, from which are derived the rules that govern the different ways in which these narratives tell their stories. In *structural* approaches, the individual works under study are commonly considered less important than the universal structures that underlie them. This tendency has opened the approach to charges of anti-**humanism.** Michel Foucault (1926–84) and other *poststructuralists* have challenged structuralists' belief in the possibility of revealing essential structures of knowledge and reality through this type of study. *See also* **semiotics, deconstruction, formalism, sign.**

subculture *See* **culture.**

subjective *See* **objective.**

sublimation Psychological concept describing the redirection of unacceptable feelings or impulses into socially acceptable behavior. For example, one might say that working long hours *sublimates* the desire to engage in adulterous exploits.

sublime Inspiring awe; impressive; moving; of high spiritual or intellectual worth. Michelangelo's painting of the ceiling of the Sistine Chapel is often cited as an example of the *sublime* in art; in nature, mountains such as Kilimanjaro have been described as *sublime.*

superego In the **Freudian** model of mental functioning, the mental agent responsible for keeping the desires of the **id** and the antisocial impulses of the **ego** in check. Religion and the law are two institutions that Freud identified as manifestations of the *superego* in society. *See also* **repression, projection.**

symbiosis In biology, a prolonged association and interdependence of two or more organisms, usually to their mutual benefit. *Parasitism* occurs when one organism benefits at the expense of another. In general usage, *symbiotic* is used metaphorically to denote a mutual dependency and benefit between people, organisms, or ideas.

taxonomy Any set of laws and principles of classification. Originating in biology, *taxonomy* includes the theory and principles governing the classification of organisms into categories such as species and phyla. Today a literary critic might compose a "taxonomy of literary styles."

teleology In philosophy, religion, history, and the social sciences, an explanation or theory that assumes movement or development toward a specific end. For instance, Christianity is profoundly *teleological* because it looks toward the second coming of Christ.

text In common academic usage, anything undergoing rigorous intellectual examination and analysis. Although commonly associated with printed or written works, *texts* may also be oral works such as speeches, visual works such as paintings, everyday objects like toys, and even human behavior. Analysis of such cultural products is often called "reading the *text*," even if the text is not a written work. *See also* **semiotics, sign.**

theory A statement devised to explain a collection of facts or observations; also, the systematic organization of such statements. *Theory* is commonly contrasted with *practice* or **praxis.**

topography The physical features of a region. In cartography and surveying, maps and charts are the graphic representations of *topography.*

totem/totemic (from the Ojibwa, a Native American tribal language) A bird, animal, or plant or a natural phenomenon that an individual or a social group holds as signifying a special meaning for and relationship with that person or group.

trope A figure of speech. In literary criticism, the term is often used to refer to any technique that recurs in a **text.** Comparing women's faces to flowers is a common *trope* in Renaissance poetry.

typology The systematic study and classification of individuals in a group according to selected characteristics. In psychology, Carl Jung (1875–1961) developed a personality *typology* that uses characteristics such as extroversion and introversion. The Myers-Briggs assessment tools, based on Jung's typologies, are used in psychotherapy and employment settings. *See also* **archetypes.**

uncertainty principle An important theory in **quantum physics** formulated by German physicist Werner Heisenberg (1901–76) that places an absolute, theoretical limit on the accuracy of certain pairs of simultaneously recorded measurements. The significance of this principle is that it prevents scientists from making absolute predictions of the future state of certain systems. Heisenberg's principle has been applied to philosophy, where it is called the *indeterminacy principle.*

unconscious In the **Freudian** theory of the mind, the repository for repressed desires, fears, and memories. Ordinarily inaccessible to the conscious mind, the repressed material in the unconscious nevertheless has a powerful impact on conscious behavior and thoughts. *See also* **id, ego, superego, projection, repression.**

valorize To give or assign a value to. *See also* **privilege.**

variable In mathematics, a *variable* is a term capable of assuming any set of values. In algebra, it is represented by a symbol such as x, y, p, q. In experimental research, the *dependent variable* is measured for change precipitated by an *independent variable* determined by the experimenter. A *random variable* is a numerical value determined by chance-driven experiment or phenomenon. The value can be predicted according to the laws of probability but is usually not known until after the experiment has been completed.

will to power (from Friedrich **Nietzsche**'s *Thus Spake Zarathustra,* 1883–85) The capacity to overcome the dictates of conventional morality in order to achieve a level of experience beyond the reach of the "common herd." The key quality of Nietzsche's *superman (Übermensch),* the *will to power* manifests itself in creativity, independence, and originality. The association of this concept with Nazism has long made Nietzsche's ideas the focus of heated debate. *See also* **Dionysian, Apollonian, Nietzschean.**

zero sum game Any competitive situation where a gain for one side results in a loss for the other side. This term originated in **game theory** but is now in common use. In a *zero sum economy,* any economic gain is offset by an economic loss.

Timeline of World History

ca. 3000 BCE City of Babylon is founded; cuneiform script, the earliest known fully developed system of writing, emerges in ancient Mesopotamia.

2500–2001 BCE Bow and arrow is first used in warfare; cotton is cultivated in Peru.

ca. 2660–1640 BCE (Old and Middle Kingdoms of Egypt) Pyramids and grand monuments such as the Great Sphinx of Giza are built as royal tributes and burial structures.

2000 BCE *Gilgamesh,* ancient Mesopotamian epic, is composed (fullest extant *written* text of this epic dates from **seventh century** BCE): theme is futile human quest for immortality.

ca. 1950 BCE Irrigation systems are in use in Chinese agriculture.

ca. 1850 BCE Oldest surviving Egyptian mathematics text shows that decimal system was in use.

1792–1750 BCE Rule of Babylonian king Hammurabi produces an orderly arrangement of written laws—the Hammurabi Code—among the first in the ancient world.

1200 BCE Olmec culture flourishes in Mexico (until **ca. 400 BCE**).

ca. 1000–80 BCE Varna system—precursor of caste system—evolves in India.

776 BCE First recorded Olympic games are held at Olympia in Greece.

ca. 750 BCE *Iliad*—the earliest surviving example of Greek literature—and *Odyssey* are composed (ascribed to Homer).

3000

2000

1000

700

600

Literary and cultural developments and events

Historical events

Advances in science and technology

Changes in everyday life

Break in timeline

551–479 BCE Life of Confucius, China's greatest philosopher

ca. 560–480 BCE Life of Buddha (Siddhartha), founder of Buddhism

508 BCE Athens becomes the world's first democracy.

ca. 500 BCE Many Old Testament books are transcribed.

ca. 500 BCE Greeks adopt Ptolemaic model of cosmos, in which the sun revolves around the earth.

461–429 BCE Reign of Pericles ushers in flowering of Athenian culture: Aeschylus, *The Oresteia* (**458 BCE**); Sophocles, *Antigone* (**ca. 442–441 BCE**) and *Oedipus the King* (**ca. 429 BCE**); Euripides, *Medea* (**431 BCE**); Aristophanes, *Lysistrata* (**411 BCE**); Plato, *Republic* (**ca. 406 BCE**).

399 BCE Greek philosopher Socrates is tried and executed for corruption of youth.

404 BCE Golden age of Periclean Athens ends with fall of Athens to Sparta.

387 BCE Greek philosopher Plato founds the Academy.

350 BCE Aristotle, student of Plato, writes *Poetics*, founds rival school, Lyceum; earliest portion of *Mahabharata* (Sanskrit heroic epic) is composed mid-century.

356–323 BCE Life of Alexander the Great, king of Macedonia, who conquers the Persian empire

ca. 300 BCE Euclid writes *Elements*, seminal work of elementary geometry.

ca. 250 BCE Archimedes, founder of mathematical physics, writes *Measurement of the Circle* (includes concept of π).

ca. 250 BCE *Ramayana* (Sanskrit heroic epic) is composed mid-century.

215 BCE Great Wall of China is built.

ca. 500–200 BCE Roman Empire encompasses the entire Mediterranean region.

500

400

300

200

100

0

23–13 BCE Roman poet Horace composes *Odes*.

27–19 BCE Roman poet Virgil composes the epic poem *Aeneid*.

8 Ovid composes *Metamorphoses*, a 15-volume poem based on Greek and Roman myths.

30 Jesus is crucified by the Romans in Jerusalem.

ca. 65–85 New Testament Gospels are composed.

300

ca. 300 Large towns exist in inland Niger Delta, later to develop into the Empire of Ghana in West Africa.

400

413–26 St. Augustine writes *City of God,* interpreting history in light of Christianity.

410 Visigoths sack Rome.

478 First Shinto shrine is built in Japan.

500

550–900 Mayan civilization reaches Late Classical phase: art, architecture, and writing flourish at dozens of city-states.

600

ca. 650–750 *Beowulf,* Old English epic, is composed.

622 Mohammed, founder of Islam, flees from Mecca to Medina, transforms Islam into religious and secular empire.

651–2 Koran or Qu'ran, the holy book of Islam, is codified.

700

718 Muslims are in control of most of Iberian peninsula; some Muslim influence remains until Christian forces gain control in **1492** with taking of Granada.

900

960–1279 Song Dynasty in China: flowering of arts and scholarship

1000

ca. 978–1026 Life span of Lady Shikibu Murasaki, Japanese author of *Tale of Genjii,* considered by many to be the world's first novel

ca. 1100 *Song of Roland,* French epic poem, is composed.

1100 **1096–1291** The Crusades, nine military expeditions in which European Christians attempt to reconquer the Holy Land (Palestine) from the Muslims, take place.

1200

ca. 1200 Zen Buddhism travels from China to Japan, becomes influential in Japanese politics, painting, landscape, and culture, especially in the tea ceremony.

ca. 1290–1918 Ottoman Empire, Muslim Turkish state comprising Anatolia, modern southeastern Europe, and the Arab Middle East and North Africa, is established.

1300 **ca. 1300–1650** Renaissance in Europe: "rebirth" of arts and culture

1307–21 Dante Alighieri composes *La Divina Commedia,* an epic poem describing his imaginary journey through heaven and hell.

1312–27 Empire of Mali in West Africa reaches its height under Kankan Musa, builder of the Great Mosque at Timbuktu.

1350

1347–51 "Black Death," an epidemic of the bubonic plague, rages in Europe, eventually claiming 25%–50% of the population.

ca. 1370–1400 English poet Chaucer composes *The Canterbury Tales,* a collection of 24 tales with dramatic links.

ca. 1350–1400 Great Zimbabwe, a fabled stone city that controlled a large part of southeast Africa in medieval times, reaches its height.

1400

1431 Joan of Arc, leader of the French army against the British in the Hundred Years' War, is burned at the stake for heresy by the British.

ca. 1438–1532 Inca empire, largest native empire of the Americas, reaches height in Central and South America; expansion ends with the Spanish invasion led by Pizarro.

1450

ca. 1455 Gutenberg Bible set and printed; Gutenberg's invention of movable type leads to book printing boom in Europe.

1453 Constantinople falls to Ottoman Turks, marking the end of the Byzantine Empire.

1484 Botticelli paints *Birth of Venus* for the Medici family of Florence.

ca. 1492 Christopher Columbus lands in the Bahamas.

1500

1499 Amerigo Vespucci lands in South America.

1503 Leonardo da Vinci, painter, inventor, and scientist, paints *Mona Lisa*.

1508–12 Michelangelo paints the ceiling of the Sistine Chapel in Rome.

1513 Niccolo Machiavelli writes *The Prince*, arguing for pragmatism over virtue in a ruler.

1517 Martin Luther's *95 Theses* introduces the Protestant Reformation in Europe.

1520 Gold, silver, and chocolate are brought from the Americas to Spain.

1532 Sugar cane is cultivated in Brazil.

1550

1593–99 Shakespeare's sonnets are published, followed by *Hamlet* (**1600–1**) and *Othello* (**1604**).

1599 Globe Theater is built in London.

1600

1603 Kabuki is first performed in Japan by female entertainer Okuni.

1605 Miguel de Cervantes Saavedra writes his masterpiece *Don Quixote*.

1608 Galileo Galilei invents astronomical telescope, provides evidence to support Nicolaus Copernicus's theory that the earth and planets revolve around the sun.

1609 Tea is first shipped to Europe from China.

1611 King James Bible is published, becomes most popular version for more than three centuries.

1614 Pocahontas, Native American princess, marries tobacco planter John Rolfe.

1619 African captives are brought to Jamestown to be servants; slave system develops over the next eighty years.

1631–1648 Taj Mahal, premier example of Mogul architecture, is built in Agra, India.

1625

1620 Pilgrims sail for America and found Plymouth Colony.

1632 Rembrandt van Rijn, prolific Dutch painter, paints his first major portrait, *The Anatomy Lesson of Dr. Tulp.*

1637 René Descartes, called by some the founder of modern philosophy, writes *Discourse on Method* (from which comes "*Cogito, ergo sum*": "I think; therefore, I am").

1642–1648 English civil war pits Parliamentary forces under Oliver Cromwell against Charles I; Charles I is defeated and beheaded in **1649.**

1650

1651 Thomas Hobbes writes *Leviathan,* portraying human life in a state of nature as "nasty, brutish, and short" and offering as a remedy a social contract in which the ruler's power—for the sake of expediency—is absolute.

1667 John Milton writes *Paradise Lost,* an epic poem describing man's "first disobedience" and the promise of his redemption.

1675

1687 Isaac Newton publishes *Principia,* in which he codifies laws of motion and gravity not modified until the twentieth century.

ca. 1688–1790 The Enlightenment, an intellectual movement committed to secular views based on reason, takes hold in Europe.

1690 John Locke publishes *Essay Concerning Human Understanding,* in which he espouses an empiricist view of philosophy (limiting true knowledge to what can be perceived through the senses or through introspection).

1700

ca. 1701 Peter the Great begins westernization of Russia.

1740

ca. 1740s Baroque music flourishes: Vivaldi, *The Four Seasons;* Bach, *Brandenberg Concertos;* Handel, *Messiah.*

1750

1755–73 Samuel Johnson publishes *Dictionary of the English Language.*

Johann Sebastian Bach

1760

1767–87 Sturm und Drang ("Storm and Stress"), a literary and intellectual movement in Germany that prefigures Romanticism (**ca. 1789–1825** in England)

1761 Jean-Jacques Rousseau publishes *The Social Contract,* in which he praises the natural goodness of human beings but insists on the need for society to attain true happiness.

1769 James Watt patents a steam engine.

1770

ca. 1770 Industrial Revolution begins, fueled by steam power: first steam-driven cotton factory (**1789**) and first steam-powered rolling mill open in England (**1790**).

1775–81 The American Revolution: hostilities begin at Lexington and Concord, Massachusettes, in 1775, although the Continental Congress will not officially vote for independence until July 2, 1776.

1780

1776 "Declaration of Independence" is approved by the Continental Congress on July 4;

Adam Smith publishes *Causes of the Wealth of Nations,* advocates regulation of markets through supply and demand and competition.

1781 Immanuel Kant publishes *Critique of Pure Reason,* an attempt at reconciling empiricism and rationalism, and for many the single most important work of modern philosophy.

1780s and 1790s Classical music flourishes: Mozart writes the opera *Don Giovanni* (**1787**); Haydn establishes the form of the symphony with *The Clock Symphony* (**1794**).

1788 Bread riots occur in France.

1789 William Blake's *Songs of Innocence,* followed by *Marriage of Heaven and Hell* (**1790**) and *Songs of Experience* (**1794**), usher in early Romanticism in England; Olaudah Equiano's *The Interesting Narrative of the Life of Olaudah Equiano, or Gustaus Vassa, the African,* one of the first slave narratives, is published.

1789–99 French Revolution transforms France from a monarchy to a modern state.

1790

1792 Mary Wollstonecraft publishes *A Vindication of the Rights of Woman,* an early work of feminism.

1793 Queen Marie Antoinette and King Louis XVI of France are guillotined.

ca. 1795–1825 English Romantic poetry flourishes with the work of William Wordsworth (**1770–1850**), Lord Byron (**1788–1824**), Percy Bysshe Shelley (**1792–1822**), and John Keats (**1795–1821**).

1798 Thomas Malthus's *An Essay on the Principle of Population* stirs interest in birth control and concerns about overpopulation.

1799 Rosetta Stone is found in Egypt, makes deciphering hieroglyphics possible; perfectly preserved mammoth is found in Siberia.

1800

1800 Alessandro Volta produces first battery of zinc and copper plates.

1803 Beethoven composes *Third Symphony (Eroica),* marking the start of his dramatic middle period.

1804–06 Lewis and Clark expedition from St. Louis to the Pacific fuels westward expansion in the USA.

1804 Napoleon becomes Emperor of France.

1807 Hegel publishes *Phenomenology of Spirit,* which introduces the concept of the "master-slave" dialectic.

1808 Goethe publishes *Part 1* of *Faust,* a drama about a man who sells his soul for knowledge and power.

1810

1812 Noah Webster's *American Dictionary of the English Language* helps standardize spelling of American English.

1813 Mexico declares independence from Spain, becomes a republic in **1824**.

1813 Jane Austen publishes her novel *Pride and Prejudice*.

1818 Mary Shelley publishes horror classic *Frankenstein*.

1820

1815 Napoleon is defeated by British and Prussian forces at Waterloo.

ca. 1821 Cherokee leader Sequoya codifies the Cherokee alphabet.

1823 Monroe Doctrine closes U.S. borders to colonial settlements by Europe.

ca. 1825 Katsushika Hokusai, great Japanese printmaker, creates *Mt. Fuji on a Clear Day.*

1830

1830–42 Auguste Comte, founder of philosophical positivism, writes *The Course of Positive Philosophy,* advocates application of scientific method to social problems.

1830 Joseph Smith founds the Church of Jesus Christ of Latter-day Saints (Mormons).

1831 Nat Turner leads a group of fellow slaves in the largest slave revolt in North America.

1833 Charles Babbage designs "analytical engine," prototype of first modern computer, based on the algebra developed by English mathematician George Boole.

1836 Samuel Colt puts revolver into mass production, revolutionizes manufacture of small arms.

1837 Ralph Waldo Emerson, American transcendentalist, delivers "The American Scholar," an address expressing American literary independence.

1837–1901 Queen Victoria reigns in England, Ireland, and India.

1838 Charles Dickens publishes *Oliver Twist,* the first of many novels that sharply criticize abuses brought on by the Industrial Revolution in England.

1839 Daguerreotypes, forerunners of modern photographs, are developed by L. M. Daguerre and J. N. Niepce in France.

1840

1840s Rise of Romantic movement in France, Germany, and Italy

1841 First university degrees granted to women in USA.

1843 Søren Kierkegaard, Christian existentialist philosopher, publishes *Either/Or.*

1843 Richard Wagner composes *The Flying Dutchman,* an opera expressing his ideal of the *Gesamtkunstwerk* ("total work of art").

1844 Samuel Morse invents the telegraph.

1847 Charlotte Brontë publishes *Jane Eyre*; Emily Brontë publishes *Wuthering Heights;* Anna Brontë publishes *Agnes Grey.*

1850

1848 Seneca Falls Convention for Women's Suffrage is held in USA; Karl Marx and Friedrich Engels write *Communist Manifesto*, a pamphlet exhorting workers to unite against capitalist oppressors.

1855 Walt Whitman publishes first edition of *Leaves of Grass,* creates a new American style for poetry.

1857 French poet Charles Baudelaire publishes *Flowers of Evil,* one of the seminal works of modern poetry.

1859 Charles Darwin publishes *On the Origin of Species,* establishes theories of evolution and natural selection ("survival of the fittest").

ca. 1860 Louis Pasteur invents pasteurization process, advances germ theory of infection, discovers rabies and anthrax vaccines (**1880s**).

1860

1860–65 Emily Dickinson writes most of her poetry, creates a new rhythm and vernacular for American verse.

1861–65 U.S. Civil War pits Northern against Southern states.

1863 "Emancipation Proclamation" frees all slaves in states rebelling against the federal government.

1865 U.S. President Abraham Lincoln is assassinated.

1865–69 Leo Tolstoy publishes *War and Peace,* an epic of the Napoleonic invasion of Russia.

1867 Universal Exposition in Paris introduces Japanese art to the West.

1867–94 Publication of Karl Marx's *Capital*, a political and economic treatise providing the theoretical basis of socialism.

1869 U.S. transcontinental railroad is completed.

1870

1874 First exhibition of French Impressionism in Paris is held; notable exponents include Monet, Renoir, Pissarro, Degas, and Cassatt.

1875 Alexander Graham Bell invents the telephone.

1877 Thomas Edison invents the phonograph.

1878 In Boston, Mary Baker Eddy founds Church of Christ, Scientist, a religion emphasizing divine healing.

1879 Thomas Edison invents the light bulb.

1880

1883–85 Friedrich Nietzsche writes *Thus Spake Zarathustra*, which expounds on the concept of *Übermensch* (superman).

1889 Eiffel Tower is built for Paris Exposition.

1890

1893 Fabian Society, a socialist group that includes Irish playwright George Bernard Shaw, is established.

1893 X rays are discovered.

1895 Louis and Auguste Lumière project brief motion pictures on a screen to a paying audience in Paris; based on Thomas Edison's technology, their Cinématographe became the prototype of the movie camera.

ca. 1895 Charles "Buddy" Bolden, New Orleans cornet player and band leader, begins playing improvised music later known as jazz.

1898 Marie and Pierre Curie isolate radium and polonium.

1900

1903 Orville and Wilbur Wright make their debut power-driven flight near Kitty Hawk, North Carolina.

1907 Albert Einstein first publishes equation $E = mc^2$, deduced from his theory of special relativity, ushering in revolution in physics and astronomy.

1907 Pablo Picasso's *Les Demoiselles d'Avignon,* first Cubist painting, leads to new artistic aesthetic.

1908 Henry Ford introduces the Model T; demand for cars induces the company to introduce assembly-line technique.

1910

1910 International Psychoanalytic Association is founded by Sigmund Freud and others; Freud's theories of the unconscious begin to gain popular recognition.

1913 *The Rite of Spring,* ballet with groundbreaking music by Igor Stravinsky and choreography by Vaslav Nijinsky, is first performed.

1914 Serbian nationalist assassinates heir to the Austro-Hungarian Empire in Sarajevo, sparking World War I.

1915 Margaret Sanger opens the first birth-control clinic in USA.

1914–21 James Joyce writes *Ulysses,* a masterpiece of modernist literature; publication in the USA is delayed until **1933** due to obscenity charges.

1915 British passenger ship *Lusitania* is sunk by German submarine, fueling American sympathy for war efforts of Britain, France, and Russia.

1917 USA enters World War I; Russian Revolution: Bolsheviks led by Vladimir Lenin seize power.

1918 Romanian poet Tristan Tzara writes manifesto for Dada, avant-garde artistic movement established in part in reaction to the senseless slaughter of World War I.

1918–19 Influenza epidemic kills 22 million worldwide.

1918 Treaty of Versailles ends World War I; death toll approaches 15 million worldwide; race riots rock major U.S. cities.

1920

1920 Nineteenth Amendment to the U.S. Constitution grants women suffrage.

ca. 1920 Arnold Schoenberg invents 12 tone system of musical composition.

1922 First Fascist government is formed by Benito Mussolini in Italy.

1920s Harlem Renaissance: flowering of African American literature and the arts, particularly jazz, centered in New York City

1924 Joseph Stalin succeeds Lenin as head of Soviet Union.

1927 Martin Heidegger publishes *Being and Time,* a founding work of existentialist philosophy; Martha Graham, pioneer of modern dance, opens a dance studio in New York.

1929 Virginia Woolf, central to the Bloomsbury literary group, publishes feminist work, *A Room of One's Own.*

1930

1927 Charles Lindbergh makes first solo, nonstop transatlantic flight; Werner Heisenberg develops Uncertainty Principle, which, together with Theory of Relativity, becomes basis of quantum physics; first successful transmission of an image via "television" occurs.

1930s The Great Depression, precipitated by a stock market crash in **1929,** begins in USA and spreads abroad; in response, President Roosevelt introduces "New Deal" measures based on Keynesian economics.

1933 Adolf Hitler becomes Chancellor of Germany, gradually assumes dictatorial power.

1931 Incompleteness Theorem is developed by the mathematician and philosopher Kurt Gödel.

1936–39 Spanish Civil War

1935 African American Jesse Owens wins four gold medals in track at the Berlin Olympics.

1941 Japan bombs Pearl Harbor and USA enters World War II.

1940

1939 World War II begins shortly after Germany's invasion of Poland; Hitler's Nazis begin program of extermination of "undesirable" elements, including dissidents, homosexuals, Gypsies, and especially Jews; 6 million Jews die in the ensuing Holocaust.

1943 Jean-Paul Sartre, existentialist philosopher, publishes *Being and Nothingness*.

1945 USA drops atomic bombs on Hiroshima and Nagasaki, Japan— World War II ends; United Nations is formed; Soviet Union occupies Eastern Europe.

1947 India and Pakistan gain independence from Britain.

1948 Mahatma Gandhi, Indian nationalist and spiritual leader, is assassinated; Pakistan-India wars ensue.

1949 Communists seize mainland China; Mao Zedong becomes first chairman of the People's Republic of China.

1950

1949 Simone de Beauvoir publishes *The Second Sex*, a groundbreaking study of women's place in society.

1950–55 Jonas Salk develops polio vaccine.

1950s–70s Height of the "Cold War," in which USA and the Soviet Union face off—mutual military buildup and threat of nuclear annihilation create a "balance of power."

1953 J. D. Watson and F. H. C. Crick determine the structure of DNA, launching the modern study of genetics.

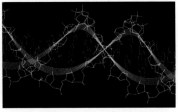

1956 Soviet Union crushes revolt in Hungary.

1959 Cuban Revolution: Fidel Castro overthrows Batista regime.

1962 Cuban missile crisis—Soviet missile-building in Cuba precipitates tense standoff with USA, ultimately resolved through diplomacy; César Chávez organizes the National Farm Workers Association (NFWA).

1960

1961 Berlin Wall erected; USA stages failed "Bay of Pigs" invasion of Cuba.

1963 Martin Luther King, Jr. delivers "I Have a Dream" speech to crowd of 250,000 at the Lincoln Memorial;

President John F. Kennedy is assassinated in Dallas.

1964 U.S. involvement in Vietnam War escalates with Tonkin Gulf Resolution; Malcolm X is assassinated in New York; Watts riots roil Los Angeles.

1966 Mao Zedong's Cultural Revolution begins, aiming to revitalize Communist zeal; Black Panther Party is founded in Oakland, California.

1968 Martin Luther King, Jr. is assassinated in Memphis, Tennessee.

1969 American astronaut Neil Armstrong becomes first man to walk on the moon.

1970

1971 East Pakistan (now Bangladesh) declares independence from West Pakistan.

1973 *Gulag Archipelego* by Alexander Solzhenitsyn is published in Paris; it is a massive study of Soviet penal system based on author's firsthand experience.

1975 Bill Gates and Paul Allen build and sell their first computer product, creating Microsoft.

1975–79 Vaccination programs against smallpox eradicate the disease worldwide.

1975 Wave of former colonies—Mozambique, Surinam, Papua New Guinea—gain independence.

1979 Islamic revolution in Iran: Shah flees, Khomeini comes to power.

1980

1981 First cases of acquired immune deficiency syndrome (AIDS) are reported in New York and California.

1982 Benoit Mandelbrot publishes *The Fractal Geometry of Nature,* contributing to chaos theory.

1986 Chernobyl nuclear power plant disaster spreads fallout over Soviet Union and parts of Europe.

1990

1989 Pro-democracy protests in Tiananmen Square, in Beijing, are quashed by government crackdown; Berlin Wall is demolished; Eastern Europe is democratized.

1991 Soviet Union is dissolved, making way for looser confederation of republics.

1995 Internet boom hits—number of people online grows geometrically.

2000

2001 Hijacked planes fly into 110-story World Trade Towers in New York City and the Pentagon in Washington, D.C. —thousands die; USA invades Afghanistan in "war on terrorism."

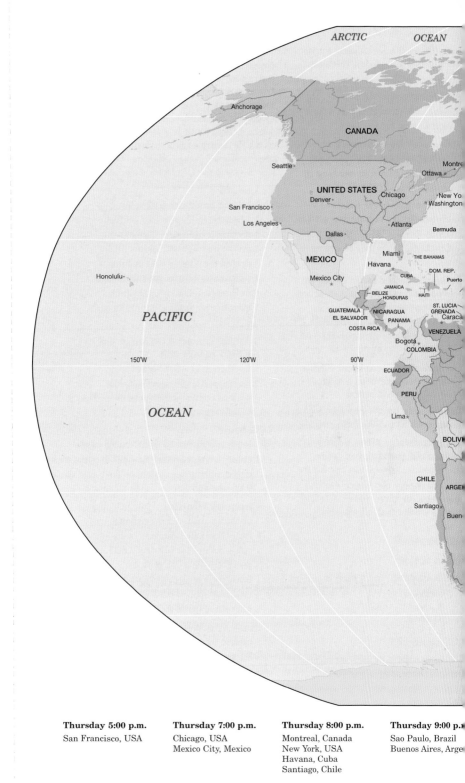

ARCTIC   OCEAN

Anchorage

CANADA

Seattle ·   Montre
                                        Ottawa ★

UNITED STATES   Chicago   · New Yo
Denver·   ★ Washington

San Francisco ·

Los Angeles ·   · Atlanta
                Dallas ·   Bermuda

Honolulu·   Miami   THE BAHAMAS
                        Havana
                                   DOM. REP.
            Mexico City   CUBA   Puerto
                ★   JAMAICA
                      BELIZE   HAITI
                        HONDURAS
            GUATEMALA   NICARAGUA   ST. LUCIA
PACIFIC   EL SALVADOR PANAMA   GRENADA   Caraca
            COSTA RICA   ★
                                   VENEZUELA
                        Bogotá·
                           COLOMBIA

150°W   120°W   90°W

                            ECUADOR

                            PERU

OCEAN   Lima ·

                                   BOLIV

                                   CHILE   ARGE

                            Santiago·
                                   Buen

MEXICO

Thursday 5:00 p.m.	Thursday 7:00 p.m.	Thursday 8:00 p.m.	Thursday 9:00 p.
San Francisco, USA	Chicago, USA	Montreal, Canada	Sao Paulo, Brazil
	Mexico City, Mexico	New York, USA	Buenos Aires, Arge
		Havana, Cuba	
		Santiago, Chile	

Quick Reference for Multilingual Writers

Many multilingual students encounter problems when they try to transfer their thoughts from one language into another. For example, some languages, like Russian and Chinese, do not include articles such as *a, an,* and *the* (English: *The flowers are beautiful*); other languages, such as Arabic and French, do not use definite articles to introduce a profession (English: *Here is the doctor*); still others, such as Spanish, include articles to indicate a generalization, whereas English does not (English: *time flies*). More tips for multilingual writers are included in the review of basic grammar in Tab 13, but here is a quick reference for dealing with some of the common issues that come up when you are transferring your first language into English.

Nouns and Pronouns

Count and Noncount Nouns

Count nouns name persons, places, or things that can be counted. Count nouns can be singular or plural.

Noncount nouns name a class of things. Usually, noncount nouns have only a singular form.

COUNT	NONCOUNT
cars	information
table	furniture
child	humanity
book	advice

Pronouns

Common Problem: Personal pronoun restates subject.

INCORRECT	My sister, *she* works in the city.
CORRECT	My sister works in the city.

Pronouns replace nouns. They stand for persons, places, or things and can be singular or plural.

Personal pronouns act as subjects, objects, or words that show possession.

Subject pronouns: I, we, you, he, she, it, one, they, who

Object pronouns: me, us, you, him, her, it, one, them, whom

Possessive pronouns: my, mine, our, ours, your, yours, his, her, hers, its, their, theirs, whose

Relative pronouns introduce dependent clauses.

Relative pronouns: that, whatever, which,

whichever, who, whoever, wh whose

EXAMPLE	His sister, *who l* came to visit.

Articles

Common Problem: Article is

INCORRECT	Water is cold. I l
CORRECT	*The* water is col

Using Articles with Count and N

Definite article (*the*): used for with all types of nouns.

The car I bought is red. [*sing*

The dogs howled at the moor *noun*]

The furniture makes the roo cluttered. [*noncount noun*]

Do not use *the* before most s nouns, such as names of peo languages, and so on.

~~The~~ Dallas is a beautiful city

Indefinite articles (*a, an*): us count nouns only.

Use *a* before a noun that beg a consonant sound.

a pencil

a sports car

a tropical rainforest

Use *an* before a noun that b a vowel sound.

an orange

an hour

an instrument

Do not use an indefinite art a noncount noun.

Water
~~A water~~ is leaking from the
      ^

No article: Plural count nouns nouns do not require *indefinite* count nouns and noncount noun *definite* articles when they refer items in a group.

Index

a, an, 376
 italicizing in titles, 485–87
 missing, 344
 rules for using, 506–7
Abbreviations, 481–84
 associated with numbers, 482–83
 capitalizing, 474–75
 familiarity of, 481–82, 483
 for grammatical terms, 373
 inappropriate, 484
 Latin, 483
 in lists of works cited, 212, 214
 for organizations, 248
 parentheses around, 482
 periods in, 466–67, 483
 plurals of, 455
 scientific, 481
 titles before names, 481
ABC-CLIO, 164
Absolute phrases
 with comma(s), 441
 definition, 527
Abstract nouns, 506
Abstracts
 in APA paper, 259, 262
 in business reports and proposals, 145–46
 of dissertations, 219, 256, 287–88
 in lab reports, 114
 MLA citation of, 219
 in periodical databases, 162
 of research papers, 259
Abstract words, 368–69
Academic Universe, 164
accept, except, 376
Acknowledgments, 117
Active voice
 compared to passive, 360–61, 417
 shifts from or to passive, 348–49
adapt, adopt, 376
Addresses, commas in, 442
Ad hominem fallacy, 30

Adjective clauses
 with comma(s), 438
 definition, 528
Adjective phrases, 439
Adjectives
 absolutes, 429
 adjective phrases, 439
 adverbs compared to, 427
 commas between, 437
 comparisons, 511
 compound, with hyphen(s) 489–90
 coordinate, 437
 cumulative, 437, 446, 512
 definition, 426, 511
 descriptive, 511
 order of, 512
 positive, comparative, and superlative forms, 428–29
 pronouns and proper nouns as, 511
 subject complements, 426–27, 511
Adverb clauses
 definition, 528
 punctuating, 445
Adverbs
 adjectives used as, 427–28
 conjunctive, 395–96, 513, 520
 definition, 426, 513
 placement of, 350–51
 positive, comparative, and superlative forms, 428–29
 relative (*where, when*), 528
Advertisements, citation of, 220
advice, advise, 376
affect, effect, 376, 495
after, 445, 528
Afterwords, citation of, 215
Agreement. *See* Pronoun-antecedent agreement; Subject-verb agreement
agree to, agree with, 376

ain't, 376, 499
Aircraft names, italics for 487
all, 402, 418
all, all of, 376, 401
all right, alright, 376
all together, altogether, 376
allude, elude, refer to, 376
Almanacs, 156
almost, most, 376
along with, 399
a lot, 376
also, 440
Alternative search engines, 167
although, 445, 447
A.M., AM, a.m., 376, 482
American Memory, 177
American Psychological Association (APA) style. *See* APA (American Psychological Association) style
among, between, 377
amoral, immoral, 377
amount, number, 377
Ampersands (&), 484
an. See a, an
Analogies, 51
Analyses
 in critical reading, 22–23
 interpretive, 94
 mapping the topic, 24, 38–39
 process of, 51
and
 comma in front of, 44, 437
 compound subjects joined by, 399–400
 incorrect semicolon with, 450
 pronoun-antecedent agreement with, 420–21
 repairing comma splices and run-ons with, 394–95
 unnecessary comma with, 444, 446–47
Anecdotes, 32

Annotating
  as critical reading
    strategy, 22
  as note-taking strategy,
    181
Antecedents
  ambiguous references
    to, 421–22
  compound, 420–21
  definition, 507
  implied references to,
    421–22
  pronoun-antecedent
    agreement, 418–20,
    423
  relative pronouns, 403
Anthologies, citation of
  APA style, 252
  Chicago style, 282
  MLA style, 211, 214
Anthropology, library and
  Internet resources
  for, 192
Antonyms, 67
anxious, eager, 377
any, 402, 418
anybody, 509
anybody, any body, 377, 401
anymore, any more, 377
anyone, any one, 377, 401
anything, 401
APA (American Psycho-
  logical Association),
  245, 247
APA (American Psycho-
  logical Association)
  style, 244–71
  capitalization, 477
  disciplines that use,
    190, 205
  explanatory notes, 258
  in-text citations, 245–50
  quotations, 458
  reference lists, 250–58
  research paper format,
    259–60
  sample paper in, 260–72
  titles, 248, 261
Apostrophes, 452–57
  with geographical loca-
    tions and organiza-
    tions, 456
  with indefinite
    pronouns, 454
  to indicate possession,
    452–54

for missing letters and
    numbers, 454–55
  misuse with plural
    nouns, 456
  in plurals, 455
  possessive pronouns *vs.*
    contractions, 456–57
Appositive phrases
  with comma(s), 439
  definition, 527
Appositives
  with colon, 450
  with comma(s), 439
  without comma(s), 445
  definition, 527
  as fragments, 392
  pronoun case in, 423
Architecture, library and
  Internet resources
  for, 192
Archive research, 176–77,
  221
ArchivesUSA, 177
Argumentative structure,
  61
Arguments
  analyzing and evaluat-
    ing, 25–28
  as college assignments,
    8–9, 35, 97–98
  conclusions in, 102–3
  counterarguments,
    100–101, 107
  determining issues,
    98–99, 105
  example of student
    paper, 104–10
  as grounds for claims,
    27–28
  introductions in, 102,
    104–5
  peer review of, 102
  reasonable stance, 99
  recognizing, 25
  revisions, 103–4
  support for thesis,
    100–101, 105–6
  thesis, 43, 99–100, 106
arise, 405
Articles (*a, an, the*)
  a, an, 344, 376, 486
  capitalized at the begin-
    ning of titles, 486
  for clarity, 344
  italicizing in titles,
    486

missing, 344
  rules for using, 506–7
  in series, 344
  the, 344, 486, 505–6
Articles, in periodicals
  APA citation style,
    252–54
  Chicago citation style,
    284–86
  COS citation style, 306
  critical reading, 21
  CSE name-year citation
    style, 298–99
  CSE number citation
    style, 302–3
  in databases, 162–63
  MLA citation style,
    214–15, 217–18, 223
  online periodicals, 223
  quotation marks around
    titles of, 460
  in reference works,
    214–15, 252
  reviews and editorials,
    218, 254
  unsigned, 218, 254
Artwork
  citation of, 227, 289
  clip art, 323
  italicizing titles of, 486
  library and Internet
    resources for, 192
as
  in comparisons, 343
  misuse of, 377
  pronoun following, 424
as, like, 377
as cited in, 249
as it were, 416
ask, 416, 525
Ask Jeeves search engine,
  167
Assignments, college. *See
  also* Writing papers
  analyzing and evaluat-
    ing arguments, 25–28
  arguments, 97–110
  case studies in the social
    sciences, 118–21
  coauthored projects,
    128–29
  common types of college
    papers, 8–9
  essay exams, 122–24
  informative reports,
    77–88

interpretive analyses,
88–97
lab reports, 113–18
learning how to
approach, 34–37
oral presentations,
124–28
personal essays, 111–13
portfolios, 129
purpose of, 35
research projects, 150
understanding, 8–9
as soon as, 445
Assumptions, in
argument, 28–29
Asterisks (*) in e-mail, 479
as well as, 399
at
to indicate time or loca-
tion, 515
misuse of, 377
ate, eaten, 407
at least, 440
Audience
appealing to, 33
in critical reading, 22
for informative reports,
78
for oral presentations,
124
questions about, 35
audience, as collective
noun, 400
Audiovisual sources, in
MLA style, 226
Auditory learners, 7
Authoritative claims, 100
Authors
APA style, 246–48
Chicago style, 279–82
COS style, 308
CSE name-year style,
296–97
CSE number style,
300–301
editors as, 214, 281
MLA style, 204–8,
212–14, 216, 218
unknown
APA style, 248, 252,
254
Chicago style, 284
COS and CSE num-
ber style, 310
MLA style, 208, 216,
218, 222

Auxiliary verbs, 501–3
awake, 405
awful, awfully, 377
awhile, a while, 377

bad, badly, 426
Bandwagon fallacy, 30
Bar graphs, 320
Base form of verbs, 404
B.C. /BC, 482–83
be
as helping verb, 360,
412, 502–3
as linking verb, 403, 524
in passive voice, 417
overworked, 360
principle forms of, 346,
405
in progressive tenses, 412
subject complements,
346
be able to, 503
be allowed to, 503
because, 445
because of, due to, 379
become, 405
before, 445
Begging the question
fallacy, 31
begin, 405
be going to, 503
being as, being that, 377
belief, believe, 377
beside, besides, 378
be supposed to, 503
be that as it may, 416
better, 378
between, among, 377
Bias
biased language, 67–68,
364–66
generic nouns and, 419
hidden assumptions,
28–29
indefinite pronouns
and, 418–19
in reference sources,
172, 174
sexist language,
364–67, 419
stereotypes, 365
Biased language fallacy,
31
Bible citations
Chicago style, 283
MLA style, 210–11, 215

Bibliographies, reference,
156, 278–79. *See also*
Citing sources
Bibliographies, working,
180
Biographies, 156–57
Biology, library, and Internet resources for, 193
Block format, for
quotations, 187
Boldface type, 318
Books
chapter citations, 301
citation models for
APA style, 250–53
Chicago citation
style, 279–84
CSE name-year style,
296–99
CSE number style,
300–301
MLA citation style, 208,
210, 212–16, 223
critical reading, 21
locating in library,
157–61
titles of
capitalizing, 447
italicizing, 486–87
title within title, in
MLA style, 216
Boolean operators, 168
both, 402, 418, 519
Brackets, 186, 470–71
break, 405
bring, 405
bring, take, 378
Brochure design, 325–27
Browsers, 10, 329
Bullets, 316, 318
Business, library and Internet resources for, 193
Business reports and pro-
posals, 145–46, 484
but, 393–94, 437
but that, but what, 378
buy, 405
by, to indicate time or
location, 515
By (in citations), 215

Call numbers, 157
Campus writing centers, 71
can, may, 378, 503–4
can't hardly, 378
capital, capitol, 378

Capitalization, 474–80
  after a colon, 480
  for emphasis in e-mails, 479
  first word of sentence, 480
  geographical regions, 478
  misuse of, in e-mail, 12, 479
  proper nouns, 475–76
  quoted sentences, 478–80
  races, ethnic groups, and sacred things, 478
  scientific names, 476, 487
  small caps, 318
  titles before names, 476–77
  titles of works, 477
Cartoons, citation of, 220
Case, objective *vs.* subjective, 425
Case, pronoun, 422–23. *See also* Pronoun case
Case studies in the social sciences, 118–21
Catalog, library, 155
catch, 405
Cause and effect, 51, 58
CBE (Council of Biology Editors) style. *See* CSE (Council of Science Editors) style
CD-ROMs, citation of
  Chicago style, 290
  MLA style, 224
censor, censure, 378
certainly, 440
cf., 483
Change-tracking, in word-processing programs, 73
Chapters, citation of, 301, 460
Charts, citation of, 220
Chats, online, 70
Checklists, for revising drafts, 62, 69
Chemistry, resources and style manuals for, 191, 193
Chicago style (*Chicago Manual of Style*), 276–95
  disciplines that use, 190, 205

in-text citations, 277–78
  research paper example, 292–95
  works-cited list guidelines, 277–78
choose, 405
chorus, as collective noun, 400
Chronological sequences, 112
Circular reasoning fallacy, 30
cite, sight, site, 378
Citing sources. *See also* References list, APA style; Works cited list, MLA style
  APA style, 250–58
  Chicago style, 278–79, 295
  COS with APA style, 307
  COS with *Chicago* style, 307–8
  COS with CSE style, 308–10
  COS with MLA style, 305–6
  CSE name-year style, 296–99
  CSE number style, 300–303
  MLA style, 212–27
Claims, in argument, 27, 29–32, 100
Classics, library and Internet resources for, 193–94
Classification, 48
Clauses *See also* Dependent clauses, Independent clauses
  adjective, 438, 528
  adverb, 445, 528
  after a colon, 480
  colons between, 450
  definition, 530
  dependent, 388–90, 438, 528–29
  if, 416, 529–30
  independent, 388–89, 392–93, 437
  modifying, 342
  noun, 528–29
Clichés, 369–70, 465
cling, 405

Clip art, 323
Clustering, to explore ideas, 38–39
CMS. *See Chicago* style
Coauthored projects, 128–29
Coherence, paragraph, 56–58
Collaboration, 69, 128–29
Collective nouns
  definition, 506
  pronoun agreement with, 420–21
  subject-verb agreement with, 400–401
Collective subjects, 400–401
Colons, 450–52
  with quotation marks, 462
  instead of a semicolon, 396
  to set off quotations, 458
Color, use of in design, 317
The Columbia Guide to Online Style (Walker and Taylor), 303
Columbia Online Style (COS). *See* COS (Columbia Online Style)
come, 406
Commas, 434–47. *See also* Commas, common misuses
  with absolute phrases, 440–41
  in addresses, 442–43
  after introductory word groups, 435–36
  with appositives, 439
  comma splices, 392–97, 447
  with contrasting comments, 441
  in dates, 442–43
  in journalism, 436
  for nonessential additions, 438–39
  in numbers, 442–43
  for omitted words or phrases, 443
  with parenthetical expressions, 440, 445
  with quotation marks, 441, 447, 462

in series, 436, 444
to set off subordinate
    ideas, 354
with titles after names,
    442
with transitional
    expressions, 440–41
with words that inter-
    rupt a sentence, 441
Comma splices, 392–97,
    447
Commas, common
    misuses, 443–47
after *although,* 447
between adjectives and
    nouns, 446
between adverbs and
    adjectives, 446
in compound word
    groups, 444
after coordinating con-
    junctions, 446–47
between cumulative
    adjectives, 437–38, 446
in front of or following a
    series, 444
after *like,* 447
before parentheses, 447
with other marks in a
    quotation, 447
to separate major sen-
    tence elements, 444
to set off restrictive ele-
    ments, 447
after *such as,* 447
committee, 400, 420
Common knowledge, 189
Common nouns, 505, 507
Communication. *See also*
    E-mail; Letters
cultural differences in, 15
online, 169–71
Communications, library
    and Internet
    resources for, 194
Community-service
    writing, 132
Comp., 218
Company names, abbrevi-
    ations with, 482
Comparatives, 428–29
compare to, compare with,
    378
Comparisons
in college papers, 49–50
making clear, 343–44

similes and metaphors,
    370–71
superlatives and, 428–29
complement, compliment,
    378
Complements
definition, 523
object, 525
subject, 403, 423, 523
Complete predicates,
    522–23
Complete verbs, 415
Compound adjectives,
    489–90
Compound antecedents,
    420
Compound-complex
    sentences, 531
Compound nouns, 453,
    489–90
plural of, 489, 494
possessive form, 453
Compound numbers, and
    hyphens, 490
Compound predicates, 392
Compound sentences
combining sentences,
    353–54
definition, 531
punctuating, 394–96,
    437, 447–48
Compound structures,
adding words to, 342–43
with comma, 437
without comma, 444–45
parallelism in, 350
pronoun case in, 423
Compound subjects,
    399–400
Compound words
dividing between lines,
    491
hyphens with, 488–89
Computers. *See* Internet;
    Online sources
Computer science, library
    and Internet
    resources for, 194
Computer software, cita-
    tion of
APA style, 258
MLA style, 225
Computer toolbars, 314–15
Concerts, citations of, 208
Conclusions
in arguments, 102–3

in case studies, 121
in informative reports,
    80–81, 86
in interpretive
    analyses, 93, 97
memorable, 186
in oral presentations, 128
paragraphs, 52–53
Concrete nouns, 368–69,
    506
Conditional clauses, 416,
    529–30
Conference proceedings,
    citation of
APA style, 258
MLA style, 219
Confidentiality, in field
    research, 175
Conjunctions
coordinating, 399, 437,
    446–47, 518
correlative, 399
definition, 518
subordinating, 518–20
Conjunctive adverbs,
    395–96, 513, 520
Connotations, 66, 368
conscience, conscious, 378
consequently, 393, 513
Context, in critical
    reading, 21
continual, continuous, 378
Contractions, 456–57
Contrary-to-fact state-
    ments, 416
Contrasting comments,
    punctuating, 441
Contrasts, 49–51
Coordinate adjectives,
    comma with, 437
Coordinating conjunctions,
    64, 353, 394, 399, 437,
    446, 518–20
Coordination, 353–56
Copyright infringement,
    188–89, 190. *See also*
    Plagiarism
Correlative conjunctions,
    399, 518–19
COS (Columbia Online
    Style), 303–9
APA style and, 306–7
Chicago style and, 307–8
*The Columbia Guide to
    Online Style* (Walker
    and Taylor), 303

COS (*continued*)
CSE name-year style and, 308–9
CSE number style and, 309–10
FAQs on, 305
information required by, 304–5
MLA style and, 305–6
could, 503–4
could of, should of, would of, 378
Council of Biology Editors. *See* CSE (Council of Science Editors)
Counterarguments, 33, 100–101
Count nouns, 17, 505–6, 507
Course of study, 3
Cover letters, 146
Credibility, 171–74, 183
criteria, criterion, 378
Critical reading
analyzing, 22–23
annotating, 22
evaluating sources, 171–74, 183–84
previewing, 21–22
summarizing, 23
synthesizing, 23–25
Critical thinking
analyzing and evaluating an argument, 25–28
evaluating hidden assumptions, 29
logical fallacies, 28, 30–31
recognizing an argument, 24
recognizing logical fallacies, 28–29
in writing papers, 24–28
Critical writing
appealing to audience, 33
checking for errors in logic, 33–34
considering opposing viewpoints, 33
making a strong claim, 29–32
selecting the topic, 29
supporting a claim with evidence, 32–33
Critiques, 98. *See also* Arguments
crowd, 400, 420

CSE (Council of Science Editors) style, 296–303
disciplines that use, 190, 205
name-year style, 296–99
number style, 299–303
sample reference list, 304
used by specific disciplines, 190, 205
Cultural studies, library and Internet resources for, 194
Cumulative adjectives
incorrect comma with, 437–38, 446
order of, 512
Cumulative sentences, 64–65, 357–58
Cyberspace, 9–11

-d, -ed, verb ending, 410
Dance, library and Internet resources for, 199–200
Dangling modifiers, 352–53
Dashes, 468–69
for change in tone or idea, 469
for nonessential independent clauses, 469
overuse of, 469
for parenthetical material, 468
quotation marks and, 463
for a series or an explanation, 468–69
data, 379, 494
Databases
citation of
APA style, 255, 257
Chicago style, 291–92
COS style, 306–9
CSE number style, 303
MLA style, 221–22
ERIC, 164, 255
library, 158–62
online, 164–65, 221–22, 291–92, 303, 306–7
periodical articles in, 162–63
Data reports, 324. *See also* Lab reports; Scientific reports
Dates
commas with, 442

numerals for, 485
slashes with, 474
Dave's ESL Café Web site, 15
Declarative sentences, 531
Deductive reasoning, 25–26
Defenses, type of critique, 98. *See also* Arguments
Definition of concepts, 48, 80
Definitions, in dictionaries, 373–74
Demonstrative pronouns, 508–9, 510
Denotations, 66, 368
Dependent clauses, 528–29
adjective, 528
adverb, 528
in complex and compound-complex sentences, 353, 531
definition, 528
as fragments, 389–90
for less important ideas, 355
noun, 528–29
Descriptions, 47–48, 59–60
Design. *See* Document design; Web design
Desk encyclopedias, 18
despite, 351
Development, paragraph, 53–54
Development, patterns for
analogy, 51
cause and effect, 52
classification, 48
comparison and contrast, 49–51
definition, 49
description, 47–48, 59–60
illustration, 49
narration, 47
process analysis, 51
Dewey Decimal system, 157
Diagrams, 322
Dialogue
paragraphs and, 457
quotation marks for, 457–58
punctuation with, 396, 461–64
Diction. *See* Word choice

Dictionaries
of American idioms and slang, 18
citation of, 282–83
definitions in, 373–74
ESL, 17–18
information in, 66, 372–73
as reference materials, 157
standard, 371–372
tips on using, 374
translation, 17
usage information, 374
word origins, 373–74
different from, different than, 379
differ from, differ with, 379
Direct address, commas with words of, 441
Direct objects
definition, 524
and pronoun case, 423
using only one, 524
Directories, search engine, 167
Disciplines
definition, 4
documentation styles for, 190–91, 205
help sheets, 155
library and Internet resources for specific, 155, 193–200
lines of inquiry in, 152
discreet, discrete, 379, 495
Discussion lists, 169–71
citing in APA style, 258
citing in *Chicago* style, 290
citing in MLA style, 224
disinterested, uninterested, 379
Dissertations
APA citation style, 256
Chicago citation style, 287–88
MLA citation style, 219
Division, 48
do
as helping verb, 501, 502
as irregular verb, 406
present-tense forms of, 399
Documentation styles
APA style, 244–71

Chicago style, 276–95
COS style, 303–10
CSE style, 296–303
deciding which to choose, 277
MLA style, 202–42
for specific disciplines, 190–91, 204, 434
Document design, 312–28. *See also* Web design
brochures and newsletters, 325–28
business letters, 141–43
computer toolbars, 314–15
consistency of, 317
headings, 318–19
integration of visuals, 323–25
organization of information, 315–16
paper format
APA style, 259
Chicago style, 291
MLA style, 228–29
standard academic, 313–14
restraint in, 317–18
template designs, 319
variations in type style and lists, 318
visuals, 319–23
don't, 398
don't, doesn't, 379
Double negatives, 429
Doublespeak, 364
Double superlatives, 429
Drafting, 42–59
idea development, 47–52
online help with, 68–70
outline preparation, 45–46, 185
paragraph development, 52–58
research papers, 184–85
thesis development, 42–44, 185–86
draw, 406
drink, 406, 408
due to, because of, 379

each, 401, 420
each and every, 379
each other, one another, 379, 509
eager, anxious, 377

eat, 406
EBSCOhost, 162–63, 164
Economics, library and Internet resources for, 194–95
-ed, verb ending, 410
Ed. / Eds., 214, 251
ed. / eds., 214, 281
Editing for clarity, 337–84
active verbs, 359–61
appropriate language, 361–67
confusing shifts, 347–49
coordination and subordination, 355–56
dangling modifiers, 353
exact language, 367–71
faulty parallelism, 349–50
misplaced modifiers, 350–51
missing words, 342–44
mixed constructions, 344–46
sentence variety, 356–59
split infinitives, 351–52
wordy sentences, 340–42
Editing for grammar conventions, 386–429. *See also* Grammar review
adjectives and adverbs, problems with, 426
comma splices, 392–97, 447
irregular verbs, 404–9
pronouns, problems with, 417–25
run-on sentences, 392–97
sentence fragments, 388–92
subject-verb agreement, 397–404
verb tenses, 410–15
Editions, citation of
APA style, 252
Chicago style, 283
MLA style, 215
Editorials, citation of
APA style, 254
MLA style, 218
Editors, citation of books by
APA style, 251–52
Chicago style, 281
CSE name-year style, 297–98
MLA style, 214

Education, library and Internet resources for, 195
effect, affect, 376, 495
e.g., i.e., 379, 483
either, neither, 379, 401, 519
Either/or fallacy, 31
either . . . or
  as correlative conjunction, 519
  parallelism with, 35
  pronoun agreement and, 420
  subject-verb agreement and, 400
Electronic mailing lists
  APA citation style for, 258
  Chicago citation style for, 291–92
  as research tools, 169–71
  MLA citation style for, 224
Electronic résumé, 141
Electronic sources. *See* Online sources
elicit, illicit, 379
Ellipses, 186–87, 472–73
else, in comparisons, 343
elude, allude, refer to, 376
E-mail
  APA in-text citation, 249
  for communication with classmates, 69
  COS citation style for, 306
  discussion lists, 169–71
  emphasis in, 479
  italics and underlining in, 486
  MLA citation style for, 211, 225
  netiquette, 11–13
  reference list citation of, 225
  in the workplace, 144–45
emigrate, immigrate, 379
eminent, imminent, immanent, 380
Emoticons, 13
Emphatic sequences, 112, 502
Enclosures, 143
Encyclopedias
  APA citation style for, 252
  Chicago citation style for, 282–83

MLA citation style for, 214–15
  as research tools, 156
Endnotes
  Chicago citations as, 277
  MLA explanatory notes as, 228
Engineering, library and Internet resources for, 195
English as a Second Language (ESL). *See* Multilingual writers
Environmental sciences, library and Internet resources for, 195
er / -est endings, 428–29
ERIC database, 164, 255
-es, -s
  forming plurals with, 489
  as verb ending, 373
ESL. *See* Multilingual writers
ESL dictionaries, 17–18
Essay exams, 121–24
Essays, quotation marks around titles, 461
et al.
  as Latin abbreviation, 483
  in APA style, 247
  in *Chicago* style, 280–81
  in MLA style, 207, 212–13
etc., 380, 483
Ethical principles in research, 175–76
Ethnic groups, capitalization of, 477
Ethos, 33
Etymology, 66
Euphemisms, 363–64
Evaluating sources, 163, 171–74, 183–84
Evaluations, 146, 149
even though, 445
every, 420
everybody, 401
everybody, every body, 377
everyone, every one, 377, 401
everything, 401
Evidence, to support thesis, 32–33
ex-, hyphen with, 490
Exact language, 367–71
Examples. *See* Illustration of ideas
except, accept, 376

Exclamation points, 463, 467–68
  as end punctuation, 467
  with quotation marks, 463
  incorrect comma with, 447
Exclamations, 358–59
Exclamatory sentences, 531
expect, suppose, 380
Expert opinions, 32–33, 100, 106–7
Explanatory notes
  APA style, 258
  below visuals, 324
  MLA style, 227–28
Explanatory structure, 61
Expletive constructions, 65
explicit, implicit, 380
Exploratory structure, 61

Facts, definition, 149
fall, 406
Fallacies, logical, 28, 30–31
False analogy fallacy, 31
family, as collective noun, 400, 420
Family relationships, hyphens in, 489
farther, further, 380
Faulty parallelism, 349–50
Faulty predication, 345–46
few, 402, 418, 509
fewer, less, 380
Field notes, 176–77
Field research, 138–39, 176–78
fight, 406
Figures of speech, 370–71
Films
  in-text citations, MLA style, 208
  library and Internet resources for, 195–96
  reference list citation of
    APA style, 256
    Chicago style, 289
    MLA style, 226
first, firstly, 380
First person, use in case studies, 119
First-person point of view, 347
FirstSearch, 164
Flaming, 12
flaunt, flout, 380

fly, 406
Focus groups, as field
  research 178
Font type and size,
  313–14, 316
Footnotes
  APA explanatory notes
    as, 258
  below visuals, 324
  Chicago style citations,
    277
  MLA explanatory notes
    as, 228
for
  comma in front of, 437
  repairing comma splices
    and run-ons with,
    394–95
Foreign terms, italics for
  487
Forewords, citation of, 215
for example, 393, 440, 451
forget, 406
forgive, 406
Formality, appropriate
  level of, 362
Formal outline, 45–46
Format of paper. *See* Document design
former, latter, 380
Fractions, 401, 484, 489
  numerals for, 485
  plural when referring to
    people or things, 401
  spelled out, hyphens
    with, 490
Fragments, sentence,
  388–92
Freewriting, to explore
  ideas, 39–40
freeze, 406
further, farther, 380
Fused sentences, 392–97,
  447–48
Future perfect progressive
  tense, 412
Future perfect tense, 411
Future progressive tense,
  411
Future tense, 411

GDCS (Government
  Documents Catalog
  Service), 164
Gender bias, avoiding
  alternating pronouns, 367

biased terms, replace-
  ments for, 366, 419
genderless nouns and
  pronouns, 67–68
in names of
  occupations, 68
parallel titles for women
  and men, 36, 68
sexist language,
  364–67, 419
use of plural, 347, 367,
  419
General Science Index, 164
General words, 368
Generalizations
  hasty, 31
  unsupported, 118–19
Generic nouns, 419
Genre selection, 36
Geographical locations,
  capitalization of, 478
Geography, library and
  Internet resources
  for, 196
Geology, resources and style
  manuals for, 191, 196
Gerund phrases
  definition, 527
  as subject, agreement of
    verb with, 404
Gerunds
  noun or pronoun before,
    424–25
  prepositions with, 515
  verbs followed by, 501
get, 380, 406
GIF (Graphics Interchange
  Format), 334
give, 406, 525
Glossary of usage, 375–84
go, 406
gone, went, 408
good, well, 380, 426
Google search engine, 167
Government, style manu-
  als for, 191
Government documents
  APA citation style, 255
  Chicago citation style,
    287
  CSE number style
    citation, 301
  MLA citation style, 218
Grammatical terms,
  abbreviations for, 373
Graphs, 320–22, 324

Grounds, in argument, 27
group, as collective noun,
  400
grow, 406

half, a half, half a, 380
hang, 406
hanged, hung, 380
Hanging indents, 213
hardly, 429
Hasty generalization
  fallacy, 31
have
  as helping verb, 501–2
  as irregular verb, 406
  perfect tenses and, 411–12
  present-tense forms, 398
have got to, 503
have to, 503
he
  alternating with *she,* 367
  avoiding generic *he,* 365
  case of, 423
Headings for papers
  APA style for, 259–61
  document design and,
    316, 318–19
  MLA style for, 228, 230
Health, library and Internet resources for, 196
hear, 406
Helping verbs
  definition, 415
  matching with main
    verb, 502–3
  missing, 415
  modal verbs as, 503–4
Help sheets, 155
herd, as collective noun, 400
herself, 382
he said, 463–64
he/she, 367
himself, 382
his/her, 367, 419
History, library and Internet
  resources for, 196–97
Home page, 329
  MLA citation style for,
    222–23
Homophones, 494–95
hopefully, 381
Hot links, 333
however
  with comma(s), 440
  as conjunctive adverb,
    520–21

however (*continued*)
with semicolon, 394,
395–96, 448–49
signal of possible comma
splice or run-on, 393
HTML (hypertext markup
language), 329, 486
HTTP (hypertext transfer
protocol), 329
Humanities, resources
and style manuals
for, 190–91, 193–200
Chicago documentation
style, 276–95
Chicago paper format,
291
MLA documentation
style, 202–42
MLA paper format,
228–29
Humanities Index, 164
hung, hanged, 380
Hyperlinks, disabling
before printing, 221
Hyphens, 488–91
compound adjectives,
489–90
compound nouns,
489–90
compound numbers, 490
in fractions, 490
with prefixes and
suffixes, 490–91
two to make a dash, 468
suspended, in series, 490
unnecessary use with
-*ly* adverbs, 490
URLs and, 221
Word division, 491
Hypothesis, 121, 152–53,
178

I vs. *me,* 423
Idea development. *See*
Development, pat-
terns for
Ideas, exploring, 37–42
Identification questions,
123
Idioms
definition, 16
dictionaries of, 18
listing of common
expressions, 516–18
prepositions in, 369, 515
use of, 369

-*ie, -ei,* spelling words
with, 492
i.e., e.g., 379, 483
if, 445
if clauses, 416, 529–30
if . . . then, 381
illicit, elicit, 379
Illustration of ideas, 49, 79
Illustrations, use of, 323
*immanent, eminent,
imminent,* 380
immigrate, emigrate, 379
immoral, amoral, 377
Imperative mood, 415
Imperative sentences,
522, 531
you as implied subject,
522
implicit, explicit, 380
imply, infer, 381
in, to indicate time or
location, 515
in, in to, into, 381
in addition to, 393, 399
in contrast to, 440
incredible, incredulous, 381
Indefinite pronouns
definition, 509
possessive form of, 454
pronoun agreement
with, 418–19
subject-verb agreement
with, 401–2
Independent clauses
with colon, 451
with comma and coordi-
nating conjunction, 437
in complex sentences,
353–54
in compound sentences,
353, 531
definition, 388–89, 530
for main idea, 353, 355
with semicolon, 447–48
vs. sentence fragments,
388–89
Indexes, periodical, 162,
164–65. *See also*
Databases
Indicative mood, 415
Indirect objects, 525
Inductive reasoning, 25–26
infer, imply, 381
Infinitive phrases, 527
Infinitives
pronoun case with, 424

split, 352
tense with, 414
verbs followed by, 501
Informality. *See* Formality,
appropriate level of
Informal outline, 45–46
Informative reports
audience for, 78
classification and divi-
sion in, 79
conclusions in, 80–81, 86
definitions in, 80, 82–83
example of student
paper, 81–88
illustration of key ideas,
79, 85
introductions in, 79,
81–82
objective stance, 78, 83
reasons for assigning, 77
thesis, 43, 78–79, 82–83
topic selection, 77–78
understanding
assignment, 8–9, 35
Informed consent, in field
research, 175–76
InfoTrac, 162
InfoTrac SearchBank, 164
-*ing* phrases. *See* Gerund
phrases
in order to, 528
in other words, 393
inside of, outside of, 381
insist, 416
instead, 440
Intensifiers, 340
Intensive pronouns, 508,
510
Interjections
comma with, 441
definition, 520
Internet. *See also* E-mail;
Internet searches;
Online sources; Web
sites
archiving, 14
chatting about ideas, 70
coauthoring online, 128
discussion lists, 169–71
evaluating sources
from, 163, 173–74
for exploring subjects, 42
extension meanings, 174
help with drafts on, 70
informational sites for
newcomers, 10–11

ISPs (Internet Service
    Providers), 10
jargon, 329
netiquette, 11–14
online collaboration, 14
online communication,
    169–71
online databases,
    164–65
online learning, 13–14
overview, 163
peer review on, 69
periodical databases,
    162–63
primary research on, 175
search engines, 164–67
tools for revising on,
    73–74
URLs, 174, 305, 329,
    473, 490
Internet searches
archives, 177
keyword, 166–69
online databases,
    164–65
search engines, 164–67
source evaluation, 163,
    174
starting points for, 166
World Wide Web, 163
Internet service providers
    (ISPs), 10
Internships, 138–39
Interpretation, definition,
    149
Interpretive analyses
clarity of purpose, 59–60
conclusions in, 93, 97
example of student
    paper, 93–97
intellectual framework
    for, 89–90, 95
introductions in, 91–92
reasons for assigning,
    88–89
support for thesis,
    92–93, 95–97
thesis, 43, 90–91, 97
thoughtful stance, 89, 96
topic selection, 88–89
understanding assign-
    ment, 8–9, 35
Interrogative pronouns
definition, 509
who, whom, 425
Interrogative sentences, 531

Interviews
    Chicago citation style, 287
    conducting, 178
    MLA citation style, 211,
        220, 227
In-text citation
    APA style, 245–50
    Chicago style, 277–78
    CSE name-year style, 296
    CSE number style,
        299–300
    MLA style, 204–11
    use of superscript num-
        bers, 277–78
Intransitive verbs
    definition, 525–26
    lie, sit, rise as, 408
Introductions
    of arguments, 102
    of case studies, 121
    citation of, 215
    of informative reports, 79
    of interpretive analyses,
        91–92
    of lab reports, 114–15
    of oral presentations, 125
    paragraphs, 52
    to quotations, 462–64
Introductory word groups,
    comma with, 435–36
Invention. *See* Ideas,
    exploring; Planning
Inversions
    for variety, 358
    subject-verb agreement
        and, 403
ironically, 381
irregardless, 381
Irregular verbs, 404–8
is. See be
is because, 346
is when, is where, 346
it, unclear reference, 422
Italics (Underlining), use
    of, 485–88
    added to quotation, 488
    in design, 318
    for emphasis, 488
    for foreign words, 487
    for ships, aircraft, etc.,
        487
    for titles of works, 486–87
    for words, letters, num-
        bers as themselves,
        488
it's, its, 381, 456, 495

Jargon, 362
Journalism, resources and
    style manuals for,
    191, 194
Journalist's questions,
    40–41
Journals. *See* Periodicals
JPG (Joint Photographic
    Experts Group), 334
J STOR, 164
jury, as collective noun, 420
Justifying margins, 314

Keyword searches,
    158–61, 166–69, 224
kind, kinds, 381
know, 406

Laboratory notebooks,
    178–79
Lab reports, 113–18
    abstract, 114
    acknowledgments, 117
    credibility, 183
    discussion, 117
    introduction, 114–15
    literature cited, 117–18
    methods and materials,
        115
    in professional journals,
        117
    reporting data, 324
    results, 115–16
    structure of, 114
Language
    appropriate, 36–37,
        361–67
    biased, 67–68, 364–65
    clichés, 369–70
    connotations, 368
    cultural differences in
        communication, 15
    within disciplines, 4, 363
    doublespeak, 363–64
    euphemisms, 363–64
    exact, 367–371
    formality, 362
    idioms, 369, 516–18
    jargon, 362–63
    nonstandard English,
        361–62
    regionalisms, 361–62
    sexist, 365–67
    slang, 361–62
    stuffy, pretentious, 362
    wordiness, 340–42

Languages, library and Internet resources for, 197
Latin abbreviations, 482
latter, former, 380
Law, style manuals for, 191
lay, lie, 381, 408–9
Learning in college, 7, 13–14
Lectures, citation of, MLA style 227
less, fewer, 380
let, 501
Letters (correspondence)
  APA citation style, 249, 254
  application, 141–44, 146
  business style, 141, 145, 451
  cover, 146
  to the editor, 135, 254
  enclosures, 143
  in-text citations of, MLA style, 211
  MLA citation style, 220–21
  personal, 221
  of praise, 135–38
  of protest, 134–37
Letters (alphabet)
  capital *vs.* lowercase, 474–80
  single letters, italics for, 488
  single letters, plural of, 455
Libraries
  books, 157–61
  catalog, 157–61
  consortia, 161
  databases, 158–61
  help sheets, 155
  reference works, 156–57
  research in, 155–62
  subject searches, 157–58
  Web sites, 155–56
Library of Congress Subject Headings (LCSH), 157–58
lie, lay, 381, 408–9
like, 444, 447
Limiting modifiers, 351
Line graphs, 322
Line spacing. *See* Spacing, line
Linguistics, style manuals for, 191

Linking verbs
  adjectives with, 427–28
  definition, 403, 524
  missing, 415
  pronoun following, 423
  subject-verb agreement and, 403
Links, in Web sites, 333, 486
Listing, to generate ideas, 37, 40
List of works cited. *See* Works-cited list, MLA style
Lists
  colons with, 450
  dash with, 468
  in design, 316, 318
  as fragments, 392
  parentheses for numbers in, 470
Listservs. *See* Discussion lists
literally, 382
Literary analysis. *See* Interpretive analyses
Literature, library and Internet resources for, 197
Literature review, 77
Location, prepositions that indicate, 518
Logical fallacies, 28, 30–31
Logical thinking
  circular reasoning, 30
  claims, grounds, and warrants, 27–28
  errors in logic, 33–34
  inductive *vs.* deductive reasoning, 25–26
  logical fallacies, 28, 30–31
Logos, 33
loose, lose, 382, 495
lose, 382, 406, 495
-ly endings, 428–29

Magazines. *See* Periodicals
Mailing lists, electronic, 258, 306
Main clauses. *See* Independent clauses
Main point. *See* Thesis
Main verb, 500–501
make, 501

man, sexist use of, 367
Manuscripts, citation of, 221
Manuscript formats. *See* Document design
many, 402, 418
Mapping your topic, 24, 38–39
Maps, citation of, MLA style, 220
Margins and spacing, 228
  APA style for, 259
  in document design, 313–14
  MLA style for, 228–29
Mass nouns. *See* Noncount nouns
Mathematics, resources and style manuals for, 191, 197
may, can, 378, 503–4
maybe, may be, 382
me vs. *I,* 423
media, medium, 494
Measurements, numerals for, 485
Measurement units, as collective subjects, 400
Medicine, resources and style manuals for, 191, 196
Memos, 144–45
Metaphors, 371
Meta search engines, 167
Methodology, in case studies 121
Methods and materials sections, in lab reports, 115
Microsoft Word, 314–15, 320
might, 503–4
Misplaced modifiers, 350–53
Missing words, 342–44
  articles, 344
  in comparisons, 343–44
  in compound structures, 342–43
  subjects, 522
  that, 343
  verbs, 415
Misuse of words, 371
MLA (Modern Language Association), 207
MLA Bibliography, 164–65

MLA Handbook for Writers of Research Papers, 204, 207, 221
MLA (Modern Language Association) style, 202–42
  authors in, 206–8
  disciplines that use, 190, 205
  ellipses in, 471–73
  explanatory notes, 227–28
  FAQs on, 206
  in-text citations, 204–11
  online sources, 209, 211, 221–25
  page numbers, citation of, 205, 459
  plurals of numbers, abbreviations, 455
  quotations in, 187, 457
  research paper format, 228–29
  sample paper in, 229–42
  underlining instead of italics in, 485–86
  works cited lists, 212–27
Modal verbs, 503–4
Modern Language Association (MLA) style. *See* MLA (Modern Language Association) style
Modifiers. *See also* Adjectives; Adverbs
  ambiguous, 351
  dangling, 352–53
  disruptive, 351
  hyphenated, 489–90
  misplaced, 350–51
  participial phrases as, 356, 527
  redundant, 340
Modifying clauses, 342
Mood, of verbs, 348–49, 415–16
MOOs (multiuser dimensions, object oriented), 15, 70, 170–71
moral, morale, 382
more, 418
more, more of, 376
more, most, to form comparative and superlative, 429
more important, more importantly, 382
moreover

with comma(s), 440
  signal of possible comma splice or run-on, 393
  with semicolon, 374, 395–96, 448
most, 402, 418
most, almost, 376
Multilingual writers
  adjectives in the correct order, 512
  American and British spellings, 494
  applying for a job, 144
  articles, 506–7
  biased language, 366
  complete verbs, using, 523
  coordination and subordination, 519–20
  dictionaries for, 17–18
  direct objects, using only one, 524–25
  gerunds, verbs followed by, 501
  grammar conventions, 387
  helping verbs, 502–3
  if clauses, 529–30
  infinitives, verbs followed by, 501
  language differences, 499
  learning in college and, 14–18
  modal verbs, 503–4
  online resources for, 15
  peer review and, 71, 102
  prepositions, 515
  present and past participles as adjectives, 512
  punctuation, mechanics, and spelling, 435
  quantifiers, 505–6
  researching, 154
  sentence parts, correct order of, 521
  subjects, only one, 522
  Web site design collaboration, 330
Multiple authors
  APA citation style
    in-text, 246–48
    reference list, 250
  Chicago citation style, 280–81
  CSE number style, 300
  MLA citation style
    in-text, 207–8

works-cited list, 212–13
Multi-user dimensions (MUDs), 170
Multivolume works
  APA citation style, 253
  Chicago citation style, 283–84
  MLA citation style, 209–10, 215–16
Music
  citation of compositions, MLA style, 226, 288–89
  library and Internet resources for, 197–98
must, 503–4
myself, 382

Name-year documentation style, CSE, 296–99
Narration, idea development through, 47
National Archives and Record Administration (NARA), 177
Navigation bars, 332–33
N.B., 482
n.d., 250
Negatives, double, 429, 513
Negators
  as adverbs, 513
  between helping and main verb, 503
  contrasting comments, commas with, 441
  double negatives, 429–30
neither, either, 379
  as indefinite subject, 401–2
neither . . . nor
  as correlative conjunction, 519
  parallelism with, 350
  pronoun agreement and, 420
  subject-verb agreement and, 400
Netiquette, 11–14
Networked classrooms, 14
never, 429
nevertheless
  with comma(s), 439–40
  signal of possible comma splice or run-on, 393
News groups, 170, 306
Newsletter design, 325–28

Newspaper Abstracts, 165
Newspapers
  APA citation style, 254
  Chicago citation style,
    286
  CSE number citation
    style, 302
  initial *the,* 486
  MLA citation style,
    217–18
New York Times Index, 165
no
  as adverb, 513
  in contrasting comment,
    441
  in double negatives,
    429–30
nobody, 401
nohow, nowheres, 382
Noncount nouns, 505–6, 507
none, 401–2
Nonrestrictive words and
  phrases, commas and
  438–39
Non sequitur fallacy, 30
no one, 401
nor
  commas in front of, 437
  pronoun-antecedent
    agreement with, 420,
    423
  repairing comma splices
    and run-ons with,
    393–94
  singular or plural verbs
    with, 400
Northern Light search
  engine, 167
not
  as adverb, 513
  in double negative,
    429–30
Note, 260, 324
Notebooks, citation of in
  MLA style, 221
Notes
  bibliographies *vs.,*
    276–78, 282
  endnotes
    Chicago style, 277
    MLA style, 228
  explanatory
    APA style, 258
    in document design,
      324
    MLA style, 227–28

field, 176–77
footnotes
  APA style, 258
  Chicago style, 277
  in document design,
    324
  MLA style, 228
Note taking
  annotations on
    printouts, 181
  avoiding plagiarism, 188
  correcting mistakes, 179
  field notes, 176–77
  laboratory notebooks,
    178–79
  paraphrasing, 182–83
  quotations, 182, 188
  from sources, 181–83
  summarizing, 183
  working bibliographies,
    180–81
nothing, 401, 509
not only . . . but also, 350,
  519
Nouns. *See also* Appositives
  abstract, 506
  as adjectives, 427
  appositive phrases, 527
  collective, 400–401, 420,
    506
  compound, 453, 489
  concrete, 506
  count and noncount, 17,
    505–6, 507
  definition, 504
  genderless, 67–68
  generic, avoiding bias, 419
  plurals, 489, 493–94, 506
  possessive, 424–25
  proper and common,
    474–75, 505, 507, 509
number, amount, 377
Number, confusing shift
  in, 347
Numbers
  abbreviations for,
    482–83
  apostrophes for
    missing, 454–55
  commas in, 442–43
  hyphens in, 490
  italicized or underlined,
    488
  page numbers, 229, 259,
    313–14
  in parentheses, 470

in scientific reports,
  114, 484
spelling out, 484–85
superscript, 277–78

Object
  case of, 425
  direct, 524–25
  indirect, 525
  of prepositions, 514
  unnecessary comma
    between subject and,
    444
Object complements, 525
Objective case, 425
Objective stance, 78
of course, 440
off of, 382
Omitted words. *See* Miss-
  ing words
on, to indicate time or
  location, 515
one, 367, 401
one another, each other,
  379, 509
one of the, 403
Online books
  Chicago citation style,
    290–91
  COS style, 306, 308
  CSE name-year style,
    297–98
  CSE number style, 303
  MLA style, 223
Online communication,
  169–71. *See also*
  E-mail
Online learning, 13–14
Online library catalogs,
  155–56
Online posting
  COS style, 308–10
  MLA style, 224–25
Online services, citation
  of work from
  COS style, 308–9
  MLA style, 224
Online sources, citing. *See
  also* Online sources,
  types of; Online
  sources, working with
  APA citation format
    in–text citation, 249–50
    reference list, 257–58
  Chicago citation style,
    290–92

COS citation style, 306-10
CSE name–year style, 297–98
CSE number style, 302–3
MLA citation format
in-text citation, 209, 211
works-cited lists, 221–25
Online sources, types of.
See also Internet; Web sites
archives, 177
CD-ROMs, 224
discussion lists, 169–71
library databases, 158–61
multi-user dimensions, 170–71
online databases, 164–65
periodical indexes, 162–63
Online sources, working with. *See also* Internet; Web sites
discipline-specific, 192–200
evaluating, 163, 173–74
keyword searches, 166–69
locating, 165–67
search engines, 164–67
starting points, 166
working bibliographies, 180
Online writing labs (OWLs), 72–73
only, 351
only one of the, 403
on the contrary, 393
on the other hand, 440
Opposing views, in argument
counterarguments, 100–101, 107
or
commas in front of, 437
pronoun-antecedent agreement with, 420, 423
repairing comma splices and run-ons with, 393–94
singular or plural verbs with, 400
orally, verbally, 383
Oral presentations
audience for, 124

conclusions, 128
direct style, 125
eye contact, 126–28
openings, 125
purpose and organization of, 124–25
rehearsals, 128
visual aids, 125
Organization names, 456
Organization of findings, 120, 315–16
Organizations, as authors
APA style, 248, 250
Chicago style, 281–82
CSE number style, 301
MLA style, 208, 213
other, in comparisons, 343
Outline preparation, 45–46, 101, 185
outside of, inside of, 381
OWLs (online writing labs), 72–73

Page numbers
APA style for, 248, 250
in document design, 313–14
MLA style for, 229
PAIS International, 165
Pamphlets, MLA citation of, 219
Paragraph patterns, *See* Development, patterns for
Paragraphs
coherence, 56–58
development, 53–54
introductions and conclusions, 52–53
quotations across, 458
topic sentences, 54–56
transitions, 58
unity within, 54–56
Parallelism
to avoid gender bias, 68, 366
faulty, 349–50
with items in a series, 349
with paired ideas, 350
in titles, 68, 366
Paraphrasing, 182–83, 186–87, 442
Parentheses
around abbreviations, 482
around numbers, 470

commas after, 470
line and page numbers within, 458
no commas before, 446
question marks within, 467
for unimportant information, 469
whole sentences within, 469–70
Parenthetical citations
APA style, 246–47
MLA style, 206
Parenthetical expressions
with comma(s), 440
with dash(es), 468
unnecessary comma(s) with, 446
Participial phrases
definition, 527
for sentence variety, 356–58
tense in, 414–15
Parts of speech, 499–521
adjectives, 511–12
adverbs, 513
conjunctions, 518–20
in dictionary definitions, 66, 373–74
interjections, 520–21
nouns, 504–7
prepositions, 514–15
pronouns, 507–10
verbs, 500–504
Passive voice
vs. active voice, 360–61, 417
definition, 524
in scientific writing, 360, 417
shifts from or to active, 348–49
Past participles
as adjectives, 512
with *be,* to form passive, 503
definition, 405
examples, 405–6, 500
in infinitives, 414
of irregular verbs, 405–7, 408
in participial phrases, 526–27
in perfect tenses, 411
of regular verbs, 405
tenses of, 414–15

Past perfect progressive tense, 412
Past perfect tense, 411–12
Past progressive tense, 411
Past tense
   definition, 405, 410–11
   of irregular verbs, 405–7, 500
   vs. past perfect, 412–13
   of regular verbs, 405, 500
Pathos, 33
pay, 406
PDF files, 249
Peer review, 69, 71, 102
Percents, 400, 485
Perfect progressive tense, 412
Perfect tenses
   definition, 411
   formation of, 502
   of infinitives and participles, 414–15
Performances, citation of
   Chicago style, 290
   MLA style, 227
perhaps, 440
Periodical Abstracts, 165
Periodicals, citing
   APA citation style, 253–55, 257
   Chicago citation style, 284–86
   COS citation style, 306, 308
   CSE name-year citation style, 298–99
   CSE number citation style, 302–3
   MLA citation style, 217–18, 223
Periodicals, as sources, 161–63
   Indexes of, 162, 164–65
Periodicals, style for titles
   capitalizing, 476–77
   initial *The,* 477, 486
   italicizing, 486
Periodic sentences, 358
Periods
   with abbreviations, 466–67
   to end statements, 466
   with quotation marks, 462
Person, jarring shifts in, 347

Personal communication, APA style for citing, 249
Personal essays, 111–13
Personal pronouns
   case of, 422–23
   definition, 508
Philosophy, library and Internet resources for, 198
Photographs, use of, 323
Phrasal modals, 503–4
Phrasal verbs, 369, 503
Phrases
   absolute, 527
   adjective, 439
   appositive, 527
   dangling, 352–53
   definition, 526
   gerund, 527
   infinitive, 527
   introductory, comma with, 435–36
   misplaced, 350–51
   noun, 526
   participial, 526–27
   prepositional, 514–15
   quotation marks around, 461–62
   restrictive *vs.* nonrestrictive, 438–39, 445
   as sentence fragments, 390–91
   subordinating, 519
   verb phrases, 500, 526–27
   wordy, 341
Physics, resources and style manuals for, 191, 198
Pie charts, 321, 324
Plagiarism
   avoiding, 188–89
   common knowledge and, 189
   of Internet sources, 13
   paraphrasing and, 183
   recognizing, 190
Planning
   asking questions, 40–41
   audience, determining, 35
   clustering, 38–39
   for essay exams, 122–23
   exchanging ideas, 42
   freewriting, 39–40
   language and voice, using appropriate, 36–37

library and Internet, using for, 42
listing ideas, 37, 40
purpose, being clear about, 35
question, writing about a, 34–35, 184–85
reviewing annotated texts and journal entries, 41
selecting genre, 36
Plays, in-text citations of, MLA style, 210
Plurals
   apostrophes in, 454–55
   to avoid gender bias, 347, 367, 419
   of collective nouns, 506
   collective subjects, 401
   of compound nouns with hyphens, 489, 494
   compound subjects, 399–400
   of *data,* 494
   of foreign words, 494
   indefinite pronouns with plural meanings, 402
   irregular, 494
   of letters, 455
   of nouns, 489, 493–94, 506
   of numbers and abbreviations, 455
   possessives of, 454
   spelling rules for, 493–94
   of words treated as words, 454–55
plus, 382
P.M., PM, p.m., 482–83
Poems
   capitalizing titles of, 477–78
   capitalizing words within, 479–80
   in-text citations, MLA style, 210
   quotation marks with titles, 460
   quotations from, 458, 459–60
   slashes to mark line divisions, 473–74
Point-by-point comparisons, 50
Point of view, confusing shifts in, 347–49

Political science,
resources and style
manuals for, 191, 198
Portfolios, 129
Possessive form
apostrophes in, 452–53
in comparisons, 343–44
of compound nouns, 453
before gerund, 424–25
joint, 454
of nouns, 424–25,
452–53
of plurals, 454
of pronouns, 508, 510
PowerPoint slides,
125–27, 324
practicable, practical, 382
precede, proceed, 382, 495
Predicates
compound predicate, as
type of fragment, 392
definition, 345, 522–23
mismatched with
subject, 345–46
Predication, faulty, 345–46
Prefaces, citation of, in
MLA style, 215
Prefixes, 490–91
Premises, in critical
reading, 25–26
Prepositional phrases
adverbial and
adjectival, 514–15
cannot be subjects,
344–45
close to words they
modify, 350
containing plural
nouns, 401
definition, 514
function of, 514
idioms, 369
restrictive *vs.* nonre-
strictive, 439
as sentence fragments,
391
Prepositions
definition, 514
gerunds with, 515
in idioms, 369, 516–17
list of common, 514
objects of, 514
with phrasal verbs, 369,
517
that indicate location, 515
that indicate time, 515

Present participles
as adjectives, 512
examples, 500
-ing (gerund) phrases,
424–25, 527
participial phrases, 527
in progressive tenses,
404, 411
Present perfect
progressive tense, 412
Present perfect tense
cause of tense shift, 348
definition, 411
vs. past tense, 412–13
Present progressive tense,
411
Present tense
definition, 404
introductions to
quotations, 412–13
for events in literary
works, 348, 413–14
for scientific facts,
413–14
subject-verb agreement
in, 397–404
Previewing, before
reading, 21–22
previous to, prior to, 382
Primary research, 175–79
definition, 149
Web site on, 172
Primary sources, repositories of, 177
principal, principle, 383,
495
prior to, previous to, 382
proceed, precede, 382, 495
Process analysis, 51
Progressive tense, 411, 502
Pronoun-antecedent
agreement, 418–21.
See also Pronoun case;
Pronoun reference;
Pronouns
avoiding gender bias,
418–19
with collective nouns, 420
with compound
antecedent, 420–21
with generic nouns,
419–20
with indefinite
pronouns, 418–19
Pronoun case (e.g., *I* vs. *me*)
in appositives, 423

in compound structures,
423
before an *-ing* noun,
424–25
after a linking verb, 423
subject or object of an
infinitive, 424
with *than* or *as,* 424
we or *us* before a noun,
424
who vs. *whom,* 425–26
Pronoun reference, 421–22
ambiguous, 421
implied, 421–22
unclear references for
this, that, which, 422
unclear references for
you, they, it, 422
Pronouns
agreement with
antecedent, 418–21
agreement with verbs,
397–404
case (e.g., *I* vs. *me*),
423–26
clear references, 421–23
contractions and, 456–57
definition, 417, 507
demonstrative, 508, 510
genderless, 67–68, 367
indefinite, 509, 510
intensive, 508, 509–10
interrogative, 509, 510
list of, 508–9
personal, 508
possessive, 508–9
reciprocal, 509, 510
reflexive, 508, 509
relative, 508, 510
sexist language and,
366–67, 418–19
shifts in person or
number, 347
who vs. *whom,* 425–26
Pronunciation, in
dictionary, 372–74
Proper nouns
as adjectives, 511
and articles, 507
capitalizing, 474–76
definition, 505
Proposals, 98, 100, 145–46.
See also Arguments
Protection of vulnerable
groups, in research,
176

Protocol, Web, 329
Psychology, library and Internet resources for, 199
PsycInfo, 165
Publication Manual of the American Psychological Association, 245, 247, 259
PubMed, 165
Punctuation, 434–73. *See also* individual punctuation marks
  with quotation marks, 461–64
  spacing in citations, MLA style, 213
Purpose, 21–22, 35

Quantifiers, 506
Question marks, 467
  incorrect comma with, 447
  with quotation marks, 463
Questionnaires, in field research, 176
Questions, to explore ideas, 40–41
Questions
  direct *vs.* indirect, 467
  do in, 502
  punctuating, 467
  rhetorical, 358–59
Quotation marks, 457–65
  avoiding plagiarism with, 182, 186, 188
  block format, omitting in, 458–60
  common errors in use of, 465
  for exact words, 457–58
  misuse in indirect quotations, 457–58, 464
  line numbers and, 458
  punctuation marks with, 462–63
  quotation longer than one paragraph, 458–59
  single, 460
  titles of papers, 465
  titles of short works, 460–61
  words used in special ways, 461

Quotations
  avoiding comma splice or run-on sentence, 396
  avoiding overuse, 187
  avoiding plagiarism with, 182, 186, 188
  block format, 187, 458–60
    in MLA style, 229, 232
    in APA style, 259, 269–70
  brackets within, 186, 470–71
  capitalization of, 478–79
  in case studies, 119
  citing in text
    APA style, 245–46
    Chicago style, 277–78
    CSE name-year style, 296
    CSE number style, 299–300
    MLA style, 204–5
  colons before, 450
  comma(s) with, 441–42, 447
  ellipses within, 187, 472–73
  indirect, 457, 478–79
  integrating, 186–87
  interrupted, 464
  introductions to, 412–13, 463–64
  in notes, 182, 188
  poetry
    slashes with, 473–74
    long verse quotations, 458–59
  within quotations, 460
  sic in, 471
  signal phrases with, 187
  that begin a sentence, 463–64
  that end with a question, 465

Races, capitalizing names of, 478
Radio Program Archive, 177
Radio programs, 226, 461
raise, 406
raise, rise, 383, 408
Random House Webster's College Dictionary, 372

Random House Webster's Dictionary of American English, 17
read, 398
Reading. *See* Critical reading
real, really, 383, 426
Reasoning
  circular, 30
  claims, grounds, and warrants, 27–28
  errors in logic, 33–34
  inductive *vs.* deductive, 25–26
  logical fallacies, 30–31
reason is because, 383
Reciprocal pronouns, 509, 510
recommend, 416
Recordings, citation of
  APA style, 256
  Chicago style, 288
  MLA style, 226
Red herring fallacy, 30
Redundancies, 340
Reference citation styles. *See* Citing sources; Documentation styles
References list, APA style, 250–58
  general guidelines for, 251
  in sample paper, 271–72
Reference tools and sources. *See* Sources
refer to, elude, allude, 376
Reflexive pronouns, 508, 510
Refutations, 98. *See also* Arguments
Regular verbs, 404–5
relation, relationship, 383
Relative adverbs (*where, when*), 528
Relative pronouns
Religion, library and Internet resources for, 199
Repeated words, 340, 443
Reports, citation of, 255, 301
request, 416
Research. *See also* Sources
  archival, 176–77
  discipline-specific sources for, 192–200

ethical principles for, 175–76
evaluating sources, 171–74
for relevance, 172–73
for reliability, 171–72
field, 138–39
hypothesis, developing a, 152–53
Internet sources, 163–69, 173–74
laboratory notebooks, 178–79
library sources, 155–63
perspective on sources, gaining a, 149
planning, 153
schedule, 151
primary and secondary sources, 149, 172
reading critically, 21–29, 171–75
research questions, choosing, 150–53
understanding purpose of, 149
working bibliography, 180
Research paper, writing, 184–90
avoiding plagiarism, 182–83, 188–89
conclusion in, 53, 186
documenting sources
APA style, 244–72
Chicago style, 276–95
COS style, 303–10
CSE name-year style, 296–99
CSE number style, 299–304
MLA style, 202–42
drafting, 185–86
introduction in, 52, 185–86
outlining, 45–46, 185
paper format
APA style, 259
Chicago style, 291
MLA style, 228–29
standard academic, 313–14
planning, 184–85
quoting and paraphrasing, 186–87
revising, 59–74

checklist for content and organization, 62
checklist for style, 69
sample papers
APA style, 259
Chicago style (partial), 292–95
MLA style, 230–42
statistics in, 188
summarizing, 23, 183
thesis, 184–85
respectfully, respectively, 383
Restrictive modifiers, incorrect comma with, 444–45
Résumés, 138–41, 146
submitting electronically, 141
Reviewing, during revisions, 61–62, 69
Reviews
APA citation style, 255
arguments in, 98
Chicago citation style, 286
MLA citation style, 218
Revising, 59–74
arguments, 103–4
for biased language, 67–68
collaborating online and in print, 68–72
checklists
for content and organization, 62
for style, 69
for content and organization, 59–62
online tools for, 73–74
online writing labs, 71–72
purpose, focusing on, 59–60
reviewing, 61–62
sentences, 62–68
for sexist language, 365–67
thesis strengthening, 60–61
Rhetorical questions, 358–59
ride, 406
ring, 406
rise, 406
rise, raise, 383, 408
Roget's thesauruses, 375

Roundabout sentences, 341–42
Run-on sentences, 392–97, 447–48

-s, -es verb forms, 409–10, 500
-s, -es word ending
with apostrophe, 453
spelling and, 493
Sacred things, capitalization of, 478
saw, seen, 408
say, 406
SchMOOze University Web site, 15
Science, resources and style manuals for, 191, 193–200
CSE name-year documentation style, 296–99
CSE number style, 299–304
Scientific method, 25
Scientific names, 476, 487
Scientific reports. See also Lab reports
data, 324
jargon, 363
numbers, 484–85
passive voice in, 360, 417
tense, 413
Scores, musical, citation of
Chicago style, 288–89
MLA style, 226
Scores and statistics, numerals for, 485
Screen numbers, citation of, 209
Search engines, 164–67
see, 406
seen, saw, 408
-self/-selves, pronouns ending with, 508
Semicolons, 447–50
after quotation marks, 462
common errors in use of, 449
joining independent clauses, 447–48
with items in series, 449
repairing comma splices and run-ons with, 394, 395–96

Semicolons (*continued*)
  with transitional expres-
    sions, 440, 448–49
Sentence fragments, 388–92
  appositives as, 392
  compound predicates,
    parts of as, 392
  dependent-clause
    fragments, 389–90
  examples as, 391–92
  identifying, 388–89
  intentional fragments,
    389
  phrase fragments, 390–91
  lists as, 392
  repairing, 389–92
  transitions and, 391
Sentences
  appropriate tone in, 62–63
  biased language, 67–68,
    69, 364–65
  choppy, 63, 354
  complete, 388–89
  complex, 531
  compound, 342, 531
  compound-complex, 531
  conditional, 529–30
  cumulative, 64–65,
    357–58
  declarative, 531
  direct *vs.* indirect, 65, 69
  exclamations, 359
  exclamatory, 531
  fragments, 388–92
  fused (run-on), 392–96
  imperative, 522, 531
  interrogative, 531
  inverted, 358
  mixed constructions,
    344–46
  order of parts, 521–26
  periodic, 358
  revising for style, 62–69
  run-on, 392–97, 447–48
  simple, 530–31
  straightforward, 341–42
  topic, 54–56
  types of, 530–31
  variety in, 63–65, 69, 356
  wordy, 341
Serial commas, 436, 443–44
Series
  articles with, 344
  commas in, 436, 443–44
  dashes to set off, 468
  parallelism in, 349

questions in, 466
  semicolons with, 449
Series of books, citation of
  in MLA style, 216
set, 406
set, sit, 383, 408
several, 402, 418
Sexist language, 67–68,
    364–67, 419. *See also*
    Bias
shake, 406
shall, 503–4
shall, will, 383
s/he, 367
Shifts
  in mood, 348–49
  in number, 347
  in person, 347
  in tone or idea, with
    dash(es), 469
  in verb tense, 347–48
  in voice, 348–49
Ship names, italics for, 487
Short story titles, 460
should, 503–4
should of, 378
sic, 470–71
sight, cite, site, 378
Signal phrases, for
    quotations, 187
  punctuating, 396, 441, 463
Similes, 370
Simple sentences, 530–31
Simple tenses, 410–11
since, 445, 528
Singular nouns and pro-
    nouns, 506
  apostrophes with, 452–53
sit, 406
sit, set, 383, 408
site, cite, sight, 378
Slang, 18, 361, 465
Slashes, 473–74
Small caps, 318
so
  comma in front of, 437
  repairing comma splices
    and run-ons with,
    394–95
Social Science Index, 165
Social sciences, resources
    and style manuals
    for, 190–91, 193–200
  APA documentation
    style, 244–71
  APA paper format, 259

Sociological Abstracts, 165
Sociology, library and Inter-
    net resources for, 199
some, 402, 418
some, some of, 376, 383
somebody, 401
someone, 401, 509
something, 401
Songs, quotation marks
    around titles, 460
Sound recordings
  APA citation style, 256
  Chicago citation style, 289
  MLA citation style, 226
Source note, 324–25
Sources. *See also* Libraries;
    Internet
  books, 157–61
  choice of documentation
    style for, 190–91
  classic and current
    sources, 150
  discipline-specific,
    192–200
  evaluating, 163,
    171–74, 183–84
  kinds of, 154–55
  periodicals, 161–62
  photocopies of, 181
  popular *vs.* scholarly,
    155, 172
  primary, 149, 172
  printouts of, 180–81
  reference works as,
    156–57
  secondary, 149, 172, 188
  type and number
    needed, 183–84
  working bibliographies,
    180
Spaceship names, italics
    for, 486
Spacing, line
  in APA style, 259
  in academic papers, 314
  in MLA style, 228–29
Specific words, 368
Speeches, citation of, in
    MLA style, 227
Spelling
  American and British,
    494
  commonly misspelled
    words, 494–96
  dictionary use, 371–74
  homophones, 494–95

i before *e* rule, 492
rules for, 492–94
spell checkers, 492
suffixes, 492–93
Split infinitives, 351–52
Stance
objective, 78
personal, 111–12
reasonable, 99
stuffy *vs.* casual, 37
thoughtful, 89
unbiased, 119
stationary, stationery, 383
Standard English, 362
Statistics, 188, 485
Stereotypes, 67, 365
Subject-by-subject comparisons, 49
Subject complements
adjectives as, 428, 511–12
definition, 524
pronoun case, 423–24
subject-verb agreement and, 403
Subjective case, 425
Subjects
collective, 400–401
case of, 422–23
complete, 521
compound, 399–400, 522
definition, 521
following verbs, 403
gerund phrases as, 404
of infinitives, 424
locating, 398–99, 402, 521–22
repetition of, 522
simple, 521
standard subject-verb combinations, 398–99
you understood, 522
Subject-verb agreement
collective subjects, 400–401
compound subjects, 399–400
gerund phrases, 404
indefinite pronouns, 401–2
relative pronouns, 403
standard subject-verb combinations, 398–99
subject complements, 403
word group separating, 398–99
subject following verb, 403

Subjunctive mood, 348, 416
Subordinate clauses. *See* Dependent clauses
Subordinating conjunctions, 353, 518–20
Subordinating words, 64, 389–90
Subordination
combining sentences with, 354
excessive, 355
to express unequal ideas, 353, 355
repairing comma splices and run-ons with, 394, 396–97
such, 445
such as, 444, 447, 451
Suffixes, 490–92
suggest, 416
Summaries
avoiding plagiarism in, 188
in critical reading, 23
dashes for, 468
in note taking, 183
transitional expressions that summarize, 58
Superlatives, 428–29
Superscript numbers, for citations, 277–78
suppose, expect, 380
sure, 383
sure and, sure to, 383
Surveys, in field research, 176
Suspenseful sequence, 112
Syllables, in dictionary, 372–73
Synchronous communication, citation of, in MLA style, 225
Synonyms
connotations *vs.* denotations, 368
repeating, for coherence, 56
using cautiously, 66–67, 368
using a thesaurus, 375
Synthesis, in critical reading, 23–25

Tables, 319–20
Tag questions, with comma, 441

take, bring, 378
Taking notes. *See* Note taking
team, as collective noun, 400, 420
Technical language, 363
Television News Archive, 177
Television programs, citing, APA style, 256–57
citing, MLA style, 226
quotation marks for episodes, 460
Template designs, 319
Tenses, 410–15
definition, 410
for infinitives, 414
irregular verbs and, 404–9
in participial phrases, 414–15
than
parallelism with, 350
pronoun case following, 424
that
in adjective and noun clauses, 528
needed for clarity, 343
as relative pronoun, 508
with restrictive clauses, 438–39
subject-verb agreement and, 403
unclear pronoun reference, 422
that vs. *which,* 383, 439
that there, 383
the
missing, 344
rules for using, 505–6
treatment in titles, 477, 486
Theater, library and Internet resources for, 199–200
their, there, they're, 383, 456–57, 495
them there, 383
then, 440
there, their, they're, 383, 456–57, 495
therefore
with comma(s), 440
as conjunctive adverb, 520–21

therefore (continued)
  with semicolon, 394, 395–96, 448–49
  signal of possible comma splice or run-on, 393
Thesaurus, 67, 368, 375
these, 508
these here, 383
Thesis
  in arguments, 99–100
  claims compared to, 27
  developing, 29–32, 43–45
  evolution of, in paper, 61
  finding through questioning, 44, 184–85
  hypothesis, 121
  in informative reports, 78–79
  in interpretive analyses, 90–91
  in research paper, 184–85
  restated in conclusion, 103
  specific, 43–44
  strong, 60–61, 91
  support for, 92–93, 185
  working, 42–43, 60
they, unclear reference, 422
they're, their, there, 383, 456–57, 495
Thinking. *See* Critical thinking
this
  as demonstrative pronoun, 508
  unclear reference, 422
this here, these here, that there, them there, 383
those, 508
though, 445–46
Thoughtful stance, 89
Time
  helping verbs that show, 501
  idiomatic uses of prepositions, 515, 518
  time of day, 451, 485
  transitional expressions that show, 58
Titles of people
  abbreviations of, 481
  in business letters, 134
  capitalization, 476–77
  with comma(s), 442
Titles of works

alphabetizing, 216, 252, 284
APA style for, 248, 259, 261
capitalization, 477
colons in, 451
initial article, 216, 252, 284
italics for, 485–87
MLA style for, 228
parallel, 68, 366
within titles, 216
for visuals, 324
of your own paper, 465
to, too, two, 383
Tone, 62–63, 69, 469
too, 383
Toolbars, computer, 314–15
Topic selection. *See also* Thesis
  case studies, 118–19
  developing the question, 34–35, 184–85
  for informative reports, 77–78
  for interpretive analyses, 88–89
  topic worth writing about, 29
Topic sentences, 54–56
Toulmin, Stephen, 27
Train names, italics for, 487
Trans., 215, 252
Transitional expressions
  for coherence, 56–58
  commas with, 395–96, 440
  definition, 56
  in conclusions, 56–57
  examples of, 58, 395
  semicolons with, 440, 448–49
Transitive verbs, 408, 417, 524–25
Translations, citation of
  APA style, 252
  Chicago style, 281
  MLA style, 215
tribe, as collective noun, 400
Trite expressions, 369–70, 465
try and, try to, 383
TV programs. *See* Television programs
two, too, to, 383

Typescripts, citation of in MLA style, 221
Type size and font, 313–14, 316

Underlining
  annotating with, 22
  for emphasis, in design, 318
  for italics, 485–88
  in MLA style, 213
uninterested, disinterested, 379
Unity, paragraph, 54–56
unless, 445, 529
unlike, 440
until, 445
URL (uniform resource locator) addresses
  breaking between lines, MLA style, 221
  citation of, 305
  definition, 329
  disabling automatic hyperlinking, 221
  slashes in, 474
  types of extensions, 174
us vs. *we,* 424, 425
Usage, glossary of, 375–84
use, utilize, 383
used to, 503
Usenet news groups, 170
utilize, use, 383

Value-laden terms, 119
verbally, orally, 383
Verbal phrases, 526–27
Verbals
  beginning fragments, 390–91
  definition, 526
  functions of, 526–27
  tense for, 414–15
Verbs. *See also* Verbs, types
  abbreviation for, 373
  complete, 415
  complete predicates, 523
  conditional, 529–30
  definition, 500
  -*d* and -*ed* endings, 410
  direct objects, 524–25
  ending in -*en,* 407
  followed by gerunds, 501
  followed by infinitives, 501
  functions, 523–25

indirect objects, 525
missing, 415
mood, 348, 416
principal forms of, 407,
500
-*s* and -*es* endings, 373
shifts in tense, mood,
voice, 347–49
standard subject-verb
combinations, 397–98
subject-verb agreement,
397–404
subjunctive mood, 348,
415–16
tenses, 347–48, 404–6,
410–15
verb phrases, 500,
526–27
Verbs, types
active *vs.* passive voice,
348–49, 359–61
helping, 415, 500–502
irregular, 404–9
linking, 403, 415, 423,
425–28, 524
main, 500–501
modals, 502–4
phrasal, 369
regular, 404–5
transitive *vs.* intransitive, 408, 417, 524–26
Versions feature, in Word,
74
Videocassettes, citation of
APA style, 256
Chicago style, 289
MLA style, 226
*Virtual Library Museums
Page,* 177
Visual aids
APA style for papers, 260
bar graphs, 320
clip art, 323
crediting sources for,
260, 324–25
diagrams, 322
integration into
documents, 323–25
line graphs, 322
MLA style for papers, 229
in oral presentations,
125–27
photographs and
illustrations, 323
pie charts, 321
references to, 323–24

tables, 319–20
in Web sites, 333–34
Visual learners, 7
viz., 483
Voice
active *vs.* passive, 114,
348–49, 359–61
choosing an
appropriate, 36–37
evaluating a writer's, 23
types of, 37
unnecessary shifts in,
348–49
Volumes, numbers with,
485

wait for, wait on, 383
walk, 405
Warrants, 27–28
was vs. *were,* 416
we vs. *us,* 424, 425
weather, whether, 383
Web design, 328–35
collaboration on, 330
contact information, 332
graphics, 333–34
JPG and GIF file
formats, 334
links, 333
maintaining interest,
329–31
navigation bar, 332–33
peer feedback on, 334–35
resources for, 335
unified look, 331
Web sites. *See also* Internet; Web design
APA citation style, 258
Chicago citation style,
291–92
COS citation style,
306–8, 310
for courses, 13
critical reading of, 21
CSE number citation
style, 303
library sites, 155–56
links in, 333, 486
MLA citation style,
222–23
on netiquette, 14
networked classrooms, 14
for newcomers, 10–11
OWLs, 72
well vs. *good,* 380
went vs. *gone,* 408

whatever, 509
when
in adjective clause, 438,
528
in concluding adverb
clause, 445
in conditional clause,
529
where
in adjective clause,
438–39
in concluding adverb
clause, 445
whereas, 445
whether, weather, 383
which
in adjective and noun
clauses, 528
as relative pronoun, 508
with restrictive and
nonrestrictive
clauses, 438–39
subject-verb agreement
and, 403
unclear pronoun refer-
ence, 422
which vs. *that,* 383, 439
which, who, whose, 383
who
in adjective clause, 528
as interrogative pro-
noun, 509
in noun clause, 528
as relative pronoun, 508
with restrictive and
nonrestrictive
clauses, 438–39
subject-verb agreement
and, 403
who, which, whose, 383
*who, whom, whoever,
whomever,* 425
whose, 438–39, 508
whose, who, which, 383
whose, who's, 457
Wildcards, in Web
searches, 168
will, 411
will, shall, 383
Wishes, 416
Women's studies, library
and Internet
resources for, 200
Women Writers Project,
177
Wordiness, 340–42

Word choice. *See also* Language
  active verbs, 359–60
  active voice, 360–61
  connotations, 368
  figures of speech, 370–71
  general words, 368
  misuse of words, 371
  specific, concrete words, 368–69
  standard idioms, 369, 516–17
  synonyms, 56, 66–67, 368, 375
Word origins, in dictionaries, 373–74
Word-processing programs, 73–74, 314–15, 320
Words referred to as themselves, 488
Working bibliographies, 180
Works cited list, MLA style, 212–27
  general guidelines for, 213
  in sample paper, 241–42
"Works Consulted" lists, 212
World Wide Web, 163. *See also* Internet; Online sources; Web sites
would, 503–4
would of, 378
Writer's notebooks for multilingual writers, 16
Writing. *See also* Writing papers
  application letters, 141–44, 146
  in college, 6–9
  for community groups, 133
  credibility of, 183
  e-mail, 11, 144–45

  evaluations and recommendations, 146
  field notes, 176–77
  freewriting, 39–40
  to get and keep a job, 138–44
  laboratory notebooks, 178–79
  to learn, 4–6
  to learn more about English, 16
  letters of praise, 135–38
  letters of protest, 134–35
  memos, 144–45
  netiquette, 11–14
  online, 9–14
  résumés, 138–41, 146
Writing for the Web. *See* Web design
Writing papers. *See also* Documentation styles; Document design; Planning
  abstracts, 259
  APA paper format, 259–60, 261–71
  arguments, 97–110
  Chicago paper format, 292–95
  critical reading, 21–25
  critical thinking, 24–28
  critical writing, 29–34
  drafting, 42–59, 185–86
  electronic submission, 229
  examples of papers, 81–88, 94–97, 229–42, 261–72
  exploring ideas for, 37–42
  formality in, 362–63
  headings and titles
    APA style for, 259–61
    designing documents with, 316, 318–19
    MLA style for, 228, 230

  informative reports, 77–78
  interpretive analyses, 88–97
  learning how to approach assignments, 34–37
  mapping your topic, 24, 38–39
  margins and spacing, 228–29, 259, 313–14
  MLA paper format, 228–29
  organization, 61–62
  outlining, 185
  page numbers
    APA style for, 259
    designing documents and, 313–14
    MLA style for, 229
  paper and printer materials, 228, 259
  paragraph development, 52–58
  plagiarism and copyright infringement, 188–90
  planning, 34–42, 184–85
  purpose, 35, 59–60
  quotations and paraphrased material, 186–87
  revising, 59–74
  slang and jargon, 362–63
  thesis selection, 184–85
  visuals, 229, 260

XML (eXtensible markup language), 329

yes, 440
yet, 393–94, 437
you, 347, 422
your, you're, 383, 457, 495

Index for Multilingual Writers

a, an
  missing, 344
  use in English, 506–7
Adjectives
  adjective clauses, 438, 528
  correct order for, 512
  descriptive, 511
  present and past participles used as, 512
  problems with, 427–28
  pronouns and proper nouns as, 511
  subject complements, 511
Adverbs, 350–51, 426–28, 513, 528
Agreement,
  pronoun-antecedent, 418-21
  subject-verb, 398–403
an. See a, an
Articles
  missing, 344
  use in English, 506–7

be, as helping verb, 502–3
Biased language, avoiding, 67–68, 364–66

Clauses, dependent, 345, 528-30
Clichés, 369–70, 464
Collaboration, 69, 128–29
Comma splices, 392–97, 447
Comma use, 434–47
Conditional clauses, 529–30
Conjunctions, 518–21
Coordination and subordination, 353–56, 518–20
Cultural differences in communication, 15

Desk encyclopedias, 18
Dictionaries of American idioms and slang, 18
Direct objects, including only one, 524–25
do, as helping verb, 502

Documentation style
  choice, 277
Double negatives, avoiding, 429

E-mail etiquette, 11–13
Employment applications, 144
ESL dictionaries, 17–18

Fragments, sentence, 388–92

Gerund phrases, 526–27
Gerunds
  following *to,* 515
  verbs preceding, 501
Glossary of usage, 375–84

have, has, or *had,* as helping verb, 502
Helping verbs, 501–3

Idiom dictionaries, 18
Idioms, list of common, 516–18
if clauses, 529–30
Infinitive phrases, 527
Infinitives, verbs preceding, 501
Interjections, 521

Jargon, 363
Job applications, 144

Language differences, recognition of, 499
Learning in college, 7, 13–14
Letters, writing for practice, 16

Mixed constructions, 344–46
Modal verbs, 503–4
Modifiers
  dangling, 352–53
  misplaced, 350–52

Netiquette, 11–13
no, use of, 513

Nouns
  collective, 506
  concrete and abstract, 506
  count and noncount, 505–6
  noun clauses, 528–29
  possessive, 506
  proper and common, 505
  singular and plural, 506

Online learning, 13–14
Online resources, 15

Participles used as adjectives, 512
Past participle, used as adjective, 512
Peer review, 71, 102
Phrases
  absolute, 527
  appositive, 527
  noun, 526
  verb, 526–27
Prepositions, 514–17
Present participle, used as adjective, 512
Pronouns
  agreement, 418–21
  antecedents, and, 507
  case, 422–25
  demonstrative, 508–10
  indefinite, 509–10
  interrogative, 509–10
  personal, 508, 510
  possessive, 508
  reciprocal, 509–10
  reference, 421–23
  reflexive and intensive, 508, 510
  relative, 508, 510
Punctuation, mechanics, and spelling, dealing with, 435

Quantifiers, with count and noncount nouns, 505–6

Researching a full range of sources, 154
Run-on sentences, 392–97

Sentence fragments, 388–92
Sentences
  order of parts in, 521–26
  types of, 530–31
Shifts, avoiding, 347–49
Slang dictionaries, 18
Spelling, American and British, 494
Subject-verb agreement, 397–404
Subordination and coordination, 353–56, 519–20

the
  missing, 344
  use in English, 506–7

Usage, glossary of, 375–84

Verbs
  complete, 415, 523
  followed by gerunds or infinitives, 501
  helping, 501–3
  intransitive, 525–26
  main, 500–501
  modals, 503–4
  mood, 416
  problems with, 404–17
  tenses, 410–14
  transitive, 524–25
  voice, 417

Web site design, 330
Wordiness, avoiding, 340–42
Word order, 521–26
Writing, usefulness of, 16

Credits

NOTES

NOTES

Abbreviations and Symbols for Editing and Proofreading

abbr	Faulty abbreviation **64**	¶	Paragraph **8d**
ad	Misused adjective or adverb **56**	*p*	Punctuation error
agr	Problem with subject-verb or pronoun agreement **53, 55a**	⌃	Comma **57a-j**
appr	Inappropriate word or phrase **47**	*no ,*	Unnecessary comma **57k-o**
art	Incorrect or missing article **69**	;	Semicolon **58**
awk	Awkward	:	Colon **59**
cap	Faulty capitalization **63**	⌄	Apostrophe **60**
case	Error in pronoun case **55c**	" "	Quotation marks **61**
cliché	Overused expression **48d**	. ? !	Period, question mark, exclamation point **62a-c**
coh	Problem with coherence **8d**	— ( ) [ ]	Dash, parentheses,
com	Incomplete comparison **39c**	. . . /	brackets, ellipses, slash **62d-h**
coord	Problem with coordination **44a, b**	*para*	Problem with a paraphrase **22b, c**
cs	Comma splice **52**	*pass*	Ineffective use of passive voice **46b**
d	Diction problem **47, 48**	*pn agr*	Problem with pronoun agreement **55a**
dev	More development needed **8c, d**	*quote*	Problem with a quotation **22b, 61b, g**
dm	Dangling modifier **43e**	*ref*	Problem with pronoun reference **55b**
doc	Documentation problem	*rep*	Repetitious words or phrases **38b**
	APA **29, 30**	*run-on*	Run-on (or fused) sentence **52**
	Chicago **33**	*sexist*	Sexist language **9d, 55a**
	COS **35**	*shift*	Shift in point of view, tense, mood, or voice **41**
	CSE **34**	*sl*	Slang **47a**
	MLA **24, 25**	*sp*	Misspelled word **68**
emph	Problem with emphasis **44**	*sub*	Problem with subordination **44c, d**
exact	Inexact word **48**	*sv agr*	Problem with subject-verb agreement **53**
exam	Example needed **8c**	*t*	Verb tense error **54e**
frag	Sentence fragment **51**	*trans*	Transition needed **8d**
fs	Fused (or run-on) sentence **52**	*usage*	See Glossary of Usage **50**
hyph	Problem with hyphen **67**	*var*	Vary your sentence structure **45**
inc	Incomplete construction **39**	*vb*	Verb problem **54**
intro	Stronger introduction needed **8d**	*w*	Wordy **38**
ital	Italics or underlining needed **66**	*ww*	Wrong word **48**
jarg	Jargon **47c**	//	Parallelism needed **42**
lc	Lowercase letter needed **63**	#	Add a space
mix	Mixed construction **40**	^	Insert
mm	Misplaced modifier **43a-d**	⌒	Close up space
mng	Meaning not clear	×	Obvious error
mood	Error in mood **54k**	??	Unclear
ms	Error in manuscript form **36a**		
	APA **31**		
	Chicago **33d**		
	MLA **27**		
num	Error in number style **65**		

Contents

TAB 1 ▪ Learning across the Curriculum

1 Your College Experience 3
2 Writing to Learn 4
3 Writing in College 6
a Common college assignments
b Understanding assignments
4 Writing Online 9
a The virtual landscape
b E-mail
c Netiquette and cyberculture
d Learning online
5 Learning in English as a Second Language 14
a Cultural differences in communication
b Using writing to learn about English
c Tools for multilingual students

TAB 2 ▪ Writing Papers

6 Reading, Thinking, Writing: The Critical Connection 21
a Reading critically
b Thinking critically
c Writing critically
7 Planning 34
a Approaching assignments
b Exploring ideas
8 Drafting 42
a Thesis
b Outlining
c Developing ideas
d Paragraphs
e Online tools for drafting
9 Revising 59
a Considering purpose
b Evaluating the thesis
c Reviewing the whole and parts
d Revising and editing sentences
e Collaborating online and in print
f Revising online

TAB 3 ▪ Common Assignments

10 Informative Reports 77
STUDENT PAPER
11 Interpretive Analyses and Writing about Literature 88
STUDENT PAPER
12 Arguments 97
STUDENT PAPER
13 Other Kinds of Assignments 111
a Personal essays
b Lab reports
c Case studies
d Essay exams
e Oral presentations
f Coauthored projects
g Portfolios

TAB 4 ▪ Writing Connections

14 Service Learning and Community-Service Writing 133

15 Letters to Get Action: Protest and Praise 134
16 Writing to Get and Keep a Job 138
a Internships
b Résumés
c Job application letters
d Writing on the job

TAB 5 ▪ Researching

17 Understanding Research 149
a Primary and secondary research
b Research and college writing
c Critical inquiry
18 Finding Print and Online Sources 153
a Kinds of sources
b Using the library
c Searching the Internet
19 Evaluating Sources 171
a Print sources
b Internet sources
c Evaluating arguments
20 Doing Research in the Archive, Field, and Lab 175
a Ethics
b Archival research
c Field research
d Lab Research
21 Working with Sources 180
a Maintaining a working bibliography
b Taking notes
c Assessing your research
22 Writing the Paper 184
a Planning and drafting
b Quoting and paraphrasing
c Avoiding plagiarism
d Documenting sources
23 Discipline-Specific Resources 192

TAB 6 ▪ MLA Documentation Style

24 In-Text Citations 204
25 List of Works Cited 212
26 Explanatory Notes 227
27 Paper Format 228
28 STUDENT PAPER IN MLA STYLE 229

TAB 7 ▪ APA Documentation Style

29 In-Text Citations 245
30 List of References 250
31 Paper Format 259
32 STUDENT PAPER IN APA STYLE 260

TAB 8 ▪ Other Documentation Styles: *Chicago*, CSE, and COS

33 *Chicago* Documentation Style 276

34 CSE Documentation Styles 296
a CSE name-year style
b CSE number style
35 Columbia Online Style (COS) 304

TAB 9 ▪ Document and Web Design

36 Document Design 313
37 Writing for the World Wide Web 328

TAB 10 ▪ Editing for Clarity

38 Wordy Sentences 340
a Redundancies
b Unnecessary repetition
c Wordy phrases
d Straightforward sentences
e Reducing clauses, phrases
39 Missing Words 342
a In compound structures
b *That*
c In comparisons
d Missing articles (*a, an, the*)
40 Mixed Constructions 344
a Mixed-up structures
b Faulty predication
41 Confusing Shifts 347
a In point of view
b In verb tense
c In mood and voice
42 Faulty Parallelism 349
a In a series
b With paired ideas
43 Misplaced, Dangling Modifiers 350
a Misplaced modifiers
b Ambiguous modifiers
c Disruptive elements
d Split infinitives
e Dangling modifiers
44 Coordination and Subordination 353
a Combining short sentences
b Subordinating less important ideas
c Ineffective subordination
d Too much subordination
45 Sentence Variety 356
a Sentence openings
b Length and structure
c Cumulative and periodic sentences
d Inversion, rhetorical questions, exclamations
46 Active Verbs 359
a Alternatives to be verbs
b Active voice
47 Appropriate Language 361
a Slang, regional expressions, nonstandard English
b Level of formality
c Jargon
d Euphemisms, doublespeak
e Unbiased language